BIG LEAGUE
Ballparks
THE COMPLETE ILLUSTRATED HISTORY

BIG LEAGUE Ballparks

THE COMPLETE ILLUSTRATED HISTORY

Gary Gillette and Eric Enders

with Stuart Shea and Matthew Silverman

M

METRO BOOKS

NEW YORK

Special thanks to Andrew Ullrich, Jeff Batzli, and Mark Levine for providing the baseball cards seen throughout this book.

Photography credits appear on page 512.

Major League Baseball trademarks and copyrights are used with permission of Major League Baseball Properties, Inc.

Book design by Kevin Ullrich

Metro Books
122 Fifth Avenue
New York, NY 10011

ISBN: 978-1-4351-1452-4

Printed and bound in China

10 9 8 7 6 5 4 3 2 1

HALF-TITLE PAGE: Children try to get a glimpse of the action at Cleveland's League Park by peeking through holes punched into the stadium gate.

TITLE PAGE: A canoe sits in idyllic McCovey Cove, just outside of AT&T Park (formerly Pacific Bell Park) in San Francisco. On game days, the cove is teeming with boaters hoping to catch a home run ball.

ACKNOWLEDGMENTS: Wooden field-box chairs are stacked haphazardly at the remnants of the Polo Grounds in August 1964, as demolition of the historic ballpark nears completion. The concrete-and-steel version of the park housed the Giants, Yankees, and Mets during its more than fifty years of existence.

TABLE OF CONTENTS: Spectators take advantage of 1926's version of "standing room only"—sitting in foul territory—at the home opener between the Chicago White Sox and the St. Louis Browns at Comiskey Park.

Acknowledgments

Not only do books not write themselves, they don't design or edit themselves either—the end product is the work of a number of very talented folks. At Metro Books, we'd like to thank Kevin Ullrich for his spectacular design work; Janice Ackerman and Melissa McKoy for finding some great photos; Lindsay Herman and Hallie Einhorn for the copyediting and proofreading; and Rich Hazelton for doing the dirty work that so often goes unappreciated. We'd also like to thank ex-honcho Nathaniel Marunas for having confidence in us when there was really no good reason to. And most of all, editor Jennifer Boudinot, for her efforts in holding this project together. She shepherded it with an enthusiasm that made working on this book a joy.

We wish to acknowledge the various writers, researchers, and historians from the past 140 years who have documented the evolution of ballparks and whose prior research helped lay the groundwork for this book, especially Michael Benson, Michael Gershman, and Philip Lowry; and all the librarians and archivists whose yeoman's work makes history books possible. Various members of the Society for American Baseball Research have done much to advance the cause of research on ballparks. SABR has our thanks…and our membership dues. It deserves yours, too.

We've been researching this book in one form or another for about a decade, and there are lots of people who helped along the way. Tim Wiles gave Eric his start in baseball and remains a friend to this day. (For his sake, we hope the Cubs finally win one someday.) Other baseball geeks whose assistance and friendship we are grateful for include Freddy Berowski, Claudette Burke, Sweet Willie Francis, Jorge Jimenez, David Jones, Jeremy Jones, Larry Lester, Rob Pendell, Gabe Schechter, Tom Shieber, Erik Strohl, and Bob Timmermann. We are also appreciative of our colleague Greg Spira and his attention to detail.

As always, our work is dedicated to people who read. Most of all, we treasure Cecilia Garibay (SS) and Vicki Gillette (GG) and the life they share with us every day. Lastly, a shout out to my parents (EE), who have always been supportive above and beyond the call, and my brother Mark, with whom I've visited sixteen of the ballparks herein—a number which will hopefully be higher by the time you read this.

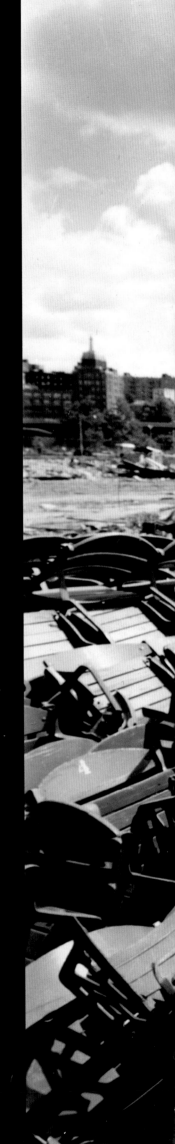

CONTENTS

Note: Because names often change, ballparks are listed by their best-known name. To find a park by a name not listed above, please see the index.

CHAPTER ONE

Pre-Ballpark Era

1845   1908

PREVIOUS PAGES:
The New York Highlanders (who will later be known as the Yankees) take the field at Hilltop Park on Opening Day 1908. Spanning from 165th Street to 168th Street in what is now the Washington Heights section of New York, the park was located on a hill overlooking the Hudson River, which could be seen from the upper seats in the left-field grandstand (if fans turned away from the field).

THE PARK ERA, 1845–1875

Before baseball developed into the organized sport we now know as the national game, the nascent exercise of baseball was pursued—literally—in parks. In the 1840s and 1850s, there were no actual baseball stadiums. To be sure, the game was played all over the new land, but it was played in open spaces, public parks, prairies, vacant lots, and on any convenient piece of ground that kids, teenagers, or even adults could find.

At the time, the sport was all about *playing*, not watching. And as remains true today for anyone playing the game in such a public space, the field conditions depended on the property. Trees, homes, fountains, and monuments were sometimes in play. Outfield fences did not exist. Dimensions were rarely uniform. Just like early players, many of us have played pick-up games in parks that don't have dimensions or fences; theoretically the game is open-ended and can reach forever in all directions. Until professionalism transformed the game, there was no need for luxury seating, tickets, or even walls to keep knot-holers out. Baseball's early wide-open spaces have lent an idyllic quality to our images of the old days: It's easy to imagine the players of the 1830s hitting a home run into a river a few hundred feet from the plate or crashing into a tree a few yards behind first base.

In the 1840s and '50s, then, the idea of a ballpark or stadium was unheard of. Folks who did come by to watch a game were watching people they knew. Games were played at this time for fun, for exercise, for the thrill of competition, and for neighborhood, club, or town superiority—rarely for money (though there were exceptions). Some clubs organized to play ball for recreation, and some reserved private grounds on which to do so. Others simply gathered regularly at vacant lots. Meanwhile, newspapers reported on the growing interest in the game with a mix of patriarchal guidance and amusement.

Most playing spaces at the time did not have enough room for what are now regulation base paths, though bases were generally equidistant, if not yet the standard 90 feet apart. Additionally, with no mass production of baseballs until the 1850s, a ball hit into the forest or a surrounding body of water could be a minor calamity. Thus, balls hit out of play—even home runs—were considered fouls. The ball itself, a handmade concoction with a rubber center, was smaller and springier than a modern baseball; it is probably more similar to a playground rubber-coated hard ball than anything else in existence today. Fielders didn't even think of using gloves, nor would they for another three decades.

Baseball rules and strategy, even from the earliest days, were highly dependent on where the game was being played. Long before the emergence of mass media, different regions of the country developed their own baseball traditions. And most every community in the land, be it city, town, hamlet, or Native American village, had playing fields where willing individuals of varying levels of skill would play some form of the game. While early baseball is often thought of today in bucolic terms, the game actually had roots in the city as well as in the countryside.

One thing the game had in common in every region was that all classes played it—the rich bankers and hardscrabble street toughs of New York; the landed gentry of the South; and the farm boys, miners, and homesteaders of the prairie. Everyone played the game, and the nation embraced baseball as its own. This democratic element was seen as very American, even though baseball was a descendent of English games. It was thought to be America's first homegrown sport, a belief that was propagated by one of baseball's first chroniclers, Henry Chadwick. Indeed, the very strength of baseball, which was to make it the national pastime by the middle of the twentieth century, was that it was *everyone's* game.

The First "Official" Baseball Game

In September 1845, Alexander Joy Cartwright, a New York banker and firefighting enthusiast, became the first to incorporate his "base ball" club and attempt to codify the rules of the nascent but very popular game. Credited over the years with developing the forerunner of modern baseball, Cartwright and his Knickerbocker club hosted on June 19, 1846, what is now known as the first recorded baseball match. In reality, however, it was far from the *first*; several recorded games of "base" had taken place in New York City at least a year before, and variants of the game had been played for many years in the East, South, and Midwest. But this particular occasion captured the popular imagination and triggered the baseball fad, leading to Cartwright's almost immediate designation as "The Father of the Game."

Cartwright's fraternity of players, New Yorkers all, fled the city in the early 1840s because available open fields were disappearing in Manhattan. These men, upper-class merchants with both the time and the money to spend on leisure, sought out bucolic ground in New Jersey, attempting to retain (or recapture) the grassy, idyllic, rural origins of the game they recalled from their youth. In this way, the early baseballists were already recalling a time gone, making organized baseball a game of nostalgia almost from the start. The players found their haven at the Elysian Fields in Hoboken, New Jersey, a well-known tourist attraction on the western shore of the Hudson River. The Knickerbockers practiced there on late weekday afternoons in 1845 and 1846, and then decided to host a match against the New York Nine on June 19.

Cartwright and other members of the Knickerbockers altered their version of baseball from informal games of "cat" played by children. The Knickerbocker game was played on a *diamond* and not a square; foul territory was defined; and the fielders could not put runners out by hitting them with a thrown ball (called *soaking*). Such a thing was considered ungentlemanly! In the earliest forms of baseball, pitchers had to serve up the ball for hitters underhanded and without much speed; strikeouts were almost unheard of except for the most inept of hitters. The point of the game was to put the ball in play, and pitchers merely served that goal instead of being the critical element of defense they would later become.

At the time, not all teams had a full complement of players—only in 1856 were the rules updated to mandate the number of players at nine. And, until 1857, games were set at a specific number of runs (usually twenty-one) rather than a specific number of innings (nine). The "home team" didn't necessarily bat first; such matters were settled by a coin flip. In fact, this tradition continued into the early days of the National League. Throughout all of these evolutionary changes, however, three outs always ended an inning.

Cartwright served as umpire for the game, which the New York Nine won 23-1. It took just four innings for the Nine to reach their limit of twenty-one runs and, after the inning, the game was stopped. Many curious society types, sports writers, friends of the players, and, most likely, gamblers showed up at the contest. As the respectable Knickerbockers began to win friends in high places, word spread of the glory of the baseball match. Players formed clubs, practiced, held banquets, and made merry. Eventually, the game reached the middle and poorer classes as well, and baseball became part of the urban experience. Both kids and adults played baseball in vacant lots or alleys, on streets and public parks, or anywhere with a spare patch of grass, asphalt, or even brick.

Baseball as Business

It was only a matter of time before the love of competition led to the establishment of a professional game. Clubs needed to pay their players, and they saw the public's passion for baseball as an opportunity to turn the new pastime into a profitable business. The honor system of admission didn't work, and, more importantly, didn't allow for stratification of the fans by ability to pay. Therefore, in order to keep out freeloaders and separate the moneyed class from everyone else, owners created structures—*ballparks* as we now know them.

At the time, the only sports venues in America were ones for horse racing, so early ballparks were modeled after racing

BELOW: In baseball's early days, there was little to no regulation, and contests took the form of informal pick-up games with spectators gathered around the field to watch. Leagues were not yet developed, and teams had any number of players, who often bet on their own games. Here, a crowd takes in a match in Newburgh, New York, in 1865.

The First Paid-Admission Game

It seems appropriate that New York City, the home of many other baseball firsts, also claims the first instance of a game where spectators were charged for the privilege of watching. Following the formation of the National Association of Base Ball Players—an aggregation of New York–area teams—in 1857, locals began asserting that their team (along with their city) was the best. To settle the question of superiority between the clubs of Manhattan and Brooklyn once and for all, the NABBP organized a match-up for the best players from the boroughs' teams to go head-to-head.

The contest generated great community interest, and the *New York Times* devoted several articles to it. On July 12, 1858, the paper reported that representatives from Brooklyn and Manhattan had selected Fashion Race Course as the site of the historic game. Located in what would now be the neighborhood of Willets Point, Queens (close to Citi Field), the site was seen as appropriately neutral, and it could hold plenty of spectators, with 10,000 seats and room for 40,000 more standing or sitting around the perimeter.

Admission, according to the *Times*, would be 10¢ per head, with all profits going to the families of fallen New York and Brooklyn firefighters. The organizers were clearly aiming for a highly refined spectator, as they ruled that no alcohol was to be sold on the grounds and no gambling would be permitted (a subtle irony for a game that was to be played at a race-track). There would also be a special section, covered by a large awning, reserved for "ladies accompanied by gentlemen."

Unfortunately, rain poured down on the day of the contest after more than 1,500 fans had arrived, forcing postponement for a week. But on July 20, 1858, baseball fans once again descended on the racecourse, eagerly anticipating the unprecedented contest. Many rode in horse-drawn carriages, which could be parked for a charge of 25¢ for a one-horse carriage and 40¢ for a two-horse coach. Others came by the Williamsburg Ferry or by the Flushing Railroad, which had scheduled extra trains to and from the game.

After the baseball clubs arrived in ornately decorated vehicles, they took the field shortly after 2:30 p.m. New York's team was made up of the best players from five teams from New York and Hoboken, while Brooklyn's "all-stars" were taken from their four National Association clubs. When the game began, fans were still streaming into the grounds after debarking from a fifteen-car train coming from Manhattan. They missed no scoring, however, as both sides were blanked until Brooklyn scored twice in the top of the second and New York answered with one in the bottom of the frame. When Brooklyn tallied four times in the fifth to take an 8-7 lead, New York came back with seven runs of its own. Down 18-17 in the bottom of the eighth, New York rallied for five and then held on for a 22-18 win.

The grandstands were filled, with carriages ringing the entire field. Inside the ring of carriages, fans stood behind other fans who were seated on the grass. The *Times* estimated that the crowd totaled more than 8,000, including nearly 500 ladies. Despite early pronouncements, both water and "lager-bier" were sold on the grounds, though no hard liquor was to be found, save for whatever the spectators smuggled in. And the anti-gambling proclamation, though well intentioned, was completely unenforceable. Still, the crowd was decorous, perhaps due to the special security detail. In addition to police officers, a force of local ballplayers (ten from each of the National Association's twenty-five clubs) were deputized to help keep the peace.

The level of interest in the game led the NABBP to schedule another match, with a third to be held if Brooklyn evened the series. On August 17, Brooklyn did just that, trouncing New York 20-8 in front of more than 6,000 spectators who were cooled by a much-welcomed drizzle. The final and decisive match was held on September 10 in front of a surprisingly small assemblage of fewer than 5,000. Brooklyn scored two in the first, but New York answered with seven in its half and never trailed again, eventually winning 29-18. Following all three games, players, club representatives, and other VIPs ate and drank to excess in the Fashion Race Course clubhouse.

grandstands. Some games were actually played at horse tracks: In the summer of 1858, "all-star" squads representing New York and Brooklyn held three matches at the Fashion Race Course in Queens. The first recorded instances of admission being charged to watch a baseball game, the matches took place in July, August, and September, and each had five to ten thousand spectators.

Soon, club owners decided to take control of their businesses, and they set out to construct their own grounds. Most parks of the time were built on inexpensive parcels of land that would now seem incredibly small, and wood construction was the norm. By the early 1860s, according to Warren Goldstein in *Playing for Keeps*, the practice of admission fees was well established. In 1861, fans paid to see a match at Hoboken's St. George Cricket Grounds, organized to benefit (i.e., to pay) stars Jim Creighton and Dickey Pearce. The next year, Brooklyn's Union Base Ball Club opened its grounds on May 15 with free admission, a band, and a special grandstand for women. Quaintly, it was thought that the fairer sex wouldn't sit on the field.

While much of baseball's recorded history focuses on what was happening on the East Coast, by the mid-1860s, clubs as far west as Illinois were playing high-level baseball in their own parks, charging admission, and beating quality eastern teams. For instance, the Cincinnati Red Stockings spent $10,000 on their park in 1868. The previous year, a club from Rockford, Illinois, hosted and defeated a DC team in a game that featured music between innings. In fact, the first major league game in baseball history took place in the Midwest—at Fort Wayne, Indiana's Hamilton Field, on May 4, 1871. The host city's Kekiongas, a charter franchise in the National Association of Professional Base Ball Players, defeated Cleveland 2-0.

The social structure of the nineteenth century was divisive, from politics to racial matters to culture right down to baseball. This birthing of baseball as we know it was painful, pitting mostly upper-class East-Coasters against the lower classes of the cities and the so-called uncultured elements of the country. The wealthy played for recreation, seeing their game as an extension of British teatime cricket and croquet matches, while the blue-collar classes saw a parallel between the struggles of their harsh day-to-day lives and the game of baseball. These less well-to-do folk relished the idea of playing to win. In the game's early days, the richer classes often sat in their carriages behind the outfielders, while the lumpen proletariat congregated in the grandstand. But even in the 1860s, baseball parks had special luxury-seating sections at higher prices, as well as discrete areas for women and even gamblers, who received special provisions during a time when gambling was a major draw for baseball. Rich people liked the game when it was played by and for their peers, while the middle and lower classes, in turn, identified with the game when the players were like *them*. The rich wanted to have luxury seating, and they got it; but owners knew they had to appeal to the *hoi polloi* as well. So they built bleachers and cheap grandstands along with the carriage views and the box seats.

Admission fees were not the only income source, of course. Concessionaires were sold licenses to hawk drinks, cigarettes, and food at baseball games almost from the beginning. The press and upper crust frowned on the consumption of alcoholic beverages at the yard, presumably because alcohol led to loosened morals among fans. However, players enjoyed the privileges of alcohol after the game—in fact, the post-game beer bash was virtually de rigeur. From the very beginning of organized ball, weekday games were played at 3:00 or even 4:00 p.m. in order to allow working men to play or attend the games after getting off their shifts or closing up the banks. Saturdays were big days for ballgames, but Sundays—at least until the 1880s—were reserved for the church and family by custom and by law. Since the papers were the only conduits of baseball news at the time, details of upcoming games were often sketchy—especially to the spectators.

The first major league, the National Association of Professional Base Ball Players, was established in 1871. Most fans of the early National Association league had become accustomed to paying a quarter to see local matches, but the advent of professionalism brought new admissions policies. The New York Mutuals' 1871 National Association home opener, at Brooklyn's Union Grounds, drew more than three thousand. Apparently, it could have drawn many more but for a last-minute hike in admission fees from 25 to 50¢. In other words, the first major league game ever played in New York City began like so many do today—with fans complaining that they'd never again return to see a game at such high prices. Of course, some of the dissatisfaction came from the fact that the visiting Troy Haymakers defeated the Mutuals 25-10, disappointing those fans who had wagered money on the Mutuals.

When charging admission caught on, it hammered home the point that fans came to games because they wanted to see their local teams win, even though the "local" teams in some cases included paid imports from other towns. The competition, not the game itself, was the draw for all but the most high-minded folks. A local park, along with uniforms and locally popular players, encouraged fans to identify with their hometown club, and at first nearly everyone was uncomfortable with the concept of "imported" talent. In fact, for many clubs, owning a ballpark was critical to remaining in competition. Peter Morris, in *Baseball Fever*, reports that in 1872, a team from Kalamazoo, Michigan, declined to play a South Bend club because the Indiana team lacked its own enclosed grounds where attendance fees could be charged. Baseball had indeed become a bona fide business.

LEFT: An 1894 promotional print of Boston's South End Grounds, which was built in 1871. The field was home to the National Association Boston Red Stockings, who would eventually join the National League and become the Red Caps, then the Beaneaters, and finally the Boston Braves. A double-decked grandstand was built on the site in 1887, but after it was destroyed by fire in 1894, the team had only enough insurance money to build a single-decked grandstand in its place.

THE GROUNDS ERA, 1876–1887

When William Hulbert and seven like-minded businessmen formed the National League of Professional Base Ball Clubs prior to the 1876 season, their plans didn't include building any new ballparks. The grounds for the first NL games were parks that had been used previously by National Association teams. Few parks built during this era had any architectural significance, and rare was it that any park lasted for more than a few seasons.

Many early ballparks, built inexpensively with low-quality wood, either burned or collapsed. On at least two occasions, such calamities occurred *during games*. Rain quickly warped and rotted the exposed "bleacher boards" as well as the wooden stands, trickling through cheap tin roofs in the covered sections. Little, if anything, was done to protect the grounds during the winter months. Many clubs couldn't practice on their home grounds in the spring after they had been frozen over the winter, covered in snow, or flooded by rain. In the days before spring training became an annual ritual, most clubs got into shape at local gymnasiums. Some of the grounds used by non-league teams, built in part to attract NL clubs to play exhibitions there, were of better quality than many league parks.

Despite the lack of care for the playing fields, some clubs had excellent business plans in place. The league's most powerful team, the Chicago White Stockings, for example, sold a limited number of season tickets (200) for $15 apiece in 1876. The season package, sold exclusively at Al Spalding's sporting goods store, guaranteed reserved seating at all thirty-five league games as well as for any exhibitions on the White Stockings grounds. Chicago's 23rd Street Grounds remained waterlogged well into April, but they were ready to play by May 10, the date of the home opener. The *Chicago Tribune* stated that the ground was "more even for short-fielding than ever before," indicating that groundskeeping had become more precise. It's not clear how many fans the 23rd Street Grounds seated, but a crowd of 8,000 was said to fill all the seats and most of the standing room areas.

Not all teams were quite as well prepared to start raking in the silver. Louisville's attractive but small park seated only 2,000. On Opening Day in 1876 against Chicago, an additional 2,000 spectators evaded the 50¢ admission charge by watching from a large hill overlooking the park. To remedy the situation for the next game, Louisville club management stretched a canvas around the outfield fences to block the freeloaders' view. But that was the least of their worries. The *Chicago Tribune* described the grounds as "sticky and soft in the outfield, and very dead all over." Meanwhile, Cincinnati's new park seated fewer than 5,000 and had rough, transplanted sod on the field—but the stands were said to be sturdy and well planned.

Among the spectators filling seats in these crude parks were more than a few gamblers. In fact, betting was such a huge part of the first days of professional ball that even the sober *New York Times* reported on it in the upper paragraphs of its game stories. While league owners officially frowned on gambling, it went on at every park, and owners tacitly understood that betting helped bring in the fans. Moreover, some of the players even engaged in open betting. If folks with money to burn couldn't make it to the park but still wanted to put a wager on the game, they could go to one of the poolrooms near each big-city ballpark. At that time, the term *poolroom* didn't mean a place to shoot billiards; it signified a place to participate in betting pools. In the 1870s, before television, radio, computers, or even the widespread use of telephones, betting parlors got the lineups, pitcher information, and game scores from the era's top method of instant communication: the telegraph. Newspapers, situated at the ballparks, transmitted inning-by-inning reports to the poolrooms, where bettors then made their wagers. But not all clubs cooperated with this practice: In 1876, the Hartford NL club refused to permit inning-by-inning telegraph transmissions from their park. The club justified this policy by claiming that in-game reports could cut down fan attendance—the same justification that would be used decades later by those opposed to live radio broadcasts, and then to television broadcasts.

The NL's Early Winners and Losers

With the national game still in its professional infancy, the novelty of a great team attracted gratuitous attention, and outrageous attendance. When Chicago's White Stockings made their Boston debut on May 30, 1876, they were greeted by what a Boston reporter called "the largest crowd ever to see a baseball game in this city." The mob went "through the gates and over the fences" and swelled onto the field in such numbers that hits into the crowd were held to one base. The final game in the series produced a paying crowd of 10,000 as well as 2,000 gate-crashers, according to the *Boston Globe*. Since NL rules awarded visiting teams one-third of the gate receipts as an incentive to make their road trips (rather than renege on their commitments as several NA clubs had done in 1875), Chicago walked away with $1,080 in receipts.

Not all clubs made the kind of cash Chicago did. So William Hulbert tightened his grip on the NL and pushed for mandatory clean-living amendments to make sure players were at the top of their games. His Western bias, a response to the perceived Eastern bias of Alexander Cartwright, turned his focus in 1880 toward the hearty, beer-loving burg of Cincinnati and its mediocre club. The *Chicago Tribune*, Hulbert's hometown paper, sniffed on February 1 of that year, "A bar will disgrace the Cincinnati grounds this year, as usual. A club that cannot live without running a saloon should quit." That month, NL owners voted to halt the playing of Sunday games, long popular in Cincinnati. The religious "blue laws" were making it difficult for games to proceed without arrests, and the high-minded continued to rail against the consumption of alcohol at ballparks as well as in clubhouses.

Prior to the 1880 season, it wasn't even certain that Cincinnati would field a club in the NL. By season's end, all but the hardiest Porktown fans had already given up after their team, disrespected by the league and playing in the ramshackle Bank Street Grounds, finished 21-59. It was no secret that the NL wanted the franchise out, both because of its poor attendance and the supposedly unsavory atmosphere. Therefore, immediately following the season, NL owners voted 7-1 to deny clubs the right to sell alcohol on their grounds. Cincinnati, predictably, refused to agree to this change in league rules, so the NL expelled the franchise, setting in motion a series of events that would change the face of the still young professional game.

The American Association, Drunks, and Ruffians

The NL's ejection of Cincinnati, plus the opportunity for profit in several large cities, led to the formation of a rival league. Magnates in Baltimore, Cincinnati, Louisville, Philadelphia, Pittsburgh, and St. Louis founded the American Association, which took the field in 1882. The National League's puritanical ways and regionalism allowed the new loop a chance to hit the ground running.

The American Association soon became known as "The Beer and Whiskey League," because unlike the NL, its ballparks were allowed to sell alcohol. In addition, each AA home team would receive *all* of its home receipts—i.e., every team for itself—and franchises could elect to play Sunday games. While these policies helped win the AA many fans, the key

reason for the new league's popularity was the low admission price of 25¢—half of what NL clubs were charging. NL club owners and their supporters groused that the AA's brand of baseball would bring in drunks, gamblers, lower-class ruffians, and social undesirables. Unfortunately for them, this haughty attitude toward the less wealthy guaranteed that they would experience grave financial problems once the new league opened for competition. And compete the AA did, signing NL stars, tweaking the rules to improve conditions for umpires, and changing ball-strike counts. What's more, the league strategically set up shop in large cities with proven fan bases, and the "rough" crowds rolled in.

Contrasts between the high-class NL and the working-class AA were particularly glaring during the 1883 season, when the new league's New York club shared the Polo Grounds with the city's NL franchise. The AA team, the Metropolitans, had first claim to the Polo Grounds, but the club's owner, John Day, had also purchased the NL's Troy Trojans and moved them into the park, too, renaming them the Gothams. The two clubs, owned by the same man, played exhibition games at the Polo Grounds prior to the regular season to drum up interest. The Gothams won seven of the eight games played for the "State Championship," indicating their on-field superiority and increasing their drawing power at the hands of their hapless AA brothers.

The grounds were large enough to accommodate two playing fields, and there were times in 1883 that both the Mets and Gothams played home games at the same park. On those days, the Mets got the worse half of the grounds— a badly rolled field with ramshackle stands—while the Gothams got the good field and the large, well-maintained grandstand. (Some sources claim that the grounds were "split" between the two clubs during the entire 1883 season,

BELOW: The AA Brooklyn Bridegrooms take on the St. Louis Browns at the Bridegrooms' Washington Park in 1887. Opened on May 12, 1883, Washington Park was located in what is now one of the most popular sections of Brooklyn: Park Slope. This photo was taken from right field, around the corner of Fifth Avenue and Third Street. For its clubhouse, the team used the Gowanus House, George Washington's headquarters during the Revolutionary War's Battle of Long Island.

ABOVE: This color print shows a game at the original Polo Grounds in Manhattan. On 112th Street, just north of Central Park, this was the first home of the National League Giants (then called the Gothams) as well as their American Association rivals, the Metropolitans. In 1911, the Polo Grounds would move about forty-five blocks north to a site along the Harlem River.

but newspaper accounts are inconclusive as to whether the grounds were divided at any time other than when both clubs were at home. Researchers have been unable to determine for certain whether the Mets ever got to play on the "good" field.) Opening Day for the NL club on May 1, 1883, drew 15,000 spectators, including former president Ulysses S. Grant and a surprising number of female fans. Even though tickets were 50¢ a pop, the talented team drew the largest throng ever to see a ballgame in New York, according to the *Times.* When the AA club opened later in the month, it drew far smaller crowds.

Even though the AA Mets and the NL Gothams shared a ballpark and an owner, their respective leagues yielded drastic differences in team management and in fan culture. The Mets were shunted to the "bad" field partly because the league was considered a substandard aggregation of its forebear, even when AA clubs did well. In addition, most analysts believe that the AA's fans, because of the affordable ticket prices and the proliferation of alcohol, were rowdier and more disruptive than NL supporters, and didn't demand the better conditions that NL fans were used to. (However, with AA parks boasting waiters that carried trays of beer steins to fans, plenty of NL fans crossed the line.) Thus, major league baseball can be seen as a microcosm of the American class divide of the times. It was a tough period in US history; people needed cheap entertainment to help them deal with the crush of late-nineteenth-century urban life. And like today, one way people blew off steam was by going to the park, sitting in the sun, having a few beers, and passionately cheering their heroes and booing their villains.

Though they were supposedly higher class, NL games were hardly free from controversy. Umpire baiting and charges of favoritism led fans to swarm the field at Washington's Swampoodle Grounds on July 30, 1886. Two months earlier, the *Sporting News*, angry at the harsh language used by some fans at St. Louis' NL Union Grounds, advocated kicking the hoodlums out of the park and tossing them in jail. "A good club or bunch of fives are the only things in the world that] hoodlums respect, and they should be given both of them with a vengeance," the paper opined.

Part of the outcry against violence was the perception that it drove ladies and their well-heeled squires away, yet a great many women found baseball to be both glamorous and exciting. They didn't generally sit in the bleachers at this time, as clubs often reserved grandstand sections for "ladies and their escorts." (Parks of the 1880s were built less like racing grandstands and more like Us or Vs, curving to allow for behind-the-plate grandstand seating and down-the-line cheaper seats.) A *Brooklyn Eagle* report of a St. Louis–Brooklyn AA game in 1889 made special mention of the crowd being so big that "the overflow of the fair sex had to find seats on the bleaching boards." The tradition of designating special "Ladies Days" began in Cincinnati in 1876 when huge flocks of women thronged to see pitcher Tony Mullane, dubbed "The Apollo of the Box." A May 1886 edition of the *Sporting News* discussed a particular female fan who wore maroon, the colors of the New York Gothams, and showed up for every one of the club's games. Speculation had her eyes fixed on either showy "Dude" Esterbrook, brainy "Johnnie" Ward, or slugging Roger Connor.

Hazards of Early Ballparks

Even if the fans were reasonably well behaved, the ballparks themselves could still be lethally dangerous. Creaky wooden bleachers, soggy fields, and smoke belching from nearby trains or factories made most of the ballparks of this era little more than overcrowded, badly maintained, dilapidated piles of kindling. The structural quality of major league ballparks had hardly improved by the 1880s, even though clubs were spending somewhat more money on them.

A good example of the sometimes harrowing conditions occurred on May 2, 1884, during Opening Day at League Park, Cincinnati's new AA playground. (The owners of Bank Street Grounds had pulled the club's lease following the 1883 season.) The bleachers collapsed just as the game ended, and several fans were seriously injured. Noted the *Cincinnati Enquirer*, "the cheap seats are not the only part of the ground that seems to be in a weak condition...the building is on new-made ground." Other wooden ballparks suffered similar fates until they were replaced by much safer, more permanent, and more expensive structures built of iron, steel, concrete, and brick. A shed overlooking Belair Lot, a Baltimore park used for the short-lived Union Association league, crumbled on July 4, 1884, tossing fans onto the field. Brooklyn's AA field, Washington Park, burned on May 19, 1889. In Cleveland, the NL's League Park caught fire during a lightning storm in 1892 and, in the same year, Rochester, New York, lost its former AA park. The Philadelphia Baseball Grounds burned to the ground on August 6, 1894, and the NL's Louisville Eclipse Park caught fire in 1899.

Many of these accidents occurred on either Opening Day, Memorial Day, or July 4, usually the only dates guaranteed to draw big crowds for most clubs—proving that the grounds were especially dangerous when maximum capacity was reached. Club owners at the time didn't buy huge parcels of land to build their ballparks, and they didn't even think of building huge grandstands because most games didn't draw anywhere near capacity crowds (moreover, most owners of the time were just plain cheap). Even after larger grounds were built, big games meant that fans would ring the playing field, cheering on their favorite players from just feet away.

BELOW: Built in 1891, Pittsburgh's third Exposition Park was the home of the NL Pirates until they moved into Forbes Field in 1909. In one famous match at the park in 1902, the Pirates played a doubleheader against the Brooklyn Dodgers after an Allegheny River flood, even though the outfield was under a foot of water. All balls hit into the standing pool were ruled singles; the Pirates took both games. This photo of the park was taken in 1914, when it was inhabited by the Pittsburgh Rebels of the Federal League, the last major league upstart, which lasted only two seasons.

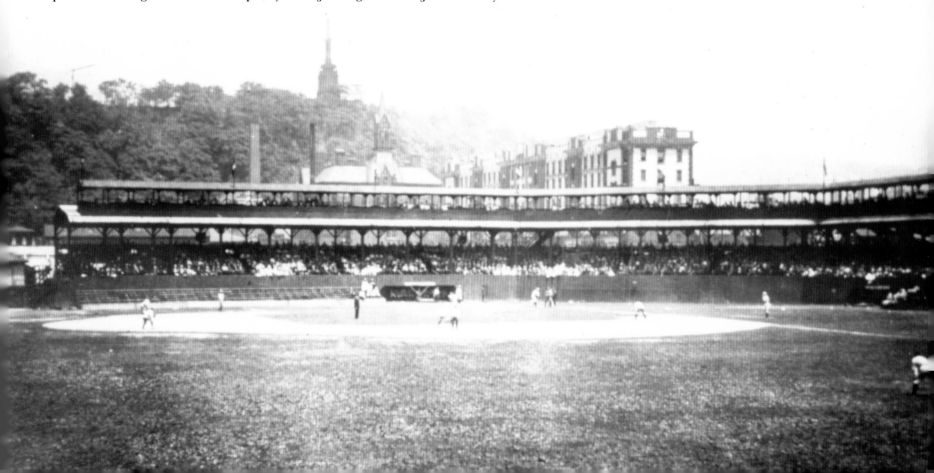

Non–Game Day Money-Makers

In order to generate extra income, clubs in all nineteenth-century leagues rented their ballparks out during long road trips. Some racetracks-turned-ballparks still held horse races, and most owners with teams out of town on Memorial Day or July 4 would host band concerts, complete with fireworks (at the time a fairly recent, and highly popular, phenomenon). Field days, races, semipro games, football scrimmages, and many other events were held at nearly all professional parks. Cleveland's NL franchise, the Blues, even turned its ballpark into a skating rink in the winter of 1880.

Of all the non-baseball attractions staged in ballparks of the era, perhaps the most unusual was held July 3 through July 5, 1886, at St. Louis' Union Grounds: a reenactment of the Siege of Vicksburg. Event organizers hung a 25,000-square-foot canvas backdrop on the field, brought in a band to play patriotic tunes, set off fireworks, and hired men dressed in period uniforms to reenact the battle. The cost of this wholesome entertainment was the same as for a ballgame, 50¢ for a grandstand seat and 25¢ for standing room.

Despite club owners' need to pick up ancillary income and their willingness to experiment, no professional club considered holding night games, even though an 1880 experiment drew much attention. For the first time, electric light was used to illuminate an evening game, which took place south of Boston between representatives of two Boston department stores. Despite the apparent efficiency of the lights, it would be another fifty-five years before major league baseball played a night game—even though the fabled Kansas City Monarchs of the Negro Leagues and various minor league teams adopted lights well before that.

Another way for clubs to generate revenue in these years was to put advertising on the outfield walls. The tradition that reached its acme with the outfield fence signs at Ebbets Field actually began in the 1880s.

Late-Century Architectural Progress

The 1880s were a time of explosive growth for the national pastime. With higher investments and potentially higher returns, owners spent more money on their venues, which in turn lasted substantially longer. Although many of the crude and impermanent parks of the early leagues were used until the first decade of the twentieth century, several new developments distinguished ballparks built in the late 1880s and 1890s. The first development was the addition of covered grandstands at wooden parks, making them more hospitable to fans and, of course, more costly to build. The second development was the gradual change from 100 percent

wood to noncombustible construction—iron, steel, concrete, and brick—making these one-time tinderboxes more fire-resistant and, ultimately, fireproof.

Perhaps the best park of the grounds era was Chicago's Lake Front Park, usually called "White-Stocking Park" or later, simply, "Base-Ball Park." Despite being nestled next to train tracks and a freight yard, Lake Front was considered a jewel, perhaps demonstrating the ragtag state of most big-league ballparks of the time. According to an 1880 letter in the *Chicago Tribune*, the White Stockings paid $1,000 per year for the land—a fairly minor investment that was made back manyfold as the team dominated the NL in the early 1880s. Fans could buy their 1880 White Stockings season tickets for $15 before April, but had to pay $17.50 afterward. Some single-game tickets, even for exhibitions, went for as much as 75¢ for the grandstand.

In 1883, Lake Front Park's seating capacity more than doubled to 8,000, with 1,800 seats designated as reserved. Team owner Al Spalding also constructed eighteen private boxes above the grandstand, starting behind home plate (for the press) and stretching down the left-field line. The boxes were meant for Spalding and other club officials, as well as any fans who wanted to pay the tariff to sit in the rarified air. Spalding's box had the first telephone line to be installed at

a ballpark. In addition to these renovations, the White Stockings built seats and aisles around the park so fans wouldn't have to traverse the field to reach seats in the outfield. And to minimize distractions for spectators, no refreshment "peddlers" were allowed to hawk their products in the crowds; instead, fans purchased their refreshments from a stand located near the park.

After just two seasons at their new palace, however, the White Stockings were evicted from their grounds by the City of Chicago. In another demonstration of baseball's general lack of clout, the municipal government granted the land on which Lake Front Park stood to the Michigan Central and Illinois Central railroads, for a passenger train depot.

Like Al Spalding, Chris Von Der Ahe, the owner of the AA St. Louis Browns (forerunners of the NL Cardinals), made his ballpark a unique expression of his own ethos and ego. Von Der Ahe, a brewer who knew little about baseball but much about running a successful saloon, bought the club in 1882 and helped turn their Sportsman's Park into a party attraction in its own right. The revamped grounds featured antecedents of modern ballpark amenities, such as picnic areas, bullpen sports bars, and a beer garden in the right-field corner where patrons could sip their brews, watch the game, and even indulge in lawn bowling.

THE WOODEN BALLPARK ERA, 1888–1908

During the 1870s and 1880s, ballparks—uneven grounds with rickety grandstands—rose and fell fairly quickly. By the end of the '80s, however, ballparks were more permanent, solid structures—though it would take another fifteen years before classic-era ballparks made of concrete and steel would open their gates.

In 1890, a group of players led by John Montgomery Ward banded together to fight the restrictive contracts imposed upon them, and formed the Players League. Though the PL was better organized than the ill-fated Union Association, and competitive on the field with the NL and AA, it lasted only one season. A year after the failed rebellion by the players, the ten-year-old American Association collapsed, weakened by five years of NL raids on its best franchises and by the three-way war among the leagues.

The National League absorbed four of the remaining AA teams and emerged as a twelve-team loop for 1892. While this hegemony was certainly good for the established NL magnates, the large number of clubs—many of them with shaky finances—quickly turned the league from triumphant to vulnerable. So, after regaining a monopoly on professional baseball, the league revised its ticket policies. Prices for the grandstand remained at 50¢, but all clubs were required to designate part of their grounds for 25¢ seats to attract more spectators. Beer sales were now permitted on the grounds, as were Sunday games if clubs wanted to schedule them (and local laws allowed it).

Despite these progressive changes, the NL monopoly quickly proved disastrous for baseball in the 1890s. With all the power concentrated in the hands of so few owners, corruption, on-field hooliganism, and lack of competitive play due to stacking the best teams with the best players made the league a farce and the national game a mockery. The final misstep by the NL's feudal barons was a major one: The league contracted only eight teams in 1900, leaving Baltimore, Cleveland, and Washington bereft of baseball—and wide open for a new pro organization, the American League.

The predictable excesses of monopoly power rotted the NL from within, but it also paradoxically helped save the game by allowing the American League to challenge the established order. As baseball transitioned into the stable, two-league setup that has lasted through the present day, ballparks continued their evolution as well. During the 1890s, the dangers of wooden ballparks—which warped in the summer rain and heat, and burned down all too often—affected several teams. The signature year for change was 1894.

Ballparks in Flames

The most acclaimed ballpark of the tumultuous 1880s was Boston's South End Grounds [II], redesigned and rebuilt to

open in May 1888. (The original Grounds had been constructed for the National Association's famed Boston Red Stockings, who became one of the NL's founding members.) The most important feature of the new South End was its beautiful, curved, double-decked wooden grandstand, festooned with conical spires that looked a bit like tepees, and with many rows of seats stretching down both lines.

But it didn't last long. On May 15, fans at South End Grounds were shocked by cries of "fire!" during the third inning of a game against Baltimore. With no rain having fallen for weeks, the wooden bleachers were dry as tinder. The slats of the bleachers burned first, then the fences caught fire, and finally, the magnificent double-decked grandstand succumbed to the flames. The park was a complete conflagration within minutes. Though the 3,500 fans in attendance evacuated the grounds without loss of life, the fire didn't stop after devouring the ballpark. Riding a harsh wind into an adjacent, impoverished neighborhood, the fire burned hundreds of crowded tenements and left 4,000 people homeless. The Boston club's damages were $75,000, and the area suffered upward of $1,000,000 in losses. The Grounds' smoldering ashes signaled the beginning of the end of the wooden ballpark era.

The Philadelphia Phillies starting playing at their National League Park, more commonly called the "Philadelphia Baseball Grounds," in 1887. The park was well appointed for its day but, like all other ballparks of the era, was constructed entirely of wood. On August 6, 1894, a fire consumed most of the park as well as some of the surrounding neighborhood. Several newspaper accounts reported that a plumber's torch caused the fire, but the August 7 *New York Times* and *Chicago Tribune* both claimed that a young "urchin" watching the ball club practice tossed a cigarette butt under the stands. No matter the cause, luck wasn't on the Phillies' side, as the weather had been dry and hot, and a stiff wind swiftly spread the flames. The fire, which began around 10:30 a.m. in the left-field side of the grandstand (called the "ladies' end" by the *Boston Globe*), quickly engulfed the wooden grandstand as well as the left- and right-field bleachers, a train shed, and nearby stables (the horses were rescued). Several houses near the corner of Broad and Huntingdon were also damaged, and some Philadelphia players lost clothes and valuables in the flames.

On August 5, just a day before the fire in Philly, a conflagration at Chicago's one-year-old West Side Grounds halted a game against Cincinnati in the sixth inning. The grandstand was nearly gutted, and the right-field bleachers, where the fire had started, were completely destroyed. The bleachers were bound by a barbed-wire fence, installed to deter fans from leaping onto the field. When the fire began, spectators in the bleachers became trapped between the flames and the fence, forcing them to either scurry for the already jammed exits or climb through the wire to reach the field and evade the fire. The ensuing panic led fans to

push each other into the sharp-tipped barbs. Several Chicago players, running from their positions, tried to pull down the metal barriers, which eventually gave way—but not until they had cut hundreds of fans. The sight of dozens of panicked men and boys with torn suits and bloody faces and hands, trying to climb through the fence and hanging like rag dolls on the wire, was enough to disgust even the most cynical of Chicago newspapermen. More than 500 people were injured by the blaze, though with 10,000 fans on hand for the Sunday contest, the injury toll could have been far worse.

After the calamitous fires in Boston and Chicago, their NL teams played at what were called the old "brotherhood" grounds of the defunct Players League: Boston's Congress Street Grounds and Chicago's South Side Park [II]. While burnt out, Philadelphia played some of its home contests at the University of Pennsylvania Field, but most of its 1894 home schedule was switched to road games.

In the wake of these events, even the squinty-eyed magnates of the game, who squeezed their dollars so tightly that the eagles screamed, began to understand that many fans wouldn't come to ballparks where they stood a very real chance of loss of life or limb by being burned, trampled, or julienned. So owners made some changes: They placed more fire extinguishers around their parks, installed more water mains on-site, and created more exits.

Of the new ballparks built in this era, few lasted very long or were historically relevant. However, when Philadelphia's National League Park opened again in May 1895, it had made a great leap forward in safety and permanence, thanks to a new grandstand made of iron. The park's innovative, cantilevered design also removed many unsightly support posts that had heretofore blocked the views of thousands of unfortunate fans. Only the seats were constructed of wood, making it the era's most revolutionary and influential ballpark. The spate of fires had finally forced the hands of the cheapskate Phillies owners. Nevertheless, indicative of how quickly things were changing at the turn of the century, by the time the park was renamed Baker Bowl in 1913, the structure had already been superseded architecturally by newer and far grander ballparks.

Greed, Egos, and the Decline of the National League
While other owners paid lip service to the concept of fire safety, none followed Philadelphia's lead and put up a new, non-wooden ballpark—no team owner was willing to build a new venue unless they truly *had* to. In the late 1890s, owners of National League teams were more interested in consolidating their feudal kingdoms than in meaningfully addressing fan safety issues. Business owners controlled the press (and, as a result, largely controlled the public dialogue), and it was a time when workers' rights had yet to be fully addressed. Baseball men ruthlessly cut player salaries and slashed other costs to the bone, attempting to extract

maximum short-term profits with nary a thought about the long-term health of their game.

As the number of major league jobs shrank after the death of the American Association, and as salaries were severely constricted after the Players League folded, winning at all costs became critical for ballplayers. The greatest cheaters of the time were the Baltimore Orioles, who finished first from 1894 to 1896, and finished second the next two years. Baltimore's hard-bitten manager and players used any available means to gain advantage—including tripping or holding opposing players, cutting corners while running bases, and abusing the umpires. Despite the resulting wins, the Orioles' style turned off a lot of fans and sportswriters, just as the AA St. Louis club's booze-filled tactics had done a decade before.

Fan interest also waned with the new "big league" NL. The twelve-team loop guaranteed that several clubs would finish forty or fifty games out of first place every year. The rampant rough behavior of players and managers, which included screaming obscenities on the field and bullying umpires, drove away many of the deeper-pocketed fans that baseball wanted desperately to attract—especially the ladies and their well-to-do escorts. "It is impossible for a respectable woman to go to the games of the National League without running the risk of hearing language which is disgraceful," baseball pioneer George Wright told the *Sporting Life* in early 1898.

What's more, during the 1890s postseason competition was treated as little more than an afterthought. With a single league, of course, there was no natural way of setting up a championship series. In the first year of the "big league," the schedule was split into two halves to enable a postseason series between the first- and second-half winners. That format elicited little interest and was dropped after 1892, leaving the league without any postseason play the next year. In 1894, noticing the gap created by the NL owners' indifference and the public appetite for a championship series, wealthy sportsman William Temple sponsored a trophy series played between the first- and second-place NL teams. The Temple Cup was a modest success, lasting three years before petering out. From 1897 to 1899, there was again no postseason competition. Then, stepping into the yawning chasm of ownership apathy, a Pittsburgh newspaper sponsored another postseason match-up between the top two teams in the regular season. The Chronicle-Telegraph Cup was a flop, however, and was discontinued after its first year.

Syndicate Ownership and the New American League
Like the fish of the famous cliché, the National League was rotting from the head as its arrogant and insular barons counted their gold while ignoring their customers. John T. Brush, owner of the NL's Cincinnati club, represented a great deal of what was wrong with baseball in the 1890s. Not only did he own Cincinnati's team, but he also owned

LEFT: Otis Clymer of the Washington Senators up to bat at the New York Yankees' Hilltop Park on Opening Day 1909. Though the game was occasionally disrupted by dynamite blasts from a nearby construction site, New York beat Washington 8-1. This was the first game in which the Yankees wore uniforms that featured the now trademark interlocking "NY" on their uniforms, seen here on catcher Red Kleinow's sleeve. "The teams did not form in a line and march across the field, as had been promised," reported the *New York Times.* "They drifted out on the ground and began cavorting around on the grass like frisky calves, though goodness knows there were some among them who haven't been calves in a long time."

BELOW: The crowd overflows at Hilltop Park on July 4, 1907, during a game versus the Philadelphia Athletics. Fans standing in fair territory were regular sights at early ballparks (especially on holidays), and ground rules were adopted to award automatic doubles or singles to balls hit into the crowd. Hilltop Park also had a unique ground rule for right field: Balls hit over the short fence blocking a large hollow in the outfield were considered home runs.

1895

NATIONAL LEAGUE PARK
Philadelphia, Pennsylvania

1898

WASHINGTON PARK [III]
Brooklyn, New York

1901

BENNETT PARK
Detroit, Michigan

COLUMBIA PARK
Philadelphia, Pennsylvania

HUNTINGTON AVENUE
GROUNDS
Boston, Massachusetts

LEAGUE PARK
Washington, DC

LLOYD STREET GROUNDS
Milwaukee, Wisconsin

ORIOLE PARK [IV]
Baltimore, Maryland

SOUTH SIDE PARK [III]
Chicago, Illinois

1902

PALACE OF THE FANS
Cincinnati, Ohio

SPORTSMAN'S PARK [II]
St. Louis, Missouri

1903

HILLTOP PARK
New York, New York

1904

LEAGUE PARK [II]
Washington, DC

stock in the New York Giants and had holdings in the Brooklyn, Pittsburgh, and Cleveland clubs, according to the *Sporting News*. If that didn't spell "conflict of interest" clearly enough, in 1898 Brush tried to buy St. Louis' AA club from Chris Von Der Ahe. Brush was, in the eyes of both those who respected him and those who didn't, one of the most powerful men in baseball—although he was not the only owner to own stock in more than one club. This kind of interlocking ownership, termed *syndicate ownership*, naturally tempted club owners to transfer their best players to whatever franchise was the owner's personal favorite or to the team that was doing the best at that particular moment.

When, before the 1900 season, the NL dropped their teams in Louisville, Washington, Baltimore, and Cleveland (three of them nearly worthless clubs ruined by syndicate ownership), President Ban Johnson of the minor Western League decided to seize the moment. Ambitious and calculating, Johnson had for some time noticed that the NL was frittering away the goodwill of the public as well as leaving fans in many cities without competitive teams. The contraction (meaning shutting down) of teams also infuriated players, who thought that the National League had guaranteed their jobs. With several open markets, plenty of former big-leaguers ready to sign, and the press on his side, Johnson declared his league, which he had run profitably since 1894, to be a "major" for the 1900 season. Renamed the American League, it fielded clubs in eight cities, including Cleveland.

The AL did well in 1900 and, encouraged by its progress as well as the press, ramped up its efforts for 1901. On August 25, 1900, the *Sporting News* editorialized, "An organization opposed to the National League will be welcome because it will mean the elevation of the game if it is successful." Now Johnson had clubs not only in Cleveland but also in former NL cities Washington and Baltimore. He moved out of smaller markets in Indianapolis, Minneapolis, Buffalo, and Kansas City, and had the chutzpah to go head-to-head with the NL in three cities by adding clubs in Chicago, Philadelphia, and Boston, and even scheduled a large number of "challenge" dates in cities with both AL and NL teams.

As with the American Association two decades earlier, once again the owners' greed allowed an upstart league to steal a march on the NL. This time, however, the new American League was here to stay. Setting its ticket prices at 25¢, half that of the NL, the new organization got off the ground with a competitive start.

New League, New Parks

The founding of what was quickly dubbed the "Junior Circuit" meant eight new big-league parks—at least *nominally* major league parks. Not all of the new grounds were top-flight; a survey of the original AL parks reveals some new, some old, and some downright awful facilities. Because major league team owners had been running their businesses with bare-bone finances, and most of them were simply cheap, many parks of the era were located in poor areas. Ballparks built in slums were products of short-term thinking that led to long-term problems; urban locations were liable to spread fires and keep the upper classes away. And some parks were situated on swampy low ground near rivers, leaving them prone to flooding after major rainstorms.

Moving out of the crowded areas and away from marshland, however, made perfect sense at the time, especially considering that trolley and train lines were running to the city limits. Capitalizing on these benefits, Washington built its new American League Park away from the downtown core of the city. This move led the *Washington Post* to state, "the day is past when ballparks could be located in the heart of a growing city," complimenting club management for building their park "on the outskirts" where access via trolleys would be easier for many fans. Most scholars tend to think of ballparks' move to the "outskirts" as a phenomenon of the 1950s and 1960s; in reality, teams have always tried to find ways to cater to customers with dollars. Washington was moving to what today would most likely be considered "suburbs"—areas reachable by public transportation and modern roads, but removed from the poorer and most congested areas of the city.

Boston's Huntington Avenue Grounds was built on a former circus midway in a poor neighborhood, just across the street from the NL club's South End Grounds. The *Boston Globe* noted that the new AL park would sport covered walkways and better-than-average player and press facilities, but also that "no effort would be made to have elaborate grandstands." Outfitted with opera chairs, the stone, steel, and wood grandstand was built to seat 2,100, with space for another 6,900 fans in the bleachers, which would feature canvas awnings for especially hot days. Charles Somers, owner of the new Boston club, touted the universally high quality of his new grounds: "We shall have accommodations that will please every one interested, from the 'fresh candy' man to the members of the 400." Like many parks of this era, the Huntington Avenue

Grounds was built incredibly quickly by modern standards: The first spade of dirt was turned on March 9, 1901, with the first game played on May 8 of that same year.

The Chicago White Stockings, who like other AL teams, borrowed their nickname from earlier NL teams, played in South Side Park. Also known as White Stockings Park, South Side was erected on a small site previously used for Union Association games in 1884, and later for cricket matches. Located four blocks south of the current U.S. Cellular Field, this was the last wooden ballpark built in Chicago. It also boasted a unique feature: grandstands built on stiltlike supports to give better visibility to the occupants. Charles Comiskey, the team's owner, expanded the park almost immediately when interest in the 1901 season exceeded his expectations. Prior to that season, local transportation officials had named a train running from downtown Chicago to the ballpark on game days "The White Sox Limited." Ban Johnson himself christened the train with a bottle of champagne on April 12.

Cleveland's new AL franchise, initially called the Blues after the defunct NL Cleveland team of the 1880s, played at League Park, former home of the NL's Spiders. In 1910, the wooden park would go through a grand renovation to bring it up to speed with the new concrete-and-steel stadiums of the time, and the team would play there (as the Indians) until 1946. The site of Detroit's Bennett Park was used for major league baseball even longer—until 1999, when Tiger Stadium closed. Originally a 6,000-seater, Bennett was a decidedly below-par facility when it opened—the field was uneven and rocks protruded from the dirt. Despite that, the

BELOW: The first home of the Boston Red Sox (then known as the Pilgrims), Huntington Avenue Grounds is suspected to have had the deepest center field in major league history, at 530 feet. Meanwhile, left field was 350 feet, left-center 433, right-center 412, and right field was 320 (with a kink in the wall that went to 353 feet). The park, which had a capacity of 11,500, hosted the first-ever World Series in 1903.

local fans were devoted. The park's namesake, Charlie Bennett, was not a wealthy owner but a former Tigers catcher who had lost his legs in a railway accident. Bennett caught the ceremonial first pitch on Opening Day in 1901.

Three more notable, though shorter-lived, AL parks opened to the public in 1901: Lloyd Street Grounds in Milwaukee, Columbia Park in Philadelphia, and Oriole Park [IV] in Baltimore. Lloyd Street previously housed the minor league Western Association Brewers and then the AL charter franchise Brewers in 1901—although the team departed for St. Louis the next season. Two minor league clubs occupied the park until 1903, when it shuttered for good. When the AL moved the Milwaukee franchise to St. Louis for 1902, the league paid to put up a new ballpark on the site where the previous Sportsman's Park had burned to the ground. That land had hosted the NA in 1875, the AA from 1884 through 1891, and the NL in 1892. Before the 1909 season, the

wooden grandstand would be double-decked and reinforced with concrete and steel. It hosted big-league ball until 1966.

Philadelphia's Columbia Park was a small but adequate facility used by the AL Athletics from 1901 through 1908. It also hosted the Athletics' rivals, the Phillies, for sixteen games after a chunk of the Huntingdon Grounds bleachers collapsed on August 6, 1903. Baltimore's Oriole Park was a new facility built on the site of the old Oriole Park. It was considered a good-looking, well-appointed park for the time. However, the franchise was eliminated when the AL moved into New York in 1903. Baltimore's International League club then occupied Oriole Park until 1915.

The new league had desperately wanted a franchise in New York, but due to Giants owner Andrew Freedman's undue influence in New York City policies, it took Ban Johnson until 1903 to find available land that Freedman didn't control. The craggy, uneven patch of ground on top of a hill on the northern tip of Manhattan would eventually be the $300,000 Hilltop Park. The wooden structure with a masonry foundation was the home of the New York Highlanders (sometimes called the Hilltoppers, and only later dubbed the Yankees), who were stuck there until 1913, when they became tenants of their NL rivals, the Giants, at the Polo Grounds. At least the hilltop location minimized the danger of having a ballpark fire affect the neighborhood, or vice-versa.

John Brush, meanwhile, had a new park built for his National League Reds. The stadium opened in Cincinnati in April 1902 and was grandiosely known as the "Palace of

the Fans." The *Chicago Tribune* called it "the finest plant in the league... furnished in every detail." The structure was fireproof, a key marketing point for the club and a sign of change in ballpark construction.

From the start, the American League benefited from built-in respectability, thanks to the decrepit state of affairs in the NL and also to the press, which had a tendency to embrace any exciting new venture. The aboveboard nature of the upstart league's owners also helped sway opinion. Three American League clubs—Baltimore, Boston, and Chicago—instituted regular Ladies' Days, which undoubtedly boosted its classy image even more. (By contrast, the NL had prohibited Ladies' Days in another misguided decision during its monopoly reign.) What's more, AL president Ban Johnson made the American flag part of the AL's official logo and stated in the early days of the new league that he wished to keep the flag in full view at all of his parks.

Meanwhile, the National League employed sneaky tactics to hamper the progress of new AL clubs. The Senior Circuit at first tried to revive the old American Association in potential AL markets. When this failed, the league then sent operatives to interfere with player signings or to drum up community opposition to the new clubs. Knowing that the NL was on their tail, the Washington club professed interest in building a new ballpark on an old circus ground. While the NL spent time trumping up citizen petitions against a park on that site, the AL club was

ABOVE: In baseball's early days, it was often easy to see a game without paying admission. Here, eager spectators peer over a wall at Detroit's Bennett Park to get a glimpse of the action.

BELOW: The Detroit Tigers take on the Pittsburgh Pirates at Bennett Park during Game 3 of the 1909 World Series—the first and only time legendary hitters Ty Cobb and Honus Wagner went head-to-head. Note the fans perched on utility poles (in the background of the photo) to watch the game without paying for a ticket. After the 1909 Series (which the Pirates would take, 4-3), temporary stands that had been erected in left field were made permanent, so that views from the tops of barns outside the park would be blocked. Today, modern parks occasionally mimic this feel: Wrigley Field allows nearby residents to rent out their rooftops to spectators (as long as the Cubs get a 17 percent cut), while San Francisco's Pacific Bell Park and Minneapolis' Target Field feature knotholes in their facades for passers-by to peek through.

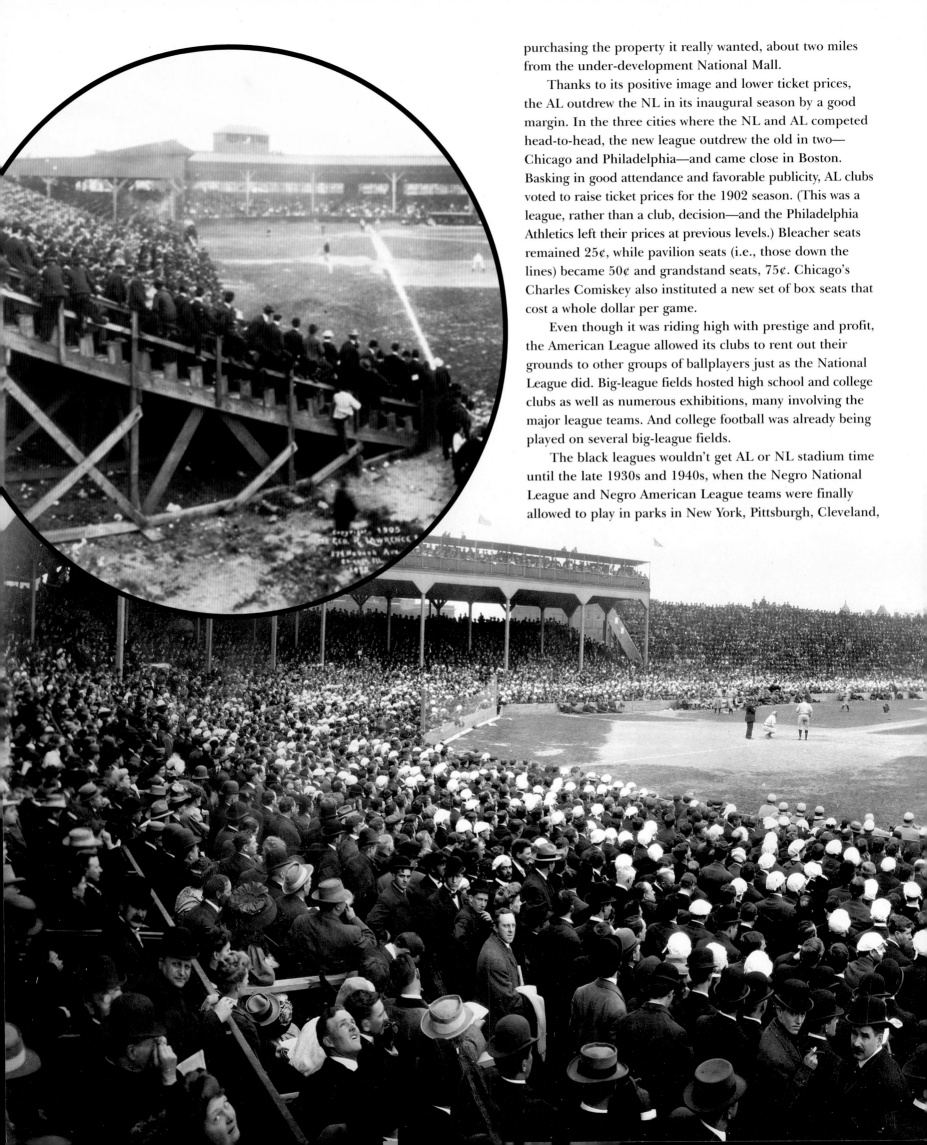

purchasing the property it really wanted, about two miles from the under-development National Mall.

Thanks to its positive image and lower ticket prices, the AL outdrew the NL in its inaugural season by a good margin. In the three cities where the NL and AL competed head-to-head, the new league outdrew the old in two—Chicago and Philadelphia—and came close in Boston. Basking in good attendance and favorable publicity, AL clubs voted to raise ticket prices for the 1902 season. (This was a league, rather than a club, decision—and the Philadelphia Athletics left their prices at previous levels.) Bleacher seats remained 25¢, while pavilion seats (i.e., those down the lines) became 50¢ and grandstand seats, 75¢. Chicago's Charles Comiskey also instituted a new set of box seats that cost a whole dollar per game.

Even though it was riding high with prestige and profit, the American League allowed its clubs to rent out their grounds to other groups of ballplayers just as the National League did. Big-league fields hosted high school and college clubs as well as numerous exhibitions, many involving the major league teams. And college football was already being played on several big-league fields.

The black leagues wouldn't get AL or NL stadium time until the late 1930s and 1940s, when the Negro National League and Negro American League teams were finally allowed to play in parks in New York, Pittsburgh, Cleveland,

Cincinnati, Chicago, and Washington. While black players were not organized into hard and fast nationwide leagues in the early part of the twentieth century, traveling teams often met local nines for high-profile matches. When, in the 1920s, the Negro National League and Eastern Colored League were formed, their clubs were forced to play in smaller, more ramshackle parks, even in major league cities.

A Day at the Game

What was it like to attend a major league baseball game at the turn of the twentieth century? With no electronic scoreboards, no public-address speakers, no lights in the park, no radio or TV coverage, and precious little grounds-keeping or equipment, the modern baseball fan would have found a day at the park in 1901 more than a bit spartan. However, even these ballparks of yore sported familiar touches. Vendors walking through the stands hawked peanuts, bottles of soda, candy, cigars, programs, and—depending on the park—beer. A man with a megaphone stood near home plate before the game and barked out the starting lineups, serving the role of the public address announcer today.

The idea of a "sellout" was almost unheard of; if more fans wanted to enter than could be seated, standing-room tickets were sold to any and all comers in excess of capacity. When there was an overflow crowd, fans who couldn't find

a place to stand would sit on fences or railings, or even clamber onto grandstand roofs and beams. Teams would often seat fans in foul territory. On holidays, when thousands more showed up than could comfortably be seated, crowds even encroached into fair territory, which called for ad hoc changes to the ground rules. In such circumstances, balls hit into the crowd were automatic doubles or, sometimes, singles.

While spectators sitting in the grandstands usually had reasonably comfortable chairs with backs, fans in the cheap seats were obligated to buy cushions if they wanted to avoid splinters. Among bleacher fans, straw hats were all the rage—especially in the summer—to prevent sunburn. Foul balls and home runs were generally thrown back from the seats because teams wanted to save money on baseballs and, thus, made a rule that fans weren't permitted to keep them. Restroom facilities were generally terrible, even as teams attempted to get women to come to the park, and aisles were rarely swept, if at all. The players and umpires generally dressed and showered in very poor facilities; most home teams had some sort of clubhouse or dressing room, its level of comfort depending on the ballpark and the generosity of the owner. Many visiting clubs had to dress in their hotels and ride to the park in their uniforms.

While there were no electronic journalists, of course, a large press corps covered ballgames. Newspapers made much

RIGHT: Fans stream into Philadelphia's Baker Bowl. Opened in 1887 as National League Park, the home of the Phillies was later renamed Baker Bowl after the team's owner, William Baker. After it burned down in 1894, the venue reopened with a double-decked grandstand constructed of brick, steel, and concrete—a fireproof design that would be copied by the Philadelphia Athletics' groundbreaking Shibe Park years later. The Phillies would stay at the park until 1938, when they, themselves, moved into Shibe.

BELOW: Rooters cheer on the home team at Baker Bowl in 1915, while two policemen keep the peace and a vendor makes a sale while still keeping an eye on the action. Especially after new, classic-era fields began to open up, Baker Bowl had some of the smallest dimensions in baseball—only 280 feet in right, and 310–320 feet in right-center. Nicknamed the "cigar box," the field was also compromised by the team's clubhouse, which sat in dead-center field and connected the left-field bleachers to the right-field wall. The clubhouse contained several large windows that faced the playing field, one of which was broken by a Roger Hornsby home run in 1929.

of their money reporting on sporting events—baseball, horse racing, boxing, billiards, and golf—often to satisfy the needs of gamblers. Most ballparks had press boxes, even before the founding of the Baseball Writers Association of America (BBWAA), because club owners saw the benefit of making it easy for newspapers to spread information about their product (and for free!). Writers sat in the open-air press boxes, sweating in the heat and freezing in the cold, bent over typewriters or pads of paper, filing their stories by telephone or telegraph. Most newspapers didn't send reporters to road games then, relying instead on telegraphed stories from reporters they hired in other cities. Eventually, advances in telephone technology made it easier to cover games from remote locations, and baseball writers would begin to travel with the teams they covered.

As the AL and NL learned to live together, finally reaching formal agreement for an annual World Series, both on- and off-the-field games grew and changed. Baseball was about to become more popular than ever before, which had much to do with a beautiful new series of ballparks that would be built beginning in 1909—ballparks that hold a unique place not only in baseball history, but in American history. After more than thirty years of dives, swamps, rock-strewn fields, hastily filled-in garbage dumps, blacktops, and racing ovals masquerading as successors to Elysian Fields, a

new spate of what would come to be called classic-era ballparks was on the horizon. Breaking new ground with their fireproof concrete-and-steel design, these venues would turn the crude baseball grounds of the past into modern civic icons. Following them would be the first ballparks known as stadiums, revered for their imposing size and unobstructed sight lines. The seating capacity of stadiums would be taken to new heights in the 1960s, '70s, and '80s, when ballpark architecture would be dominated by multipurpose concrete monstrosities. These superstadiums, some of which were enclosed by domes, became known as "cookie-cutter" parks for the striking similarity of their bowl-like shapes and symmetrical fields covered in fake turf. Beginning in the 1990s, however, baseball clubs and ballpark architects would come to see the error of their ways. Turning away from the often impersonal nature of the superstadiums, they drummed up a feeling of nostalgia by looking to the past for inspiration. Thus began the retro ballpark era, which brought baseball back outdoors to natural-grass parks usually featuring beautiful views of the surrounding city (as well as plenty of amenities for the well-heeled fan). Through their design and old-fashioned feel, these modern stadiums recall the classic fields—glories of their time that would help create some of the most durable and compelling sports mythology ever experienced in the United States.

BELOW: Built in 1902, Cincinnati's grand Palace of the Fans was the second ballpark (after Philadelphia's National League Park, later known as Baker Bowl) to use steel and concrete in its construction. The grandstand, however, was still made from wood. Here, an overflow crowd of 18,712 spectators fills the park on April 14, 1909, in a game against the Pittsburgh Pirates. The rows of fans along each foul line are part of "Rooters' Row," the section of the park where beer-drinking was allowed.

Ballparks of the Negro Leagues

As baseball clubs composed of white men began to form and inhabit green spaces across America, so too did black teams. However, while the white teams were able to build bigger and better parks as public interest grew and money began flowing in, black teams struggled. Among the many challenges facing the Negro Leagues during their heyday was finding proper facilities at which to play their games. Black teams, most of which operated on shoestring budgets, usually lacked the capital to build their own stadiums, so they had to rent them—and sometimes, they weren't even allowed to do that. Yankee Stadium, for instance, was famously off-limits to Negro League clubs until 1930. Fortunately, other major league teams were more accommodating. Washington's Griffith Stadium hosted Negro League games in 1924 and served as weekend home to the Homestead Grays beginning in 1937, and African-American fans in the nation's capital were delighted to sit in box seats to watch the Grays instead of segregated bleachers to watch the moribund Senators.

Chicago's Comiskey Park served as the site for the annual East-West Game, the biggest gala in Negro League baseball, beginning in 1933. "Oh, man, it was quite an affair," former Kansas City Monarch Buck O'Neil recalled. "The Illinois Central train and the City of New Orleans would put on a couple of extra cars, and they would bring people and pick 'em up in Memphis and all the way up. The New York Central would put on a couple of extra cars in New York City, and the Santa Fe Chief would put on a couple of extra cars coming out of California, picking up people along the way. It was quite an evening. I'll tell you what it was like: It was like a Joe Louis prizefight. Everybody was there, all of the dignitaries."

But most Negro League games were played in considerably less glamorous conditions than the East-West Game. One of the greatest teams of the 1910s, the New York Lincoln Giants, played at a tiny facility, the Catholic Protectory Oval. The Bacharach Giants played at an Atlantic City dog track. The Baltimore Black Sox played on a decrepit field they leased from the B&O Railroad. The Detroit Stars rented Mack Park, whose white owner neglected it to such a degree that the roof collapsed in 1929, injuring 100 fans.

Even when teams managed to secure adequate facilities, they usually did not control the stadium themselves, which resulted in scheduling difficulties. The Grays, for instance, had to work their schedule around those of the Pirates and Senators, the owners of Forbes Field and Griffith Stadium, respectively. The Monarchs did the same, playing at Muehlebach Field whenever the minor league Kansas City Blues were out of town. (Of course, the Monarchs generated much of their revenue on the road, pioneering night baseball by transporting a set of portable floodlights with them from town to town.)

Even Rube Foster—the founder of the Negro Leagues, and their most prominent entrepreneur—didn't own his own stadium. His Chicago American Giants played at Schorling Park, owned by Foster's white partner, John Schorling. Schorling had acquired the wooden stadium, formerly known as South Side Park, from his father-in-law, Charles Comiskey, whose White Sox played there until 1910 when Comiskey Park opened.

In 1922, the St. Louis Stars built one of the few stadiums ever constructed specifically for the Negro Leagues. Stars Park, located at the corner of Compton Avenue and Market Street in midtown St. Louis, had a capacity of 5,000–10,000 fans. According to historian Ann Morris in *Lift Every Voice and Sing: St. Louis African-Americans in the Twentieth Century*, Stars Park occupies a unique place in history: In 1929, it became the first ballpark in America to install permanent lighting for night baseball. Many years after the park's demise, former Stars legend Cool Papa Bell described it to author John Holway:

> It was a wood park. At first it didn't have a top on it. I guess it could seat around 5,000 people. It had a wood fence around it, and people almost cut that fence down by cutting peepholes in it. In right field they had a house sat on a corner there, must have been about 400 feet down the line. In left was a car shed. Down the line was 269 feet, then it would slant off to center around 500 feet. By the car barn was a track running beside there. If a right-hand hitter could pull the ball he could hit it up on that shed, but they had to hit it high—about 30 feet high. The car shed was the wall. Where the car shed ended, there you had a fence. There was plenty of room out there in center field; there wasn't anybody going to hit it out of there.

Despite its vast expanse in center field, Stars Park became famous for the short left-field porch described by Bell. Right-handed sluggers such as Mule Suttles and Willie Wells became adept at lofting shallow fly balls over the roof of the trolley car shed, resulting in booming home run totals. By one count, in 1929 Wells hit twenty-seven homers in eighty-eight official league games, a Negro Leagues single-season record. Longballs were so prevalent that during some years, balls hit over the car barn were considered ground-rule doubles. Stars Park's heyday was brief: The Negro National League collapsed in 1931 at the onset of the Great Depression, and the ballpark was sold to the city of St. Louis. Today, the site remains a baseball diamond, serving as the home field of the Harris-Stowe State Hornets, a historically black university competing at the NAIA level.

Stars Park was modest and homey, but those two qualities were steadfastly avoided by Gus Greenlee, builder of the most famous Negro Leagues park. Greenlee, a Pittsburgh gambling kingpin who also owned the legendary jazz club The Crawford Grill, decided in 1930 to dabble in baseball. He bought a local

LEFT: From 1923 to 1932, the legendary Hilldale club had their own grounds, Hilldale Park, located in Yeadon, Pennsylvania. Here, they pose in front of their scoreboard in 1925, the year they won their third Eastern Colored League pennant and their first Negro League World Series. Though the site, in the suburbs of Philadelphia, now holds a supermarket, a marker was placed on it in 2006 to honor the team.

BELOW: Before the 1910 season, Rube Foster, manager and pitcher for the Chicago Leland Giants (later the American Giants), took his team on an extensive tour of the South. Here, the team makes a stop in Foster's hometown of Calvert, Texas, and plays in front of an overflow crowd, said to be the largest ever to see a baseball game in that town. The next season, Foster's team will move into the White Sox's vacated South Side Park. Foster, considered one of the best pitchers in black baseball, will later go on to cofound the Negro National League and become its first president.

semipro team and set about transforming it into a championship caliber Negro League team. Naming the club the Crawfords after his famous nightclub, he purchased an empty lot at 2500 Bedford Avenue, which was owned by the Empress Brick Company and already used for occasional sandlot games. On this site he built mighty Greenlee Field, which used 75 tons of steel and 14 rail cars of cement, along with a facade of handsome red brick. Greenlee spared few expenses on the $100,000 park. Black players, usually forced to dress before arriving at white-owned parks that denied them access to facilities, were finally able to enjoy spacious locker rooms for both the home and visiting teams. The players were impressed not only by the amenities, but also the quality of the playing surface. Recalled Cool Papa Bell: "It was beautiful. It had lots of grass. It felt like you were playing in a major league park. The best thing for me was the big outfield. Plenty of room to run."

Greenlee Field's inaugural game on April 10, 1932, was attended by Pittsburgh's mayor, the city council, and, of course, Greenlee himself. "Gus made his entrance in a red convertible," historian Mark Ribowsky wrote in *A Complete History of the Negro Leagues*. "Surrounded by a marching band, he received a standing ovation from the capacity crowd of six thousand. Clad in a white silk suit and tie, Gus walked to the pitching mound and threw out the first pitch." The Crawfords won the game 1-0 behind a Satchel Paige shutout, scoring the lone run in a dramatic ninth inning. By year's end, some 119,000 fans had passed through the Greenlee Field turnstiles—65,000 of them for baseball and the rest for various other events, including a memorable football game between Wilberforce and West Virginia State for the black college championship.

Soon, according to some reports, the Crawfords were drawing 200,000 fans a year for baseball games alone—and this at the height of the Great Depression. Greenlee installed lights for night games, and kept the fans entertained with sometimes bizarre promotions, such as a pregame race between Jesse Owens and a racehorse (Owens won). However, according to Rob Ruck, author of *Sandlot Seasons: Sport in Black Pittsburgh*, "the ball park Greenlee built never achieved the level of patronage to turn a profit." Greenlee's tendency to hire white employees to work at the ballpark, Ruck asserts, turned off the African-American audience, which soon drifted away. Also, "the Depression undercut attendance, as did the failure of builders to install an awning over the grandstand, which could have shielded fans from inclement weather." In 1938, Greenlee Field, after just six years of existence, fell to the wrecking ball, replaced by a housing project, the Bedford Dwellings. "A purer racial interest should have been manifested to keep Greenlee Field out of the list of failures," wrote John L. Clark, a *Pittsburgh Courier* columnist and former Crawfords employee. "Greenlee field joins the list of...enterprises which should not be again attempted in this city for the next 100 years."

In fact, that is exactly what happened, not only in Pittsburgh, but around the country. Sobered by the failure of Greenlee Field and two other stadiums in which Negro Leagues teams had invested significant renovation funds—Dyckman Oval in New York and Hilldale Field in Darby, Pennsylvania—team owners decided that any further investment in ballparks was unwise. Never again would a ballpark be built specifically for a Negro League team.

LEFT: Bonnie Serrell of the Kansas City Monarchs tries to make it to first before Buck Leonard of the Homestead Grays makes a play at Griffith Stadium in 1942 or '43. The Grays played their home games at DC's Griffith and Pittsburgh's Forbes Field from 1939 to 1948. Because of its higher capacity, most weekend games were played at Griffith.

BELOW: Game 1 of the first Colored World Series, at Philadelphia's Baker Bowl on October 3, 1924. The Kansas City Monarchs of the Negro National League would triumph over the Hilldale Daises of the Eastern Colored League in the ten-game series (increased from nine games after Game 3 tied in thirteen innings). In an attempt to garner interest in the Negro Leagues, games during the '24 Series were held not only in Philadelphia and at Kansas City's Muehlebach Field, but in Baltimore and Chicago as well.

CHAPTER TWO

Classic Fields

1909   1915

Eight years after the advent of the American League completely redrew the map of the national pastime, baseball was about to experience another sea change. At the start of the 1909 season, the Philadelphia Athletics moved into glorious new Shibe Park, instantly hailed as the game's crown jewel. Shibe, along with 1909's other entries into the ballpark canon—Forbes Field in Pittsburgh (which some folks liked even more than Shibe) and St. Louis' rebuilt Sportsman's Park—ushered in baseball's first great ballpark era: the classic fields.

Between 1909 and 1915, thirteen state-of-the-art ballparks opened, and would eventually house every team in the American and National Leagues (Shibe, Sportsman's, and the Polo Grounds housed both AL and NL clubs). The profound impact of these baseball palaces is demonstrated by their longevity: ten of these parks hosted baseball for fifty years or more, and two still do. These intimate, idiosyncratic fields defined the growing national game in a way not seen again until the retro ballpark boom of the 1990s—which took its cues directly from the classic field era.

The classic fields had one major defining characteristic: they were fireproof. Built of brick, concrete, and steel, the parks were immune to the kinds of disasters that had plagued their wooden predecessors, from stands crumbling under the weight of large crowds to fires ravaging the entire park (and sometimes, parts of the surrounding neighborhood). With a more permanent, sturdier design and ramps to move people quickly up and down the grandstand, the parks were easier for spectators to navigate. They were also more comfortable for the players, who now had locker rooms both at their home parks and when traveling.

Club owners hoped that these classy new ballparks would lead to a higher-income fan base, and to that end every effort was made to make the parks opulent and luxurious, from designing impressive rotundas to installing the latest technological advances, such as elevators. Even the teams in older ballparks felt the pressure to spruce up for 1909, with nearly every field undergoing some sort of renewal as owners began to realize that the ballpark itself could be an attraction, even if the team was mediocre.

It was clear, at least to American League owners, that building a new ballpark on one's own grounds was now a key to staying financially competitive. They were restricted, however, by what land was available and what they wanted to spend. Many parks were built where their predecessors had happened to be, while others, such as Fenway Park, were constructed on cheap land that no one else wanted. Because these ballparks were squeezed in to fit on small and frequently odd-shaped parcels, the fields had unique and often quirky dimensions, and ground rules specific to each park were developed out of necessity.

By 1912, seven of the eight AL teams had new parks; and in 1913 the last holdout—the New York Yankees—moved into the Giants' Polo Grounds, which had been rebuilt with concrete and steel after a major fire in 1911. The National League owners were slower to understand the impact of the change wrought by Shibe and Forbes. In 1912 they had only three concrete-and-steel parks of their own. The Boston Braves, the final team to build a park during the era, played at the site of their original South End Grounds until they moved into Braves Field in 1915. The Cubs got a new park only after the upstart Federal League went bust and they inherited Weeghman Park (later called Wrigley Field) in 1916. The Cardinals and the Phillies, meanwhile, didn't move into the homes of their crosstown AL rivals until 1920 and 1938, respectively. The grand parks that were quickly erected by the American League helped it to gain even more prominence, and soon its reputation as a rowdy junior league would all but vanish.

Once a club owner took the plunge and built his own ballpark, he always tried to find ways to make it as profitable as possible. In the 1920s and '30s, one of the ways owners could ensure a return on their investment was to rent out their fields to professional football teams, which were just starting to be formed. This relationship would see a direct reversal during the superstadium era, when mutipurpose stadiums were built to house both teams but had the needs of football (by then the more popular sport) in mind.

Aside from renting out their homes for football, boxing, and other sports, baseball owners also allowed entertainers to put on shows on nongame days. Traveling "hippodrome" shows—proto-vaudeville acts with animals, singers, and fireworks—often set up shop in big-league parks when the host clubs were on the road.

At the time, "hippodroming" also had another meaning— throwing games. While people had been betting on games since the beginning of baseball, and many people within the industry knew that some corrupt players would take money

from gamblers, the situation came to a head when a Chicago grand jury indicted several White Sox players for throwing the 1919 World Series. Fans began to lose their confidence in the game, and baseball was in deep trouble.

Luckily, an unexpected trailblazer named Babe Ruth was reaching national prominence just in time to bring some much-needed sunshine to the national pastime. Ruth, perhaps the most charismatic sports star of all time, was funny and talented, gargantuan in both spirit and size. Traded to the Yankees prior to the 1920 season, the "Sultan of Swat" was talked about everywhere, as Joe DiMaggio, Ted Williams,

Jackie Robinson, Willie Mays, Mickey Mantle, Mark McGwire, and Barry Bonds would be later. The arrival of such a superstar with such a bat transformed the game from its focus on pitching, defense, and speed (a period of time now referred to as the "deadball era") to a game of home runs and high batting averages. As part of that transformation, vast Yankee Stadium, the "House That Ruth Built," would become baseball's newest Taj Mahal in 1923, ushering in the stadium era of major league ballparks. The unprecedented construction boom of the classic fields era had ended, yet the lifetimes of these seminal ballparks would far outlast their builders.

SHIBE PARK

Philadelphia, Pennsylvania

Athletics (AL) 1909–1954, Phillies (NL) 1938–1970

Connie Mack Stadium (1953–1976)

OPPOSITE: An aerial view from the southwest shows Shibe Park two days before Game 1 of the 1930 World Series between the Philadelphia Athletics and the St. Louis Cardinals. Connie Mack's team would defeat the opponent in six games to win their second consecutive world championship. Note the trolley lines along Lehigh Avenue in the foreground and the dense row house neighborhood of North Philadelphia just beyond Shibe. Despite what looks like a large parking area across North 21st Street (on the left side of the photo), the lack of available parking around Shibe/Connie Mack would become a major problem after World War II, when most fans would no longer be arriving by public transit.

In the first decade of the twentieth century, baseball was more successful than ever before: the newly formed American League had doubled the number of major league teams, a "World's Series" of baseball was inaugurated, and the popular song "Take Me Out to the Ball Game" was a bona fide hit. The game had gone from a casual pastime played in city parks to a revered sport, referred to as a "comparatively perfect flower of our sadly defective civilization" by the *Saturday Evening Post*. But it wasn't until the opening of magnificent Shibe Park that the first shot was fired in the revolution that would completely alter the physical landscape of the game.

In Philadelphia, it was only a matter of time before a battle would begin; with both the National League Phillies and the American League Athletics calling the city home, it was one of the largest markets in the major leagues. The teams had been sharing the same turf since the birth of the American League in 1901, when the Athletics had been founded by sporting goods magnate Ben Shibe and ingenious manager Connie Mack. After Mack's bid to bring some of the Phillies' best players to his own team was blocked by the Pennsylvania Supreme Court, he settled for simply getting them out of town by sneakily engineering a trade that took them to the Cleveland Blues. After that maneuver, the "Mackmen" consistently outdrew the Phillies, even though disgruntled NL New York Giants owner John McGraw had claimed they would never be profitable, nicknaming them the "White Elephants." After cheekily adopting a white elephant as their logo, in 1905 the Athletics stampeded off with their second AL pennant in three years, and Ben Shibe decided to build them a new park—one that would surpass all others in scale and scope and, more importantly, would allow him to sell twice as many tickets as Columbia Park, the Athletics' home at the time.

Refusing to skimp on costs by buying cheap property, Shibe selected a site just six blocks west of the Phillies' Baker Bowl. For the first time ever, a US city exercised eminent domain to secure a space to build a ballpark. After two blocks of houses on the site were bulldozed, William Steele & Sons began building the park that would bear Shibe's name in March 1908. In dramatic contrast to the plain brick and wood exteriors of the parks that had preceded it, Shibe Park featured French Renaissance pavilions more befitting a government building or major railroad station. Though it

FRANK "BLIMP" HAYES

"JOE" MARTY

GRANNY HAMNER
shortstop PHILADELPHIA PHILS

MAX BISHOP

BIG LEAGUE CHEWING GUM

ABOVE: Members of the 1914 Athletics pitching staff stand in front of a dugout just before the start of the season. From left to right are utility player Billy Orr; pitchers Herb Pennock, Weldon Wyckoff, Joe Bush, and Bob Shawkey; and centerfielder Amos Strunk. Future Hall of Famer Pennock would become known as "the Knight of Kennett Square," after his birthplace in nearby Chester County. The twenty-year-old left-hander went 11-4 in twenty-eight games that season, as the Athletics captured their fourth AL flag in five years. But it would be Philadelphia's last pennant-winning season until 1929.

BACKGROUND: Spectators watch from the stands down the right-field line at Game 2 of the 1913 World Series. The Athletics will defeat the Giants in five games.

would soon be surpassed in size by Forbes Field and others, Shibe was then by far the largest ballpark in the United States, with seating for more than 20,000—two-thirds more than the typical major league park of the time.

The $500,000 ballpark was also the first to be designed with safety in mind. To avoid the kinds of disasters that had afflicted nearby Baker Bowl, as well as most of the previous generation of firetrap wooden parks, Shibe's lower stands were made of reinforced concrete, the upper deck constructed of steel, and the entire structure was faced with brick. Seven grandstand and eight bleacher exits were installed to aid in quick evacuation if necessary.

On April 12, 1909, the baseball palace opened with 30,162 fans (well beyond the park's official capacity) crammed into the new venue, and thousands more turned away. The *Philadelphia Inquirer* called the new grounds "the largest, the handsomest, and the best equipped pavilions and bleachers ever devoted to sports in this or any other country"—an opinion shared by the fans, who were used to rickety wooden structures with uncomfortable benches and numerous poles blocking their sight lines, rather than real seats that had been arranged so that few had obstructed views.

Having started the grand ballpark revolution, the Athletics watched as other teams followed their pioneering lead and erected their own new parks. Yet most of these teams had one thing the Philadelphia clubs didn't: the ability to play ball on Sundays. For years, Connie Mack had been futilely petitioning lawmakers because Sunday games—the best attended match-ups in the major leagues, save for holidays—were prohibited in the state of Pennsylvania on account of the Christian Sabbath. In 1926, after a local exhibition honoring the city's sesquicentennial was allowed to charge admission on Sundays, Mack attempted to take matters into his own hands.

On August 22 of that year, the gates of Shibe Park opened for its first Sunday game. Though 12,000 fans came out to see their White Elephants win, protests from local killjoys forced Philadelphia mayor Freeland Kendrick to rule that

ABOVE: Crowds gather outside Shibe Park, at the corner of West Lehigh Avenue and North 21st Street, on October 9, 1914—the day of Game 1 of the World Series against Boston. The "Miracle Braves" will sweep the heavily favored Athletics in the Fall Classic, prompting an angry Connie Mack to purge his club, trading or selling off most of his best players. Mack will send five future Hall of Famers (Eddie Collins, Frank Baker, Chief Bender, Eddie Plank, and Herb Pennock) packing within a year, resulting in a string of seven consecutive last-place finishes for Philly.

LEFT: These architectural drawings show the ground-floor concourse and lower-deck seating of Shibe Park.

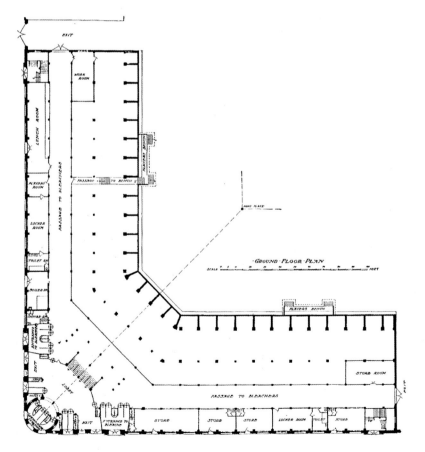

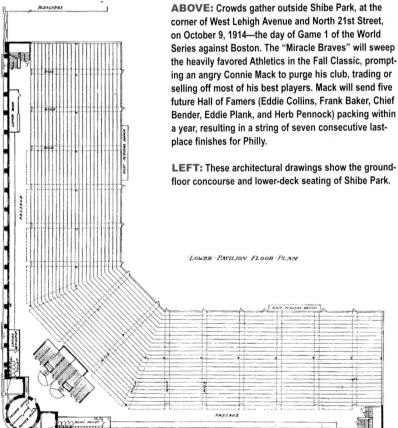

NEW PAVILION FOR THE AMERICAN LEAGUE BASE BALL CLUB, PHILADELPHIA, PA.
WILLIAM STEELE & SONS COMPANY, ARCHITECTS AND BUILDERS.

baseball on the Sabbath violated state law. However, the Great Depression softened men's hearts—or at least helped them see the economic benefits of Sunday ball—and, in 1934, Mack got his wish when the State of Pennsylvania allowed each city to vote on whether to uphold the blue laws. In both Pittsburgh and Philadelphia, the referenda passed easily, and Sunday baseball finally became a reality in the Keystone State.

Aside from the advent of Sunday baseball, the biggest baseball event in the 1930s in Philadelphia was the Phillies' becoming permanent tenants of Shibe Park. However, despite Sunday receipts and a National League team, Shibe Park's fortunes began to decline. Mired in on-field and economic hopelessness—the club could boast but a single pennant in fifty-five years of play—the Phillies had become the NL's perennial doormat club. Their AL counterparts were consistently wretched as well. Though the Athletics had captured three World Series in the first five years of Shibe Park's existence, from 1935 to 1946 they finished last or next to last every year but one. The fans stayed away in droves, and Shibe—now festering as other ballparks were expanded or spiffed up—began to look like a drafty old warehouse.

In the 1950s, the demographics of the United States began to change as people began to move to the West and the South, as well as from older industrial cities into the suburbs. Baseball redistributed itself to match the times, allowing troubled franchises to move for the first time in a half-century. With the floodgates now wide open, the Mack family sold their tarnished patrimony to corrupt Chicago businessman Arnold Johnson, who moved the refugee A's to Kansas City in 1955, where they played in a renovated minor league park (Municipal Stadium).

Left with only one team playing in a venue that had been new and wondrous in the 1910s, but was no longer fashionable nor aging gracefully, Philadelphia fans began to clamor for a new ballpark. Unfortunately, funding and logistics curbed the project for years. In 1958, rumors had the Phillies looking to ditch the city for the suburbs of New Jersey, supposedly for a park near the Garden State Race Track. Then in the early 1960s, the Mack family did what would have once been unthinkable: They sold the pioneering ballpark to Jerry Wolman, owner of the Philadelphia Eagles, who had played at Shibe in the '40s and '50s.

By this time, a new revolution in baseball stadiums had begun. Thanks to pro football's exploding popularity, the needs of NFL and AFL teams were largely framing the public discourse about stadiums.

Multipurpose superstadiums were opening up in cities across the country, and Wolman hoped Philadelphia would be next. However, even though Philadelphia voters approved a $25 million loan for a new stadium in 1964, the Phillies rejected the plans because the new facility would be, in their opinion, more advantageous for the Eagles. Nonetheless, that decision may have been shortsighted, as the result was pretty much the same: the Phillies would eventually leave Shibe for Veterans Stadium—a multipurpose facility that was designed around the gridiron instead of the diamond—but would first suffer through another six seasons in a thoroughly outmoded park.

Venerable Connie Mack Stadium (nee Shibe Park) finally closed its worn and tattered gates for good on October 1, 1970, seventeen years after the first talk of replacing it and sixty-one years after its opening. The old ball yard rotted away while the Phillies rose to power in their new park; the neglected venue was finally demolished six years later. Still, Shibe Park is remembered today as the grande dame of the classic fields, a glorious ballpark that changed the face of the national pastime.

OFFICIAL SCORE CARD

10¢   10¢

Philadelphia

Athletics

1937

1914 Manager Connie Mack, furious at the Athletics' World Series loss to the "Miracle Braves," starts breaking up his powerful club by selling MVP Eddie Collins to the White Sox.

August 15, 1915 Braves Field opens in Boston. It's the last of the thirteen classic fields built during the great ballpark boom that started with Shibe Park in 1909.

1921 Connie Mack's eviscerated Athletics finish last for the seventh consecutive year, losing one hundred games for the fifth time in that horrible stretch.

TIMELINE: SHIBE PARK

1909

Shibe Park opens on April 12. The first concrete-and-steel stadium, it is instantly hailed as the greatest park of its time, ushering in the modern era of ballpark construction. It opens with a symmetrical configuration of 360 feet down the lines, 393 in the alleys, and a staggering 515 to center.

ABOVE: Fans watch a 1910 game at Shibe Park from row house rooftops across North 20th Street.

May 18, 1912

Athletics Slaughter Ersatz Tigers The Athletics take on a team of amateurs when the real Tigers walk off the field an hour before the game. Three days earlier, Ty Cobb was suspended for climbing into the stands and brawling with a heckling fan in New York. As the Tigers walk out in solidarity with their star teammate, the majority of the 15,000 in attendance cheer. Then word spreads that Tigers manager "Hughie" Jennings is looking for last-minute replacements to avoid a $5,000 fine. Not surprisingly, once on the field, the A's destroy the team of amateurs and Tigers coaches in Tigers uniforms. The professionals will return to play their next game after a threat of expulsion from AL president Ban Johnson. As for the amateurs, each gets $50, and only one ever plays again.

Athletics 24, Tigers 2

April 12, 1909

Tragedy on Opening Day While Shibe's Opening Day is a financial success as well as a competitive one—with Eddie Plank cruising to victory in front of 30,162 fans—it ends tragically as Philadelphia catcher "Doc" Powers crashes into the grandstand wall while trying to catch a pop-up. (Powers was the club's regular catcher in 1901, playing thereafter as a reserve behind stalwart Ossee Schreckengost, mostly when Hall of Famer Eddie Plank was on the mound.) The veteran—who is also a medical doctor—suffers a grievous intestinal injury and leaves the game in the seventh inning. Despite three operations, Powers will pass away two weeks later.

Athletics 8, Red Sox 1

October 16, 1911

The Athletics Hit It Big In a rematch of the 1905 World Series (when they didn't score a single earned run against New York), the Athletics finally get a big hit. In the sixth inning of Game 2, Frank Baker cracks a tie-breaking, two-run homer against Rube Marquard. When Baker hits another crucial home run the next day against Christy Mathewson, the third baseman is dubbed Frank "Home Run" Baker. The A's will win in six games, becoming the first AL team to repeat as world champions.

Athletics 3, Giants 1

PHILAD
AMERICAN LEA

January 14, 1922 The victim of a car accident, Ben Shibe dies at the age of eighty-four. His son Thomas succeeds him as president of the Athletics.

1925 The Eastern Colored League Hilldale Daisies, playing in the Philly suburb of Yeadon, win the Negro World Series in a rematch against the Kansas City Monarchs after losing to them in 1924.

1928 The Philadelphia Stars, playing at Passon Field, win the Negro National League pennant. No Negro League games were ever played at Shibe Park.

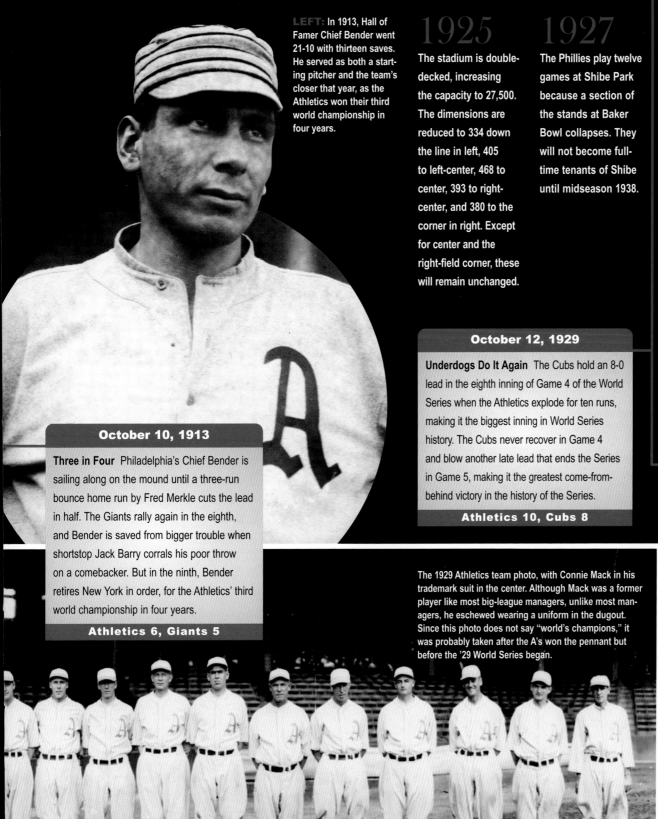

LEFT: In 1913, Hall of Famer Chief Bender went 21-10 with thirteen saves. He served as both a starting pitcher and the team's closer that year, as the Athletics won their third world championship in four years.

1925

The stadium is double-decked, increasing the capacity to 27,500. The dimensions are reduced to 334 down the line in left, 405 to left-center, 468 to center, 393 to right-center, and 380 to the corner in right. Except for center and the right-field corner, these will remain unchanged.

1927

The Phillies play twelve games at Shibe Park because a section of the stands at Baker Bowl collapses. They will not become full-time tenants of Shibe until midseason 1938.

1934

Connie Mack's tireless effort finally defeats the state blue law that effectively prohibited baseball on Sundays—a law that had been rigorously enforced since 1794. The first legal Sunday baseball game in Philadelphia is an exhibition game between the Phillies and Athletics.

1935

To spite the owners of nearby buildings who built bleachers on their rooftops and were charging admission to watch games, an iron fence is constructed in right field on top of the concrete. It nearly triples the height of the wall from 12 to 34 feet, and blocks the view across 20th Street.

October 10, 1913

Three in Four Philadelphia's Chief Bender is sailing along on the mound until a three-run bounce home run by Fred Merkle cuts the lead in half. The Giants rally again in the eighth, and Bender is saved from bigger trouble when shortstop Jack Barry corrals his poor throw on a comebacker. But in the ninth, Bender retires New York in order, for the Athletics' third world championship in four years.

Athletics 6, Giants 5

October 12, 1929

Underdogs Do It Again The Cubs hold an 8-0 lead in the eighth inning of Game 4 of the World Series when the Athletics explode for ten runs, making it the biggest inning in World Series history. The Cubs never recover in Game 4 and blow another late lead that ends the Series in Game 5, making it the greatest come-from-behind victory in the history of the Series.

Athletics 10, Cubs 8

October 8, 1930

The Cardinals Get a Series Pounding The Athletics win the World Series in six games against the Cardinals. Though he had pitched seven innings in the previous game, George Earnshaw shows up the Cardinals' Wild Bill Hallahan 7-1. It is the last of Connie Mack's five world championships, although he will win one more pennant.

Athletics 7, Cardinals 1

The 1929 Athletics team photo, with Connie Mack in his trademark suit in the center. Although Mack was a former player like most big-league managers, unlike most managers, he eschewed wearing a uniform in the dugout. Since this photo does not say "world's champions," it was probably taken after the A's won the pennant but before the '29 World Series began.

IIA "ATHLETICS"
ENNANT WINNERS "1929"

COPYRIGHT BY J. BODZIAK PHILADELPHIA, PA.

June 3, 1932

Lou Gehrig Hits Four Homers Lou Gehrig becomes the first American Leaguer to hit four home runs in a single game. When the record was set in the National League it was also done in Philadelphia—at the place later known as Baker Bowl—by Ed Delahanty of the Phillies, on July 13, 1896.

Yankees 20, Athletics 13

A Heckling Hero

Heckling—even directed against the game's biggest stars—has been part of baseball from the game's earliest days. Barry Bonds has nothing on Honus Wagner, who was so mercilessly taunted by Boston's "Royal Rooters" in the 1903 World Series that they made up a song about him. Babe Ruth, despite his status as a national icon, also received some of the nastiest insults ever visited on a player, even amidst his famous "called shot."

While many players have been famously heckled, perhaps the most famous heckler is Pete Adelis, a former newsboy who hung out at the ball yard on 21st and Lehigh so long (and loudly) in the 1940s that he gained the nickname "The Leather Lung of Shibe Park." The portly Adelis actually began his heckling as a hot-dog vendor at the park—ripping on the hometown players as he peddled his meats. Phillies management finally convinced their foghorn-voiced employee to razz the opponents—and a star was born.

Connie Mack, realizing he had a weapon on his hands, gave Adelis season passes and kept him at the ballpark as often as possible. And in 1948, the New York Yankees actually hired the boisterous heckler (with the Athletics' consent) to come to the Big Apple for a few days and give the business to the visiting Cleveland Indians.

Though Big Pete dropped from the headlines once the A's left for Kansas City, he left a legacy that even razzers today can learn from. Herewith, reprinted from the *Sporting News*, are Adelis' Seven Rules for Rooting:

1. No profanity.
2. Nothing purely personal.
3. Keep pouring it on.
4. Know your players.
5. Don't be shouted down.
6. Take it as well as give it.
7. Give the old-timer a chance; he was a rookie once.

1936 After selling superstar Jimmie Foxx to the Red Sox in the off-season, the Athletics take the field without one regular left from their 1929–31 pennant-winning teams.

June 12, 1939 The National Baseball Hall of Fame opens its doors in Cooperstown, New York, inducting twenty-six Hall of Famers, including Connie Mack.

1938

The Phillies move out of Baker Bowl and into Shibe Park for good on July 4.

1939

The first American League game under the lights is held on May 16 against Cleveland.

Athletics fans crowd the grandstand before Game 3 of the 1929 World Series against the Cubs. Philadelphia will lose this game but win the world championship in five games.

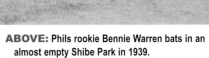

ABOVE: Phils rookie Bennie Warren bats in an almost empty Shibe Park in 1939.

LEFT: Bing Miller of the Athletics is tagged out at home by catcher Muddy Ruel of the Senators in a 1925 game. Washington will win the AL pennant by 8½ games over Philadelphia that year.

OPPOSITE: The last-place Mets face the fifth-place Phillies at the stadium on September 10, 1963.

1950 In Connie Mack's last season as manager, the once-proud Athletics finish last in the AL for the tenth time in sixteen years.

September 13, 1953 Former Negro League pitcher Bob Trice debuts with the Athletics, who become the fourth AL club to integrate. Trice will go 9-9 with Philly that season.

1961 The AL expands to ten teams, adding the Los Angeles Angels and the new Washington Senators, the latter replacing the club that moved to Minnesota in 1960 to become the Twins.

1940

The NFL's Philadelphia Eagles become the third tenant at the park. They will play here through 1957.

1953

The park is renamed Connie Mack Stadium for the man who ran the Athletics for fifty years and retired as manager at the age of eighty-seven.

1954

The Athletics play their final game in Philadelphia on September 19. They are sold by the Mack family and move to Kansas City.

1956

A "new" scoreboard is installed. It is actually the old one from Yankee Stadium.

1961

Beer is sold at the park for the first time.

1970

The shrine in Philly closes its doors forever. Much of the structure burns down in 1971 before the hulk of a stadium becomes home to a junkyard. After the remains of the stadium are leveled in 1976, a megachurch is built on the site in 1990.

September 28, 1941

The Kid Hits .406 Ted Williams completes a 6-for-8 doubleheader with a 2-for-3 nightcap against rookie Fred Caligiuri, giving him a legendary .406 average. But The Kid almost didn't play that day: In the first game of the series, he had gone 1-for-4, putting him at .3995. Manager Joe Cronin gave him the option to sit out the season-ending twinbill, since his average would round up to .400. Williams famously demurred, and his .406 season average will never be topped. Caligiuri, who debuted earlier in the month, will never win another game.

Athletics 7, Red Sox 1

August 17, 1957

Worst Seat in the House Philadelphia's Richie Ashburn, known for his ability to foul pitches off, accomplishes an unparalleled feat when he hits the same woman twice in one at-bat. The unfortunate victim—Alice Roth, the wife of *Philadelphia Bulletin* sports editor Earl Roth—is hit in the face with Ashburn's first foul ball. As paramedics tend to her broken nose, Ashburn fouls again, and this time the ball hits Roth as she is being removed on a stretcher. None of Roth's injuries are permanent, but Ashburn's odd record will be.

Phillies 3, Giants 1

October 1, 1970

Last Game In the tenth inning, Oscar Gamble singles in Tim McCarver for the final run at Connie Mack Stadium. The 2-1 victory enables the Phils to avoid last place by half a game, but it is the hunt for souvenirs that causes many of the 31,822 fans on hand to swarm the field and tear it apart.

Phillies 2, Expos 1

SPORTSMAN'S PARK

St. Louis, Missouri

Browns (AL) 1909–1954, Cardinals (NL) 1920–1966

Busch Stadium (1954–1966)

"PEPPER" MARTIN

OPPOSITE: With the Cardinals in first place, 1½ games ahead of the Dodgers, a near-capacity crowd of 31,468 fills Sportsman's Park for the first game of a day-night doubleheader between the two rivals on September 21, 1949. The separate-admission night game would pack in even more fans. The Redbirds win the first game 1-0, but lose the nightcap 5-0. Brooklyn will pull ahead a week later and take the NL pennant by one game over the Cardinals.

Sportsman's Park, when it is remembered at all in the annals of the classic fields, is recalled fondly as the home field for both teams in a gripping wartime World Series, the setting for some of Bill Veeck's strangest stunts, and the first field to be christened with the name of a beer. While the venue was home to the Cardinals for forty-six years, it is often forgotten that Sportsman's Park was originally built for that other team who played in the prosperous Gateway to the West—the St. Louis Browns.

The Browns were owned by shrewd businessman Robert Hedges, who had purchased the franchise—then the Milwaukee Brewers—after the team's inaugural season in 1901. The next year, he moved them to the Gateway City and rechristened them the Browns, after the defunct NL team that used to play there. During the 1902 season, the newcomers finished a relatively close second in the American League, and managed to outdraw the resident Cardinals by 17 percent—no mean feat considering that the Cardinals had already been playing in St. Louis for twenty years and had the better home park!

Feeling their oats, the Browns decided to build a new concrete-and-steel stadium on the site of their current home (also called Sportsman's Park). Though only two such structures—Shibe Park in Philadelphia and Forbes Field in Pittsburgh—were scheduled to open in 1909, it was clear that grand new fields were the way of the future, and Hedges was willing to build one, even if it came at great personal anguish. "This is the last ballpark I will ever build," the *Sporting News* quoted him as saying. "None who has not had the experience can estimate the care, worry, and annoyance that attach to the equipment of a modern baseball plant." Wanting to finish the park as soon as possible, Hedges even declared that the bleacher seats at Sportsman's should remain heat-warped wooden slats, even though they had been known to afflict unlucky spectators with splinters.

While the bleacher seats were barely nice enough for fans looking to see a game on the cheap, the box seats were only for the well-to-do—selling for the pricey amounts of $1.00 to $1.50, according to their proximity to the field. The high prices led some fans to balk at attending, but the new Sportsman's, which opened on April 14, 1909, was far

ELDEN AUKER

LARRY JACKSON

pitcher ST. LOUIS CARDINALS

ABOVE: The original tenants at Sportsman's Park, the Browns, are pictured here in 1909. The club placed seventh in the American League that year, a frequent fate for the St. Louisans: from 1901 through 1919, the Browns finished above fifth in the AL only twice.

RIGHT: This undated aerial photo of Busch Stadium, facing southwest, was taken in the mid- to late 1950s. Sportsman's Park was renamed in 1954, after Gussie Busch bought the Cardinals and the ballpark. The centerfield bleachers (in the lower foreground) had been closed that year, reducing the park's capacity to below 31,000.

better than the outmoded and hard-to-get-to League Park (later Robison Field) where the Cardinals played.

Eventually St. Louisans had no choice, as the Cardinals reluctantly moved into Sportsman's Park in July 1920. To take advantage of the attendance boom in both leagues after the end of World War I, the capacity was increased to 34,000 from 25,000 by expanding the second deck all the way down the foul lines. This tricky feat was accomplished

by moving the existing outfield pavilions in foul territory past the left- and right-field fences, and constructing permanent concrete bleachers in center field.

They didn't know it at the time, but the Cardinals' decision to move into the superior park is part of what made the franchise legendary. With more seats and nicer accommodations, Sportsman's was a fitting home for a permanent powerhouse. However, Sportman's holds the unfortunate distinction of

being the last major league park to keep a Jim Crow section, which wouldn't be done away with until 1944. What's more, the seats denoted for African Americans in the right-field bleachers were blocked by a large screen, preventing the fans from catching home run balls. (Oddly enough, despite the segregation in the stands, the Browns were one of the more progressive teams in terms of integration, mostly because the strapped team dove right into the new market for inexpensive former Negro Leaguers.)

In the three decades after the move to Sportsman's Park, the Cardinals won nine pennants and six world championships. Their AL landlords, however, became a perpetual laughing-stock after the 1920s, not winning a single pennant except at the end of their war-depleted 1944 campaign. "Even the Browns," the saying of the times went, could contend when the best players were inducted into the military for wartime service. And although they won only 89 of 154 games, the phrase proved true as the Browns squeaked past the Tigers on the final day of the season and made it to the World Series for the first time. But there was a fly in the ointment—the team they were playing was none other than the St. Louis Cardinals, who had bulldozed through the Senior Circuit to a 105-49 record for their third consecutive pennant. It was the third and last time that the World Series would be staged at a single venue (the Yankees and Giants had tussled at the Polo Grounds in 1921 and 1922), and the earth-toned Cinderellas capitulated to their scarlet elder sisters after a surprisingly exciting October Classic.

After the war, the Browns fell back into their cellar-dwelling ways, exacerbating the already tense relationship between them and their more fortunate tenants, while the care of Sportman's Park fell between the cracks. In 1951, the Browns' perpetual financial difficulties led to iconoclast Bill Veeck buying the sad-sack team for a bargain price after he had to sell his powerful Cleveland Indians to fund a divorce settlement. The maestro's famous promotional stunts—including hosting a "grandstand managers" night, in which fans voted on strategy moves via placards, and sending little person Eddie Gaedel up to bat during a game

against the Tigers—drew enthusiastic publicity, but couldn't pull the team out of its tailspin. Worse, Veeck's eccentricities earned him the ire of his fellow owners, resulting in the AL blocking his proposed move to Baltimore. Two years later, the isolated and desperate owner was forced to sell both his club and his ballpark.

Under new ownership by a group of Baltimore businessmen, the Browns were finally able to get out of town, and became the Baltimore Orioles in 1954. Sportsman's Park was sold to Cardinals owner and Anheuser-Busch brewery magnate Gussie Busch, who failed to get league approval to rename the stadium after his best-selling beer. League officials, thinking that naming the field "Budweiser Stadium" would be tacky, did allow Busch to name the stadium after himself, and one year after the stadium was christened "Busch Stadium," Busch beer was invented by the crafty owner.

After that, the story of the old St. Louis field ended like many of its Classic-Era brethren. Busch Stadium soldiered on into the mid-1960s, when it was replaced by a multipurpose stadium bearing the same name. Rarely remembered as the home of a historic field, the site presently contains a baseball diamond for the Herbert Hoover's Boys' Club.

ABOVE: A standing room–only crowd at Sportsman's watches the opening game of the 1946 World Series between the Red Sox and the Cardinals. The ballpark's capacity was listed as 34,500, but 36,218 tickets were sold that day—even though hundreds of seats were normally reserved for the out-of-town working press. Boston won the game 3-2 on Rudy York's tenth-inning home run.

1908 Vaudeville star Billy Murray scores a huge hit with his rendition of "Take Me Out to the Ball Game."

1911 A jury awards former Browns manager Jack O'Connor his would-be salary of $5,000, after he is fired because of allegedly coaching his players to help Cleveland's Nap Lajoie set a 1910 batting record (and win a car).

1909

The St. Louis Browns open the new Sportsman's Park on April 14. The old ballpark was rebuilt with reinforced concrete and steel, creating a modern facility holding more than 17,000. It measures 368 feet down the line in left and is 335 to the line in right. Center is vast, estimated at 430 feet.

October 9, 1910

The Decks Are Stacked for Lajoie Universal dislike of Detroit's Ty Cobb manifests itself on the field in St. Louis, where his Tigers aren't even playing. With the race between Cleveland's Nap Lajoie and Cobb for who will get the best batting average down to the wire, St. Louis manager Jack O'Connor purposely plays rookie third baseman Red Corriden deep. Lajoie, who tripled his first time up, lays down six more bunt hits during the twinbill. He also bunts for a sacrifice and is given a hit on a wild throw. The trickery costs O'Connor his job—a 47-107 mark for the club doesn't help—and it still doesn't give Lajoie the batting title. With an average of .383, Cobb is awarded the title by .007, and both players are presented Chalmers automobiles. However, a records discrepancy discovered decades later will prove that Lajoie actually had the higher average, at .384. Commissioner Bowie Kuhn decides Cobb's title should stand. It only seems fair, given how Lajoie got those extra hits.

**Browns 7, Naps 4;
Naps 3, Browns 0**

1912

A second deck is built down the first and third base lines.

1920

The Cardinals abandon Robison Field and move into Sportsman's Park. They share the facility with the Browns for thirty-three years, longer than any other pair of major league teams. The Cards will outdraw the host Browns in all but one season after 1925.

1925

Stands are double-decked all the way to the foul poles, with a covered pavilion in fair territory in right field.

October 3, 1920

Gorgeous George Hits 257 The Browns' George Sisler collects his 257th hit of the season in a rout of the disgraced White Sox, who just had eight players indicted for their part in the 1919 World Series fix. Sisler, a pitcher turned first baseman, even tosses a scoreless inning of relief. Sisler's hit total will go unmatched for eighty-four years, until Ichiro Suzuki of the Seattle Mariners breaks Gorgeous George's mark in 2004. However, Ichiro will do it in a 162-game schedule while Sisler, with a .407 batting average to Ichiro's .372, does it in just 154.

Browns 16, White Sox 7

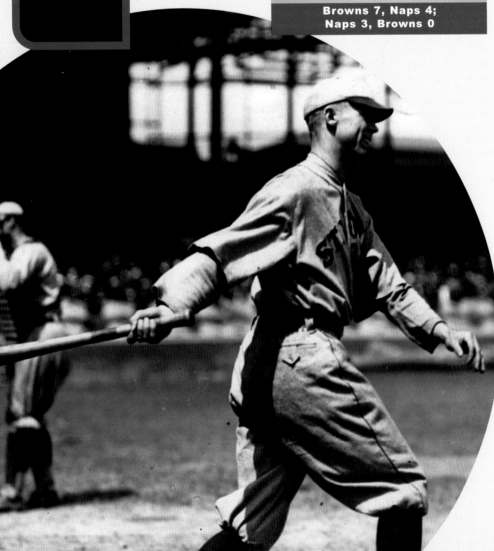

LEFT: Browns future Hall of Famer George Sisler practices his swing, probably during his rookie season of 1915. The icon of the Browns, Sisler boosted the normally bottom-feeding club in the 1920s, when it finished in the first division seven times in the decade.

CAP: 1926 (Cardinals).

1926 The Cardinals win their first NL pennant in Rogers Hornsby's only full season as player-manager, then defeat the Yankees in seven games in the World Series. The Redbirds will win the pennant again in '28 and '30.

1930 The Negro National League St. Louis Stars win their second NNL championship, two years after their 1928 title, never playing a game in Sportsman's.

1940 The Cardinals hold the first All-Star Game at Sportsman's, with the NL blanking the AL, 4-0, on Max West's three-run, first-inning homer off Red Ruffing.

1929

A screen is installed over the right-field pavilion; balls that hit it are in play. It remains until 1955.

1940

Lights are installed. The Browns flip the switch on May 24, losing to Cleveland and Bob Feller. The Cardinals debut at night in St. Louis on June 4, in a loss to Brooklyn.

October 10, 1931

Pepper Ends the Athletics' Streak After winning the two previous World Series, including one against the Cardinals, the Athletics' dynasty comes to an end—but not without a fight. The Cardinals take a 4-0 lead early in Game 7, thanks to a wild pitch, an error, and a two-run home run by George Watkins. Ready to close it up in the ninth, the Cardinals just miss turning a double play that would have ended the Series and given spitballer Burleigh Grimes the shutout. The A's follow with a walk and a single, and then pinch hitter Doc Cramer singles in two runs. With the tying runs on base, Wild Bill Hallahan takes Grimes' place on the mound, and gets Max Bishop to fly out to Cardinal favorite Pepper Martin. The Cards take the Series, and Martin, hitless in the final game, bats .500 in twenty-four at-bats in the Series. The A's, winners of nine pennants and five World Series in their first thirty-one years under Connie Mack, will not win another title in their last twenty seasons under their owner-manager. The Cards will defeat the Tigers in the World Series three years later, as brothers Paul and Dizzy Dean win four games for St. Louis.

Cardinals 4, Athletics 2

October 4, 1944

An All–St. Louis Series It's the first World Series game in the history of the Browns, and they are the visiting team in the stadium they own. Since the Browns and the Cardinals share Sportsman's Park, there are no travel days or restrictions. During the game, the Browns get just two hits—they come consecutively, and the second is a two-run homer to right field by George McQuinn. Browns pitcher Denny Galehouse doesn't allow a run until the ninth inning and the Browns win, 2-1. Jack Kramer will pitch a 6-2 masterpiece for the Browns in Game 3, but the Cardinals will ultimately take the last three from their landlord to win the championship.

Browns 2, Cardinals 1

BACKGROUND: Crowds arrive outside right field before the first World Series game ever played at Sportsman's. Game 1 of the 1926 Series pits player-manager Rogers Hornsby's Cardinals against Babe Ruth's and Lou Gehrig's Yankees.

1944

Sportsman's Park becomes the last major league stadium to integrate its seating. In October, the only all–St. Louis World Series is held at Sportsman's. The landlord Browns lose to the tenant Cardinals, one of seven world championships (in ten tries) the Cards win at the park.

October 15, 1946

Slaughter's Speed Beats Pesky's Throw In one of the most angst-filled games in Red Sox history, the Cards blow a 3-1 lead in the eighth inning of Game 7. Harry "The Cat" Brecheen relieves Murry Dickson with runners on second and third, nobody out, and the top of the Boston order coming up. Though Wally Moses and Johnny Pesky strike out, Dom DiMaggio doubles off the wall to tie the game. But then in the bottom of the eighth, with Enos Slaughter on first and two down, Harry Walker hits a shot to left. Generations of Red Sox fans will argue whether shortstop Pesky hesitated on the throw (and if it cost the Series), but Slaughter's speed is what allows him to round the bases and just beat the throw to the plate. The Cat allows two hits to start the ninth, but he retires the next three batters to win his third game of the Series. For the Cardinals it is the conclusion of the greatest run in franchise history: twenty-one seasons, nine pennants, and six world championships.

Cardinals 4, Red Sox 3

LEFT: The Cards' Enos Slaughter slides home with the winning run in the 1946 World Series at Sportsman's Park.

BELOW: The Cards and Yankees face off in the Fall Classic two years in a row, 1942 and 1943. In '42, the Cardinals beat the Yanks in five games for the world championship; the Bronx Bombers return the favor the following year.

BELOW, INSET: This sequence shows how one-armed outfielder Pete Gray would make a play in the field: he'd catch the ball, toss it up in the air, drop his glove, then grab the ball as it was falling and prepare to throw.

1953

New Cardinals owner August Busch buys the stadium from Browns owner Bill Veeck. The brewer tries to rename it Budweiser Stadium, but the other owners demur on such crass commercialism. He calls the stadium Busch and the next year unveils a new beer by the same name. A mechanical Busch eagle flaps its wings when a Cardinal homers. On September 27, the Browns play their final game in St. Louis before relocating to Baltimore.

April 17, 1945

Pete Gray Takes the Field One-armed outfielder Pete Gray makes his major league debut with the defending AL champion Browns. He singles once (off Les Mueller) in four at-bats, and handles no chances in the outfield. St. Louis beats the Tigers 7-1 for their ninth straight Opening Day win—a major league record that the 1975–83 Mets will tie. Runners take advantage of the relatively long time it takes Gray to transfer the ball from his specially made glove to his left hand, but during the season he fans just eleven times in 234 at-bats, and hits .218. Despite playing only in the final year of World War II, he is one the best-remembered players on a forgotten team.

Browns 7, Tigers 1

April 13, 1954 On Opening Day at Sportsman's, the Cardinals become the sixth NL club to integrate when black first baseman Tom Alston takes the field.

July 9, 1957 The AL beats the host NL, 6-5, in the third and last All-Star Game played at the park.

1963 Stan Musial becomes the first Cardinal to have his uniform number (6) retired. During his career he won MVP three times and was elected to the All-Star team twenty times.

1960

The NFL Cardinals, relocated from Chicago, join the baseball Cardinals at Busch. They will play at the park through 1965.

1966

The season opens at the old Busch, but the new Busch is soon ready. The Cardinals play their final game at the old stadium on May 8. A helicopter flies home plate to their new home.

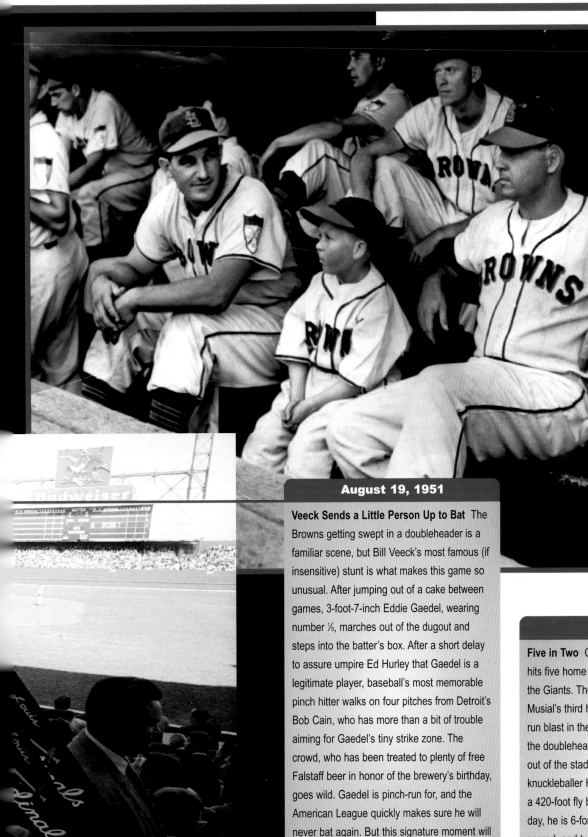

October 15, 1964

The Boyer Brothers' Blasts In each of the four previous Yankees-Cardinals World Series, the visiting team won the clincher, but the pattern is finally broken in St. Louis. With the Cardinals up 6-0 in the middle innings, the Yankees strike back with a three-run homer by Mickey Mantle. Ken Boyer, who won Game 4 with a grand slam, homers for an insurance run in the seventh. It's a good thing, too, as an exhausted Bob Gibson, the Series MVP, allows home runs in the ninth to Clete Boyer and Phil Linz (in between registering a new record with thirty-one strikeouts for the Series). Clete's blast marks the first time two brothers homer in the same Series game. The Cards have their seventh world championship, their third against the Yankees.

Cardinals 7, Yankees 5

August 19, 1951

Veeck Sends a Little Person Up to Bat The Browns getting swept in a doubleheader is a familiar scene, but Bill Veeck's most famous (if insensitive) stunt is what makes this game so unusual. After jumping out of a cake between games, 3-foot-7-inch Eddie Gaedel, wearing number ⅛, marches out of the dugout and steps into the batter's box. After a short delay to assure umpire Ed Hurley that Gaedel is a legitimate player, baseball's most memorable pinch hitter walks on four pitches from Detroit's Bob Cain, who has more than a bit of trouble aiming for Gaedel's tiny strike zone. The crowd, who has been treated to plenty of free Falstaff beer in honor of the brewery's birthday, goes wild. Gaedel is pinch-run for, and the American League quickly makes sure he will never bat again. But this signature moment will be remembered far longer than the Browns or venerable Sportsman's Park.

Tigers 6, Browns 2

May 2, 1954

Five in Two Cardinals hero Stan Musial hits five home runs in a doubleheader against the Giants. The Cards win the first game on Musial's third home run of the game, a three-run blast in the eighth inning. In the nightcap of the doubleheader, he hits two balls completely out of the stadium against future Hall of Fame knuckleballer Hoyt Wilhelm. Musial also hits a 420-foot fly ball for an out. At the end of the day, he is 6-for-8 with eight RBIs, six runs scored, and two walks. In attendance is eight-year-old Nate Colbert, who, eighteen years later, will become the only player in history to match the feat.

**Cardinals 10, Giants 6;
Giants 9, Cardinals 7**

ABOVE: Stunt pinch hitter Eddie Gaedel—all sixty-five pounds of him—sits on the Browns' bench in 1951 during his moment in the limelight.

FORBES FIELD

Pittsburgh, Pennsylvania

Pirates (NL) 1909–1970

Though the former site of Forbes Field has been re-graded, paved over, built upon, and completely bisected by a new street, it still remains a place of pilgrimage for many baseball aficionados. After visiting Forbes' last home plate and what's left of its outfield wall, reverent baseball fans find the bronze plaque in the sidewalk that marks the spot where, in the final game of the 1960 World Series, Bill Mazeroski's stunning leadoff home run in the bottom of the ninth soared over the head of the Yankees' Yogi Berra at the left-centerfield wall. Coming as it did on the last pitch of the last game of the 1960 season, the home run was not only the coup de grace in one of the biggest October upsets ever, but also marked the end of an era in baseball. The next year, expansion teams would be added, and Major League Baseball would begin its spread to the West. Forbes Field, an outmoded relic amongst new parks like Candlestick Park and the Astrodome, would be torn down ten years later.

When construction first began on Forbes Field on March 1, 1909, baseball had just seen expansion of a different kind—eight years earlier, a new league had fought its way into the majors, with one of its star teams, the Philadelphia Athletics, becoming one of Pittsburgh's cross-state rivals. This new "American League" not only sold tickets for half the price, they had stolen more than a hundred players from the National League—including such big-name talent as Nap Lajoie and Cy Young. To the further dismay of Pirates president Barney Dreyfuss, in 1906, the new Philadelphia franchise announced plans to open the first state-of-the-art baseball arena—the opulent, innovative Shibe Park—in Philadelphia. But Dreyfuss wasn't about to let his cross-state competition from a supposedly inferior league steal the headlines. After hearing about the projected scope of Shibe Park, he decided to build an even bigger and more upscale ballpark for the Pirates, both to honor his top-rated National League team and to increase his profits by drawing in crowds eager to experience the national pastime in the lap of luxury.

Less than four months after the cornerstone was laid, Forbes Field was ready to give the American League a run for its money. Upon the venue's opening, it was hailed as the grandest ballpark yet—as it should have been, since it cost a million dollars to build: twice as much as Shibe. "It is impossible to properly describe Forbes Field. It requires a personal visit to permit one to understand just how big and magnificent it is," Ralph Davis wrote in the *Sporting News*. During the first game, in which the Pirates faced off against the Cubs, he wrote, "the thousands in attendance…spent most of the afternoon looking about them, to gain some adequate conception of the magnitude of the undertaking just completed." The day's 36,388 attendance broke what was believed to be the all-time record (set the previous year at a raucous Pirates-Cubs showdown in Chicago), and even though the Cubs defeated the hometown nine, 3-2, the fans were euphoric. Especially so was one Pittsburgh gambler who had garnered $80 betting against the Bucs. His magnanimous gift to winning pitcher Ed Reulbach was a single quarter—particularly fitting since 25¢ was the price of the cheapest seats, which were wedged into a small bleacher section in right field. Most seats—aimed at the higher-income fans—were priced at 50¢ or more, a risky policy in a time when a table seat for Ziegfeld's Follies in New York was just a dollar.

But Forbes had the goods to back up the price. Other than Shibe Park, there wasn't a single outdoor sports facility comparable to Forbes, with its imposing double-deck construction, steel frame, and huge seating capacity. And the modern marvels! The ballpark's upper deck, which seated 5,500, not only drew considerable praise for its awe-inspiring views of the field, but for the installation of upper-deck restrooms so that fans didn't have to descend all the way to the lower deck for bathroom breaks. (Maids were even on hand to assist ladies in their facilities.) Rather than the usual stairways, an innovative series of inclined ramps allowed large throngs of fans to move easily between the upper and lower decks. In addition, two elevators—the first ever seen in a ballpark—were provided for quick access. The lower deck contained a grand walkway that the *Chicago Tribune* reported was "nearly as long as three city blocks and as wide as most streets." Public telephones, still relatively novel, were

Fans take in the stunning new Forbes Field on Opening Day, June 30, 1909. Well-known American Olympic track star Martin Sheridan said, after visiting Forbes in 1909, that the park was much larger and more impressive than Shepherd's Bush Stadium in London where the Olympic Games had been held the previous year.

BELOW: Called "Dreyfuss' folly" because it was located so far from downtown, Forbes Field still found an audience. Here fans arrive by horse-drawn carriage in 1909, the park's inaugural season.

installed by the Bell System at kiosks on the lower level. Only the view from the press box brought boos. On the park's Opening Day, sportswriter Ring Lardner complained, "You can almost see the playing field from the press stand….Honus Wagner looks like an insect!" The new era of concrete-and-steel stadiums had begun, and the Pirates proudly took their place as one of the top-drawing teams in the nation.

But with new parks sprouting up in St. Louis, Chicago, and Cleveland, Pittsburgh's palace quickly began to lose its shine. Though the Pirates' attendance levels at the beautiful

new ballpark had risen 40 percent in 1909, they quickly dropped back down to their pre-Forbes levels—and for the next fifteen years the park consistently drew below the NL average. In the mid-1920s, the Bucs returned to contention, and like most parks, Forbes was able to pull in the numbers when their team played well. Fans paid the high prices to see their home team take on the American League in the 1925 and 1927 World Series, but after the great Pirates teams of the 1920s aged away, Forbes Field would go more than thirty years (until the famous bout with the Yankees) without a World Series.

But the club's poor performance didn't stop Barney Dreyfuss from making a buck off his expansive edifice. Before his death in 1932, Dreyfuss raised plenty of money by renting out the park to traveling circuses, vaudeville shows, and other such lowbrow amusements; and beginning in 1939, Forbes Field (along with Washington's Griffith Stadium) hosted one of the greatest Negro League teams in history—the Homestead Grays. The dominant Grays featured a devastating duo of Hall of Famers: catcher Josh Gibson and first baseman Buck Leonard, two of the most powerful sluggers baseball has ever seen. Owner Cum Posey's legendary Grays won eight Negro National League pennants and three Negro World Series in the ten seasons they played at Forbes before the collapse of the NNL in 1948.

In the 1950s, as the Pirates began fielding weak teams that rank among the worst in major league history, the splendor of Pittsburgh's Palace faded like a neglected resort hotel. Given that nobody was expecting to see good baseball, there had been little pressure to expand the park or improve its amenities over the years. Soon the fans—just like their rivals in Philadelphia—wanted a new ballpark.

A proposal to replace Forbes Field was floated in 1948, and even though a site was finally chosen in 1958, the city of Pittsburgh couldn't free up the funding for another ten years; construction didn't begin until April 1968. An anachronism in the era of multi-use stadiums with fake grass and enormous parking lots, venerable Forbes Field hosted its final Pirates game on June 28, 1970. This time, the Bucs swept the visiting Cubs in a doubleheader, and afterward thousands of fans helped with the park's demolition by tearing numbers from the scoreboard, ripping phones out of the booths, and yanking electrical wires out of the walls. Souvenirs of a more official nature were given away in a postgame ceremony.

The following year, the park was damaged by fires and torn down, but a large portion of the red brick outfield wall survives on the University of Pittsburgh campus, still near Forbes' last home plate, scarred by untold numbers of spiked feet and entombed in Lucite in a hallway floor. Along with the plaque that marks Maz's 1960 home run, these silent souvenirs now stand as postmodern archaeological relics of a grand baseball palace that was once Pittsburgh's pride.

ABOVE: This remarkable upper-deck view shows Forbes' huge foul territory behind home plate; its tall, freestanding light towers along the ivy-covered brick outfield wall; the main scoreboard in the left-field corner; and the city's Schenley Park behind left field and center field. Here, the Pirates play the Giants in October 1966.

1909 The American Tobacco Company manufactures the White Borders series of baseball cards, which includes the instant-classic T206 Honus Wagner, and sells them along with packs of cigarettes. Still a red-hot collectors' item to this day, the Wagner card sold for a record $2.8 million in 2007.

1915 Player-manager Fred Clarke, who led the Pirates to four NL titles and racked up a .315 career batting average, retires after sixteen years with the team.

September 17, 1917 Pirates shortstop Honus Wagner, nick-named the "The Flying Dutchman," plays his last game at age forty-three at Forbes.

1909

The Pirates christen the park on June 30. The land was cheap and the stadium is deep: 360 feet to the line in left, 447 in center, and 376 to the right-field line.

July 17, 1914

Twenty-One Innings Babe Adams of the Pirates and Rube Marquard of the Giants each pitch twenty-one innings. Adams, one of the stingiest pitchers in history, doesn't allow a single walk. Finally, a home run by Larry Doyle breaks the knot and New York wins, 3-1. Adams will make his next start on four days rest and beat Boston, but Marquard will go on to lose his next (and final) ten decisions.

Giants 3, Pirates 1

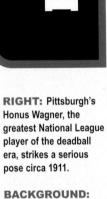

RIGHT: Pittsburgh's Honus Wagner, the greatest National League player of the deadball era, strikes a serious pose circa 1911.

BACKGROUND: From behind home plate, this 1911 photo shows Forbes' original wooden outfield walls and the scoreboard in right field. The right-field grandstand in fair territory won't be built until 1925; the familiar brick outfield wall won't be built until after World War II.

October 8, 1909

Forbes First Series A crowd of 29,264 sees Game 1 of the World Series—the first Series game at Forbes Field. Manager Fred Clarke goes with rookie Babe Adams, who allows a first-inning run but keeps Detroit scoreless the rest of the game. Detroit's George Mullin, a twenty-nine-game winner during the season, allows Clarke's game-tying home run in the fourth inning, but the Bucs end up taking the game on three unearned runs.

Pirates 4, Tigers 1

October 20, 1920

The Pirates Salvage a Triplebill Played to determine who gets the third-place money— it goes to the Reds—the last tripleheader of the majors is held at Forbes Field. After dropping the first two by scores of 13-4 and 7-3, Pittsburgh takes number three. The Pirates drag themselves onto a train that night and win the season finale in Chicago the next afternoon.

Pirates 6, Reds 0

August 5, 1921

Pirates Beat the Phillies Over Radio The Pirates score three times in the eighth to beat the Phils, but the big achievement is off the field: the first major league radio broadcast is heard over KDKA in Pittsburgh, with Harold Arlin, who also broadcast the first football game (Pittsburgh vs. West Virginia), at the microphone. KDKA becomes the world's first commercial radio station to schedule broadcasts of baseball games on a regular basis.

Pirates 8, Phillies 5

1927 The Pirates win a tight NL pennant race before being swept in the World Series by perhaps the best team in baseball history, the "Murderers' Row" Yankees.

1932 After slugging seventy-five homers with the Negro National League Homestead Grays in '31, the legendary Josh Gibson joins the NNL Pittsburgh Crawfords. Gibson will die tragically at age thirty-five, months before Jackie Robinson breaks the major league color barrier in 1947.

May 24, 1935 The era of night baseball begins at Crosley Field in Cincinnati. Forbes will be electrified five years later in 1940.

1925

A double-decked grandstand is added in right field, increasing capacity from 25,000 to 41,000. Distance down the line is reduced by 76 feet.

1930

The distances in left and center are increased to 365 and 435, respectively. The cavernous area to the left of center is reduced 5 feet to 457.

1932

A screen is added in right field to discourage "cheap" home runs.

1933

The Pittsburgh Pirates football team (renamed the Steelers in 1940) is founded. They play at Forbes Field through 1963.

1934

A granite memorial to late owner Barney Dreyfuss is erected near the exit gate to mark the twenty-fifth anniversary of Forbes Field. It will later be moved to Three Rivers Stadium.

1938

A press box, known as the Crow's Nest, goes up on top of the roof behind home plate.

October 15, 1925

Pirates Sail Ahead in the Rain Muddy Forbes Field is magical for the Pirates, who become the first team to win a World Series after going down three games to one. Washington shortstop Roger Peckinpaugh, the AL MVP, homers to snap a tie in the eighth, but his two errors (his last of eight miscues in the Series) undo the Senators. Worse still are the rain and fog, which make it impossible to find a fly ball hit by Pirate Kiki Cuyler. After much discussion amongst the umpires, it's ruled that the ball bounced into the stands, doubling in two runs. Relief pitcher Rey Kremer benefits from the comeback, and the Pirates have their first world championship since 1909.

Pirates 9, Senators 7

May 25, 1935

Babe's Last Home Run Babe Ruth has one last bit of magic left, as he launches three home runs at Pittsburgh. The final one, which some estimate flies a whopping 600 feet, is the last of his 714 career blasts and the first to clear the right-field grandstand at Forbes. Despite this remarkable accomplishment, the inept Braves still can't win. Future Hall of Famer Waite Hoyt, the Bambino's former teammate with both the Red Sox and the Yankees, picks up the win for Pittsburgh in relief.

Pirates 11, Braves 7

CUYLER PIT.

6424-4

BATTER
BALL STRIKE
OUT
INFIELD

ABOVE: Pittsburgh outfielder Kiki Cuyler poses on the field with his cudgel in 1925. Cuyler hit .357 that year and led the NL with twenty-six triples as his Pirates won the franchise's second world championship, beating Washington in seven games in

July 11, 1944 In the twelfth Midsummer Classic, the NL defeats the AL 7-1 at Forbes, as Pittsburgh's Rip Sewell pitches three hitless innings.

December 21, 1947 The Philadelphia Eagles beat the Steelers 21-0 for the Eastern Division title in the only NFL playoff game Forbes Field will ever host.

April 17, 1955 Hall of Famer and Pirates fan favorite Roberto Clemente makes his big-league debut in a Sunday doubleheader against the Dodgers.

1939

The legendary Homestead Grays of the Negro Leagues begin play at Forbes Field. (They also play out of Griffith Stadium in Washington.) The Grays will host games at Forbes through 1948.

1940

Lights are added, and the first night game is held June 4.

1943

Although no advertisements ever appear on the ballpark walls, a promotion for war bonds, in the form of a wooden statue of a marine, is added. The giant statue is 32 feet high and 15 feet wide, and stands against the wall in left field for the last three months of the season.

1946

Brick walls replace concrete; ivy is planted at the base of the new outfield wall.

1947

Box seats are added behind home plate. Slugger Hank Greenberg joins the team, and the bullpens are moved from foul territory to left field, bringing the fence 30 feet closer (51 feet nearer in left-center). "Greenberg Gardens" doesn't do much for the aging, right-handed slugger, but Ralph Kiner will hit 175 home runs at Forbes Field as a Pirate.

1954

With the trade of Ralph Kiner, the shortened left field, subsequently dubbed "Kiner's Korner," comes down. The bullpens go back to foul territory, and left field reverts to its previous distance. A new left-field scoreboard that rises 25½ feet high makes it even harder to hit home runs.

1955

An 18-foot-high statue of Honus Wagner is erected outside the stadium in Schenley Park. It will later be moved to Three Rivers Stadium, and then to PNC Park.

May 28, 1956

Long's Long Run Dale Long of the Pirates goes deep against Brooklyn's Carl Erskine in a 3-2 Pittsburgh win. It is his eighth home run in as many games, a record that will stand until Don Mattingly ties it in 1987. During Long's binge, the Pirates are 7-1 and pitcher Bob Friend picks up three wins. However, the streak will come to and end in the following game, when Brooklyn's Don Newcombe skunks the Pirates, including Long.

Pirates 3, Dodgers 2

LEFT: Looking a little melancholy, the Cuban All-Stars pose in front of an empty grandstand at Forbes Field sometime in 1942. Within a few short years of Jackie Robinson's entry into the major leagues, empty grandstands would become the norm at Negro League games. By the mid-1950s, the all-black game would just about disappear.

July 7, 1959 Forbes hosts the first of two All-Star Games played this year; the second game is scheduled for August 3 at Los Angeles Memorial Coliseum. In Forbes' second and last Midsummer Classic, the NL beats the AL 5-4.

October 3, 1970 Umpires strike for the first time, and AAA umps are called in for the Reds-Pirates playoff game.

1971 Led by Roberto Clemente, the Pirates take the Baltimore Orioles in seven games during the World Series.

October 13, 1960

Losing Pirates Win the Series Coming into the Series, the Yankees were on a fifteen-game winning streak, while the Pirates, whose last World Series appearance was a sweep at the hands of the Yankees in 1927, hadn't won a Series game in thirty-five years. In the deciding Game 7, the Pirates rally from a 7-4 deficit in the eighth inning, only to blow the lead in the top of the ninth. But when Bill Mazeroski homers in the bottom of the ninth off Ralph Terry, Game 7 is ended on a home run for the first time in World Series history, and Pittsburgh is sent into unmatched celebration. The home run isn't the only historic World Series event: Bobby Richardson is the first MVP from a losing team, as the Yankees doubled Pittsburgh's scoring output despite losing the Series. Yankees manager Casey Stengel will be "retired" after the season, even with seven world championships since 1949.

Pirates 10, Yankees 9

1970

The grand park closes June 28 with a double-header against the Cubs, the same team the Bucs played to open the place. No pitcher ever tossed a no-hitter in nearly 5,000 games at Forbes Field.

1971

The park is torn down, but portions of the left-field wall remain. Home plate is encased in plastic in the floor of the Forbes Quadrangle building on the University of Pittsburgh campus.

CAP: 1970 (worn by Dock Ellis).

LEFT INSET: Bill Mazeroski, the Steel City's new hero, approaches home plate after hitting his historic walk-off home run.

RIGHT INSET: Pirates fans swarm over the field and scoreboard to grab souvenirs after the last game is played at Forbes Field on June 28, 1970.

BACKGROUND: Pittsburgh players leave the field seconds after the last out at Forbes is recorded—and just before the fans spill out of the stands and trash the historic ballpark.

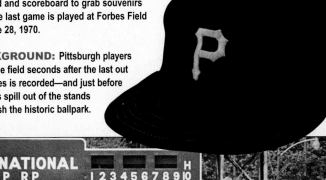

LEAGUE PARK

Cleveland, Ohio

Indians (AL) 1910–1946

Dunn Field (1920–1926)

Before artificial turf, retractable domes, and even lighting for nighttime games, what made new baseball stadiums impressive and revered was sturdy, fireproof concrete and steel. These state-of-the-art building materials, which had instantly become the industry standard with the erection of Shibe Park in 1909, were just what Cleveland's rickety League Park needed to draw in crowds in the rapidly growing sixth-largest city in the United States. The cost: a modest $300,000, 40 percent less than Shibe Park and less than half the price of the new Comiskey Park being raised on Chicago's South Side. Cleveland got its new-and-improved stadium on the cheap, and it showed. As nondescript as its name, League Park was without question the least successful of the classic field–era parks. In fact, only twenty-two years later, it would be the first of that era to see its replacement rising across town. It was also unique in two other ways, both negative: It was the only modern field never to be illuminated, and the only field of its time that was never substantially expanded.

When the gates first opened on April 21, 1910, however, Cleveland had high hopes for its refurbished park. More than 18,500 shivering patrons braved freezing weather to come out to see the Naps (as the Indians were known until 1915) on Opening Day—by far the biggest crowd ever to turn out for a baseball game in Cleveland. All concerned politely said that it was a grand new park, though maybe not quite in the class of Shibe or Forbes...but what could one expect from the relatively small expenditure? The grandstands were now concrete and steel, a new entrance more efficiently handled traffic flow, and the playing surface had an improved grading, but these innovations were not exactly at the level of the grand palazzos built to house the national game in Philadelphia, Chicago, and Pittsburgh. Though it was lacking in luxury, what the new League Park did have was plenty of good seats for the middle-income fan. For only 50 to 75¢, patrons could snag one of the more than 18,000 grandstand or pavilion tickets—a huge offering for a park that had a relatively small capacity of 21,000.

But the Indians couldn't even fill the small number of seats, as the team was beset by a combination of poor play, poor management, and bad luck. The tribe continued its pre–League Park losing streak and captured only one American League pennant and one world championship (in 1920) in its first twenty-two seasons at the park. In 1932,

they began playing their home games at the cavernous new Lakefront Stadium (later to be renamed Municipal Stadium and then Cleveland Stadium), built a few years earlier by the City in a vain attempt to forge a partnership with the team's owner, Alva Bradley. Though they moved between League and Lakefront from 1932 to 1946, the Indians didn't take up permanent residence in the city's mammoth white elephant until the team's new owner, Bill Veeck, negotiated a deal with the City beginning with the 1947 season.

Most of the concrete and steel so proudly assembled in League Park was demolished in 1952, with the city preserving the field for amateur baseball. While the site—which still holds the ticket booths and a small part of the grandstand—had been poorly maintained and virtually forgotten (a state historical marker designating the site of League Park wasn't erected until 1979), the city of Cleveland has now proposed rebuilding part of League Park, using some bricks from the original structure. Though a large amount of money has yet to be secured for the project, the city has appropriated several million dollars for it, and supporters are optimistic. In what can only be termed an odd twist of history, this failed classic field may be resurrected once again.

JOSS CLEVELAND

"ROLLIE" HEMSLEY

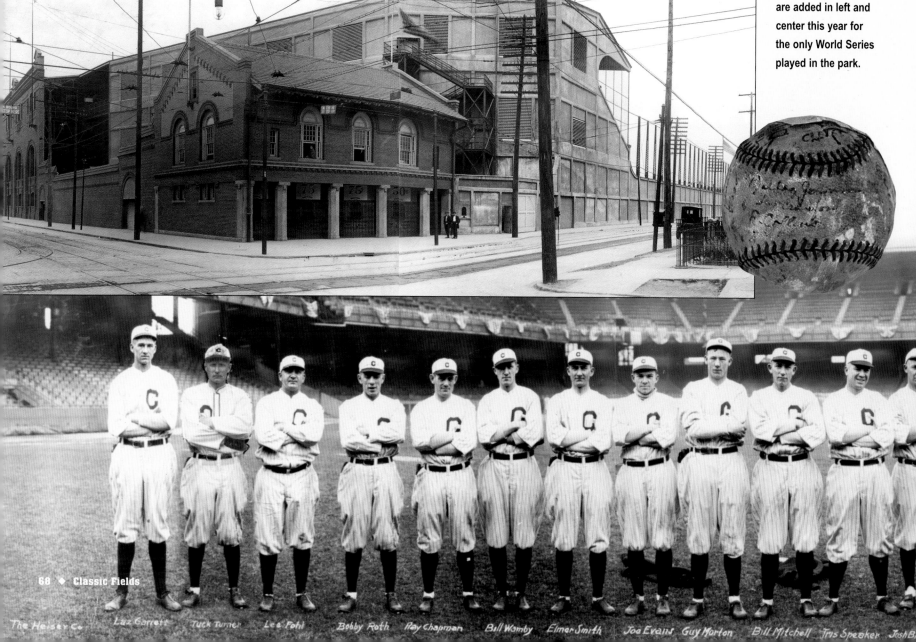

1916 The Red Sox trade Tris Speaker to Cleveland, where "the Grey Eagle" will spend the next eleven years, leading the Indians to their first world championship in 1920 as player-manager.

April 6, 1917 The United States enters World War I, fighting in Europe until November 1918. Baseball will play abbreviated schedules in 1918 and 1919.

August 16, 1920 In a pennant-race showdown against the Yankees, Indians shortstop Ray Chapman is struck in the head by a Carl Mays fastball. He dies the next morning at age twenty-nine.

1910

Cleveland's ballpark is rebuilt in concrete and steel with a brick exterior. Opening Day capacity is 21,000, and the field dimensions are 385 feet to left field, 420 to center, and 290 to right.

September 27, 1914

Nap on the Job Napoleon Lajoie, namesake of the Cleveland Naps, collects his 3,000th hit with a first-inning double against New York—the third player in baseball history to reach the milestone figure. After starting his career 0-13, Cleveland's Guy Morton gets his first major league win. The game is one of Lajoie's last with Cleveland; he will soon depart for Philadelphia, where he will play his final two years for Connie Mack's Athletics. As a result, the Cleveland team will be renamed the Indians.

Naps 5, Yankees 3

BELOW, LEFT: This undated composite photo shows League Park from behind the right-field grandstand, facing the team office building and ticket offices at the corner of 66th and Lexington. The premises is now part of a city park and recreation center, which includes the site of the original League Park diamond and the office building, renamed "League Park Center." Though poorly maintained, a portion of the first base grandstand along East 66th Street remains today.

BELOW, RIGHT: This autographed baseball dates back to League Park's "Addie Joss Day" on July 24, 1911, an exhibition game that pitted Cleveland against a squad of AL All-Stars. Staged as a benefit for Addie Joss' widow, Lillian, and their two children, the event raised $12,914. The well-respected and very popular Joss had died on April 14 from tubercular meningitis, two days after his thirty-first birthday. Joss led the AL in ERA twice and hurled two no-hitters in his career. Though he only played for nine seasons, Joss was elected to the Hall of Fame in 1978 after the ten-year minimum was waived by the Veterans Committee. Note faded signatures of Hall of Famers Walter Johnson, Sam Crawford, and E. (Eddie) Collins, from top to bottom.

1920

Recessed bleachers in left field make the playing field's dimensions even more vast. It's now 408 feet to left-center field and 431 to the power alley just left of center, yet right field is only 290 with a 44-foot-high fence, complete with protruding beams. The park is renamed Dunn Field after the team's new owner, but will revert back to League Park in 1927. Bleachers are added in left and center this year for the only World Series played in the park.

1939 The Baseball Hall of Fame opens in Cooperstown, New York.

1947 The Cleveland Buckeyes win the Negro American League pennant but fall to the Negro National League New York Cubans in five games during the Negro World Series.

1932

Cavernous Cleveland Municipal Stadium opens on the lakefront in July. The Indians play every 1932 game at the new 78,000-seat ballpark, but will alternate between it and League Park for most of the next fourteen years.

1939

The Negro American League's Cleveland Bears begin a two-season residence at the park. In 1943, the NAL's Buckeyes will move in, playing at the park through 1948 and then in 1950.

1946

League Park hosts its last major league game on September 21. It will be demolished in 1951.

LEFT: Cleveland's "natural" and one of the greatest pitchers in history, Bob Feller served in the Navy for more than three years during World War II. "Rapid Robert" is seen here in March 1943, donning cold-weather battle dress on the battleship *Alabama*. Though better known for her participation in many battles in the Pacific, the *Alabama*'s first wartime service was actually with the British Home Fleet, assigned to protect Lend-Lease convoys headed to the Soviet Union on the "Murmansk Run." Feller supervised a crew manning twin 40-mm Bofors antiaircraft guns, like those in the background. Unlike many major leaguers, who kept playing as long as they could before being drafted, Feller enlisted the day after Pearl Harbor—despite having a deferment due to his father's illness.

October 10, 1920

A Rare Triple Play Although Game 5 of the World Series is a rout, fans witness three important firsts in Series history. In the first inning, Cleveland's Elmer Smith hits the first grand slam ever in the World Series. And in the fourth, Indians hurler Jim Bagby smashes a homer of his own, the first ever hit by a pitcher in Series play. Although Bagby is roughed up for thirteen hits, he gets out of every jam—thanks in part to the most famous play in League Park annals. With nobody out in the fifth, Brooklyn pitcher Clarence Mitchell hits a line drive up the middle. The ball is snagged by lunging shortstop Bill Wambsganss, who steps on second base to double off Pete Kilduff and then tags the stunned Otto Miller, who had been running from first. It's the first unassisted triple play in Series history, and only the second in the majors during the twentieth century. Two days later, Stan Coveleski will toss a shutout here to clinch the Indians' first world championship.

Indians 8, Robins 1

May 17, 1925

Speaker in the House Cleveland player-manager Tris Speaker gets his 3,000th career hit against Washington's Tom Zachary. He will finish his career with 3,514 hits, second only to Ty Cobb, and remains the all-time doubles leader with 792.

Senators 2, Indians 1

RIGHT: Two women prepare scorecards for a game in League Park in 1940. The woman on the left is operating a machine that "saddle stitches" the scorecard into a booklet (i.e., staples them through the folds of the pages).

BELOW: The 1916 Indians line up for a panoramic photo at League Park. Third from left is manager Lee Fohl. The image of third baseman Terry Turner (labeled here as "Tuck"), second from left, was spliced into the negative after the photograph was taken.

August 11, 1929

Five Hundred and Counting In just his tenth season as a full-time hitter, Babe Ruth slugs his way into uncharted territory. The Bambino smashes his 500th career home run at League Park off the Indians' Willis Hudlin. Ruth is the first to reach the 500 milestone, and his career total is more than double that of the second-place home run hitter.

Indians 6, Yankees 5

y Chanelle Jack Graney ma Larry Tom Daley Jim Bagby Ed Klepfer Herbert Kelley Stanley Coveleski Ivan Howard Steve O'Neill Chick Gandil Rip Hagerman Fritz Coumbe

THE HEISER CO.

COMISKEY PARK

Chicago, Illinois

White Sox (AL) 1910–1990

White Sox Park (1967–1975)

BILLY PIERCE
pitcher CHICAGO WHITE SOX

OPPOSITE: Fans pour into Comiskey Park on July 11, 1950, for the second All-Star Game ever held there. The first, in 1933, was also the first All-Star Game in major league history. The brainchild of Arch Ward, a sports writer for the *Chicago Tribune*, the first All-Star Game was to be a one-time event as part of Chicago's centennial celebration. The exhibition was such a hit, however, that it became an annual affair. The 1950 contest, the first Midsummer Classic to ever go to extra innings, featured Jackie Robinson, Pee Wee Reese, and Stan Musial for the NL, and Yogi Berra, Larry Doby, and Ted Williams for the AL. The lone player from the White Sox, pitcher Ray Scarborough, never made it onto the field. Meanwhile, Ted Williams ran into the wall while chasing a hit off Pittsburgh's Ralph Kiner and broke his elbow. The National League won the game (4-3 in fourteen innings), and Williams was out of commission until September.

On July 11, 1990, just months before Comiskey Park closed its doors forever, the Chicago White Sox held what is believed to be the first ever "Turn Back the Clock" day at a big-league park. The exploding scoreboard sat dark and unused, lineups were announced by megaphone, popcorn was sold for a nickel, and the players donned the black-and-white pinstripes of their 1917 counterparts. The hugely successful promotion didn't just help spark a new industry for vintage jerseys—it was a fitting tribute to a storied ballpark. In 1917, Comiskey Park was still several years from the breaking of the "Black Sox" gambling scandal, which would be a very public loss of innocence for the national pastime. Still further in the future lay the racial unrest of the 1970s, some of which took place on Comiskey's very field, reflecting the forces tearing not only at the city of Chicago but at the nation as a whole. In 1917, baseball was still relatively pure, and the Sox—one of the nation's top-drawing clubs—not only had the best team in the league, but one of the best parks in the world.

Comiskey Park first opened its gates on July 1, 1910, just nine years after the Chicago White Sox (initially called "The White Stockings") became one of the first teams in the brand-new American League, cofounded by Sox owner Charles Comiskey. Comiskey took a handful of players from his former team in St. Paul, along with some stars from the rival National League, and set up shop at Chicago's South Side Park, a risky site for a sport that had been much more popular on the west side of town. Known for being as hard-nosed as he was frugal, Comiskey (often called "The Old Roman" by the press) was also a magnetic personality who loved nothing more than winning. After his players won the AL pennant in the league's opening year of 1901 and again in 1906 (along with the newly christened "World's Series"), Comiskey decided to reach deep into his pockets to build a park worthy of the team—and his family name.

The park went up in just 3½ months, on land purchased from former Chicago mayor John Wentworth. On Opening Day, fans streamed into Comiskey Park serenaded by a brass band, and gazed in wonderment at its size and scope. With its large footprint, gleaming concourse lined with lush ferns, and innovative exterior wall design—allowing sunlight to

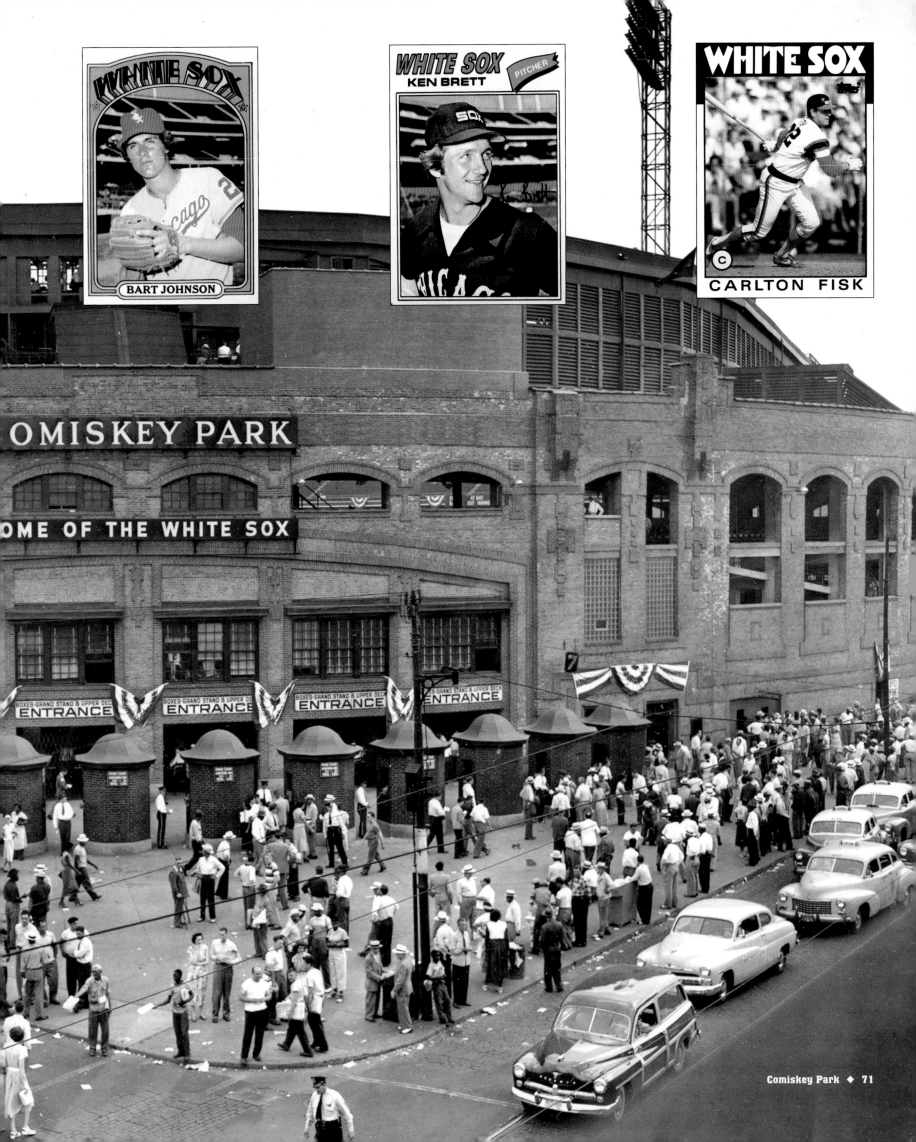

WHITE SOX

BART JOHNSON

WHITE SOX
KEN BRETT
PITCHER

WHITE SOX

CARLTON FISK

COMISKEY PARK

HOME OF THE WHITE SOX

ABOVE: Comiskey cost $750,000 to build and went up quickly, especially considering the cool Chicago spring and a five-week steelworkers' strike that hampered the building process, forcing the contractors to finish a huge portion of the work in the last two weeks. Fans, accustomed to the lousy accommodations of South Side Park, were thrilled to see the new structure rising at the corner of 35th and Shields, east of the famous stockyards.

stream through the structure behind left and right fields—fans naturally felt that they were in the greatest of the new ballparks: the "Baseball Palace of the World," as the display ads called it.

Comiskey's complex layers of box, reserved grandstand, general admission, and bleacher seating charmed yet baffled the spectators used to the much simpler wooden ballparks. The stadium initially seated more than 32,000, featuring a double-decked covered grandstand from dugout to dugout, a single deck down each foul line, and a deep (rather than steep) bleacher section with thousands of the best cheap seats in the country. These 25¢ seats didn't have reserved seating, of course, but they did feature small wooden dividers that allotted each fan a certain amount of space. This fan-friendly improvement meant that the section had a defined capacity, and spectators would no longer end up being squeezed like sardines into a tin (or, in this case, steel) box at oversold games.

Comiskey was also responsible for another innovation—this one on the field. Previously, ballparks had been shoehorned into small parcels of land that made an even layout impractical, if not impossible. But because Charles Comiskey had purchased such a large amount of real estate to build the park, he was able to create the first major league field that remained symmetrical throughout its lifetime. Because of all the space—and star Sox moundsman Ed Walsh, who vetted the design—the field had vast, pitcher-friendly dimensions of 363 feet down both lines and 382 feet to the power alleys.

Things were good for the Sox in the first decade at their revolutionary new park, and such players as Eddie Collins and Joe Jackson, not to mention a bullpen full of talented pitchers, helped the Sox take the championship again in 1917. But the wake of the 1919 Black Sox scandal upset their good fortune. With most of their great players banished from the game forever, the Sox were now bereft of talent in the new era of power baseball, when a seasoned power-hitter was a must for a winning team. Meanwhile, the Chicago Cubs cemented their love affair with the Windy

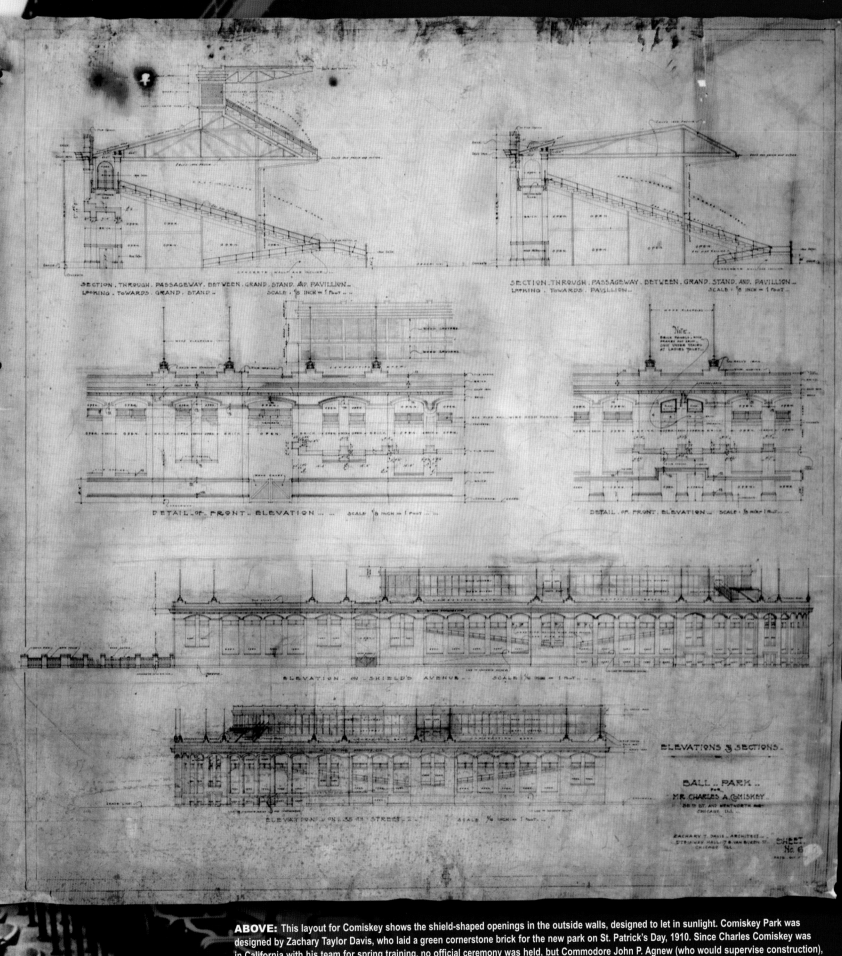

ABOVE: This layout for Comiskey shows the shield-shaped openings in the outside walls, designed to let in sunlight. Comiskey Park was designed by Zachary Taylor Davis, who laid a green cornerstone brick for the new park on St. Patrick's Day, 1910. Since Charles Comiskey was in California with his team for spring training, no official ceremony was held, but Commodore John P. Agnew (who would supervise construction), AL president Ban Johnson, dozens of fans, and several local politicians were on hand to witness the event. The next day, the *Chicago Daily Tribune* ran a story with the subhead "'Commy' Not There, But Other Baseball Notables Are Present."

BACKGROUND: The *Chicago Daily News* snapped this photo during the construction of Comiskey Park in 1910.

City by fielding a competitive team in their intimate, likeable park. Casual fans began to transfer their allegiance to the Cubs or stayed away altogether, and the Sox's cadre of loyalists wasn't enough to keep their very large venue from feeling rather drafty. The Sox, who drew 43 percent more fans than average in the first two decades of the league's existence, were now drawing 11 percent below the league norm. One of the AL's flagship franchises was crumbling, a decline that would take three decades to reverse.

In the 1930s and 1940s, while the White Sox suffered through loss after loss, there was one source of excitement at Comiskey Park: the blossoming Negro Leagues. On the edge of a thriving black community on the South Side (as opposed to Wrigley Field's exclusively white neighborhood), Comiskey drew fans in for its annual East-West All-Star Game, as well as many important blackball exhibition contests. African-American fans, press, celebrities, and players from all across the country gathered in Chicago, a mecca of black culture full of jazz clubs, restaurants, and stores that served the black population. Crowds crammed into Comiskey, cheering loudly for Negro League heroes at a time when ovations rarely rang for the major leaguers.

However, as they entered the fifties the Sox did finally get their fans back, first with some inspired playing and then with some inspired stunts. Led by manager Paul Richards and popular stars like Nellie Fox, Sherm Lollar, Billy Pierce, and Luis Aparicio—along with former Negro Leaguers Minnie Minoso and Larry Doby—the Sox enthusiastically battled the Yankees' juggernaut throughout the 1950s. They were the Go-Go Sox, so called for their speed and base-stealing prowess (in an era when plodding, station-to-station baseball was more typical), and fans began to trickle back to Comiskey Park to see their hardscrabble, blue-collar brand of baseball.

In 1959, the Sox came under new ownership, helmed by promotional genius Bill Veeck. Back in Cleveland in the late 1940s, Veeck had sponsored numerous "special" days, giving away everything from radios to nylon stockings, while also encouraging celebrities and unique personalities to hang out at the park. Though he was only around for three years until health problems forced him to sell, Veeck's attention-getting gambits at Comiskey reached new heights, as he cheekily invited Fidel Castro to Opening Day, put a spaceship full of little people dressed as aliens on the field, and tried out other "ballpark as carnival" stunts. The most popular by far, however, was the world's first exploding scoreboard. At a cost

of $350,000 (a gigantic sum in 1959), Veeck installed ten mortars that launched fireworks after every White Sox home run. Opponents hated it, but Chicago fans loved it so much that it became a signature element of the ballpark, later also featuring rotating pinwheels and flashing lights. The tradition of home run fireworks was adopted by many other teams, and continues today at the current home of the Sox, U.S. Cellular Field.

But the fun of a new scoreboard—as well as the White Sox's solid performance—could only last so long. As the 1960s began to wane, so did the Sox. Following a heartbreaking loss that knocked the Sox out of one of the greatest pennant races ever at the end of the 1967 season, the team was decimated as its veterans aged out and its young prospects came to naught. Bill Veeck returned as owner, but such gimmicks as having the players wear shorts received a tepid response from fans; he also garnered the irritation of other owners, many of whom had been scorned by his 1961 tell-all autobiography. Attendance dipped sharply as concerns about the safety of the adjacent Bridgeport and Armour Square neighborhoods kept many Chicagoans from coming out to the park. The South Side was simply no longer the place to be for baseball.

In 1979, Veeck's son, Mike, decided to help the park "go young" by staging a "Disco Demolition Night" with local DJ Steve Dahl. What started with chants of "Disco sucks!" evolved into drunk and stoned fans rushing the field, and ended with an all-out riot that brought racial tensions to a boil. The ill-fated promotion, along with years of poor tickets sales, gave fuel to the idea that Veeck's time was past, and he was forced to sell in 1981. Comiskey's fate was sealed when the park was bought by shrewd operators

Jerry Reinsdorf and Eddie Einhorn. The new owners were aggressive businessmen (Reinsdorf in real estate, Einhorn in television) who quickly decided they needed a new ballpark and started trolling for public funding.

There were certainly legitimate arguments that Comiskey had outlived its usefulness. Even though a good amount of cash had been spent in the early 1980s to refurbish the park, chunks of concrete fell from the upper deck in right-center field on Opening Day in 1986. After turning the screws on the state government, Reinsdorf and Einhorn got their money, and the Sox broke ground for the new park on May 7, 1989. Residents living south of Comiskey Park, most of them black and poor, were bought out and relocated, and McCuddy's, a legendary neighborhood bar that had served beers to players all the way back to Babe Ruth, was torn down.

Comiskey Park closed after the Sox's final home game, on September 30, 1990, ending eighty-one years of baseball at the historic park. In a particularly pointed—as well as pointless—gesture, armed policemen on horses were on-site to deny fans the chance to run around on the field, even though Comiskey was scheduled for demolition. In a tip of the hat to the past, the new stadium, criticized by many as being "soulless," was also named Comiskey—at least at first—and the Sox moved across the street for a fresh start in a new park.

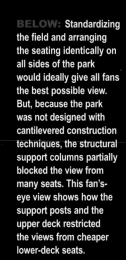

BELOW: Standardizing the field and arranging the seating identically on all sides of the park would ideally give all fans the best possible view. But, because the park was not designed with cantilevered construction techniques, the structural support columns partially blocked the view from many seats. This fan's-eye view shows how the support posts and the upper deck restricted the views from cheaper lower-deck seats.

TIMELINE: COMISKEY PARK

1910

The White Sox open their new stadium on July 1. The symmetrical park measures 363 feet down the lines, 382 in the gaps, and 420 to center field.

1918

The Cubs use the stadium during the World Series, the second of three straight World Series played at Comiskey.

1922

The Chicago Cardinals bring NFL football to Comiskey. The Cardinals will call Comiskey home off and on through 1958, though they'll spend most of the '30s at Wrigley Field.

1927

The stadium is double-decked and wooden bleachers are replaced with concrete and steel. Capacity increases to 52,000.

October 9, 1919

Rocked Baseball Disgusted with poor treatment and low wages from owner Charles Comiskey, the Chicago "Black Sox" throw the World Series. In Game 8 of the best-of-nine series, pitcher Lefty Williams loses his third Series game, not even making it out of the first inning. Cincinnati's Hod Eller cruises through the White Sox lineup with only one exception, and the Sox lose 10-5. The Reds walk away with the championship, and seven players on the Sox walk away with heavier pockets. Though gossip that the game was fixed is already running rampant, it will be almost a year until anyone is indicted and the players confess to their dirty deed.

Reds 10, White Sox 5

ABOVE: Pants Rowland (right), White Sox manager from 1915 through 1918, talks to his ace knuckleball pitcher Eddie Cicotte during a 1917 game.

September 27, 1920

Black Sox Banned Dickie Kerr shuts out the Tigers for his twentieth win of the season, making him the fourth pitcher on the White Sox to win twenty or more games. (The 1971 Orioles will be the only other team ever to have four twenty-game winners.) Joining Kerr in the club are Red Faber (twenty-three wins), Lefty Williams (twenty-two), and Eddie Cicotte (twenty-one), but two days later Williams and Cicotte are indicted for conspiracy to fix the 1919 World Series. The 1920 White Sox are just one game behind Cleveland with three games remaining when the eight "Black Sox" are suspended by Charles Comiskey (seven for fixing the game, one for knowing about it.) With Kerr the only pitcher to win in the final series, Chicago finishes two games behind the Indians. The eight players, though later acquitted in court, will be banned from baseball for life.

White Sox 2, Tigers 0

July 6, 1933

First All-Star Game The MLB All-Star Game, the brainchild of Chicago Tribune sports editor Arch Ward, debuts as an attraction for the World's Fair. Forty-nine thousand fans pour into Comiskey to see the AL prevail behind Lefty Gomez, who also scores the first run in All-Star competition. Fittingly, Babe Ruth cracks the first home run and also makes a great running catch in right field in the eighth inning. The game is so popular it is made an annual event.

AL 4, NL 2

BACKGROUND: Construction begins on Comiskey Park in the spring of 1910.

1927 The Negro National League Chicago American Giants win their second consecutive Negro World Series. Their home field, South Side Park, was formerly the home of the White Sox.

January 15, 1942 President Franklin Delano Roosevelt pens what will be known as the "green light letter," telling Baseball Commissioner Kenesaw Mountain Landis that in the face of World War II, "I honestly feel that it would be best for the country to keep baseball going."

1950 In the second All-Star Game at Comiskey Park and the first to go to extra innings, the National League wins 4-3.

1939
Lights are added, and the first night game in Chicago is played on August 14.

1941
The Negro American League Chicago American Giants begin playing at the park, and will call Comiskey home through 1952.

1947
Centerfield bleachers are eliminated to make it easier for batters to see.

August 26, 1934

Eastern Superiority In the second annual East-West Game (the Negro Leagues' All-Star exhibition), the two greatest pitchers in black baseball at the time combine to lead the East to a thrilling victory. Slim Jones, a 6-foot-6 lefty in the midst of what will be a 32-4 season, starts the game for the East and pitches three scoreless innings. He's relieved by Harry Kincannon, who in turn gives way to the brilliant Satchel Paige in the sixth. The game is a scoreless tie until the eighth, when the East's Cool Papa Bell walks, steals second, and scores on Jud Wilson's two-out bloop single. Paige seals the victory by shutting out the West over the last four innings of the game, striking out five.

East 1, West 0

July 5, 1947

Doby Breaks the AL Color Barrier The American League color barrier is broken when twenty-three-year-old Larry Doby pinch-hits for the Indians at Comiskey Park. By 1978, Doby will not only have followed Jackie Robinson as the second black player, but Frank Robinson as the second black manager: Bill Veeck, who signed Doby with the Indians in 1947, will eventually elevate him to manager of the White Sox in 1978.

White Sox 6, Indians 5

INSET LEFT: Chuck Klein races out of the batter's box during the 1933 All-Star Game at Comiskey Park, the first Midsummer Classic ever played.

INSET ABOVE: Josh Gibson slides into home after being tagged out by catcher Ted "Double Duty" Radcliffe during the 1944 Negro Leagues' East-West All-Star Game at Comiskey Park. Radcliffe's West team will beat Gibson's East team 7-4. The highlight of summer for Negro League fans, the East-West Classic was frequently played at Comiskey Park.

BACKGROUND: The White Sox walk onto the field before a 1917 World Series game. With the US at war in Europe, the team dons special patriotic togs during the Fall Classic: the blue "Sox" letters on the jerseys are outlined in red, the giant "S" speckled with thirteen stars, and their socks boast red and blue stripes. Chicago will beat the New York Giants in six games for the world championship, the club's last until 2005.

CAPS: 1940, 1985, 1971.

1950

Bullpens are moved from foul territory to behind the center-field wall.

1951

A large scoreboard is built in center field between the left- and right-field bleachers. It does not start exploding until Bill Veeck buys the club in 1959.

1967

The park is renamed White Sox Park only to be changed back to Comiskey Park after the 1975 season.

1969

AstroTurf, dubbed "Sox Sod," is installed in the infield, while grass is still used in the outfield. This odd situation remains until Bill Veeck buys the team (for the second time) in 1976.

October 1, 1959

Sox Slaughter the Dodgers For the first time in two generations, the White Sox are in the World Series. They certainly play like they belong, taking an 11-0 laugher. Eight straight White Sox players reach base in the fourth inning, with two Dodgers errors thrown in. Ted Kluszewski hits a two-run homer in both the fourth and fifth innings while knocking in five runs to support Early Wynn.

White Sox 11, Dodgers 0

September 12, 1976

A Hit for an Old-Timer Minnie Minoso, who debuted in 1949, becomes the oldest player in history to get a hit. One of the most productive White Sox during his heyday in the 1950s, the popular player came out of retirement for three games at the request of his old benefactor, Bill Veeck. In the second inning of the first game of a doubleheader, the fifty-year-old singles against California's Sid Monge. He ends up going 1-for-8 with two strikeouts from the nine hole as the designated hitter. (Minoso will come back again in 1980, but go hitless in two tries.)

White Sox 2, Angels 1

BELOW: Tom Seaver, age forty, throws a pitch for the White Sox in a 1985 game at Comiskey. The future Hall of Famer spends 2½ years with Chicago.

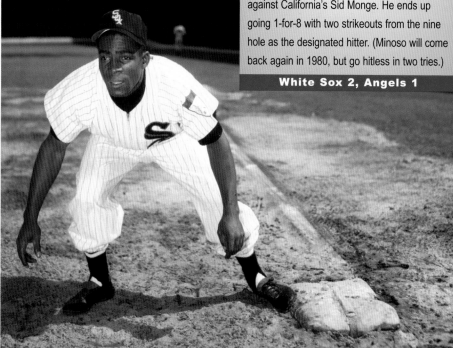

TOP: In another of Bill Veeck's famous stunts, "midget spacemen" arrive via helicopter to present ray guns to diminutive Sox middle infielders Luis Aparicio and Nellie Fox before a 1959 game against Cleveland. One of the actors in the space suits is none other than Eddie Gaedel!

MIDDLE: Fan favorite Minnie Minoso strikes an action pose at first base during his debut season with Chicago in 1951. He is the Sox's first black player. African-American Sam Hairston joins the club after him, on July 21, 1951.

OPPOSITE, BOTTOM: The "new Comiskey" (now U.S. Cellular Field) rises across 35th Street from its more modest predecessor in 1990. The towering height of the upper deck in the new park ends up being deemed a huge mistake, and the White Sox will later spend millions of dollars to tear off the top six rows of nosebleed seats and install a new "retro" roof to make the park feel more intimate.

1977 Nicknamed "the South Side Hitmen," the '77 Sox record a banner year, breaking the team's home-run record with 192 on the season and finishing third.

1983 Comiskey hosts its third and last All-Star Game, which the AL wins 13-3. The Sox win the AL West title and draw two million fans for the first time.

BELOW: Comiskey undergoes demolition after the 1990 season.

1979

Along with other park innovations, Bill Veeck installs a shower in center field and a picnic area under the bleachers where fans can look out at the game.

1990

As the larger, new Comiskey next door casts a shadow over the old park, the original goes out with a Sox win on September 30. Old Comiskey is demolished and turned into a parking area for new Comiskey.

May 9, 1984

The AL's Longest Game The longest game in American League history takes two days and twenty-five innings to play. While the game falls one inning shy of the major league record, the 8:06 contest takes more than twice as long as the Brooklyn-Boston twenty-six-inning tie of 1920. This game has more drama, too. Both teams score twice in the ninth to force extra innings, and then the game is suspended after seventeen innings with a score of 3-3. Then in the twenty-first, each team scores three times. The game ends suddenly in the twenty-fifth when Harold Baines homers off Chuck Porter of the Brewers. The teams then play their regularly scheduled game, and the Sox take that one, too, 5-4.

White Sox 7, Brewers 6

July 12, 1979

More than Disco is Demolished Disco Demolition Night is the worst backfire ever for a Veeck promotion. The brainchild of owner Bill Veeck's son, Mike, the night is promoted by disco-adverse DJ Steve Dahl, who encourages listeners to bring disco albums to the game to be burned on field. Dahl's fans, many considered "strange" by regular game attendees, appear in droves. Mayhem ensues once Dahl appears on field after the first game, and thousands of fans swarm onto the field. They tear up the grass and refuse to budge until the police show up in riot gear; the umpires forfeit the second game to the Tigers.

Tigers 4, White Sox 1

GRIFFITH STADIUM

Washington, DC

Senators (AL) 1911–1961

National Park (1911–1920)

OPPOSITE: On March 17, 1911, fire destroyed the second version of Washington's wooden American League Park. The team's loss was only $20,000, as the park was just about ready to succumb to its own decrepitude anyway. The Senators immediately announced that a partially rebuilt park would be ready for Opening Day, but that construction would continue into May. The result was Griffith Stadium, shown here with faded gridiron striping in left field. Griffith fit into the neighborhood like the center piece of a jigsaw puzzle, with a portion of the centerfield wall jutting inward to leave space for a tree and several houses, whose owners were unwilling to sell.

Just two miles north of the White House, in a ballpark whose "Presidential Box" hosted presidents from Taft to Kennedy, played a team that inspired the saying, "First in war, first in peace, and last in the American League." In the nation's capital, from 1911 to 1961, Griffith Stadium was home to the American League Senators, a flawed team ruled by one of baseball's most famous family dynasties.

But before it would bear the name of the family who ran it, Griffith Stadium was known by several other official and non-official names—National Park, American League Park, and even just League Park. Though a ballpark had occupied the corner of Georgia Avenue and W Street since 1891, it wasn't a full-fledged concrete-and-steel edifice until April 12, 1911, when it reopened to 16,000 cheering fans. The April opening was no small feat—less than a month earlier, fire had destroyed the most recent version of the wooden park after a plumber's torch set fire to some papers under the stands. Though the small fire began in the daylight and was quickly noticed, because the plumbers had shut off the water mains in order to do their work, the blaze quickly grew, destroying the dilapidated ballpark, several buildings, and a nearby lumberyard.

But amazingly, the stadium was rebuilt by Opening Day, thanks to 800 men working eight-hour shifts around the clock. Just like the Polo Grounds, which would also be rebuilt after a fire in 1911, the concrete-and-steel lower deck was completed first, with the upper deck added during the season. Both parks had odd dimensions and inconvenient quirks. However, the deep pockets of the New York franchise allowed the Giants to field a team so good no one cared about the less-than-ideal stadium, while the tenuous finances of the Washington franchise would doom its team—and its new concrete-and-steel home—to being an easily forgettable entry in the annals of baseball history.

Without the money to pay top players, even a new ballpark couldn't help the flagging Senators. In their first season at the rebuilt park, the club finished seventh out of eight, marking the ninth consecutive season that they had finished last or next to last, and lending even more credence to the "First in war" quip that sportswriter Charles Dryden had adapted from Henry Lee's famous eulogy for George

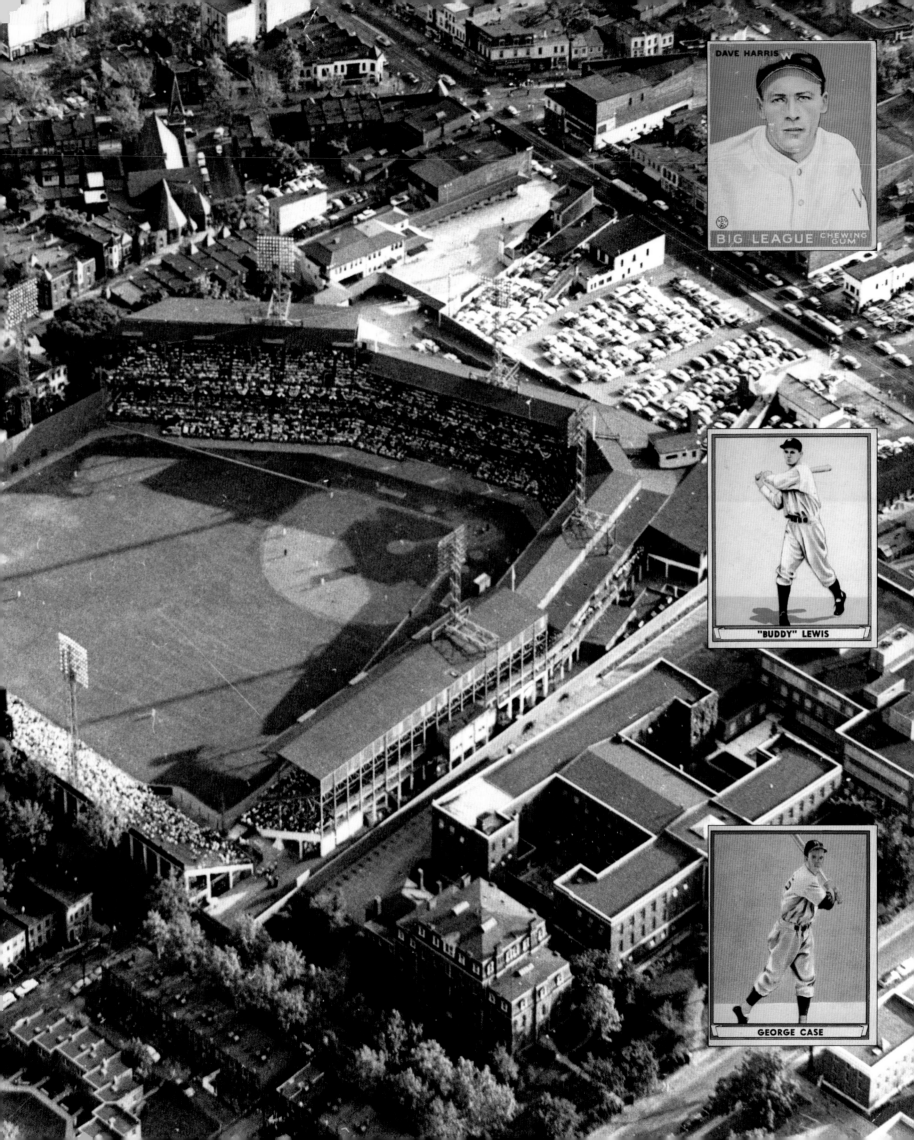

DAVE HARRIS

BIG LEAGUE CHEWING GUM

"BUDDY" LEWIS

GEORGE CASE

Washington. However, the next year, the club's fortunes began to improve. For the first time in their history, the Senators ended the season in second place, a feat they would repeat the next year. Much of the team's newfound success was attributed to a new hire: manager Clark Griffith, the stadium's eventual namesake.

Griffith, whose imposing presence would dominate the history of the club for more than four decades, managed the Senators for nine years, and became the club's majority owner in 1920. Griffith had been involved with the American League since its inauguration in 1901—first as a player-manager for the Chicago White Sox and New York Yankees (nee Highlanders), then as a manger for the Cincinnati Reds. When forty-two-year-old Griffith arrived in Washington in 1912, he had already had the nickname "The Old Fox" for eighteen years.

The halcyon days of the Senators lasted through 1933, the last year they ever won a pennant. During this time they even won a World Series—in 1924, thanks to the pitching of the immortal Walter Johnson. But the Senators' on-field performance—and fan attendance—quickly plummeted thereafter. Under Griffith, the Senators were essentially a mom-and-pop shop, and as the

team sank into a permanent underclass in the American League, it seemed as though providing good jobs for his extended family (including a batboy gig for his adopted nephew Calvin) was far more important to Griffith than fielding a competitive team or treating his players well.

Since they weren't winning any ballgames, Griffith stooped to such gimmicks as hosting an annual "Joke Game" at the end of the season where everyone played out of position. And when stunts didn't get people into the stands, the Griffith family filled their coffers in a multitude of other ways, including renting out the park to local high school teams. In 1937, when the Boston Redskins of the young National Football League relocated to Washington, they naturally became tenants of the park. Griffith, determined to keep them as tenants, offered them priority for September playing dates—assuming his team would be buried by that point in the season. This plan backfired badly in 1945, when the Senators fielded a surprisingly contending team, and had to play

the last five games on the road, then sit idle for a week while the rest of the league finished the season! Despite being known as a racist, Griffith also rented his park to Negro League teams as early as 1924, making the stadium's most notable tenant the dynastic Homestead Grays of 1939 to 1948. Had they been given a chance, the legendary team—which featured Hall of Fame sluggers Josh Gibson and Buck Leonard—could have easily trounced their land-lords. However, when the Negro National League collapsed in 1948, the Senators (like the White Sox and several other AL clubs), chose not to strengthen themselves by picking up African-American talent. Instead, the Griffiths scouted lowly paid Latin American players—but unlike the White Sox, they were unable to capitalize on the infusion of Latino talent to return to the first division.

Meanwhile, as the hapless and hopeless Senators played in an increasing outmoded stadium, Clark Griffith, followed by former batboy and new owner Calvin, looked for a way out of poorly drawing Washington, DC. Finally, after the 1960 season, just as the organization was starting to assemble a talented group of young ballplayers, the team packed up and left for greener pastures in Minnesota. Major League Baseball—unable to bear not having a ball club in the nation's capital, but also staving off an antitrust lawsuit—granted the District of Columbia an expansion team for the 1961 season.

Since the revolutionary new District of Columbia Stadium (later RFK Stadium) wasn't ready in time, the brand-new Washington Senators played their inaugural season at fifty-year-old Griffith Stadium. The last games at the park—a doubleheader between the new Senators and the old Senators, now the Minnesota Twins—were attended by only 1,498 fans. On April 9, 1962, the second-generation Senators moved into their new home and continued their predecessor's pitiful performance by finishing last in the American League. Meanwhile, the original team responsible for inspiring the embarrassing slogan flourished in its new home, vaulting all the way to second place, and eventually winning the pennant in 1965. That same year, forgotten Griffith Stadium was unceremoniously torn down, without even a marker left behind to denote the capital city's first concrete-and-steel home for the national pastime.

TOP: Walter Johnson watches the Senators beat the damn Yankees 1-0 behind the pitching of Stan Coveleski on June 25, 1925, at Griffith. Coveleski went 20-5 that year at age thirty-five, while Johnson was 20-7 at age thirty-seven. The two future Hall of Fame right-handers led the original Senators to the second of only three AL pennants in sixty seasons in Washington.

MIDDLE: The Homestead Grays play the New York Black Yankees at Griffith, circa 1940, during the decade when the Grays split home games between Pittsburgh's Forbes Field and Washington's Griffith Stadium (1939–48). The Grays won eight Negro National League pennants in that decade, along with three Negro World Series.

BOTTOM: The American League All-Star team takes the field at the start of the 1937 Midsummer Classic on July 7. The AL won the fifth annual All-Star Game 8-3. The next and last All-Star match-up at Griffith will be played in 1956.

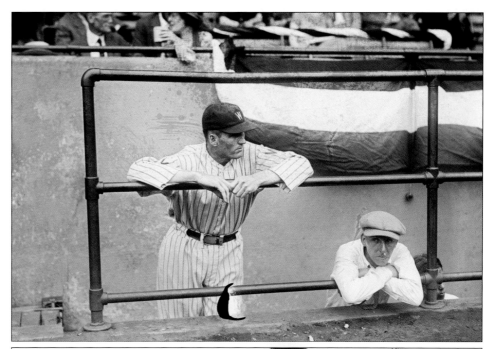

1914 The Federal League begins play in the majors, competing with the established American and National Leagues. The FL will last only two seasons, folding after 1915.

1918 DC officials begin to allow baseball games on Sunday, supposedly because of wartime needs.

1920 Babe Ruth hits fifty-four home runs for the Yankees, shocking the baseball world and effectively ending the Deadball Era, though not in spacious Griffith Stadium.

TIMELINE: GRIFFITH STADIUM

1911

On April 12, President William Howard Taft begins a new tradition by throwing out the ceremonial first pitch at League Park. The new field is massive: 407 feet down the left-field line, 391 to left-center, 421 to center, 378 to right-center, and 328 down the right-field line. Houses neighboring the property cause some strange angles in the outfield, and a 31-foot-high wall is erected in right to protect them.

August 26, 1912

The Big Train is Derailed Thanks to a technicality in the rules, Walter Johnson's American League–record winning streak comes to an end after sixteen straight victories. Johnson enters the game in relief with Washington and St. Louis tied at 2, and two Browns runners on base. Johnson immediately allows a run-scoring single to Pete Compton for the winning margin. Under NL rules, the loss would have been assigned not to Johnson, but to the pitcher who allowed the runners to reach base. However, AL rules at the time dictated that the reliever was the losing pitcher even if the winning run was scored by an inherited baserunner. It won't matter in the end, as two days later Johnson will lose his next start to the Browns anyway. However, he'll go on to win a remarkable thirty-three games for the year, and after the season the AL will change its inherited runners rule to match the NL's.

Browns 4, Senators 3

1920

League Park is renamed Griffith Stadium after manager and owner Clark Griffith. The stadium is double-decked down to the foul poles, raising capacity to 32,000.

1921

The Washington Senators, a short-lived football team, play their only season in the American Pro Football Association (as the future NFL was then known) at Griffith Stadium.

1925

The world champion Senators move the fence back all the way to 424 feet down the left-field line. This distance will fluctuate for the rest of the stadium's existence, but the other dimensions will remain stable except for center field being moved in by 13 feet in 1959.

May 15, 1918

I Hear the Train A-Comin' Walter Johnson tosses the longest shutout in major league history, an eighteen-inning, 1-0 masterpiece against Chicago's Lefty Williams. The marathon game comes just four days after Johnson shut out Cleveland, also by a 1-0 score. Over the course of his career, "The Big Train" will win five games of thirteen innings or longer. In 1918 alone, he garners fifteen extra-inning decisions despite the season's being shortened due to World War I.

Senators 1, White Sox 0

RIGHT: The defending world champion Washington Senators—the first and only time that phrase can be used—line up on Opening Day, 1925, at Griffith Stadium. Note the lack of uniform numbers: Cleveland will add numbers for the first time in 1929, before they are adopted by all clubs in the 1930s.

1924 Griffith Stadium becomes home to the Eastern Colored League Potomacs. Launched in 1923, the ECL was the second major league for African-American ballplayers, competing with the three-year-old Negro National League.

LEFT: Walter Johnson warms up at Griffith before the 1924 season. This is Johnson's eighteenth season in the majors, and the first year he'll make it to the World Series. At age thirty-six, "the Big Train" leads the league in winning percentage, starts, shutouts, strikeouts, and ERA, posting a 23-7 record with a 2.72 ERA and winning his second AL MVP award.

ABOVE: Washington's 1933 AL pennant winners, posing at Griffith Stadium before the World Series. Four future Hall of Famers played for the Senators that year: forty-three-year-old Sam Rice (front row, far left), Goose Goslin (front row, third from left), twenty-six-year-old player-manager Joe Cronin (front row, fourth from right), and Heinie Manush (back row, center). The 1933 Fall Classic will end in defeat for the Senators, who will lose to the New York Giants four games to one.

October 10, 1924

Stone Cold Luck In Game 7 of the World Series, the bounces finally go Washington's way—literally. With two outs in the eighth, Senators player-manager Bucky Harris ties the game when his ground ball hits a pebble and takes a wild bounce over the head of eighteen-year-old third baseman Freddie Lindstrom. Walter Johnson, the aging legend who has lost his only two starts during this Series, enters in the ninth and pitches four tense but scoreless innings. In the bottom of the twelfth, Giants catcher Hank Gowdy drops a pop-up when his foot gets caught in his discarded mask; Muddy Ruel, given a second chance, lines a double. After Johnson reaches on an error, Washington's Earl McNeely hits a grounder that looks to be a sure double play ball. Unbelievably, this grounder also hits a pebble and bounces over Lindstrom's head, bringing in the run that makes the Senators world champions.

Senators 4, Giants 3

October 10, 1925

Did He or Didn't He? In the third game of the World Series, with President Calvin Coolidge looking on, Senators right fielder Sam Rice makes one of the most mysterious and controversial catches in baseball history. With the Senators leading 4-3 and Washington relief ace Fred Marberry on the mound in the eighth, Pittsburgh's Earl Smith launches a long drive to right field. Rice, who has just switched from center to right field, dashes toward the fence, leaps into the stands after the ball—and disappears. After a long pause he emerges with the ball in his glove, and is ruled to have made the catch despite the Pirates' vehement arguments that a hometown fan placed the ball in the mitt. Rice will refuse to answer questions about the game-saving catch for the rest of his life, but he does give a sealed letter to Hall of Fame officials with instructions to open it upon his death. When Rice passes away in 1974—nearly half a century after the infamous catch—the letter's contents will finally be revealed: "At no time did I lose possession of the ball."

Senators 4, Pirates 3

May 24, 1935 The first major league night game is played under newly installed lights at Crosley Field. By 1948 every field in the majors (except Wrigley Field) will be illuminated.

July 7, 1937 Griffith Stadium hosts the fifth annual All-Star Game. The Yankees' Lou Gehrig shines, homering and driving in four runs in the 8-3 AL victory.

1937

The NFL's Redskins relocate from Boston and become tenants of Griffith Stadium. They will play here through 1960.

ABOVE: President Franklin Delano Roosevelt prepares to throw out the first pitch at Griffith Stadium for the defending AL champion's home opener on April 24, 1934. To FDR's left are Clark Griffith, Senators owner; Joe Cronin, Senators player-manager; and Bucky Harris, Red Sox manager. All three are future Hall of Famers.

RIGHT: Hall of Fame slugger Buck Leonard of the Homestead Grays shows off his fearsome swing in a 1938 game against the New York Cubans. From 1937 until 1948, Leonard anchored the Homestead lineup, joined by legendary home run hitter and Hall of Famer Josh Gibson for nine of those seasons.

LEONARD   LOUD
                            CU

CAP: 1922.

BELOW: A big crowd fills Griffith Stadium sometime between 1921 and 1932. The two classic fields that opened in 1911—Griffith and the Polo Grounds—were hastily built after major fires, which differentiated them from the carefully planned ballparks erected at the start of the classic field era (1909–10) and those that opened during the keeping-up-with-the-Joneses period (1913–15). At Griffith, the lack of planning showed in many ways, a prime example being the upper deck past first and third bases, added for the 1921 season, which was substantially higher than the original second deck behind home plate.

1939

The Homestead Grays of the Negro National League begin alternating their games between Griffith Stadium and Forbes Field, usually playing their high-drawing weekend games at Griffith. They will migrate between DC and Pittsburgh through 1948.

1941

Lights are added, and Griffith's first night game is played on May 21.

June 18, 1942

A Good Day to Be a Pitcher In a battle between the Negro Leagues' two marquee teams, pitchers dominate not only on the mound but also at the plate. The Monarchs' Hall of Fame pitching duo, Satchel Paige and Hilton Smith, achieves nine scoreless innings, while Homestead lefty Roy Partlow throws nine scoreless of his own. The defensive gem of the day, meanwhile, is pulled off by Josh Gibson, who decoys baserunner Willie Simms and tags him out after tricking him into trying to score standing up. The Monarchs finally take a 1-0 lead in the tenth when Smith, an excellent hitting pitcher, singles home a run. But in the bottom of the inning, as 28,000 fans begin to head for the exits, the Grays mount a comeback. A walk, a stolen base, and a Jud Wilson single tie the score. Partlow, the Homestead pitcher, follows with a 400-foot triple into the left-field corner for a walk-off win.

Grays 2, Monarchs 1

August 4, 1945

No Ordinary Batting Practice Pitcher World War II veteran Bert Shepard makes his major league debut in a mop-up relief role in a 15-4 blowout by the Red Sox. It's the only game the left-hander will ever pitch in the majors, but that's just a small part of the story. A pitcher in the minors before the war, Shepard was shot down over Germany and lost the lower part of his right leg. A fellow prisoner at Stalag IX-C fashioned an artificial leg, and Shepard worked out on it every day. When he was sent back home in 1945 in an exchange of prisoners unable to fight, a War Department official arranged for him to meet Senators owner Clark Griffith. Hired as a batting practice pitcher, Shepard tossed three innings in an exhibition against Brooklyn played in lieu of the All-Star Game. Today, with the Senators losing big in the second game of a doubleheader, manager Ossie Bluege figures it can't hurt to bring Shepard into a real game. Bert pitches the rest of the way, allowing three hits and just one run in 5⅓ innings, while striking out two. His lone day as a major leaguer is an inspiration to the thousands of veterans maimed during World War II.

Red Sox 15, Senators 4

1946

The Senators draw one million fans for the only time at Griffith Stadium. A giant scoreboard in right-center field, featuring a huge National Bohemia beer ad on top, makes the height of the fence 41 feet.

August 15, 1941

The Senators Just Can't Win The Senators hold a rare 6-3 lead on the Red Sox in the bottom of the eighth inning when play is stopped by rain. After a forty-minute delay, the game is called in favor of the Senators. Red Sox manager Joe Cronin—Clark Griffith's nephew-in-law and former manager of the Senators—argues that the game has only been called because the Senators don't have a grounds crew, and thus didn't protect the field with a tarp as required. AL president Will Harridge upholds the Red Sox's protest and the forfeit goes to Boston. The Senators drop into last place, but they will pull themselves into a sixth-place tie by season's end.

Red Sox 9, Senators 0 (forfeit)

BELOW: Joe DiMaggio raps a single off Washington pitcher Red Anderson in the second game of a doubleheader on June 29, 1941. "The Yankee Clipper" extended his hitting streak to forty-two consecutive games, breaking George Sisler's AL record of forty-one games set nineteen years earlier.

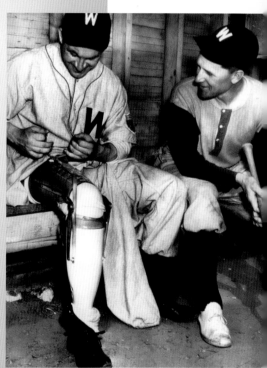

ABOVE: Washington pitcher Bert Shepard, left, tightens the brace on his prosthesis as manager Ossie Bluege watches. Between games of a doubleheader on August 31, 1945, Shepard was awarded the Distinguished Flying Cross, the military's second-highest medal. After the war, he both played for and managed the National Amps, a team of amputee veterans.

September 6, 1954 Black Cuban outfielder Carlos Paula integrates the Senators with his Griffith debut. Calvin Griffith's Senators will employ many Latinos but few African-American ballplayers.

July 21, 1959 Pumpsie Green makes his debut for the Red Sox, finally integrating all sixteen big-league clubs.

October 1, 1961 Roger Maris hits his controversial sixty-first home run, breaking Babe Ruth's record and igniting a backlash against offensive play.

1954

The bullpen in left field is moved in front of the fence, cutting the distance there to 388 feet.

1956

Additional rows of bleachers are added in left field, knocking the distance down to 350 feet.

July 10, 1956

An All-Star Slugfest The All-Star Game turns into a home run derby for four future Hall of Famers. Willie Mays and Stan Musial go deep for the NL, while American Leaguers Mickey Mantle and Ted Williams homer in consecutive sixth inning at-bats against yet another future Hall of Famer, Warren Spahn. It's the fourth career All-Star home run for Williams, the second for Mantle, and the sixth (and last) for Musial. Mays' two-run shot off Whitey Ford is his first; he'll hit two more over the next twenty-one All-Star Games. Pittsburgh's Bob Friend gets the win over Chicago's Billy Pierce in front of 28,843 spectators in the second and final All-Star Game played at Griffith Stadium.

NL 7, AL 3

1960

The Senators play their last game at Griffith Stadium before leaving for Minnesota.

1961

The new expansion Senators provide a quick hello and a final goodbye. The last major league game at the stadium is played (ironically, against Minnesota) in front of just 1,498 fans on September 21.

1965

Griffith Stadium is demolished. Howard University Hospital will eventually be built on the site.

RIGHT: National League All-Stars Stan Musial of the Cardinals and Willie Mays of the Giants both homered during the NL's 7-3 victory in the twenty-third Midsummer Classic on July 10, 1956, at Griffith Stadium. Musial, thirty-five, was in his fifteenth big-league season; Mays, only twenty-five, was in his fifth year in the majors.

BELOW: Elwood Quesada, the first owner and president of the expansion Washington Senators, watches a Redskins football game at Griffith on November 20, 1960, with his son Ricci. Quesada was a World War II veteran and retired Air Force lieutenant general, a Lockheed executive, President Eisenhower's special advisor for aviation, and the first administrator of the Federal Aviation Administration before he bought the expansion franchise.

The Senators
The National Game from the Nation's Capital
1963
AMERICAN LEAGUE OFFICIAL PROGRAM AND SCORECARD
15¢

May 26, 1961

Something Old, Something New In something of an awkward match-up, the former Washington Senators—who left for Minnesota after the 1960 season—return to their old stomping grounds as the Twins. Their opponents are the new Senators, the expansion franchise formed to replace them. Fans at Griffith Stadium find themselves rooting against almost exactly the same roster they'd cheered on the year before. But Mickey Vernon, a five-time All-Star and one of the greatest players in the annals of the old Senators, has been hired to manage the new version. In a bit of sweet revenge, Washington's Joe McClain outduels Minnesota's Jim Kaat, and the new Senators will sweep the series from the Twins and move ahead of them in the standings.

Senators 4, Twins 3

September 25, 1965 The former Washington Senators, now the Minnesota Twins, win their first AL pennant.

A young scoreboard operator peers out of a slot in Griffith's wooden scoreboard, located in the right-centerfield wall, on July 3, 1956. The Senators will go on to win the game 6-5 in front of a "crowd" of 2,118. Baseball commissioner Bowie Kuhn often spoke fondly of his youth, when he also served as a scoreboard operator in Washington.

POLO GROUNDS

New York, New York

Giants (NL) 1911–1957, Yankees (AL) 1913–1922, Mets (NL) 1962–1963

CARL HUBBELL

OPPOSITE: This eastward view shows the Polo Grounds from Coogan's Bluff in Harlem, with the South Bronx visible in the distance beyond the Harlem River. This Polo Grounds never held a polo match, and was actually the fifth place to carry the name: In 1883, the Giants (then called the Gothams) and the American Association Metropolitans played at side-by-side fields formerly used for polo. In 1889–90, two more adjacent fields called the Polo Grounds were constructed farther uptown for the Giants and a team of the same name in the Players League. After these parks burned to the ground, this concrete-and-steel version was born, and would be home to the NL Giants for more than half a century.

No other baseball park brings to mind sepia-toned images of baseball greats gone by more than the storied Polo Grounds, unquestionably one of the most celebrated houses of the game. Home at one time or another to Willie Mays, Babe Ruth, Christy Mathewson, Mel Ott, Bobby Thomson, and a stable of other players whose on-field feats made major league baseball legendary, the Polo Grounds packed in fans—or simply drew them to nearby Coogan's Bluff where they could catch a glimpse—to bear witness to some of the grand old game's most thrilling moments. Built in 1911, with what would now be considered strange dimensions and plenty of quirks, the Grounds would host major league baseball for forty-nine of the subsequent fifty-three years.

Of course, the 1911 Polo Grounds was not the first ballpark in New York City with that name. The original, which saw its first baseball game in 1883, was located between 110th and 112th streets in Manhattan, and (unlike its successor) was formerly used for playing polo. In 1889, the Giants moved farther into Harlem—up to 157th Street—onto land leased from the estate of Mrs. Harriet Coogan (whose surname provided the moniker for the famous bluff). Had the New York club owned the land, it might have invested in building a safer grandstand, but instead, their outdated wooden home fell prey to a ballpark's biggest enemy: fire.

On April 13, 1911, the day after the nation's capital had celebrated the opening of its new ballpark, the Giants had their second bout of the season at the Polo Grounds—a routine loss to the Phillies, except for a meager fire involving a large pile of discarded peanut shells, which had to be extinguished by groundskeepers. Whether this very peanut shell pile or something else in the concession area was to blame, a full-blown conflagration later broke out that evening around midnight, beginning in right field and engulfing the ballpark in just twenty minutes. The Polo Grounds was almost a total loss, with only the clubhouse and the left-field bleachers salvaged.

The blaze, called "a red-hot argument in favor of steel and concrete construction" by the *Sporting News*, cost the Giants hundreds of thousands of dollars not just in damaged property, but in game receipts. Because the prosperous club was forced to temporarily move into shabby Hilltop Park—home of their poorer cousins, the Yankees—the number of tickets they could sell went down drastically. Hilltop Park was so much smaller

GUS MANCUSO

BIG LEAGUE CHEWING GUM

HARRY "GUNBOAT" GUMBERT

WAYNE TERWILLIGER

second base NEW YORK GIANTS

Wayne Terwilliger

that the Giants' move affected not only their own bottom line but that of all the other National League clubs—used to pulling in big numbers at the Grounds—as well. However, the homeless Giants only had to play twenty-eight games at Hilltop, and on June 28 moved back into the Polo Grounds, even though the reconstruction was only partially finished. The park-in-progress opened with a 16,000-seat capacity, all in the lower deck, and work on the upper deck continued throughout the summer, except during games. Even though he had acted because of the calamity, wealthy Giants owner John Brush decided to rebuild the park in a far grander fashion. After all, his club shared the biggest market in the country, more than double the next largest, Chicago, and nine times larger than Pittsburgh, which boasted the beautiful new Forbes Field.

While still working as quickly as possible to raise the new edifice, the Giants' boss looked all the way back to ancient Rome for the grand flourishes that would live up to his self-anointed royal status. By the start of the 1911 World Series (which the club lost to the Athletics), the new field was surrounded by an exquisite marble facade of bas-relief baseball figures and coats of arms for each NL club. Members of the sporting press called the park the best sporting facility ever built, or that ever would be built. And while that designation may have been the result of reporters who were predisposed to hang the "greatest" title on anything from the Big Apple, the new ballpark was both beautiful and functional. The grandstand seated 9,150 in the upper deck and 15,915 in the lower, and had ramps instead of stairs to save room and speed up pedestrian traffic. So magnificent was the new stadium that Brush tried to name it after himself, but its old moniker stuck. (Because there were two diamonds at the park's original location, many historians consider this version

of the Polo Grounds the fourth to carry the name. Other baseball researchers consider it the fifth, because there were also two adjacent diamonds at the 157th Street location before the fire.)

In 1913, the Yankees started a trend that would later be followed in St. Louis and Philadelphia—moving into the home of their crosstown competitors. The lordly Giants were once again sharing the field with their weaker rivals, this time at a grander venue. But this relationship would ultimately change, when the Yankees made what would be one of the most famous deals in baseball, one that would alter the course of history. In January 1920, the Yankees acquired Babe Ruth from the Boston Red Sox, and were immediately lifted into contention. That season, the Babe hit an astonishing fifty-four home runs, as the Yankees became the first team ever to draw more than a million fans. Ruth's team reprised that previously unheard-of feat in their next two years at the Polo Grounds. And even though the Giants defeated the Yanks in both the 1921 and 1922 World Series (the first between two teams sharing the same park), the record gates gave the Yankees' owners a good reason to leave the Polo Grounds and build their own palace.

The Yankees prospered in their new eponymous stadium just across the Harlem River. Meanwhile, the Giants brought five World Series to the Polo Grounds between 1923 and 1937. New York was blessed with two great teams, and attendance levels at both premier parks remained high. By the 1940s, however, the Yankees had eclipsed their former landlords, finishing first five times between 1940 and 1949, while the Giants spent most of the decade in their league's lower division.

The venerable Polo Grounds was by then hardly an ideal place for baseball. The cavernous, horseshoe-shaped arena resembled a football stadium that had been converted

RIGHT: Giants and Phillies players survey the charred rubble after the wooden (fourth) Polo Grounds was destroyed in a fire on April 13, 1911. The event led to the rapid construction of its concrete-and-steel successor, which would host the Giants until 1957. While the new park was under construction, the Giants played twenty-eight games at Hilltop Park, the deteriorating home of the Yankees.

RIGHT: The Giants and Boston Braves take the field on Opening Day 1923, while the marble facade is still to be renovated during a left-field expansion.

BELOW: With the Polo Grounds' marble facade in all its glory, the Giants face the Red Sox in Game 4 of the 1912 World Series. Boston will take the game and proceed to win the Series four-games-to-three with one tie.

for baseball use, not the purpose-built showcase for baseball it was supposed to be. Unlike later fields, it had been squeezed into the land that was available, so it measured a short 280 feet down the left-field line and a scant 257 down the right-field line, with the often-changing center-field fence anywhere from 480 to 505 feet. As a result of its unusual configuration, a ball hit over the portion of the outfield fence closest to home plate was a home run, but a ball hit higher and farther to almost the same point was in play. In addition, the home team bullpen was located in fair territory in left-center, and the clubhouses were in deep center field, so players had to walk the entire length of the playing field after the game to take their showers and change.

These idiosyncrasies seemed almost commonplace when state-of-the-art ballparks were just beginning to be squeezed in where their predecessors sat, but they would soon be considered major inconveniences as mammoth stadiums became standard. But even though they were playing in an aging park, the Giants still had some fight left in them. In 1954, the team captured their first world championship in twenty-one years by upsetting the powerful Cleveland Indians, who had set an AL record that season by winning 111 games. Willie Mays' jaw-dropping catch in center field during Game 1 at the Polo Grounds—a staple of every historical highlight reel worth its celluloid—served notice to the AL that the National League, loaded with newly signed African-American stars, was ready to emerge from its slumber after half a century of being dominated by the junior league.

Nevertheless, the ascent of the immortal Mays and the Giants' exciting rivalry with the Brooklyn Dodgers couldn't obscure the dry rot that had set in under Giants owner Horace Stoneham. Like so many other postwar owners, Stoneham had refused to invest in his own home, a penny-wise but pound-foolish attitude that was cemented once the Boston Braves cashed in on taxpayers' largesse in Milwaukee and moved out to the Midwest. As they watched the newly christened Milwaukee Braves rise to power both in standings and attendance, baseball barons in other cities decided that to draw bigger crowds, it would be cheaper to move than to renovate their aging mansions, which needed substantial refurbishment after four or more decades of service.

While fans drifted away from the deteriorating Polo Grounds, Stoneham began actively scouting new homes for the Giants, and in the late 1950s became a willing accomplice to Brooklyn Dodgers owner Walter O'Malley. O'Malley had plans to move his New York team to California, and needed another team on the West Coast so that his new Los Angeles

Dodgers would have an opponent to play that was closer than St. Louis. The coming together of the two New York owners quickly became a grand opera whose climax saw both clubs simultaneously move to the West Coast at the end of the 1957 season.

Five days after the Dodgers sang their swan song at Ebbets Field, the Giants played their last game at the Polo Grounds, losing by a score of 9-1 to the Pittsburgh Pirates. As the game ended, fans tried to grab a cap or a glove by chasing the players through center field as they scurried to the safety of the clubhouse. With a mixture of sadness and anger, the fans tore up chunks of the field, swore at the heavens, and promised that if they couldn't see the New York Giants, they would never to go to a baseball game again.

Some never did. Yet many others became loyal followers of the expansion New York Mets, born five years later, despite the fact that the team would inhabit a different borough and a completely different style of ballpark. A terrible club for the first seven years of their existence, the Mets planned on occupying a new, city-owned superstadium in the Flushing section of Queens. While their Shea Stadium slowly rose, however, the Mets made do at the Polo Grounds. The rotting hulk was no more attractive nor fan-friendly than it had been when the Giants took flight, but it did give the tremendously popular Mets their start. For two seasons, the lucky National Leaguers competed with the ghosts of baseball greats gone by, surrounded by flickering memories of the sublime games that had played out on its greensward.

CAP: 1947 (worn by Mel Ott).

ABOVE: Giants players hurry up the steps to their clubhouse in center field to escape over-eager fans after their last game at the Polo Grounds on September 29, 1957. The Giants lost to the Pirates 9-1 in their swan song under Coogan's Bluff, in front of only 11,606 loyal fans. Bobby Thomson (number 21), author of the "shot heard round the world," leads the procession five steps below the cameraman on the landing.

March 17, 1911 One month before the fire at the Polo Grounds, Washington, DC's American League Park burns down. It will reopen on April 12, and later be renamed Griffith Stadium.

1911

After succumbing to a fire on April 13, the Polo Grounds is rebuilt in concrete and steel and reopens on June 28. Though capacity has been more than doubled to 34,000, the dimensions of the field remain the same: 277 feet to the left-field line, 500 feet to center, and 258 feet to the corner in right. Work on the concrete-and-steel upper deck continues when games aren't being played.

July 3, 1912

Marquard Gets Nineteenth Win Rube Marquard ties the record of former Giant Tim Keefe with his nineteenth consecutive victory of the season. He outduels the Brooklyn Dodgers' Nap Rucker in the first game of a doubleheader to give the Giants their fifteenth consecutive win (they'll win the second game, too). New York's streak will end the next day, and Marquard's string will be snapped when Chicago hands him his first loss of the year on July 8.

Giants 2, Dodgers 1

Lefty pitcher Rube Marquard in front of the Polo Grounds' box seats in 1912, the year of his historic nineteen-game winning streak. Marquard signed with the Giants in 1908 for the unprecedented salary of $11,000 per year, and his on-field success led to off-the-field celebrity: he endorsed products, wrote a newspaper column, starred in a silent film, and launched a popular traveling vaudeville act with future wife Blossom Seeley.

CAP: 1915 (worn by Christy Mathewson).

1911 While their park is being rebuilt, the Giants play twenty-eight games at the Yankees' decrepit Hilltop Park.

1913 The Giants win the NL pennant for the third year in a row, but lose their third-straight World Series title.

1920 The Red Sox sell slugger Babe Ruth to the Yankees for $100,000 and a hefty loan, forever changing the course of baseball in the Big Apple.

1913

The Giants return the favor of the Yankees' having let them play at Hilltop Park back in 1911 by allowing the crosstown rivals to move into the Polo Grounds. The Yanks will stay for ten seasons.

August 16, 1920

Deadly Ball In a singular, horrifying moment, Ray Chapman is killed by a pitch. Yankees submarine pitcher Carl Mays beans the Cleveland shortstop, known for crowding the plate. Carried off the field at the Polo Grounds, he dies the next day. His death will lead to the establishment of a rule requiring umpires to replace balls when they become dirty (though batting helmets won't become compulsory until more than thirty years later). The incident will also result in bringing young shortstop Joe Sewell to Cleveland. Mays, known for his surliness and disliked by both teammates and foes, will pitch another five years and have a brilliant career. Yet, he will never get more than a handful of votes for the Hall of Fame.

Indians 4, Yankees 3

BELOW: The wooden precursor to the concrete-and-steel version of the Polo Grounds that would be reconstructed in 1911. Because of the curve of the grandstand down the left-field line, the corner of the stands was actually in fair territory, as were the bullpens behind it. The bullpens of the new Polo Grounds, built a year after this photo was taken, were also in play.

BELOW: Boys hang out in the trees on Coogan's Bluff in 1902, trying to watch a game at the original Polo Grounds for free.

1921

The left-field line is extended by almost 10 feet to 287, the deepest it will ever be. Left-center and right-center measure 455 and 449, respectively.

October 5, 1921

Everyone Feels at Home at the Series The Yankees and Giants play the first one-city World Series since 1906, and the first between two teams sharing the same park. They alternate home and away for each of the eight games in the best-of-nine series (the last World Series that is not a best-of-seven). Carl Mays kicks it off with a shutout of the "home team" Giants, but much to the relief of manager John McGraw, the Giants will rally to take the last three games and win the Series, with help from pitcher Art Nehf, who will toss a shutout in Game 8.

Yankees 3, Giants 0

May 5, 1922 Ground is broken on a new ballpark for the Yankees in the Bronx, right across the Harlem River from the Polo Grounds.

1929 The Giants introduce a public address system, the first of its kind in major league baseball.

1925

Expansion is completed during the season, pushing capacity to 55,000 for baseball. The NFL Giants are founded and move in. Almost 70,000 cram into the stadium to see Red Grange and the Chicago Bears on December 6, assuring the franchise's future. The NFL Giants will remain at the Polo Grounds until 1956.

September 28, 1930

Best of the Rest Despite going hitless in a ten-inning season-ending victory, Bill Terry still finishes at .401, becoming the last National League player to bat over .400. The Giants, one of six National League teams to bat .300, finish the season with the highest batting average of the twentieth century at .319. (The Phillies set the all-time mark, batting .350 in 1894, another offensively explosive year.)

Giants 7, Phillies 6

October 5, 1922

Daylight Earnings Time The last tie in post-season history is called in Game 2 of the Series. Umpire George Hilderbrand and Commissioner Kenesaw Landis get booed by the crowd after calling the ten-inning game too dark to play at 4:46 p.m., and are accused of forcing a fifth game simply to make more money. Fans are so outraged that Landis declares that the profits from the tied game will be donated to charity. The Giants go on to clinch the world championship with Art Nehf on the mound (for the second year in a row); it is the last of three Series that manager John McGraw will win.

Giants 5, Yankees 3

September 10, 1922

Goodbye American League The Yankees turn away thousands at the gate for what will be the last American League game at the Polo Grounds. An estimated 40,000 lucky fans get in to see the doubleheader sweep of the Athletics. The Yankees will return once more in 1922 after a long, season-ending road trip and fall to the Giants in the World Series at the Polo Grounds, but the team, a better draw than their landlord Giants, will do just fine in their new surroundings starting in 1923.

Yankees 2, Athletics 1

LEFT: Dubbed "Little Napoleon" for both his stature and his imperious manner, John McGraw managed the Giants for thirty years (from 1902 to 1932), leading them to ten NL pennants and three world championships.

BELOW: A huge crowd attends an October 1910 game at the expanded wooden Polo Grounds.

OPPOSITE: Billy Jurges of the Cubs sprints to first base as the Giants' Bill Terry makes the stretch to record the out during a 1935 game.

June 1, 1932 After running the Giants for thirty years, during which time the team won ten pennants and three World Series, John McGraw resigns as manager due to health problems. First baseman Bill Terry takes the reins, and McGraw will pass away two years later.

1934 The football Giants play the Chicago Bears in the championship at the Polo Grounds. In what will be known as the "Sneakers Game," the Giants wear basketball shoes to help combat the icy turf and freezing temperatures. They win 30-13.

October 3, 1933

The Pitchers Have It At the height of the Great Depression, the Giants see their first World Series in nearly a decade. Though they won only ninety-one games during the season, the Giants have one of the strongest pitching staffs in baseball: hurlers Freddie Fitzsimmons, Hal Schumacher, and Carl Hubbell have combined for a 2.20 ERA during the season, and will improve to 1.73 during the Series. Today Hubbell, who's enjoying the best season of his career, gets the Giants off to a good start, striking out ten and giving up not a single earned run. The offense is anchored by Mel Ott, who collects four hits and three RBIs, and hits a home run in his first at-bat. The Giants will put forth another fine pitching performance tomorrow night at the Polo Grounds for a 6-1 win, then take the Series in three more games in Washington. The Senators won't see another pennant until 1965, after they move west and change their name to the Minnesota Twins.

Giants 4, Senators 2

July 10, 1934

Star Pitching The high score of the second All-Star Game makes it sound like it's all about hitting, but the game is really about Carl Hubbell. King Carl famously fans five American League greats in succession: Babe Ruth, Lou Gehrig, Jimmie Foxx, Al Simmons, and Joe Cronin. Hubbell leaves with a 4-0 lead, but the AL pounds his replacements. Mel Harder is the pitching star on the other side, entering with a one-run lead in the fifth and permitting just one hit the rest of the way.

AL 9, NL 7

POLO GROUNDS

YANKEE STADIUM

BOB LENNON
outfield NEW YORK GIANTS

1940

The Giants, who had refused to play at night at Crosley Field in 1935, host their first night game on May 24.

1949

The site, which was under the Harlem River in the nineteenth century, keeps getting flooded, so the field is raised 4½ feet to help with drainage.

1957

The Giants play their final game at the Polo Grounds on September 29. They move to San Francisco in 1958.

LEFT: This aerial view from the mid-1950s faces northwest from the Bronx, showing both Yankee Stadium in her prime and a deteriorating Polo Grounds on the opposite side of the Harlem River.

BELOW: This view from the right-field grandstand shows a packed house for a 1955 game at the Polo Grounds.

RIGHT: Truly a-Mays-ing is this sequence of shots following Willie Mays as he makes "The Catch" during the eighth inning of Game 1 of the 1954 World Series. After an unbelievable over-the-shoulder grab at full gallop—on Vic Wertz's longball into deep center field—Mays instantly whirls and throws a strike to the infield, holding the runner at first and falling down after uncorking the throw. Larry Doby, on second, advances to third on the play but does not score, and the Giants will go on to win the game in the tenth.

1   2   3   4

February 23, 1960 Demolition begins on Ebbets Field in Brooklyn.

October 12, 1963 At the Polo Grounds, the National League takes the American League, 5-2, at the first and only Hispanic-American All-Star Game, which stars Minnie Minoso, Roberto Clemente, Luis Aparicio, Orland Cepeda, Juan Marichal, and others.

October 3, 1951

The Shot Heard Round the World The most famous game in Polo Grounds history is far from a sellout, with a Wednesday afternoon crowd of only 34,320. After having been thirteen games behind the Dodgers on August 11, the Giants came back to tie for the pennant, prompting a three-game playoff. In the last of the three, Jackie Robinson's first-inning single off Sal Maglie produces the only run until the home seventh, when Bobby Thomson's sacrifice fly ties the score. Brooklyn immediately regains the lead with three in the eighth, thanks to a wild pitch and RBI-singles by Andy Pafko and Billy Cox. Dodgers pitcher Don Newcombe tires in the bottom of the ninth when Whitey Lockman doubles in a run to put the tying runs in scoring position. As Ralph Branca comes in to face Thomson, there is one out. Revelations fifty years after the fact of an intricate sign-stealing system (utilizing a high-powered telescope) will mar the Giants' comeback story, but nothing will change what happened on the 0-1 pitch that Thomson turns into the "shot heard round the world." Russ Hodges radio call for the ages tells all, "The Giants win the pennant! The Giants win the pennant!"

Giants 5, Dodgers 4

ABOVE: Bobby Thomson is mobbed by his joyous teammates after his shot won the 1951 NL playoffs and the pennant for the Giants at the Polo Grounds.

September 29, 1954

Mays' Amazing Catch The Cleveland Indians, who set an American League record for 111 wins, are worth two runs in the first inning of Game 1 of the World Series…and nothing more. Vic Wertz, whose triple had given Cleveland the early lead, steps up in the eighth inning of the tied game and launches a shot to the deepest reaches of the massive Polo Grounds. Willie Mays races with his back to the wall and makes the most celebrated catch of his career—and perhaps ever. Mays walks and steals second in the tenth off Bob Lemon, and after an intentional walk to Hank Thompson, pinch hitter Dusty Rhodes pulls a fly ball just long enough to reach the cozy seats. Wertz's blast would have been a homer and Rhodes' fly an out in Cleveland, but the Polo Grounds makes it happen. The Giants will shock the Indians in four games.

Giants 5, Indians 2

1960

Professional sports returns to the Polo Grounds, sort of. The terrible Titans of the newly formed American Football League draw sparse crowds, but they will play here for four seasons, changing their name to the Jets in 1963.

1962

National League baseball returns to New York and to the Polo Grounds. The Mets stumble their way to the worst record of the twentieth century, yet the team establishes a base of former Giants and Dodgers fans that they will take with them to Shea Stadium two years later.

1963

The Mets play their final game at the park on September 18. Demolition will begin on the Polo Grounds on April 10, 1964, a week before Shea Stadium opens, using the same wrecking ball used to tear down Ebbets Field. The ballpark will be replaced by Polo Grounds Towers, four thirty-story apartment buildings.

Miserable Mets relief pitchers huddle under blankets in the bullpen at the Polo Grounds during a 1962 game. Even if the weather hadn't been bad, the pitchers would have had reason to feel sorry for themselves, toiling for a team that would lose 120 games.

Bringing Down the House

"This time, there are no reprieves for the Polo Grounds," said a United Press International staff member on April 10, 1964, as workers wearing Giants jerseys began to demolish the grounds at Coogan's Bluff, ignominiously leveling the old stomping grounds of the Giants, Yankees, and Mets. The wrecking ball—cruelly painted to resemble a baseball—was the same orb of steel that had taken down Ebbets Field four years prior.

Today, the wrecking ball doesn't play as big a role: for the most part, parks are blown up rather than torn down. Or, rather, blown *in*, by being imploded with dynamite. Atlanta–Fulton County Stadium was laid to rest in 30 seconds, while Three Rivers Stadium crumbled in just 19. Veteran's Stadium came down with the help of 3,000 pounds of explosives, and left 50 pounds of dirt and twisted steel (and space for 5,000 parking spots) in its wake.

Though the blasts used to down a structure may appear simultaneous, most parks are destructed with a series of domino-like detonations. Afterward, nearby structures are tested for integrity. When Cinergy Field was imploded, the *Cincinnati Enquirer* reported, "As the final chunk of Cinergy's 22,500 tons of steel fell, inspection crews raced to the $280 million Great American Ball Park—literally an arm's length away from Cinergy's outfield wall—to see if the Reds' new home had sustained damage." The $5.7 million the city paid for Cinergy's demolition was well spent—neither the new park or the nearby Roebling Suspension Bridge had a scratch.

But sometimes there are bigger problems than just the surrounding structures. For Seattle's Kingdome, built to last a millennium but razed after only twenty-four years, the problem was the strength of the arch design used to construct it. The stadium was too structurally sound to destroy from the bottom up, and simply detonating the dome would cause its 25,000 pounds of concrete to hit the ground all at once, resulting in a virtual earthquake. Ultimately, it was imploded in six pie piece–like sections, with beams in place to "cushion" the earth from the blow. In 16.8 seconds, the Kingdome appeared, in the words of the *Seattle Post-Intelligencer*, like a "sunken soufflé," leaving a dust cloud more than 500 feet high that "sent people scrambling like extras in the Blob movie." In the end, it still registered a 2.3 on the Richter scale.

RIGHT: Workers dismantle what remains of Cincinnati's stately Palace of the Fans in November 1911, one month after the nine-year-old ballpark's last game. Palace of the Fans was the second park (after Philadelphia's Baker Bowl) to use steel and concrete in its foundation. However, like many parks built before the classic fields era, its wooden grandstand burned to the ground. The Reds' new home, Crosley Field, will be built on the same site in less than a year and open for the 1912 season.

BELOW: A wrecking ball painted like a baseball, the same one used at Ebbets Field four years earlier, smashes a concrete wall at the Polo Grounds in 1964.

RIGHT: The Polo Grounds undergoes demolition in late July 1964. The centerfield clubhouse, with its large Rheingold beer ad, has not yet fallen to the wrecking ball.

OPPOSITE: Three years after the Brooklyn Dodgers played their last game at Ebbets Field, demolition began in 1960. Although the diamond had all but vanished by the time this photo was taken, still standing is the famous Schaefer beer advertisement on the Ebbets scoreboard, which would eventually be recycled for use in a minor league park.

WRECKING OLD GRANDSTAND AT BALL PARK - CIN, O.

Specialized demolitions like the Kingdome's can cost up to $9 million—money some cities don't have to spend. When the building of their most recent Busch Stadium went over budget, St. Louis harkened back to the days of the Polo Grounds and simply hired workers to rip down the old stadium, wrecking ball and all. And Montreal's Stade Olympique, built on top of a subway line, may be awaiting its inevitable fate for some time to come. Teams have found a way, however, to save on costs and spare fans a bit of the heartache of watching their old ballpark come down: selling pieces of baseball history. If you'd like a pair of seats from the Mets' most recently destroyed home, it will only cost you $869. With a high-capacity stadium like Shea, it just might pay for its own demise.

OPPOSITE, TOP: One day shy of its twenty-fourth birthday, Seattle's concrete Kingdome is imploded on March 26, 2000, even though Seattle still owes $26 million on the structure. The blast, which was broadcast on Seattle's three major networks and in New York's Times Square, required 21.6 miles of detonation cord in order for the person pushing the button to be out of harm's way.

OPPOSITE, BOTTOM: St. Louis' Busch Stadium [II] is demolished the old-fashioned way in December 2005, making it one of the last concrete super-stadiums to go.

RIGHT: This sequence of photos shows the implosion of Three Rivers Stadium in Pittsburgh on February 11, 2001. Crowds gathered on the banks of the Allegheny River well before the 8:00 a.m. detonation to watch, and a fireworks show was put on afterward. A raffle, held for the honor of hitting the button that would bring the structure down, was won by sixteen-year-old Joseph King, who told the Associated Press, "This is the greatest day of my life. I heard the bangs, and it seemed like forever before it went down."

CROSLEY FIELD

Cincinnati, Ohio

Reds (NL) 1912–1970

Redland Field (1912–1933)

In Cincinnati, one of major league baseball's oldest homes, a small piece of land near the confluence of Mill Creek and the Ohio River once held a classic field hailed by the *Chicago Tribune* as "the most perfectly designed of all." Redland (later Crosley) Field had no gingerbread facades or fancy flourishes, but it was well built and spacious. The first major league park to host nighttime ball, it was abandoned only when the property it sat on—which had been the site of a major league field since 1884—was no longer deemed to be in a desirable part of town.

Built after its wooden predecessor, Palace of the Fans, burned to the ground, Redland Field opened on April 11, 1912, with an oversold 10-6 rout of the Chicago Cubs. Cleverly figuring that two openings were better than one, the Reds also held an official dedication on May 18—not coincidentally, when the top-drawing Giants were in town. That day, gates to the new stadium opened at noon even though the game didn't start until 3:00. Bands played, dignitaries gave speeches, and—most importantly to the Reds—many thousands of dollars worth of concessions were sold before the first pitch.

Seating only 23,500, fewer than most other fields of its time, Redland was complete and well-appointed. It had been an awfully long time since anyone in the Queen City had seen a nice, new ballpark, and much was made of its consideration for the fans' comfort as well as its facilities for the players. The Reds' dressing room was so luxurious that it had a separate lounge with a pool table and a reading room. And in what may have been a first, there was a "sunken garage" for fans to park their cars. On the other side of the complex, fans arriving by trolley were greeted by an attractive flower garden. However, the facade of the $400,000 edifice was less stunning: its walls of pressed brick gave the structure the look of an upscale office building more than that of a grand ballpark.

When they moved into their classy new stadium, the Reds were recovering from a drought that had seen them win only one pennant in twenty-nine years. But beginning in 1919 with their infamous World Series win over the crooked White Sox, their luck turned around. That win would quickly be deemed a fix, but it heralded the start of an eight-year stretch during which the club finished in the first division all but once. After that, however, during the Great Depression, the Reds fell back into their losing ways, finishing last for four consecutive

"VANDY" VANDER MEER

TONY PEREZ
3rd Base

REDS

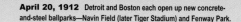

1912

Redland Field opens on April 11. A flood earlier in the month, one of several great floods that will plague the park over the years, causes grounds crews to work frantically to get the field ready for Opening Day. The original dimensions are 360 feet down the left-field line, 420 to center, and 385 down the right-field line.

1919

York Street behind left field is closed and bleachers are added for the World Series. This will be the only time the city allows the street to be closed for temporary seating.

ABOVE: Willie Mays is up at the plate during a July 1961 Reds-Giants game at Crosley Field. By this time, the Superior Towel & Linen Service building beyond left-center field had been demolished to make way for more parking spaces. The building had featured an advertisement on the side that promised batters who hit the sign a free Siebler-brand suit. Mays won the most suits of any visiting player at seven. The Reds' best-dressed player was Wally Post, who won eleven suits.

seasons beginning in 1931. Though their attendance never dipped too low, perhaps thanks to their tradition of offering cheap beer and keeping their grounds well maintained, the Reds saw a stroke of good fortune when local radio pioneer Powel Crosley Jr. bought the team. In addition to renaming the field after himself, Crosley brought enterprising changes to the Reds in the form of plane-travel for away games and a new rooftop press box for reporters. But his biggest innovation was in illumination.

Previously, several minor and Negro League clubs had experimented with night baseball, but Crosley was the first to bring lighting to the major leagues, spending more than $50,000 to bathe his ballpark in 924,000 watts of radiance. (Previously, the best-lit park had been San Francisco's Seals Stadium, which boasted just 310,000 watts.) The artificial sunshine came from eight light towers, four of them attached to the grandstand roof and two at the base of the outfield walls in left- and right-center. On May 24, 1935, the Reds lit up the sky over Crosley Field with their General Electric installation, with a switch flipped by none other than President Franklin D. Roosevelt, sitting in his office in Washington, DC. Except for a few holdouts, everyone marveled at the new era in baseball. More than 20,000 fans—about four times the average—showed up to see the Reds defeat the Phillies, 2-1. The field offered another first for baseball as well: the practice of painting numbers on the outfield walls—"so the spectators may readily ascertain how far drives carry," the staid *Sporting News* sniffed.

Crosley Field changed little in the last three decades before its closing in 1970, aside from the installation of a 58-foot-tall scoreboard in 1957. By the 1950s, the venerable park was obsolete, with outdated facilities and not enough parking; and by the 1960s—like many old ballparks—Crosley had become increasingly irrelevant as its neighborhood declined. After exploring various options, including moving to a site near the Kings Island amusement park in southern Ohio, owner Bill DeWitt decided to sell the team in 1966 rather than commit to the city's plan to move the Reds into a multipurpose facility, Riverfront Stadium.

Sad that Crosley was closing, hometown fans cheered long and loud as their heroes won a dramatic 5-4 finale over the Giants on June 24, 1970. As St. Louis had done four years earlier, Cincinnati had a helicopter fly Crosley Field's home plate over to the team's new venue. For Reds' fans, the contrast between quaint Crosley and the new superstadium was akin to moving from a homey ranch house to a modern, yet sterile, mansion. Crosley Field sat abandoned while a local fan bought the scoreboard and moved it to his Kentucky farm, where it soon rusted out. Though the original site near the confluence of Mill Creek and the Ohio River is now an industrial park, Crosley Field's classic look has been recreated in suburban Blue Ash, Ohio—right down to the period ads on the scoreboard. Part of an amateur diamond at a community center, the park is a nostalgic tribute to Cincinnati's first concrete-and-steel home for baseball—a good, hardworking field with plenty of fans.

September 1918 With the United States deep into World War I, the final month of the season is cancelled when the government announces that it will draft baseball players.

September 20, 1920 The Reds' 1919 World Series championship is forever tainted by the Black Sox scandal, when it's revealed that Chicago's second-place team had thrown the Series in exchange for cash.

May 28, 1935 During a game at Crosley Field, Babe Ruth trips on the left-field incline, falls on his face, and storms off the field. He will retire five days later.

June 2, 1921

It's Outta Here In the park's tenth season, the first major league player finally hits an outside-the-park home run at Redland Field. The Reds' Pat Duncan achieves the feat on June 2, just eleven days after John Beckwith, a slugger for the Negro American League's Chicago American Giants, became the first man to clear the wall.

Reds 8, Cardinals 5

May 24, 1935

Let There Be Light The Reds host the Phillies in the first major league game ever played at night, a 2-1 Cincinnati victory. At the urging of innovative Reds President Larry MacPhail, President Franklin D. Roosevelt flips a switch at the White House in Washington to turn on the floodlights in Cincinnati. A couple of months later, the Reds will host another first—the first woman to hit a ball during a major league game—when local burlesque star Kitty Burke runs onto the field, snatches a bat from Babe Herman, and somehow convinces Cardinal's pitcher Babe Herman to lob her an underhanded throw. Though she never makes it to first base (at least, not on field), Burke will go on to brag about her feat prominently in her show, while the Reds will play one night game against every NL team in 1935.

Reds 2, Phillies 1

1934

At the urging of Reds president Larry MacPhail, new team owner Powel Crosley Jr. names the ballpark after himself.

1937

In January, nearby Mill Creek and the Ohio River overflow and flood the entire neighborhood, submerging Crosley under 21 feet of muddy water.

October 1, 1919

Place Your Bets When Chicago pitcher Eddie Cicotte hits Morrie Rath with a pitch to open this best-of-nine World Series, it's a secret signal to gamblers that the fix is in: Several White Sox players have agreed to throw the Series. More money is instantly bet on sudden favorite Cincinnati, which was a three-to-one underdog just days earlier. The game remains tied for a couple of innings before Cicotte and shortstop Swede Risberg fail to turn an easy double play and the Reds get five straight two-out hits, including a two-run triple by pitcher Dutch Ruether, to take a 6-1 lead. Lefty Williams, Chicago's pitcher the next day, will be only slightly less obvious in throwing that game.

Reds 9, White Sox 1

BELOW: Hapless Morrie Rath spent six seasons in the majors. After playing in a total of forty-nine games for the Athletics and Indians over two years, he was traded to the White Sox in 1912. In 1913 he was sent back down to the minors, and didn't return until his 1919 debut with Cincinnati. At the start of the World Series, he was hit with a pitch by former teammate Eddie Cicotte to signal that the fix was in, and was sent back down to the minors the next year.

RIGHT: This view from the west shows Crosley Field during the flood of 1937, the worst in the state's history. After eighteen days of rain, sleet, and hail that January, Crosley was buried beneath 21 feet of water, while the river rose to a record 79 feet high. Water covered 60 percent of Cincinnati, and 100,000 were left homeless.

BACKGROUND: An early night game is played at Crosley Field around 1935.

July 6, 1938 In the sixth annual All-Star Game, the NL defeats the AL 4-1 at Crosley Field. Crosley will host the Midsummer Classic again in 1953.

1939 Behind Bucky Walters' twenty-seven wins and Paul Derringer's twenty-five, the Reds take their first NL pennant in twenty years before getting swept in the World Series by the Yankees.

1938

Home plate is moved forward 20 feet, additional seats are added to the lower deck, and upper decks in left and right field are added. Crosley's new dimensions are 328 feet down the left-field line, 387 to center, and 366 in right. Capacity is now 33,000.

1939

Crosley becomes the first stadium to mount screens on the foul poles to make it easier for umpires to judge home runs.

October 8, 1940

A Red-Letter Day A crowd of 26,854 witnesses the only world championship the Reds will ever win on this field. Detroit and Cincinnati have alternated wins throughout the World Series, and the pattern says Detroit should take Game 7. The Tigers take a 1-0 lead in the third, but Cincinnati's Jimmy Ripple doubles in the tying run in the seventh, and Billy Myers, the lowest-hitting regular on either team (.130), hits a sacrifice fly to bring in the go-ahead run. Reds ace Paul Derringer then finishes off the Tigers for Cincinnati's first non-fixed world championship. The unlikely hero of the Series is Jimmie Wilson, a forty-year-old coach who is pressed into catching duty after backup catcher Willard Hershberger commits suicide in August and regular back-stop Ernie Lombardi is injured in September. Wilson bats .353 for the victorious Reds while stealing the only base of the Series.

Reds 2, Tigers 1

1946

The "Goat Run," a new seating area, is built in front of the right-field stands to aid home run hitting. It will be removed and re-added intermittently through 1958. When it's in place, the distance to right is 342 feet; when removed, as it is permanently after 1958, the distance is 366 feet.

May 13, 1947

Reese Shows His Support Amid howls from many of the 27,000 spectators, Jackie Robinson plays his first game in Cincinnati. The abuse is so harsh that Brooklyn shortstop Pee Wee Reese, a Southerner from nearby Louisville, Kentucky, who has family and admirers at the stadium, walks over and puts his arm around Robinson as a gesture of support. "You could have heard the gasp from the crowd as he did it," Dodgers pitcher Rex Barney will write years later. A statue commemorating the moment will eventually be built in front of KeySpan Park in Brooklyn.

Reds 7, Dodgers 5

BELOW: Rookie left-hander Johnny Vander Meer, age twenty-two, poses as if he were about to hurl a pitch in this 1937 photo.

RIGHT: Taken during the 1940 World Series against Detroit, this photo shows a prominent advertisement for beer—the Queen City's signature product—in left center. Note the bend in the left-field line as it ascends the famous terrace in front of the outfield wall.

June 11, 1938

Vandy's First No-No Wild left-hander Johnny Vander Meer throws the first no-hitter by a Reds pitcher in twenty years, walking four Boston batters and striking out three. Cincy third baseman Lew Riggs fields Heinie Miller's ground ball for the final out. It will be a much shorter wait for the next Reds no-hitter, as Vander Meer, remarkably, will hurl another one four days later in Brooklyn. In 1947, Vander Meer's teammate Ewell Blackwell will come tantalizingly close to matching Johnny's back-to-back no-hitters before giving up a single in the ninth inning. The feat remains unmatched.

Reds 3, Bees 0

April 17, 1954 Black players Nino Escalera and Chuck Harmon both pinch-hit in the seventh inning of a game at Milwaukee, thus integrating the Reds.

1961 The Reds win their first NL pennant in twenty-two years behind MVP Frank Robinson. They will fall to the Mantle-Maris Yankees in five games in the World Series.

1965 In one of the worst trades in baseball history, the Reds deal thirty-year-old Frank Robinson to the Orioles for pitcher Milt Pappas and two other players.

1947

Pay phones are removed from the park to cut down on betting.

1961

The red brick facade is painted white. With buildings in the surrounding West End torn down for parking, a large net is erected in left field to protect windshields from home run balls. The Reds boast that Crosley is the only "air-cooled" park in the major leagues, with jet fans using "patented Westinghouse air-injector rings" to make the customers more comfortable.

1965

The centerfield fence is raised almost 10 feet using mostly plywood and old ping-pong tables. A line is drawn where the wood meets the existing concrete, and balls hitting above the line (on the wooden portion) are home runs. The rule is soon changed so the ball has to clear the 23-foot fence entirely.

1970

The Reds play the final game at Crosley Field on June 24. Afterward, home plate is transported to Riverfront Stadium by helicopter.

1972

Used as an auto impound lot since its closing, Crosley Field is torn down. Sitting on the wrecking ball operator's lap, helping to strike the first blow, is future Reds player Pete Rose Jr.

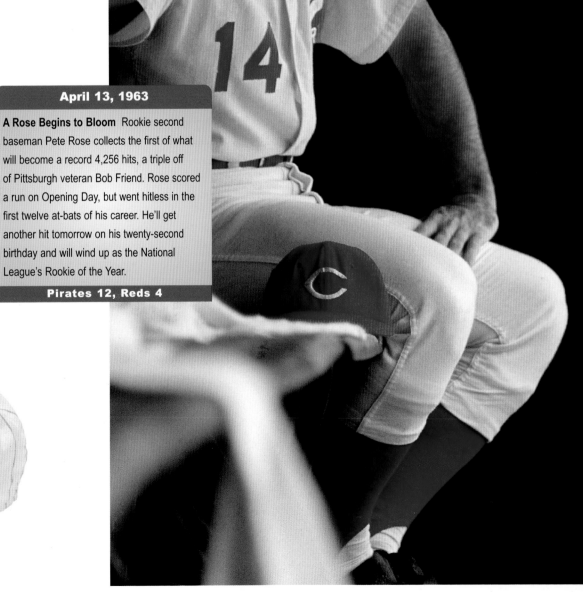

RIGHT: A young Pete Rose (a.k.a. "Charlie Hustle") peers intently out of the Reds dugout in this photo from the late 1960s. Rose will have played for the Reds for sixteen seasons by the time he goes free agent and transfers to the Philadelphia Phillies for an unprecedented $3.2 million over four years.

CAPS: 1951, 1965.

April 13, 1963

A Rose Begins to Bloom Rookie second baseman Pete Rose collects the first of what will become a record 4,256 hits, a triple off of Pittsburgh veteran Bob Friend. Rose scored a run on Opening Day, but went hitless in the first twelve at-bats of his career. He'll get another hit tomorrow on his twenty-second birthday and will wind up as the National League's Rookie of the Year.

Pirates 12, Reds 4

FENWAY PARK

Boston, Massachusetts

Red Sox (AL) 1912–present, Braves (NL) 1914–1915

Celebrated Fenway Park has transcended its destiny of being a home for a team with some of the worst luck in history, and has become hallowed ground for any baseball fan—Red Sox lover or hater. Perhaps the epitome of the classic field era, Fenway Park has housed the Sox for nearly 100 years, and has survived—even thrived—while all of its sister fields have been abandoned. However, many of the features we now associate with this grande dame of major league ballparks, such as the Green Monster, the oddly configured "upper deck," and the outfield bullpens, came to life long after the park opened.

In 1911, two years into the concrete-and-steel ballpark revolution, Beantown's Red Sox needed a new home. Huntington Avenue Grounds, where they had been playing for the past decade, was quickly becoming obsolete; with seating for only 9,000 and very few rules in place for over-flow crowds, fans would spill onto the field, barely held back by velvet ropes. This led not only to fans inserting themselves into on-field arguments, but outlandish ground rules like awarding triples for balls hit into the fans but not all the way to the fence. Furthermore, AL president Ban Johnson had just pushed through a new rule, to take effect the following year, that would require all ballparks to be outfitted with dressing rooms for both the home and road clubs. Since teams visiting the Sox still had to dress at their hotels and ride the trolley out to the Grounds in uniform, the Sox would have had to add on to their park as it was.

So to control the fans and give the Sox a bigger, modern ballpark, Red Sox owner John Taylor began scouring the city for a site for the new park. He found it in a cheap, swampy area of Boston called The Fens and began building immediately. The $650,000 Fenway Park opened on April 20, 1912, after Opening Day was canceled twice due to rain (and the fact that the team's newly ordered tarpaulin hadn't arrived in time to protect the field from a torrent). Even in the second decade of the twentieth century, when all ballparks were small compared to today's standards, Fenway's fans were especially close to the action. It had long been a Boston custom to build compact parks with seats near the field, as all previous Boston parks—the notable exception being the second incarnation of the Braves' South End Grounds, which had burned in 1884—did not have an upper deck. Fenway Park carried on the tradition, with a deep, single-deck

grandstand and a large bleacher section. On Opening Day, however, 27,000 spectators crammed into the park to see the Sox take the Yankees in eleven innings, with the fans who didn't have seats crowding behind a rope drawn around the outfield.

The Red Sox continued to prosper on their new field, thanks to superstar pitcher Smoky Joe Wood, a fantastic outfield anchored by legendary centerfielder Tris Speaker and left fielder Duffy Lewis—whose mastery of the strange incline of left field gave it the moniker "Duffy's Cliff "— and the potent pitching and then revolutionary power

hitting of Babe Ruth. Boston won the World Series in Fenway's debut season, then proceeded to bring home three more world championships before the unutterable mistake that would bring ruin to Beantown and glory to Gotham.

After the sale of Babe Ruth and numerous other players before the 1920 season, the Red Sox struggled to win on-field while their management struggled to make money off the field. In spring 1929, they announced that they were considering vacating Fenway—though it was not yet twenty years old—in order to become co-tenants with their more successful National League counterparts, the Braves, whose fourteen-year-old Braves Field was much larger. As a trial run, the Sox began playing their Sunday games (which were prohibited by law at Fenway because of the park's proximity to a church) at Braves Field, which they continued to do regularly through 1931 and on four occasions in 1932. Interest in Fenway Park seemed to be waning, but the next year a new Red Sox era would dawn.

Prior to the 1933 season, the strug-gling Sox were purchased by thirty-year-old Tom Yawkey. Yawkey, whose name now emblazons the street that borders the stadium, would become one of history's staunchest advocates for Fenway Park. Like many owners of the time, he had baseball in his blood. His uncle, Bill Yawkey, who had adopt-ed him after the death of his parents, was a co-owner of the Detroit Tigers,

and was hunting buddies with Ty Cobb. As legend would have it, it was Cobb who encouraged the young Yawkey to buy a ball club with his trust money.

Though Yawkey freely admitted he didn't know much about baseball (for that he entrusted general manager Eddie Collins), he wasn't afraid to pour money into the team, including an estimated $250,000 to renovate the festering Fenway Park. He began by replacing temporary seating along the third base line that had been erected and never replaced after a 1926 fire burned down the bleachers in foul territory in left field. However, during construction prior to the 1934 season, the park caught fire again. Yawkey promised that Fenway would be ready for Opening Day, and after workers labored through an unseasonably cold winter to the tune of an additional $5,000, the park opened up with 10,000 more seats, concrete-and-steel bleachers, and new press facilities, soon considered by the writers of the day to be the best in the AL. There was also a major change to the field—Duffy's Cliff had been bulldozed, and a 37-foot, left-field wall had been constructed. It wouldn't be until 1947 that the wall would be stripped of its advertisements and painted green.

The same year that the "Green Monster" was born, Fenway finally added lights, becoming the third-to-last major league park to do so. As was the case with other classic ballparks like Wrigley Field, Fenway didn't change much after that, with the exception of the addition of seats to squeeze in a few more bodies. Seats were added to the roof of the grandstand, including a glassed-in seating area behind home plate with two vertical levels of seating on either side of it, giving the rooftop somewhat of a Globe Theater look.

Despite these various modifications, Fenway's facilities were outmoded and well below average in terms of fan comfort, even though most of the seats were close to the action and the park was quite easy to get to. During the late 1990s, with the Sox still struggling under the oppressive Curse of the Bambino, the club's ownership—now helmed by John Harrington, the head of Yawkey's trust—began to debate the merits of opening up a new ballpark across Yawkey Way. Although the Massachusetts legislature authorized $100 million for the construction of a new venue, with another $200 million to be contributed by the City of Boston, the plans to replace Fenway failed—partly due to opposition led by an organization called Save Fenway Park, which picketed games, lobbied officials, and kept the public informed of proposals regarding the Sox's beloved home.

Whether it was the team's euphoric 2004 World Series win or public pressure, on March 23, 2005, officials announced that Fenway was here to stay. "The Red Sox will remain at Fenway Park for the long term," stated the team's chief executive, Larry Lucchino. "There is a kind of magic in the place—an energy and a history that is impossible to duplicate." So America's most beloved ballpark remains, albeit with plans intact to add new ladies restrooms, widen the concourses, and free up space around the park. One of the only parks to have obstructed views, a pre-1950 manual scoreboard, an in-play ladder, and no parking lot, it's the oldest ballpark still in use in the major leagues, and many would say that it's the best.

CAPS: 1935, 2002.

BELOW: A young, lean Fenway Park at the end of its second season, unencumbered by the extensive superstructure built onto the roof in its later years.

April 20, 1912 Detroit's Navin Field (later Tiger Stadium) opens on the same day as Boston's new ball yard. The premiere of both parks is knocked out of the headlines by the sinking of the *Titanic*, which happens on the same day.

1912 The Red Sox tally 105 wins and take the AL pennant with help from fastballer Smoky Joe Wood, who posts a 1.91 ERA for the season.

1914 The Red Sox purchase pitcher Ernie Shore, catcher Ben Egan, and nineteen-year-old Babe Ruth from the minor league Baltimore Orioles for $8,000. Beginning with the Sox in mid-July, Ruth will hit in only five games and pitch in four during his first major league season.

1912

The Red Sox take on the Yankees in the first game at Fenway Park on April 20. The park is 321 feet down the line in left (up the incline dubbed "Duffy's Cliff" to a 25-foot-high wall), 488 to center, and 314 to the line in right. A portion of deepest right-center is listed at 550 feet from home plate.

RIGHT: The 1912 Red Sox pose at the World Series. Jake Stahl's crew went 105-47 that year, winning the pennant by fourteen games over Washington before beating John McGraw's famed New York Giants in an exciting eight-game Series for Boston's second world championship.

October 16, 1912

Giants Botch World Series At the top of the tenth inning of the deciding Game 8 of the World Series, the Giants have every reason to believe they will continue their come-from-behind two-game winning streak to take the Series. Fred Merkle has just singled in the go-ahead run to give his New York Giants a 2-1 lead, and pitcher Christy Mathewson, who went eleven innings without a decision (partly due to five New York errors in Game 2), is on the mound. But then, sure-handed centerfielder Fred Snodgrass famously drops a fly ball. Next, an easily catchable foul pop-up by Tris Speaker drops in the midst of three players. Given another chance, Speaker singles in the tying run, Larry Gardner hits a sacrifice fly that brings in the winning run, and the Sox win their first Series at Fenway.

Red Sox 3, Giants 2

BELOW: A packed Fenway Park hosts the National League's "Miracle Braves" in the 1914 World Series. (The Braves moved to Fenway late in the 1914 season to accommodate bigger crowds.) In this October 12 game, the Braves top the Athletics 5-4 in twelve innings. The Braves will close out their sweep at Fenway the next day.

1914

The Boston Braves abandon the South End Grounds for Fenway Park in September, and stay for the World Series. They'll call Fenway home for part of the 1915 season, as well. The Red Sox will, in turn, play the Series at the Braves' new field in 1915 and 1916, as well as Sunday games from 1929 through 1932.

June 23, 1917

Babe Starts No-hitter Brawl Babe Ruth never finishes a no-hitter during his short but remarkable pitching career, but he does start one—as well as a small brawl. In perhaps the strangest beginning to a no-hitter in history, Ruth walks Washington leadoff man Ray Morgan to start the first game of a doubleheader. Ruth is so livid at umpire Brick Owens' call that he rushes him, and when the ump ejects him, Ruth punches him on the side of the head as he walks off the field. Eddie Foster is thrown out stealing on relief pitcher Ernie Shore's first pitch, and Shore retires the next twenty-six batters. He is credited with the fourth perfect game ever pitched, although that distinction will be removed by MLB more than seven decades later because of the leadoff walk. And Ruth? He gets a ten-day suspension.

Red Sox 4, Senators 0

1914 The Boston Braves earn the nickname "Miracle Braves" after their tremendous come-from-behind season. At 35-43 on July 18, they end the season in first place and take the pennant, as well as the World Series in four games against the Athletics.

December 26, 1919 The Sox sell Babe Ruth to the Yankees for $125,000, the highest amount ever paid for a player. Attendance at the Yankees' Polo Grounds doubles, and the signed contract will be sold to a collector for $996,000 eighty-six years later.

ABOVE: This photograph was taken from Fenway's right-field grandstand in late September 1914. Because of its age, Fenway is one of the only parks in the majors to still have seats that are obstructed by support columns. In 2005, Sox management stopped discounting obstructed-view tickets. Yet, according to the *Boston Globe*, they've received few complaints.

LEFT: Twenty-four-year-old Babe Ruth during his last season with the Sox, 1919.

1933 Tom Yawkey buys the Red Sox and enlists Eddie Collins, then working for the Philadelphia Athletics as a manager and occasional player, as his vice president and general manager.

1926

Bleachers along the left-field line burn down in a May fire. Management doesn't replace the stands, which allows left fielders the unique opportunity of catching foul balls behind the third-base grandstand.

1933

The Boston Braves football team relocates to Fenway from Braves Field after one year, and becomes the Boston Redskins. The club will move to Washington in 1937 because of owner George Preston Marshall's fury over lack of fan support.

1934

Fenway undergoes renovation. Duffy's Cliff is removed and owner Tom Yawkey replaces it with a 37-foot-high wall just 310 feet from home plate (for many years it is erroneously listed as 315 feet away). Center field is at 389 feet, with a 17-foot-high wall that serves as a batter's eye (meaning it helps players at bat see the ball better). Right of center is 420 feet.

TOP: Boston firefighters battle the 1934 five-alarm blaze that consumed much of Fenway Park during its off-season renovations. More than 150 workers were on the site when the fire started on cold, snowy January 5. The fire jumped Lansdowne Street and destroyed several businesses located across from the park.

BOTTOM: Fenway's fabled main entrance, pictured here in 1914, sits on Jersey Street. In 1977, the narrow strip will be renamed Yawkey Way to honor former team owner Tom Yawkey.

October 30, 1940 President Franklin Roosevelt gives a famous speech at Fenway during his re-election campaign, stating, "I have said this before, but I shall say it again and again and again: Your boys are not going to be sent into any foreign wars."

September 28, 1941 At Shibe Park, Ted Williams attains a season average of .406 on the last day of the season. In 2002, the Sox will rename their glassed-in luxury seating area the "406 Club," but will later sell the naming rights to the EMC Corporation.

1942 Johnny Pesky begins with the Sox, getting 205 hits in his rookie year. Fellow Sox broadcaster and former teammate Mel Parnell, making fun of Pesky's short home runs hit past the marker, will later nickname the right-field foul pole "Pesky's Pole."

1936

A 23-foot-high net is erected atop the fence in left field to protect bystanders on Lansdowne Street.

RIGHT: Born Robert Moses Groves, Lefty Grove would be inducted into the Hall of Fame in 1947.

BELOW: Hall of Famer Jimmie Foxx, the famed "Double X," bats for the Olde Towne Team at Fenway in 1937. Foxx is in the midst of an off year during which he hits "only" .285 with thirty-six homers and 127 RBIs. He'll rebound the following season to win his third AL MVP Award, batting .349 with fifty homers and 175 RBIs.

1940

The bullpens are moved in front of the right-field bleachers, trimming distances to 304 down the first base line and 382 in right-center. The bullpens become known as "Williamsburg," after Ted Williams who arrived the previous year.

July 25, 1941

A Hot Win for Lefty At the age of forty-one, Lefty Grove tosses all nine innings in 90° heat to beat the Indians. The win puts him in the 300 club, and is the last win of his career, although he will start six more games. At the end of the season, Grove will retire after seventeen years in the majors with a .680 winning percentage and the fifth most wins in history.

Red Sox 10, Indians 6

The Most Famous Wall in Baseball

When aging Fenway Park received a major upgrade before its 1934 season, no one could have guessed that the most revered aspect of the new construction would be a big, blank wall. The "Green Monster," as it came to be known, wasn't exactly unprecedented—several parks of the era had such walls—but Fenway's iconic left-field boundary remains more than seventy-five years later, and is now as much a part of Boston as historic Faneuil Hall.

When Tom Yawkey bought the Red Sox in 1933, he hired Osborn Engineering, which had recently built Yankee and Cleveland Stadiums, to give the dilapidated ball grounds an upgrade. The reconstruction cost upwards of $750,000, an amount that included rebuilding the left-field grandstand after an overturned cement heater started a five-alarm fire. Along with repairing and reconfiguring the grandstand, Yawkey flattened left field, the formerly slanted "Duffy's Cliff" named for famed outfielder Duffy Lewis. What he famously built in place of its 25-foot-high, left-field fence became the bane of left fielders and an imposing challenge for hitters across the American League.

The 37-foot-high structure of concrete and tin-covered wood was at first, like the rest of the park, plastered with advertisements. But in 1947, the wall was painted green, and soon the name "Green Monster" crept into the lexicon. The first national reference to the term may have come in the May 15, 1957, issue of the *Sporting News*. In an article describing Yawkey's habit of taking batting practice at Fenway, opposing pitchers—intimidated by the huge, lurking wall just 310 feet away—are credited as referring to it as such.

Since its construction, the Monster has housed a hand-operated scoreboard. Of course, in 1934, almost all scoreboards were manual, but Fenway's retention of a low-tech, hand-op board was considered quaint by the 1960s. Today, however, it is seen as an affectionate throwback, and some newer parks, including Minute Maid Park and Coors Field, have also incorporated fence-based scoreboards. The board, which takes three people to operate, has traditionally shown both AL and NL out-of-town scores (except from 1976 to 2002, when NL games were deleted), and the initials of Tom Yawkey and his wife Jean run down the center in Morse code.

The Red Sox didn't even have an electric scoreboard until 1976, when the club built a centerfield message board. At that time, the Red Sox also replaced the original Monster with a hard plastic version. Players as well as fans view the Green Monster as the signature of Fenway Park. Over the years, hundreds of players from Jimmy Piersall to Manny Ramirez (who is also rumored to have relieved himself inside during a pitching change) have walked through a small door into the scoreboard's operating area and signed the inside walls. And in 2003, boxes called "Monster Seats" were affixed atop the wall, allowing fans to have a bit of the Green Monster action as well.

July 9, 1946 After a year off from All-Star competition because of World War II travel restrictions, the Game returns. The AL trounces the NL, 12-0, at Fenway Park.

1950 Ted Williams becomes the highest paid baseball player to date when he re-signs his contract with the Red Sox for $125,000 per year.

1951 Curt Gowdy begins his fifteen-year career broadcasting for the Sox. In 1966, he'll leave to host NBC's Game of the Week, and will be awarded the Baseball Hall of Fame's Ford Frick Award in 1984.

1944

The football team the Boston Yanks join the NFL. They will play at Fenway through 1948, when they fold.

1946

Seats begin to be added to the roof, eventually becoming Fenway's upper deck of sorts.

1947

The wall in left field is stripped of its advertisements and painted green, and is soon dubbed the "Green Monster." On June 13, Fenway hosts its first night game, against the White Sox.

OPPOSITE: Writer John Updike called the Green Monster "a compromise between man's Euclidean determinations and nature's beguiling irregularities."

BELOW: Duffy's Cliff in left field is leveled after the 1933 season during construction of what would eventually be known as the Green Monster. The construction shown here will burn in the great fire of January 1934, but will be rebuilt by that year's Opening Day.

RIGHT: As viewed from the roof behind home plate, the left-field wall in September 1946 is covered with advertisements. In 1947, the wall will lose its billboards and be painted its now-familiar green color, giving rise to the famed Green Monster.

July 21, 1959 The Red Sox become the last major league team to integrate when Elijah "Pumpsie" Green pinch-runs in a game versus the White Sox at Comiskey Park.

September 28, 1960

Williams Bids MLB Adieu Exactly nineteen years after he hit .406, Williams homers in his final major league at-bat when he whacks the ball into the right-field bullpen off Baltimore's Jack Fisher. Even after he is replaced in left field during the next inning, Williams refuses to tip his cap. His record of 521 home runs puts him third on the all-time home run list of the day, behind only Babe Ruth and Williams' former teammate Jimmie Foxx. John Updike, who is in the crowd, immortalizes the occasion with his story "Hub Fans Bid Kid Adieu."

Red Sox 5, Orioles 4

1961 With the addition of the Anaheim Angels and the expansion Washington Senators, the American League increases the season to 162 games to accommodate ten teams.

BELOW, INSET: Call him what you may—"The Kid," "Teddy Ballgame," "The Thumper," "The Splendid Splinter"—but many believe that Ted Williams was the best hitter who ever lived.

1963

The AFL Boston Patriots play their first home game at Fenway. Denied by Fenway and Harvard originally, the Pats played their first three seasons at Nickerson Field, the same site as old Braves Field. Once at Fenway, they will stay through 1968.

October 1, 1967

Sox Bring It Down to the Wire The Red Sox win one of the tightest American League races in history on the season's final weekend. A five-run Boston sixth helps Jim Lonborg beat Dean Chance in a battle of twenty-game winners. Carl Yastrzemski clinches the Triple Crown with a 4-for-4 performance. And Sox fans pour into Kenmore Square to celebrate Boston's first pennant in twenty-one years.

Red Sox 5, Twins 3

BELOW: Workers transform Fenway Park into its pigskin incarnation, as they set up for a Boston Patriots game against the Oakland Raiders on October 11, 1963—only the second home game for the AFL Patriots at Fenway. At left, temporary bleachers are being erected in left field, and the under-construction Prudential Tower is visible over the right-field bleachers. Fenway has also hosted both Boston College and Boston University football games.

October 21, 1975

The Famous Game 6 Game 6 of the 1975 World Series is the game that all Game 6s—and all other World Series games—are judged against. After three days of rain, the anticipation was building, and after Boston's Fred Lynn hits a three-run homer in the first and Reds starter Gary Nolan is knocked out in the third, it looks like the Sox might win the game in a romp. But Cincinnati ties it in the fifth, and the game eventually goes to extra innings. The Reds use eight pitchers over the course of the evening, including Rawly Eastwick, who allows another three-run homer (to Bernie Carbo), and ending with Pat Darcy, who surrenders Carlton Fisk's famous foul-pole drive, complete with "go fair!" arm waving. In between, Dwight Evans makes one of the greatest catches and throws in Series history.

Red Sox 7, Reds 6

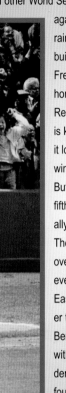

ABOVE: Fred Lynn (left) and Carlton Fisk celebrate after Fisk hits the winning home run in Game 6 of the 1975 World Series.

RIGHT: A toilet paper streamer flies behind number 8, Fenway favorite Carl Yastrzemski, as he heads for first base after rapping his 3,000th hit, against the Yankees on September 12, 1979.

October 2, 1978

Bucky Dent's Defining Moment The game would not have even been necessary in today's wild card era, but this one-game playoff for a division title means everything, especially for Boston fans hoping to break the Curse of the Bambino. In the top of the seventh inning, Bucky Dent's pop fly catches the net over the Green Monster and shatters Boston's dreams of finally beating the Yankees in a do-or-die struggle. Dent gains an off-color middle name throughout New England, joining home-team pitcher Mike Torrez and manager Don Zimmer as those who are forever held in contempt by followers of the Olde Towne Team.

Yankees 5, Red Sox 4

September 7, 1978 The dreaded Yankees come to town for a four-game series against the Sox, who are ahead of their rivals by four games. The Yanks will outscore the Sox 42-9 in an outright massacre, tying the pennant race with twenty games left to play.

May 25, 1984 The Red Sox retire the numbers of Joe Cronin and Ted Williams, 4 and 9 respectively. They now hang on the right-field facade of Fenway Park along with the retired numbers of Bobby Doerr, Johnny Pesky, Carl Yastrzemski, Carlton Fisk, and Jackie Robinson.

September 12, 1979

Yaz Hits the Record When Carl Yastrzemski gets a single against Jim Beattie, it is his 3,000th career hit, making him the first AL player to collect both 3,000 hits and 400 home runs. (Stan Musial, Henry Aaron, and Willie Mays had done it in the NL.) The game is delayed fifteen minutes for a speech, and Yaz is congratulated by both teams. Jim Dwyer pinch-runs and scores the game's final run.

Red Sox 9, Yankees 2

1989 One of the most beloved baseball movies of all time, *Field of Dreams*, is released. In one of the few scenes filmed outside of the Iowa-Illinois area, Kevin Costner takes James Earl Jones to a ballgame at Fenway Park.

1995 The Sox nab the AL East title with an 86-58 record. First baseman Mo Vaughn will win AL MVP honors, but Boston will be swept in the newly created AL Division Series by Cleveland.

1997 Nomar Garciaparra begins his first full season with the Sox, winning Rookie of the Year, getting nominated to the All-Star team, and batting .306 with ninety-eight RBIs and thirty home runs.

1989

The 600 Club, a glassed-in seating area, is built atop the roof behind home plate, and the press box is then rebuilt on top of it. The club, later renamed the .406 Club and then the EMC Club, is believed by many players to affect wind patterns, making it tougher to hit home runs.

1997

Much to the distaste of advertising-adverse fans, a huge Coke bottle is affixed to the top of the light tower in left field. It will be removed in 2008 to make way for more Coke-themed advertising when that section of the stands is dubbed "Coca-Cola Corner."

April 29, 1986

Clemens Strikes Out Twenty Roger Clemens fans twenty Mariners to set the all-time record for a nine-inning game. Four M's whiff three or more times, including Ken Phelps, who finally puts a bat on the ball to ground out, ending the game. Clemens is 4-0 and will win twenty more games to earn the league MVP and Cy Young awards.

Red Sox 3, Mariners 1

July 13, 1999

Ted's Tribute All-Stars from both leagues and from the All-Century team surround eighty-year-old Ted Williams in an impromptu tribute at The Kid's home park. When the game starts, the admiration switches to the mound, where Pedro Martinez strikes out the first four batters and throws so hard that he winds up on the disabled list a few days later. Still, Pedro is the game's MVP and is the overwhelming choice for Cy Young. (He'll just miss winning the league MVP in a controversial vote.)

AL 4, NL 1

ABOVE, RIGHT: "Rocket" Roger Clemens, twenty-three years old but already at the top of the game, poses against the left-field scoreboard on May 1, 1986, two days after he fanned twenty hapless Seattle batters at Fenway to set a record.

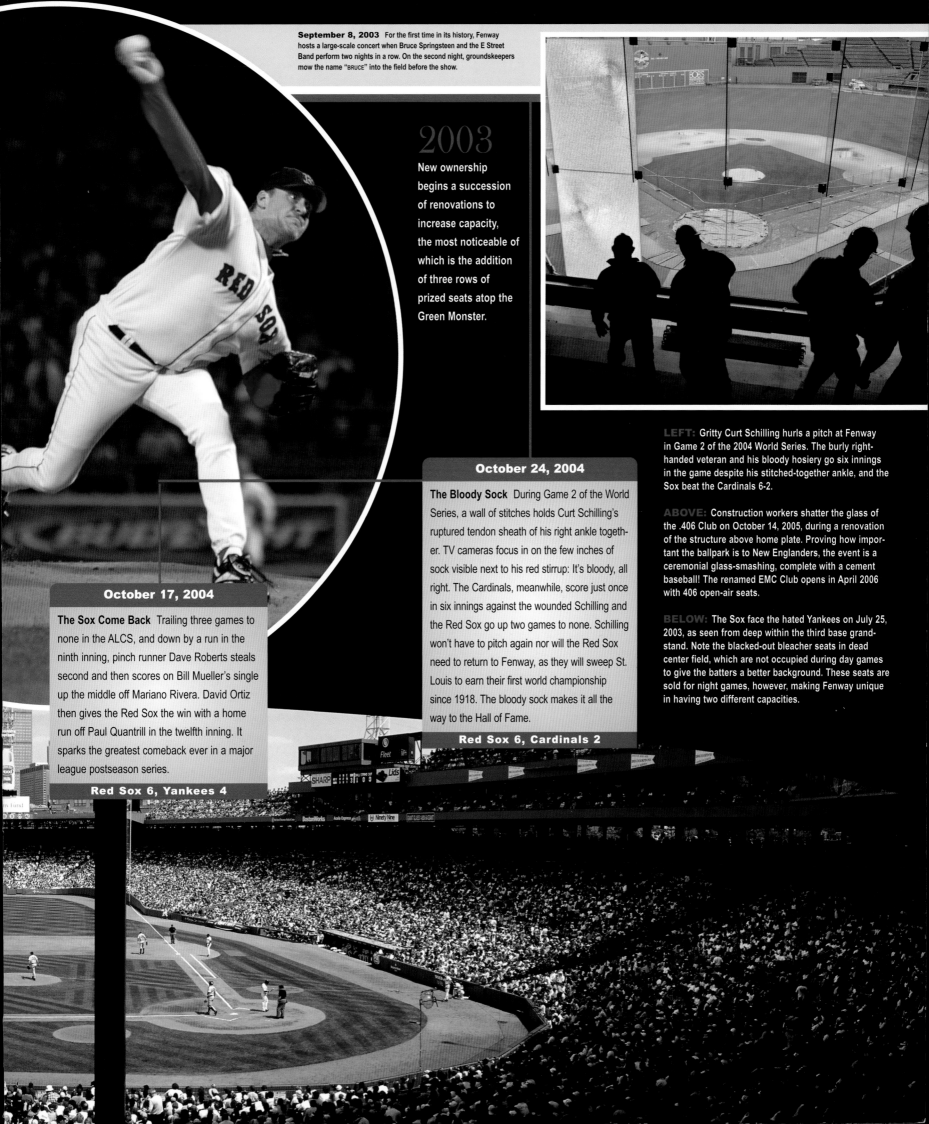

September 8, 2003 For the first time in its history, Fenway hosts a large-scale concert when Bruce Springsteen and the E Street Band perform two nights in a row. On the second night, groundskeepers mow the name "BRUCE" into the field before the show.

2003

New ownership begins a succession of renovations to increase capacity, the most noticeable of which is the addition of three rows of prized seats atop the Green Monster.

LEFT: Gritty Curt Schilling hurls a pitch at Fenway in Game 2 of the 2004 World Series. The burly right-handed veteran and his bloody hosiery go six innings in the game despite his stitched-together ankle, and the Sox beat the Cardinals 6-2.

ABOVE: Construction workers shatter the glass of the .406 Club on October 14, 2005, during a renovation of the structure above home plate. Proving how important the ballpark is to New Englanders, the event is a ceremonial glass-smashing, complete with a cement baseball! The renamed EMC Club opens in April 2006 with 406 open-air seats.

BELOW: The Sox face the hated Yankees on July 25, 2003, as seen from deep within the third base grandstand. Note the blacked-out bleacher seats in dead center field, which are not occupied during day games to give the batters a better background. These seats are sold for night games, however, making Fenway unique in having two different capacities.

October 24, 2004

The Bloody Sock During Game 2 of the World Series, a wall of stitches holds Curt Schilling's ruptured tendon sheath of his right ankle together. TV cameras focus in on the few inches of sock visible next to his red stirrup: It's bloody, all right. The Cardinals, meanwhile, score just once in six innings against the wounded Schilling and the Red Sox go up two games to none. Schilling won't have to pitch again nor will the Red Sox need to return to Fenway, as they will sweep St. Louis to earn their first world championship since 1918. The bloody sock makes it all the way to the Hall of Fame.

Red Sox 6, Cardinals 2

October 17, 2004

The Sox Come Back Trailing three games to none in the ALCS, and down by a run in the ninth inning, pinch runner Dave Roberts steals second and then scores on Bill Mueller's single up the middle off Mariano Rivera. David Ortiz then gives the Red Sox the win with a home run off Paul Quantrill in the twelfth inning. It sparks the greatest comeback ever in a major league postseason series.

Red Sox 6, Yankees 4

2006 David Ortiz sets a club record by hitting fifty-four home runs during the season.

2007 The Sox pay a record-breaking $5.1 million for the right to negotiate with Japanese superstar Daisuke Matsuzaka. They then sign a six-year, $52 million deal with the ace pitcher.

2007

The Sox announce several new changes to the park, including more standing-room-only space. The most noticeable change is the Dunkin' Donuts billboard in right-center field that reads, "Welcome to Fenway Park" in Japanese.

September 1, 2007

Beginner's Luck Clay Buchholz, in just his second major league start, throws a no-hitter at Fenway. The Red Sox give him plenty of support at the plate and in the field, with rookie second baseman Dustin Pedroia preserving the bid with a diving stop in the seventh inning. The twenty-three-year-old Buchholz gets Nick Markakis looking at a curve to end the game as the fans go wild. It is the seventeenth no-hitter in Red Sox history and the third in major league annals by a pitcher making his first or second career start. Jon Lester, a cancer survivor, will add yet another Red Sox no-hitter the following year, tossing one against the Royals in Boston on May 19, 2008.

Red Sox 10, Orioles 0

October 21, 2007

Out On a High Note The Red Sox cap a pennant-winning rally against the Indians by taking Game 7 of the ALCS. After winning the opening game and then dropping three straight to Cleveland, the Red Sox outscore the Indians over the final three games by a count of 30-5. Though the final out is a formality, the game ends dramatically as Coco Crisp dashes back to the 420-foot mark and makes a spectacular catch against Casey Blake, crashing into the fence and then into the ground. Japanese import Daisuke Matsuzaka wins Game 7 for his new team, but Josh Beckett, who won twice—including Game 5 with Boston's back to the wall—is the series MVP. The Red Sox will go on to sweep the Colorado Rockies for their seventh world championship (each against a different NL team).

Red Sox 11, Indians 2

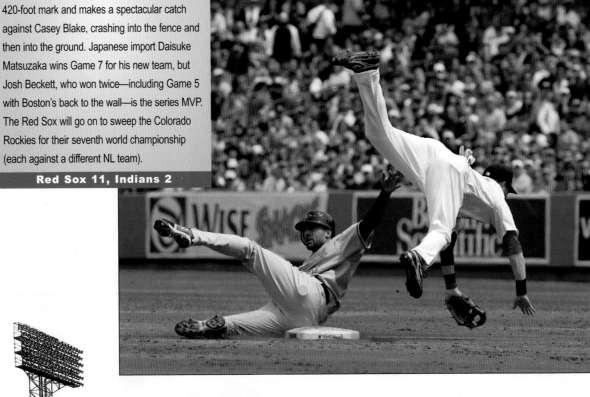

BELOW: Dustin Pedroia goes airborne over a sliding Nick Markakis of the Orioles at Fenway Park on May 12, 2007. Pedroia completes the double play, the Sox slaughter the visitors by a score of 13-4, and the pint-size second-sacker goes on to win the AL Rookie of the Year Award.

BELOW: This June 2008 photo shows Fenway's old-fashioned wood-and-metal chairs as well as the extensive modern additions to the rooftop down the first base line.

October 6, 2008

A New Streak Though last night the Angels ended an eleven-game postseason losing streak to Boston (which dated back to 1986), the Sox immediately start a new streak. Tonight they beat Anaheim in the Division Series for the third time since 2004, and for the second time in walk-off fashion. Angels shortstop Erick Aybar botches a suicide squeeze in the top of the ninth on a controversial call that saw Jason Varitek tag the runner out at third before dropping the ball as he hit the ground. The Red Sox stage a rally in the home ninth. Rookie Jed Lowrie singles in Jason Bay, who slides home headfirst for the winning run in Game 4.

Red Sox 3, Angels 2

October 16, 2008

Rally Rousers After many in Red Sox Nation leave the park and turn off their TVs, Boston stages the greatest postseason rally since the 1929 World Series. Down 7-0 (including two inherited runs against maverick closer Jonathan Papelbon) and about to be pushed aside in the ALCS in five games, the Red Sox counter with four runs in the bottom of the seventh—a Dustin Pedroia single to right that drives in Jed Lowrie, and then a three-run shot by David Ortiz (1 for 17 before that at-bat) that quickly closes the gap. An inning later, a two-run homer by JD Drew makes it a one-run deficit and Coco Crisp then knocks in the tying run. The game is an out from going into extra innings when an Evan Longoria error puts the go-ahead run at second base and Drew drives in the game winner. The series heads back to Tampa Bay and the Red Sox will force a Game 7 before falling short in their quest for their third 3-1 postseason comeback since 2004.

Red Sox 8, Rays 7

BELOW: Hub favorite Kevin Youkilis backhands a ground ball off the bat of Evan Longoria during the eighth inning of Game 4 of the 2008 ALCS against Tampa Bay.

The Grass Is Always Greener

In 1991, baseball fans across the United States breathed a sigh of relief as new Comiskey Park opened with a major change from the current breed of parks: natural sod. Starting in the mid-1960s, many fields—whether indoors or out—had been fitted (or retrofitted) with artificial turf, and their outfields were uniformly green and cut. During this time, owners saved money by having little to no grounds crew, since the "ground" rarely required more than a periodic cleaning.

For Fenway Park's natural grass, groundskeeping has never been so easy. Like most parks of its era, the field was built on substandard land that nobody else wanted. Infielders routinely dealt with bad hops due to the uneven surface. It was not unusual for garbage from former dump sites to be found under the grass at some parks. Improvements developed surprisingly slowly given the enormous popularity of the game, with the most important changes occurring only in the last thirty years. A field that would have been acceptable in 1940, or even 1970, would be woefully inadequate today. When Fenway was built, the task of groundskeeping consisted of merely rolling out the infield and cutting the grass. Today, the concept of basic maintenance has vastly changed, as the landscaped design of the field has become more intricate. Many clubs crosshatch their grass for visual effect, and each postseason provides an opportunity to insert attractive patterns on the field, such as the team's logo, using special mower blades.

Maintaining the grounds requires a lot more work than just making the grass look

BELOW: Manny Ramirez trudges through intricately designed left field during an August 2007 game at Fenway.

good. Keeping it dry is an even more difficult task. Modern stadiums have always been built with pipes underneath the surface to facilitate flow, but current drainage systems have benefited from sophisticated and careful research, not to mention decades of trial and error. (Ironically, two of the biggest innovators of grounds maintenance—Roger Bossard in Chicago and George Toma in Kansas City—developed some of the largest advances in drainage control and water conservation during the days when artificial turf was used throughout the industry.) Today, it's not unusual for a baseball field to drain an inch or more of rain per hour, a necessity to prevent injury to players—and injury to the wallets of owners, who like to avoid rained-out games and makeup doubleheaders.

The condition of the ground—including the occasional intentional overwatering or undercutting—is also a contributing factor to a team's performance. Clubs trying to defend against Dodgers speedster Maury Wills were known to water down their base paths (especially leading from first base) to cut his speed. And keeping infield grass high to either aid a team's bunters or help a ground-ball pitching staff remains a legitimate strategy.

The job of groundskeeper requires specialized skills in lawn care, foul-line layout, infield and warning track maintenance, and even design, not to mention the strength to roll the tarpaulin out after every game and during rain delays. Luckily, the heads of grounds crews across the country (including Detroit's Heather Nabozny, the first female head groundskeeper in the majors) have better-paid staffs than ever before, as well as the latest equipment to keep fields in top shape—even during the off-season. Gone are the days when clubs spray-painted slow-growing outfield grass during April. Now, teams rotate new sod every year, sometimes *during* the season. With care like this, it's guaranteed that not only will teams have a field their fans can enjoy, but that players won't find any surprises underfoot. It's been a long time since Chicago's star shortstop Luke Appling dug out chunks of crockery from underneath the field of the original Comiskey Park in the 1930s, more than two decades after the park opened.

LEFT: Groundskeepers tend to Wrigley Field in 1924, years before the park's signature ivy-covered brick wall was built.

BELOW: African Americans—who wouldn't be able to play for the Senators for another three decades—prepare the Griffith Stadium diamond for the 1924 World Series, the first in Washington's history.

TIGER STADIUM

Detroit, Michigan

Tigers (AL) 1912–1999

Navin Field (1912–1937), Briggs Stadium (1938–1960)

RIGHT: Hailed as "The Greatest Tiger of Them All," Tyrus Raymond Cobb stands in front of a dugout early in 1914. The AL's best and most famous player, he had already won the batting title seven years in a row.

OPPOSITE: This aerial photo of Tiger Stadium (then called Navin Field) was taken during Game 2 of the 1935 World Series. Behind future Hall of Famers Mickey Cochrane, Charlie Gehringer, Goose Goslin, and Hank Greenberg—who broke his wrist in this game and would not play for the rest of the Series—the Tigers defeated the Cubs in six games. The *Sporting News* summarized the Series thusly: "While neither team excelled overall, the conquerors at least (and at last) won their first World Series."

Note the field's double-decked grandstand, the single-decked pavilions with roofs in the left- and right-field corners, and the huge amount of bleacher seating in fair territory in left and right fields. Invigorated by Detroit's first championship in '35, owner Frank Navin made plans to expand the park, although those plans wouldn't be executed for another three years. Over the decades, many of the houses visible in this photo would be demolished, with their vacant lots serving as off-street parking.

Known simply as "The Corner," the intersection of Michigan Avenue and Trumbull Street in Detroit has been a haven for professional baseball longer than any other site—since 1886, when it was the home field of the Western League Tigers. In 1901, the team became the American League Tigers, and eleven years later a concrete-and-steel stadium was built on the site for $200,000. The fate of the field at The Corner was always tied to that of the city around it. As Detroit grew, so did its ballpark. And when Detroit's fortunes began to crumble, talk turned to abandoning the storied field. But it wouldn't go down without a fight, as its fans staged a battle almost as historic as the field itself.

The new concrete-and-steel stadium opened on April 20, 1912—the same day as Boston's Fenway Park—with fans attended to by ushers in tidy uniforms and matching caps, and peanut and popcorn vendors in clean-cut, pressed khaki suits. The park seated 23,000 and was laid out in a large single deck, with the grandstand, box seats, and even the pavilions down the left- and right-field lines designed to be in the shade at all times. Spectators wanting to bask in the sun would sit in the concrete bleachers—an immensely popular location throughout the park's history, especially on "Bat Day," when fans were given free bats and took to rhythmically banging them on the decking. ("Bat Day" was eventually discontinued when it was discovered that the banging might pose a threat to the structure.)

For most of the park's run, the fans had plenty to cheer—or bang—about. Over the years, talented players like Ty Cobb, Charlie Gehringer, Hank Greenberg, Hal Newhouser—and later Al Kaline, Norm Cash, Mickey Lolich, and Willie Horton—called Tiger Stadium home. The Tigers won the World Series in 1935, 1945, and again in 1968, the year the ballpark saw more than two million fans enter its gates. In

1984, Detroit had their last Series win at the stadium, with a little help from Kirk Gibson's famous homer in the eighth inning of Game 5.

The park on The Corner went through several owners, and with them, numerous improvements and name changes. Before 1912, it had been called Bennett Park, after a catcher who had lost his legs in a train accident. Then it changed to Navin Field, named for team owner Frank Navin, who not only erected the first concrete-and-steel structure for the Tigers, but also built a second deck and a press box on the roof in 1923. After the team's first World Series win and Navin's death in 1935, the remaining shares of the team were purchased by co-owner Walter Briggs. In addition to renaming the park after himself, Briggs brought capacity to 58,000 by adding even more upper-deck sections, razing an adjacent street in the process and completely encasing the field. And after John Fetzer bought out the Briggs heirs in 1960, the field was renamed Tiger Stadium and several improvements were made, including repair work to the third deck and press area after a 1977 fire, the installation of new chairs, and the addition of a $2 million scoreboard in 1980. Fetzer also had the brilliant idea of selling Tiger Stadium to the City of Detroit for $1, then leasing it back for thirty years, leaving the city with the bill for maintenance and renovation (with help from the fans, who paid a 90¢ surcharge on every ticket).

While the stadium changed, so did the city around it. A prosperous hub for automobile manufacturing when the stadium was built, Detroit became the "Arsenal of Democracy" in World War II. But in the 1960s, the city's fortunes began to decline. In 1967, the city was afflicted with race riots, and the Tigers found themselves locked in a four-way battle for the AL title. In an ugly coda to one of the greatest pennant

AL SIMMONS

BARNEY McCOSKY

AL KALINE
DETROIT TIGERS
OUTFIELD

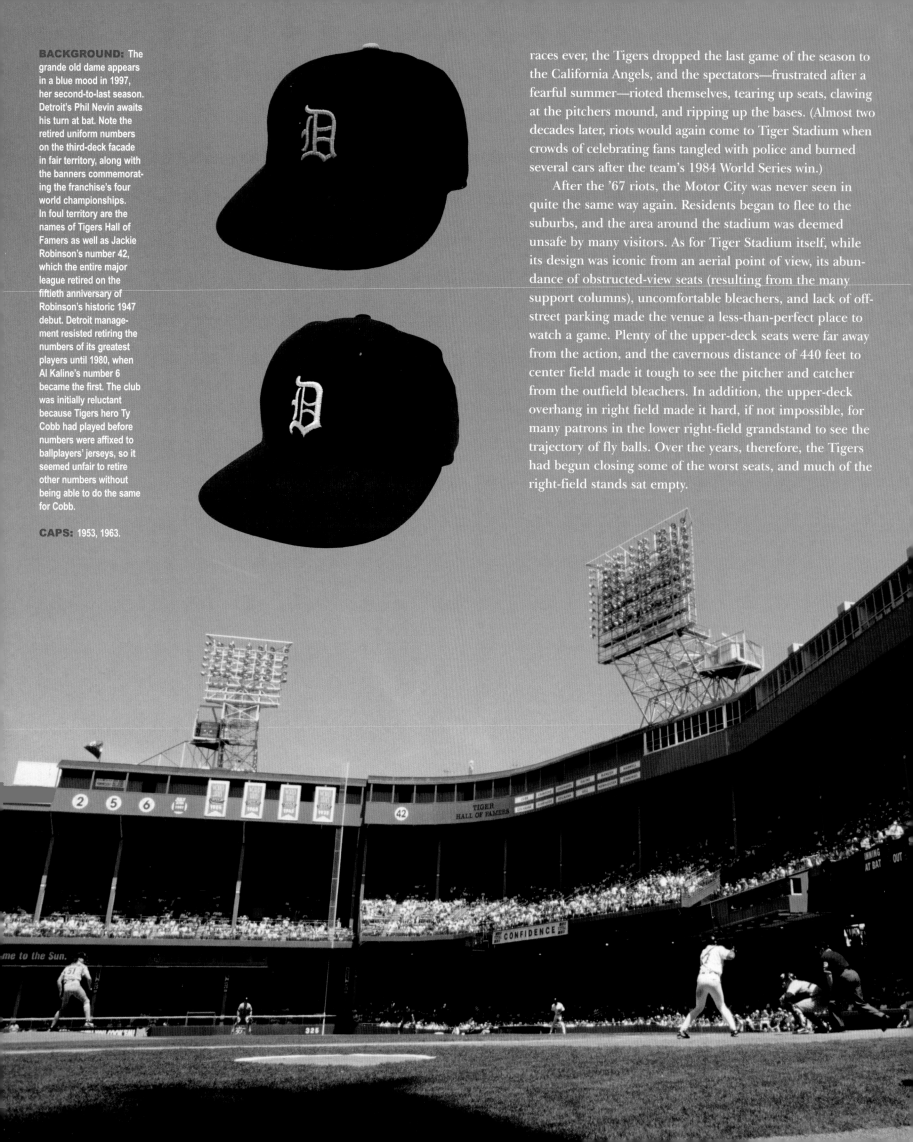

BACKGROUND: The grande old dame appears in a blue mood in 1997, her second-to-last season. Detroit's Phil Nevin awaits his turn at bat. Note the retired uniform numbers on the third-deck facade in fair territory, along with the banners commemorating the franchise's four world championships. In foul territory are the names of Tigers Hall of Famers as well as Jackie Robinson's number 42, which the entire major league retired on the fiftieth anniversary of Robinson's historic 1947 debut. Detroit management resisted retiring the numbers of its greatest players until 1980, when Al Kaline's number 6 became the first. The club was initially reluctant because Tigers hero Ty Cobb had played before numbers were affixed to ballplayers' jerseys, so it seemed unfair to retire other numbers without being able to do the same for Cobb.

CAPS: 1953, 1963.

races ever, the Tigers dropped the last game of the season to the California Angels, and the spectators—frustrated after a fearful summer—rioted themselves, tearing up seats, clawing at the pitchers mound, and ripping up the bases. (Almost two decades later, riots would again come to Tiger Stadium when crowds of celebrating fans tangled with police and burned several cars after the team's 1984 World Series win.)

After the '67 riots, the Motor City was never seen in quite the same way again. Residents began to flee to the suburbs, and the area around the stadium was deemed unsafe by many visitors. As for Tiger Stadium itself, while its design was iconic from an aerial point of view, its abundance of obstructed-view seats (resulting from the many support columns), uncomfortable bleachers, and lack of off-street parking made the venue a less-than-perfect place to watch a game. Plenty of the upper-deck seats were far away from the action, and the cavernous distance of 440 feet to center field made it tough to see the pitcher and catcher from the outfield bleachers. In addition, the upper-deck overhang in right field made it hard, if not impossible, for many patrons in the lower right-field grandstand to see the trajectory of fly balls. Over the years, therefore, the Tigers had begun closing some of the worst seats, and much of the right-field stands sat empty.

In 1972, Fetzer announced that the club was looking for a new home, but voters didn't approve the financing. Instead, Fetzer was forced to spend his money on upgrades and repairs to the park after the 1977 fire. While attendance slumped in the '80s, a PR campaign combined with behind-the-scenes machinations began to convince the people of Detroit that Tiger Stadium was falling down—and that tax-payers' money was needed to build a new ballpark. Domino's Pizza mogul Tom Monaghan, who bought the team after the 1983 season, also began looking for a new site for a ballpark, though he hadn't made much progress by the time he sold the club to rival pizza baron Mike Ilitch of Little Caesars a decade later.

Whether or not to build a new stadium had become a heated debate around the city. Though the park had obvious shortcomings, old-time fans pointed to the need to preserve local history, the lack of funding the suffering city had to build a new park, and the aesthetic values of the old stadium, which were being mimicked by new retro ballparks across the country. Those in favor of building a new ballpark downtown felt that it might revitalize the struggling district and improve the image of Detroit.

Fueled mostly by a deep-rooted love of Tiger Stadium and its tradition, but also by anger at the distortions and false-hoods the club and city officials had been spinning to bolster their case, a group of Tigers fans banded together to fight for their beloved park. The battle between the Tiger Stadium Fan Club (as they were known) on one side, and the team owners and the city government on the other, was both lengthy and bitter. While the Fan Club and its allies offered alternate plans to renovate the existing stadium and got the park put on the National Register of Historic Places, Ilitch obtained enough money from the state and county to build a new stadium, and ground was broken in 1997.

Even with a trip to the Michigan Supreme Court, the battle was effectively over. The new field, Comerica Park, opened in 2000, and baseball at The Corner ended at the end of the 1999 season. But is it over for good? Though wrecking balls have already begun swinging, the fate of the original 1912 structure is unknown. Still fighting for the legendary stadium that represented the history of Detroit on its field, the Tiger Stadium Fan Club raises money little by little from baseball fans around the country who see a value in keeping a bit of the park alive. And it's easy to see why. As *Time* magazine's Walter Shapiro Chicago wrote several years before the last game at the park, "Watching a game in Detroit is a graduate course in capturing the magic of the old-time ballparks. Unlike the ivy-clad perfection of Wrigley Field or the self-congratulatory ugliness of Fenway Park, Tiger Stadium represents the last remaining link with baseball before it became too self-conscious." Or as former Tigers rookie Bob Melville simply put it, "the whole place smelled like baseball." Even with weeds growing in its out-field and pieces of memorabilia pulled from its walls long ago, it probably still does.

INSET: Tigers owner Walter O. "Spike" Briggs Jr., who took the helm after his father passed away in 1952, watches workers remove seventy-five box seats from right-field foul territory in December 1954. Briggs ordered the change after Detroit's promising rookie Al Kaline injured his knee running into the protruding grandstand while playing right field that season.

1917 Ty Cobb stars in the critically panned film *Somewhere in Georgia*, essentially playing himself.

1921 Ty Cobb is appointed manager of the club while still an active player. Moreover, he proceeds to hit twelve home runs this season, his career high.

1912

Navin Field opens to an overflow Opening Day crowd of 24,384. Built on the same location as Bennett Park, where professional baseball has been played since 1896, the new field is 345 feet in the left, 467 to center, and 370 in the right.

1923

The grandstand is double-decked from first base to third base; capacity increases to 30,000.

1924

The Tigers draw more than one million fans, becoming the first team other than the Yankees to do so.

July 13, 1934

The Bambino Breaks New Ground Babe Ruth, who had shrugged off a meeting with Detroit owner Frank Navin the previous winter to discuss the possibility of managing the Tigers, makes history in Detroit anyway. Ruth, already the only player with more than 400 career home runs, starts another new club with his 700th four-bagger. With the victory, the Yankees leapfrog the Tigers and take over first place, although Detroit will eventually capture the pennant. Lou Gehrig has to leave the game with a lumbago seizure, but he'll keep his consecutive games streak going the next day by batting leadoff against the Tigers (he'll be listed as the shortstop) and then departing for a pinch runner after his first-inning single.

Yankees 4, Tigers 2

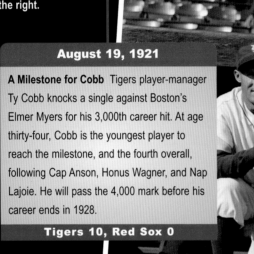

August 19, 1921

A Milestone for Cobb Tigers player-manager Ty Cobb knocks a single against Boston's Elmer Myers for his 3,000th career hit. At age thirty-four, Cobb is the youngest player to reach the milestone, and the fourth overall, following Cap Anson, Honus Wagner, and Nap Lajoie. He will pass the 4,000 mark before his career ends in 1928.

Tigers 10, Red Sox 0

LEFT: Detroit's 1935 version of Murderers' Row includes (from left) Leon "Goose" Goslin, "Hammerin' Hank" Greenberg, and "the Mechanical Man" Charlie Gehringer. Led by the three future Hall of Famers, each of whom will score more than one hundred runs and drive in more than one hundred RBIs for the season, the '35 Tigers will lead the league in offense and outscore the second-place Yankees by 101 runs. Greenberg will drive in 170 runs (the eighth-highest single-season RBI count ever) while leading Detroit to its second consecutive pennant and first world championship.

1930 Star centerfielder Norman "Turkey" Stearnes and the Detroit Stars, playing at Hamtramck Stadium after Mack Park burned down, lose a seven-game Negro World Series to the St. Louis Stars.

1934 After an unsuccessful courtship with Babe Ruth, Tigers president Frank Navin signs Philadelphia Athletics catcher Mickey Cochrane as player-manager. Cochrane leads the team to two consecutive World Series, in 1934 and 1935, winning the championship in 1935.

December 8, 1941 After having been discharged from the army earlier in the year, Tigers' "Hammerin' Hank" Greenberg re-enlists the day after the bombing of Pearl Harbor. He is the first ballplayer to leave the game to serve in World War II.

October 9, 1934

Dizzy with Excitement The Tigers, playing in their first World Series since 1909 and the first ever played at Navin Field, are trounced by St. Louis in Game 7. The crowd (and the game) begins to get ugly when the Cardinals score seven times in the third inning to knock out Tigers starter Elden Auker and put the game out of reach. When the Cards' Joe Medwick triples in another run in the sixth, he slides hard and becomes entangled with Tigers third baseman Marv Owen. Angry about the run-in with Owen and the losing game, fans start pelting Medwick with rotten fruit and other garbage when he returns to his spot in left field, and he's forced to take cover in the dugout three times. Finally, Commissioner Kenesaw Mountain Landis orders Medwick removed from the game for his own safety. Pitcher Dizzy Dean, meanwhile, holds the Tigers scoreless for the duration of the game.

Cardinals 11, Tigers 0

BELOW: In this 1909 Detroit team portrait at Bennett Park (precursor to Tiger Stadium), Ty Cobb is the leftmost player in uniform. Slugger Sam Crawford is seventh from the left (with the unbuttoned sweater) and manager Hughie Jennings is second from right (without a sweater). Jennings' Tygers—as they were frequently labeled in the press—won AL pennants in 1907, 1908, and 1909 but lost all three World Series.

October 7, 1935

Sweet Revenge After twenty-seven years, the Tigers finally get a World Series rematch with the Chicago Cubs, who humiliated them in both the 1907 and 1908 Series. The Tigers lead the Series three-games-to-two as they return to Navin Field for Game 6. With the game tied in the bottom of the ninth with two outs, Goose Goslin's hit scores player-manager Mickey Cochrane, finally giving Detroit its first world championship. Tommy Bridges, who managed to pitch around a leadoff triple in the top of the inning, is the winning pitcher.

Tigers 4, Cubs 3

1938

The park's name is changed to Briggs Stadium, and completion of the upper deck all the way around the playing field brings capacity to a peak of 58,000. The NFL's Lions move in.

May 2, 1939

Gehrig's Farewell In the Motor City, the Iron Horse finally takes a rest. Lou Gehrig, weakened by the fatal nerve disease amyotrophic lateral sclerosis, removes himself from the lineup for the first time in 2,130 games. The announcement is made on the loudspeaker at Briggs Stadium before the Yankees' 22-2 rout of the Tigers. Gehrig will officially retire from playing two months later, and will never play another game. The legendary player will end his career with a lifetime average of .340 and a total of 493 home runs and 1,995 RBIs. Two years later, at the age of thirty-eight, he will die from the disease that will eventually bear his name.

Yankees 22, Tigers 2

July 8, 1941

Teddy Ballgame Wins Again Briggs Stadium hosts the first of its three All-Star Games, and thanks to Ted Williams, it ends up being one of the best Midsummer Classics ever played. Pittsburgh's Arky Vaughan becomes the first player to homer twice in an All-Star Game, giving the NL a 5-3 lead entering the bottom of the ninth. After the AL loads the bases, Joe DiMaggio barely beats out what would have been a game-ending double play grounder. The game ends soon enough, though, as Williams crushes a Claude Passeau pitch off the right-field roof and dances around the bases to the cheers of 54,674 spectators.

AL 7, NL 5

ABOVE: Yankees legend Lou Gehrig watches from the visitors' dugout at Tiger Stadium on May 2, 1939. It is on this day that the "Iron Horse" takes himself out of the Yankees' lineup after 2,130 consecutive games.

1960 Radio and television entrepreneur John Fetzer purchases the Tigers ball club from the Briggs family. His first plan of action is to rechristen the ballpark "Tiger Stadium."

1968 Detroit's Denny McLain becomes the second and last pitcher in history to win thirty-one games in a season. Known as the "Year of the Pitcher," 1968 saw 21 percent of all games finish as shutouts.

1970 Tigers ace and future felon Denny McLain is suspended three times—for gambling, dousing sportswriters with water, and carrying a gun onto a plane.

1948

Thirteen years after the introduction of night baseball to the major leagues, Briggs Stadium becomes the last American League park to host its first game under the lights.

BELOW: Left-hander Mickey Lolich delivers a pitch during Game 5 of the 1968 World Series. With Detroit facing elimination, the durable sinkerballer saves the Tigers' bacon, striking out eight to beat St. Louis. Lolich, who pitched for most of 1968 in the shadow of MVP and thirty-one-game-winner Denny McLain, will be named World Series MVP.

FAR RIGHT: Al Kaline starts his swing on September 14, 1974, against the Yankees. Kaline will go 3-for-4 with a homer and three RBIs on this day. Later in the month, he'll record his 3,000th career hit before retiring at the end of the season.

1961

In its final name change, the park is renamed Tiger Stadium.

1968

On their way to the World Series, the Tigers draw two million fans for the first time.

October 7, 1968

Brock's Baserunning Adventures Thirty-four years after the 1934 Classic, St. Louis and Detroit face off in another memorable World Series. The Cardinals, needing a win in Game 5 to wrap up the Series, score three runs in the first inning, but the Tigers respond with two in the bottom of the fourth. In the next inning, the Cards' Lou Brock—who was thrown out stealing earlier in the game—makes another baserunning error. Brock tries to score standing up on a single to left, but is tagged out by catcher Bill Freehan on Willie Horton's great throw. Tigers pitcher Mickey Lolich, meanwhile, starts the home seventh with a single, and later scores on Al Kaline's two-run single. Lolich's second complete game of the Series gives Detroit a 5-3 win. Three days later, his third complete game win will clinch the championship for the Tigers.

Tigers 5, Cardinals 3

July 13, 1971

Reggie's Light Tower Homer Twenty years after a record six home runs were hit at the 1951 All-Star Game in Detroit, six are hit again. This time, however, they are all hit by future Hall of Famers: Johnny Bench, Hank Aaron, Reggie Jackson, Frank Robinson, Harmon Killebrew, and Roberto Clemente. Jackson's legendary blast off Dock Ellis in the third inning is one of the longest home runs in baseball history, hitting the top of the light tower on the right-centerfield roof. Robinson's homer in the same inning makes him the first player to homer for each league in the All-Star Game. The AL wins 6-4, its only All-Star win between 1962 and 1983.

AL 6, NL 4

October 12, 1972 Manager Billy Martin goads an old Tigers team to an AL East Division title, but the Tigers lose to Dick Williams' Athletics in a close ALCS.

December 10, 1972 American League owners agree to institute designated hitters for a three-year trial.

1979 Fifty-three games into the season, Detroit fires new manager Less Moss, despite his winning record, to hire the Big Red Machine's former skipper Sparky Anderson.

June 28, 1976

The Bird Takes Flight Mark "The Bird" Fidrych puts on a memorable show at Tiger Stadium during his first nationally televised game. The eccentric, frizzy-haired rookie is famous for talking to the baseball while on the mound, and on this day the ball is a good listener. Fidrych is nearly unhittable, beating the Yankees 5-1 as a packed house roars its approval. Just over two weeks later, Fidrych will start the All-Star Game in Philadelphia.

Tigers 5, Yankees 1

1972

A bond issue fails, ending plans for a multipurpose domed stadium on the downtown Detroit riverfront.

1974

The Detroit Lions play their final game at Tiger Stadium.

1977

A February fire destroys the press box; the box is replaced and the lighting system upgraded. After the city acquires ownership, it will replace all of the original green wooden seats with blue plastic ones over the next three years.

1980

Obscene chanting by rowdy fans leads the team to close the bleachers for two weeks.

ABOVE: Mark "The Bird" Fidrych engages in his patented mound-grooming ritual at Tiger Stadium on June 28, 1976. An amazing 47,855 fans show up on this Monday night to see the red-hot Fidrych run his record to 8-1, more than twice the crowd for the game on June 29. The out-of-nowhere rookie will go 19-9 for the year and win the AL Rookie of the Year Award. Subsequently, though, the twenty-one-year-old right-hander will be hampered by arm trouble and win only ten more games in his career.

RIGHT: Kirk Gibson celebrates after smashing a homer off the Padres' Goose Gossage in the final game of the 1984 World Series at Tiger Stadium. Gibby's second home run of the game makes the score 8-4 and effectively clinches the world championship for Detroit.

October 14, 1984

Captain Kirk's Big Day With the Tigers needing one more win for a world championship, Kirk Gibson blasts a two-run homer in the first inning and follows it up with a three-run blast in the eighth. The latter hit comes against Padres relief ace Goose Gossage, who refuses to walk him with first base open. Gibson's blasts, both upper-deck shots, rescue Dan Petry from a poor start to give the Tigers their first world championship since 1968. Alan Trammell, who hits .450, is Series MVP and Sparky Anderson becomes the first manager to win a world championship in both leagues. It's the fourth and final title for Tiger Stadium, and a riot ensues in downtown Detroit.

Tigers 8, Padres 4

1987 In the Tigers' last hurrah of the 1980s, the club wins the AL East but is upset by the Twins in the ALCS.

1992 Pizza baron Mike Ilitch of Little Caesars buys the struggling Tigers from Domino's pizza baron Tom Monaghan. Detroit's pizza dynasty began when Monaghan purchased the club from media magnate John Fetzer in 1984.

October 4, 1987

Tanana Clips Toronto's Wings Capping off one of the most exciting pennant races in recent memory, Detroit wins the AL East thanks to Frank Tanana's 1-0 shutout of the Blue Jays. Larry Herndon's second-inning homer provides the only run of the game. The Tigers, who were trailing Toronto by one game upon entering the three-game series on the season's final weekend, win each game by one run to take the title. Their good fortune dates back to August 12, when they traded minor leaguer John Smoltz to Atlanta for veteran-hurler Doyle Alexander. Alexander went 9-0 from that point on, including the first win of the climactic Toronto series. Detroit ends the season on a 34-18 run.

Tigers 1, Blue Jays 0

1999

With the team set to move to Comerica Park, Tiger Stadium hosts its last game. The stadium will remain padlocked for years, unused and empty.

2007

The City of Detroit announces its intention to demolish Tiger Stadium if a viable plan to renovate and reuse it cannot be found. A massive auction of memorabilia and fixtures—including 20,000 seats—from the stadium is held on eBay.

2008

The Old Tiger Stadium Conservancy, entrusted by the city with the responsibility for finding a way to save Tiger Stadium, persuades the city to delay demolition several times.

September 18, 1996

Twenty Strikeouts, Take Two Roger Clemens ties his own ten-year-old major league record by striking out twenty Tigers in a masterful 4-0 shutout. Detroit, which had lost its 100th game of the season the previous night, manages just five hits off Clemens, who walks none even while throwing an unbelievable 151 pitches. It's the last victory in a Red Sox uniform for Clemens, who will end the season with a 10-13 record.

Red Sox 4, Tigers 0

BELOW: Representative of the many sentimental banners unfurled by fans at Tiger Stadium's last game on September 27, 1999, this homemade sign reads, "Good Bye Old Girl."

TOP: A worm's-eye view of Tiger Stadium in May 2008 shows the dandelions around the pitcher's mound and the stands along the third base line. Some of the aluminum cladding below the third-deck press box has fallen away, and many of the lower-deck seats have been removed and auctioned off on eBay.

MIDDLE: A rainbow appears over the left-field corner during the dismantling of Tiger Stadium in August 2008.

BOTTOM: Taken sometime after the closing of Tiger Stadium, this photo shows the view of the deteriorating diamond from deep in the upper-deck grandstand in right field.

EBBETS FIELD

Brooklyn, New York

Dodgers (NL) 1913–1957

OPPOSITE: This gorgeous aerial view from the 1950s shows the dense Flatbush neighborhood surrounding Ebbets. Visible are the fading ballpark's signature entrance and sign, its left-field grandstand and centerfield bleachers, and its right-field wall and scoreboard. Facing north, the photo shows Sullivan Place running from left field down the first base line and Bedford Avenue running behind right field. Flatbush Avenue and, beyond it, Prospect Park are three blocks to the west.

Although gone for more than half a century, Ebbets Field remains firmly ensconced in the hearts of baseball fans, unquestionably one of the most famous and fondly remembered parks in the history of the game. In the hurly-burly of midcentury Brooklyn, the "Boys of Summer"—Jackie Robinson, Gil Hodges, Roy Campanella, Pee Wee Reese, Duke Snider, Carl Furillo, Carl Erskine, Don Newcombe, and others—played legendary baseball in what now seems like a ridiculously small field on a tiny sliver of land. When "Dem Bums" finally left Brooklyn for the Golden West, Dodgers fans, who saw the national pastime not just as a game, but as an integral part of the fabric of their lives, were shaken to the core. The move signaled the end of an era, both for Brooklyn and for baseball.

Forty-five years earlier, on October 5, 1912, a different era had come to an end when the team played its last game at the aging Washington Park. "Auld Lang Syne" was sung after the last out as the Dodgers prepared to move into what was being referred to as their "million-dollar plant": Ebbets Field. Owner Charles Ebbets had been planning to build a new park since 1908, when he first heard of plans for ambitious new parks in Philadelphia and Pittsburgh. But unlike the Athletics or the Pirates, who broke with tradition to install their new baseball palaces in desirable places, Ebbets hewed to the old paradigm of going cheap. Bit by bit, he bought parcels of land in an area of Flatbush called "Pigtown" due to its former use as a garbage dump. Finally, Ebbets had enough real estate, and ground was broken in early 1912.

By the end of February 1913, Ebbets was showing reporters around the new structure, amazing them with the park's comfort and quality, especially in the dressing rooms and offices (regarded as the best ever included in a ballpark). Since it had taken longer than expected to acquire the land, Ebbets was able to build his eponymous monument with full knowledge of what had been done at the other state-of-the-art fields—and improve on them. Shibe Park's impressive cupola now seemed a bit underwhelming compared to Ebbets' enormous marble rotunda behind home plate. Like Shibe's, it served as the main entrance for the park and held the team's offices above. But at Ebbets, it was larger and more grandiose. The floor was a marble mosaic, and the ceiling was not only painted like a dark sky with stars and clouds, but also featured a giant chandelier made of baseball bats and globes painted to look like baseballs.

LUKE "HOT POTATO" HAMLIN

JOE BLACK
pitcher BROOKLYN DODGERS
Joe Black

ROY CAMPANELLA
catcher BROOKLYN DODGERS
Roy Campanella

BACKGROUND: Second-line pitcher Ray Caldwell of the Yankees pitches to an unidentified Dodger during the first exhibition game at Ebbets Field on April 5, 1913.

LEFT: Genevieve Ebbets, daughter of Dodgers owner Charles Ebbets, throws out the first ball at the opening of Ebbets Field on April 5, 1913, before an exhibition game against the Yankees. The first game to count at Ebbets will be played four days later, with the Phillies shutting out the Dodgers 1-0 on April 9.

GAME ON EBBETS FIELD

Ebbets also provided one of the earliest examples of a batter's eye, an innovation that didn't find universal acceptance until the 1950s. It was painted dark green "for the benefit of batters," the *New York Times* explained, "following the custom which has become quite popular of late years." Unlike 1912's single-level debutantes, Navin Field (later Tiger Stadium) and Fenway Park, Ebbets' grandstand was double-decked from its opening—except in the outfield, which allowed fans to sit for free on a hill past the left-field fence that had a clear line of sight into the park. The piece of land on which Ebbets rose was so compact that the right-field fence was just 301 feet from home plate (62 feet longer than the minimum distance at the time). Center field and left field were much deeper. The *Washington Post* reported that Ebbets Field would seat 30,000 fans and that the park would have no stairways, since ramps were perceived as innovative and cool.

To bolster his claim that his park would be the most comfortable and commodious, Ebbets purchased thousands of umbrellas and stored them at the park for fans to use in soggy weather. But although the seats were dry, they weren't cheap. Both AL and NL rules mandated that each park have some affordable seats, but Ebbets bucked the custom of having a large bleacher section and announced shortly before the park opened that there would only be a small number of 25¢ seats. He blamed the new fire-safe regulations for the high prices: "The demand of the fans is for safe, secure, and comfortable accommodations. The club owners must provide suitable stands, and under the laws of the Building Department, they must be steel, stone, and concrete. Thus the cost is greatly increased."

Bleachers or not, the new park was an instant success, even though AL president Ban Johnson deliberately created conflicting games at the Polo Grounds, booking strong clubs against the Yankees on twenty-nine dates when the Dodgers were at home during their first season. Known as the "Holiday King," Ebbets was one of the first baseball moguls to embrace the concept of special days, and hosted as many as possible—including "Orphans' Day," which, according to the *Times*, was "celebrated with the presence of all the children from the various orphan asylums of Brooklyn, together with three bands."

On the field, the Dodgers struggled through the Great Depression, until they emerged as a perennial NL power in

the 1940s under the skillful leadership of general manager Branch Rickey. The Dodgers' postwar battles with the hated Yankees transfixed the city and the nation at large as the star-studded teams of "Willie, Mickey, and the Duke" played their way into legend. Meanwhile, Rickey signed a new player to the team: Jackie Robinson. Robinson broke through the color barrier with grace, dignity, and 175 hits (including 12 home runs) in 151 games. In 1947, Robinson's first year with the team, not only was an annual attendance record set at Ebbets, but the Dodgers also shattered the single-game attendance record at every NL stadium they visited, except for Crosley Field. When the Baseball Writers Association of America decided to start awarding a Rookie of the Year prize, Robinson was their first pick.

In 1950, Branch Rickey's shares in the team were purchased by Walter O'Malley, a co-owner for the previous five years who, along with Rickey, had bought out a portion of the shares held by the Ebbets estate. Known for his shrewd business sense, O'Malley worried about the future, even when his money-making Dodgers became still more lucrative after winning the Series in '55. Ebbets Field was deteriorating badly after forty years, and Flatbush was becoming less safe. Brooklyn had fallen on tough times (as had most older, industrial areas), while the relocation of the Braves, Browns, and Athletics into virgin territory began to redraw the map of major league ball. Looking at the new, taxpayer-financed venues built for these struggling teams—even Milwaukee, for goodness sake, had a nicer and more profitable stadium than his—O'Malley turned green with envy. The strong-willed owner of the NL's best team wanted the same for his club and was willing to pay $6 million for it—provided, that is, that the City of New York acquired (at great taxpayer expense) the property needed to build his grand vision of a domed stadium in downtown Brooklyn. No longer were destitute teams the only ones looking for greener pastures—and greener profits.

Despite his vision, power, and iron will, O'Malley met his match in unmovable and inscrutable Robert Moses, the urban planning czar who had to approve a new park. After protracted and contentious negotiations between the club and the city government broke down, O'Malley was left with two options: accept a city-built and -owned stadium in

OPPOSITE, TOP LEFT: Dodgers players haul a giant American flag into the Ebbets outfield on Opening Day, April 14, 1914. That year the team becomes known as the "Robins" in the press, thanks to their new manager Wilbert "Uncle Robbie" Robinson. The name will stick until 1932, when Max Carey takes the helm and the moniker switches back to the Dodgers.

OPPOSITE, TOP RIGHT: An Opening Day parade marches through the Ebbets outfield. Advertisers could buy billboard space at the park through the Mr. Brook of Brooklyn company, whose sign is seen behind the band.

ABOVE, LEFT: The left-field bleachers are crowded on this day in 1922, even as the Robins trudge through a losing season. Brooklyn will finish sixth with a 76-78 record.

ABOVE, RIGHT: Hungry spectators line up for hot dogs outside Ebbets Field.

an undesirable section of Flushing in the borough of Queens, or try to move elsewhere. When representatives of Los Angeles made it known that they wanted a major league team, O'Malley sprang into action. A born power broker, he knew the league would never approve of a single team relocating to the West Coat, where it would be hard to schedule games with far-away rivals. So he seduced Horace Stoneham, the owner of the New York Giants, to go west with him, where he would get better, subsidized accommodations (and fatter profits) in San Francisco.

On September 24, 1957, in the last game ever played at Ebbets Field, the Dodgers beat the Pirates 2-0 in front of only 6,702 fans. The team moved to burgeoning California, bringing the home plate from Ebbets Field with them. The Dodgers' epic relocation opened new vistas for the game and had a profound effect on professional sports in America. But an entire generation of NL fans' hearts were broken in Gotham. As Dave Anderson, the last writer to cover Dem Bums for the *Brooklyn Eagle*, opined in the *New York Times* almost half a century later, "Without the baseball team that was its identity, Brooklyn hasn't been the same since."

CAP: 1950.

OPPOSITE: From top to bottom, these images show Ebbets' main concession area, press lounge, and concession area behind home plate. Once seen as luxurious, these areas began to be criticized for being too small once Yankee Stadium opened.

BACKGROUND: Fans line up outside Ebbets before Game 1 of the 1920 World Series against Cleveland, the next-to-last best-of-nine Fall Classic. The Indians end up winning this game 3-1 in a match-up of two future Hall of Fame pitchers, Cleveland's Stan Coveleski and Brooklyn's Rube Marquard. Spitballer Coveleski will go on to win two more games in the Series, and Cleveland will prevail 5-2 for the championship.

TICKET HOLDERS
LOWER TIER BOXES
AND
LOWER RESERVED SEATS · ROWS 1 to 9
ENTER HERE
GATES 6 & 7 ON LEFT
GATES 8 & 9 ON RIGHT

The Game Comes Alive

When Harold Arlin, sitting in the stands at Forbes Field in 1921, was the first ever to broadcast a baseball game on the airwaves, only a few hundred radios were even in range of Pittsburgh's KDKA to hear the groundbreaking transmission. But it didn't take long for baseball on the radio to catch on. The next year, the World Series contest between New York's Giants and Yankees was beamed to an estimated one million people by the city's WJZ.

Almost three decades later, the Giants would again make radio history, this time in a pennant race against the Dodgers that ended in Bobby Thomson's surprising three-run homer in the ninth inning. The moment was broadcast round the world by the Giants' Russ Hodges: "There's a long drive...it's gonna be...I believe...the Giants win the pennant! The Giants win the pennant! The Giants win the pennant! The Giants win the pennant! I don't believe it! The Giants win the pennant!" The broadcast—filled with palpable excitement—is now embedded in the memories of millions of fans who aren't even old enough to remember the game. In this way, radio announcers don't just tell listeners the score; they're storytellers who help fans visualize the game, the verbal embodiment of the action unfolding on the field.

Over the years, Ebbets Field saw some of the greatest announcers in baseball history. In 1939, Red Barber took the seat in the Dodgers' press box, and the city began adopting his curious phrases like "sittin' in the catbird seat" and "tearin' up the pea patch." He later went on to team up with a fellow Southerner, Mel Allen, to announce for the Yankees, and the two won the first ever Ford Frick Award for excellence in baseball broadcasting in 1978.

In 1948, Ernie Harwell became the first broadcaster to be traded for a player when Dodgers president Branch Rickey got him from the Atlanta Crackers in exchange for catcher Cliff Dapper. After filling in for an ailing Barber, Harwell went on to announce for the Tigers for forty-two years, becoming known for his folksy style and such idioms as "he stood there like the house by the side of the road," and "excessive window shopping!—he looked at one too many." But no one enlivened Midwestern baseball quite like Harry Caray, who worked for the Cardinals, White Sox, and then Cubs, where he sang "Take Me Out to the Ball Game" in a manner as delightfully obnoxious as his huge glasses and outspoken criticism of bad plays.

However, the best-known announcer of all time may be Vin Scully, who took the mic at Ebbets after Harwell moved on, and has been with the Dodgers ever since. After bringing the game to life for more than half a century, in 2005 he was named history's best baseball announcer in the book *Voices of Summer: Ranking Baseball's 101 All-Time Best Announcers* by Curt Smith, who told the *Washington Post* that he was inspired to write the book when he heard Scully describe a runner on second as "a tiny ship looking for safe harbor." So beloved is Scully that many people bring radios to Dodger Stadium just to hear the Irish tenor weave the action into an exciting story. As Scully himself said when announcing Sandy Koufax's perfect game in 1965, "There's 29,000 people in the ballpark, and a million butterflies."

TOP: In this 1926 photo, KDKA radio announcer Louis Kaufman is flanked by Pittsburgh's 1925 world champions—manager Bill McKechnie (far left), Lee Meadows (left), Pie Traynor (right), and Kiki Cuyler (far right).

BOTTOM: Pioneering broadcaster Graham McNamee did the first World Series radio play-by-play in 1923 on NBC. McNamee had previously worked for WEAF in New York City (later WNBC and WRCA; now WFAN). He was inducted into the American Sportscasters Association Hall of Fame in 1984.

BELOW: Flamboyant broadcaster Harry Caray strips down to his boxer shorts and socks in the Busch Stadium broadcast booth during a sweltering Astros-Cardinals game on July 9, 1966. The game-time temperature was recorded at 101°.

ABOVE: Red Barber posing at the mic in the early 1950s, broadcasting a Dodgers game for WOR-TV. WOR telecast all Brooklyn home games from 1950 to 1954; in '55, the network also started covering select away games.

BELOW: For fifty-nine years, Vin Scully—photographed here in the broadcast booth at Shea Stadium—has been behind the mic for the Dodgers, starting with Brooklyn in 1950.

1914 The Dodgers hire Wilbert Robinson as their manager. "Uncle Robbie" will manage Brooklyn for eighteen years, and the team will get a new nickname: the Robins.

1916 The Robins win the franchise's first NL pennant, but in the World Series they fall prey to Boston's Ernie Shore, Babe Ruth, and Dutch Leonard in five games.

April 18, 1925 Charles Ebbets dies of heart failure at age sixty-six. His successor, Ed McKeever, will pass away eleven days later due to pneumonia. Manager "Uncle Robbie" Robinson will take the helm after the double tragedy.

1913

After Charles Ebbets insists the schedule be rearranged, Ebbets Field opens on April 9, before the official Opening Day. Original dimensions are a generous 419 feet down the left-field line and 450 to center, but only 301 to the 38-foot-high wall down the right-field line. Capacity is 18,000.

September 16, 1924

An Even Dozen St. Louis first baseman Jim Bottomley collects a record 12 RBIs during the Cardinals' pounding of the Robins. He singles home two runs in the first, doubles in another in the second, and hits a grand slam in the fourth after Brooklyn manager Wilbert Robinson intentionally walks Rogers Hornsby to face Bottomley instead. "Sunny Jim" then smacks a two-run homer in the sixth, knocks a two-run single in the seventh, and delivers a final run with a single in the ninth. Bottomley breaks the mark of 11 RBIs in a game set in 1892 by Wilbert Robinson—the very same Robinson who insisted on pitching to him.

Cardinals 17, Dodgers 4

September 13, 1925

Dazzy Dazzles Dazzy Vance tosses the first no-hitter at Ebbets Field, handcuffing Philadelphia by a 10-1 score. The third time's the charm for the Brooklyn ace, who twice before has failed to put the finishing touches on a no-hit masterpiece (once with two outs in the ninth). Philadelphia's only run of the day is scored by the superbly nicknamed Nelson "Chicken" Hawks, who five days earlier got the only safety in Dazzy's one-hitter.

Dodgers 10, Phillies 1

1926

Bleachers are added in the outfield, expanding capacity to 28,000. Distance down the left-field line is reduced to 383 feet.

The Dodgers face Pittsburgh on August 2, 1913. Brooklyn will go on to finish sixth in Ebbets' inaugural season.

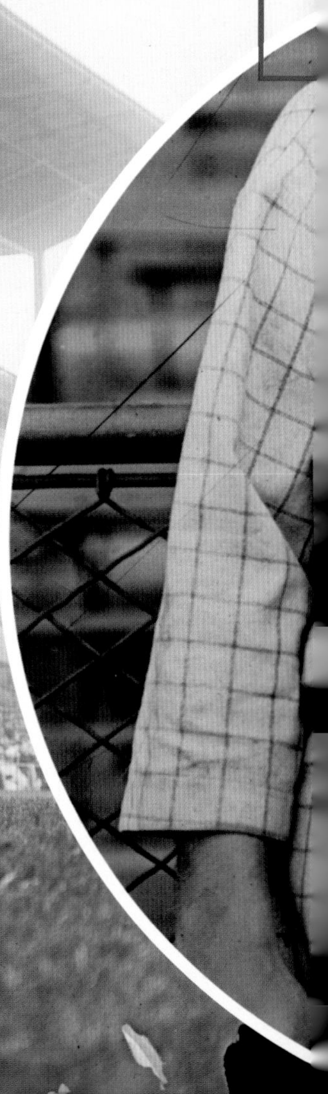

1929

A press box, forgotten when the stadium was built, is finally added. Reporters previously occupied the first two rows of the upper deck.

1931

Stands in left and center field are double-decked after the season, and the distance down the left-field line is reduced to 353 feet for 1932.

1936

The Dodgers add box seats in center field in the 1936–37 off-season. Capacity reaches 35,000.

June 15, 1938

Dandy Vandy Nearly 39,000 fans turn out for the first night game ever played at Ebbets Field, and end up bearing witness to an even more historic moment. With batters having trouble adjusting to the newfangled lights, Cincinnati's Johnny Vander Meer, a wild, hard-throwing lefty, does the unthinkable by tossing his second consecutive no-hitter. Vandy makes it thrilling by walking eight Dodgers, including three in the ninth, before getting the last two outs with the bases loaded. As an appetizer, the fans also see Dodgers rookie Ernie Koy beat Jesse Owens in a 100-yard dash before the game—albeit with a 10-yard head start.

Reds 6, Dodgers 0

August 15, 1926

Base is Loaded During Wilbert Robinson's tenure as manager, his Robins became known as the "Daffiness Boys" for their frequent comic mishaps on the field. In one of Ebbets Field's most amusing moments—and the signature moment of the "Uncle Robbie" era—the Robins end up with Dazzy Vance, Chick Fewster, and Babe Herman on third base simultaneously. Herman, whose long hit would forever be remembered as "doubling into a double play," is called out for passing a baserunner. Fewster thinks he's out, too, so he walks away—only to be tagged out. The Robins wind up sweeping a doubleheader from the Braves, but for years, whenever someone informs a Brooklyn fan that his team has three men on base, the inevitable reply will be: "Which base?"

Dodgers 4, Braves 1

October 5, 1941

One Strike Away With the Dodgers one strike away from winning Game 4 to even the World Series at two games apiece, heartbreak rears its ugly head. New York's Tommy Henrich strikes out for the apparent last out of the game, but Dodgers catcher Mickey Owen mishandles the late-breaking pitch from relief ace Hugh Casey. Henrich races to first safely, goes to second on Joe DiMaggio's hit, and both men score on Charlie Keller's double. The Yankees eventually score four runs off the hard-luck Casey, who loses his second straight game in relief. Brooklyn will lose the final Series game the next day, the first of six heartbreaking Fall Classic losses to the hated Yankees.

Yankees 7, Dodgers 4

ABOVE: Pittsburgh's great and beloved star Honus Wagner doffs his chapeau as the crowd behind the visitors' dugout responds in kind. At age fifty-nine, Wagner was in his first year as coach for the Bucs; he would coach the team for eighteen years.

LEFT: Brooklyn shortstop Ivy Olson poses in the club's new (and rare) checked uniform in 1916. The checked home togs were abandoned after one season, while the club's checked road uniforms lasted for another year.

August 26, 1939 The Dodgers face off against the Reds at Ebbets Field in baseball's first televised major league game.

October 1, 1946 With the Dodgers and Cardinals having tied for the pennant, the first playoff game in major league history is played at Ebbets Field. The Cards win the best-of-three playoff by taking the first two games.

1945

Branch Rickey announces the formation of a new Negro League, the United States League, as well as the new Brooklyn Brown Dodgers, who call Ebbets Field home. In 1935 Ebbets had been the home of the Negro National League Eagles before they moved to Newark, New Jersey.

April 15, 1947

A New Era On a cold, gray New York day, only 25,263 fans attend on Opening Day to witness the most significant game in Ebbets Field history. When Jackie Robinson trots out to his first base position, he becomes the first African American to play in the major leagues since 1884. Dodgers president Branch Rickey looks on with approval as interim manager Clyde Sukeforth, who scouted Robinson for the Dodgers, writes out the historic lineup card. (Leo Durocher, the Dodgers' regular manager, has been suspended for the year for associating with gamblers.) Robinson goes 0-for-3, but scores a key run after reaching base on an error as the Dodgers win, 5-3.

Dodgers 5, Braves 3

LEFT: A Brooklyn groundskeeper cuts the grass at Ebbets on October 2, 1946. The Dodgers will lose their second straight playoff game to St. Louis the next day, giving the Cardinals the NL pennant after the first ever tie for first place in baseball history.

BACKGROUND: Shown here on the street outside Ebbets Field in 1947, the iron-willed Jackie Robinson changed baseball—and America—forever when he debuted with the Dodgers that year.

October 3, 1947

Just One Hit Bill Bevens, a journeyman pitcher for the Yankees, sets a new World Series record by walking ten batters in a game, but that's rendered irrelevant by the fact that, with two outs in the bottom of the ninth, he has also held the Dodgers hitless. With two men on base—both of them having walked—pinch hitter Cookie Lavagetto comes to the plate as Brooklyn's last hope. Remarkably, Lavagetto doubles home both runners, breaking up Bevens' no-hitter and giving the Dodgers a 3-2 walk-off victory. The dramatic blow evens the Series at two games apiece, but the Yankees will eventually take it in seven. Neither Bevens nor Lavagetto will ever play in the major leagues again after the Series.

Dodgers 3, Yankees 2

ABOVE, LEFT: In preparation for the 1949 All-Star Game at Ebbets, workers install additional temporary press facilities in the grandstand behind home plate. The NL will lose to the AL 11-7, with reserve player Joe DiMaggio collecting two hits and three RBIs. However, this day in baseball will become historic for another reason: It is the first Midsummer Classic to allow black players to participate.

ABOVE, RIGHT: Left out of the field's initial construction in 1912, a press box was finally installed at Ebbets in 1929.

August 31, 1950

A Gentle Giant In a rout of the Boston Braves, Gil Hodges becomes the sixth major league player to hit four home runs in a game. Hodges hits each homer off a different pitcher. He nearly adds another homer (which ends up going for a long single) and collects nine RBIs in the contest. A hulking first baseman known for his defensive prowess and gentle personality, Hodges will cement his place in New York baseball history when he manages the "Miracle Mets" to the 1969 world championship

Dodgers 19, Braves 3

October 1, 1951

Thomson v. Branca, Round One Thanks to a homer by Bobby Thomson off Dodgers pitcher Ralph Branca, the Giants win the first game in a best-of-three playoff for the National League championship. As fate will have it, it's the last game played at Ebbets Field this year. The Giants, who had trailed Brooklyn by thirteen and a half games in August, used an intricate sign-stealing system to propel them on a remarkable run that ended in a tie for the pennant. In the ninth inning of the third and final playoff game at the Polo Grounds, Dodger manager Chuck Dressen will bring in Branca to face Thomson despite today's Game 1 homer. When Branca mislocates a fastball, Thomson will send the ball into the left-field stands, immediately ending Brooklyn's season and putting an exclamation point on perhaps the most exciting pennant race in baseball history.

Giants 3, Dodgers 1

LEFT: The Dodgers face the reviled Yankees in a 1949 World Series game at Ebbets. In the ninth inning of Game 5, the field's lights are turned on so play can continue into the night—marking the first World Series game played under lights. That night also marks the end of the Dodgers' season, as they lose to the Yanks in five games.

April 20, 1948 Former Negro League catcher Roy Campanella makes his debut for Brooklyn. "Campy" will win three MVP Awards with the Dodgers before an auto accident ends his career in 1958.

1953 The Boys of Summer win a franchise-record 105 games, finishing 13 games ahead of Milwaukee before losing to the Yankees in the Fall Classic.

1956 The Dodgers win their last pennant in Brooklyn, but fall to the Yankees in a seven-game World Series marked by Don Larsen's perfect Game 5.

October 7, 1952

Martin Saves the Day It is perhaps the most famous infield pop-up in the history of baseball. With the Yankees on the verge of winning the World Series, leading Game 7 by a 4-2 score, Brooklyn loads the bases in the bottom of the seventh. Yankees manager Casey Stengel, in a surprise response, summons lefty Bob Kuzava to make his first appearance of the Series. With two outs, Kuzava induces a pop-up from Jackie Robinson, but neither Kuzava, catcher Yogi Berra, nor first baseman Joe Collins can spot the ball against the bright sky. With time running out, rookie Billy Martin saves the game by dashing in from his position at second base to grab the ball as it's about to hit his shoe tops. Kuzava cruises the rest of the way as the Yanks capture the Series.

Yankees 4, Dodgers 2

September 30, 1955

Bums No More The Dodgers, losers of all seven World Series in which they've played, drop the first two games of the Series in the Bronx. Back home in Brooklyn for Game 3, a 2-0 first-inning lead evaporates, but the Dodgers grab the lead back in the bottom of the second and never look back, winning 8-3 behind young southpaw Johnny Podres. Manager Walter Alston will use six different starting pitchers for the first six games, but for Game 7 he will go back to Podres—and Podres pitches a shutout, thereby ending Brooklyn's run of postseason futility and finally making heroes of "Dem Bums."

Dodgers 8, Yankees 3

1957

The Dodgers play their final game at Ebbets Field on September 24 against Pittsburgh. They will begin the 1958 season as the Los Angeles Dodgers.

1960

Demolition of Ebbets Field begins on February 23. An urban housing complex called the Ebbets Field Apartments will take its place.

RIGHT: A jubilant Johnny Podres swings from the top of his dressing cubicle in the Yankee Stadium visitors' clubhouse on October 4, 1955. The twenty-three-year-old lefty shut out New York in the seventh game of the '55 World Series, giving the long-suffering Dodgers their first world championship.

BACKGROUND: A full house at Ebbets Field for the 1949 World Series.

BELOW, INSET: The last ball thrown at Ebbets Field is now part of the Hall of Fame's collection.

Take Me Out...
for Some Giveaways

The ballpark "experience" has come a long way from the first few decades of the 1900s, when fan appreciation took the form of special days during which various local organizations—trade unions, good-fellow societies, ethnic associations, and groups hailing from a particular player's hometown—could parade the field, saluting themselves and awarding gifts to their favorite players. While this gift-giving practice died out in the 1970s (not coincidentally coinciding with the advent of free agency and higher salaries), today's fans have come to expect the best that their team's marketing department can provide: Electronic scoreboard graphics, coordinated "waves," FanCams, and posh restaurants (sushi with your beer?) have become de rigueur.

Baseball fans have never been a shy lot, with America's favorite pastime offering up endless opportunities for spectators to "express" themselves—for better or worse. Perhaps nowhere was this audience participation so intensely felt than at Ebbets Field, where even the most important game days featured their share of goofballs and cranks, many of whom chose to communicate their opinions musically. There was softball-star-wannabe and Ebbets Field regular Hilda Chester, who after having a heart attack was advised by her doctor to stop shouting at the games, so she banged her frying pan instead. This could only be matched by the Brooklyn Sym-Phony Band, a group of fans who toted anything that would make a noise to the first row behind the dugout, playing memorable renditions of "Three Blind Mice," aimed at one unpopular umpire after another. And on August 15, 1951, everyone got in on the act for the Dodgers' "Music Depreciation Day," when all fans toting an instrument were admitted for free; one of the first discounted admission promotions, this gimmick was simply a ploy to get a local musicians' union to stop making noise about the amateur band members needing to be part of their organization.

What proved a better, and more profitable, promotion than free tickets was attracting fans to the games with giveaway merchandise. The year 1951 saw the first "Bat Day" in St. Louis when the Browns' owner gave away bats to each child who came to the game with an adult in tow. "Ball Day" and "Jacket Day" followed soon after—just the beginning of all conceivable types of "freebies," among them autographs, photos, and team-emblazoned caps and shirts. And what says turn-of-the-millennium baseball more than cuddly little stuffed animals? Crowds have almost rioted in the stands over gratis Beanie Babies and Precious Moments figurines. Some baseball clubs now have more promotional days than not, with the bleachers awash in free merchandise festooned with team—and corporate—logos. Luckily for the players, no free frying pans have been given out—yet.

May 12, 1956

"Oisk" Strikes Again In the confines of tiny Ebbets Field, holding a team hitless was harder than finding a seat on a subway at rush hour. But on this momentous day the Dodgers' Carl Erskine becomes the only pitcher to throw two no-hitters at cozy Ebbets, skunking the hated Giants, 3-0, while walking just two. "Oisk," as he is affectionately known in Brooklynese, also pitched an Ebbets Field gem during the 1953 World Series, striking out a Series-record fourteen Yankees in Game 3.

Dodgers 3, Giants 0

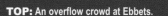

TOP: An overflow crowd at Ebbets.

BOTTOM: More than 2,400 fans showed up with instruments on "Music Depreciation Night."

WRIGLEY FIELD

Chicago, Illinois

Whales (Federal League) 1914–1915, Cubs (NL) 1916–present

Weeghman Park 1914–1918, Cubs Park 1919–1925

LARRY BOWA   SS

OPPOSITE: Nothing delights Wrigleyville more than a sunny afternoon game. Nicknamed the "Friendly Confines," the venerable Wrigley Field wins accolades for how close fans are to the field—even if they are watching from the roofs of nearby buildings.

Nestled in a neighborhood dubbed "Wrigleyville" on the North Side of Chicago, fabled Wrigley Field may not have seen many championships, but it's a must-visit for any baseball fan. With its ivy-covered walls, manual scoreboard, and spectators scattered across the tops of nearby buildings, it's earned the nickname the "Friendly Confines"—even if those in the stands aren't always so friendly to visiting players. Adding to its charm is its high number of afternoon games— a necessity until lights were added in 1988. But whether a game is taken in under the sun or under the stars, it's hard not to feel the history inside Wrigley Field, the second-oldest park in the majors.

When it opened in 1914, the ballpark wasn't yet called Wrigley Field, and it wasn't even the home of the Cubs. Along with baseball commissioner Kenesaw Mountain Landis, the park was one of the only lasting legacies of the short-lived Federal League, an eight-team renegade outfit engineered to directly challenge the National and American Leagues. The ill-fated Federal League got much of its pep—and much of its cash—from Chicago owner "Lucky" Charley Weeghman, a restaurateur who was one of the first baseball moguls to know that customer service and fan comfort are much easier to guarantee than a winning team. Weeghman's FL franchise, the Whales, needed a place to play, so Lucky Charley built them one. And fast!

The new park went up in near-record time, with its ground-breaking on March 4 and its opening just nine weeks later, despite an unseasonably cold spring. Weeghman had made his fortune from quick-lunch restaurants in downtown Chicago, and he applied many of his hard-won business principles to baseball, becoming one of the first—if not *the* first—to open concession stands to eliminate the blight of annoying vendors blocking the view of the game. Weeghman also kept the new park's aisles swept and its restrooms clean in order to encourage the ladies (and their escorts) to attend. Starting in 1916, he even allowed fans to keep foul balls hit into the stands—an unheard-of and very popular policy at the time.

When built, Weeghman Park was a single-deck facility that seated 20,000. A majority of those seats (13,000) were located in the grandstand, with another 4,000 in the pavilions down

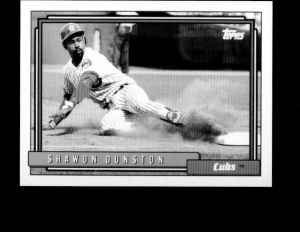

SHAWON DUNSTON

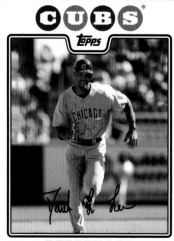

DERREK LEE

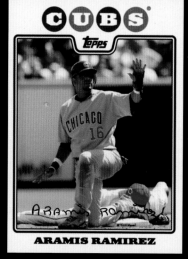

ARAMIS RAMIREZ

ABOVE: Workers prepare Wrigley Field for the opening of the 1961 season by trimming the famous vines and painting the centerfield scoreboard. Against the wall, rolls of fresh sod await unfurling.

RIGHT: The left-field upper deck before lights and the rooftop press box were added in 1988.

LEO DUROCHER
Manager

the foul lines and 3,000 in the bleachers. Despite its age and extensive renovations, the park's original lower-deck design is still recognizable today. Architect Zachary Taylor Davis, also the designer of Comiskey Park, planned the structure to accommodate eventual double-decking and expansion. Though other classic fields suffered as they aged from the constraints imposed by their limited footprint, Weeghman had purchased enough property to allow for plenty of refurbishing over the decades—even if it required moving the left-field stands on rollers to create more room for seats behind home plate, as was done during a 1923 renovation.

When the AL and NL brokered a deal to shut down the Feds after the 1915 season, they agreed to let two FL owners, Weeghman and St. Louis' Phil Ball, buy into their exclusive leagues. Weeghman, long rumored to have been interested in the Cubs, was finally allowed to purchase the club from Charley Murphy, who had made nothing but enemies during his tenure in the NL. Weeghman relocated his newly acquired Cubs from their decrepit West Side Grounds to his beautiful new park on the North Side, which he renamed Cubs Park. Like Charles Ebbets in Brooklyn, Weeghman—who had competed with two established major league clubs during his years in the FL—saw to it that nearly every home game was designated a special day for some group or other, whether it be ethnic groups, friends of local players, school organizations, or others. This helped ensure that when the Cubs moved in for 1916 a strong neighborhood fan base was already there to welcome them.

Even after chewing-gum king Bill Wrigley bought a controlling interest in the Cubs in 1918, the park flourished, mainly because, like Weeghman, Wrigley wasn't afraid to spend significant amounts of his treasure to upgrade the

facility. The stands were double-decked, and attendance rose throughout the Roaring Twenties. In 1927, the team became the first NL club to draw a million fans in one season, and continued to do so through 1931. Fans at Wrigley were enthusiastic, even downright rowdy, and they still are today. When they're not singing, cheering, or heckling, Wrigley spectators have been known to throw baseballs, beer, or anything else that's handy at players—which is easily accomplished thanks to their proximity to the field. The bad behavior hit a peak at a drunken Opening Day riot in 1970, which caused management to install a wire basket on the outer perimeter of the outfield wall to keep bleacher fans from leaping onto the field. Though they hadn't yet earned their "party people" reputation, Cubs fans in the '30s were well on their way.

In 1932, PK Wrigley took over when his dad Bill passed away. PK was no old-fashioned baseball tycoon—he was a marketer! And so, whether or not they were having a winning season (and they usually weren't), "Beautiful Wrigley Field" became the Cubs' selling point. Wrigley figured out how to make his park one of the best in baseball, not only by keeping it clean and well-appointed, but by spending a significant amount of time and money designing a brilliant new outfield structure. Breaking the old rules, the Cubs raised the bleachers well above the field level, giving the fans in the cheap seats a better view while allowing the club to use the space under the elevated seats to store groundskeeping equipment, batting cages, and the like. In addition, Wrigley and his lieutenant, Bill Veeck Jr., had bittersweet vines and ivy planted on the outfield walls. The lush Boston ivy—also featured on the left-field wall at Forbes Field— eventually overgrew the sparser bittersweet to create Wrigley's now world-famous look. Decades later, the ivy motif was adopted for deep center field on the South Side at U.S. Cellular Field, but the plant is still considered Wrigley's signature.

Another cornerstone of the park's appeal for many decades was its schedule of 100 percent afternoon games. Unlike the club's other signature elements, however, the uniqueness of day baseball was somewhat of a fluke. In a little-remembered moment in December 1941, the Cubs were reluctantly preparing to install lights to spur attendance when the Japanese attacked Pearl Harbor. PK Wrigley, distinctly uncomfortable with night baseball anyway, used the tragedy as an excuse to donate the lights and their towers to the War Department, and staunchly declared that night baseball would never be played at his park so long as he was alive. The Cubs remained daytime-pure at home for another forty-seven years, until after Wrigley died and his son William sold the team to the Windy City's dominant newspaper, the *Chicago Tribune*, in 1981. The sale, which financed the taxes on the Wrigley estate, marked the end of one of the last family dynasties in the game. With the club and the park in new hands, lights were a foregone conclusion—the only question was how to overcome local opposition.

Although many fans felt that installing lights would upend the last bastion of traditional afternoon games, and

LEFT: On game days, Chicago trolleys displayed signs like this one, from the Baseball Hall of Fame.

TOP: Traffic congestion was a problem at Wrigley Field even during the early days. Here, a crowd crosses West Addison Street as lines of cars head north on Clark Street. This shot was most likely taken during the 1929 World Series.

MIDDLE: A July 2003 view at dusk of the back of the centerfield scoreboard, as seen from Murphy's Bleachers across Waveland Street.

BOTTOM: Cubs left fielder Alfonso Soriano at the plate during a Brewers-Cubs game on July 1, 2007.

Wrigleyville residents worried about nighttime crowds causing vandalism, the Tribune Company ultimately won. The impetus came in 1984, when the Cubs rebounded to become surprise NL East champions, and no-nonsense commissioner Peter Ueberroth declared that the Cubs would have to play World Series home games at Comiskey Park under the lights. The Cubs' unprecedented collapse in the NLCS made it a moot point that year, but by 1988, the team had convinced much of the Chicago City Council that night baseball would be good economics. To demonstrate, they secured an agreement from MLB to host the 1990 All-Star Game—which would bring an estimated $40 million to the city—if lights were installed. After a long and bitter battle, which even saw some in Wrigleyville fighting to move the newly avaricious Cubs out of the neighborhood, the result was still predictable: on February 25, 1988, the city council approved the installation of lights for use in eight games in 1988, then eighteen games annually through 2002. Perhaps the baseball gods were sending a signal of their displeasure when the first night game, on August 8, was rained out. Nevertheless, over the years, night games at Wrigley have become a pleasant diversion from the routine of day ball, and the Cubs have expanded the number of evening events per season to twenty-five.

The playing of night games wasn't the only club policy that was radically revamped by the new corporate management. Wrigley patrons had long enjoyed a generous day-of-game ticket sale policy, with thousands of tickets held back rather than being sold as season tickets. The Tribune Company quickly changed that, eventually making every seat in the park eligible for season purchase. Ticket prices steadily rose at Wrigley—with the help of sixty-seven new luxury boxes—even as the Cubs continued to wallow below .500 for most of the 1980s and 1990s. In 2005, the Cubs took the plunge into tiered-game pricing along with several other high-profile clubs. Game days were denoted as "prime," "regular," or "value" dates, with the last category available for only six bargain games in April and May. Two years later, there were many more "prime" than "regular" games—which not only defied logic but forced fans to pay an outrageous $42 for bleacher seats at any game in June and July and most in August.

The Tribune Company sometimes engendered great controversy as it gradually modernized its precious jewel, and fans were even more worried when universally loathed Sam Zell took over the company and threatened to sell the naming rights to the stadium. Even still, Wrigley Field is one of the most beloved of all major league parks. Whether you're paying high prices for a "prime" game at night, or bumming in the bleachers on a weekday afternoon, you can still soak up a bit of baseball history while sitting in some of the best seats in the majors—and maybe even lob some Cracker Jacks at an opposing player while you're at it.

1915 After finishing second in the FL's inaugural season, Weeghman's Whales win the pennant by a .001 margin in winning percentage, the closest pennant race in history.

1918 The Cubs win the NL pennant over the Giants by 10½ games but lose the World Series to Babe Ruth's Red Sox in 6 games.

1920 The first major Negro League, the Negro National League, is founded in Chicago. The NNL will last until 1931, but is never allowed to play in Wrigley Field.

TIMELINE: WRIGLEY FIELD

1914

The Chicago Whales of the Federal League, owned by Charles Weeghman, open pristine new Weeghman Park on Chicago's North Side with dimensions of 310 to the left, 400 to center, and 350 down the right-field line.

1916

Weeghman takes over the NL's Cubs as part of an agreement with the major leagues after the folding of the Federal League. He moves the team from West Side Grounds into his own Weeghman Park.

1918

Chewing-gum magnate William Wrigley Jr. purchases a controlling interest in the Cubs and renames the field Cubs Park before the 1919 season.

1921

The NFL's Chicago Staleys, who will later change their name to the Bears, play their first professional football game at Cubs Park.

1923

The Cubs expand the ballpark by putting the third base stands on rollers, moving them north, and creating more seats behind home plate. Capacity jumps from 20,000 to 32,000.

LEFT: Southpaw Hippo Vaughn following through with a pitch in Wrigley Field. Vaughn pitched for the Cubs from 1913 to 1921, winning twenty games five times.

BELOW: Off-season reconstruction work at Wrigley Field, most likely between the 1926 and 1927 seasons, when a partial upper deck was added on the third base side.

May 2, 1917

Double No-Hitter For the only time in major league history, two pitchers—Chicago's Jim "Hippo" Vaughn and Cincinnati's Fred Toney—go through nine innings without allowing a hit. Larry Knopf's tenth-inning single for Cincinnati is the first hit of the game. Knopf scores the game's only run when Vaughn grabs Jim Thorpe's grounder but throws it wildly past catcher Art Wilson. In the bottom of the inning, Toney completes his no-hitter and emerges with a 1-0 win.

Reds 1, Cubs 0

April 14, 1925 Chicago institution WGN broadcasts its first regular-season Cubs game with Quin Ryan at the mic.

1929 After coasting to the NL pennant by 10½ games over the Pirates, the Cubs are defeated by the Athletics in 5 games in the World Series.

1925
A section of left-field bleacher seats is removed to prevent cheap home runs.

1926
The park's name is changed from Cubs Park to Wrigley Field.

1927
With a new partial upper deck down the third base line, the Cubs become the first NL club to draw one million fans in a season.

1928
The upper deck is expanded down the first base line.

October 1, 1932

Did He or Didn't He? In one of the most-talked about plays in baseball history, Babe Ruth calls his shot—or doesn't—in Game 3 of the World Series. All day long, the Cubs players have been razzing Ruth and vice versa. Things come to a head in the fifth inning, when Ruth (who already has one homer in the game) pauses in the middle of his at-bat and makes a motion with his arm. Whether he's gesturing at the pitcher, Charlie Root, or pointing at the centerfield bleachers because he intends to hit the ball there is a question that will be discussed until the end of time. Regardless, Ruth then blasts a long home run to center, spawning one of the game's greatest legends. He taunts and heckles the Cubs as he rounds the bases. The next batter, Lou Gehrig, follows with his second home run of the game. The Yankees win 7-5, and finish off the sweep the next day.

Yankees 7, Cubs 5

ABOVE: At a charity game in 1931, Chicago catcher and future Hall of Famer Gabby Hartnett autographs a baseball for Al Capone's son Sonny, with Al Capone looking on from the boy's left. "You are no longer allowed to have your picture taken with Al Capone," baseball commissioner Kenesaw Mountain Landis wired Hartnett, according to William McNeil in his biography of the popular player. Hartnett's cheeky reply: "OK, but...you tell him."

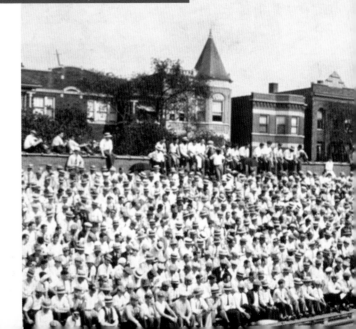

ABOVE: Cubs slugger Hack Wilson takes a mighty hack at Wrigley, sometime between 1927 and 1931. Wilson set the NL record with fifty-six home runs in 1930, one that stood for almost seventy years until it was shattered by Sammy Sosa and Mark McGwire in 1998. In '30, Wilson also drove in 191 runs, a major league record that stands today.

RIGHT: In the early days of modern baseball, overflow crowds often sat on the edge of the field, as in this 1929 photo.

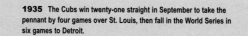

1935 The Cubs win twenty-one straight in September to take the pennant by four games over St. Louis, then fall in the World Series in six games to Detroit.

1938 The Cubs win ten consecutive late-September games, taking the NL flag by two games over Pittsburgh. The Yankees then sweep the Cubs in the Fall Classic.

1937

Wrigley Field as we know it today comes into existence. The bleachers are expanded and raised to their present height, and a giant hand-operated scoreboard is installed in center field, where it will remain for more than seventy years. Boston ivy and bittersweet are planted at the base of the outfield wall by an eager young employee named Bill Veeck Jr. Boston ivy will later overtake the bittersweet.

ABOVE: The last legal spitballer, Burleigh Grimes played for seven different teams during his professional career, including the Cubs from 1932 to 1933.

RIGHT: An aerial photo of Wrigley Field in 1938, with its new bleachers in place.

LEFT: Vines are planted along the Wrigley Field outfield wall in 1937.

September 28, 1938

Homer in the Gloamin' One of the best-remembered Cubs games of all time is nearly called due to darkness. Trailing the Pirates by half a game in the standings, the pesky Cubs rally to tie the game in the sixth and again in the eighth. With sunset approaching, the umpires agree that the ninth will be the last inning, and if the game ends in a tie the two teams will play a doubleheader the next day. Cubs player-manager Gabby Hartnett comes to bat against Pittsburgh's Mace Brown with two outs and the bases empty in the bottom of the ninth. If he makes an out, the game is over. But Brown hangs a curveball, and Hartnett rips it over the fence for a walk-off homer that sends the Cubs into first place for good.

Cubs 6, Pirates 5

December 21, 1941 At the NFL Championship at Wrigley Field, the Bears slaughter the New York Giants, 37-9, in front of 13,341 fans—the smallest attendance ever at a championship game.

July 8, 1947 A pinch-single by Stan Spence drives in the winning run in the seventh in the first All-Star Game played at Wrigley. The final score is 2-1, AL

1941

The Cubs prepare to install lights at Wrigley Field, but the Japanese attack on Pearl Harbor leads owner Philip K. Wrigley to donate the steel light towers to the War Department.

RIGHT: Lines wrap along Sheffield Avenue on October 9, 1945, as fans queue up to buy tickets to World Series Game 7. Although tickets went on sale at 8 a.m., fans had started lining up around 6 p.m. on the previous day. The Cubs will go on to lose the game to the Tigers, 9-3.

1942

Because the Wrigleys do not allow Negro League games at the park, Satchel Paige becomes the first African American to play at Wrigley Field when he appears in a military fundraiser game during World War II.

1943

Women take the field at Wrigley for the first time, playing in the All-American Girls Professional Baseball League, a wartime project of PK Wrigley. A women's exhibition game is played under a bank of temporary lights, the first such event in the ballpark's history.

May 13, 1958

Musial's Milestone Needing only one more to reach 3,000, Stan Musial had planned on waiting a day—when the Cardinals would be at home—before making his record-breaking hit. He changes his mind, however, in the sixth inning, when his Cardinals are trailing the rival Cubs, and pinch hits for the pitcher. With two strikes on him, "Stan the Man" knocks a Moe Drabowsky breaking ball into left field, an RBI double. St. Louis rallies to win, 5-3, and Musial will go on to hit a career total of 3,630.

Cardinals 5, Cubs 3

October 6, 1945

This Ain't No Petting Zoo Thanks to a smelly goat, the Cubs acquire a stench that will linger over the franchise for more than sixty years. With most able-bodied players off at war in 1945, Chicago had captured the 1945 pennant on the strength of twenty doubleheader sweeps and the pitching of midseason pickup Hank Borowy, and were leading the World Series two games to one. But before Game 4, the team denies entry to local tavern owner Billy Sianis and his pet goat. Both owner and goat have tickets, but Cubs officials decide the animal's foul odor will bother the other fans. Sianis places a curse on the Cubs, vowing that the team will lose the Series and never win another pennant. Indeed, the Cubs lose the game, 4-1, and the Series, 4 games to 3. Although Sianis will later lift his curse, the team will not appear in a World Series for the next sixty-plus years.

Tigers 4, Cubs 1

The Birth of the Bleacher Bums

On September 21, 1966, a mere 530 spectators showed up at Wrigley Field on a Wednesday afternoon to watch the Cubs beat the Reds. In the left-field bleachers, on the thin slats of wood with no protection from the harsh Chicago weather, sat only ten hardy fans, who sang, cheered, and jibed the visiting players. The rowdy group formed a club, and by the next year, "Bleacher Bums" had become part of the Chicago lexicon.

The original Bums were crude, obnoxious, funny, and loyal. They dressed up—many in yellow construction hats (undoubtedly borrowed from someone's workplace)—and adopted political chants ("The whole world is watching!") to yell from the stands. Some even drank with Cubs players; others went on road trips. By 1969, the beer-guzzling, opponent-razzing, coed group had expanded to thousands, bringing life to the venerable park's cheap seats.

Wrigley Field's bleacherites had always had a wild streak. Fans who could only afford bleacher seating were working-class and often prone to carousing, cussing, and gambling. During the 1910s and '20s, they regularly tossed bottles, trash, and seat cushions onto the field to protest bad calls, and would sometimes engage in gamesmanship like shining mirrors at visiting players. And they didn't always stick to the bleachers: during one May game in 1922, driven mad by a fierce, pounding rain, they actually jumped the fence and ran onto the field, trying to reach the dry grandstands.

By the 1970s, the original Bleacher Bums had begun drifting apart, but there were plenty of leather-lunged, fanatical youngsters to replace them. So notorious was the group that a play, called *Bleacher Bums*, was put on by Chicago's Organic Theater Company after its members (including Joe Mantegna and Dennis Franz) visited the bleacher seats for a few games. The production (and later, the TV movie) helped popularize the rowdy aesthetic of the bleacher section, and soon the seats were the most popular in the park.

However, in the 1990s, Cubs ownership forever altered the dynamics of the fan base by changing ticket pricing to make the bleacher tickets among the most expensive. In trying to capitalize on baseball's ultimate bleacher experience, the Cubs effectively destroyed the conditions that had created it. But die-hard fans now priced out of the seats made for them can take heart: they can still curse, gamble, and drink in front of the TV in any bar in Wrigleyville.

BACKGROUND: A view of the packed (and be-hatted) centerfield bleachers on July 27, 1929, as the Cubs sweep a doubleheader against the Phillies.

The bleachers are often filled until they are standing room only, as in this photo from July 2003. The park's signature scoreboard, with flags stretched out in the breeze, stands above the fray.

July 30, 1962 The AL beats the NL, 9-4, in the thirty-fourth Midsummer Classic—the second All-Star Game of the summer and the last of the two-ASG format.

1969 In first place in the NL East from Opening Day until September 10, the Cubs swoon in the late-summer heat, finishing eight back of the Miracle Mets.

1960

The Cubs get a new clubhouse in the left-field corner, using the only remaining space available on the property. A quarter of the grandstand is also rebuilt.

1963

A temporary fence is installed atop the centerfield wall to cut down enemy home runs, but is soon taken down.

1970

A wire basket is added around the outfield wall, and balls hit inside count for four bases. While this results in a few more home runs, its main purpose is to protect players from fans.

May 12, 1970

A Great Day for Baseball Ernie Banks connects for his 500th career home run against Atlanta's Pat Jarvis, becoming the eighth major leaguer to reach the mark. Atlanta's Rico Carty retrieves the prized ball for Banks after it pops out of the left-field bleachers. Carty also extends his own hitting streak to thirty games, but the Cubs tie the game in the ninth on a Billy Williams homer and win it in the eleventh on a Ron Santo hit. Banks will finish with 290 career home runs at Wrigley, more than any other player.

Cubs 4, Braves 3

ABOVE: Ace right-hander Ferguson Jenkins strikes a confident pose at Wrigley. Jenkins pitched for the Cubs from 1966 to 1973 and from 1982 to 1983. He was elected to the Hall of Fame in 1991.

CAP: 1971.

LEFT, TOP: "Mr. Cub," Ernie Banks, tips his cap to the adoring faithful at Wrigley after slamming his 500th career home run.

LEFT, BOTTOM: A "speedwalk" moving ramp transports Cubs fans up to the upper deck in right field in 1956. (They will have to walk back down.) The newfangled but unnecessary device was first used on July 22, 1956. Plagued with problems, it will be dismantled circa 1960.

May 17, 1979

Kingman vs. Schmidt With the wind blowing out at Wrigley, the Phillies and Cubs combine for a major league record-tying eleven home runs as Philadelphia holds on for a 23-22 victory. Each starting pitcher gets exactly one batter out. Every starting position player for the Cubs has at least one hit and one RBI, and Bill Buckner drives in seven. Dave Kingman homers three times for Chicago, but he is trumped by the Phillies' Mike Schmidt, whose second home run of the day is the game-winner in the tenth against relief ace Bruce Sutter.

Phillies 23, Cubs 22

August 24, 1971   Ernie Banks hits his 512th and final home run against the Reds at Wrigley. He will be inducted into the Hall of Fame three years later.

1984   Midseason acquisition Rick Sutcliffe goes 16-1 to lead the Cubs to the NL East title. After winning the first two NLCS games at Wrigley, the Cubs lose three straight in San Diego to blow the pennant.

1989   Don Zimmer's Cubbies take the NL East title by six games but lose to Roger Craig's Giants in five games in the NL Championship Series.

1971

After fifty seasons at Wrigley, the Bears move to Soldier Field. Neither the Cubs nor the Bears improve.

June 23, 1984

The Sandberg Game In the heady days of June 1984, about a week after trading for ace pitcher Rick Sutcliffe, the Cubs use an appearance on NBC's "Game of the Week" to show the nation that they're very much for real. Chicago erases a 9-3 deficit, cutting it to one run in the ninth before Ryne Sandberg ties the game with a homer off All-Star reliever Bruce Sutter. Willie McGee doubles home two runs in the tenth to complete a cycle, but in the bottom of the inning Sandberg homers off Sutter again to re-tie it. Backup infielder Dave Owen finally wins it for the Cubs with a bases-loaded single in the eleventh, but the contest will go down in Cubs lore as "The Sandberg Game." The future Hall of Famer ends the day going 5-for-6 with two game-tying homers and seven RBIs.

Cubs 12, Cardinals 11

1988

After a long battle with local residents, night baseball finally comes to Wrigley when lights are installed.

August 9, 1988

Lights, Camera, but No Action After years of being the only major league park without night baseball, Wrigley Field finally gets lights. Mike Bielecki throws the first nighttime pitch at the park, and the record book says Mark Grace owns the first hit after dark at Wrigley. A pounding rainstorm the night before had washed out what was supposed to be the first night game at Wrigley, with the Cubs leading Philadelphia 3-1 in the fourth inning (as if anyone needed further evidence that the Cubs were cursed). Under a clear sky tonight, the Cubs will score four times in the seventh and hold on for a 6-4 win in front of a sellout crowd of 36,399.

Cubs 6, Mets 4

1989

At the cost of $14 million, the Cubs install a new press box, a permanent upper-deck concession stand, an upper-deck balcony, and sixty-seven luxury boxes, which they rent out for $45,000–$65,000 per season.

BACKGROUND: Wrigley Field during the first inning of the first night game on August 8, 1988, with the famed Chicago skyline in the background. Although it is the last field to illuminate, fans and local residents still raised objections to the addition of lights. Despite the rosy sunset, the historic game will be rained out in the fourth inning.

July 10, 1990 Despite playing in the Friendly Confines, the NL All-Stars manage only two hits and lose to the AL stars, 2-0, in the sixty-second Midsummer Classic.

1992 Wrigley Field is featured in the popular film *A League of Their Own*, with signs redone to read "Harvey Field," the fictionalized moniker of the easily recognizable park.

September 18, 1999 In a loss to the Reds at his home park, Sammy Sosa becomes the first player in major league history to hit sixty homers in back-to-back seasons.

May 6, 1998

Wood Whiffs the World Twenty-year-old rookie Kerry Wood, in just his fifth major league start, becomes the first National League pitcher to strike out twenty batters in a game. The fireballer from Texas ties the major league record held by fellow Texan Roger Clemens, who had fanned twenty twice before in the American League. Only Bob Feller, at seventeen, had ever fanned as many batters as his age. Wood also pitches a one-hitter, the only hit being a questionable infield single that shortstop Jeff Blauser is unable to field. Only 15,758 are in the Wrigley Field stands to witness Wood's historic performance.

Cubs 2, Astros 0

2002

The Cubs install a dark mesh fence to block the view from privately owned buildings across the street, which have turned into money-making machines for their owners, but not for the Cubs. The two sides later work out a deal to share the lucrative pie.

ABOVE: Cubs idol Sammy Sosa slams his sixty-second home run in the ninth inning on Sunday, September 13, 1998. Sosa also hit his sixty-first home run that day in Chicago's 11-10 win over Milwaukee. Cardinals slugger Mark McGwire had broken Roger Maris' record five days earlier.

RIGHT: Cubs fireballer Kerry Wood grimaces as he hurls a pitch to the first batter of the Astros-Cubs game on May 2, 2000. Wood goes six innings, fanning four and allowing only one run in his first start after missing the 1999 season due to elbow surgery.

September 28, 1998

Trachsel Tames the Giants The first one-game playoff in Wrigley Field history quickly changes from rout into nail-biter in the ninth inning. Gary Gaetti and Matt Mieske help the Cubs jump out to a 5-0 lead with two RBIs each, and Steve Trachsel carries a no-hitter into the seventh. However, Cubs manager Jim Riggleman uses worn-out starters Kevin Tapani and Terry Mulholland to relieve in the ninth, and San Francisco scores three times. Finally, Chicago's most overworked pitcher, closer Rod Beck, induces the Giants' Joe Carter to pop up in his final career at-bat to end the game. The Cubs' Wild Card–clinching victory is the last game they will win in 1998.

Cubs 5, Giants 3

October 14, 2003

Bartman Lives in Infamy In the long and frustrating history of the Cubs, no game leaves an emptier place in more hearts than Game 6 of the 2003 NLCS. Cubs ace Mark Prior is rolling, leading 3-0 with one out in the eighth inning—five outs from the Cubs' first World Series since 1945. Florida then proceeds to send twelve men to the plate and score eight runs, the most in an NLCS inning in eighteen years. The most important miscue in the inning is an error by Cubs shortstop Alex Gonzalez, without which five of the Marlins' eight runs would not have scored. But it's Cubs fan Steve Bartman who takes the spotlight after he gets to a fly foul before Moises Alou, and incurs the abomination of Cubs fans the world over (though it's usually forgotten that he didn't reach onto the field, but was merely trying to catch a ball hit into the stands, as is every fan's right). The Marlins will win the next night's game 9-6 and head to the World Series, while Bartman will get a security-guard escort out of the stadium, beers pelting him all the way.

Marlins 8, Cubs 3

January 22, 2009 Sam Zell announces the pending sale of Wrigley Field and the Cubs (subject to MLB approval) to billionaire Cubs fan Tom Ricketts for $900 million.

2004 Wrigley Field is granted limited landmark status by the Chicago City Council.

2006 Wrigley Field opens for the season with a newly remodeled and greatly expanded bleacher section. It is the first serious renovation of the outfield seats in nearly seventy years.

ABOVE, LEFT: The foul fly that will live in Cubs lore forever: Cubs left fielder Moises Alou reaches for the ball as fan Steve Bartman does the same in Game 6 of the 2003 NLCS.

LEFT: Fans get a great view of Wrigley from "skybox" seating across Waveland Avenue behind left field in August 2008.

BACKGROUND: At one of the most beautiful parks in the majors, the emerald green of Wrigley's field is surrounded by an amethyst sky as dusk fades into night.

BRAVES FIELD

Boston, Massachusetts

Braves (NL) 1915–1952

National League Park 1936–1940

OPPOSITE: On October 6, 1948, Braves Field is jammed with 40,135 fans for the opening game of the World Series between two major league teams each referred to as "the Tribe." Hometown hero Johnny Sain will outpitch Cleveland Indians superstar Bob Feller. This was the only Braves World Series the stadium saw. However, the Red Sox moved their home games for the 1915 and 1916 World Series to Braves Field—even though Fenway was less than five years old—because of the NL ballpark's greater capacity.

Venerable Fenway Park has been synonymous with Boston for so long that it's hard to imagine another major league field sharing the hearts of Beantown baseball fans. But from 1915 to 1952, Boston's other big-league team—the Braves—had their own state-of-the-art park, on the banks of the Charles River. Built to be the pinnacle of the new concrete-and-steel ballpark movement, Braves Field was the biggest park yet (if not the brightest), and held some of the largest crowds in baseball history when it opened. However, the stadium's popularity would fade as quickly as that of its home team, and it would soon be abandoned as its tenants moved west.

The building of Braves Field had taken a miracle, which came in the form of the greatest come-from-behind season in the history of major league ball. In 1914, the inept Braves, who hadn't had a winning season since 1902, were languishing in their customary position—last in the NL. But in mid-July, the lackluster team suddenly began to play first-rate baseball, taking seven of eight on the road before coming home to win eleven of thirteen. Fans began jumping on the surging Braves' bandwagon, and the team's decrepit old South End Grounds didn't have enough room to seat them. So the team moved into two-year-old Fenway Park with their cross-town rivals in September, while team president James Gaffney looked into upgrading their existing field.

By the end of the year, the "Miracle Braves" had obliterated the rest of the NL, taken the heavily favored Philadelphia Athletics in a four-game sweep in the World Series, and excited fans not just in Boston but across the country. In January, Gaffney had a miracle of his own when he was saved from drowning in quicksand while hunting at the plantation of manager George Stallings. Perhaps his brush with death resulted in an epiphany, because later that month Gaffney reversed course on building a new park. Citing both the small size of the South End lot and its increasing rent, he decided to build an entirely new home for his Braves, and soon acquired property in the Allston section of Boston. Formerly a golf course, the land was bordered by Commonwealth Avenue, Babcock Street, and the Boston & Albany Railroad tracks, which ran alongside the Charles River.

Gaffney hired Osborn Engineering, which had built most of the new concrete-and-steel parks, to draft a plan. According to the *Sporting News*, Gaffney looked to Detroit's Navin Field,

"BABE" DAHLGREN

"GENE" MOORE

TOP: A Boston player signs autographs for a group of young fans atop the bat rack at Braves Field—formally known at the time as National League Field and informally known as the "Bee Hive"—in 1938. The sad-sack Braves were renamed the Boston Bees in 1936 as Braves Field was also re-branded, with both reverting to the tradition-al name Braves in 1941.

MIDDLE: Braves players lounging in the home clubhouse in 1939.

BOTTOM: Female pages and ushers pose for the camera at Braves Field in the early 1950s.

"the last word in new ball parks," as the primary inspiration for his own design. The result was Braves Field, a single-decked park that cost more than $800,000 and seated an amazingly large crowd of 43,250. That was nearly double the capacity of Shibe Park, which was by far the largest park when it had opened six years (and a baseball revolution) earlier. The number of seats was also so much higher than Fenway Park's that the Braves' former landlords decided to play their World Series games there during its first two years of existence.

An overflow crowd of 47,000—then the largest audience ever to see a major league game—filled every available inch of standing room for the debutante field's coming-out party on August 18, 1915. The grandstand seated 19,000, with another 19,000 seats in pavilions situated down the foul lines. The bleacher seats, of which there were only 5,250, were located in a special section in right field, as far away from the action as possible. Gaffney had wanted a park that favored triples and inside-the-park home runs, and that's what he got, with the left field wall 400 feet away, a 440-foot center field, and a 500-foot chasm in right-center. In the first year of the park's existence, only eight home runs were hit, and none made it over the fence.

As the years went by, the park began to empty out as the team got further away from its 1914 miracle. The Braves finished second in 1915, third in 1916, and then tumbled back into the nether regions of the NL. The small section of bleacher seats earned the nickname "The Jury Box" when a reporter attending a game noticed that only twelve people were sitting in the section. In 1928, responding to fan demand for home run hitters like the Yankees' Babe Ruth, the Braves erected gargantuan bleacher sections down the left and right field lines as well as temporary bleachers in left and center, reducing home-run distances by more than 200 feet. However, the seats resulted in *visiting* players blasting so many dingers that the club quickly ordered the temporary stands dismantled. After that, field dimensions were rejig-gered almost every year, with the park earning the dubious distinction of becoming the field that altered its dimensions more than any other during its history.

With a losing team and the opening of a nearby racetrack siphoning off some of the stadium's most common spectators—gamblers—the Braves were desperate to get fans into the stands. A contest to rename the team was held, and from 1936 to 1940 the club was called the "Bees," and its stadium (although officially called "National League Park") was known as the Bee Hive. The better-known and more effective stratagem that the team employed in the 30s, however, was the signing of a new player: Babe Ruth himself. Ruth had his eye on managing, and Braves owner Emil Fuchs promised him a managing position later and the positions of vice president and assistant manager for the 1935 season. But Ruth soon discovered that what Fuchs really wanted was a star to play at exhibition games, and perhaps even some of Ruth's own fortune to help bail out the team. So after two months of pushing his aging body through the paces, Ruth called it quits—or Fuchs fired him, depending on whom you believe. Either way, Fuchs couldn't keep his team solvent and soon it passed into the hands of Lou Perini.

Perini did have a feasible plan for making money—moving the team to Milwaukee. Though attendance surged as the club climbed to third in '47 before capturing the NL pennant in '48, Perini was determined to move, and the Braves played their final season in Boston in 1952. By the time of the team's last game there on September 21, the long-rumored move to Wisconsin had turned into a badly kept secret that gave fans even less of a reason to come out to the ballpark. Only 8,822 spectators (the second-biggest crowd of the season) bothered to show up at the Braves' wake. The team, which had played in Boston under many different names, dating back to the National Association in 1871, became the first to change cities since the Baltimore Orioles became the New York Highlanders in 1903. The land was sold to Boston University, and the Red Sox have ruled Boston baseball ever since.

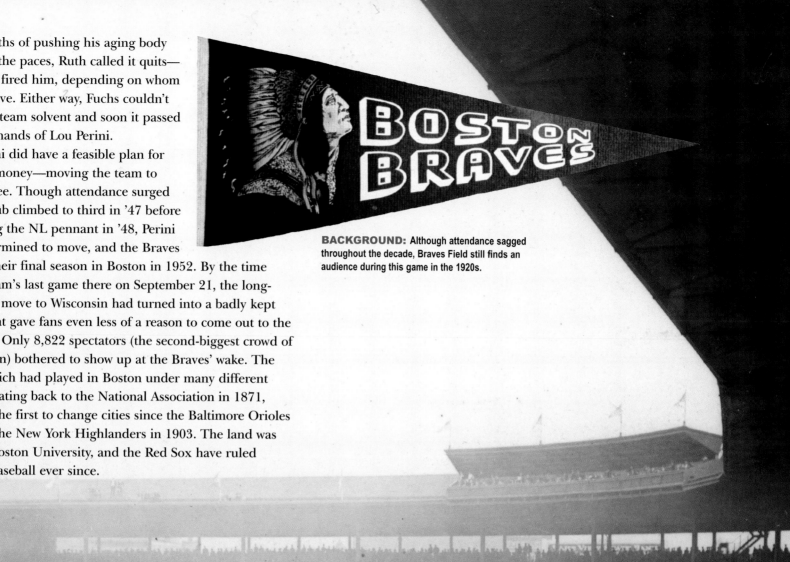

BACKGROUND: Although attendance sagged throughout the decade, Braves Field still finds an audience during this game in the 1920s.

1916 The Braves go 89-63, finishing third in the National League, only four games back of Brooklyn. They won't finish this high again until 1947.

1920 The first major Negro League, the Negro National League, is founded in Chicago. Negro League ball will continue into the 1950s, but no important black team will ever represent Boston.

1924 The Braves lose exactly one hundred games for the third consecutive year on their way to a streak of ten consecutive losing seasons from 1922 to 1931.

1915

Braves Field opens on August 18 as the first major league stadium with more than 40,000 seats. Built on the site of a former golf course, the park plays like a very long par five: 400 feet to left and 440 in center, with a staggering 500 to right-center.

October 12, 1915

Sox Feel Right at Home The Red Sox, playing their World Series home games at Braves Field because of its larger capacity than Fenway Park, win their third straight 2-1 decision over the Phillies. Remarkably, winning pitcher Ernie Shore's 2.12 ERA will be the highest of the three pitchers Boston uses in the Series. The Sox will clinch the Series with a 5-4 victory at Baker Bowl in Game 5.

Red Sox 2, Phillies 1

October 9, 1916

Babe's Big Game After allowing a first-inning run, Red Sox hurler Babe Ruth proceeds to shut out Brooklyn for the next thirteen innings while also driving in a run of his own. Sox pinch hitter Del Gainer, in his only appearance of the Series, delights the partisan crowd of 47,373 when he ends the game with a walk-off double in the fourteenth. Ruth will go on to pitch 29⅔ consecutive scoreless innings in World Series play, a record that will stand until 1961. Three days after Ruth's heroic effort, Ernie Shore allows just three hits in the clincher for Boston. While Braves Field is the only stadium to host a World Series in its first two years of existence, there will be no more championships won here; the Boston Braves' lone Series title came at Fenway Park in 1914.

Red Sox 2, Dodgers 1

1928

The Braves add 6,000 seats in left and center field. With the Braves having finished last or next to last in the league in attendance every year since 1922, the move is made not to accommodate more fans, but to increase home runs by reducing the size of the spacious playing field. The new bleachers are removed and distances lengthened in midseason.

1929

The Boston Bulldogs call Braves Field home during their single year of existence in the NFL.

August 1, 1918

My Kingdom for a Run The Pirates and Braves play scoreless baseball for twenty innings before Pittsburgh manages to scratch across two runs in the top of the twenty-first. Losing pitcher Art Nehf goes all twenty innings, taking one of the toughest losses in baseball history. Nehf will be traded to the Giants in 1919 and pitch on four straight pennant-winning teams under John McGraw. His record for most shutout innings in a game will last less than two years before being broken by Joe Oeschger in the same ballpark.

Pirates 2, Braves 0

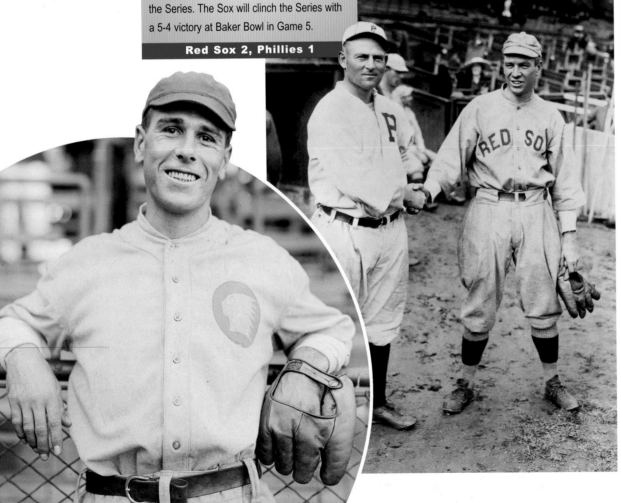

FAR LEFT: A smiling Fred Snodgrass poses in the Braves' new road togs in 1916.

LEFT: Stars Gavvy Cravath of the Phillies and Tris Speaker of the Red Sox shake hands for the camera before Game 3 of the 1915 World Series at Braves Field.

July 7, 1936 Braves Field hosts the fourth annual All-Star Game, the only Midsummer Classic ever played there. The NL stars defeat the AL, 4-3.

1933

An NFL version of the Boston Braves debuts at Braves Field. They move to Fenway after one year and change their name to the Redskins before relocating to Washington in 1937.

1936

Boston's National League club changes it name to the Bees and the park is re-christened National League Park, a.k.a. the Bee Hive. Both names revert back to Braves in 1941.

1941

The distance to deepest right-center field, is cut drastically to 401 feet.

May 1, 1920

The Longest Game In the longest game in major league history, the Braves and Robins play an excruciating twenty-six innings before the game is called due to darkness, with the score tied 1-1. Remarkably, both pitchers—Brooklyn's Leon Cadore and Boston's Joe Oeschger—last all twenty-six innings. Oeschger shuts out the Robins for the last twenty-one frames, topping Art Nehf's record set two years earlier. The game lasts a remarkably brief three hours, fifty-one minutes before the sun sets on a cold, wet New England day. Brooklyn's next two games will be losses lasting thirteen and nineteen innings, respectively, but the Robins will rebound to win the 1920 pennant. The Braves win their next six in a row after the marathon tie, but will finish in seventh place.

Braves 1, Dodgers 1

ABOVE: Bees players pose while sitting on the third base grandstand wall at the park in April 1939.

April 16, 1935

Return of the Bambino Babe Ruth returns to Boston, making his National League debut before more than 25,000 spectators, the largest-ever Opening Day crowd at Braves Field. The Babe doesn't disappoint, belting a long home run off Giants ace Carl Hubbell. However, Ruth, in his twenty-second major league season, soon begins showing signs of age, and will announce his retirement shortly after a three-homer performance in Pittsburgh in May. The moribund Braves will average less than 3,000 fans per game the rest of the year, and lose an embarrassing 115 games—a modern mark that won't be topped until the New York Mets enter the league in 1962.

Braves 4, Giants 2

ABOVE: Babe Ruth choosing his weapon in front of the dugout during the Braves–Red Sox City Series in 1935. The two Boston clubs played a City Series each spring from 1925 to 1953, except in 1928. A tired forty-year-old Ruth hit only .181 in seventy-two at-bats with the Braves during the regular season before retiring.

BACKGROUND: View from the left-field corner—looking toward the Boston & Albany Railroad tracks and the Charles River behind center field—of a near-capacity crowd at Braves Field on June 13, 1937.

1946 The Braves get pitcher Johnny Sain back from the Navy at the start of the season, with Warren Spahn being discharged from the Army in midseason.

April 28, 1946 The Braves play a doubleheader against the Phillies at Fenway Park due to "paint issues" at Braves Field. Their game at Fenway the previous day had been rained out.

1946

Lights are installed, fir trees are planted beyond the centerfield fence, and the field is slightly rotated to the right. Many Opening Day fans go home with a souvenir on their pants—the new coat of green paint on the seats in some sections is still wet.

1948

A 68-foot-high score-board is added in left.

September 14, 1948

Praying For Rain As the Braves try to map out their beleaguered pitching rotation for the rest of the pennant drive, a legendary phrase enters the baseball lexicon. On this day, the *Boston Post* runs a poem by sports editor Gerald C. Hern: "First we'll use Spahn / then we'll use Sain / Then an off day / followed by rain." Manager Billy Southworth's rotation runs almost true to poetic form, except it is Johnny Sain, not Warren Spahn, who beats the Phillies to give Boston a 4½ game lead in the standings. Combined, the two ace pitchers will start eleven of Boston's final sixteen games of the year, and the saying "Spahn and Sain and pray for rain" will endure long after the players retire.

Braves 10, Phillies 3

ABOVE: Braves Field scoreboard in left field, ready to "light up" for a preseason City Series tilt between the Red Sox and Braves in the late 1940s or early 1950s.

CAP: 1948.

June 19, 1942

Big Poison's Big Hit The Braves' Paul Waner becomes the seventh player in major league history to collect 3,000 hits, banging out the milestone knock against his former team. "Big Poison," who amassed 2,868 hits in his fifteen years as a Pirate, singles against Pittsburgh's Rip Sewell for his historic hit, but the Pirates win 7-6 in eleven innings. Waner had initially appeared to collect his 3,000th two days earlier when he smashed a grounder that was mis-handled, but he signaled to the press box that he didn't want hit number 3,000 to be a questionable one, so the scoring was changed.

Pirates 7, Braves 6

RIGHT: Young rookie lefty Warren Spahn demonstrates his high-kicking form in spring training, 1942. After serving in the Army in World War II from 1943 to 1946, Spahn went on to win 356 games while pitching for the Braves from 1946 to 1964 in Boston and Milwaukee.

April 27, 1947 More than a decade after the Bambino's last game, as a Boston Brave, 58,000 fans celebrate "Babe Ruth Day" at Yankee Stadium.

July 12, 1949 Club owners agree that all parks will now feature warning tracks around their perimeters, to warn outfielders before they crash into a wall.

April 18, 1950 Negro League veteran Sam Jethroe makes his major league debut at age thirty-two, integrating the Braves. He will win the 1950 NL Rookie of the Year Award.

1952

The club plays its final game at its eponymous park on September 21. Only 1,885 home runs were hit during the nearly 2,800 games played at the park.

1960

The site of Braves Field is reconfigured for football; Boston University, the AFL's Boston Patriots, and the USFL's Boston Breakers all eventually play there. Part of the stands and a building from Braves Field remain at the renamed Nickerson Field, which is now part of the BU campus.

October 6, 1948

Home of the Braves In Game 1 of the World Series, Johnny Sain outduels Cleveland fireballer Bob Feller, allowing four hits while Feller allows only two in a classic, 1-0 game. Because the 1914 Braves won their championship at Fenway Park, this is the first Fall Classic game ever won by the Braves at Braves Field—and also, unfortunately, the last. The Indians will win both remaining games on this field, including the Series-clinching Game 6. The major leagues' two Native American–themed teams will not face each other again until the 1995 World Series, by which time the Braves will have moved to Atlanta.

Braves 1, Indians 0

TOP: Aerial photo of a capacity crowd at Braves Field sometime between 1928 and 1935. Note the rows of fans, five or more deep, standing on the field behind ropes.

LEFT: Third baseman Eddie Mathews posing for a photo in 1952. Mathews played his rookie season in Boston that year, then went on to play fourteen years in Milwaukee and Atlanta for the Braves.

BACKGROUND: Demolition of the left-field stands at Braves Field by Boston University in 1955. A few parts of Braves Field, including some of the right field bleachers, survive today as part of Nickerson Field, the BU football, soccer, and track facility.

Stadiums

1923   1962

In 1923, the Yankees moved out of the cramped Polo Grounds and across the Harlem River to the South Bronx. Unlike with previous ballparks, which were squeezed into whatever parcel of land happened to be available, they had plenty of room to build a grand edifice the likes of which no one had ever seen. With their triple-decked wonder a whole new era of stadium construction was born. The virtually instantaneous iconic status of impressive Yankee Stadium caused most ball clubs to henceforth call their new homes "stadiums." In an age that saw the birth of talking motion pictures, radio, and commercial airplane travel, more modest words like "grounds," "field," or "park" suddenly seemed quaint. A decade earlier, the trend in building major league ballparks had been to replace wooden structures with fireproof parks of concrete and steel that weren't much bigger than their predecessors. In the 1920s and beyond, clubs began to move their parks where they could greatly increase their size, and thereby, their capacity.

After Yankee Stadium opened in 1923 and Cleveland Stadium in 1932, no more major league parks were built until the years after the end of World War II, when professional baseball was more successful than ever before. The US economy was expanding, and middle-class Americans now had the ability to enjoy the fruits of their labor in ways they never could before the war and during the Depression. Automobile sales skyrocketed, millions of new homes were built, and suburbs sprouted up everywhere as Americans flocked to ballgames in record numbers.

From 1949 to 1953, however, attendance began to slump as families bought TVs in huge numbers and started staying home to watch them. In the mid-1950s, attendance began to recover, largely because of franchise relocation. For the first time in half a century, clubs were allowed to change cities. Team owners realized that instead of putting forth their own capital to make improvements on their deteriorating ballparks, or trying to get funding to build new ones in their hometowns, they now had an easier choice. They could move to a new city, where residents would be excited about a major league team coming to town—and would approve public financing for a new park. The only question was where. Oftentimes, owners made decisions based on neither the best interests of their team nor of their fans but solely on which municipal or county government was promising the biggest pot of cash. Making the switch from risk-taking entrepreneurs to subsidy-dependent businessmen, owners would send their teams packing to areas where they could dip into the public treasury.

Beginning in 1953, teams from New York and Brooklyn headed to the burgeoning West while the Boston Braves moved to Milwaukee, the Philadelphia A's moved to Kansas City, and the St. Louis Browns became the Baltimore Orioles. Once they arrived in their new hometowns, various accommodations were made. In Kansas City and Baltimore, minor league parks were refurbished to make room for the big leagues. In Milwaukee, the Braves had County Stadium already waiting for them, as the city was the first to build a park in an attempt to lure a major league team—a practice that would become commonplace in the superstadium era. In California, the new home of the Giants and Dodgers, teams played in existing parks temporarily while their new palaces—Candlestick Park and Dodger Stadium—were being built. Dodger Stadium, one of the best specimens of the stadium era and one of the most beloved ballparks in the United States, still stands today.

Thanks to the popularity of the automobile, team owners were no longer constricted by the need for easy public transportation, and searched for plots of land that could contain large stadiums that would hold huge baseball crowds, and thus, hopefully, result in increased ticket sales. Plus, the large venues could host concerts and other forms of entertainment as well. While ballparks used to be part of the fabric of the cities that surrounded them, they were now on the fringes of cities and even in nearby suburbs, encased in parking lots. These concrete behemoths, with no local flavor to draw upon, were largely defined by the teams that played in them—for better or for worse. Although the new stadiums tended to lack individual touches that set them apart or made the ballpark experience special, they set attendance records again and again. Their large capacities, together with the addition of lights—which allowed games to be scheduled at night, when more people were available to attend them—set the stage for the most lucrative decade baseball had ever seen. To keep pace with the new stadiums, the remaining classic-era fields began remodeling, stuffing in seats as fast as they could upgrade the structure to fit them. Baseball was booming, and owners and their government sponsors began to search for a way that they could get even more money out of their grand showcases. Soon they began looking at another booming sport—football—for their answer.

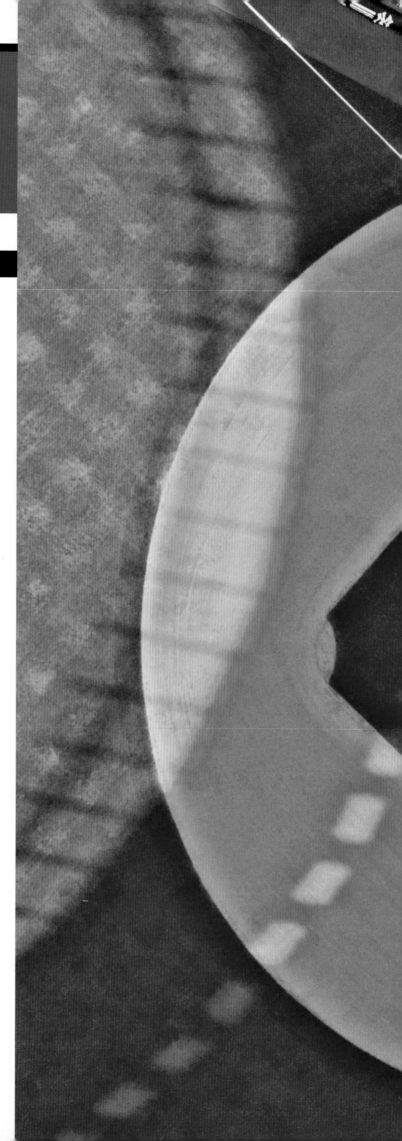

YANKEE STADIUM

The Bronx, New York

Yankees (AL) 1923–2008

The merits of the New York Yankees and their famous former field can be debated by fan and foe, but what can't be disputed is that Yankee Stadium has seen more history than any other ballpark. In its eighty-six years of existence, it saw thirty-seven World Series, had eighteen 100-win seasons, and was the home field for more than two dozen future Hall of Famers. The first ballpark to be called a *stadium* from its inception, the "House That Ruth Built" reached iconic status almost immediately upon opening, and helped launch a new era in baseball.

Before they had their own stadium, the Yankees had been sharing the New York Giants' commodious Polo Grounds on the northern end of Manhattan. Long time rivals of the Giants, in 1919 the Yankees had recently begun to reach new heights of popularity and on-field success, thanks to recent acquisition Babe Ruth. With Waite Hoyt, Carl Mays, and Bob Meusel also on hand, the soon-to-be-famous Yankees had developed by the early 1920s into a powerhouse, and the Giants wanted them out of their park.

In 1921, Giants manager and part-owner John McGraw served his AL tenants an eviction notice. It is said that he believed he could eliminate them altogether because he thought they wouldn't be able to find another site in Manhattan. The Yankees may not have been able to find another suitable place in Manhattan, but they certainly weren't through. A parcel of land directly across the Harlem River in the South Bronx was purchased from the Astor estate, and despite a brutally wet winter, Yankee Stadium was quickly built and ready for use by the 1923 season.

From the moment it was conceived, the new park truly was the House That Ruth Built. In an early example of building one's home park to suit one's talent, the Yankees constructed their new palace to help the left-handed-hitting Ruth swat more home runs. While the right-field foul line would be almost 40 feet longer than that of the horseshoe-shaped Polo Grounds by 1924, straightaway right field in the Bronx was much closer than at the Polo Grounds. The deepest part of the outfield (left of center) was cavernous at more than 500 feet, earning the nickname "Death Valley." In February 1923, just prior to leaving for spring training, Ruth took a tour of his new home and, in street clothes, clubbed a pitch, thrown by a local sportswriter, into the right-field seats.

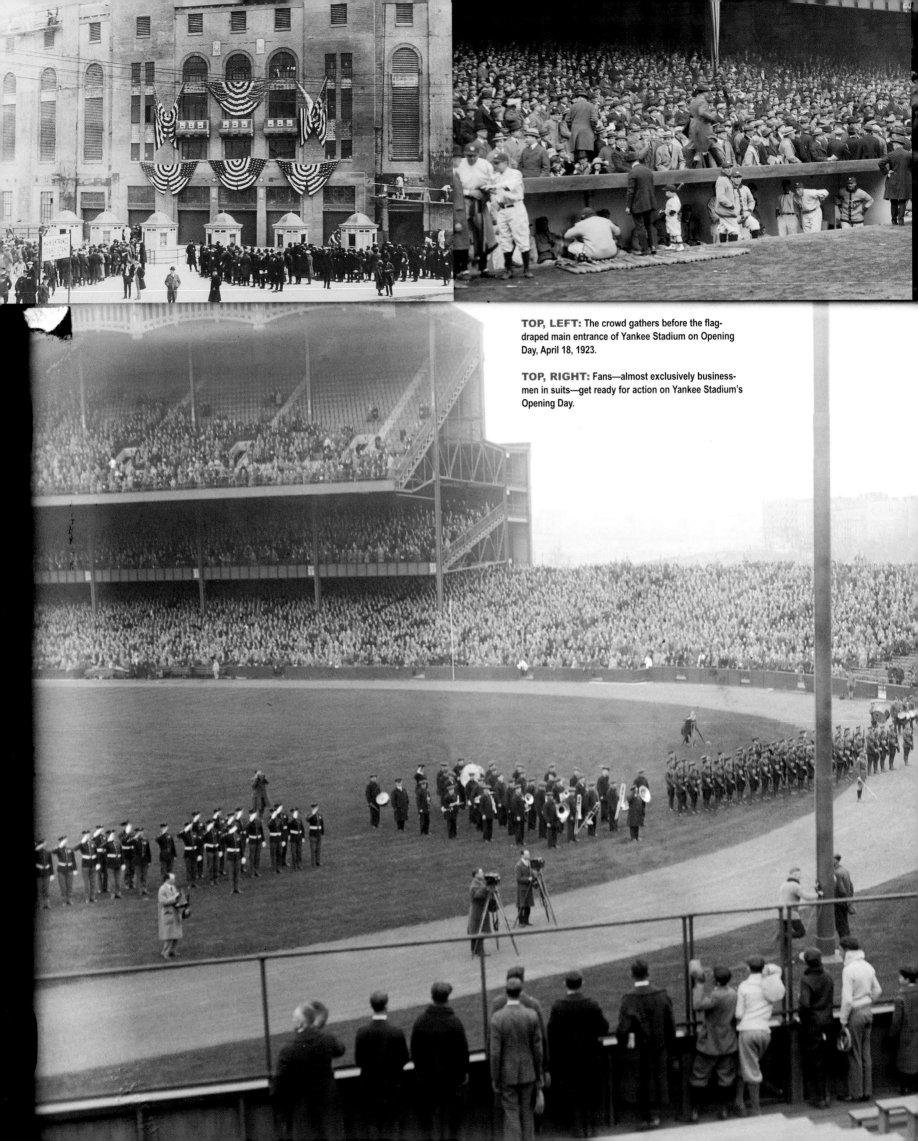

TOP, LEFT: The crowd gathers before the flag-draped main entrance of Yankee Stadium on Opening Day, April 18, 1923.

TOP, RIGHT: Fans—almost exclusively businessmen in suits—get ready for action on Yankee Stadium's Opening Day.

ABOVE: The Senators-Yankees game on April 24, 1923, is attended by a bevy of VIPs. From left: Postmaster General Harry New, Dr. Charles Sawyer (presidential physician), Albert Lasker (part-owner of the Cubs and pioneering advertising executive), Yankees owner Jacob Ruppert, and President Warren Harding.

He'd repeat the feat again on April 18, hitting a three-run homer in the third inning on Opening Day against his former team, the Red Sox. John Philip Sousa and the Seventh Regiment band entertained the crowd before the game, and Governor Al Smith threw out the first ball. The Yankees announced that a record-breaking 74,217 fans had attended, although the *Sporting News* later disputed the figure, pointing out that the stadium's capacity was 60,000 at the most.

Ruth's grand new domicile featured a degree of architectural splendor unprecedented for a ballpark. But Yankee Stadium was certainly no ordinary ballpark. It was a *stadium*—the first to feature three stately decks and a palpable vastness upon entering. A 15-foot-high copper frieze, soon to be the park's signature element, lined the roof of the top deck. Baseball teams finally had a place to play that had all the grandeur of the huge soccer and track stadiums in Europe and some of the larger college football stadiums stateside.

The imposing new stadium in the Bronx wasn't used solely for major league baseball, of course. Yankee Stadium followed the Polo Grounds' lead by regularly hosting boxing matches, and a 15-foot-deep vault with telephone and telegraph wires was constructed under second base for use during the events. Respected sportswriter Joe Vila and others decried the trend of renting parks for boxing matches, stating that the rental fees weren't worth the loss of publicity as a result of having to share the sports pages. Beginning in 1930, the Yankees also leased their stadium to the Negro Leagues, and over the next two decades hosted many four-team doubleheaders. Football teams, too, made use of the park, with two teams from upstart leagues (both called the Yankees) playing in the stadium before the NFL Giants moved in from 1956 to 1973.

For the first forty years of Yankee Stadium's existence, the team embarked on an epoch-making winning streak, unrivaled in any sport before or since. Beginning with Babe Ruth and Lou Gehrig, then moving on to Joe DiMaggio and Bill Dickey, and finally starring Mickey Mantle, Roger Maris, and Yogi Berra, the club thrived with a steady stream of awesome talent and no shortage of fans, even before their crosstown rivals the Giants and Dodgers fled to California in 1958.

Beginning in 1932, these baseball greats were immortalized in Monument Park, an area at the end of left-center field that featured in-play statues of Ruth, Gehrig, and late manager Miller Huggins. The area was subsequently moved behind the fence, and came to feature six monuments—including one honoring those lost on September 11, 2001—and twenty-two plaques devoted to Yankees players, owners, managers, and others—including popes who celebrated masses at the stadium.

But the Yankees' championship streak wasn't as immortal as it appeared. Following consecutive World Series defeats in 1963 and 1964, the club fell from grace in 1965, tumbling to the second division and finishing last the next year. On September 22, 1966, Yankees TV announcer Red Barber pointed out that only 413 fans were at that day's game at Yankee Stadium. (Barber sealed his fate—his contract was not renewed.) After watching the club continue to struggle through the late 1960s, CBS, the club's owners, floated plans to move to New Jersey if Yankee Stadium, owned by the City of New York, wasn't modernized. So the two parties organized a deal to renovate the old ballpark, which hadn't had a substantive change to its structure or grounds since 1937, when second and third decks had been built down the right-field line. On August 8, 1972, the Yankees signed a thirty-year lease to stay in their eponymous park, which would be renovated after the stadium's fiftieth anniversary season of 1973.

In order for the city to tear apart and reconstruct Yankee Stadium, the team vacated the Bronx for two years, taking up residence at Shea Stadium, the home of the Mets, during the 1974 and 1975 seasons. While having to visit Flushing was certainly an emotional trauma for Yankees fans, the work done back in the Bronx was worth the hassle. The venerable park reopened in April 1976 with space for about 10,000 fewer fans (making the new capacity 54,028), but with larger and more comfortable seats in bright blue plastic. Double-width escalators transported fans to the upper decks, and the old support pillars and posts, which blocked views from many seats, had been removed. Gone was the copper facade that once rang the park; in was a sleek, but not overly modern, design that featured a white-painted concrete replica of the frieze over the bleachers in center field. The playing surface was also smaller—center field was shortened to a more reasonable 417 feet—although left-center field remained defiant of power hitters at 430 feet.

Yankees fans were happy to see the beautiful renovations, which were said to have cost the city as much as $75 million. They were even happier that new owner George Steinbrenner had entered baseball's newfangled free-agent derby with abandon. Thanks to his burning desire to win, and his deep pockets, the Yankees regained their standing as the game's greatest franchise. But even with their winning ways, many team members—and regular New Yorkers—weren't fans of the tough-as-nails boss. Steinbrenner became known for being rash in his decisions to fire people, unpredictable in his policy-making (he introduced a rule forbidding players to have beards), and less-than-courteous to employees, reporters, and fans. He was famously lampooned on *Seinfeld*, and twice suspended from baseball—once for illegal contributions to Richard Nixon's re-election campaign, and once for paying a gambler for information about Yankees star Dave Winfield. "The Yankees' owner audited the team from moment to moment," wrote Buster Olney in his 2004 book *The Last Night of the Yankee Dynasty*, "like a caffeinated rent-a-cop monitoring a Wal-Mart through security cameras."

It came as no surprise, then, that the owner everyone loved to hate decided that his team would leave their historic home. On June 15, 2006, the Yankees announced plans to open a new state-of-the-art stadium across the street from the old one in 2009. Fans were relieved that their beloved team wouldn't be moving out of the city, but most felt that

CAPS 1930, 1986, 1999.

the new field—also called Yankee Stadium—was simply an excuse to put more money in Steinbrenner's pockets. Though the park would offer more amenities and perks, such as wider concourses and a martini bar, many felt that abandoning the original Yankee Stadium wasn't worth it, even if most of the money to build the new park was coming directly from the team. The final game in the House That Ruth Built took place on September 21, 2008. "The new Yankee Stadium will never be like this one," a spectator told the *New York Times*. "It's kind of like when you fall in love. You fall in love once, and you fall in love with one stadium."

RIGHT: Yankees great, fan favorite, and grandmaster of the English language, Yogi Berra stands at home plate during ceremonies on September 21, 2008, before the last game at Yankee Stadium.

1925 Babe Ruth takes two months off for stomach trouble, and the Yankees finish the season at 69-85, after going 89-63 the previous year. The papers call it "the bellyache heard round the world."

1927 and 1928 With a stacked lineup known as "Murderers' Row"—which includes Babe Ruth, Lou Gehrig, Earle Combs, and Tony Lazzeri—the Bombers mutilate their competition and win back-to-back World Series.

April 16, 1929 The Yankees become the first team to permanently add numbers to all their uniforms. Babe Ruth takes number 3 because he bats third in the lineup.

TIMELINE: YANKEE STADIUM

1923

Yankee Stadium opens across the Harlem River from the Giants' Polo Grounds. The park that will quickly become known as "The House That Ruth Built" has been constructed with left-handed sluggers in mind, with the right-field corner just 255 feet away. The left-field line measures just 255 feet, but quickly juts out to 455 in left-center and 515 just left of center. Dead-center is 490 feet away, and right-center is 429.

June 1, 1925

The First of Many Lou Gehrig begins a consecutive games streak that will surpass current teammate Everett Scott's record and reach 2,130 games before ending due to illness. Gehrig is sent to the plate as a pinch hitter for Pee Wee Wanninger, who is subbing for Scott at shortstop. Lou will get the start tomorrow and stay in the lineup every day for fourteen years. During that time he'll play through a broken toe, a broken thumb, and lumbago so bad that he will be carried off the field in Detroit. (The day after that he will be the leadoff hitter, listed as the shortstop, and will be removed after singling in the first inning.) He'll also amass a career 8,001 at-bats, 493 home runs, and a .340 average before he is forced to leave the field permanently in 1939.

Senators 5, Yankees 3

BELOW, LEFT: "The Bambino," pictured here with his war club in the early 1930s, had quite a resume. Credited for "building" Yankee Stadium, the superstar revolutionized the way baseball was played, introducing the power-based game with his shocking fifty-four homers in 1920.

BELOW: The streets around Yankee Stadium are clogged with traffic on April 18, 1923—the day of the season opener against Boston, not to mention the park's grand opening. New York will defeat its historical rival 4-1, with Babe Ruth hitting the first home run in the Yankees' new palace.

1926

A second New York Yankees team—this one in the American Football League, and featuring Red Grange—begins play at Yankee Stadium. When the league folds after one season, the Yankees join the NFL and play two more years at the stadium.

September 30, 1927

Ruth Hits His 60th With first base open, Babe Ruth hits his sixtieth home run of the year against Washington's Tom Zachary to break a 2-2 tie in the eighth inning. Ruth, who is already baseball's career home run leader, breaks the single-season record for the fourth and final time. Ruth's seventeen home runs in September are also a record, and will remain the highest monthly total until Rudy York cranks eighteen in August 1937. Today also marks the 934th and final major league appearance for the greatest pitcher of all time, Washington's Walter Johnson, who pinch-hits for Zachary and flies out to Ruth. The Yankees, having long ago clinched the pennant, earn their 109th victory of the season. They'll get number 110, a league record, the next afternoon.

Yankees 4, Senators 2

1928

Second and third decks are added to left-center field, raising capacity to 67,000 and enabling the exaggeration-prone Yankees to draw the first reported crowd of 80,000 in big-league history. The reconfiguration moves the left-field fence, which had been moved to 281 feet in 1924, even farther away at 301 feet. Straightaway right field is 367, but it is only 295 down the right-field line.

October 1, 1932 At Wrigley Field, Babe Ruth gestures toward center field while at bat in Game 3 of the 1932 World Series—his infamous "called shot"—and he proceeds to smack a homer into the centerfield bleachers.

May 3, 1936 The Yankee Clipper, a.k.a. Joseph DiMaggio Jr., makes his rookie-season debut with the Bronx Bombers. He'll become the first rookie All-Star ever, and lead the Yanks to the next four World Series titles.

September 9, 1934

Satch vs. Slim In the first of what will become a popular series of four-team doubleheaders at Yankee Stadium, a quartet of the Negro Leagues' best squads duke it out: the Chicago American Giants versus the New York Black Yankees, and the Philadelphia Stars versus the Pittsburgh Crawfords. Chicago beats New York in the opener, but it is the nightcap that will be remembered as a classic duel between the Negro Leagues' two best pitchers, Slim Jones and Satchel Paige. Philadelphia's Jones works on a perfect game until the seventh, when Pittsburgh's Oscar Charleston singles to break it up. The score stands at 1-1 entering the ninth, which the teams know will be the last inning due to impending darkness. When Philadelphia gets a man on third in the bottom of the inning, the exhausted Paige manages one last burst of strength, striking out his seventeenth and eighteenth batters of the day to end both the inning and the game. The 1-1 tie will be regarded by many as the greatest Negro League game ever played.

American Giants 4, Black Yankees 3; Stars 1, Crawfords 1

1932

The first monument at Yankee Stadium, in honor of the late manager Miller Huggins, is dedicated on May 30 and placed on the field of play in deepest left-center.

1937

Second and third decks are built down the right-field line, and outfield bleachers are added. Capacity is now more than 71,000.

LEFT: The incomparable Satchel Paige poses for the photogs at Yankee Stadium in 1943, his sole season with the New York Black Yankees. Despite Paige's presence, the Black Yankees would go 2-21 in Negro National League play that year.

BELOW, LEFT: Twenty-one-year-old Joe DiMaggio as he appeared on his rookie card from 1936, when the Yankee Clipper broke in by hitting .323 with 29 homers and 125 RBIs in 138 games.

BELOW: Lou Gehrig signs autographs at Yankee Stadium on June 22, 1939, before the White Sox–Yankees game. Gehrig had played his last game on April 30, but the fan favorite was still suiting up and coming to the ballpark.

July 4, 1939 Yankees legend Lou Gehrig says, "I consider myself the luckiest man on the face of the Earth" in his farewell speech at Yankee Stadium. Diagnosed with amyotrophic lateral sclerosis—which will become known as Lou Gehrig's disease—he will pass away two years later at age thirty-seven.

1943 After having lost to the Cardinals in the 1942 Fall Classic, the Yanks beat the Cards four-games-to-one in a rematch. They'll regain the title again in '47 and yet again in '49, both times against their inter-borough rivals, the Brooklyn Dodgers.

1946

Yankee Stadium's first game under the lights is played on May 28, and thanks to the attendance boost from night games, the Yankees become the first team to draw 2 million fans. Meanwhile, the New York Black Yankees of the Negro National League begin a two-season run at Yankee Stadium, while the New York Yankees of the All-America Football Conference begin what will be a four-season run.

1950

The NFL's New York Bulldogs, with many of the defunct AAFC Yankees players, move to Yankee Stadium and change their name to the New York Yanks. They last two years before departing for Dallas.

October 5, 1953

Five in a Row The Yankees capture their record fifth straight world championship, three of which have come at the expense of the Brooklyn Dodgers. Casey Stengel has now won the World Series in each of his five years as Yankees manager. The Dodgers trail 3-0 for most of Game 6, but Carl Furillo's two-run homer in the ninth off Allie Reynolds ties the game. In the bottom of the inning, however, Billy Martin's single off Dodgers reliever Clem Labine brings home Hank Bauer with the Series-winning run. The hit is Martin's record-tying twelfth of the Series, and he also leads all players with eight RBIs.

Yankees 4, Dodgers 3

BACKGROUND: From way up in the third deck in right field, fans watch the Yankees take on the St. Louis Cardinals during the 1942 World Series. Note the silhou-etted view through the section's copper-frieze facade as well as how high the seats are above the right-field foul pole, which can be seen in the lower left corner.

October 2, 1949

Boston Creamed The Red Sox came to New York needing to win just one of the season's final two games to clinch the pennant, but the Yankees win both in dramatic fashion. After rallying from four runs down to take the series opener on October 1, Casey Stengel's Yanks explode for four runs in the eighth inning of the second game. Boston rallies for three in the top of the ninth, but Yankees right-hander Vic Raschi nails the door shut to clinch New York's sixteenth pennant since 1921. They'll soon win their twelfth World Series as well. This marks the second straight year the Red Sox, skippered by former Yankees manager Joe McCarthy, have lost the pennant in their final game of the season.

Yankees 5, Red Sox 3

ABOVE: Baseball fans cling to the overhead pipes on the second level of Yankee Stadium during Game 6 of the 1947 World Series against the Dodgers. The Bums will win this game, knotting the Series at three games apiece—but they will lose Game 7 to the lordly Yankees the next day.

1951 Longtime Yankees announcer Bob Sheppard begins his stint behind the mic at Yankee Stadium, and will hold the post until the park closes.

1956

The NFL's New York Giants move to Yankee Stadium, leaving the Polo Grounds two years before the baseball Giants do. The Giants will play football at Yankee Stadium until 1973.

1960

The club installs 135 loge seats with carpeted floors, waitstaff, hot beverages, and telephone service.

October 1, 1961

Roger and Out In the final game of the year, Roger Maris hits his sixty-first homer to right field off Boston's Tracy Stallard, breaking Babe Ruth's beloved single-season record. However, Maris' record is met with widespread skepticism since he's been helped by the recent addition of eight extra games to the season. Remarkably, only 23,154 fans attend. The record-breaking ball is caught by nineteen-year-old Brooklynite Sal Durante, who will later sell it to a restaurateur for $5,000. Maris' blast is the only run of the game, giving the Yankees their 109th win—the most victories they've posted since the famed Murderers' Row club won 110 in 1927. Mickey Mantle, the local favorite who kept pace with Maris in the home run race for most of the year, misses the season's final week due to injury. He finishes with fifty-four homers.

Yankees 1, Red Sox 0

October 8, 1956

Larsen is Perfect Don Larsen, a mediocre pitcher who bombed in World Series Game 2, pulls off the unexpected by hurling the greatest game in Series history—a perfect game victory over the befuddled Brooklyn Dodgers in Game 5. Larsen, who was knocked out of Game 2 in the second inning, fans seven and throws just ninety-seven pitches in retiring all twenty-seven hitters he faces. Mickey Mantle has the first hit of the game for the Yankees, a fourth-inning homer just inside the right-field foul pole. Mantle also makes the toughest catch of the day, a one-handed grab in deep center field on a Gil Hodges drive in the fifth. The last out of the game is pinch hitter Dale Mitchell, who is controversially called out on a questionable third strike. It will be the only no-hitter thrown in the first one-hundred-plus years of postseason play.

Yankees 2, Dodgers 0

ABOVE: Roger Maris watches from the batter's box as his sixty-first home run sails into the right-field stands on Sunday, October 1, 1961, the last day of the season.

TOP: A Yankees scorecard from 1956.

ABOVE, RIGHT: The iconic image from Don Larsen's perfecto is not Mickey Mantle's great catch nor Dale Mitchell caught looking at a questionable game-ending third strike. It's Yogi Berra jumping into Larsen's arms after the last out of the unprecedented game.

Vital Organs

With all the press about the differences (or lack thereof) between the old and new Yankee stadiums, one aspect that wasn't discussed until way after Monument Park had been uprooted and moved across the street was whether or not the new stadium would feature an organ player.

Yankee Stadium had an organist beginning in 1965, and in 1967, the job was taken over permanently by Eddie Layton. Layton—who claimed to have invented the lead-up melody to "Charge!"—switched teams (so to speak) when he was hired off a CBS soap opera to work at the network-owned Yankee Stadium. He held the post for thirty-six years, and upon his retirement told the *New York Times*, "I've had my day. Playing with 50,000 watts of power, what rock star has an amplifier like that? I play for up to 56,000 people a night. Not even Madonna has done those kind of numbers."

These days, stadium organists are becoming rarer and rarer. Few new stadiums feature organs; those that do often limit organ music to an occasional sound effect and the seventh inning stretch. Money isn't the issue—in fact, organ companies have been known to donate instruments for the publicity. The real fear is that the old-fashioned sound will scare off young people. As the MLB website quotes a fan commenting on his ten-year-old son, "He associates more with the rap and the three songs they put up on the scoreboard to choose from. That's society now."

Luckily, society at some stadiums still means full-time organ players. Gary Pressy has been playing at Wrigley Field since 1986, and Nancy Bea Hefly has been playing for the Dodgers since 1988. Cleveland's Jacobs Field features an organ player, as does Kauffman Stadium in Kansas City; and Dolphin Stadium's one redeeming feature may be its organ player, Lowery Ballew, who has played for the club since its debut season. He previously played for the Braves, who now use pre-recorded organ sounds.

Though you're less likely than ever before to hear the custom-made melodies of a baseball organ, it's rare for a club to fire their beloved player since the sound of the pipes is seen as a tradition among baseball purists. Most teams wait until their organist retires or a new stadium is built, conveniently without a spot for a 100-pound Hammond. The Giants gave up a pipe player when they moved from Candlestick to Pac Bell Park. And when the Phillies moved into the organless Veterans Stadium, Paul Richardson ended his thirty-five-year career after he was relegated to playing in the concourse before and after games.

But there is hope yet. In 2003, the Diamondbacks added an organ player due to fan demand. And as for the Yankees? With a Hammond right behind home plate in their new stadium, it could be a long time before their organists have to face the music.

ABOVE: Eddie Layton, the master of Yankee Stadium's Hammond organ for almost four decades, tickles the keys in his signature captain's hat. From 1967 to 1985, he also played the electronic pipes at Madison Square Garden for the NBA Knicks and NHL Rangers, leading to this popular trivia question: Who was the only man to play for the Yankees, Knicks, and Rangers?

June 8, 1969 The Yankees retire Mickey Mantle's number 7 on "Mickey Mantle Day" at the stadium. The career Yankee was a sixteen-time All-Star, twelve-time pennant winner, seven-time World Series champion, and three-time MVP.

1967

The stadium's exterior is painted blue and white.

October 10, 1964

Mantle's Last Hurrah In the ninth inning of World Series Game 3, Mickey Mantle hits Cardinals reliever Barney Schultz's first pitch into the right-field stands for a walk-off home run. It is Mantle's sixteenth career World Series homer, pushing him past Babe Ruth for the all-time lead. Mantle will hit two more homers in what will be his twelfth and last World Series. The Yankees take a 2-1 Series lead, but St. Louis will win Games 4, 5, and 7 to capture the world championship. Oddly, both teams will have new managers shortly after the Series ends. The Yankees, upset at losing the Series, will fire Yogi Berra and hire the manager who beat them, the Cardinals' Johnny Keane. St. Louis will hire coach Red Schoendienst to replace Keane, while Berra will become a coach for the New York Mets.

Yankees 2, Cardinals 1

ABOVE: Mickey Mantle holds his game-winning home-run ball from Game 3 of the 1964 World Series at Yankee Stadium. The Mick is embracing Yanks starting pitcher Jim Bouton, who pitched a complete game and allowed only one run. Though Mantle hit .333, scored eight runs, and drove in eight during the seven-game loss to St. Louis, he was not selected Series MVP. That honor rarely goes to a player on the losing team. The '64 season was Mantle's last great year, as he hit .303 with thirty-five homers and 111 RBIs—three figures he would never approach again.

1973

The Yankees play their final game at the original Yankee Stadium on September 30. They will play at Shea Stadium for two years while their ballpark is rebuilt from the ground up.

1976

The much smaller and drastically different Yankee Stadium reopens in April. The new dimensions are 312 feet down the left-field line, 387 to left-center, 430 to just left of center, 417 to center, 385 to right-center, and 310 down the right-field line. The Yankees christen the rebuilt park with their first pennant in twelve years.

ABOVE: Football fans pack Yankee Stadium on a fall afternoon in the late sixties or early seventies for an NFL Giants game. The Giants played in the Bronx from 1956 through 1972—plus one home game in 1973 before reconstruction began—before moving across the Hudson River to New Jersey's Meadowlands.

BELOW: The historic stadium undergoes a complete renovation from 1974 to 1975. As seen in this photo taken from a crane behind center field, the old structure has been stripped down to its concrete-and-steel bones.

1979 Thirty-two-year-old Yankees catcher and team captain Thurman Munson is tragically killed when his twin-engine Cessna Citation crashes in a field at the Akron-Canton Airport in Ohio.

July 24, 1983 Kansas City Royal George Brett has his game-winning two-run homer against the Yankees revoked when Yanks manager Billy Martin accuses him of using an illegal amount of pine tar on his bat. Known as the "Pine Tar Incident," the decision will later be reversed.

1988 Lou Piniella is named manager of the team for the second time, after Billy Martin is let go for the fifth (and final) time.

October 14, 1976

Chambliss Wins the Pennant In this best-of-five ALCS, everything comes down to the ninth inning of Game 5. After Kansas City's George Brett ties the game in the eighth with a clutch three-run homer off Yankees southpaw Grant Jackson, New York's Chris Chambliss unties it with a walk-off, series-winning homer in the ninth. Fans and players immediately storm the field, preventing Chambliss from completing his circuit around the bases, but the run still counts and the Yankees win. It is their first pennant in twelve years and comes in their first season playing in the newly renovated Yankee Stadium. They will, however, get swept in the World Series by the Cincinnati Reds.

Yankees 7, Royals 6

October 18, 1977

Three Swings, Three Homers In one of the greatest feats of showmanship in the game's history, Reggie Jackson establishes his legend as "Mr. October" by homering on three consecutive swings in Game 6 of the World Series. Jackson's three home runs come off three different pitchers, and he becomes the only player besides Babe Ruth to homer three times in a Series game. (Ruth did it in both 1926 and 1928.) Factoring in Reggie's four-pitch walk in the first inning, and the homer he hit in his final at-bat of Game 5, he has now hit four home runs on four successive swings. New York's Mike Torrez, meanwhile, pitches a complete game to give the Yankees their first championship since 1962.

Yankees 8, Dodgers 4

1988

Field dimensions are altered for the final time. Center field is shortened to 408 feet. However, distances are lengthened to 318 down the left-field line, 314 down the right-field line, and 399 to left-center. Right-center remains at 385.

RIGHT: "Mr. October," a.k.a. Reggie Jackson, stirs up the crowd and earns his sobriquet with his record-tying third home run of the game on October 18, 1977, in Game 6 of the Fall Classic. Dodgers catcher Steve Yeager and home plate umpire John McSherry watch the historic moment.

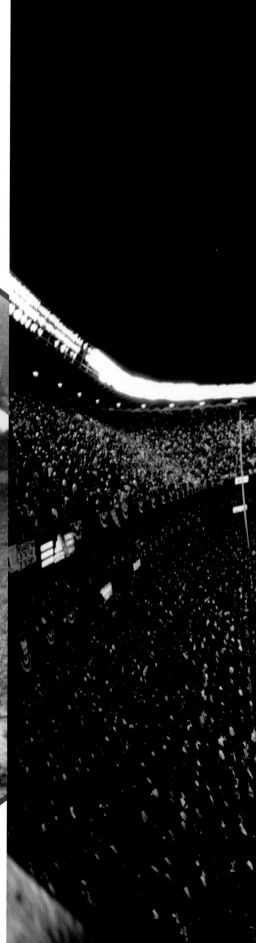

August 12, 1994 The Major League Baseball Players Association goes on strike in protest of the club owners' plans to institute a salary cap. The '94 World Series and more than 900 games are canceled as a result.

October 26, 1996

A Pristine Wetteland The Yankees, who opened the World Series by losing the first two games (at home, nonetheless), sweep the final four to win their first world championship since 1977. In Game 7 the Yankees' Jimmy Key pitches into the sixth inning, Mariano Rivera throws two hitless frames, and John Wetteland gets the save in the ninth. The Braves muster only three hits, and leave the tying and go-ahead runs on base when Mark Lemke pops up to end the Series. Wetteland, with a save in all four Yankees wins, will be named Series MVP, but will soon sign with the Texas Rangers as a free agent.

Yankees 3, Braves 2

1998

On April 13, several hours before game time, a 500-pound concrete-and-steel joint falls off the upper deck and crashes into the lower stands, forcing the Yankees to postpone two games, swap a home series with the Tigers, and reschedule a game against the Angels to take place at Shea Stadium.

ABOVE: Don Mattingly greets Jack Clark at home plate after Clark slammed a two-run homer against the White Sox on May 11, 1988. The Yanks will go on to win the match-up 12-2.

BACKGROUND: The Mets and Yankees line up for the national anthem before Game 1 of the 2000 World Series on October 21. The Yanks will edge out their rivals from Queens in twelve innings, then take the Series in five games.

October 21, 1998 New York defeats San Diego to win the
first of three consecutive World Series—three of four titles under
Joe Torre's management.

October 30, 2001 President George W. Bush throws out the first
pitch of Game 3 of the World Series at Yankee Stadium. Due to postpone-
ments following the September 11 terrorist attacks, the "November Series"
ends on November 4 when the Diamondbacks beat the Yankees 4-3.

October 16, 2003

Too Little, Too Late Just when it seems like
the Red Sox might finally break the eighty-four-
year-long "Curse of the Bambino," everything
falls apart for them in the eighth inning of ALCS
Game 7. Boston takes a 5-2 lead into the inning
and has one of the greatest pitchers of all time,
Pedro Martinez, on the mound. But after the
fatigued Martinez allows three consecutive hits
to the Yankees, he seems done for the night.
However, he talks manager Grady Little into
leaving him in the game—and immediately
allows a game-tying double to Yankees catcher
Jorge Posada. The game remains tied until
the bottom of the eleventh, when knuckleballer
Tim Wakefield takes the mound for Boston.
Wakefield's first pitch is blasted into the left-field
stands by Aaron Boone (who is batting just .161
in the postseason) for a pennant-winning home
run. The Yankees will be knocked off by the
Florida Marlins in the World Series, while the
stunned Red Sox will fire Little for waiting one
batter too long to call on his bullpen.

Yankees 6, Red Sox 5

2001

**Additional handicapped
seating is placed
behind the fence in left
field, with Plexiglas
windows cut into the
fence and a protective
net affixed overhead.**

ABOVE: Red Sox manager Grady Little visits Pedro
Martinez on the hill during Game 7 of the 2003 ALCS.
Star hurler Martinez allows the Yankees to tie the game
with a three-run rally in the eighth, and New York goes
on to win in the eleventh. Shortly after the Sox lose the
series, Little loses his job.

BELOW: Derek Jeter walks underneath the famous
"I want to thank the Good Lord for making me a
Yankee" sign in the tunnel that leads to the Yankees'
dugout. After the last home game at the park, Jeter
admitted to stealing the sign as a keepsake.

2002 Yankees games begin to be broadcast on the YES (Yankees Entertainment and Sports) Network, which is partially owned by the team.

2006 The Yankees win their ninth consecutive AL East title, and finish the regular season with ninety-seven wins—the sixth straight year they've finished with ninety-five or more wins.

2008

The Yankees play their last game at the stadium on September 21. Unfittingly for a park that saw thirty-seven World Series, this year the stadium won't see the postseason.

July 15, 2008

All-Stars, All Night With both sides having used sixty-three players and down to their last pitchers, Michael Young's deep fly brings in Justin Morneau just ahead of Brian McCann's tag in the bottom of the fifteenth inning. It's a thrill ride getting there. The American League rallies to tie it in the eighth on rookie Evan Longoria's hit. After Dan Uggla commits two of his record three errors to help load the bases with no one out in the tenth, Aaron Cook gets out of the jam. George Sherrill leaves the bases full of National Leaguers in the twelfth. Meanwhile, twenty-three pitchers come in from the Yankee Stadium bullpens, including local hero Mariano Rivera, who gets Uggla to ground into a double play with men on the corners (Uggla fans his other three times up). AL skipper Terry Francona has pegged MVP right fielder JD Drew as his next pitcher if the game lasts much longer, while NL manager Clint Hurdle has tabbed third baseman David Wright as his emergency hurler. Brad Lidge takes the loss, the only one he will suffer in the entire season. Scott Kazmir gets the win in the longest All-Star Game ever.

AL 4, NL 3

ABOVE: Opening ceremonies kick off the seemingly never-ending 2008 All-Star Game at Yankee Stadium on July 15. Clocking in at four hours and fifty minutes, the game is the longest in the history of the Midsummer Classic. The AL's Justin Morneau scores in the fifteenth inning to edge out the NL 4-3—at 1:30 the following morning.

LEFT: New Yankee Stadium takes shape alongside its aging predecessor in this 2007 photo. Note the enormous footprint of the new park as compared to the compact site of the old one.

CLEVELAND STADIUM

Cleveland, Ohio

Indians (AL) 1932–1933, 1937–1993

Lakefront Stadium 1932–1937, Cleveland Public Municipal Stadium 1938–1964

OPPOSITE: Cleveland Stadium is packed to the rafters for a doubleheader against the Yankees on September 12, 1954. The '54 Indians were cruising to a then-record 111 wins and the AL pennant. In its glory days, when the team was a perennial contender in the AL from 1948 to 1956, Cleveland drew pretty well. On this Sunday, as they sweep the twinbill against New York for victories number 103 and 104, the crowd of 86,563 is not only the largest ever in the stadium's history, but the largest for any regular-season doubleheader at any park.

Situated on reclaimed land on the shore of Lake Erie adjacent to downtown, Cleveland's gigantic precursor to its popular Jacobs Field was known as Lakefront Stadium, Municipal Stadium, Cleveland Stadium, and most commonly in its later years as "The Mistake by the Lake." Cavernous, architecturally vacuous, and rarely home to a winning team, the stadium that would come to be known as the worst of its era was also the last new big-league venue to open for two decades.

It may seem strange to have constructed a new ballpark during the Great Depression, but the city of Cleveland decided to build Lakefront Stadium in 1928 (before the crash). Lakefront had the distinction of being the first park ever built using public money. Though the park was an attempt to forge a partnership between the city and the Indians' owner, Alva Bradley, negotiations over the lease almost kept the project from getting off the ground. It took until more than a month into the 1932 season before the two parties reached an agreement, and the Tribe didn't play its first game at the mammoth new structure until July 31 of that year. The 35,000 programs that were printed for Opening Day were quickly exhausted as 80,284 fans, then said to be the largest crowd ever at a ballgame, jammed Lakefront to see the Indians christen the new park with a contest against the Philadelphia Athletics.

Built for size and not specifically to accommodate baseball, the park was utilitarian, with symmetrical distances from the plate and without interesting design elements. Lakefront was so big that typical ticket pricing schemes didn't work. Some of the seats, including the "bleachers," were so far away from the action that fans were almost immediately allowed to pay bleacher prices to sit in the grandstand, closer to the diamond. The venue's sheer size made it difficult to keep clean, and decades of playing before small crowds engulfed by 50,000 or more empty seats saddled the stadium with a gloomy atmosphere and a terrible reputation.

After only one full season on the lake, the Indians decided to return to League Park in 1934, where the stands looked fuller and they kept every dollar of the gate rather than sharing with the city. In 1936 the Indians came back to Lakefront for one game only, followed by fifteen games in 1937 and eighteen in '38. From 1939 to 1946, however,

BOB LEMON
pitcher CLEVELAND INDIANS

MAX
ALVIS
3rd Base

INDIANS

INDIANS
RAY FOSSE

CATCHER

because of Lakefront's larger size, most of the team's weekend and holiday games (thirty to fifty each year) were played at the white elephant.

After World War II, customer-focused maverick Bill Veeck bought the club and finally got things rocking on the shore of Lake Erie. Veeck's unheard-of schedule—chock-full of giveaway days and promotional stunts—brought legions of fans to the park (now called Municipal Stadium), and his 1948 world champion Indians drew more than 2.6 million spectators, shattering the record. From 1948 to 1956, Cleveland fielded a strong team with a great pitching staff, and won another pennant in 1954. But after 1959, sadly, the club, unable to compete with the dynastic Yankees, dropped off the map as Ohio fans mostly deserted the Indians. During the 1964 season (which also saw the final renaming of the stadium), the Indians—struggling to draw even half the major league average—entertained bids from groups in Seattle, Dallas, and Oakland to move the team. In October, however, the club announced that it would stay put. Not coincidentally, the lease with the city had been reworked to the Indians' benefit in several ways. First, it reduced the threshold on which the Indians paid a share of ticket revenue to the city. Second, the city agreed to make needed improvements, including a new press box and a Stadium Club. The threat of losing the team also scared the TV affiliate that broadcasted their games into increasing rights payments for 1965 by $140,000. Two years later, the city installed a new lighting system.

Still, public attitude toward the stadium was abysmal, and it was even further dimmed by a bizarre riot in 1974. On June 4—10¢ beer night at the park—the Tribe was taking on the Texas Rangers, after their previous series (in Arlington) had included a bench-clearing brawl. Already rowdy and drinking the virtually free beer flowing from concession taps, fans (one of them naked) ran onto the field and created such a scene that the tied game was forfeited to the Rangers, who were standing in the visitor's dugout holding bats for protection. Instead of accepting responsibility for their promotion, Cleveland VP Ted Bonda and GM Phil Seghi—both of whom had left the park before the incident—blamed the players for overreacting and the umpires for losing control of the crowd.

The rest of the Cleveland Stadium story was not much brighter. The Mistake continued to sit, mostly empty, by the lake while the Indians stumbled. (The team had a ghastly twenty-seven seasons with losing records between 1960 and 1993.) Even attempts to roll back prices in the early 1970s couldn't get fans to support their badly managed, unexciting club.

Only in 1986, with all of baseball enjoying an attendance boom, did the Indians finally start to clear a million customers per year consistently.

Mercifully, Cleveland was one of the first cities to jump on the retro ballpark bandwagon, and in May 1990 voters approved a "sin tax" on alcohol and cigarettes to finance a new sports complex that would include the gorgeous Jacobs Field. The new park was well received by fans and sportswriters alike. Not that it took much to be better than Cleveland Stadium. On the day of its opening, *Sports Illustrated* noted Jacobs Field's differences from its predecessor: "The infield was level, the outfield had no football hash marks, and the manager wasn't afraid to drink the tap water." Cleveland fans finally had a beautiful park to watch baseball in, and attendance numbers, as well as the team's performance, made one of the biggest turnarounds in baseball history.

As for Cleveland Stadium, it remained the home of the NFL Browns until 1995, and was later destroyed. In 1998, portions of the rubble were sunk half a mile offshore in Lake Erie. The Mistake *in* the Lake is now two artificial reefs, home to smallmouth bass, yellow perch, and other fish oblivious to the fact that they're swimming through a piece of baseball's past.

July 3, 1931 Two days after it's dedicated, Lakefront Stadium holds its first sporting event: a heavyweight championship boxing match between Max Schmeling and William "Young" Stribling.

December 16, 1945 The Cleveland Rams win their first NFL championship, a victory over the Redskins, 15-14, at home. It's the last game they will play at the stadium before relocating to Los Angeles.

1946 Thirty-two-year-old showman Bill Veeck purchases the Cleveland Indians; during his short tenure, he acquires star Larry Doby, the first African American in the American League, and leads the team to a pennant and World Series title in 1948.

1932

Though it has been open for more than a year, Lakefront Stadium hosts its first Indians game on July 31, drawing what is, at the time, the largest crowd in baseball history. Dimensions are 322 feet down each line, 435 to the power alleys, and 470 to center.

1937

After three seasons of playing almost exclusively at League Park, the Indians return to Lakefront for fifteen games.

1938

The stadium is renamed Cleveland Public Municipal Stadium.

1939

Lights are added to newly renamed Cleveland Public Municipal Stadium, and the NFL's Cleveland Rams move in for three seasons.

1946

The All-America Football Conference's Cleveland Browns begin play at Municipal Stadium. They will join the NFL in 1950 and will call the stadium home through 1995.

1947

After the Indians have spent a decade playing weekday and Saturday day games at League Park but night, holiday, Sunday, and other assorted games at Municipal Stadium, new owner Bill Veeck moves his club into the big park for good. He erects a wire inner fence that is more hitter-friendly: 320 feet down the foul lines, 365 to the power alleys, and 410 to center.

OPPOSITE, LEFT: Cleveland TV station WEWS prepares to broadcast the first televised Indians game on May 15, 1948. The Indians waded cautiously into the television era, one of three big-league teams (along with the Red Sox and White Sox) that waited until 1948 to broadcast any games. Only the Pirates held out longer.

OPPOSITE, RIGHT: This 1954 aerial view of Cleveland Stadium shows the industrial nature of the lakefront; the downtown business district is just out of the image to the left, separated by a railroad cut. The area west of the stadium (in the upper right) will later be converted to parking.

BELOW: This April 1931 image of under-construction Lakefront Stadium shows the latticework of structural steel, common in the classic fields of the previous era, which allowed the upper decks to be built close to the field. However, this design also obstructed views, with many fans in both the lower- and upper-decks having to crane their necks to follow the game. And because Lakefront was so large and not specifically built for baseball, it ended up with the worst combination: lots of steel columns blocking views from seats that weren't even close to the field.

July 17, 1941

Yankee Clipper Gets Clipped Joe DiMaggio's record hitting streak ends at fifty-six games in front of more than 67,000 fans. Indians pitchers Al Smith and Jim Bagby get the official credit, but the real hero is third baseman Ken Keltner, whose two remarkable defensive plays finally stop the Yankee Clipper. DiMaggio reached fifty-six the previous day by going 3-for-4 across town at League Park. He'll hit in sixteen more consecutive games after today. If not for Keltner, DiMaggio's already impressive streak could have reached an unthinkable seventy-three games.

Yankees 4, Indians 3

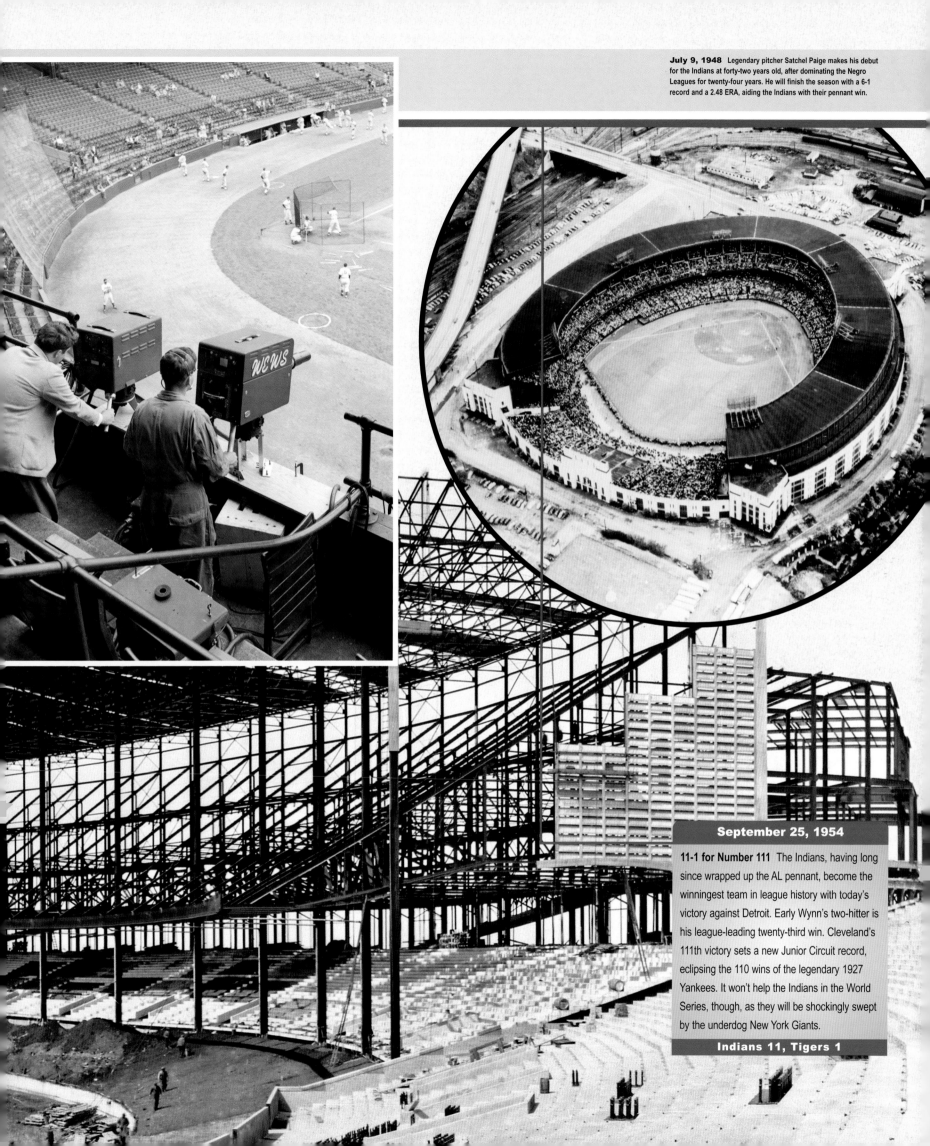

September 25, 1954

11-1 for Number 111 The Indians, having long since wrapped up the AL pennant, become the winningest team in league history with today's victory against Detroit. Early Wynn's two-hitter is his league-leading twenty-third win. Cleveland's 111th victory sets a new Junior Circuit record, eclipsing the 110 wins of the legendary 1927 Yankees. It won't help the Indians in the World Series, though, as they will be shockingly swept by the underdog New York Giants.

Indians 11, Tigers 1

1960 Indians manager Frank Lane trades 1959 AL home run leader Rocky Colavito to the Tigers for Harvey Kuenn, who led the league in batting the previous year. The trade will subsequently be blamed for triggering the decades-long "Curse of Rocky Colavito."

1975 Frank Robinson—Triple Crown–winner, two-time MVP, twelve-time All-Star, and 1971 All-Star MVP—becomes the first African-American manager in the history of Major League Baseball when he takes the helm for the Indians as player-manager.

1989 The film *Major League* debuts in theaters; with a cast that includes Charlie Sheen, Wesley Snipes, and Tom Berenger, the comedy follows a rag-tag Cleveland Indians ball club on their haphazard quest for the pennant. However, the movie was filmed at Milwaukee's County Stadium.

1965

The park is renamed Cleveland Stadium.

1975

The loge boxes are upgraded by the city to include closed-circuit televisions, refrigerators, ice service, and private restrooms.

1984

The fence is moved back 20 feet in left and right field and 10 feet in left-center and right-center.

June 4, 1974

Fans on the Field In the most infamous promotion in franchise history, unruly Indians fans riot and cause the Tribe to forfeit a game to the Texas Rangers. Fueled by an intense rivalry and an ill-advised promotional gimmick—unlimited quantities of 10¢ beer—fans are rushing the field by the third inning. One man runs into right field, removes his clothes, and streaks across the outfield before being arrested. In the bottom of the ninth, with the Indians rallying and the score tied 5-5, two more fans race onto the field and try to steal right fielder Jeff Burroughs' cap. Other fans soon join the fracas as players and umpires run to Burroughs' aid; one moron hurls a metal chair, hitting Cleveland pitcher Tom Hilgendorf in the head. Finally, security forces manage to clear the field, but then another fight breaks out near the mound, causing head umpire Nestor Chylak to declare the game a forfeit to the Rangers.

Rangers 9, Indians 0 (forfeit)

May 15, 1981

A Perfect Night On a damp, chilly night, a paltry crowd of just 7,290 witnesses the second perfect game in Indians history as Len Barker retires all twenty-seven Toronto batters he faces. Barker's is the tenth perfect game in major league annals, and the first since Catfish Hunter's in 1968. The Blue Jays manage to hit only five balls out of the infield, including Ernie Whitt's fly to Indians centerfielder Rick Manning to end the perfecto. Cleveland becomes the first franchise to throw more than one perfect game; Hall of Famer Addie Joss tossed one in 1908.

Indians 3, Blue Jays 0

ABOVE: Described by Indians PR Director Bob Dibasio as "a red, furry thing," "The Baseball Bug" mascot entertains fans at Cleveland Stadium in 1981. The Indians had several other mascots during their tenure at Cleveland Stadium, including "The Duck" and "Tom E. Hawk," who performed a dance to "Shake Your Tail Feather."

BELOW: Fans cheer at the 1981 All-Star Game, played at Cleveland Stadium on August 9, the latest date of any Midsummer Classic due to the players' strike. (The regular season resumes the next day.) The NL beats the AL 5-4 in front of a crowd of 72,086—the record for an All-Star Game.

August 9, 1981

An End to the Strike After a fifty-day players' strike in midseason, the owners and players' union agree on a contract and the season resumes—starting with the All-Star Game, which, prior to the strike, had been scheduled for July. Jack Morris throws the first pitch to Pete Rose in front of an All-Star record crowd of 72,086. Indians pitcher Len Barker, who tossed a perfect game in this stadium some three months earlier, retires all six men he faces. Game MVP Gary Carter hits two home runs, but the biggest blast belongs to Mike Schmidt, whose two-run shot in the eighth off Rollie Fingers turns a one-run NL deficit into a one-run lead. Winning pitcher Vida Blue throws a hitless seventh for the NL, and his resume now includes an All-Star win for each league. Nolan Ryan and Bruce Sutter also toss perfect innings to stave off any comeback as the Senior Circuit wins its tenth straight All-Star Game.

NL 5, AL 4

1993

The Indians play their final game at Cleveland Stadium on October 3, before moving into brand-new Jacobs Field a few blocks away. The Browns will remain through the 1995 season, after which the team will relocate to Baltimore. The stadium will be torn down in November 1996.

May 26, 1993

Get Your Head in the Game For all the criticism he gets, Jose Canseco can no longer be accused of not using his head. In one of the great blooper moments of all time, the Texas right fielder drifts back to attempt to catch a long drive by Cleveland's Carlos Martinez. When Canseco turns his head to take a look at the wall, the ball skims off the top of his glove, hits him square on top of the head, and bounces over the fence for a home run. Canseco has a tough day all around, going 0-for-3 and getting thrown out stealing in the Indians' 7-6 win.

Indians 7, Rangers 6

ABOVE: The signs tell the story at Cleveland Stadium's last baseball game on October 3, 1993. Fittingly, the Indians are shut out by the White Sox 4-0, finishing in sixth place in the AL East, nineteen games off the pace.

BELOW: The Indians play at their oft-criticized "Mistake by the Lake" in May 1992. While the stadium was being built, a state-of-the-art grass growing system was installed under the field. The underground heating tubes were supposed to stimulate the grass, causing it to grow more quickly. It's hard to say whether or not it was successful.

COUNTY STADIUM

Milwaukee, Wisconsin

Braves (NL) 1953–1965, Brewers (AL, NL) 1970–2000

As modest as it was, blue-collar Milwaukee's County Stadium had a seismic impact on the history of the national pastime, one equaled by only a handful of other ballparks, even though no one usually includes it with the likes of Shibe, Wrigley, Yankee Stadium, or Camden Yards. The significance of the park certainly didn't come from its utilitarian design, which included a plethora of temporary outfield bleachers, a double-decked grandstand reminiscent of Cleveland Stadium, and symmetrical dimensions; nor did it result from the fact that it was the first ballpark to be built with lights for nighttime games. Milwaukee's bellwether ballpark revolutionized baseball by being the first to be built specifically to lure a major league team. However, after only thirteen seasons, the popular Braves moved yet again, leaving County Stadium virtually empty until the Brewers came to town.

In the booming, *Father Knows Best* 1950s, the American sports landscape was being redrawn as baseball expanded its geographic footprint, moving west in a pell-mell rush to escape deteriorating ballparks landlocked in downtown or even inner-city neighborhoods. While much of the impetus to relocate franchises after World War II resulted from powerful national trends such as suburbanization and the rapid growth of the West, another prime factor was the willingness of local governments to subsidize big-league teams.

One such government was that of the City of Milwaukee, which built a new stadium with public money on the fringe of its limits, conveniently accessible by car from the burgeoning suburbs. Giving up the hope of revitalizing their fan base in Boston, the Braves were finally lured west, and played their first game in Milwaukee on April 6, 1953, in an exhibition match versus their former crosstown rivals, the Red Sox.

The Braves were such an instantaneous success in Milwaukee that capacity at County Stadium was expanded by almost 7,000 seats during its inaugural season. High attendance continued as the surprisingly good team won the NL pennant in 1957 and 1958—taking the '57 World Series from the hated Yankees in one of the biggest October upsets in history. Following the record-breaking attendance in the 1950s, however, crowds fell off—partially due to the club's failure to win in 1959 and 1960, but mostly because of the typical downturn any relatively new franchise experiences. No team can continue to draw record throngs forever, but Braves management was disappointed by

the decline and blamed Milwaukee fans. Although attendance remained above the NL average and was incredibly healthy for a market that small, local media—goaded by Braves management—began to report on the public's waning interest in the team. Speculation about why fans had fallen out of love with their club became a blame game that made things worse.

Perhaps the Braves should have pointed the finger at themselves. For one, they had priced beer too high, and had caused a revolt in 1959 by banning fans from bringing in their own. Worse, they refused to televise games—even *road* games—in the hopes of attracting more people to the park. The plan backfired, resulting instead in the team's not gaining enough followers. (The Braves finally began televising games in 1962, three years before leaving Milwaukee. Ironically, upon their move to Atlanta, Ted Turner would begin broadcasting almost all of their games to a national audience, greatly increasing their fan base.)

In 1963, disgruntled Braves fans began to hear rumors that their hometown team might be moving. As planning, and then construction, for Atlanta's new stadium proceeded, the atmosphere in Milwaukee got gloomier. During the 1965 season, the Braves were either booed or ignored in Milwaukee; no company would buy sponsorships on the club's radio broadcasts for fear of being targeted as supporters of owners now scornfully regarded as carpetbaggers.

After thirteen seasons in their adopted home—only four of which had mediocre attendance—the Braves packed their bats and moved south. The City of Milwaukee filed suit against the team, claiming that the move was illegal, and even spent money to keep County Stadium painted, cleaned, and ready, just in case. In March 1966, Wisconsin judge Elmer Roller ordered the Braves back to Milwaukee. The first adjudication ever that baseball had violated its antitrust exemption, it went ignored by NL owners and had little effect. Opening Day 1966 passed with the Braves happily ensconced in their new home, and County sat empty.

The ballpark hosted twenty White Sox games from 1968 to 1969, as Chicago's owners kicked around the idea of moving and baseball boosters in Milwaukee tried to keep themselves visible. Meanwhile, used-car dealer (and future MLB commissioner) Allan H. "Bud" Selig worked tirelessly to bring major league baseball back to his hometown of Milwaukee. When he

JOE TORRE catcher

PAUL MOLITOR Brewers

ROBIN YOUNT Brewers

March 14, 1954 After left fielder Bobby Thomson breaks his ankle during a spring-training game, Hank Aaron makes his major league debut for the Braves. Aaron will bat .280 with thirteen home runs during his rookie year.

1953

On April 14, the Braves host the first major league game played in Milwaukee since 1901. County Stadium's symmetrical dimensions measure 320 feet down the foul lines, 355 to left and right field, 397 to the power alleys, and 404 to center. The NFL's Green Bay Packers will also play selected games here every season through 1994.

The great baseball town of Milwaukee once again had a club to call its own, and the Brewers, by the late 1970s, had captivated the city. They smartly introduced a popular family ticket plan in 1973, and increased capacity to more than 50,000. The field dimensions themselves did not change the entire time the Brewers played at the park; at 392 feet, County Stadium sported some of the deepest power alleys in postwar baseball.

In 2001, an aging County Stadium was razed to make way for parking for the Brewers' new home, Miller Park. But long before it went, the park that had changed the landscape of baseball changed one more thing about the national pastime. The first stadium built amidst a parking lot, it also became the first ballpark to find itself host to scores of tailgating parties before and after games. Braves—and later, Brewers—fans made parking-lot beers and bratwursts a baseball tradition, and even the players (and at least one Brewers manager—George Bamberger) sometimes attended postgame tailgating parties. These parties are one of the reasons why historic County Stadium is fondly remembered by both Braves and Brewers fans for its hometown, unpretentious, and celebratory atmosphere.

BACKGROUND Popular sluggers and future Hall of Famers Eddie Mathews (41) and Hank Aaron (44) walk to the home clubhouse for the last time on September 22, 1965, after losing to the Dodgers 7-6 in eleven innings. The Braves have ten more games to play on the road before closing out their sad final season as Milwaukee's baseball team.

heard in late 1969 that the Seattle ownership group was dangerously low on cash, he jumped at the chance to buy the foundering, one-year-old Seattle Pilots. Even though the American League didn't want a team to shift cities after just one season, owners were forced to allow the sale—finalized on April 1, 1970, while the Pilots were at spring training—because no Seattle-area backers came forward with a commitment to get a new park built. A maze of lawsuits, restraining orders, and bankruptcy proceedings concluded with Selig's group purchasing the club for $10.8 million.

1954

Capacity is expanded to 43,000, and the Braves become the first National League team to draw more than 2 million fans, a figure they will surpass in four consecutive seasons. The right-field distance is shortened to 315 feet.

September 23, 1957

Aaron Wins the Pennant Hank Aaron clubs a two-run homer in the eleventh inning to clinch the NL pennant for the Braves, sending a packed County Stadium into ecstasy. His forty-third homer of the year gives the Braves their first pennant since 1948 and their first in Milwaukee. Aaron will hit one more home run before year's end, claiming his first home run title with forty-four and also leading the league with 132 RBIs. He will be voted the NL MVP and help the Braves to their first world championship win since 1914.

Braves 4, Cardinals 2

October 6, 1957

Milwaukee's First Series Win A day after the Braves were blown out in the first World Series game ever played in Milwaukee, they pull off one of the most thrilling comebacks in franchise history. It's Game 4, and Milwaukee holds a 4-1 lead until the ninth inning, when 2 two-out singles precede a game-tying blast by New York's Elston Howard. The Yankees score again in the top of the tenth on a triple by Hank Bauer to go on top. But when the Braves bat in the bottom of the inning, Johnny Logan doubles in the tying run and Eddie Mathews, batting with first base open, hits a two-run homer to win it. Warren Spahn goes all ten innings for the win, while the Yankees use five different pitchers.

Braves 7, Yankees 5

1961

Perini's Woods—a copse of spruce and fir trees planted behind the centerfield fence in 1954—is razed in order to add bleachers.

1962

The distances to both left and right field are extended to 362 feet.

1965

The Braves relocate for the second time in a relatively short span, playing their final game in Milwaukee on September 22. They'll start the '66 season in Atlanta.

May 26, 1959

Harvey's Invisible Pitches The greatest game ever pitched at County Stadium—or perhaps anywhere—bizarrely turns into the biggest hard-luck loss in history. Pittsburgh lefty Harvey Haddix has just twirled twelve perfect innings against the Braves when Don Hoak commits an error in the bottom of the thirteenth and ends the perfect game. And there's more to come: After Eddie Mathews sacrifices to put Felix Mantilla on second, Hank Aaron is walked intentionally. Joe Adcock then blasts a pitch over the right-centerfield fence for Milwaukee's first hit, an apparent game-winning home run. However, Aaron runs off the field too soon and Adcock passes him on the basepaths, negating the homer. Officially it goes as a double, but the first run still counts, and the Braves win.

Braves 1, Pirates 0

CAP: 1950s-era (worn by Warren Spahn).

LEFT: Hank Aaron crosses home plate after slamming a three-run homer during Game 4 of the 1957 World Series. Aaron's blast gives the Braves a 4-1 lead over the Yankees in the fourth inning. Though New York will later tie the game, Milwaukee ends up winning it 7-5 in the tenth to tie the Series at two games apiece. Braves stalwarts Wes Covington (43), Eddie Mathews (41), and Johnny Logan (in front of the batboy at right) greet Hammerin' Hank.

Baseball Lightens Up

The first stadium to open in the second half of the twentieth century, County Stadium was also the first to have lights installed as it was being built. By 1953, the year the park debuted, all fields in Major League Baseball but one were illuminated—the only hold-out being Wrigley Field, which didn't get lights until 1988.

The Braves were the first major league team to play a game at night, but not in Milwaukee. In 1927, while the team was still in Boston, they played a team of amateurs in a General Electric–staged demonstration game. Even in 1927, nighttime ball wasn't a new concept. In 1880, some enterprising amateurs played the first documented game under artificial light, at Oceanside Park in Hull, Massachusetts. In 1909, the Reds' Garry Herrmann had installed a primitive lighting system at the Palace of the Fans for use by amateur clubs. And Negro League teams, far more versed in having to find ways to bring out fans, began playing under lights in the early '20s. Necessity being the mother of invention, the famed Kansas City Monarchs even traveled with their own portable lighting system, powered by a 250-horsepower generator and carted from city to city on eleven trucks.

The first major league field to install permanent lights was Cincinnati's Crosley Field. In 1934, wealthy Reds owner Powel Crosley Jr. was keen to get turnstiles clicking at his newly purchased stadium, and turned to nighttime ball as a way to get more white-collar spectators who worked during the day (and had more disposable income) into the park. But NL owners weren't convinced that night ball was a good idea. So Reds GM Larry MacPhail lobbied representatives from each of the seven teams, promising to play one night game against each of them that would bring in Sunday-size crowds. As the share of gate receipts received by NL owners was quite significant in the 1930s, money eventually prevailed and the NL voted unanimously to allow night baseball at Crosley Field—just as long as Crosley and MacPhail didn't try to make any extra cash by staging nighttime exhibition games with AL teams.

Crosley shelled out more than $50,000 for a General Electric installation, and on May 24, 1935, the Reds took on the Phillies under 924,000 watts. Even though some of the ballplayers and a few local scribes doubted a revolution was at hand (the lordly New York Giants even refused to play under lights), the so-called Bible of baseball, the *Sporting News*, was giddy with excitement over night ball, claiming that the new innovation would help save the game in tough economic times. In the next seven years, nine of the fourteen major league teams installed lights, and the rest of the clubs would follow after World War II. By 1984, Commissioner Peter Ueberroth proclaimed that no World Series would be held at a park without lights. It would be four more years before Wrigley Field would be illuminated, but County Stadium, like every other ballpark that came after it, was ready for prime time from day one.

CAP: 1987.

RIGHT: This view from the upper deck shows off County's clean sightlines and simple postwar design as the Brewers face the Reds on September 28, 2000. Though this game, County Stadium's swan song, drew 56,354 fans, the previous two games drew only around 28,000 each, and fewer than 15,000 showed up the previous Saturday. That was to be expected, however, for a club finishing its eighth-straight losing season.

1976 One of the many concerts held at County Stadium throughout the years, the Kool Jazz Festival begins its five-year run at the park. It includes such big-name talent as BB King, Al Green, the Temptations, and Smokey Robinson.

1968

With no team in Milwaukee, the White Sox host the first American League game ever played at County Stadium. Chicago will play nine home games in Milwaukee in 1968 and eleven in 1969.

1970

The Seattle Pilots, after just one year of existence, pack up and move to Milwaukee shortly before the season starts. Renamed the Brewers, the team debuts at County Stadium on April 7. The playing field retains the same dimensions it had when the Braves left.

1973

County Stadium is expanded to hold 54,000. The addition blocks views of the games from the nearby National Soldiers Home and Veterans Administration Hospital, but creates a home for team mascot Bernie Brewer. From high atop the outfield stands, he slides into a giant fake beer mug whenever a Brewer homers.

July 31, 1988 The World Wrestling Federation's WrestleFest 1988 is held at the stadium. The highlight of the show is Hulk Hogan defeating André the Giant in a steel cage match.

1994 MLB expands to three divisions per league, and as part of the realignment, the Brewers move from the American League to the National League.

July 25, 1999 Robin Yount becomes the first player to be inducted into the National Baseball Hall of Fame as a Brewer.

October 10, 1982

Something Big Is Brewing In a desperate battle between two teams looking for their first World Series berth ever, the Brewers become the first major league team to rally from a two-games-to-none deficit to win a best-of-five play-off series. Milwaukee hits just .219 in the series with eight errors, and manages only six hits in the deciding Game 5—but the hits come at key moments. After the Angels take a 3-1 lead in the top of the fourth inning, the Brewers' Ben Oglivie, who has two of Milwaukee's four errors of the day, homers to make it a one-run game. An inning later, Cecil Cooper singles home the tying and go-ahead runs. After California puts the tying run on second in the ninth, Pete Ladd, subbing for injured relief ace Rollie Fingers, induces a Rod Carew groundout to end the game. The crowd goes wild as the Milwaukee Brewers win their first—and only—AL pennant.

Brewers 4, Angels 3

1984

The bleachers are rebuilt and a giant sound tower is added, eliminating Bernie Brewer's home and sending him into retirement until 1993.

2001

After the Brewers move next door, County Stadium is demolished to create a parking lot for the new Miller Park.

September 9, 1992

Yount Makes History The best player in Brewers history, two-time MVP Robin Yount becomes just the seventeenth player to record 3,000 career hits when he singles in the seventh inning off Cleveland's Jose Mesa. The thirty-six-year-old, a Brewers regular since he was a teenager, is the third-youngest player to reach the 3,000-hit mark, behind Ty Cobb and Hank Aaron. Pat Listach, who next month will become the first Brewer to be named Rookie of the Year, drives in two runs as the Brewers take a 4-3 lead into the ninth. But a two-out, two-run error by Milwaukee closer Darren Holmes brings home the tying and go-ahead runs for Cleveland. Yount ends up making the last out of the game, sending the crowd of 47,589 home with bittersweet memories.

Indians 5, Brewers 4

October 3, 1999

Brewing Up a Storm Although the paid attendance is announced as 55,992, torrential rain keeps all but a few thousand devoted fans away from the final game of the 1999 season. Because the game is needed to determine whether the Reds will play a one-game tiebreaker against the Mets, the two teams wait for almost six hours to get in the game, scheduled to be the last ever at County Stadium. (However, a fatal crane accident will push the opening of Miller Park back one year.) The game finally begins with standing water all over the field, which splashes up with every step taken in the outfield. Cincinnati wins it with help from Greg Vaughn, who launches a three-run homer in the third inning, and Pete Harnisch, who records his sixteenth victory of the season. The Reds will lose to the Mets the next night in the wild card playoff game.

Reds 7, Brewers 1

ABOVE: County Stadium in its final season while its successor, Miller Park, undergoes construction in the background. Note how County Stadium—which once seated more than 54,000—is dwarfed by its replacement, which seats 11,500 fewer fans. Because of a crane accident during Miller Park's construction that killed three ironworkers in July 1999, the opening of the new park was delayed by one year.

MEMORIAL STADIUM

Baltimore, Maryland

Orioles (AL) 1954–1991

The man who was responsible for major league baseball being played at Memorial Stadium never actually made it to Baltimore. Bill Veeck, who owned the St. Louis Browns, was looking to move the team, and he had his eye on the Charm City and its recently renovated park. Memorial Stadium, built in 1950, was home to minor league baseball and had housed the NFL Colts since 1953. But Baltimore was looking to add an MLB franchise—still a bigger draw than the NFL—to its roster. Assuming they had a deal with Veeck, the City issued $6 million in bonds and greatly expanded the stadium, constructing a second deck and adding light towers (which wouldn't be installed until after Opening Day).

AL owners weren't opposed to the Browns leaving St. Louis. But they were opposed to Veeck, who had brought some of the most questionable promotional stunts to baseball and was outspoken in his desire to revise the league's television policy. In a ploy to rid the AL of the infamous owner entirely, the group obstructed Veeck's deal for six months, until a group of Baltimore-based investors finally convinced him to sell the club. Veeck eventually became the owner of the White Sox, while the Browns—now called the Orioles—had a new city, new ownership, and a new park.

The Baltimore Orioles played their first game at Memorial Stadium on April 15, 1954. Though the park's vast feel made the already struggling team even less interesting to watch, the Orioles managed to draw more than a million fans in their inaugural season. In their years at Memorial Stadium, they would not only become truly competitive, but would also alter their park to create a more intimate, higher quality setting for baseball.

First, they reduced the distance of the long power alleys in both left and right. Then in 1961, the huge foul territories were made smaller by the addition of box seats, which also necessitated new dugouts. During the 1970 season, the stadium was graced with a new scoreboard in left-center field. And in the mid-1970s, the upper deck's splintering benches were finally replaced. Meanwhile, the Orioles were playing some of the best baseball in the franchise's history. From 1968 to 1985, the team had eighteen consecutive winning seasons, and in 1981, they called up Iron Man Cal Ripken Jr., who would play the first half of his record-breaking career at Memorial.

DAVE McNALLY

BROOKS ROBINSON
BALTIMORE ORIOLES
3rd BASE

MIKE TORREZ
PITCHER ORIOLES

But even still, the park was far from evergreen. Many seats had obstructed views, thanks to bulky concrete support columns. The structure wasn't adequately accessible to the disabled. And both team office space and (worse) public restrooms were not in sufficient supply. In 1984, the Colts skipped town for Indianapolis and a stadium that was built to better suit football. By 1986, the O's had sunk into a funk, finishing last for the first time since they moved to Baltimore.

With the Colts out of the picture and the Orioles in need of a shot in the arm, baseball boosters began campaigning for a new, baseball-only stadium that would give their team a beautiful, fan-friendly place to play. And on April 6, 1992, they got their wish when watershed Oriole Park at Camden Yards opened and ushered in the retro ballpark era. Memorial Stadium returned to its previous life as a home to a minor league team, and eventually also housed the Baltimore Ravens football team for two years until their stadium was completed in 1998.

When Memorial was shuttered, it was the seventh-oldest park in the major leagues. Still, it took until 2000 for demolition of the structure to begin, due to community and political jockeying over the new use for the site, as well as over the issue of whether the stadium, which had become a symbol of Baltimore, should even be destroyed. Thankfully, the plaque that gave the stadium its name—a memorial to war veterans—was preserved and incorporated into a similar display at Oriole Park at Camden Yards. It reads: "Dedicated as a memorial to all who so valiantly fought in the world wars with eternal gratitude to those who made the supreme sacrifice to preserve equality and freedom throughout the world—time will not dim the glory of their deeds."

TIMELINE: MEMORIAL STADIUM

December 27, 1959 In a rematch of the previous year's championship game at Yankee Stadium, the Baltimore Colts top the New York Giants 31-16 at Memorial Stadium in the twenty-seventh NFL Championship.

1954

Memorial Stadium, completed in 1950, has a second deck added for major league baseball. (The NFL's Colts were already playing there by 1953.) The addition isn't completed by Opening Day, but a capacity crowd of nearly 47,000 still fills the park. Dimensions are 309 feet down the lines, 446 to the power alleys, and 445 to center field.

September 17, 1955

The Brooks Robinson Era Begins The first great homegrown Oriole, future Hall of Famer Brooks Robinson makes his major league debut. The eighteen-year-old Arkansan, signed as a second baseman just three months earlier, comes up from the minors to fill in at third base for the injured Billy Cox. Robinson goes 2-for-4 in the win over Washington, but will go 0-for-18 the rest of the year. Nonetheless, he'll wear an Orioles uniform for twenty-three years, win sixteen consecutive Gold Gloves, and set the all-time record for games played at third base. The "Human Vacuum Cleaner" will be named the AL MVP in 1964 and will be the hero of the Orioles' 1970 World Series triumph over Cincinnati.

Orioles 3, Senators 1

December 9, 1965 The O's trade pitcher Milt Pappas to Cincinnati in exchange for slugger Frank Robinson, who will be a key contributor to the World Series–bound club in '66.

May 8, 1966 In a game against the Cleveland Indians, Frank Robinson becomes the only player ever to hit a ball out of Memorial Stadium. The spot where the home run flies over the single-decked left-field stands will later be marked with a flag that reads "HERE."

1970 The Orioles' bullpen is nearly invincible, boasting three pitchers with twenty or more wins during the season—Mike Cuellar, Dave McNally, and Jim Palmer.

1956

The distances are reduced to 405 feet to the power alleys and 425 to center field. The concrete fences down the lines will always remain 309 feet.

1958

The second reduction of the dimensions in two years makes the distances 380 feet to the power alleys and 410 to center field. These measurements will fluctuate through-out the park's life.

RIGHT: Brooks Robinson, known as the "Human Vacuum Cleaner" for his sensational play at the hot corner, shows the umpires as well as the rest of the world that he caught Johnny Bench's line drive with another diving stop in Game 3 of the 1970 Fall Classic. Robinson also hits a home run that day and will finish the Series with a .429 batting average, seventeen stolen bases, and nine hits in five games.

October 9, 1966

Another Day, Another Shutout Baltimore clinches its first world championship before 54,458 adoring fans, beating the Dodgers in Game 4 1-0 for the second day in a row. It's the third straight shutout for Orioles pitchers, who never allowed Los Angeles to score after the third inning of Game 1. Dave McNally, who allowed the only Dodgers runs in that first game, blanks them this time, clinching the title in a mere one hour, forty-five minutes. The game's only run comes on Frank Robinson's second homer of the Series. Robinson wins the Series MVP, and as the first Triple Crown winner in a decade, he will also be named the regular season AL MVP. Orioles manager Hank Bauer, winner of seven world championships as a player, now gets a ring as a skipper.

Orioles 1, Dodgers 0

October 15, 1970

Cuellar Clinches the Title The Orioles complete their World Series destruction of Cincinnati, blowing out the Reds in Game 5 to clinch the second world championship in franchise history. For the third time in the Series, the Reds take an early lead only to squander it. After Cincinnati scores three in the first, Frank Robinson gets Baltimore back in the game with a two-run homer against his former team. RBI singles by the light-hitting Mark Belanger and Paul Blair then give the Orioles the lead, which they will later pad when the Reds' bullpen falters. Mike Cuellar, Baltimore's Cuban-born ace, allows no runs and just two hits over the game's final eight innings.

Orioles 9, Reds 3

LEFT: Pitcher Dave McNally and catcher Andy Etchebarren celebrate the O's Game 4 win against the Dodgers in the 1966 World Series. Orioles pitchers had a stranglehold on the opposing team's offense, serving up a combined 0.50 ERA for the Series.

October 17, 1971

Clemente Dominates the O's After losing the 1969 World Series to the Mets, Baltimore is knocked off by another NL underdog when the Pirates win Game 7 by a narrow 2-1 margin. Series MVP Roberto Clemente—who has spent the past nine days dazzling the nationwide television audience with his prodigious hitting, daring baserunning, and powerful throwing—hits a crucial homer in the fourth inning. Jose Pagan, a fellow Puerto Rican, drives in the winning run in the eighth for Pittsburgh.

Pirates 2, Orioles 1

ABOVE: A peculiar sight at a sports arena: A single-engine plane sits in the upper deck of Memorial Stadium after crashing into the stands on December 19, 1976. The incident occurred just moments after a playoff game between the Baltimore Colts and the Pittsburgh Steelers. Luckily, since the Steelers lost 40-14, most fans had already left the park and there were no major injuries.

1983

The Colts play their last game as a Baltimore team.

1991

The Orioles play their final game at Memorial Stadium on October 6.

October 12, 1983

The Phils are Bephuddled The Orioles have been bad in first games all year long, losing on Opening Day, in Game 1 of the ALCS, and now in Game 1 of the World Series. But each time it comes out all right in the end, including today, when the Orioles beat the Phillies to tie the World Series at one game apiece. John Lowenstein hits a key home run for Baltimore, while pitcher Mike Boddicker not only collects an RBI, but shuts down Philadelphia on three hits and one unearned run. The Orioles will clinch the championship on the road in Game 5.

Orioles 4, Phillies 1

BELOW: Orioles shortstop Cal Ripken Jr. hurdles Cleveland's Andy Allanson as he throws to first to complete a double play on August 12, 1987. Despite Ripken's three hits and three runs scored, the O's will fall to the Indians 8-6. The hometown hero will spend his entire twenty-year career with Baltimore, during which he'll break Lou Gehrig's fifty-six-year-old record for most consecutive games played (2,632) in 1995 and make the All-Star team nineteen times.

May 30, 1982

Ripken's Streak Begins In an otherwise non-descript game, rookie third baseman Cal Ripken Jr. goes 0-for-2 with a walk in the first of his record 2,632 consecutive games played. The entire Orioles team, meanwhile, manages only one hit against Toronto pitchers Jim Gott and Roy Lee Jackson. Although nobody knows it yet, in 1995 Ripken will surpass Lou Gehrig's record of 2,130 straight games, previously thought to be unbreakable. In the process, Ripken will cement his legendary status by winning a world championship, a Rookie of the Year award, and two AL MVP awards, as well as surpassing the 3,000-hit and 400-homer milestones.

Blue Jays 6, Orioles 0

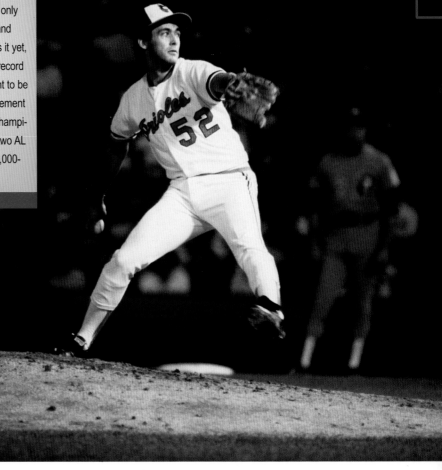

1983 O's catcher Rick Dempsey snags the World Series MVP award, after smacking three clutch doubles and a homer against the Phillies.

1986 Longtime manager Earl Weaver (a.k.a. the Earl of Baltimore), famous for his flamboyant and witty outbursts on the field, retires after seventeen years with the Orioles.

1991 Star shortstop Cal Ripken Jr. has a killer year at the plate, batting .323 with 34 homers and 144 RBIs, and bringing home both the regular-season and the All-Star MVP awards.

1993

The Orioles' new Double A farm team, the Bowie Baysox, call Memorial Stadium home for one season while their own ballpark is being constructed.

1996

NFL football returns to Memorial Stadium, as the relocated Cleveland Browns change their identity to the Baltimore Ravens.

1997

The Ravens play their final game at Memorial on December 14. Demolition will begin in 2000.

LEFT: The Orioles face the Tigers in the last game at Memorial Stadium on October 6, 1991. Detroit sails to an easy 7-1 win, but the real action takes place after the final out: O legends Frank Robinson, Jim Palmer, Brooks Robinson, Dave McNally, and scores of others take the field to commemorate the occasion. Home plate is transported to the new Oriole Park at Camden Yards via limousine and a tuxedo-clad grounds crew.

BELOW: "Wild Bill" Hagy, the O's most celebratory and celebrated fan, cheers on his home team from atop the Orioles' dugout during Game 2 of the 1979 World Series against the Pirates. The Orioles will lose the game (and the championship), but Hagy's undying enthusiasm will continue to be an inspiration to fans and the ball club in the '80s, as it has been during the '70s. A taxi driver by day, the beer-bellied icon is known for leading "The Roar from 34" in his seat in the upper deck, as well as frequent invitations to cheer on the O's dugout. After Wild Bill's death in 2007, the Orioles created a fan award in his honor, The Wild Bill Hagy Award.

October 6, 1991

Birds Fly the Coop A crowd of 50,700 comes to bid a bittersweet farewell to Memorial Stadium on the day it hosts its final major league game. The beloved nest of the Birds—and of legendary Johnny Unitas' departed NFL Colts—closes its run with yet another Orioles loss, their ninety-fifth of the year. Detroit's Frank Tanana throws the park's final pitch, while Mike Flanagan is the last Oriole on the mound. Cal Ripken goes 0-for-4, but will win his second AL MVP award despite playing for a sixth-place club.

Tigers 7, Orioles 1

OPPOSITE: Mike Boddicker on his way to victory during Game 2 of the 1983 World Series against the Phillies.

CAP: 1982 (worn by Jim Palmer).

MUNICIPAL STADIUM

Kansas City, Missouri

Athletics (AL) 1955–1967, Royals (AL) 1969–1972

CAP: 1959.

OPPOSITE: Municipal Stadium, pictured here in 1960, made an old-fashioned (i.e., very small) footprint in a neighborhood east of downtown Kansas City. The thirty-two-year-old venue was greatly expanded to accommodate pseudo-big-league ball when the A's immigrated from Philadelphia in 1955; however, it still seated barely 30,000 when the Kansas City Athletics played their first home game.

New team owner Arnold Johnson had announced that he would expand Blues Stadium (as it was known until 1954) to a capacity of 45,000, if needed. But the Athletics' miserable play voided any need for those extra seats—they finished sixth in their first season in KC, then dropped into the AL basement with a 52-102 record in 1956. However, the A's did draw almost 1.4 million in their inaugural year in Missouri, compared to the Philadelphia Athletics' peak attendance of 945,076 in 1948.

Originally constructed in 1923, Kansas City's Municipal Stadium had hosted minor league and Negro League teams for decades under the names Muehlebach Field, Ruppert Stadium, and Blues Stadium. In 1955, the park became the major league home of the newly relocated Athletics, where they played until they moved (yet again) to Oakland in 1967. Municipal Stadium would have been perfectly suitable for major league baseball when it first opened and even through the 1940s. In the 1950s, it was outmoded, but not dreadfully so. But by the mid-1960s, it was hopelessly inadequate, both for the Athletics and for the Royals, who moved in after the A's left town.

In 1955, Arnold Johnson purchased the Philadelphia Athletics from the Mack family, and relocated the sad-sack team halfway across the country to Kansas City. At the cost of about $2.5 million, Municipal Stadium was double-decked and improved, including the addition of an old scoreboard purchased from Braves Field. Unfortunately, the Athletics played as badly in their new home as they had in their last two decades at Philadelphia's Shibe Park.

Johnson managed his American League club as little more than a farm team for the mighty New York Yankees, to the detriment of the game and every other club in the league. The A's limped along as nearly every good player they produced miraculously ended up in pinstripes in the Bronx, while the profits from these one-sided deals went into Johnson's deep pockets. Meanwhile, the Yanks "farmed out" promising young players to KC for experience, then conveniently re-acquired them a few years later. This unholy alliance between the two franchises went on until Johnson's death in 1960, after which Charles O. Finley bought the team.

Eccentric and ultracompetitive, Finley put his personal stamp on everything he could. He changed the club's uniforms to a shocking combination (by baseball's conservative standards) of wedding-cake white, Fort Knox gold, and kelly green, with white leather spokes completing the ensemble. He brought in sheep to graze the grassy berm beyond the right-field wall and changed the team mascot to a live mule who, when he wasn't wandering around the stadium, accompanied Finley to parties and press events. He had his grounds crew install a mechanical rabbit in the ground behind home plate. Named Harvey, he popped up with a basketful of baseballs whenever the umpire needed replenishment. Promotional stunts abounded at the stadium, including having players enter the park in limousines or on the backs of donkeys. After trying unsuccessfully to gain league permission to shorten the distance to Municipal Stadium's right-field fence to the length of Yankee Stadium's, Finley fooled around with either the distances or heights of Municipal's outfield fences—often both—every year between 1961 and 1967. That kind of flux certainly didn't help his players learn how to handle the ballpark's oddities, but the A's were so bad it didn't really matter.

Finley had plenty of innovative ideas—and although many of them were crazy, some of them made for good marketing. Unfortunately, he countered everything he did to win fan attention with threats to move, ill-advised trades (and tirades), and bush-league behavior that embarrassed the residents and fans of Kansas City. After the 1967 season, he finally got his wish to move and vacated Missouri for Oakland.

Notwithstanding the fact that they failed to reach .500 even once, the Athletics had more than average support during their brief stay in Missouri, considering the size of the market. Still, many baseball lovers on both banks of the Missouri River were happy to see the team go, especially when Kansas City was awarded an expansion club for 1969. As soon as the Athletics had left for California, powerful US senator from Missouri Stuart Symington had angrily threatened to look into repealing Major League Baseball's antitrust exemption. To pacify him and retain a presence on the Great Plains, the AL moved quickly to give Kansas City an expansion team. The newly created Royals were forced to play from 1969 to 1972 in old Municipal Stadium, but the field was promptly forsaken when sparkling Royals Stadium opened for business in 1973. Three years later, the fifty-three-year-old Municipal Stadium was leveled to the ground.

HARRY SIMPSON
outfield KANSAS CITY A'S

DAN PFISTER
K. C. ATHLETICS PITCHER

JIM HUNTER
pitcher

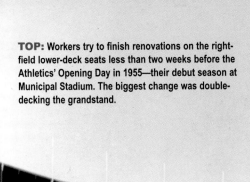

TOP: Workers try to finish renovations on the right-field lower-deck seats less than two weeks before the Athletics' Opening Day in 1955—their debut season at Municipal Stadium. The biggest change was double-decking the grandstand.

BOTTOM: The Negro National League champion Kansas City Monarchs and Eastern Colored League champion Hilldale Daisies pose for this fabulous portrait at the stadium—then called Muehlebach Field—before Game 1 of the first ever Colored World Series in 1924. Rube Foster, standing in street clothes between the two clubs, was owner of the Chicago American Giants and the prime mover behind the formation of the NNL—not to mention a great pitcher in his own right.

October 11, 1924 The Kansas City Monarchs host the first of three straight home games during the first Colored World Series at Muehlebach Field. The Monarchs will take two of the three games against the Hilldale Daisies, but will ultimately lose the ten-game series.

1955

As major league baseball returns to Kansas City for the first time since 1889, a second deck is added to Municipal Stadium (originally built in 1923 as Muehlebach Field). Dimensions are just 312 feet to the left-field line, 347 to right, 382 to the power alleys, and 430 to dead center.

1956

Fences are moved back in left (330 feet) and right (352) fields, but center field is shortened to 421. Attendance surpasses 1 million for the last time.

April 22, 1959

This One Goes to Eleven A blowout loss at the hands of the "Go-Go" Sox signals that it's going to be another long year in Kansas City. The A's take a quick 6-1 lead, but squander it in the seventh as Chicago manages the seemingly impossible feat of scoring eleven runs with just one hit. The A's help by shooting themselves in the foot, making three errors on the first three plays of the frame while walking ten batters, including eight with the bases loaded. Chicago's Johnny Callison collects the inning's only base hit, and is also hit by a pitch for good measure. The A's will finish mired in seventh place for the third straight season, while the White Sox will go on to win their first pennant in forty years.

White Sox 20, A's 6

July 11, 1960 The NL All-Stars defeat the AL, 5-3, at Municipal Stadium in the first of two Midsummer Classics held in 1960. Former KC Monarchs player Ernie Banks, now with the Chicago Cubs, is picked as the game's MVP.

1961

New owner Charles O. Finley builds a picnic area in left field and a petting zoo in right, which includes the mascot mule he names after himself. Other additions include "Harvey," a mechanical rabbit that pops up out of the ground to supply umpires with new baseballs, and "Little Blowhard," a device that blows compressed air across home plate to keep it tidy.

LEFT: A new bank of floodlights is installed atop the grandstand roof on February 28, 1955, in preparation for the first American League game in Kansas City. Of course, the legendary KC Monarchs of the Negro Leagues had already played major league–caliber ball in the city for more than three decades.

RST COLORED WORLI
OCT. 11, 1924

December 1960 After having attempted to purchase the Athletics (when they were based in Philadelphia), Tigers, White Sox, and Angels, Charles O. Finley buys a controlling interest in the Kansas City Athletics from the estate of Arnold Johnson. He'll buy out the rest of the investors within a few months.

September 17, 1964 During their first US tour, the Beatles open a concert at Municipal with Little Richard's "Kansas City." Charles Finley, who paid the group an unprecedented $150,000, prints his name above the band's on the tickets, most of which also feature a photo of him in a Beatles wig.

December 19, 1976 Led by Jim "Catfish" Hunter and John "Blue Moon" Odom, the A's go on a pitching streak that will last 45½ scoreless innings.

1963

The Dallas Texans, the defending AFL champions, relocate to Kansas City and are renamed the Chiefs. Temporary bleachers are set up in the outfield, pushing capacity for football to 49,000. They'll move to Arrowhead Stadium in 1971.

1965

Convinced that the Yankees' success comes from their short porch in right field, Finley builds a 296-foot right-field porch identical to that of Yankee Stadium. After two preseason games, the league orders the A's to take it down. Finley complies reluctantly, pushing the fence back to the minimum 325 feet and labeling it his "One-Half Pennant Porch."

RIGHT: A's shortstop Bert Campaneris takes the mound in the seventh inning on September 8, 1965; he's on his way to becoming the first big leaguer to play all nine positions in a single game.

September 8, 1965

The Little Shortstop That Could With the A's long out of the pennant race, the team draws 21,576 fans to watch a never-before-tried publicity stunt: Bert Campaneris, normally Kansas City's shortstop, plays all nine positions in one game. Campaneris moves to a new spot each inning, starting at shortstop, and in the first inning he scores the first run of the game after walking and stealing second. Campy plays second base in the second, third in the third, and then moves across the outfield from left to right. His sixth-inning error in right field allows California to score the go-ahead run, but he flawlessly handles his other six plays during the game. After playing first base in the seventh, Campaneris takes over on the mound in the eighth with the A's trailing 2-1. He allows a run, a hit, and two walks, but strikes out Angels second baseman Bobby Knoop. Campaneris completes his day by catching the ninth inning, but is injured when he tags out the Angels' Ed Kirkpatrick in a home plate collision. After Campy leaves the game, the A's rally to tie it in the bottom of the ninth, but the Angels pull out the win in thirteen innings. Though always a versatile player, Campaneris will never play first base, right field, pitcher, or catcher again.

Angels 5, A's 3

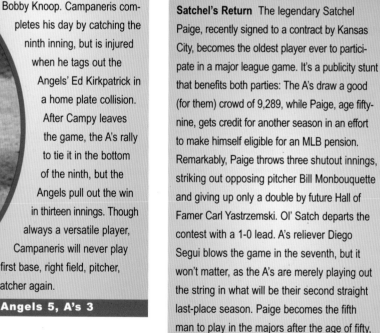

September 25, 1965

Satchel's Return The legendary Satchel Paige, recently signed to a contract by Kansas City, becomes the oldest player ever to participate in a major league game. It's a publicity stunt that benefits both parties: The A's draw a good (for them) crowd of 9,289, while Paige, age fifty-nine, gets credit for another season in an effort to make himself eligible for an MLB pension. Remarkably, Paige throws three shutout innings, striking out opposing pitcher Bill Monbouquette and giving up only a double by future Hall of Famer Carl Yastrzemski. Ol' Satch departs the contest with a 1-0 lead. A's reliever Diego Segui blows the game in the seventh, but it won't matter, as the A's are merely playing out the string in what will be their second straight last-place season. Paige becomes the fifth man to play in the majors after the age of fifty, following Nick Altrock, Jim O'Rourke, Charley O'Leary, and Jack Quinn. Minnie Minoso will join the club in 1976.

Red Sox 5, A's 2

LEFT: Fans stream into Municipal Stadium during the Athletics' first season in Kansas City in 1955. The offices and ticket windows are located in a stand-alone building behind right field at the corner of 22nd Street and Brooklyn Avenue.

ABOVE: Seemingly ageless Satchel Paige sits in his rocking chair in the A's bullpen on September 25, 1965, alongside a nurse the Athletics hired as part of the publicity stunt. This appearance, his last in the big leagues, occurs twelve years after he last pitched in the majors, for the St. Louis Browns.

June 9, 1967 Twenty-one-year-old Reggie Jackson makes his major league debut with the A's. The future "Mr. October" will be instrumental in the team's postseason success once they move to Oakland.

July 4, 1968 Brazilian soccer team Santos, featuring international star Pelé, faces off against the Kansas City Spurs of the North American Soccer League in an exhibition match at Municipal Stadium attended by 19,296.

1971 In their third year of existence, the Royals have their first winning season, finishing second place in the AL West.

September 27, 1967

The Last Hurrah The Athletics finally play a part in a pennant race, sweeping a late-season doubleheader from Chicago to effectively end the White Sox's bid for the AL pennant. The two games are also the last contests the A's will play in Kansas City as the home team; beginning in 1968, they'll be known as the Oakland A's. Remarkably, the A's defeat the pitchers with the two best ERAs in the AL during the respective ends of this doubleheader. In the opener, Pat Dobson defeats Gary Peters, 5-2. In the nightcap, A's rookie Catfish Hunter tosses a 4-0 shutout against the Sox and Joel Horlen. The seemingly paltry crowd of 5,325 is actually more fans than the A's have drawn to a game in nearly a month. The doubleheader loss drops the White Sox from second place to fourth, leaving a tie for the pennant as their only hope. They'll be eliminated the next day, and the Boston Red Sox will win the AL title for the first time in twenty-one years. The Athletics, meanwhile, will close out their dubious tenure as a Kansas City franchise by losing four straight at Yankee Stadium.

A's 5, White Sox 2;
A's 4, White Sox 0

1967

The A's draw 726,639 fans during their final season in Kansas City. They'll start the next season in Oakland.

1969

The newly formed Kansas City Royals move into Municipal Stadium and draw 902,414 fans, more than any Kansas City A's club since 1959.

1972

The final major league game is played at Municipal Stadium on October 4. The team moves to Royals Stadium (much later known as Kauffman Stadium) for the 1973 season, and Municipal will be torn down in 1976.

LEFT: A crowded Municipal Stadium seen from above in the mid-1950s.

BELOW: This postcard depicts the Kansas City Royals at Municipal Stadium.

April 8, 1969

Royals Flush Minnesota After a year's absence, major league baseball returns to Kansas City as the expansion Royals make their debut. Wally Bunker throws the franchise's first pitch to Minnesota's Ted Uhlaender. Lou Piniella, on his way to winning the Rookie of the Year award, leads off the bottom of the inning with the first hit in franchise history, a double. He soon rounds the bases to score the Royals' first run on a single by Jerry Adair. The 17,688 fans are treated to free baseball on Opening Day, as the game goes twelve innings before the Royals win it on an RBI single by Joe Keough—who, fittingly, was originally drafted by the Kansas City Athletics in 1965.

Royals 4, Twins 3

CANDLESTICK PARK

San Francisco, California

Giants (NL) 1960–1999

3Com Park at Candlestick Point 1995–1999

WILLIE MAYS

OPPOSITE: The Giants beat the Cardinals 3-1 in the first game ever played at Candlestick Park, on April 12, 1960. Winning pitcher "Toothpick" Sam Jones hurls a three-hit complete game, and the immortal Willie Mays doubles and scores two runs. Willie McCovey, the 1959 NL Rookie of the Year who will ultimately become even more popular than Mays in San Francisco, goes 1-for-3 while playing first base. Orlando Cepeda, the 1958 NL Rookie of the Year, goes 2-for-3 with a triple and three RBIs while playing left field. The Giants will win the NL pennant in their third season at Candlestick, in 1962, and finish second for five consecutive years in the late 1960s.

Though it is remembered fondly by music fans as the site of the last Beatles concert, Candlestick Park is remembered not-so-fondly by baseball fans as being one of the worst stadiums in history. It was a beautiful place to take in a game on a sunny afternoon, but the weather was rarely so cooperative. Thanks to wind, fog, and cold caused by nearby San Francisco Bay, games at the park were often blooper-filled disasters for those on the field and frigid tests of endurance for those in the stands. Still, in the 1960s, Candlestick Park gave the newly relocated Giants a place to win over a fresh (although freezing) fan base.

When they moved into Candlestick, the Giants had been in San Francisco for two years, after having skipped town with fellow New York team the Dodgers. Though the Giants moved in 1957, the $5 million bond issue for a new MLB park in San Francisco had been approved back in November 1954. It had two contingencies: that the building of the park not commence until the city acquired a team and that the bond be paid back in five years. So, while the Giants took up temporary residence at the minor league Seals Stadium—an intimate, single-decked structure with inadequate parking and seating for only about 23,000—the city frantically set about building a suitable home for its team in two years.

San Francisco had promised Giants owner Horace Stoneham a 40,000-seat stadium with 12,000 parking spaces. Such a space required at least 75 acres, and there were few site choices in the rapidly growing City by the Bay. Soon, a finger-shaped piece of land on the western shore of San Francisco Bay was chosen. Called Candlestick Point, the land wasn't ideal, but the majority of it was owned by construction tycoon Charles Harney, who Stoneham knew he could get on board. Harney, who was certain the park would be named after him, sold the land for more than it was worth and hired architect John Bolles to design the structure that would go on it, even though Bolles had little experience in building stadiums.

There were problems from the start. The park was saddled with two Grand Jury investigations regarding business deals pertaining to its construction. Teamsters went on strike, and the stadium failed to pass its first fire inspection because of inadequate exits. The state-of-the-art heating system, designed

DAVE KINGMAN

Brett Butler

WILL CLARK

to have 35,000 feet of iron pipe installed 1 inch into the concrete, was actually installed 5 inches into the concrete, rendering it useless. Foul poles were accidentally placed in fair territory (and wouldn't be moved back until after the first season). The cost to construct the park went over budget by $10 million, and not surprisingly, the stadium wasn't finished in the time mandated by the bond issue. When a contest was held to name the stadium, Harney lost in a landslide to Candlestick Park.

The first game at the Stick was held on April 12, 1960. Vice President Richard Nixon, who threw out the first ball, proclaimed, "San Francisco can say this is the finest ballpark in America!" As with many other things, Nixon was wrong. When the site had originally been chosen, officials had toured it in the morning; however, in the later hours, there was a strong wind coming from the bay. The park's position made the breeze worse—it was later discovered that if it had been constructed only a few hundred yards away, winds might not have been such a problem. As it was, it was hard not to notice the almost hurricane-like gusts that barreled through. Home runs were made into pop-ups (and vice versa), and outfielders circled under fly balls waiting for them to drop. Players had caps blown off their heads and peanut bags seemed to hover in midair. With no heating in the stands, fans suffered in the cold and fog, and by the 1980s were being given "Croix de Candlestick" pins for sticking it out until the end of the game. To make matters worse, there was a sewage dump nearby, and the wind blew the disgusting smell into the park, giving it the nickname "Candlestink" until the facility was finally relocated.

Players hated the park, especially slender reliever Stu Miller, who was blown off the pitcher's mound by a gust of wind during the 1961 All-Star Game (a balk was ruled). In a 1983 poll, major league players voted Candlestick the worst park to play in, and the New York Mets' Keith Hernandez

had a clause added to his contract that prevented the team from trading him to the Giants. Most people believe Willie Mays could have increased his 660 career home runs if not for the cold wind blowing from left-center—although he actually hit slightly more homers at home than on the road while playing at Candlestick from 1960 to 1971.

In 1971, San Francisco spent $16.1 million to double-deck and fully enclose the park. Although the reason behind the expenditure was to raise capacity to accommodate the football 49ers moving in, engineers predicted that it would completely eliminate the wind problem. Unfortunately, they were wrong—the wind remained, although now it swirled around even more unpredictably.

During the 1971 expansion, trendy new AstroTurf was also added to the field for the benefit of the football players. The next year, it went all turf, with only dirt sliding pits around the bases. "Having AstroTurf wasn't our idea in the first place; it was the 49ers'," Giants Director of Scouting Jack Schwartz told the *Sporting News* in 1978. But according to Schwartz, once the plastic was installed, the baseball club wanted it to remain because of the time it took to get a grass field in shape for baseball after the rigors of a football game. Eventually, however, the gridders tired of the fake stuff, and, prior to the 1979 season, Candlestick reverted to old-fashioned grass and dirt, thereby becoming the first park to have a complete plastic surface installed, then ripped out.

Though their park was less than ideal, the Giants spent four decades in its windy confines. After voters rejected ballot measures in 1987, 1989, 1990, and 1992 to build the beleaguered team a new park, in 1995 new owner Peter Magowan secured private financing to construct a $357 million park near downtown. Though the 49ers stayed behind, the Giants moved into beautiful Pacific Bell Park for the 2000 season. Fans packed Candlestick on September 30, 1999, for the last Giants game ever played there. It was a summery, fog-free day.

of Candlestick Park's heating system, which caused his box seats to be too cold. After having Arctic explorers testify in court that they were colder at Candlestick than on the tundra, he is awarded the $16,000 price of his season tickets.

the Dodgers. The longtime rivals meet in a best-of-three playoff, with the Giants taking two games and the pennant.

1960

Candlestick Park opens on April 12. The stadium has open views of the water from center to right field—and lots and lots of wind. Original dimensions are 397 to left- and right-center and 420 to dead-center field. After one year, the dimensions will be shortened to 365 to left-center, 410 to center, and 375 to right-center.

CAP: 1965.

BELOW: On the first Opening Day at Candlestick, fans disembark from boats on the tidal flats of San Francisco Bay, and a packed parking lot surrounds the brand-spanking-new park. The 1960 debut game brings a capacity crowd of 42,269.

July 11, 1961

Blowin' in the Wind The All-Star Game comes to San Francisco for the first time, and befitting this ballpark best known for its strong gusts, the wind steals the show. With a 3-2 lead in the ninth inning, NL manager Danny Murtaugh sends Stu Miller, a Giants pitcher, in to relieve Sandy Koufax. Trying to close out the game before his hometown fans, Miller pitches from the stretch position with two runners on base. A sudden gust of wind blows him off the pitcher's rubber, moving him only slightly, but the movement is enough for a balk to be called, advancing the runners to second and third. The balk is followed by three errors, allowing the American Leaguers to tie the game and send it into extra innings. But the NL comes back to win it in the tenth, as hits by Hank Aaron, Willie Mays, and game MVP Roberto Clemente help make Miller the winning pitcher.

NL 5, AL 4

and .398 on-base percentage.

form a concert at Candlestick Park. The show will be the band's final public performance, and will last only thirty minutes (and eleven songs).

the Giants' first Cy Young award with an ERA of 2.85.

A Game of Inches In one of the most exciting World Series Game 7s ever played, the only run of the day scores on a double-play grounder by Tony Kubek in the fifth inning. Matters come to a head when the Giants stage a thrilling—but ultimately frustrating—ninth inning rally. Matty Alou leads off the inning with a bunt single, but the next two Giants batters strike out. Willie Mays, representing San Francisco's last chance, smashes a double to right field, but an outstanding defensive play by Roger Maris holds the speedy Alou at third base. The next batter is dangerous left-handed slugger Willie McCovey. Strategy dictates that the Yankees should either walk McCovey intentionally or bring in a southpaw to face him, but Yankees manager Ralph Houk does neither, instead allowing his tiring starter, Ralph Terry, to face the future Hall of Famer. McCovey hits a blistering line drive toward second base, and the Yankees' Bobby Richardson reaches up and snags it for the final out of the season, hanging on to the ball even though the impact nearly knocks him off his feet. It is the closest the Giants will come to a world championship in their forty years at Candlestick.

Yankees 1, Giants 0

July 2, 1963

Legendary Pitching Faceoff Future Hall of Famers Juan Marichal and Warren Spahn tangle in a marathon sixteen-inning pitcher's duel that becomes one of the most famous regular-season games in baseball history. When Giants manager Alvin Dark tries to remove Marichal from the game, the twenty-five-year-old ace—who threw a no-hitter just two weeks earlier—insists he will remain as long as the forty-two-year-old Spahn does. Willie Mays finally wins it with a one-out, walk-off home run in the sixteenth. Marichal will finish the year with twenty-five wins, 248 strikeouts, and a 2.41 ERA in a staggering 321⅓ innings pitched.

Giants 1, Braves 0

ABOVE: Nope, this ain't Texas, pardner. But these fans in a box on Candlestick's press level are all wearing cowboy hats as they take in a game in 1960.

RIGHT: The bitter Giants-Dodgers rivalry spawned many fights—both on the field and in the stands—but this bloody brawl on August 22, 1965, is the most famous. LA pitcher Sandy Koufax charges the Giants' Juan Marichal (27), who has just clubbed LA catcher John Roseboro on the head with his bat. Giants coach Charlie Fox (left) tries to restrain Koufax as umpire Shag Crawford pushes Marichal away. Roseboro had thrown a ball close to Marichal's head—allegedly in retaliation for two struck batters earlier in the game—and Marichal responded by whacking back. The fight devolved into a fourteen-minute, bench-clearing melee on the field, and Marichal was subsequently suspended and fined.

June 25, 1968 At the age of twenty-one, Bobby Bonds makes his major league debut at Candlestick Park. His first hit ever is a grand slam against the Dodgers' John Purdin. His son Barry will debut for the Pirates eighteen years later.

1969 Willie McCovey wins the MVP Award after finishing the season with a league-leading 126 RBIs and 42 home runs. When the Giants move into Pacific Bell Park, they'll rename the part of the bay behind the right-field wall "McCovey Cove."

May 3, 1972 Willie Mays plays his last game in a Giants uniform at Candlestick Park, going 2-for-3 against the Mets. The Giants legend will be traded to the Mets after three more games, making his first appearance with his new team on May 14—fittingly, at Candlestick.

August 22, 1965

Marichal Goes Batty In perhaps the signature moment of the Dodgers-Giants rivalry, Juan Marichal attacks Los Angeles catcher John Roseboro by pounding him over the head with a bat until blood runs down his face, a brutal incident that lands Roseboro in the hospital and earns Marichal an eight-date, ten-game, suspension in the middle of the pennant race. The chaos appears to distract the usually brilliant Dodgers hurler Sandy Koufax, who walks two and allows a three-run homer to Willie Mays in a 4-3 loss that drops his season record to 21-5. Marichal will later claim that he attacked Roseboro in self-defense because the Dodgers catcher was whizzing his return throws to Koufax too close to Marichal's head. Roseboro will not only admit to the charge, but will actively campaign to help get Marichal into the Hall of Fame years later.

Giants 4, Dodgers 3

September 17, 1968

Consecutive No-Hitters In "The Year of the Pitcher," offense has never been harder to come by than during today's game at Candlestick Park, where Giants ace Gaylord Perry tosses a no-hitter but barely defeats the league's best pitcher, Bob Gibson, 1-0. Tomorrow the Cardinals' Ray Washburn will turn the tables on the Giants, no-hitting them at Candlestick by a 2-0 score. Surprisingly, only three other no-hitters will be thrown throughout the majors during this low-scoring season.

Giants 1, Cardinals 0

1971

The arrival of the NFL's 49ers spurs a major renovation. The stadium is fully enclosed in the 1971–72 off-season. AstroTurf is installed, except on the infield basepaths, which will be turfed over one year later. Movable stands are installed in order to switch back and forth easily between baseball and football configurations. Candlestick's baseball capacity is now 58,000, an increase of more than 15,000.

1979

The AstroTurf is removed and replaced by grass, making Candlestick the first ballpark to pull up its artificial turf and go natural again.

1982

The distance to center field is reduced to 400 feet.

October 3, 1982

Little Joe's Big Hit In a game that shows the ferocity of the Giants-Dodgers rivalry, a packed Candlestick Park revels in the Giants' knocking Los Angeles out of the pennant race on the last day of the season. Joe Morgan's dramatic three-run homer off Dodgers reliever Terry Forster hands the NL West title to the Atlanta Braves. Eleven years later the roles will be reversed and the Dodgers will knock out the Giants in Los Angeles, thanks to the power hitting of rookie catcher Mike Piazza. Once again, Atlanta will be the beneficiary of the rivalry.

Giants 5, Dodgers 3

May 4, 1975

One in a Million According to calculations by Commissioner Bowie Kuhn's office, Houston's Bob Watson scores the one millionth run in major league history in the first game of a doubleheader at Candlestick Park. Coincidentally, it is also the one hundredth season that major league baseball has been played. In future years, retroactive audits of old records will make it clear that Watson's run was not actually the one millionth, but he will remain widely credited with the accomplishment.

Giants 8, Astros 6

October 9, 1989

The Giants Win the Pennant The largest baseball crowd in Candlestick history, 62,084, sees the Giants clinch their first NL pennant in twenty-seven years. San Francisco trails the Cubs entering the seventh inning of NLCS Game 5, but Giants first baseman Will Clark triples and scores on Kevin Mitchell's sacrifice fly to tie the game. An inning later, Chicago's Mike Bielecki walks the bases full, bringing Clark to the plate with two outs. After reliever Mitch Williams is brought in to face him, Clark fights off two difficult two-strike pitches before singling to center to give the Giants the lead. Chicago stages a two-out rally in the ninth, but it fizzles when Ryne Sandberg grounds out against Giants relief ace Steve Bedrosian. Clark is named MVP of the series.

Giants 3, Cubs 2

October 27, 1989

The Earthquake Series Resumes Ten days after the Loma Prieta earthquake devastated the Bay Area, killing sixty-seven people and postponing Game 3 of the World Series, the area's two teams take the same field they were evacuated from on October 17. Although Candlestick Park suffered minor damage in the 7.1 magnitude quake, it is declared structurally sound and the Series is allowed to go on. The pitchers look rusty after so much time off; four A's hit home runs, including Dave Henderson, who blasts two. Dave Stewart wins his second game of the Series, and tomorrow he will be named MVP of what has become known as the "BART Series," after the local mass transit system. It will be the last World Series ever played at Candlestick.

A's 13, Giants 7

October 17, 1989 Just before Game 3 of the World Series, the Loma Prieta earthquake hits San Francisco. The Series is postponed for ten days to assess and take care of the damage from the quake, a 7.1 on the Richter scale. The stadium sustains only minor damage, and no spectators are injured.

1992 Longtime fan Peter Magowan buys the team, saving it from the clutches of potential buyers who would like to move the team to St. Petersburg, Florida. Magowan will spearhead the building of the Giants' new home, Pacific Bell Park.

ABOVE: Candlestick Park is closed for inspection the day after the Loma Prieta earthquake on October 17, 1989. The quake occurred just before Game 3 of the World Series, and the remaining games were postponed for ten days while the damage was cleaned up and the park was made safe for fans. Game 3 finally commenced on October 27, and Oakland finished its sweep of San Francisco in Game 4 on October 28.

The second deck in the outfield, seen in this 1999 photo, made the park even worse for baseball. Added during the 1971–72 off-season, it was meant to increase capacity for football, but it also trapped the already detrimental winds inside the stadium.

1993

A padded outfield wall replaces the eyesore chain-link fence in the outfield.

1994

Capacity is increased to 63,000, with new box seats cutting down slightly on foul territory.

1996

Candlestick Park becomes the first major league stadium to sell its existing name to a corporate sponsor when it is renamed 3Com Park at Candlestick Point.

1999

The Giants play their final game at Candlestick Point on September 30 before moving into a new retro-style ballpark at China Basin. The 49ers remain at the old stadium, which will be renamed San Francisco Stadium in 2002 and Monster Park in 2004.

April 12, 1993

A Barry Good Team The Giants open their home season with new ownership, a new manager, a new left fielder, and a brand-new team—the expansion Florida Marlins—as their opponent. After years of rumors that the Giants would relocate to St. Petersburg, Florida, the team stays put when it is purchased by Peter Magowan. Almost immediately, Magowan hires rookie manager Dusty Baker and lures two-time NL MVP Barry Bonds away from the Pittsburgh Pirates with a lucrative free-agent contract. Before the home opener, Bay Area icons Tony Bennett and the Grateful Dead perform before 56,689 adoring fans. Bonds homers in his first home at-bat as a Giant, and Darren Lewis singles in the winning run for San Francisco in the eleventh inning.

Giants 4, Marlins 3

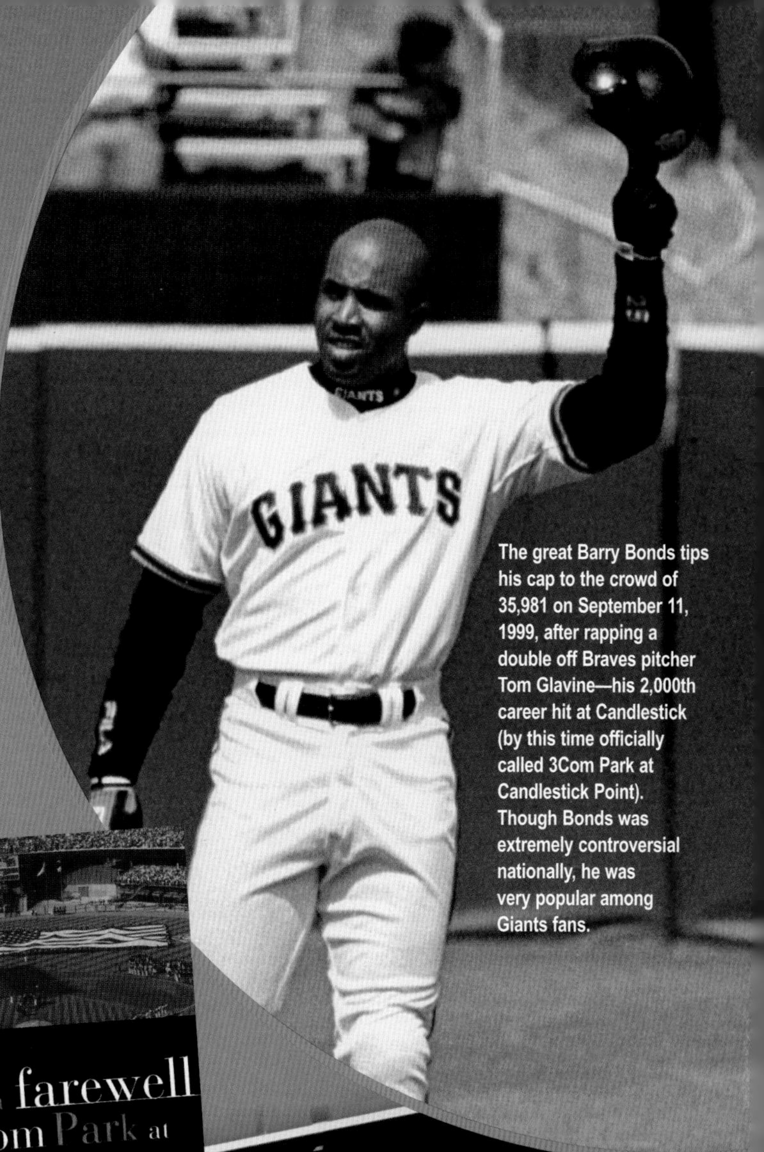

The great Barry Bonds tips his cap to the crowd of 35,981 on September 11, 1999, after rapping a double off Braves pitcher Tom Glavine—his 2,000th career hit at Candlestick (by this time officially called 3Com Park at Candlestick Point). Though Bonds was extremely controversial nationally, he was very popular among Giants fans.

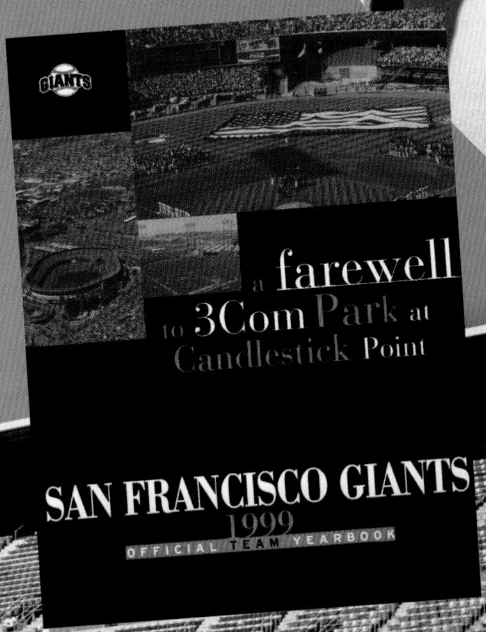

a farewell
to 3Com Park at
Candlestick Point

SAN FRANCISCO GIANTS
1999
OFFICIAL TEAM YEARBOOK

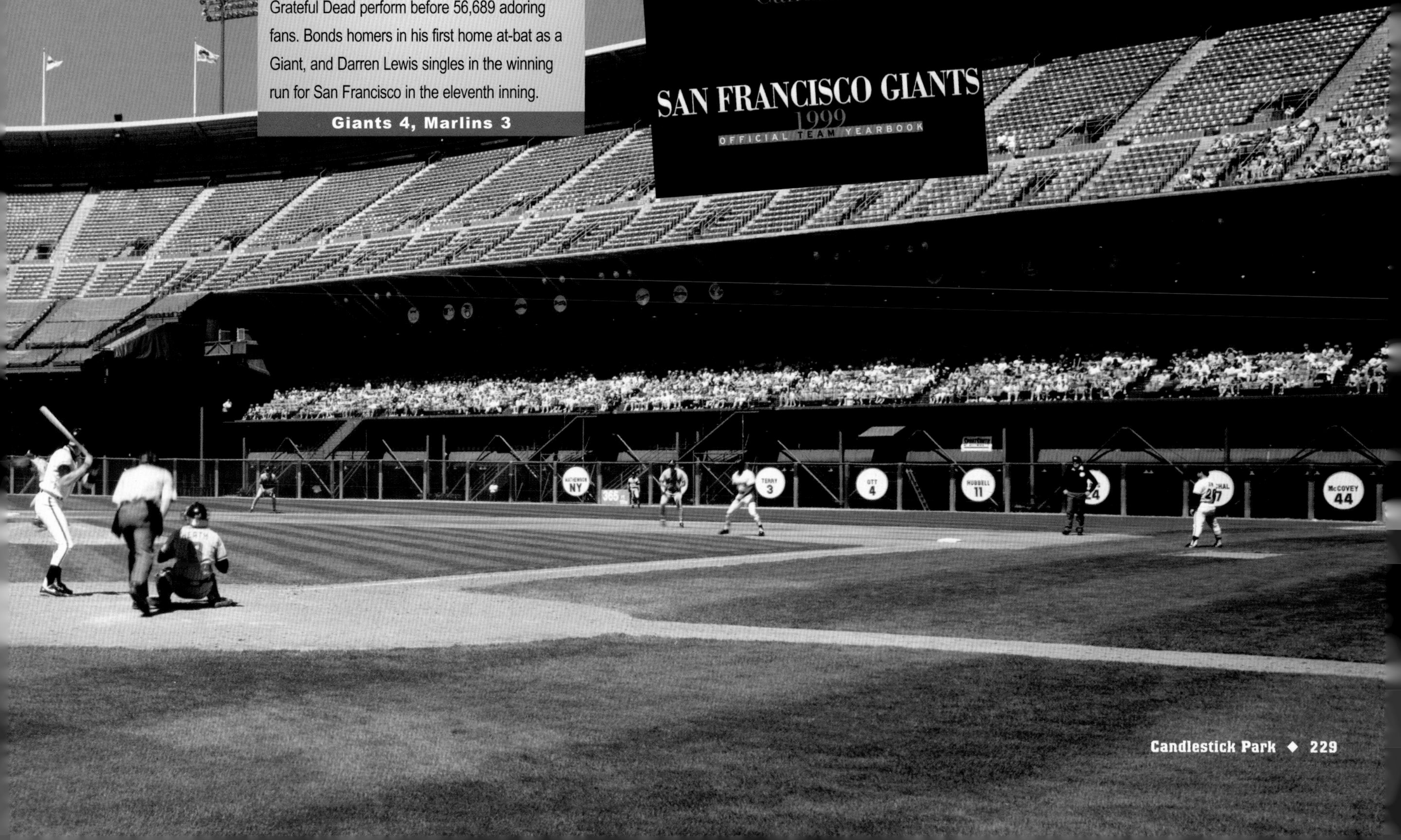

METROPOLITAN STADIUM

Bloomington, Minnesota

Twins (AL) 1961–1981

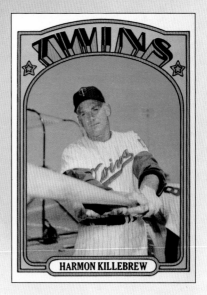

HARMON KILLEBREW

OPPOSITE: This 1965 photo, taken from the upper deck behind home plate, shows Metropolitan Stadium's new double-decked bleachers in left field, the scoreboard in right-center, and the parking lots ringing the stadium. Note how undeveloped the site was in the 1960s, despite housing a top-tier ball club. The Twins jumped from sixth place in 1964 to win the AL in '65 with an iconic club built around slugger Harmon Killebrew, batting champion Tony Oliva, and MVP shortstop Zoilo Versalles.

As baseball moguls hopscotched around the country in the 1950s and '60s looking to move their teams "wherever the people are as green as the money" (as flimflam man Harold Hill says in the *Music Man*), they settled into several minor league parks. Some of these parks merely served as way stations while new venues were being erected, while others were expanded into permanent homes. Of this latter kind, Metropolitan Stadium was by far the most successful. Although the stadium was not particularly original, it is remembered fondly by millions of Twins fans, mostly thanks to the great baseball played within its confines.

Metropolitan Stadium began its life as a minor league park, home of the Minneapolis Millers from 1956 to 1960. In 1961, when Washington owner Calvin Griffith moved his Senators west to become the Minnesota Twins, the Millers moved out and Metropolitan added more seats. This addition, plus an in-season expansion down the right-field line, brought capacity from 18,000 to close to 40,000.

Griffith's decision to move came just in time for his developing club to give the Twin Cities an exciting team throughout the 1960s. (At the same time, a cruel joke was played on long-suffering Senators fans, as they watched their new baseball team, the expansion Senators, dive quickly to the bottom of the AL, just like their predecessors.) Enthusiastic fans filled the Met to the rafters to cheer on such sluggers as Harmon Killebrew, Bob Allison, Don Mincher, and Earl Battey, all of whom had come with the club from DC. The 1965 AL MVP, Zoilo Versalles, had also made his first appearance, at the age of nineteen, in Washington; and the Twins' two top pitchers, Camilo Pascual and Jim Kaat, were Washington refugees as well. They, along with slugger Tony Oliva and the rest of the '65 Minnesota club, won 102 games and the AL pennant, falling only in Game 7 of an exciting World Series to an unhittable Sandy Koufax. Throughout the decade, the Twins drew well above the AL attendance average, peaking at more than three times the league average in '65 after factoring in their small market. Unfortunately, after winning the first two AL West titles in 1969 and 1970, the Twins drifted into mediocrity for more than a decade. Attendance followed that trend, dropping to less than half the league norm.

BERT
BLYLEVEN
MINNESOTA TWINS
PITCHER

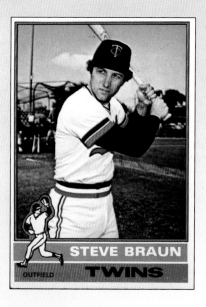

STEVE BRAUN
OUTFIELD
TWINS

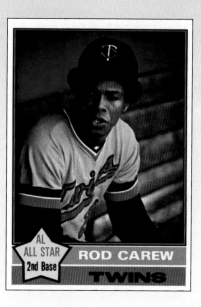

AL
ALL STAR
2nd Base
ROD CAREW
TWINS

TOP: Metropolitan Stadium undergoes construction in October 1955. The park's ground-breaking on June 20, 1955, was almost delayed. A farmer who owned property on the site, claiming he hadn't been paid, created a wall of agricultural equipment along his property line, which ran through the future infield. He was eventually mollified, however, and the construction went on as planned.

BOTTOM, LEFT: TV legend Ed Sullivan (right) sits in the Met's incomplete upper deck with stadium commissioner Bill Boyer in 1956; meanwhile, construction crews get the park ready for the Triple-A Minneapolis Millers.

BOTTOM, RIGHT: The Met's first base dugout as it appeared during the stadium's construction in April 1956, just before the Minneapolis Millers' first home game. An official name for the stadium would not be decided upon until that July.

OPPOSITE: In December 1960, the minor league Metropolitan Stadium is less than a year away from its major league christening. The sixty-one-year-old refugee Washington Senators and the expansion NFL Vikings will move into their new digs on April 21 and September 10, respectively.

Following a similar evolutionary path as most fields, Metropolitan grew and changed to fit the needs of its tenants. A decent-size, friendly—if spare—park with wire fences throughout its life, the Met also hosted the NFL's Vikings, and regrettably, many compromises were made to accommodate them, to the Twins' detriment. It was the Vikings who really controlled the park, and the Vikings' demands for a bigger venue with artificial turf that ultimately drove both teams into the unappealing Metrodome in 1982. As patronage dropped and the expectation of a new stadium grew, maintenance was slighted and the Met became downright shabby in its later years.

In retrospect, Metropolitan Stadium—which was not in Minneapolis proper, but in the nearby suburb of Bloomington—exemplified an important trend of the stadium era. Cities, led by explosive middle class growth, began to abandon ballparks in the older, industrial parts of town in favor of suburban settings on the fringe of the city or in the suburbs. Surrounded by vast parking lots that catered to the increasingly dominant automobile-centered culture, these ballparks were no longer planned around public transportation systems that made it possible for fans to reach the park easily by bus, trolley, or train.

It was also a telling sign of ballpark trends to come that after Metropolitan was deserted, it was demolished, in 1985, as part of the site of the super-gigantic Mall of America. As such, it presaged the parks of the 1990s and 2000s, which morphed into retro parks–cum–outdoor shopping malls that focused on entertaining the customer in any way possible, regardless of how that entertainment related to the game itself. Even still, there are no doubt plenty of people in the Twin Cities who would rather get the chance to take in a game at the old Met than go on any shopping spree.

TIMELINE: METROPOLITAN STADIUM

1962 Herb Carneal begins broadcasting for the Twins. He'll win the Ford C. Frick award in 1996 and be the voice of the team until his death in 2007.

September 9, 1962 Twenty-four-year-old Tony Oliva makes his major league debut with the Twins. He'll play only nine games in 1962 and seven in 1963 before being called up permanently in 1964.

1961

Having opened in 1956, Metropolitan Stadium is expanded from 18,000 to 30,000 seats upon the arrival of the Twins, who play their first game here on April 21. Seats are added in mid-season, making the capacity more than 39,000. Dimensions are 329 feet down the lines, 402 to the power alleys, and 412 to center field. The NFL's Vikings also make their debut here, on September 10.

April 21, 1961

Old Team, New Beginning The Twins play their first game in Minnesota—and their opponents, appropriately enough, are the Washington Senators, the expansion team created to take their place in the nation's capital. Until this year, the Twins themselves had been called the Senators, playing their home games at Washington's Griffith Stadium. Today nearly 25,000 Minnesotans—about 6,000 short of a sellout—come to Metropolitan Stadium to see the home team lose to the Senators, as Twins pitcher Camilo Pascual allows two runs in the top of the first inning. The first Twins batter is shortstop Zoilo Versalles, who will be named American League MVP four years later when he leads Minnesota to the pennant.

Senators 5, Twins 3

1964

With the All-Star Game—and, as it turns out, the World Series—coming in 1965, a second deck of left-field bleachers is installed after the season, raising capacity to 45,000 by mid-season 1965. The height of the fence is raised to 12 feet, except in center, where it stays at 8 feet.

October 14, 1965

KKKKKKKKKKKoufax Sandy Koufax shows why he's the best pitcher of his generation, as he shuts down the Twins with a masterful performance in Game 7 of the World Series. Like his opponent, Jim Kaat, Koufax is starting on just two days' rest, but he nonetheless allows only three hits while striking out ten Twins batters, including Bob Allison to end the game. Kaat, meanwhile, gives up a Lou Johnson homer off the foul pole to lead off the fourth, and an RBI single to Wes Parker later in the inning. It's the second shutout in four days for Koufax, who was forced to miss his Game 1 start because it fell on the Jewish holy day of Yom Kippur. He is named Series MVP as the Dodgers capture their third world title since moving to Los Angeles seven years earlier. This is the only World Series home game the Twins will lose during the twentieth century; they will go 11-1.

Dodgers 2, Twins 0

July 13, 1965

A Star-Studded Contest The All-Star Game is held in Minnesota for the first time, and the AL squad features six members of the first-place Twins. But it's a long day for the AL, as NL stars Willie Mays and Joe Torre homer in the top of the first inning. Willie Stargell adds another in the second off Minnesota pitcher Mudcat Grant. The AL comes back in the fifth thanks to Twins players Jimmie Hall, who starts the rally with a walk, and Harmon Killebrew, who hits a game-tying homer. In the seventh, however, a Ron Santo single gives the NL a lead it will not relinquish. The winning pitcher is Sandy Koufax, but the MVP is Juan Marichal, who threw three scoreless innings to start the game.

NL 6, AL 5

ABOVE: An early-1960s postcard image shows a packed Metropolitan Stadium. Note the football press box in the upper deck down the first base line.

RIGHT: The 1965 Twins, "The Boys of Summer" for the Upper Midwest, pose for their team photo at the Met. In the last row, pitcher Camilo Pascual is third from the left, Jim Kaat is fifth, Zoilo Versalles is seventh, Harmon Killebrew is tenth, and Tony Oliva is at the far right. Twenty-one-game-winner Jim "Mudcat" Grant is second from the end in the middle row; and manager Sam Mele is seventh from the left in the front row.

1973 The Twins finish in third place, but lead the league at the plate with 1,521 hits and a .270 batting average.

December 20, 1979 Ground is broken on what will be the Twins' new home, the Hubert H. Humphrey Metrodome.

1992 Mall of America opens on the former site of Metropolitan Stadium. In the indoor theme park that will come to be known as Nickelodeon Universe, a home-plate-shaped plaque commemorates where the stadium once stood.

1965

The dimensions become vast, as the fence is pushed back to 435 feet in left-center field and 430 in right-center and center. In their only pennant-winning campaign at the Met, the Twins draw a team record 1.46 million fans.

1975

The distances in left and center field are reduced to 350 and 410 feet, respectively, allowing fans to stand behind the chain-link outfield fence. Right-center remains a distant 430 feet from home plate.

1977

Dimensions are reduced for the final time to 406 feet in left-center field and 402 in center. Right-center field is 410, and the right-field distance is increased by 5 feet to 370.

June 26, 1977

Carew Reaches .400 It's Rod Carew T-Shirt Day at the Met, and the guest of honor responds by collecting four hits, scoring five runs, and driving in six. At day's end, Carew's average is .403, and he appears poised to become the first player since Ted Williams in 1941 to bat .400 in a full season. In one of the great slugfests in Twins history, Glenn Adams tops Carew with eight RBIs to help the Twins to a 19-12 win over Chicago. Minnesota's Tom Johnson gives up seven runs in relief but nonetheless gets credit for the win; he'll amass sixteen relief wins by the end of the year. Carew, meanwhile, will eventually fall short of the .400 mark at .388, but will take home both the AL batting title and MVP as consolation prizes.

Twins 19, White Sox 12

1981

Never well cared for, the stadium falls into disrepair in its final season, and only 16,000 fans attend the last game of the strike-torn season on September 30. The Vikings, whose machinations are forcing both teams to move indoors for 1982, play their final game at the Met on December 20.

1985

Metropolitan Stadium, the first ballpark built after World War II to be abandoned by both its MLB and NFL teams, is razed to clear space for Mall of America.

August 10, 1971

Killebrew Reaches 500 Harmon Killebrew becomes the first Twin, and the tenth player overall, to hit 500 career home runs. Killer's milestone blast comes in the first inning, and he later hits number 501 to tie the game in the sixth. Both shots come against Baltimore's Mike Cuellar, who nonetheless wins the game in the tenth after Baltimore's Merv Rettenmund hits a tie-breaking homer. All told, Killebrew will hit 244 of his 573 career home runs at Metropolitan Stadium, and will rank fifth on the all-time homer list when he retires in 1975.

Orioles 4, Twins 3

CAP: 1978 (worn by Rod Carew).

LEFT: Harmon "Killer" Killebrew watches his 500th career home run—and guaranteed ticket to Cooperstown—sail out of the Met on August 10, 1971.

BELOW: On December 20, 1981, the Vikings play their last game in snowy Bloomington to a packed house. The Kansas City Chiefs beat the hometown eleven by a score of 10-6. The Twins had finished their career at the Met in front of a sparse crowd three months earlier.

DODGER STADIUM
Los Angeles, California
Dodgers (NL) 1962–present, Angels (AL) 1962–1965

OPPOSITE: Newly renovated Dodger Stadium displays its pastel charms on June 4, 2006, during a Sunday afternoon game between the Phillies and the Dodgers. Weather at the start of the game is a sunny Southern California 98°. The Dodgers have sold 48,270 tickets to a typically late-arriving crowd, but the home team will lose to Philadelphia 6–4. Note the field-level box seats between the dugouts and down both foul lines, which have dramatically cut down on foul territory and made the venerable park much less friendly to pitchers.

In the first eight days of October 1959, the Los Angeles Dodgers took on the Chicago White Sox in the first World Series played on the West Coast. While packing their home games sky-high with fans at the gargantuan LA Coliseum, the Dodgers managed to out-speed the Go-Go Sox in an exciting six-game series. Their unexpected win brought instant credibility to California baseball and electrified scores of true-blue Angelenos, who rejoiced not only at having their very own ball club, but a ball club that *won*.

Only a few weeks earlier, the team had broken ground on its future home, just north of downtown Los Angeles in a hilly area called Chavez Ravine. The edifice to arise there, Dodger Stadium, would open to universal acclaim, and more than forty-five years later it still remains one of the true jewels in the national pastime's crown. Thoroughly modern, with clean architecture, top-flight concession facilities, and acres of land surrounding it, it's also a park that never gets in the way of the baseball being played there. Like a Hollywood star with a top-notch plastic surgeon on retainer, Dodger Stadium never seems to age, existing in a state of perpetual youth.

The stadium's secret is that it was designed so well that it didn't have to be altered to remain a first-class venue. Large, clean, and blessed with 16,000 parking spaces and good sight lines (even from the very high upper deck), the stadium opened in April 1962 at a cost of nearly $18 million. To clear the land for the stadium, the city forcibly relocated the low-income residents (most of them Latino) from Chavez Ravine, even though the property had been given to the city by the federal government with the stipulation that it be used for public housing. The controversial referendum on the land transfer passed by approximately 25,000 votes, and Dodgers owner Walter O'Malley purchased the property for a song.

O'Malley's grand monument was built into the side of a hill; its below-grade field allowed its upper decks to be cantilevered, so nary a support post mars the views of the field. The park's field-level boxes, built between the dugouts, were an innovation, as were the field-level auxiliary scoreboards located down each foul line. Fans were immediately charmed by the attractive scoreboards, the pastel color scheme, the

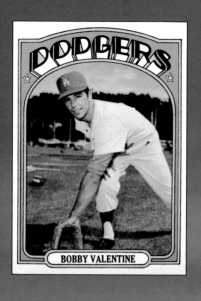

BOBBY VALENTINE

STEVE SAX

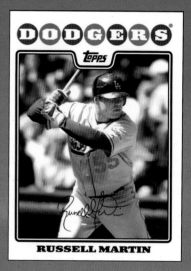

RUSSELL MARTIN

The Colossal Coliseum

Though it is much better known for being the only venue to host the Olympics twice (in 1932 and 1984), the Los Angeles Memorial Coliseum was also the home of the Dodgers for four years. While they were waiting for Dodger Stadium to rise, the newly relocated team played at the Coliseum from 1958 to 1961. Built in 1923, the Coliseum had been used primarily for track-and-field and football, and was not well suited for baseball. The fans were seated far from the action, and the field had the oddest dimensions in the major leagues, with a distant 440 feet to right-center, a brutally long 390 feet to straightaway right field, and at the other extreme, a minuscule 250 feet to left field. In an attempt at making it harder to hit home runs, a 42-foot-high screen was erected behind left field, but an astonishing 193 home runs were hit (8 to right, 3 to center, and 182 to left) during the Dodgers' first season at the stadium. The geography of the park tremendously altered the way the game was played, with the Death Valley in right punishing lefty power hitters and hastening the end of star centerfielder Duke Snider's productivity. ("Duke, they killed you!" Willie Mays was reported to have said laughingly upon seeing the right-field fence.)

Of course, there was a reason team owner Walter O'Malley picked the Coliseum over the minor league Wrigley Field, which many agreed was more suitable for baseball: crowds. The Olympic-size stadium held more than 92,000, and the park was often almost filled to capacity as fans streamed in to check out the new hometown team. "Lead me to the bank," said Yogi Berra when asked about the prospect of playing a Series at the gigantic park and having to spot the ball amidst a sea of white shirts. "I'll find those pitches if I have to feel for them."

In 1959, the stadium hosted an All-Star Game, and the same year, the team brought the World Series to its new city. On May 7, an MLB attendance record was broken when 93,103 fans packed in for an exhibition game between the Dodgers and the Yankees to honor paralyzed Dodgers star Roy Campanella. In 2008, the Dodgers did it again, when they spent $500,000 to create a facsimile of the original field and hosted 115,300 spectators for a Red Sox–Dodgers exhibition game to celebrate the fiftieth anniversary of the team's move to LA. Duke Snider was one of a dozen Dodgers who originally played at the field who returned for the event. "It was not, or ever will be, a baseball stadium," Snider commented, "even though baseball was played there."

BELOW: A crowd of 78,672 packs the LA Coliseum for the pregame ceremonies before the first Dodgers home game in California. The opponents are the Dodgers' traditional rivals, the Giants, who leapt from the East Coast to the West Coast in tandem with the former Bums from Brooklyn. LA beats San Fran 6-5 in the inaugural game.

views of the surrounding palm trees and the San Gabriel Mountains, and the ever-popular Dodger Dogs—and they continue to be charmed to this day.

The experience of the Dodgers' tenants in the 1960s, however, was not so wonderful. In 1961, the American League had expanded into Los Angeles with a franchise owned by performer Gene Autry. When Dodger Stadium opened for business, Autry's Angels reluctantly moved out of the minor league Wrigley Field—with its small dimensions and even smaller capacity—and into Chavez Ravine, which is what the Angels called Dodger Stadium while they were playing there. The Dodgers began turning the screws on their tenants in various subtle and not-so-subtle ways. The Angels' ticket windows were installed near the site's garbage dump, and Autry was billed for groundskeeping and landscaping that the Dodgers would have done anyway. The Angels began an immediate search for a suitable home of their own, eventually leaving the city and moving deep into the soon-to-boom suburban Orange County.

The record of the Dodgers in LA, however, has been one of almost unbroken prosperity. They became the second major league team to draw 2 million paying customers in a year in 1959, and they thrived even more in Dodger Stadium, drawing more than 2.75 million fans in 1962 and leading the NL in attendance by a wide margin in the stadium's first five years of existence. In 1978, the Dodgers achieved a first by shattering the 3-million fan mark. Then, over the next thirty seasons, they again drew more than 3 million fans a remarkable twenty-two times, leading the NL in attendance virtually every season until Colorado joined the league in 1993. It helped that the Dodgers held the line on ticket prices from 1958 to 1975, with their $3.50 boxes, $2.50 reserved seats, and $1.50 general admission tickets becoming even better bargains over the years. But no matter what the prices, the Boys in Blue have maintained a loyal fan base. Even the recent drought since the Dodgers' last World Series (the club's longest since the twenty-one-year gap between Brooklyn's NL pennants in 1920 and 1941) hasn't stopped the team from drawing well.

And with good reason! Dodgers management has always prided itself on first-class treatment of its fans and spotless maintenance of its park, and has found that with a fan-focused attitude and a fresh coat of paint between every season, it has to do little else to pull in dedicated onlookers (although they may come late and leave early).

Even the park's dimensions have been changed much less often than in most long-lived stadiums. Distances to the fences have been altered only twice: pulled in by 10 feet in center and the power alleys in 1969, and pushed back by 15 feet in the power alleys in 1983. The seating has changed little, too. The permit granted for the construction of the stadium was for an entertainment venue seating a maximum of 56,000; therefore, although the Dodgers have added seats down the foul lines as well as in back of the plate in recent seasons, seats in other portions of the park have been removed or closed off so as not to violate the capacity imposed by the city license.

For most of its history, Dodger Stadium has been a pitcher's park, often an extreme one. The archetypal Dodgers teams in LA were built around the pitching of hard throwers, such as Sandy Koufax and Don Drysdale, with their hurlers depending on good defense and always getting a boost from their home park. Hitters, on the other hand, have faced a stadium that has large, symmetrical dimensions and a hitting background that has never been that good. In recent years, however, as the club added super-premium seating from first to third base and behind home plate, the park became more of a neutral venue as its foul territory shrank.

Being located so close to Tinseltown, Dodger Stadium has naturally played host to the filming of numerous movies, TV shows, and commercials, from an episode of *Mr. Ed* to the CGI-loaded *Transformers*. Even some car-racing scenes from the 1966 Elvis pic *Spinout* were filmed in the parking lot. And on game days, there's never a shortage of celebrities at the ballpark—in fact, star-watching in the stands has become almost as important as watching the baseball stars on the field.

With all the glitz and glamour, it's not surprising that the current ownership is planning to add two outdoor pavilions filled with shops, restaurants, a Dodgers museum, and other diversions that, as the *Los Angeles Times* put it, "undermine—in the most tasteful possible way, of course—how quickly fans can get from their cars to their seats." Still, Dodger Stadium remains a model of how to build a modern stadium that depends neither on nostalgia nor on multifunctional utilitarian design. When it opened at the end of the stadium era, Dodger Stadium was one of the best places in all the land to watch a ballgame. Half a century later, the venue, now the third-oldest park in the major leagues, still is.

TIMELINE: DODGER STADIUM

1963 A stellar pitching staff, led by lefty legend Sandy Koufax and Don Drysdale, helps the Dodgers sweep the Yankees in four games to win their first World Series championship on the left coast.

1966 Sandy Koufax and Don Drysdale re-sign their contracts after negotiating jointly through an agent, an almost unprecedented move. Each nearly doubles his salary, with Koufax receiving $130,000 and Drysdale $115,000 for one year.

1962

A capacity crowd of more than 52,000 attends the opening game at Dodger Stadium between the Dodgers and Reds on April 10. A week later, only 18,000 see the Los Angeles Angels make their own home debut at the stadium. The park is a pitcher's paradise, with lots of foul territory and dimensions of 330 feet down the lines, 380 to the the power alleys, and 410 to center.

1965

The Angels, who have changed their name from the Los Angeles Angels to California Angels, host their final game at Dodger Stadium—which they call "Chavez Ravine" in order to spite the Dodgers—on September 22.

September 9, 1965

Two Teams, One Hit In the greatest day for pitchers in Dodger Stadium history, Sandy Koufax and Chicago's Bob Hendley allow just one hit between them. The game's only run scores in the fifth when Dodger Lou Johnson walks, is sacrificed to second, steals third, and scampers home on a wild throw by catcher Chris Krug. Johnson later doubles in the seventh to break up the double no-hit bid. Koufax fans fourteen, including the last six batters of the game. The dominating lefty turns in the eighth perfect game in history, and his fourth no-hitter in as many years.

Dodgers 1, Cubs 0

ABOVE: The "Big D," Don Drysdale, delivers a pitch during Game 4 of the 1965 World Series at Dodger Stadium. Drysdale will strike out eleven on the way to a 7-2 victory over the Twins, tying the Series at two games apiece. LA will win the Series in seven games.

October 24, 1972 Trailblazing Dodger Jackie Robinson suffers a fatal heart attack at age fifty-three; he is buried in Cypress Hills Cemetery in his adopted hometown of Brooklyn.

1974 Slugger Steve Garvey, one-fourth of the Dodgers' "fabulous four" infield, nabs the NL MVP with a .312 average, 21 homers, 200 hits, and 111 RBIs.

1977 and 1978 In his first two seasons as manager, Tommy Lasorda leads the Dodgers to back-to-back pennant wins. However, LA ends up losing to the New York Yankees in both World Series.

October 6, 1966

Sandy's Last Stand Sandy Koufax is not as sharp as usual in Game 2 of the World Series, losing to the Orioles on a four-hitter by Jim Palmer. It's the first of three straight shutouts by the Baltimore staff on their way to a stunning Series sweep. Although none of the 55,947 fans in the stands realize it, this is the final game Koufax will ever pitch. Just thirty years old, he will retire in November because of an arthritic left elbow, prematurely ending one of the greatest pitching careers in history. The numbers in his final season include twenty-seven wins, twenty-seven complete games, a 1.73 ERA, and 317 strikeouts in 323 innings—all of which lead the major leagues.

Orioles 6, Dodgers 0

1969

Home plate is moved 10 feet closer to the outfield, reducing the dimensions all the way around (except down the foul lines).

1973

The height of the main outfield fence is reduced from 10 feet to 8 feet. However, the fences down the foul lines will remain less than 4 feet high throughout the stadium's history.

BELOW: Sandy Koufax, the immortal lefty, pitches in the first inning of Game 2 of the 1966 World Series against Baltimore. During what will be his last game, the soon-to-retire star is tagged for six hits and four runs in six innings, as the Dodgers are shut out by twenty-year-old Jim Palmer on the way to being swept by the underdog Birds in the Fall Classic.

September 22, 1974

Marshall's Plan: 100 Games Pitched Mike Marshall becomes the only major league pitcher to hit triple digits in games pitched in one season. The Dodgers' iron man reliever hurls one inning to get a win over San Diego (no save). For the year, Marshall will toss a record 208⅓ innings out of the bullpen and become the first reliever ever to win the Cy Young Award.

Dodgers 6, Padres 5

CAP: 1970.

June 8, 1968

Big D's Streak Snapped Don Drysdale allows his first run in nearly a month, snapping his major league–record scoreless streak at 58 consecutive innings. Phillies pinch hitter Howard Bedell drives in the run with a sacrifice fly in the fifth inning, spoiling Drysdale's bid for a seventh consecutive shutout. It will be the only RBI of the season for Bedell. Drysdale's streak had nearly ended two starts earlier when he plunked San Francisco's Dick Dietz with the bases loaded, but the umpire ruled that Dietz had not attempted to avoid the pitch as required by the rules. Given a reprieve, Drysdale retired Dietz and went on to break Walter Johnson's record of fifty-five consecutive scoreless innings. Drysdale's record, widely considered unbreakable, will stand for only twenty years, until it is broken by fellow Dodger Orel Hershiser in 1988.

Dodgers 5, Phillies 3

1981 Fernando Valenzuela's killer screwball and dynamic pitching jump-start "Fernandomania" in Los Angeles, and the hurler finishes the season with Rookie of the Year and Cy Young awards—the first player to win both in the same season.

1985 The Dodgers win the NL West for the second time in three years, but lose to the Cardinals in six games in the first year of the expanded National League Championship Series.

1978
The Dodgers become the first team to draw 3 million fans in a season.

1980
The Dodgers install the first Diamond Vision full-color scoreboard in the major leagues.

1983
The distance to the power alleys is increased to 385 feet, but dead-center field stays at 400 (even though the 400 marking is removed from the fence).

1984
Baseball is played as a demonstration sport for the 1984 Olympics, and Dodger Stadium plays host for future Dodgers ace Ramon Martinez, who takes the mound for the Dominican Republic.

April 25, 1976

Monday Saves the Flag Cubs outfielder Rick Monday becomes a national hero when he runs in and snatches an American flag away from two fans who are attempting to burn it in protest on the outfield grass. Monday's fourth-inning rescue makes him a symbol of patriotism in this bicentennial year. The next day, the Illinois State Legislature decrees that May 4—a Tuesday, alas—will be Rick Monday Day in the state. Monday will later become a star with the Dodgers.

Dodgers 5, Cubs 4

ABOVE: Rick Monday grabs a lighter-fluid-soaked American flag from two protesters who ran onto the field at Dodger Stadium during the April 25, 1976, game against the Cubs.

BELOW: On a fall day in Southern California, the Yankees take on the Dodgers in the 1978 World Series. LA wins the first two games at home before losing the next four in a row to the Bombers.

October 25, 1981

Reuss Rolls Over Yankees The Dodgers catch comeback fever, having rallied from deficits to defeat the Astros and Expos in the first two rounds of playoffs, and carrying that momentum into the World Series against the hated Yankees. With the Series even at two games apiece, New York lefty Ron Guidry holds the Dodgers scoreless until the seventh inning of Game 5. But Pedro Guerrero and Steve Yeager hit consecutive homers to give Los Angeles a 2-1 lead, and Jerry Reuss goes the distance on the mound to give the Dodgers the Series edge. Back in New York, they'll win the championship in Game 6, thanks to the efforts of the only tri-MVPs in Series history: Guerrero, Yeager, and Ron Cey.

Dodgers 2, Yankees 1

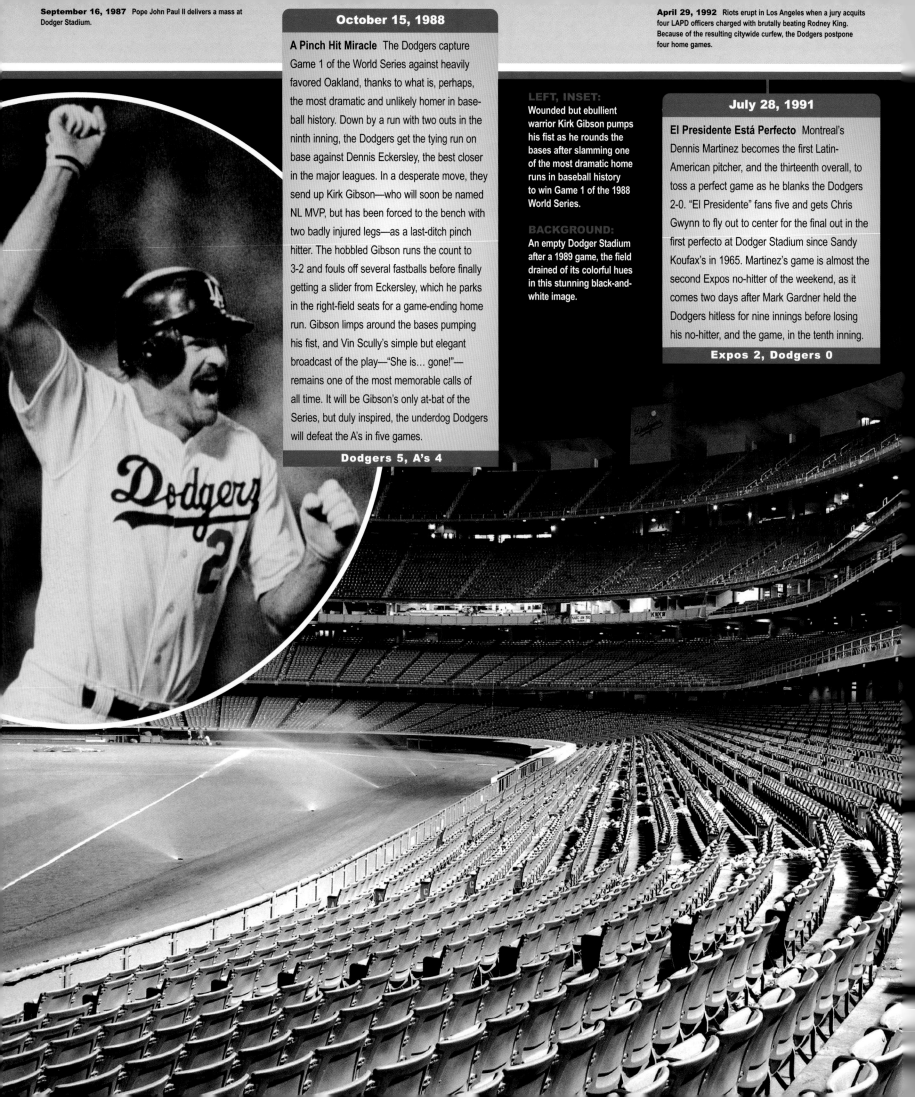

September 16, 1987 Pope John Paul II delivers a mass at Dodger Stadium.

October 15, 1988

A Pinch Hit Miracle The Dodgers capture Game 1 of the World Series against heavily favored Oakland, thanks to what is, perhaps, the most dramatic and unlikely homer in baseball history. Down by a run with two outs in the ninth inning, the Dodgers get the tying run on base against Dennis Eckersley, the best closer in the major leagues. In a desperate move, they send up Kirk Gibson—who will soon be named NL MVP, but has been forced to the bench with two badly injured legs—as a last-ditch pinch hitter. The hobbled Gibson runs the count to 3-2 and fouls off several fastballs before finally getting a slider from Eckersley, which he parks in the right-field seats for a game-ending home run. Gibson limps around the bases pumping his fist, and Vin Scully's simple but elegant broadcast of the play—"She is… gone!"—remains one of the most memorable calls of all time. It will be Gibson's only at-bat of the Series, but duly inspired, the underdog Dodgers will defeat the A's in five games.

Dodgers 5, A's 4

LEFT, INSET: Wounded but ebullient warrior Kirk Gibson pumps his fist as he rounds the bases after slamming one of the most dramatic home runs in baseball history to win Game 1 of the 1988 World Series.

BACKGROUND: An empty Dodger Stadium after a 1989 game, the field drained of its colorful hues in this stunning black-and-white image.

April 29, 1992 Riots erupt in Los Angeles when a jury acquits four LAPD officers charged with brutally beating Rodney King. Because of the resulting citywide curfew, the Dodgers postpone four home games.

July 28, 1991

El Presidente Está Perfecto Montreal's Dennis Martinez becomes the first Latin-American pitcher, and the thirteenth overall, to toss a perfect game as he blanks the Dodgers 2-0. "El Presidente" fans five and gets Chris Gwynn to fly out to center for the final out in the first perfecto at Dodger Stadium since Sandy Koufax's in 1965. Martinez's game is almost the second Expos no-hitter of the weekend, as it comes two days after Mark Gardner held the Dodgers hitless for nine innings before losing his no-hitter, and the game, in the tenth inning.

Expos 2, Dodgers 0

August 10, 1995

Dodgers Thrown Out, Balls Thrown In In the ugliest fan-related incident in Dodger Stadium history, the Cardinals are awarded a victory by forfeit over the Dodgers on Ball Day. All day long, home plate umpire Jim Quick repeatedly makes what the Dodgers view as highly questionable ball and strike calls. Finally, in the bottom of the ninth, both Eric Karros and Raul Mondesi are ejected for arguing balls and strikes with Quick, and manager Tommy Lasorda soon follows. An angry faction of the 53,361 on hand—many drawn by the free baseballs and the fact that rookie sensation Hideo Nomo is pitching—litter the field with more than 200 souvenir balls. After a ball whizzes dangerously near the head of Cardinals outfielder Brian Jordan, the umps order St. Louis, ahead 2-1, off the field and hand the Cardinals the first major league forfeit since the disastrous 1979 Disco Demolition Night at Comiskey Park.

Cardinals 9, Dodgers 0 (forfeit)

November 6, 1996 Outfielder Todd Hollandsworth is voted NL Rookie of the Year with a .291 batting average, twelve home runs, and fifty-nine RBIs. He is the fifth consecutive Dodger to earn the title.

April 12, 1999 A game at Dodger Stadium is rained out for the first time in eleven years and 856 games.

1995

A state-of-the-art playing surface, a grass called Prescription Athletic Turf, is installed. It is the first change to the playing field since the park's opening.

July 5, 2004

Gagne Finally Blows One Eric Gagne's amazing streak of eighty-four consecutive saves—thirty more than the previous record held by Tom Gordon—finally comes to an end against Arizona. With one out in the ninth and the Dodgers leading 5-4, Arizona's Chad Tracy drives in the tying run with a grounder barely out of the reach of defensively challenged first baseman Olmedo Saenz. Gagne nonetheless gets a standing ovation from the home fans for his remarkable streak, which has lasted nearly two years, since August 28, 2002. During that time, the tying run reached third base against Gagne only once. His numbers during the streak include 43 hits and 141 strikeouts in 87⅔ innings pitched, with a 0.82 ERA. The Dodgers come back to win the game in ten innings anyway, 6-5.

Dodgers 6, Diamondbacks 5

April 23, 1999

Tatis' Taters Fernando Tatis' major league career will never amount to much, but he memorably etches his name in the record book during the second inning of this Cardinals rout. The St. Louis third baseman becomes the only player ever to hit two grand slams in one inning—and even more remarkably, both come off the same pitcher, the beleaguered Chan Ho Park. Tatis' first slam erases Park's 2-0 lead, and the second one sends him to the showers, down 11-2.

Cardinals 12, Dodgers 5

Dodgers reliever Eric Gagne hurls two hitless and scoreless innings against the Astros at Dodger Stadium on July 10, 2004. Just five days earlier, Gagne had ended his mind-boggling streak of eighty-four consecutive saves when the Diamondbacks beat out the Dodgers 6-5 in Los Angeles.

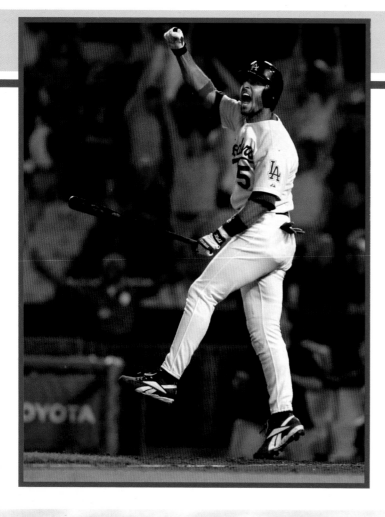

2001 Dodgers right fielder Shawn Green slugs forty-nine homers and eighty-four extra-base hits—both club records.

January 29, 2004 Real estate mogul Frank McCourt purchases a controlling interest in the team from Fox Entertainment Group and Robert Daly. His wife, Jamie, will become vice chairman and president; his son, Drew, will run the marketing department.

2006

The Dodgers replace nearly all the seats in the stadium and add a new section of luxury box seats directly behind home plate, which dramatically reduces foul territory. The color of the seats is changed from royal blue back to the original light pastel colors used when the stadium first opened. The existing baseline boxes are remodeled to feature small counters for a retro box seat effect.

September 18, 2006

4+1=First Place The greatest regular season game ever played at Dodger Stadium is an epic contest between two teams battling for the NL West title. The Dodgers erase an early four-run deficit against Padres ace Jake Peavy, but then proceed to give the lead back, and Los Angeles trails 9-5 entering the bottom of the ninth. Jeff Kent leads off with a home run and JD Drew follows suit, after which the Padres bring in legendary closer Trevor Hoffman to slam the door. But the first batter against Hoffman, Russell Martin, also homers. So does the next batter, Marlon Anderson, who raises his arms in triumph as he watches his game-tying blast leave the yard. It is only the fourth time in history a team has hit four consecutive homers, and the first time it's been done in the ninth inning to tie a game. The pesky Padres retake the lead in the top of the tenth, but in the bottom of the inning, Nomar Garciaparra launches a two-run walk-off homer to cap off the Dodgers' third dramatic comeback of the evening. The legendary "4+1" victory leapfrogs the Dodgers over the Padres into first place.

Dodgers 11, Padres 10

2008

Dodgers owner Frank McCourt announces plans for a $500 million makeover to the park and its surrounding area, which will include restaurants, shops, and a Dodgers museum all encased in a tree-lined promenade outside the park. The Los Angeles City Council approves a resolution to rename the area "Dodgertown" and give it its very own zip code.

ABOVE: Nomar Garciaparra roars in triumph after hitting a two-run walk-off homer in the tenth inning to defeat the Padres on September 18, 2006. LA had tied the game in the ninth on four consecutive round-trippers. The win put the Dodgers in first place in the NL West, a half game ahead of San Diego.

BACKGROUND: Taken from above the stadium parking lot, this photo offers a view of downtown LA on the Dodgers' Opening Day 2006, just after the extensive renovations carried out that year. The marriage of the transplanted Dodgers with their beautiful Elysian Fields stadium has been the most successful in baseball history, much like the Bronx Bombers and Yankee Stadium.

Manny Ramirez runs the basepaths at Dodger Stadium during Game 3 of the NLCS against Philadelphia. Ramirez goes 1-for-2 on the day, with two walks, two runs, and an RBI in LA's 7-2 victory. The Phillies, however, will have the last laugh: They'll end up taking the series in five games, even though Manny bats .533 with two homers and seven RBIs.

Buy Me Some Peanuts and Bobblehead Dolls

When the Brooklyn Dodgers migrated to Los Angeles in 1958, the team inadvertently brought to baseball a new multibillion-dollar marketing and sales bonanza. Where once a baseball "souvenir" meant a cap, a badge, or maybe a small pennant, the wild world of baseball marketing was about to explode with all types of memorabilia, from posters and cigarette lighters to T-shirts and the soon-to-be-ubiquitous bobblehead dolls, thanks largely to longtime concessionaire Danny Goodman.

Goodman had been involved with ballpark concessions since the age of thirteen, when he quit school to sell hot dogs and soda pop at Milwaukee's Borchert Field. By the time the Dodgers arrived in LA, Goodman had already built up an audience for baseball in Los Angeles with his infectious enthusiasm and innovative ideas. At the age of twenty-five, he was the king of California concessions, managing them at every California- and Pioneer-League park in the minors and working as concessions manager and advertising director for the Pacific Coast League's Hollywood Stars. The jovial promoter organized baseball-themed testimonial dinners, bringing his showbiz pals (Jack Benny, Ronald Reagan, and Dean Martin among them) out to salute the game's heroes. He also set up free clinics at the Stars' Gilmore Field, where youngsters got tips from the players, loaded up on soda and hot dogs, and—most importantly—got into the habit of visiting the ballpark. When the newly relocated major league team needed someone to pioneer their advertising and concessions operations, Goodman was the obvious choice.

As vice president and director of advertising and promotion for the Dodgers, Goodman brought the team's souvenir operation in-house, and was savvy enough to realize—and capitalize on the fact—that local fans would buy almost anything featuring the Dodgers' logo: caps, straw hats, pen and pencil sets, "autographed" baseballs (long-rumored to have been forged), jackets, posters, glossy yearbooks, antenna balls, and just about any item that could be monogrammed. The team did gangbusters at the souvenir tables at the gargantuan LA Coliseum, and Dodger Stadium was designed to accommodate more than a dozen souvenir stands. If you wanted a Dodgers bugle, a Duke Snider doll, or a record of Vin Scully calling the last inning of Sandy Koufax's perfect game, Goodman had it in stock at the park. He also carried the *Sporting News*, the daily papers, camera film, and lots of food. In addition, a mail-order business sold novelties to Dodgers fans worldwide.

Eventually, other professional sports leagues began to notice the extra revenue pouring into the Dodgers' coffers and realized that they too could virtually print money by licensing their teams' logos to various manufacturers—thus giving rise to the sports apparel business.

At the time of Goodman's death in June 1983, he was still on the job, as the Dodgers' director of advertising, novelties, and souvenirs. More than 500 people attended his funeral, confirming his status as a giant in the development of sports marketing, and the man that modern marketing execs should thank for his vision, hustle, and shameless desire to peddle *anything*.

RIGHT: Never one to pass up an opportunity to make a sale, concessionaire extraordinaire Danny Goodman sold recordings of Dodgers broadcaster Vin Scully calling Sandy Koufax's perfect game long after it happened.

Danny Goodman
Concessions
Dodger Stadium

Side 1

33⅓ RPM

Last Inning Sandy Koufax
Perfect Game
Actual Reproduction as narrated by Vince Scully

CHAPTER FOUR
Superstadiums
1961 — 1991

It is no coincidence that the first of baseball's infamous cookie-cutter ballparks, DC Stadium (later renamed RFK Stadium), was constructed largely with Washington's NFL team in mind. The exploding popularity of the nation's newer, more violent pastime in the 1960s created a demand for larger pro football stadiums, and in many cases the local baseball team piggybacked its way to a new home. In such cities as San Diego, Pittsburgh, and Cincinnati, among many others, a series of nearly identical multipurpose stadiums sprang up. Characterized by circular concrete shapes, artificial turf, massive seating capacities, poor sight lines, and dreary aesthetics, these superstadiums collectively represent the most regrettable era in the history of ballparks.

Constructed mostly between 1961 and 1971, the cookie-cutter parks "rank among the more dreadful examples of late-modernist American architecture," *New York Times* architecture critic Christopher Hawthorne wrote. "Though these postwar stadiums, mostly charmless concrete bowls surrounded by oceans of parking-lot asphalt, were never beloved by fans of any sport, they were particularly ill-suited for baseball. Modernist architecture is about symmetry, contemporaneity, and the idea of universal solutions; its marriage with baseball, easily the most idiosyncratic and traditional of sports, was doomed from the start."

Modernist architecture—an international trend that exploded in the 1920s and became the nation's predominant style in the post–World War II era—was largely concerned with simplification of design and rejection of ornamentation. Modernists believed that function was infinitely more important than form. "Modernism claimed to have supplied a definitive answer to the question of beauty in architecture: the point of a house was not to be beautiful but to function well," wrote Alain de Botton in *The Architecture of Happiness*. "Yet…we are in the end unlikely to respect a structure that does no more than keep us dry and warm. Of almost any building, we ask not only that it do a certain thing but also that it look a certain way, that it contribute to a given mood.… We may hope that it will connect us to the past or stand as a symbol of the future."

This was exactly where the superstadiums went wrong: They neither connected baseball fans to the past nor pointed toward the future. In their eagerness to achieve the ultimate utilitarian goal—the ability to be employed for baseball, football, and pretty much anything else—architects, team executives, and public officials shunted aside all concerns about the response that such bleak aesthetics might elicit in fans. Perhaps it is coincidence, but it happens that the period from the mid-1970s through the mid-1980s—the time when multipurpose stadiums were at their most ubiquitous—was an era of nearly unprecedented brawling, drunkenness, and general unpleasantness at ballparks. "Between 1977 and 1983 I never went to a major league game at which I was not seated next to a loud, obnoxious drunk," historian and stat guru Bill James once wrote. "I went to very, very few games in that era at which there was not a fight that broke out somewhere in the vicinity of my seat.…There were frequent incidents of fans throwing things at players, pouring beer on players. Drunken fans would run onto the field." Is it possible that de Botton's thesis—that a building's architecture greatly influences the happiness, or lack thereof, of its inhabitants—helps explain this era of lawlessness and unrest in the stands? It seems far-fetched, but one wonders.

The parks built during the superstadium era were best known for the massive amount of cash that could be earned by herding people into them. To that end, owners sought to make costly rainouts a thing of the past with enclosed stadiums, beginning with the Astrodome in 1965. Though enclosed parks further shut off fans from their surroundings, they did allow stadiums to be built in locations where it otherwise might be too hot, cold, or rainy to be financially viable. But they came with a learning curve. Some teams, like the Montreal Expos, never quite got their retractable roof working properly, while the Astros quickly discovered that it was impossible to grow grass inside their "Eighth Wonder of the World," even if it did have a plethora of windows. The latter issue led to the use of AstroTurf, which soon became a defining feature of superstadiums whether they had roofs or not.

With the bowl shapes and drab concrete exteriors of the cookie-cutter ballparks, few could distinguish one from another. Even on the playing field itself, predictability and homogeneity were the hallmarks. "I stand at the plate in Philadelphia," slugger Richie Hebner once said, "and I don't honestly know whether I'm in Pittsburgh, Cincinnati, St. Louis, or Philly. They all look alike." Symmetrical dimensions made outfield play less a carefully learned skill, and more an exercise in pure athleticism. This, along with the synthetic grass, spurred a sea change in the way the game was played. Balls bounced much faster, much higher, and much truer than on real grass, which led to the reemergence of speed as a vital element of baseball. Base hits reached gaps faster, which meant faster outfielders were necessary. Grounders reached infielders faster, which meant faster baserunners were necessary. Eight of the top nine individual stolen base seasons in modern history were achieved in cookie-cutter parks between the years 1974 and 1987. Though artificial turf was widely viewed as an abomination, the exciting style of play it engendered could not be denied. "The new stadiums defined a new brand of baseball," James wrote. "And a great brand of baseball it was. Don't get me wrong: I have nothing good to say about artificial turf. But the baseball of the 1970s, which was derived in part from the artificial turf that was then so popular, was a wonderful brand of baseball....It was a game that put the full athletic ability of the players on display in a way that was very satisfying, very exciting. Attendance boomed."

By 1982, seventeen of the twenty-six major league teams were playing in what were essentially football stadiums. Ten played on fake grass. Four played in cavernous domes. Soon after the last of these stadiums was built, fans began to notice a curious thing. These concrete donuts, for all the architectural lip service paid to their modern utilitarianism, were not much good for watching baseball. The round shape, combined with a playing surface large enough to accommodate the gridiron, invariably resulted in a massive amount of wasted foul territory. Fans accustomed to the cozy environs of the golden age ballparks found themselves sitting much farther away from the action than ever before. Attendance numbers swung wildly. These parks, with capacities far greater than those of their predecessors, packed in the fans for marquee games. But at less desirable contests, the atmosphere resembled that of a giant circular morgue. For instance, one 1973 Astros-Padres game drew 1,413 fans—a number even most minor league teams would scoff at—to 45,000-seat San Diego Stadium. Team executives knew something had to change, but nobody was quite sure what that was until April 6, 1992. That afternoon Baltimore unveiled its glorious new retro ballpark, Oriole Park at Camden Yards, and the cookie-cutter stadiums were soon consigned to their well-deserved place in the dustbin of history.

BELOW: The newly minted Washington Nationals play their first game in what was once known as DC Stadium on April 14, 2005. Renamed RFK Memorial Stadium in 1969, the multipurpose facility housed the Washington Senators from 1962 to 1971, and was used for football, soccer, and concerts after that team moved to Texas. When the Nationals came to town, they spent their first three years in the aging stadium while their beautiful new retro ballpark was being built.

RFK MEMORIAL STADIUM

Washington, DC

Senators (AL) 1962–1971, Nationals (NL) 2005–2007

District of Columbia Stadium (1961–1968)

An austere structure that sheltered two eternally moribund teams, RFK Stadium is remarkable mostly for being the earliest example of baseball's most unfortunate architectural trend: the "concrete donut." Opened in 1961, it was the first stadium built for both baseball and football, a money-saving innovation that soon spread to St. Louis, Cleveland, Cincinnati, and other major league cities. Like most of these multipurpose superstadiums, RFK was better suited to the odd dimensions of football, and its two baseball teams used it for only as long as it took them to find more inviting homes. The expansion Washington Senators played here for a decade before escaping to the greener pastures of Texas, while the Washington Nationals used it as a temporary home for three years after moving from Montreal. In its thirteen years as a major league facility, RFK housed only one winning team, and even that club, the 1969 Senators, managed only to finish fourth.

In the 1950s, Major League Baseball, which had not seen a franchise relocate since 1915, suddenly abounded with teams moving to new cities. Boston, St. Louis, Philadelphia, Brooklyn, and Harlem all lost teams, and DC officials were determined to keep their team in town with a new alternative to crumbling Griffith Stadium. Though Washington Senators owner Calvin Griffith refused to agree to move into the proposed stadium, a $6 million budget for the new edifice was approved. (Appropriately for the nation's capital, the budget would eventually mushroom to $21 million, with the final tab totaling $22.7 million.) But while the stadium got mired in delays due to bidding and construction, Griffith finally got the OK from the American League to leave town anyway, and moved his club to Minnesota, renaming it the Twins.

With the sport booming economically, however, the AL and NL decided, for the first time ever, to create new teams from scratch. With the brand-new ballpark already underway, the AL awarded an expansion franchise to Washington. This team would also be called the Senators, and would begin play in 1961, picking up where its predecessor had left off. While the old Senators would go on to spend much of the 1960s contending for pennants in Minnesota, the new version would become the weakest franchise in the league.

TED WILLIAMS
Manager

SENATORS

SENATORS

HOWIE KOPLITZ   pitcher

FRED VALENTINE

OUTFIELD
SENATORS

From the start, District of Columbia Stadium—the first and only ballpark owned by the federal government—was intended to be a thoroughly modern, jet-age structure suitable for both baseball and football. Movable stands placed on rollers allowed the seats to be repositioned between baseball and football games, albeit at a steep cost of $40,000 per transfiguration. A hydraulic lift even allowed the pitcher's mound to be raised and lowered. The design of the circular stadium was so complicated, however, that construction wasn't completed until several months after Opening Day, forcing the Senators to use shabby old Griffith for their 1961 games.

DC Stadium finally opened for business on October 1, 1961, when the Washington Redskins hosted the New York Giants. Six months later, the new Senators moved in, although their fans found the new ballpark hardly worth the wait. The park featured a "formal, pretentious, martial, classically antiseptic, and cold style," which gave the impression that it had been "designed by Stalin," wrote baseball historian Philip Lowry. Indeed, the personal and intimate atmosphere that fans had come to expect from major league ballparks was shattered by DC Stadium, where fans were so far away from the action that the players looked like ants from most seats. Because of the space needed for football, the regular grandstand seats were much farther away from the diamond than fans were used to, and since the ground-level space behind the outfield fence was used for storage, there was no lower deck of bleachers ringing the field.

In January 1969, DC Stadium was renamed Robert F. Kennedy Memorial Stadium after the promising young senator who had been assassinated the previous summer. In 1962, Kennedy, as US attorney general, had forced the Redskins to integrate their football team or risk losing their lease at the federally owned stadium. The stadium's baseball tenants never faced any such problems, but neither did they field competitive teams. The Senators lost more than a hundred games in each of their first three years in the stadium,

and even during its inaugural season of 1962 the park drew a paltry average of 9,122 fans per game. Despite the presence of such memorable characters as prodigious slugger Frank Howard and celebrity manager Ted Williams, the Senators never topped a million in attendance during their tenure at RFK.

A healthy crowd of 14,460 did show up, however, for the Senators' final game in Washington before they moved to Texas in 1972. Unfortunately, most attended in order to express their outrage regarding the team's departure toward Bob Short, the wealthy, well-connected owner who seemed to spend lavishly on everything in his life except his baseball team. The crowd threw confetti and debris from the stands, and a fan-made banner reading "Short Stinks" was unfurled from the left-field balcony until it was removed by stadium personnel to a chorus of boos. Feeling uneasy about the fans' demeanor even though they had a rare lead of 7-5, the Senators emptied out their bullpen, and finally, with two outs in the ninth, a torrent of spectators ran onto the field, forcing the umpires to declare a forfeit in favor of the Yankees. The near-victory turned into a loss that seemed a perfectly appropriate ending for the stumblebum Senators franchise. The next year, they would move into Arlington Stadium and become the Texas Rangers.

Although it wouldn't house a baseball team for the next thirty years, RFK stayed as busy as ever. The Redskins continued to call it home until 1996, and a legendary 1973 concert featuring the Grateful Dead, the Band, and the Allman Brothers drew an estimated 100,000 fans—almost triple the number that the Beatles had attracted to the stadium in 1966. In the late 1990s, RFK developed a reputation as one of the nation's premier soccer venues. In addition to serving as home field for the best-known American soccer club, DC United, it also hosted the 1994 World Cup and 1996 Summer Olympics soccer matches.

Baseball finally returned to the nation's capital in 2005, when the Washington Nationals, nee Montreal Expos, came to town. A franchise so destitute that it had been purchased collectively by the other twenty-nine teams when no suitable buyer could be found, the Nationals surprisingly played .500 ball during their inaugural season under popular manager Frank Robinson. Just as importantly, they were successful at the box office, drawing about three times more fans than the Senators had before skipping town. Instead of the barren, empty feeling of the 1960s, the stadium's atmosphere during the twenty-first century was positively electric at times. When it was full, fans could feel the stands noticeably swaying back and forth, an eerie artifact of the grandstand's hollow (but safe) construction. Baseball's return to RFK was only temporary, however, as the Nats' move to DC had been contingent upon the construction of a new $611 million stadium on the banks of the Anacostia River. The Nats moved into their palatial new home in 2008, leaving creaking old RFK to continue shaking and swaying to the gyrations of soccer fans.

April 15, 1964 Construction begins on Turnpike Stadium in Arlington, Texas, which will eventually become the home of the Senators franchise in 1972.

December 4, 1964 Slugger Frank Howard, who will become the best player in Senators history, is acquired from the Dodgers for pitcher Claude Osteen.

April 10, 1967 Lyndon Johnson throws his third and final ceremonial first pitch at RFK. The Senators lose 8-0, and have now lost LBJ's three games by a combined score of 19-2.

1962

The Senators play the first major league game at District of Columbia Stadium on April 9. The majors' first circular baseball stadium measures 335 feet down the lines, 385 to the power alleys, and 410 to center.

1968

The power alleys are shrunk slightly to 381 feet in left-center and 378 in right-center.

July 10, 1962

Maury Steals the Show MLB holds two annual All-Star Games for the fourth and final time, and this year's first contest is awarded to DC Stadium. A crowd of 45,480, including President John F. Kennedy, watches the NL win thanks to the baserunning exploits of the Dodgers' Maury Wills, a DC native. Wills doesn't even enter the game until the sixth inning, but he dominates on the bases, stealing a bag, going from first to third on a hard single to left, and scoring two of his team's three runs. Wills wins the first-ever All-Star Game MVP; after the season he will also add the NL MVP to his trophy case. The losing pitcher is Camilo Pascual, who began his career as a Washington Senator before moving with the club to Minnesota in 1961. Dick Donovan, who threw the first pitch in the history of the expansion Senators, pitches two innings as a representative of Cleveland. The only Senators All-Star, Dave Stenhouse, does not play.

NL 3, AL 1

June 12, 1967

A Twenty-Two Inning Marathon It's an extremely long Monday for the White Sox and Senators, who battle through twenty-two innings over six hours and thirty-eight minutes before the home team finally pulls out a win. The game ends at 2:43 a.m., prompting the league to adopt a curfew stating that no inning may begin after 1:00 a.m. The White Sox take a lead in the tenth, but the Senators match it in the bottom of the inning on a Ken McMullen single, two wild pitches, and a sacrifice fly. Paul Casanova, who catches all twenty-two innings for Washington, finally ends it with a bases-loaded single, sending home what few fans remain from the original crowd of just 7,236. Bob Humphreys pitches three scoreless innings and gets the win over John Buzhardt, who throws eight innings of one-run relief for Chicago.

Senators 6, White Sox 5

PEOPLES DRUG STORES
THE PRESCRIPTION STORES

ABOVE: John F. Kennedy throws out the first pitch at DC Stadium (which would later be renamed for his brother Robert) before the All-Star Game on July 10, 1962. At Kennedy's left is baseball commissioner Ford Frick and at his right is Hubert Humphrey, then the director of the president's Food for Peace program.

CAP: 1970.

FAR RIGHT: There weren't many smiles during Ted Williams' tenure as Senators manager. He was named AL Manager of the Year in his 1969 debut season, but lost more than ninety games in each of the following two years. He was finally fired in 1972 after losing one hundred games during the franchise's first season in Texas.

December 3, 1968 The Senators are purchased by Bob Short, treasurer of the Democratic National Committee.

1969 The Senators' Dick Bosman wins the AL ERA title with a 2.19 mark.

1970 After enjoying the first winning season in team history in 1969, the Senators collapse to a 70-92 mark.

1969

The park is renamed Robert F. Kennedy Stadium in honor of the slain senator and presidential candidate.

October 1, 1969

A Fantastic Finish The expansion Senators sweep the season's final series from the Red Sox to finish up their most successful campaign in Washington with an 86-76 mark. Senators pitcher Joe Coleman takes only one hour, forty-seven minutes to dispatch the Sox, holding them hitless after the fourth inning. Carl Yastrzemski hits his fortieth homer of the season in the top of the first, but Washington's Mike Epstein upstages Yaz with a three-run dinger, his thirtieth of the year, in the bottom of the inning. Rookie skipper Ted Williams will be named AL Manager of the Year for his startling turnaround of the moribund Senators, who enjoy impressive seasons by Dick Bosman (the AL ERA champ at 2.19) and slugger Frank Howard (who finishes fourth in MVP voting).

Senators 3, Red Sox 2

1971

The expansion Senators, who have been playing in Washington since 1961, move to Texas and become the Rangers.

BELOW: As his family looks on, sixteen-year-old Joseph Kennedy speaks at the 1969 dedication ceremony during which DC Stadium is renamed after his late father, Robert F. Kennedy.

September 30, 1971

Loved Not Wisely, But Too Well With the Senators having announced that they'll move to Texas after the season, the last American League game in Washington ends in an ugly forfeit. The Senators take a 7-5 lead in the eighth on a pinch-hit single by Tom McCraw—the last hit ever by a Washington Senator—and a sacrifice fly by Elliott Maddox. Joe Grzenda throws the final pitch in Senators history, but never gets to finish the game. With Washington just one out away from a memorable victory, many of the 14,460 fans storm onto the field and begin picking it apart for souvenirs. With the home team unable to restore order on its own field, the umpires declare the Yankees winners by forfeit. Although the statistics count, no winning or losing pitcher is assigned, robbing southpaw Paul Lindblad of the distinction of being the last man ever to win a game for the Senators. Grzenda, for his part, will finally get to make another pitch for Washington thirty-four years later, when he throws out the ceremonial first ball at the home opener of the newly relocated Nationals.

Yankees 9, Senators 0 (forfeit)

LEFT: Upper-deck fans unfurl a banner directed at Senators owner Robert Short during the team's infamous final game at RFK in 1971. The game will be forfeited to the Yankees with the Senators just one out away from a victory, due to rowdy fans rushing the field. "When first base was lifted and carried away, you could tell it was all over," reported the *Washington Post.* "No one on the field cared."

1971 Jim Bouton's controversial tell-all *Ball Four* is published. In addition to exposing the behind-the-scenes bad behavior of the major leagues, he recounts his first big-league win—a shutout against the Senators.

June 19, 1994 RFK hosts its first World Cup game. Norway defeats Mexico 1-0.

August 3, 2002 RFK hosts its first Major League Soccer All-Star Game. DC United's own Marco Etcheverry is named game MVP.

1982

More than a decade after the last Senators game was played here, RFK hosts the first annual Cracker Jack Old-Timers Baseball Classic. The AL beats the NL 7-2, thanks largely to a shocking home run by seventy-five-year-old Luke Appling off Warren Spahn. The event will be held three more times at the stadium, through 1985.

1996

The Redskins, winners of three Super Bowls in thirty-six seasons at RFK, play their final game here on December 21. They will move into Jack Kent Cooke Stadium, later known as FedEx Field.

2005

Washington gets an MLB team after going without for thirty-three years, but RFK's dimensions are essentially the same as before: 336 feet down the lines, 380 to the power alleys, and 410 to center, making it an extremely pitcher-friendly park.

2008

The Nationals leave RFK for brand-new Nationals Park; RFK Stadium remains in use for the DC United soccer team and special events.

April 14, 2005

Third Time's the Charm A crowd of 45,596 witnesses baseball's return to the nation's capital, as the Washington Nationals—known for the prior thirty-six seasons as the Montreal Expos—play their first home opener at RFK Stadium. President George W. Bush renews the tradition of having the commander in chief throw out the first pitch on Opening Day in Washington. The first two runs are brought across on a fourth-inning triple by Washington third baseman Vinny Castilla. The Nats defeat another recently born team, the Arizona Diamondbacks, as pitcher Livan Hernandez outduels ex-Expo Javier Vazquez. It is the first big-league game played at RFK in more than 12,000 days, and Washington is the first city in modern times to be given three chances to support a major league team.

Nationals 5, Diamondbacks 3

ABOVE: Three different seats in RFK Stadium's upper deck were painted white to mark the landing spots of three long homers by Frank "Hondo" Howard, the greatest hitter in team history.

RIGHT: Nationals lefty John Halama throws a pitch against the Cardinals during the team's debut season in 2005.

ABOVE: Alfonso Soriano celebrates on September 16, 2006, by uprooting second base after becoming the fourth player in major league history to reach forty homers and forty steals in the same season. Soriano's jersey is sent to the Hall of Fame, but 2006 turns out to be his only season in a Nats uniform. He signs an eight-year, $136 million deal with the Cubs after the season.

SHEA STADIUM

Queens, New York

Mets (NL) 1964–2008, Yankees (AL) 1974–1975

OPPOSITE: The Mets take on their biggest rivals, the Phillies, in a 2003 day game at Shea Stadium. With left-handed slugger Jim Thome at the plate, the Mets are deploying an unusual shift in which three infielders play to the right of second base. Note the airplane above the centerfield flagpole; it is about to land at nearby LaGuardia Airport. A signature of Shea Stadium over the years was the constant stream of takeoffs and landings from the airport, which in 2007 serviced about 25 million passengers. Although the airplane noise was sometimes a distraction for the players on the field, pilots and their passengers loved to peek into Shea from above, and there was even a special route—called the "expressway visual approach" among aviation professionals—which allowed for the best view of the playing field. "We make a sweeping turn around Shea Stadium to land, and you bank the airplane and out of the corner of your eye you can see the scoreboard and the players," American Airlines pilot Joe Romanko told the *New York Times* in 2008. Also note the evidence that this picture was taken after September 11, 2001: in the faux New York skyline atop the scoreboard, a memorial ribbon has been placed where the World Trade Center once stood.

Few ballparks have squeezed as much action into so short a lifetime as Shea Stadium. In its four-and-a-half decades the giant ballpark in Flushing hosted a World's Fair, a mass given by Pope John Paul II, and concerts by the Beatles, The Rolling Stones, and Bruce Springsteen. As for baseball, Shea housed the best of teams (the 1986 Mets), the worst of teams (the mid-1960s Mets), and everything in between. Most memorably, it was the backdrop that defined the 1969 Mets, perhaps the most lovable and unlikely World Series champions of all time.

After New York City lost two-thirds of its major league teams when the Giants and Dodgers moved west in 1958, it didn't take long to get one back. Almost immediately, Mayor Robert Wagner, who was up for re-election, appointed corporate lawyer Bill Shea to head a commission charged with returning the National League to New York. When attempts to lure the Phillies, Reds, and Pirates to the Big Apple failed, Shea turned his attention to a wild new scheme. Along with legendary executive Branch Rickey, Shea and other businessmen formed the Continental League, a new major league that planned to debut in 1961 with one of its franchises located in New York. Frightened at the prospect of losing their monopoly over the national pastime, MLB owners quickly moved to co-opt the new league. As part of the resulting agreement, New York was awarded an expansion franchise to begin play in the National League in 1962.

As the Mets played two miserable years at Harlem's old Polo Grounds, city officials set about building their new home: a grand $25.2 million structure in the Flushing Meadows section of Queens. (The same site had earlier been offered to, and rejected by, Brooklyn Dodgers owner Walter O'Malley in an effort to keep that team in New York.) Located on Flushing Bay just east of LaGuardia Airport, Flushing Meadows was the site of a marsh and garbage dump before being converted into parkland for the 1939–40 World's Fair. As it happened, the ballpark's opening would coincide with another World's Fair, the 1964 version, also held in Flushing Meadows. In gratitude for his efforts in bringing the Senior Circuit back to New York, city officials named the new ballpark after Shea.

Although superficially resembling Dodger Stadium, Shea was outfitted with hydraulically movable stands so its co-tenants, the New York Jets of the American Football League, could also play there. "It's a beautiful stadium, well planned, a fine place to play baseball," said Pittsburgh manager Danny Murtaugh, whose Pirates beat the Mets in Shea's inaugural game. "I like everything about it." In an effort to differentiate themselves from the buttoned-down Yankees, the Mets made a conscious effort to imbue the ballpark experience with sound and color. A large scoreboard in right field featured a faux New York City skyline. In center field, a big apple would emerge from a top hat and light up whenever a Met homered. The circus atmosphere was augmented by brightly colored plastic seats, which were yellow at field level, beige in the loge, white in the club level, blue in the mezzanine, and green in the upper deck. Even the Mets' uniforms were a colorful mishmash of New York's baseball past, borrowing blue from the Dodgers, orange from the Giants, and pinstripes from the Yankees.

The fan-friendly effort worked, as the Mets outdrew the Yankees in each of the first twelve years of Shea's existence, even though the Yankees were a winning team and the Mets were usually awful. From the beginning, it was clear that Shea would draw an entirely different species of fan from Yankee Stadium. Mets fans were younger, wilder, and louder. They didn't mind the deafening roar of jets landing on nearby runways, which quickly became a signature of the park. Willing to root for a team full of lovable losers, the fans filled the stands with colorful banners and homemade signs saluting their heroes, another Shea signature which eventually spread to other sporting venues across the nation.

On a few famous occasions, though, Mets fans went too far. When New York defeated Pittsburgh to clinch the 1973 pennant, a mob rushed the field, ripped up the turf, and made off with the bases, turning the playing surface into a wasteland that required groundskeepers to work around the clock to repair it in time for the World Series. Thirteen years later, as the Mets prepared to clinch their next division title, memories of the ugly 1973 scene still lingered. "I hope they don't tear down our park," first baseman Keith Hernandez said, "because we've got to play in it." When the Mets won the division-clinching game on September 17, 1986, thousands of fans nonetheless rushed the field in defiance of the hundreds of extra security guards hired for the occasion. "They sang and danced and yelled for more than half an hour," the *New York Times* reported, "and gouged huge chunks of the playing field."

After being treated as a second-class franchise by the Yankees for much of their existence, the Mets must have relished the irony in 1974 when the Bronx Bombers came begging, hat in hand. A massive renovation of Yankee Stadium was going to leave the pinstripers in need of a temporary home for two years, so they moved in as tenants of the Mets. The Yanks soon found that their left-handed sluggers were powerless away from the short right-field porch of The House That Ruth Built. Their best hitter,

Bobby Murcer, managed just two homers at Shea after hitting nineteen the previous year at Yankee Stadium. In 1975, the final year of the Yankees' residency, Shea served as home to no fewer than four major league franchises: the Mets, Yankees, Jets (who'd played there since 1964), and the New York Football Giants, who moved in while their new stadium in New Jersey's Meadowlands was being constructed. Although scheduling four pro teams in one stadium was difficult, it proved possible because of a clearly defined pecking order. The Mets, the main tenants, got first priority, followed by the Yankees, then the Jets, the permanent football tenants. The Giants got whatever dates were left over, and were forced to play two of their home games on Saturdays instead of Sundays.

The Giants and Yankees moved out in 1976, followed by the Jets in 1984, leaving the Mets as Shea's sole occupants. By 2007 the stadium, once the shining jewel of Queens, had become an oft-criticized relic with outdated facilities. A new stadium, Citi Field, was constructed in Shea's parking lot with the team moving in in 2009. Though the new field was designed to be a luxurious modern update of Ebbets Field, as fans prepared for the Mets' move they couldn't help but be nostalgic. After all, Shea Stadium had been synonymous with Mets baseball for most of the team's existence—for better or for worse.

INSET: No baseball stadium was ever as intimately tied to homemade banners as Shea Stadium. Rarely seen in baseball until the birth of the Mets, banners became popular during the team's infancy at the Polo Grounds and really began to take off after the move to Shea. Here, Jack Moses, Steven Blumhof, Alfred Grab, and Ronald Einziger pose with their winning banner at Shea's first "Banner Day," in 1964. Wilbur Huckle, despite never making it out of the minor leagues, was a fan favorite at Shea, if only because of his delightful name.

"Banner Day" at Shea

Now a staple of any baseball game, homemade signs were not always commonplace. But at Mets games, it's long been a custom for fans to show affection for their lovable losers by bringing homemade signs and banners to the park. When the tradition began, during the Mets' miserable first two years at the Polo Grounds, most teams didn't approve of such antics—in fact, the crosstown Yankees forbade banners altogether. But the Mets saw fan participation as a sign of loyalty—and a selling point. Beginning in 1964, their first year at Shea, the Mets hosted an annual "Banner Day." Fans with homemade signs were allowed to march around the warning track, with others cheering or booing the best and worst signs.

Through the early 1990s, the Mets held the event between games of a scheduled Sunday doubleheader. But with the death of the twinbill, the Banner Day walk was moved to precede a weekend afternoon contest. Messages ranged from simple—"Go Mets!"—to more clever—"I'd Bet My Testes On the Metsies"—and were scrawled on all types of materials.

The players would often judge the best sign. Mets reliever Tug McGraw recalled to ESPN that he judged the contest during his rookie season: "Before the game, Ed Kranepool comes up and says, 'Hey, McGraw, you're a lucky guy....We voted you to be the judge for Banner Day.' I said, 'Really? Hey, that's great.' Two hours later—when I was still sitting in the dugout and there were 200 or 300 banners still to come—I realized it wasn't such a great honor. But I remember that my first year, I picked the winning banner: 'To Error is Human. To Forgive Is a Mets Fan.' How could you ever forget that one?"

As the Mets fumbled, the signs got even less complimentary, with the *New York Times* citing the highlights from 1993's Banner Day: "It's Lonely at the Bottom," and "I Made This Banner Just to Get on the Field." Soon thereafter, Banner Day quietly disappeared, but memories of the fun event remain with Mets fans, far sweeter than the memories of the legendary Shea Stadium potato knish.

CAP: 1971.

LEFT: The Mets take on the Montreal Expos in a July 2, 2003, game, which they will lose 11-4. Pitching for New York is Pedro Feliciano; batting for Montreal is Endy Chavez, who will strand the runners by striking out with the bases loaded. The large baserunner on first is Expos pitcher Livan Hernandez, who has just laid down a bunt single.

1964 Famed mascot Mr. Met, a humanoid figure with a baseball for a head, debuts at Shea.

August 15, 1965 The Beatles play at Shea Stadium, ushering in the era of stadium rock. The landmark event draws 55,000, at that time the most people to ever see a single rock concert.

1964

Shea Stadium opens as the Pirates visit on April 16. The original dimensions of the symmetrical park are 341 feet down the lines, 371 to the power alleys, and 410 to center, with a capacity of 56,000. The Mets host their only All-Star Game this season, and the New York Jets also make their debut at Shea, which they will call home through 1983.

July 9, 1969

Tom is Terrific Tom Seaver comes as close as a Mets pitcher ever has to throwing a no-hitter, retiring the first twenty-five Cubs before rookie Jimmy Qualls singles to left. Seaver then retires the last two Cubs to complete the first of five one-hitters he'll pitch in his Mets career. He won't get his no-hitter until 1978, when he'll be wearing a Cincinnati Reds uniform. The Mets, meanwhile, will still be searching for their first no-hitter nearly four decades later. The game itself is crucial in establishing the Mets as legitimate contenders, as the former laughingstock franchise moves within 3½ games of first place.

Mets 4, Cubs 0

October 16, 1969

A Miraculous Finish The Mets complete their miracle season by overcoming a 3-0 deficit to win Game 5 of the World Series against Baltimore. In the sixth, New York skipper Gil Hodges gains his team a key baserunner when he proves a pitch hit Cleon Jones in the foot by pointing out a shoe polish stain on the baseball. Donn Clendenon follows with a home run, then light-hitting infielder Al Weis ties it with a homer in the next inning. After Ron Swoboda drives in the go-ahead run, southpaw Jerry Koosman holds off Baltimore in the last few innings to complete what may be the most unlikely world championship in history.

Mets 5, Orioles 3

RIGHT: Emergency lights flood the stadium on July 13, 1977, after a blackout has swept across the city. Lenny Randle was up at bat and the Chicago Cubs were beating the Mets 2-1 at the bottom of the sixth inning when the stadium went dark at 9:34 p.m. Power will be restored to the city twenty-four hours later, but the game won't finish until September 16 when the Cubs will win 5-2.

June 21, 1964

A Perfect Holiday In the first game of a Father's Day doubleheader, Jim Bunning tosses the first perfect game in the major leagues since 1922 and the first in the National League since 1880, mowing down the Mets in their new stadium before a crowd of 32,026. New York will finally get its first hit of the day in the third inning of the nightcap, a single by Joe Christopher off Rick Wise in an 8-2 Philadelphia win.

Phillies 6, Mets 0

The Phillies' Jim Bunning delivers the final pitch of his perfect game against the Mets on Father's Day 1964. Pinch hitter John Stephenson is about to strike out.

December 10, 1971 The Mets make their most lamented trade, sending wild young pitcher Nolan Ryan and three others to the Angels for shortstop Jim Fregosi.

May 31, 1977 Joe Torre makes his major league managerial debut and in the process becomes the first player-manager in Mets history.

September 20, 1973

Willie Says Goodbye On the day that beloved Mets outfielder Willie Mays announces his retirement, his team makes a move toward first place. With the game tied in the thirteenth, Pittsburgh's Dave Augustine blasts a ball to left with a man on first. Mets left fielder Cleon Jones turns to look as the ball hits the top of the wall, but instead of bouncing over the fence as physics would seem to dictate, it caroms to Jones, who throws to Wayne Garrett, who fires to rookie Ron Hodges, who tags out stunned baserunner Richie Zisk. Hodges then singles in the winning run for the Mets in the bottom of the inning. New York, which was in last place at the end of August, will take over first the next night and eventually take the NL pennant with just eighty-two wins.

Mets 4, Pirates 3

1974

Due to reconstruction at Yankee Stadium, the Yankees play the first of two years at Shea.

1975

Shea Stadium is now home to the Mets, Yankees, Giants, and Jets. The four teams play a total of 173 games this year at Shea.

1978

The fence is extended to each foul line to make it easier for umpires to judge home runs, reducing the distance by 3 feet.

ABOVE, LEFT: Jerry Koosman embraces Jerry Grote after the 1969 Mets win perhaps the least likely world championship of all time.

BELOW: Left-hander Jerry Koosman poses in 1968, his first full major league season, during which he wins nineteen games for the Mets. Koosman will go on to win 140 games as a Met, more than anyone besides Tom Seaver or Dwight Gooden.

June 3, 1980 With the first overall pick in the Amateur Draft, the Mets select Los Angeles high school outfielder Darryl Strawberry.

June 15, 1983 The Mets trade Neil Allen and Rick Ownbey to St. Louis for former NL MVP Keith Hernandez.

1980

The unique orange-and-blue steel panels are removed from the stadium exterior and the first annual catchphrase—"The Magic Is Back"—appears outside the stadium. A picnic area in left field is also added by new owners Nelson Doubleday and Fred Wilpon.

1981

An enormous top hat is installed in center field. A "big apple" emerges from it every time a Met hits a home run.

1982

A 35-by-26-foot Diamond Vision screen is installed in left-center field.

April 5, 1983

Back and Better Than Ever The exile is over, as prodigal son Tom Seaver returns to the Mets after an ill-advised trade to Cincinnati nearly six years earlier. As a crowd of 46,687 roars its approval, Tom Terrific opens the season by striking out Pete Rose. Seaver throws six shutout innings, but rookie Doug Sisk gets the win in relief when Mets right fielder Mike Howard breaks the scoreless tie with a single in what will be his final major league at-bat.

Mets 2, Phillies 0

1983

Tom Seaver

OFFICIAL SCORE BOOK

Mets '85 SCHEDULE

BACKGROUND: Shea Stadium on July 25, 2007. For fans with enough cash, the Shea Stadium experience often included illicit access to prime seating. Ushers in the sections of box seats around home plate were known to solicit tips of $20 to $50, in exchange for which they would guide fans to the empty seats of season-ticket holders who likely would not be in attendance that day.

October 25, 1986

The Curse Continues In the game that Shea will be most remembered for, Red Sox fans watch their hopes for a long-awaited world championship slip through Bill Buckner's legs in Game 6 of the World Series. With Boston just six outs away from its first title since 1918, manager John McNamara pinch-hits for ace Roger Clemens in the top of the eighth. Clemens' replacement, Calvin Schiraldi, proceeds to give up the tying run in the bottom of the inning. Boston scores twice in the tenth to retake the lead, but the Mets threaten again in the bottom of the frame. Gary Carter, Kevin Mitchell, and Ray Knight all hit singles before Boston reliever Bob Stanley throws a wild pitch that ties the game. Stanley induces a harmless grounder from Mookie Wilson, but the ball skips through the legs of the gimpy Buckner, allowing Knight to score the winning run. The Mets will rout the Sox in Game 7 to wrap up their second world title.

Mets 6, Red Sox 5

May 22, 1998 The Mets acquire Mike Piazza in a memorable trade, sending Preston Wilson and two minor league pitchers to the Marlins.

June 26, 1998 For the first time ever, the Yankees play at Shea Stadium as the visiting team. They defeat the Mets in an interleague battle, 8-4.

1992

Outfield distances are changed for the last time, as the alleys are deepened by 7 feet.

1998

Due to crumbling concrete at Yankee Stadium, both the Mets and Yankees host games at Shea on April 15, the first time two leagues have played games in the same stadium on the same day. Both New York teams win.

October 17, 1999

Grand Slam Single The Mets and Braves stage a fifteen-inning NLCS marathon that has the sweeping highs and lows of a TV miniseries. New York scores twice in the first inning of Game 5 on John Olerud's home run, but doesn't score again for another thirteen frames. The Braves, who can capture the pennant with a victory, tie things in the fourth but are then held scoreless by seven subsequent Mets pitchers. Atlanta squanders countless opportunities, leaving nineteen runners on base and getting a runner gunned down at home plate to end the thirteenth. The Braves finally break through in the fifteenth, scoring on Keith Lockhart's triple off rookie pitcher Octavio Dotel. The Mets rally in the bottom of the inning, though, tying the game on a bases-loaded walk issued by Atlanta hurler Kevin McGlinchy. As rain continues to fall in the game's fifth hour, New York's Robin Ventura blasts a pitch over the fence for what appears to be a walk-off grand slam. Mobbed by his teammates, Ventura never finishes running around the bases, and his hit is officially downgraded to a game-winning single. The Braves, despite the deflating loss, will win the pennant in Game 6.

Mets 4, Braves 3

ABOVE: One of the most joyous moments in Mets history: Ray Knight scores to win Game 6 of the 1986 World Series.

RIGHT: In the second-to-last game of the 2008 season, Carlos Delgado keeps his eye on the ball after hitting a sacrifice fly to drive in a run against the Marlins.

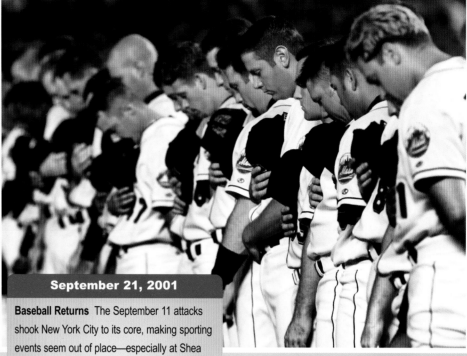

2000

Two extra rows of seats on the field that were added during the 1999 playoffs become permanent.

October 8, 2000

Can't Keep Up With Jones A day after Benny Agbayani won Game 3 of the Division Series with a thirteenth-inning home run, Robin Ventura kicks off Game 4 with a two-run homer in the first inning. That's all Bobby Jones needs, as the Mets hurler pitches a one-hit shutout marred only by a fifth-inning Jeff Kent double. Jones also issues two walks in that inning, but escapes trouble by retiring Giants pitcher Mark Gardner with the bases loaded. There are only three Giants baserunners for the day, and Jones' masterpiece propels the Mets to the NLCS, where they take the Cardinals in five games, setting up a memorable Subway Series against the Yankees.

Mets 4, Giants 0

September 21, 2001

Baseball Returns The September 11 attacks shook New York City to its core, making sporting events seem out of place—especially at Shea Stadium, which was used as a staging area for rescue workers. After a ten-day layoff, the Mets host the first outdoor sporting event in the city since the catastrophe. After some early struggles the Mets have moved themselves back into the NL East race, but that's far from most people's minds this night. Mike Piazza, who has always possessed a flair for the dramatic, hits a two-run homer in the eighth inning to bring New York back from behind and offer some small measure of enjoyment to the city's grieving residents.

Mets 3, Braves 2

ABOVE: The Mets observe a moment of silence on September 21, 2001, at the first game played in New York after the September 11th attacks.

CAP: 2000.

BACKGROUND: Shea Stadium's exterior, which was remodeled in 1980 to make it more colorful.

September 30, 2007

Glavine Hooked by Marlins The Mets, who have had a death grip on first place throughout most of the season, complete a spectacular September collapse by losing the final game of the year, which allows Philadelphia to capture the NL East title. Just seventeen games earlier the Mets held a commanding seven-game lead, but after today's loss they'll go home empty-handed. New York starter Tom Glavine wastes no time in blowing the game, retiring only one batter as the Marlins bat around and score seven times in the first inning.

Marlins 8, Mets 1

July 2008 Billy Joel plays two star-studded concerts at the stadium. The second closes with special guest Paul McCartney, who first played at Shea in 1965 during the height of Beatlemania.

BACKGROUND: Left-hander Johan Santana throws a pitch in 2008, the year after he was acquired by the Mets in one of the biggest trades in franchise history.

2008

The Mets play their last game at Shea. They will head to Citi Field, which is being constructed next door.

September 28, 2008

A Sad Farewell For the second straight year, the Marlins, who have already been eliminated, knock the Mets from postseason contention on the final day of the season. Just as with the last game of the year in 2007, all the Mets have to do is beat the Marlins to force a one-game playoff. That point is moot when the Marlins use back-to-back home runs by Wes Helms and Dan Uggla—the last round-tripper at Shea Stadium forty-four years after Willie Stargell hit the first—to break a seventh-inning tie. Matt Lindstrom retires Ryan Church for the final out of both the season and in the history of Shea. A parade of dozens of former Mets greats takes the field after the game. As the climax of a poignant, bittersweet ceremony, each player touches home plate for the last time. The greatest Met, Tom Seaver, throws a final pitch to Mike Piazza and they exit through the centerfield gates. Shea goodbye, forever.

Marlins 4, Mets 2

TOP LEFT: Citi Field (foreground), constructed just beyond Shea's centerfield fence, opened in 2009.

BOTTOM LEFT: José Reyes, the Mets' dynamic shortstop, runs the bases in 2007.

ATLANTA–FULTON COUNTY STADIUM

Atlanta, Georgia

Braves (NL) 1966–1996

Atlanta Stadium 1965–1976

When it opened, Atlanta Stadium, at just over a thousand feet above sea level, had the highest elevation of any major league park. Known as "The Launching Pad" thanks to the fly balls that flew over its fences with alarming frequency, the batter's park fueled the late-career renaissance of Hank Aaron, who broke Babe Ruth's career home run record here in 1974. The home of the first big league team in the Deep South, the stadium would later be the backdrop to some of the more outlandish antics of a celebrity owner, and, beginning only a few years before its destruction, house a dynastic pitching staff described by historian Bill James as "probably the best in the history of baseball."

Before Hank Aaron and the Braves came to town, Atlanta had never had major league sports. In the 1960s, the city was continuing to be one of the most rapidly growing urban areas in the South, developing a mass transit system and new public facilities. One of these public facilities was Atlanta Stadium, an $18 million structure built just south of downtown to lure both a major league baseball team and a football team. In 1965, the city was awarded an NFL expansion franchise, the Atlanta Falcons, and an MLB team, the Braves, who had been playing in Milwaukee since 1953, but whose ancestry can be traced back to the 1869 Cincinnati Red Stockings, baseball's first ever pro team. The Braves—now the first ever pro team in the South—christened Atlanta Stadium with a 1965 spring-training game against the Tigers. A year later, after a bitter court battle with the Wisconsin government, they moved in for good.

Like most parks of its era, Atlanta Stadium was drab and unrepresentative of its locale—once inside, you could be Anywhere, USA. Similar parks existed or would soon exist in San Diego, Pittsburgh, Philadelphia, Cincinnati, Washington, St. Louis, and Oakland. Unlike the ones in those cities, though, Atlanta's at least had the benefit of real grass (albeit poorly maintained grass—the notoriously bumpy field didn't get a full-time groundskeeper until 1989). The seating bowl fit nearly 60,000 spectators for football and about 8,000 fewer for baseball, almost all of whom were far from the action. Still, in the first few years of the stadium, fans came in droves to see the Braves, more for the novelty of the experience than the quality of the team.

Atlantans finally had something to cheer about in 1969, when the team won the NL West title with a roster that featured Aaron, Orlando Cepeda, Felipe Alou, and knuckle-baller extraordinaire Phil Niekro. Aaron in particular seemed to love Atlanta Stadium, and in return was beloved by its denizens. After spending the first twelve years of his career in Milwaukee's County Stadium, a hitter's graveyard, Aaron now found himself playing in a park that actually inflated offense instead of depressing it. Though Aaron arrived in Atlanta at an age when most hitters begin to decline precipitously (thirty-two), he managed to average thirty-nine homers per year in his first eight seasons at Atlanta Stadium. On April 8, 1974, he provided the ballpark's greatest moment when he knocked his record-breaking 715th homer into the left-field bullpen. Even Aaron's heroics, however, couldn't bring fans out to watch a losing team. In 1973, when Aaron spent all year chasing Ruth's record, the Braves nonetheless averaged just 9,885 fans per game.

By 1976 Aaron was gone, and the most familiar face at Atlanta–Fulton County Stadium (as it was renamed that year) became the Braves' new owner, TV mogul Ted Turner. Turner, who buddied up to players and fans alike, quickly became famous for his off-the-wall promotional stunts, from wet T-shirt contests to an ostrich race featuring none other than Turner himself riding one of the birds. After deciding jerseys should display his players' nicknames, he outfitted number 17 Andy Messersmith with a jersey featuring the word "channel"—thereby turning him into a walking billboard for Turner's Channel 17, which broadcasted Braves games nationally. In 1977, he even named himself field manager, lasting one game before baseball officials barred him from the position.

Turner's goofiness served to draw attention away from the product on the field, where the Braves had become the laughingstock of baseball, finishing last eight times in fifteen years. The Braves also became the target of increased criticism from Native Americans, who took exception to the stereotypical caricatures and gibberish-filled cheers employed at the ballpark. In 1986, Turner eliminated Chief Noc-a-Homa, the headdress-wearing mascot located on a platform above left field who would whoop and dance around his tepee whenever

the Braves homered. But even into the 1990s the fans—including Turner's super-progressive wife, Jane Fonda—performed the ludicrous "Tomahawk Chop," a phony war chant accompanied by hand motions, which the Braves had usurped from the Florida State University Seminoles.

After finishing in last place yet again in 1990, Atlanta made a remarkable turnaround in 1991, becoming the first team ever (along with the Minnesota Twins) to go from last place one year to the World Series the next. Thanks to the sure hand of manager Bobby Cox and a superb farm system overseen by general manager John Schuerholz, the Braves appeared in fourteen consecutive postseasons, a period of sustained success unprecedented in baseball history. The dynasty was led by three top-shelf pitchers who defied the hitter-friendly characteristics of their home park: Greg Maddux, Tom Glavine, and John Smoltz, each of whom won at least one Cy Young Award during Atlanta's remarkable run. Their winning ways brought the fans back to the ballpark. After never before averaging more than 27,000 fans per game, the Braves surpassed 35,000 each year from 1992 to 1996, the last five years of the park's existence. After the 1996 Summer Olympics ended in Atlanta, the Braves converted the new Centennial Olympic Stadium, located next to Fulton County Stadium, into a baseball park. Soon after hosting its final event, Game 5 of the World Series, Fulton County Stadium was demolished and turned into a parking lot for the new field. Though gone, the park is not entirely forgotten— brick paths in the asphalt denote the base and foul lines, with plaques showing where the bases once sat. A portion of the outfield fence and left-field bullpen still exist, with a giant baseball-shaped plaque baldly listing the event that made the stadium famous: "HANK AARON HOME RUN / 715 / April 8, 1974."

April 12, 1966 Brave Eddie Mathews makes his Atlanta debut, making him the first player in modern history to play with the same franchise in three different cities.

April 8, 1974

July 25, 1972 Atlanta Stadium hosts its only All-Star Game. The NL defeats the AL 4-3, with help from Hank Aaron's two-run homer off Gaylord Perry in the sixth.

1966

On April 12, the Braves play their first regular-season game in Atlanta Stadium, becoming the first major league team south of Washington DC. With their home field at nearly a thousand feet above sea level, the Braves also become the team with the highest elevation. Batted balls carry well in the 325-385-402 dimensions, leading fans to nickname the park "The Launching Pad." The NFL's Falcons will play the first game in their history here on September 10.

1967

The distance to the outfield corners is pushed back to 330 feet. Chief Noc-a-Homa's tepee is built, giving a new home to the team's Native American–caricature mascot. The tepee stands on a 20-foot-high platform behind the left-field fence. It will move around over the years, but will be removed in 1982 to squeeze in more seats, although subsequent losing streaks will lead to its brief return.

Hammerin' Hank Makes History After months of media hoopla, death threats, hate mail, and debate over his record's legitimacy, Hank Aaron finally hits the home run that vaults him over Babe Ruth as baseball's career leader. Aaron's 715th homer comes off the Dodgers' Al Downing, and is caught in the Atlanta bullpen behind the left-field fence by Braves reliever Tom House. A few fans run onto the field to accompany Aaron around the bases, and a Monday night national TV audience watches as teammates serenade him in an eleven-minute celebration on the field. Although Aaron professed his desire to set the record in Atlanta, Commissioner Bowie Kuhn ordered him to play at least twice in the opening series in Cincinnati, where he homered once to tie Ruth's mark. The Babe's record lasted fifty-three years (since 1921); Aaron's will last thirty-three years until Barry Bonds breaks it in 2007 amid a cloud of steroids-related controversy. A permanent marker will be placed on the spot where Aaron's 715th landed in the bullpen.

Braves 7, Dodgers 4

BELOW, INSET: Hank Aaron is congratulated by Tom House, the relief pitcher who caught Aaron's 715th homer when the ball sailed over the left-field fence into the Braves' bullpen.

BOTTOM: Aaron batting on April 4, 1974, the day he ties Babe Ruth's record with his 714th career homer at Cincinnati's Riverfront Stadium. Aaron will break the record four days later at his home stadium.

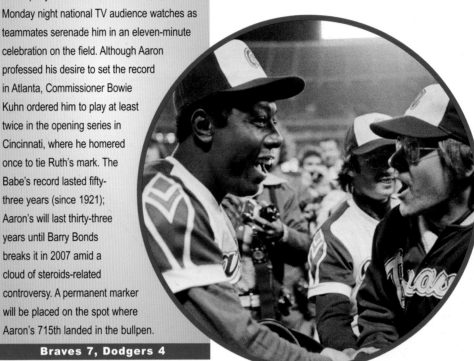

OPPOSITE, BACKGROUND: Atlanta Stadium was built about two miles southwest of Ebenezer Baptist Church, where the Rev. Martin Luther King Sr. served as pastor and where funeral services were held for King's murdered son in 1968. The stadium's site was selected in part because it was located between downtown and the mostly black Summerhill district; city leaders wanted the ballpark to serve as a buffer between downtown businesses and the impoverished neighborhood. The Braves made a point of using their African-American stars, including Hank Aaron, to establish goodwill with Summerhill residents during 1966, the team's first season in Atlanta. However, residents were still angry at local government for demolishing housing to build the stadium, among other things, and riots broke out on September 6 when a white policeman shot a fleeing Summerhill resident.

May 11, 1977 Exasperated owner Ted Turner names himself Braves manager. He lasts one game, a 2-1 loss, before being banished from the dugout by Commissioner Bowie Kuhn.

1983 Dale Murphy becomes the first Brave to win back-to-back NL MVP awards.

July 6, 1986 Braves first baseman Bob Horner ties a major league record by hitting four home runs in a game at the aptly nicknamed "Launching Pad."

1976

Ted Turner purchases the team, and the stadium's name is changed to Atlanta–Fulton County Stadium.

1983

The outfield fence is raised from six feet to ten feet high as Plexiglas now tops the wire fence.

CAPS: 1974, 1983, 1987.

BELOW: While Game 1 of the 1982 NLCS in St. Louis is delayed by rain, Braves manager Joe Torre passes the time puffing on a stogie in the visitors' bullpen. The Braves will fall to the Cardinals in a three-game sweep.

July 4, 1985

Fireworks Night Appropriately, the most bizarre game in Atlanta–Fulton County Stadium history comes on Fireworks Night, as the Braves and Mets play nineteen innings and combine for twenty-nine runs, forty-six hits, twenty-two walks, five errors, and thirty-seven men left on base. The game is delayed twice by rain, and neither starter lasts past the fourth inning, marking the shortest outing of the year for eventual NL Cy Young winner Dwight Gooden. Though only a few of the original 44,947 fans are still left after the six-hour-and-ten-minute-long game, the Braves nonetheless keep their promise to shoot off fireworks. The 4:00 a.m. blasts awaken nearby residents, some of whom initially fear that the city is under attack.

Mets 16, Braves 13

1991

The Falcons play their final outdoor game in Atlanta on December 15. They'll move into the new Georgia Dome in 1992.

October 5, 1991

From Last to First The Braves, who were 9½ games behind at the All-Star break, beat the Astros to clinch at least a tie for the NL West title. While the Braves celebrate their own win, the scoreboard shows that the Giants have just shut out the Dodgers to give the Braves their first division title since 1982. John Smoltz goes all the way as Atlanta wins its eighth straight game. The Braves' ninety-four wins are their most since their 1957 world championship season in Milwaukee. Atlanta will go on to battle the Minnesota Twins in the World Series; they'll be the first two teams in baseball history to play in the Series after finishing in last place the previous season.

Braves 5, Astros 2

October 14, 1992

Orlando's Magic Hit For the second straight season a Braves-Pirates NLCS comes down to the seventh game, and this time it ends on one of the most dramatic and unlikely hits in baseball history. In the bottom of the ninth with two outs, the Pirates still lead by a run, but the Braves have the bases loaded for pinch hitter Francisco Cabrera, a third-string catcher who has batted just ten times all year. Remarkably, Cabrera singles to shallow left. The tying run scores easily from third, and the plodding Sid Bream chugs around from second in an attempt to score the winning run. Barry Bonds' weak throw arrives a split second too late, and Bream slides safely below the tag with the pennant-winning run. The Pirates, soon to lose Bonds and Drabek to free agency, will still be searching for their next winning season sixteen years later.

Braves 3, Pirates 2

September 11, 1991 The Braves throw the first combined no-hitter in NL history, split amongst newbies Kent Mercker (six innings) and Mark Wohlers (two), and closer Alejandro Peña.

1993

During batting practice before the Braves' July 20 game, a fire erupts in a luxury suite adjacent to the press box when a Sterno heat canister used for catering is left unattended and sets the suite's curtains ablaze. After firefighters put out the flames by running hoses from the parking lot through the concourses on golf carts, the game goes on, delayed by ninety minutes—and with a portion of the stands sectioned off for the press.

October 3, 1993

103 is Not Enough The Braves complete a 51-17 second half and emerge the winners of what is perhaps baseball's most exciting pennant race since the start of divisional play. After acquiring slugging first baseman Fred McGriff in a midseason trade with the Padres, Atlanta overcomes a ten-game deficit in the NL West to pull even with the San Francisco Giants. Tom Glavine's twenty-second win of the year helps the Braves complete a season sweep of the expansion Rockies. It's the Braves' 104th win of the year, but they must still wait for the outcome of the Giants-Dodgers game before they can celebrate. Out west, rookie Mike Piazza leads the Dodgers in a 12-1 pounding of Giants starter Salomon Torres, which gives the Braves their fifth and final NL West crown. Atlanta will move to the NL East in 1994, and the Giants' 103 wins will remain the most for a second-place team in the divisional play era.

Braves 5, Rockies 3

October 28, 1995

Justice For All Tom Glavine pitches the Braves to the title in Game 6 of the World Series, making them the first Atlanta team to capture a major professional sports championship—and the first baseball franchise to win the World Series in three different cities. Glavine allows only one hit in eight masterful innings, and David Justice's home run off Jim Poole stands up as the only run of the game. Mark Wohlers relieves Glavine and retires the Indians in the ninth, getting Carlos Baerga to fly to center for what will be the lone championship in Atlanta's fourteen consecutive playoff appearances under Bobby Cox.

Braves 1, Indians 0

1996

The baseball portion of the Summer Olympics is held in the stadium. The final MLB game at the stadium is played on October 24, making it the first ballpark whose last game is a World Series contest.

TOP: Fire rips through Atlanta–Fulton County Stadium's press box and luxury suites before a game on July 20, 1993.

BOTTOM: Fans pack the stadium to watch the Braves take on the Indians in the 1995 World Series. This championship was the first since 1979 in which each team had the best record in its league.

ASTRODOME

Houston, Texas

Astros (NL) 1965–1999

In an era when many games were still played in the afternoon, outdoor baseball never could have worked in Houston, where the summer heat and humidity kept everyone inside—except the giant mosquitoes, which Dodgers pitcher Sandy Koufax once described as "twin-engine jobs." The Houston Colt .45s immediately realized this when they joined the majors in 1962. So while the newly minted team endured three seasons at sultry Colt Stadium, the only major league park built to be temporary, the Colts laid plans for a spectacularly innovative ballpark, which would be marketed as "The Eighth Wonder of the World." The Astrodome opened in 1965 as the first domed stadium ever built, and it rocketed the team from tenth to second in NL attendance. Over the years it became America's most prestigious sporting venue, hosting football and basketball games, rodeos, tennis matches, and even political conventions. Though it spawned many imitators and ushered in a new era of stadium architecture, the Dome grew obsolete by the late 1990s, when the Astros abandoned it to hop on the retro ballpark bandwagon.

Before the Dodgers moved to Los Angeles, owner Walter O'Malley had briefly considered building a domed stadium—designed by geodesic dome inventor Buckminster Fuller, no less—in the borough of Brooklyn. But that dream never came to pass, and it took Judge Roy Hofheinz to finally build baseball's first indoor park. Hofheinz, a flamboyant former mayor, was Houston's most visible political figure and one of its most ardent sports fans. In 1960, Hofheinz and his partner, oil mogul Craig Cullinan Jr., were awarded an expansion National League franchise (to begin play in 1962) based on the promise of delivering a new ballpark. Projected to cost $15 million and open in 1963, Harris County Domed Stadium instead ended up costing taxpayers $31.6 million and opening in 1965. Part of the delay was caused by the US Defense Department, which had originally intended to fund and build a $2 million bomb shelter underneath the massive structure, but later backed out.

The stadium was a sweetheart deal for the powerful Hofheinz, who paid the county $750,000 per year to rent the stadium, a figure that included full subleasing rights. Judge Roy even went so far as to have a luxurious apartment built for himself in the right-field stands. Over the stadium's forty-year lease Hofheinz and his company, the Houston Sports Association, would make a mint subleasing the stadium to

Colt Stadium: A Mosquito Heaven

Colt Stadium—Houston's temporary home for baseball while the gargantuan Astrodome was being constructed—wasn't Texas-sized, but it certainly had plenty of Texas heart. Christened with .45-caliber blanks rather than shovels at its ground breaking, the stadium also featured the popular Fast Draw Saloon and usherettes in bright, color-coded uniforms to guide fans to seats that matched the colors on their tickets: orange for box seats, turquoise and chartreuse in the reserved section, and flamingo pink for the bleachers. The single-tiered stadium, which featured a large playing field that was 360 feet down both foul lines and 427 in the power alleys, also had the biggest dugouts in baseball as well as a separate press box for any female reporters who happened by.

While the Astrodome was being assembled beyond the park's first base grandstand, players battled in the oppressive heat, which often reached over 100°. After almost a hundred fans had to be treated for heat stroke during a Sunday game, MLB rescinded their rule against Sunday-night games, and on June 9, 1963, a major league baseball game was played on a Sunday night for the first time. Worse than the heat were the swarms of mosquitoes that plagued fans and players alike at Colt Stadium. The pests were so bad that the field had to be sprayed by groundskeeping crews between innings and insect repellant was available at concession stands.

After 2½ years at the bug-infested park, the team played their last game as the Colt .45s on September 27, 1964, with a twelve-inning victory over the Dodgers. Only 6,246 fans—less than a fifth of the park's capacity—were in attendance. Colt Stadium was painted gray, so that it wouldn't show up in aerial photos of the team's grand new home, before it was dismantled and shipped south in the early seventies to be put to use by a Mexican League team.

BELOW: Colt Stadium, the only modern major league ballpark built specifically as a temporary structure, was the home of the Astros from 1962 to 1964, while the Astrodome was under construction next door. "I said to myself, 'These people are talking through their hats, they will never start the 1962 season here—not in this marshland,'" MLB treasurer Charley Segar told the *Houston Chronicle* after Colt Stadium opened. "I have never been so wrong in my life. The people behind this place deserve tremendous credit. This may be a temporary stadium, but I have never seen one so colorful." However, the park proved less than a hit with local fans, and the first major league game played in Houston didn't even sell out.

anyone who needed a large venue and was willing to pay for it. The cavernous park covered 9½ acres and was 208 feet tall, high enough to fit a twenty-story skyscraper inside. It featured the latest in modern conveniences, including opulent office space, cushioned seats, fifty-three luxury boxes, and a gigantic, $2 million scoreboard that entertained fans with baseball-themed cartoons. Most importantly, it was fully air-conditioned, a necessity for fans trying to escape the sweltering heat.

Meanwhile, Hofheinz's baseball team needed a futuristic name to match its futuristic stadium. Although the Colts seemed the perfect nickname for a Texas team—after all, it could refer to a horse, a gun, or a beer—the team sought to embrace Houston's newfound identity as the capital of America's space program. When the team changed ballparks in 1965, it also changed its name to the Houston Astros, leading the stadium to be informally dubbed the Astrodome.

Although the Astrodome was a huge hit, not everything was well planned. Its roof consisted of a metal framework supporting panes of translucent Lucite, which, theoretically at least, would allow light to shine through and grass to grow on the field. But from the moment the park opened, fielders complained about blinding reflections from the roof that made catching pop flies a hazardous adventure. After one year under these conditions, the Astros solved the problem by tinting the ceiling panels so that they blocked the sunlight. This not only required the team to increase the artificial lighting dramatically—sucking up as much electricity as a 9,000-person city—but also caused the Bermuda grass to shrivel and die (even more so than before). So for the 1966 season, the field was laid with a synthetic grass invented by Monsanto Industries. This fake grass soon became famously known as AstroTurf.

The stadium's gigantic dimensions, combined with the artificial lighting, served to severely depress hitting. The 390-foot power alleys, the longest in the league, were where fly balls went to die. Although the Astros of the sixties and early seventies featured such outstanding batters as Jimmy Wynn, Joe Morgan, and Cesar Cedeno, the park deflated their hitting stats and made them look less outstanding than they really were. This in turn led Astros management to underestimate the ability of its own players, and to trade many of them, including Morgan, for pennies on the dollar. For pitchers, conversely, the Astrodome was a dream come true. Larry Dierker, Houston's franchise pitcher, was a case in point. In neutral stadiums, Dierker was a mediocre hurler, posting a 50-70 lifetime record

with a 4.04 ERA. At home in the Dome, however, Dierker was an ace, going 89-53 with a 2.73 ERA. In 1969, Houston became the first major league team to have its pitching staff strike out 1,000 batters in a season. Astros pitchers also hurled six no-hitters here over the park's thirty-five years, including Nolan Ryan's record-breaking fifth in 1981.

From the very beginning Hofheinz had envisioned the Astrodome as America's premier multipurpose facility, and that is exactly what it became. In 1968, the Houston Oilers of the American Football League moved in, and would remain tenants until moving to Tennessee in 1997. From 1968 to 2003, the Dome hosted the Houston Livestock Show and Rodeo, advertised as the second-largest rodeo in the world. In 1968, it was the site for college basketball's "Game of the Century," a showdown between the first-ranked UCLA Bruins and second-ranked Houston Cougars. The first college basketball game ever to be televised nationally, it was attended by a record 52,963 fans. Most of them went home happy when the Cougars' Elvin Hayes led Houston to a 71-69 victory, snapping the epic forty-seven-game winning streak of Lew Alcindor and UCLA.

Over the years the stadium also hosted University of Houston football, the Bluebonnet Bowl football game, six concerts on Elvis Presley's comeback tour, the 1971 NCAA Final Four, professional soccer, and innumerable other events. One of these was perhaps the most famous tennis match of all time, the 1973 "Battle of the Sexes" in which Billie Jean King defeated Bobby Riggs. In 1992, the Astrodome was even the site of the Republican National Convention, during which the GOP renominated Houston resident George H.W. Bush as its presidential candidate and the Astros were forced to play twenty-six consecutive road games. In 2005, the Dome housed a decidedly less-privileged group when it became the primary destination for victims evacuated from New Orleans after Hurricane Katrina. About 25,000 evacuees lived in the Astrodome for two weeks until more permanent housing could be found.

By then, alas, the world's first domed ballpark was a relic no longer being used by any major sports team. The futuristic stadiums of the sixties had fallen out of favor as fans realized that, for all their convenience and practicality, they were sterile and drab places to watch games. The new craze was a retro style that attempted to combine the homey feel of classic ballparks with the moneymaking techniques of modern ones. The Astros moved to their new Enron Field after the 1998 season, and for a decade afterward the Astrodome stood vacant for the most part. (There were whispers about turning it into an upscale hotel.) The revolutionary stadium—which costs the county $1 million in annual maintenance—has become a white elephant, its future remaining in limbo.

September 22, 1964 Heralded pitching prospect Larry Dierker makes his major league debut on his eighteenth birthday, but loses to the Giants 7-1.

July 9, 1968 The Astrodome hosts its first All-Star Game. The NL wins 1-0 on a run scored by its first batter of the game, Willie Mays.

November 29, 1971 In the most lamented trade in Houston's franchise history, Joe Morgan, Jack Billingham, César Gerónimo, and two others are shipped to Cincinnati.

1965

Baseball takes a step forward—or backward—with the first indoor major league game on April 12. The Astrodome's field measurements are 340 feet down the lines, 375 to the power alleys, and 406 to center, but the dead air and poor lighting are killers of offense. The 45,000-seat stadium measures 208 feet from floor to roof.

RIGHT: After escaping hot, humid Colt Stadium, the Astros installed a massive air-conditioning system—another of the Dome's major league firsts. The system used six thousand tons of cooling capacity to circulate two million cubic feet of air per minute.

The speakers visible in the center of this photo hung from the ceiling at 117 feet above the playing field. The stadium's ground rules specified that any batted ball striking a speaker in fair territory was a live ball—a rule that came into play on June 10, 1974, for Philadelphia slugger Mike Schmidt. Schmidt hit a high drive that would easily have been a home run had it not hit a speaker 329 feet from home plate. The ball bounced back onto the playing field and the bewildered Schmidt was held to a single.

1966

After a year of struggling to make grass grow indoors, the Astros hire Monsanto Industries to lay down a type of fake grass that quickly becomes known as AstroTurf. It is the first artificial playing surface in the major leagues.

1968

The AFL's Oilers move in, becoming the first football team to call a dome home. The Astrodome also hosts the largest crowd ever to witness a basketball game, as 52,963 watch number-one-ranked UCLA fall to number two Houston, 71-69, ending the Bruins' 47-game winning streak.

April 15, 1968

The Longest Day Some Mondays just seem to go on forever, and so does this Monday night ballgame at the Astrodome. Houston and the Mets tango in the longest NL game ever played to completion, a twenty-four-inning epic lasting six hours and six minutes. The first twenty-three innings of the game represent the longest period that two teams have ever been scoreless. The first four batters in the Mets lineup combine to go 2-for-39, and each team strands sixteen runners while collecting just one extra-base hit. Both starting pitchers are brilliant, with Tom Seaver hurling ten scoreless innings for New York and Don Wilson throwing nine for Houston. Eleven more pitchers are used before the game finally ends on a bases-loaded error by Mets second baseman Al Weis in the bottom of the twenty-fourth. Houston's Wade Blasingame gets the win, while Les Rohr, who will pitch only two games all year for the Mets, takes the loss.

Astros 1, Mets 0

1969

The height of the outfield wall is reduced from 16 to 12 feet, and will dip further to 10 feet in 1977.

January 5, 1975 In what is officially ruled an accident, longtime Astros pitcher Don Wilson dies in his garage with his car's motor running.

1973

The Astrodome hosts the famous "Battle of the Sexes," a tennis match between fifty-five-year-old Bobby Riggs and twenty-nine-year-old women's champion Billie Jean King. Billie Jean wins easily in front of 30,000 spectators and a worldwide television audience.

The Birth of Fake Turf

When players walked onto the field at the Astrodome on Opening Day 1966, they were met with an even bigger adjustment than playing indoors: the entire infield had been replaced with artificial grass.

Chemgrass—quickly dubbed "AstroTurf"—was a nylon grass substitute that had been invented by Monsanto Industries, a chemical company, in 1964 for use in city playgrounds. Made of super-heated nylon woven into a carpet-like material, the turf arrived in 220-foot-long, 14-foot-wide strips that were then zippered together and held in place by underground hooks. Although this surface looked like (very bright) grass, it didn't act much like it.

When players and engineers had tried out a test sample of AstroTurf earlier in the year, they found that balls bounced at erratic angles—a

AstroTurf and its many imitators have state-of-the-art features to aid in drainage and durability. Still, the majority of players and fans prefer natural grass.

problem caused by all of the rigid fibers on each strip lying in the same direction, and easily fixed by turning the turf around so that the ball would bounce with the grain, rather than against it. But players still complained that the ball occasionally produced "bad hops," especially when it hit the zippers between strips.

Even though the players were less than thrilled with it, AstroTurf was hailed not only as the newest space-age advancement—gleefully installed by J. Edgar Hoover for his own front "lawn"—but as the wave of the future for ballparks across the United States. Soon, new parks in Pittsburgh, Cincinnati, and Philadelphia opened, looking like "the world's biggest pool table," as Cubs skipper Leo Durocher called the Astrodome. (Such an outspoken hater of AstroTurf was Durocher that when the Astros replaced their outfield with the stuff during the All-Star break, they mischievously shipped a chunk of the "real thing" to Chicago with their regards.)

As AstroTurf became more and more common in baseball fields around the country—in 1985 almost half the major league stadiums didn't have real grass—players began complaining about higher incidents of injuries on the field. However, researchers found no proof to back up their accusations, aside from more occurrences of rug burn and "turf toe," a toe sprain that is easily caused when pressure is put on the calf while the tips of the toes are on a rigid surface. More importantly to owners, though, fans were growing weary of the artificial surface; and along with the eradication of multipurpose, cookie-cutter stadiums, so too came the pulling out of AstroTurf, even for teams like the St. Louis Cardinals, whose fleet-footed team thrived on the easy tread of the surface.

Now, only a couple of stadiums use artificial turf: a new-and-improved version made of a softer, more flexible polyethylene-polypropylene blend called FieldTurf. And although owners may lament the higher cost to maintain a "real" field, fans and players alike seem glad that artificial fields are mostly a thing of the past.

LEFT: One of the Astrodome's first superstars, Cesar Cedeno is pictured here in 1971, his first full season. The following year Cedeno will explode with a superb campaign, batting .320 with twenty-two home runs and fifty-five stolen bases—truly eye-popping numbers in the cavernous stadium.

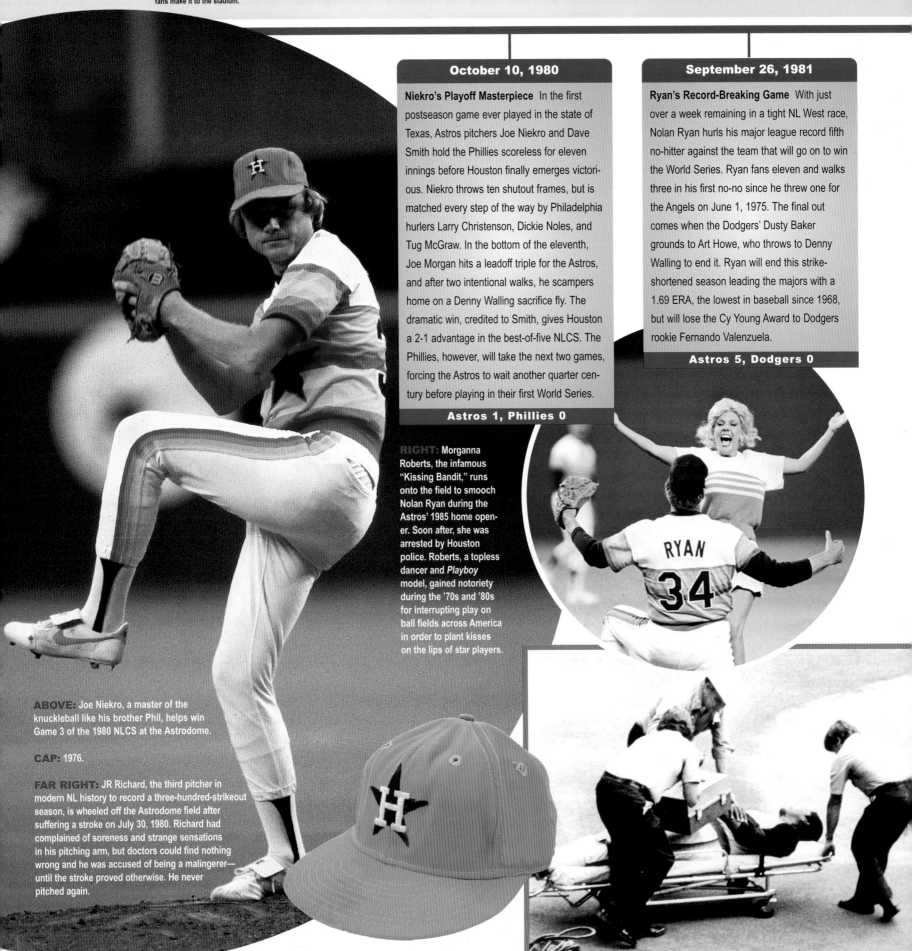

June 15, 1976 Baseball's first indoor rainout occurs when massive rainstorms prevent umpires from making it to the Astrodome for a game against Pittsburgh. Only the players and a couple of dozen fans make it to the stadium.

November 19, 1979 The Astros make free-agent pitcher Nolan Ryan the first million-dollar player in baseball history.

April 8, 1984 The Astros' twenty-five-year-old star shortstop Dickie Thon is hit in the eye by a Mike Torrez fastball. He'll recover, but his career never will.

October 10, 1980

Niekro's Playoff Masterpiece In the first postseason game ever played in the state of Texas, Astros pitchers Joe Niekro and Dave Smith hold the Phillies scoreless for eleven innings before Houston finally emerges victorious. Niekro throws ten shutout frames, but is matched every step of the way by Philadelphia hurlers Larry Christenson, Dickie Noles, and Tug McGraw. In the bottom of the eleventh, Joe Morgan hits a leadoff triple for the Astros, and after two intentional walks, he scampers home on a Denny Walling sacrifice fly. The dramatic win, credited to Smith, gives Houston a 2-1 advantage in the best-of-five NLCS. The Phillies, however, will take the next two games, forcing the Astros to wait another quarter century before playing in their first World Series.

Astros 1, Phillies 0

September 26, 1981

Ryan's Record-Breaking Game With just over a week remaining in a tight NL West race, Nolan Ryan hurls his major league record fifth no-hitter against the team that will go on to win the World Series. Ryan fans eleven and walks three in his first no-no since he threw one for the Angels on June 1, 1975. The final out comes when the Dodgers' Dusty Baker grounds to Art Howe, who throws to Denny Walling to end it. Ryan will end this strike-shortened season leading the majors with a 1.69 ERA, the lowest in baseball since 1968, but will lose the Cy Young Award to Dodgers rookie Fernando Valenzuela.

Astros 5, Dodgers 0

RIGHT: Morganna Roberts, the infamous "Kissing Bandit," runs onto the field to smooch Nolan Ryan during the Astros' 1985 home opener. Soon after, she was arrested by Houston police. Roberts, a topless dancer and *Playboy* model, gained notoriety during the '70s and '80s for interrupting play on ball fields across America in order to plant kisses on the lips of star players.

ABOVE: Joe Niekro, a master of the knuckleball like his brother Phil, helps win Game 3 of the 1980 NLCS at the Astrodome.

CAP: 1976.

FAR RIGHT: JR Richard, the third pitcher in modern NL history to record a three-hundred-strikeout season, is wheeled off the Astrodome field after suffering a stroke on July 30, 1980. Richard had complained of soreness and strange sensations in his pitching arm, but doctors could find nothing wrong and he was accused of being a malingerer—until the stroke proved otherwise. He never pitched again.

July 15, 1986 In the Astrodome's second All-Star Game, the Dodgers' Fernando Valenzuela ties Carl Hubbell's hallowed record by striking out five consecutive batters.

June 3, 1989 After seven hours and fourteen minutes of play, the Astros beat Los Angeles with a single off emergency pitcher Jeff Hamilton in the twenty-second inning. It was longest game (by time) in Astrodome history.

September 30, 1991 All-star catcher Craig Biggio plays his first game at second base, a position switch that will help send him to the Hall of Fame.

1985

The outfield dimensions are shortened for the only time in the Astrodome's history. It's now 325 feet down the lines, and 400 to center. Power alleys remain 375 feet.

July 11, 1985

Another Ryan Milestone Nolan Ryan becomes the first pitcher to record 4,000 strikeouts when he fans ex-teammate Danny Heep before a crowd of 20,921. Ryan, ironically, began his career with the Mets, who will forever regret trading him for shortstop Jim Fregosi in 1971. The Astros take an early lead, but a seventh-inning single by Gary Carter ties the game, and The Ryan Express will not be involved in the decision. Houston eventually wins it in the twelfth on a Bill Doran walk-off single.

Astros 4, Mets 3

In 1986, Mike Scott became the first pitcher ever to clinch a playoff spot with a no-hitter. After nearly a decade of mediocrity, Scott blossomed into a Cy Young winner virtually overnight, leading to widespread accusations that he was illegally scuffing the ball. Scott's explanation was that he'd mastered a new pitch, the split-fingered fastball, and nobody was ever able to prove otherwise.

October 15, 1986

The 16-Inning Thriller In the longest ever postseason game, the Mets outlast the Astros in a sixteen-inning thriller considered one of the most exciting contests ever played. The Astros score three runs in the first and hold that 3-0 lead through eight innings, but the game is merely half over. In the top of the ninth, Mets rookie Lenny Dykstra leads off with a pinch-hit triple. After a Mookie Wilson single and a Keith Hernandez double, pitcher Bob Knepper is removed in favor of closer Dave Smith, who allows a game-tying sacrifice fly to Ray Knight. The game remains tied until the Mets push across a run in the top of the fourteenth, but Houston's Billy Hatcher re-ties it in the bottom of the inning with a home run off Mets relief ace Jesse Orosco. New York comes back to score three runs in the sixteenth, but the Astros still refuse to give up. In the bottom of the sixteenth they score twice, putting the tying and winning runs on base with two outs. But Orosco, in his third exhausting inning of relief, summons enough strength to strike out Kevin Bass to end the game and clinch the NL pennant for the Mets. It's Orosco's third relief win of the series, but the MVP award goes to Astros ace Mike Scott—who sat on the bench all game long, hoping to start a seventh game that will never be played.

Mets 7, Astros 6

September 25, 1986

Scott Sends Astros into Orbit Mike Scott becomes the first pitcher ever to clinch a postseason berth with a no-hitter, blanking the Giants 2-0 to give Houston the NL West title. With his dramatic thirteen-strikeout performance, Scott also cinches the Cy Young Award. He will become the second Astros pitcher (after JR Richard) to record a 300-strikeout season. Scott puts a perfect game out of reach by hitting Dan Gladden with a pitch leading off the game, but will issue only two walks on the day. In the final game of the year, Will Clark's seventh-inning double will break up Scott's bid for consecutive no-hitters.

Astros 2, Giants 0

December 10, 1991 The Astros trade former Arizona Wildcats basketball star Kenny Lofton to Cleveland for backup catcher Eddie Taubensee.

1989

A $60 million football-inspired renovation replaces the original scoreboard with two Diamond Vision screens and adds seats ringing the upper level, bringing capacity to 54,000.

1991

Padded outfield walls are extended to the top of the stands, nearly doubling the height of the fence to 19½ feet.

September 8, 1993

Kile Stymies the Mets In yet another memorable Astros-Mets game, right-hander Darryl Kile no-hits New York in what will be the last no-no pitched at the Astrodome. Kile strikes out nine, walks one, and allows an unearned run in the fourth inning. The Mets' Butch Huskey, making his major league debut, strikes out all three times against Kile and also makes an error at third base. For the Astros, Ken Caminiti and Andujar Cedeno hit solo homers and Luis Gonzalez drives in two runs. Although the Mets are on their way to a 59-103 record, their worst showing since 1965, it is the first time in eighteen years they have been no-hit.

Astros 7, Mets 1

ugust 1992 The Astrodome plays host to the Republican
ational Convention, while the Astros go on a twenty-six-day road trip.

July 31, 1998 Houston trades for Mariners ace Randy Johnson,
who will go 10-1 with a stunning 1.28 ERA the rest of the season.

2005 The Astrodome, which is still used for various civic events,
serves as a temporary home for victims of Hurricane Katrina who have
been relocated from New Orleans.

June 13, 1999

Dierker Collapses With Houston leading San Diego 4-1, the game is halted in the eighth inning when Astros manager Larry Dierker collapses in the dugout due to a grand mal brain seizure. He will undergo brain surgery and, remarkably, end up missing only twenty-seven games before returning to the helm. Interim manager Matt Galante will go 13-14 during Dierker's absence. Meanwhile, the suspended game will resume on July 23 with Dierker in the dugout and Houston's Billy Wagner ready to take the mound. The manager is in good shape, but the closer is shaky. Wagner allows two ninth-inning homers, but holds on for the 4-3 victory.

Astros 4, Padres 3

1996

The Oilers host their final game in Texas on December 15 before moving to Tennessee, where they will eventually be renamed the Titans.

1999

The futuristic stadium closes down just before the end of the century, as the Braves end the Astros' tenure by eliminating them in Game 4 of the Division Series. The stadium draws 2.7 million fans in its final season, its highest total ever.

2005

The Astrodome, which is still used for various civic events, serves as a temporary home for victims of Hurricane Katrina who have been relocated from New Orleans.

OPPOSITE: The Astrodome as it appeared during its first 1965 exhibition game (top) and on Opening Day 1997 (bottom). The most notable change in the thirty-two-year interim (besides the fake turf) was the addition of a wraparound upper deck. An out-of-town scoreboard was also added on the left-field wall, and banners for championships and retired numbers were hung from the rafters.

TOP, INSET: Manager Larry Dierker celebrates with his players.

LEFT: Third baseman Ken Caminiti waves to fans after the Astros clinch the 1999 NL Central title. It is the last regular-season game to be played at the Astrodome.

LEFT: This 1967 photo clearly shows the seams between the long swatches of newly installed AstroTurf, which caused many bad hops at the Astrodome.

ANAHEIM STADIUM

Anaheim, California

Angels (AL) 1966–present

Edison International Field (1998–2003), Angel Stadium (2004–present)

OPPOSITE: Anaheim Stadium is jam-packed for its grand opening, an exhibition game against the San Francisco Giants on April 9, 1966. The stadium's design and structure make it nearly a carbon copy of Dodger Stadium, but the legendary Big A—which serves triple duty as a landmark, scoreboard support, and Chevron advertisement—gives the park a distinctive feel. Located in then-rural Orange County, the stadium was built atop the site of four former farms: an alfalfa farm, an orange and eucalyptus farm, and two corn plots.

In the four decades since they moved into Anaheim Stadium, the Angels have undergone a stunning transformation. Once a laid-back, also-ran team that was content to mimic the Dodgers in hopes of siphoning off fans, the Angels have now become one of the mightiest powers in baseball. Their stadium, too, has undergone massive face-lifts, morphing from a modest suburban ballpark into a monstrous football stadium and then back again. Along the way the Angels became the first—and, if sanity prevails, the last—major league team to employ four different geographic designations while remaining in the same area. Originally they were the Los Angeles Angels, in 1966 they became the California Angels, in 1997 the Anaheim Angels, and in 2005 (ludicrously) the Los Angeles Angels of Anaheim.

After playing their inaugural season of 1961 in a converted minor league park, Wrigley Field in South Central LA, the Angels spent 1962–65 as rent-paying tenants in Walter O'Malley's new baseball palace, Dodger Stadium. However, not wanting to appear subservient to the club that many viewed as their older brother, the Angels refused to call it Dodger Stadium. Instead, whenever they used it, they called it Chavez Ravine—mischievously poking a stick at O'Malley. "There is nothing I wouldn't do for Walter O'Malley, and nothing he wouldn't do for me," Angels owner Gene Autry said. "I am quite sure we will go through life doing nothing for each other."

Tired of riding O'Malley's coattails, the Angels aimed for Walt Disney's instead. On the advice of Disney (who sat on the team's advisory board), the Angels in 1966 moved to Anaheim, a quiet citrus-growing village thirty miles south of Los Angeles which had been transformed into a tourist mecca with the opening of Disneyland eleven years earlier. Suddenly, Anaheim was one of America's biggest boomtowns, with businesses springing up right and left. The population exploded from 14,500 in 1950 to more than 100,000 by 1960. The Angels were arriving at just the right time, and baseball fit in perfectly with Disneyland's—and Anaheim's—claim to be "the happiest place on Earth."

CALIFORNIA PITCHER

NOLAN RYAN ANGELS

ANGELS

ROD CAREW

JIM ABBOTT

G. ANDERSON

Previous baseball games in Anaheim had been played at City Park and La Palma Park (constructed in 1939 as the spring home of the Philadelphia Athletics), but such facilities were nowhere near large enough for a major league team. On August 31, 1964, ground was broken for Anaheim Stadium. The city of Anaheim hired Del Webb, the construction mogul who co-owned the Yankees, to build the park because his company was the only one of four bidders that guaranteed an on-time finish.

The Angels' dislike of the Dodgers didn't deter them from attempting to build a copy of Los Angeles' ballpark. Architect Nobel Herzberg's design for Anaheim Stadium was a transparent attempt to re-create Dodger Stadium, with the same wraparound grandstand curving gently around the foul poles, the same short metal fences in the right- and left-field corners, the same slanted roof, the same palm tree décor, and the same three-tiered design (an upper and lower deck with a smaller loge section in between). But although it resembled Chavez Ravine visually, it seemed to be missing some of the magic of that green cathedral. For one thing, Dodger Stadium had a magnificent setting: near downtown Los Angeles, yet on top of a hill and surrounded by forest and mountains. Anaheim Stadium, by contrast, was built on the former site of a cornfield, next to an orange grove in a rural area where the roads had not yet been paved.

Still, the Angels' ballpark had a lot going for it. Fans had unobstructed views of the field from everywhere in the park, a rarity at the time. Anaheim Stadium's central feature was a giant, steel letter A with a halo around it, representing the team's logo, which rose 230 feet in the air behind the left-field fence. Halfway up, the A held a state-of-the-art scoreboard. Visible from five nearby freeways, it served as a larger-than-life advertisement for Angels baseball and also gave the stadium its most enduring nickname, "The Big A."

At first, players disagreed on whether the stadium would benefit pitchers or hitters more. Angels pitching ace Dean Chance complained that baseballs "carry out of here like golf balls," but infielder Jim Fregosi countered with a claim that the park was "designed for pitchers." It was Fregosi who turned out to be correct, as The Big A allowed a below-average level of offense every year until its 1979 renovation. Initial capacity was 43,204, with that number slated to increase to more than 50,000 once outfield bleachers were added. The city expected to make its money back by keeping 7.5 percent of ticket sales during the Angels' thirty-five-year lease, and also by luring a pro football team to play in the stadium. But the football team failed to materialize, and the Angels' attendance fell off. After having led the AL in ticket sales during the stadium's debut season, the Angels had fallen to tenth by 1974. By then the city had lost more than $1.3 million in expected revenues and was trying unsuccessfully to sell the stadium.

Relief came in 1979, when the NFL's Los Angeles Rams agreed to move from the LA Coliseum to Anaheim. Along with the Rams, however, came the inevitable football renovation that sapped Anaheim Stadium of its charm. The massive refurbishment increased capacity by more than 20,000, but also turned the stadium into a faceless mass of concrete. The seating bowl was completely enclosed, cutting off views of the Orange County hills and orchards once visible in the distance. Even the famous Big A was a casualty of the renovation. Not tall enough to be seen over the new seating deck, it was moved to the parking lot, an appropriately forgotten symbol of a team that was now an afterthought in its own ballpark.

In 1997, with the Rams having previously abandoned Anaheim for St. Louis, the Walt Disney Company, which now owned the Angels, embarked on an ambitious $117 million renovation to retrofit the stadium for baseball. Twenty-eight million was recouped by selling the stadium's name to Edison International, an energy company, while the city pitched in another $20 million. Disney paid the rest of the bill. In return for the public funds, the team agreed to change its name to the Anaheim Angels and to play in the ballpark until at least 2017. When Edison dropped out of its twenty-year naming rights contract after just seven years, the park was renamed Angel Stadium.

The renovation went swimmingly. The football seats in the outfield were mercifully removed, replaced by a giant scoreboard and a Disneyesque waterfall with water running over fake boulders. The outer facade was given a makeover in an adobe-style motif subtly reminiscent of the Angels' original home, Wrigley Field. The new look was enthusiastically received by fans, transforming the ballpark back into a great place to watch a ballgame (though alas, the Big A still sat forgotten in the parking lot).

In 2000, the Angels' now-legendary mascot, the Rally Monkey, made its first appearance at Edison Field. With the Angels trailing a game 5-4 in the bottom of the ninth, the scoreboard operator played a video clip of a dancing monkey (taken from the movie *Ace Ventura: Pet Detective*) accompanied by the words "Rally Monkey!" The Angels came back to win the game, and a phenomenon was born. The ubiquitous monkey was given credit for leading Anaheim to the 2002 world championship, and a plush version sold at the ballpark became a must-have for young Angels fans.

The Rally Monkey contributed to the lively ballpark atmosphere fostered by Arte Moreno, the Walt Disney lookalike who purchased the Angels from the Disney Company in 2003. One of Moreno's first acts as owner was lowering beer prices, which was followed by reductions in other concession items as well as souvenirs and certain tickets. Moreno also opened his pocketbook to sign big-money free agents like Vladimir Guerrero, and his habit of sitting in regular seats and commingling with fans won him a reputation as a man of the people. Under the guidance of the wildly popular Moreno, Angel Stadium became a genuine destination for the first time, instead of just a place

for Orange County fans to go when they didn't feel like driving all the way to Dodger Stadium. Despite boldly challenging the Dodgers' status as Southern California's number one team, the Angels haven't yet managed to top their rivals' attendance in any given year. In 2003, though, the Angels' 3.06 million fans fell just 2.5 percent shy of the Dodgers' total, a better showing than anybody had ever expected for the upstart team from Orange County.

1970 Alex Johnson wins the AL batting title, becoming the first (and still the only) Angel ever to do so.

September 28, 1974 Nolan Ryan pitches his third career no-hitter, but only 10,872 witness it at Anaheim Stadium.

September 23, 1978 Angels outfielder Lyman Bostock, a .311 career hitter, is murdered at age twenty-seven in Gary, Indiana.

TIMELINE: ANAHEIM STADIUM

1966

The Angels' first Opening Day at Anaheim Stadium occurs on April 19. The baseball-only park holds 43,204, with dimensions of 333 feet down the line, 375 in the alleys, and 406 to center. There are no seats beyond the outfield fence, but a 230-foot-tall letter A supports a giant scoreboard.

September 27, 1973

Ryan Tops Koufax It takes eleven innings, but Nolan Ryan fans sixteen Twins in his final start of the season to inch past Sandy Koufax's modern single-season strikeout mark, 383 to 382. Ryan ties the mark with his fifteenth strikeout of the game in the eighth inning, but doesn't break it until he punches out Rich Reese with two outs in the eleventh to top Koufax's 1965 mark. Pinch hitter Richie Scheinblum's RBI double in the bottom of the inning gives the Angels and Ryan a 5-4 win. Only 9,100 fans attend the history-making game, and many of them have gone home by the time the game ends. Two years later, Ryan will tie Koufax's no-hitter record by throwing his fourth, against the Orioles.

Angels 5, Twins 4

TOP: Nolan Ryan strides off the mound after his record-breaking 383rd strikeout of 1973. The crowd gave Ryan a four-minute standing ovation.

BOTTOM: Nolan Ryan hurls a pitch during the ninth inning of his record-tying fourth no-hitter on June 1, 1975.

OPPOSITE, BOTTOM: Wally Joyner stretches in the on-deck circle during a 1986 game. The Angels rookie took baseball by storm that season, batting .321 with twenty-one homers over the first ninety-four games of his career. Note the completely enclosed upper deck, a hallmark of Anaheim Stadium's football configuration from 1980 to '96. A discoloration line is visible where the old stands end and the new ones begin.

September 17, 1984

Reggie's Big Hit The Angels, who start the day half a game behind the Royals in the AL West, are shelled by Kansas City in Anaheim. The day's biggest hit, though, belongs to an Angel. Reggie Jackson connects for his 500th career home run, becoming the thirteenth player to reach this exclusive club. Reggie's benchmark homer comes seventeen years to the day after he hit his first career home run—also at the Big A—while a member of the Kansas City Athletics. Jackson's seventh-inning blast wins him an extended standing ovation from 28,862 Angels fans, and also spoils Royals southpaw Bud Black's shutout bid. It's one of just three hits Black allows on the day.

Royals 10, Angels 1

1974

The fences are moved out about 5 feet all the way around. In 1976, the dimensions will return to almost exactly the 1966 measurements, and will remain the same for twenty years.

1980

With the NFL's Rams moving to Orange County, Anaheim Stadium becomes a multipurpose facility. To prepare it for football, the stadium is completely enclosed and 22,000 seats are added, making the new capacity 64,000 for baseball and almost 70,000 for football. The Big A structure now barely peeks over the top of the outfield stands.

RIGHT: Reggie Jackson acknowledges the crowd after blasting his 500th career homer.

September 25, 1979

Angels Finally Make Playoffs California's Frank Tanana defeats the three-time defending AL West champions, the Kansas City Royals, to clinch the first division title in Angels history. Brian Downing singles home two runs on the night, including AL MVP-to-be Don Baylor in a three-run second inning. Although the Angels' 88-74 record would be good for only fifth place if they played in the AL East, they reach base and score more frequently than any other major league team. California becomes only the third expansion team (after the Mets and Royals) to reach the postseason.

Angels 4, Royals 1

August 4, 1985

Carew Knocks No. 3,000 Rod Carew collects his 3,000th career hit, a single to left field, in a 6-5 Angels win. Fittingly, it comes against the Minnesota Twins, the club for which Carew won seven batting titles in twelve seasons before being traded to California in 1979. The thirty-nine-year-old's historic knock against lefty Frank Viola gets him a long ovation from 41,630 enthusiastic Angels fans. California blows an early three-run lead, but rallies to win the game on Brian Downing's eighth-inning RBI single. Carew will amass fifty-three more hits before retiring at season's end, and his .280 batting average will be his lowest mark since 1968.

Angels 6, Twins 5

June 1, 1988 The Angels draft Jim Abbott, a pitcher born without a right hand, in the first round. He'll win eighteen games for California in 1991.

July 15, 1994 The Disney remake *Angels in the Outfield* is released. Although the on-field action was filmed at Oakland Coliseum, the exteriors were shot at Anaheim Stadium, where the movie takes place.

May 15, 2003 Arte Moreno purchases the Angels, becoming the first ever minority owner of an MLB team.

1994

The Rams host their last game in California on Christmas Eve; they will move to St. Louis in 1995.

1997

Anaheim Stadium embarks upon its second drastic renovation. During the nearly two-year rebuilding, parts of the stadium are closed, reducing capacity by almost half to 33,000.

1998

The rebuilt and renamed park emerges as Edison International Field of Anaheim, with a new concourse, rock garden, fountain, grassy batter's eye extending from left to center field, and massive scoreboard in right. Bleachers are located in both left and right fields, and capacity returns to its pre-Rams level of 45,000. The Big A structure is moved into the parking lot, out of view from the stands. The new dimensions are 300 feet down each line, 370 to left and right fields, 396 to left-center, and 408 to center.

October 12, 1986

Henderson's a Hero Just when it looks as if the Angels will reach the World Series for the first time ever, the most gut-wrenching moment in franchise history rears its head. With California up by three in the ninth inning of ALCS Game 5, Don Baylor—one of the best hitters in Angels history—homers for his new team, the Red Sox, off Mike Witt. Three batters later, Angels manager Gene Mauch calls on his fatigued closer, Donnie Moore, to retire Boston's Dave Henderson for the last out of the game. Henderson, however, hits a miraculous two-run homer to give the Red Sox the lead. The Angels tie it back up in the bottom of the ninth, but fail to score again after loading the bases with one out. In the eleventh inning Henderson comes through once more, hitting a sacrifice fly off Moore to bring home Baylor with Boston's winning run. The 64,223 fans at the Big A leave stunned. As it turns out, this will be the Angels' final home game of the year; they'll lose the Series after the teams return to Boston.

Red Sox 7, Angels 6

RIGHT: Angels starter Jarrod Washburn puts all his effort into a pitch during the opening inning of Edison Field's first World Series game—Game 1 against the Giants in 2002. Washburn and the Angels end up losing, 4-3, but will go on to capture the Series nonetheless.

April 8, 2009 After pitching six shut-out innings in his fourth major league appearance, twenty-two-year-old Nick Adenhart is tragically killed by a drunk driver on his way home from the game.

October 10, 2005

Yankees Go Home Despite losing eventual Cy Young winner Bartolo Colon to injury after just one inning pitched, the Angels persevere and topple the favored Yankees in the decisive Game 5 of the Division Series. Rookie Ervin Santana replaces Colon and gives the Angels 5⅓ passable innings, outpitching Yankees star Mike Mussina, who is unable to hold a 2-0 lead. The key moment comes on what appears to be a routine fly ball hit by Adam Kennedy, but Yankees outfielders Bubba Crosby and Gary Sheffield collide and the ball drops between them for a two-run triple. Los Angeles catches another break when the Yankees' Robinson Cano is called out for interference after seemingly reaching base on a third-strike wild pitch. New York threatens in the ninth, but the door is nailed shut by Angels closer Francisco Rodriguez, who helps his club eliminate the Yankees for the second time in four years.

Angels 5, Yankees 3

October 26, 2002

A Legendary Comeback The Giants seem to be on their way to their first world championship since moving to San Francisco, holding a 5-0 lead in the seventh inning of Game 6. But Anaheim's Scott Spiezio cuts it to 5-3 with a three-run home run in the seventh, and a Darin Erstad homer makes it 5-4 in the eighth. The tying and go-ahead runs move into scoring position on an error by left fielder Barry Bonds, leading Giants manager Dusty Baker to bring in relief ace Robb Nen. With the famed "Rally Monkey" performing its antics on the scoreboard, the first batter Nen faces, Troy Glaus, doubles in both runners to give the Angels a 6-5 lead. Anaheim's Troy Percival then retires the Giants in the ninth to tie the Series at three games apiece. The Angels will go on to take Game 7 behind rookie pitcher John Lackey, winning the championship for the first time in their forty-two year existence.

Angels 6, Giants 5

2005

The team dubs itself the Los Angeles Angels of Anaheim—a name that will lead to not only widespread derision, but also a courtroom battle with the Anaheim city government. The team name stays, and the name of the stadium is changed to Angel Stadium of Anaheim.

ABOVE: Yankees outfielders Gary Sheffield (left) and Bubba Crosby collide with each other—and the Angel Stadium wall—while trying to catch a fly ball hit by the Angels' Adam Kennedy during 2005 Division Series Game 5. The ball, visible inside the Z in "zoo," drops for a key two-run triple, helping the Angels to win the decisive game and end New York's season.

BACKGROUND: The Yankees' Hideki Matsui flies out against Anaheim's John Lackey on August 22, 2007. The catcher is Jeff Mathis, the third baseman is Maicer Izturis, and the left fielder about to catch the ball is Reggie Willits. The Angels are bludgeoned by New York, 8-2, but will finish the season with ninety-four wins, identical to the Yankees' total.

BUSCH STADIUM [II]

St. Louis, Missouri

Cardinals (NL) 1966–2005

Busch Memorial Stadium 1966–1983

The first multipurpose concrete bowl in the National League, Busch Stadium [II] served as home to the baseball Cardinals through 2005, the football Cardinals until their departure for Phoenix in 1987, and the first few home games of the newly relocated Rams in 1995. Along the way, the stadium would witness three separate Cardinals mini-dynasties: one fueled by the sterling pitching of Bob Gibson, another by the baserunning and defensive wizardry of Ozzie Smith, and the last by the prodigious hitting of young Albert Pujols.

When the Browns escaped St. Louis in 1954, the Cardinals became the city's sole major league team. However, they were left with a run-down ballpark and a middling team, resulting in attendance figures that rarely rose above the middle of the pack. In 1964, the year the team won its first World Series in nearly two decades, ground was broken for a new stadium in downtown St. Louis. The site was just blocks away from the soaring Gateway Arch (also under construction), which would become the city's best-known landmark. On May 12, 1966, the Cardinals played their first game at new Busch Memorial Stadium, beating the Atlanta Braves 4-3 in twelve innings before 46,048 fans. That year the new stadium also hosted the All-Star Game.

Busch II (as it's often called to distinguish it from its predecessor, Sportsman's Park, which was called Busch Stadium during its final decade of existence) resembled its concrete, cookie-cutter brethren in most aspects. A tall, perfectly round bowl, the simple two-deck structure was free of any obstructions, lending a certain egalitarianism to the seating arrangement. Designed by architect Edward Durrell Stone—who would later design such impressive modernist landmarks as the Kennedy Center in Washington, DC—Busch was undeniably more attractive than the other concrete bowls built during its era. Its circular roof was connected to the upper deck by a row of ninety-six small arches, echoing the Gateway Arch, which from certain vantage points was visible behind the left-field stands. And for fans with other interests, the International Bowling Museum, which later added a Cardinals Hall of Fame, was located right across the street.

Busch II held just over 50,000 people, quite a bit more than Sportsman's 34,000. The increase in seating came just

CARDINALS

BOB GIBSON

OZZIE SMITH Cardinals

in time, too, as the Redbirds won a memorable world title over the Boston Red Sox in 1967, setting a new franchise attendance record of 2.1 million in the process. With a lineup featuring legendary players Lou Brock, Bob Gibson, Roger Maris, and Orlando Cepeda, the Cardinals of the late '60s were one of the most integrated teams in the country. The charismatic team and glamorous new stadium helped allow Cardinals fans to move on from the ugly racial history symbolized by Sportsman's Park. (African-American fans had been banned from Sportsman's main grandstand until the mid-1940s, and in 1947 the Cardinals had voted to strike rather than play against Jackie Robinson.)

Although the Busch II era started off well for the Cardinals, things headed downhill after the team lost the 1968 World Series. Popular announcer Harry Caray was fired, always penurious owner Gussie Busch became even more tightfisted, and the club found itself embroiled in baseball's biggest controversy of the day when Gold Glove–winning centerfielder Curt Flood sued the team and demanded the right to free agency. Flood never played for the Cardinals again, and the outfield grass he had so expertly covered was ripped up in 1970, replaced by AstroTurf to make things easier for football. In 1977 the

infield grass was also replaced with synthetic turf, completing the ill-advised transformation of Busch from charming modern stadium into drab gray donut. In addition to its aesthetic deficiencies, the turf also radiated heat, and field temperatures routinely soared well above 100°F during the sweltering St. Louis summers. Brock, for one, was forced to resort to putting aluminum foil in his baseball shoes to help keep his feet cool.

Players found other adjustments necessary as well. Although turf generated truer bounces than real grass, the occasional wacky hop would occur when a ball hit the seams joining different pieces together. The hard surface also caused the ball to bounce much higher, so outfielders had to be wary of balls suddenly caroming over their heads. Infielders, meanwhile, had to improve their reaction times, as grounders zoomed across the carpet. Sinkerball specialist Frank Linzy, who didn't fare well in a short stint with the Cardinals, later told the *Sporting News*: "I got them to hit the ball on the ground. But anytime you do that on artificial turf, two things can happen. It will go right at somebody or it will likely go through." But above all, the reason most players hated playing on the artificial turf was that they believed it caused more injuries, especially to the knees, than real grass did.

Now forced to play baseball in a stadium that catered to football, the Cards made do as best they could. Conventional wisdom held that in order to win on synthetic grass, a team should be composed of speedsters who could turn the wild outfield bounces into doubles and triples. Studies by the legendary statistician Bill James refuted this theory, but Whitey Herzog, who served in the rare dual capacity of manager and general manager, nonetheless set about constructing a team full of fleet-footed players. "It's true his teams were built with an eye towards the parks they played in," longtime Braves manager Bobby Cox said of Herzog, "but they also played outstanding defense and were built around great pitching, and those are the kind of things that play well in any park." Led by speed-burning stars Ozzie Smith and Willie McGee, Herzog's Cardinals won the World Series in 1982. Three years later, after adding speedy rookie Vince Coleman and slugging first baseman Jack Clark, they came within an umpire's blown call of winning another title. In 1987, the Cards won the pennant but lost the World Series again, this time to the underdog Minnesota Twins.

After the football Cardinals flew the coop in 1987 and the Rams followed suit in 1995, the team was free to turn Busch Stadium back into a baseball park. The turf was replaced by real grass in 1996, a handsome hand-operated scoreboard was added, and during its last decade of existence Busch again became the underrated jewel it had once been. In 1997, the team traded for home-run hero Mark "Big Mac" McGwire, whose pursuit of the single-season homer record in '98 drew record crowds to Busch, even for batting practice. Thanks to a sponsorship agreement with McDonald's, the section of left-field stands where many of McGwire's clouts landed was officially named "Big Mac Land."

Led by McGwire and brilliant young slugger Albert Pujols, St. Louis made the playoffs five times in the stadium's final six seasons. Their only World Series appearance, however, resulted in a sweep by the Boston Red Sox in 2004. In the new millennium Busch appeared nowhere near as outmoded as places like Riverfront, Three Rivers, or Veterans stadiums, but ownership nonetheless insisted on a new park that could generate untold new revenue streams. Throughout the 2005 season, a new version of Busch Stadium went up next door while the Cardinals played out the string in the old concrete bowl. Busch II's era ended with the 2005 NLCS, as the Houston Astros celebrated their NL pennant on the field after defeating the Cardinals in Game 6. The stadium was soon demolished and the site slated to turn into the retail equivalent of a concrete bowl stadium—Ballpark Village, a mixed-use development containing condos, restaurants, and a large mall.

CAP: 2001.

The inimitable Ozzie Smith does his trademark backflip while taking the field at Busch Stadium for Game 2 of the 1987 NLCS against San Francisco. Although he began his career with the Padres, Smith became a Cardinal before the 1982 season when the two teams swapped star shortstops. Heavy-hitting Garry Templeton, whose best years were behind him, went to San Diego, while the light-hitting defensive whiz known as "the Wizard of Oz" came to St. Louis. During the fifteen seasons Smith called Busch Stadium home, he improved his batting tremendously, cemented his status as a first-ballot Hall of Famer, and became the Cardinals' most beloved player since Stan Musial.

BELOW: When it opened in 1966, Busch Stadium [II] was the first stadium built by the Cardinals franchise since Robison Field's wooden grandstand debuted in 1893. The round tower seen in so many images of Busch [II] is the Millennium Hotel, a twenty-eight-story building with a rotating restaurant, Top of the Riverfront, located on the top floor. In this 2005 photo, taken the day after Busch [II] hosted its final game, the nearly complete Busch Stadium [III] can be seen directly to the south. The extreme size difference between the two structures was typical of the retro ballpark era, during which new stadiums almost always had significantly smaller capacities than the older ones.

July 12, 1966 Busch Stadium II hosts the All-Star Game, which is won by the NL 2-1 in ten innings.

1968 The Cardinals' Bob Gibson posts a 1.12 ERA, the lowest in the majors in fifty-four years.

April 16, 1978 The Cards' Bob Forsch no-hits the Phillies at Busch.

TIMELINE: BUSCH STADIUM [II]

1966

The Cardinals christen Busch Memorial Stadium on May 12. Dimensions are 330 feet down the lines, 386 to the power alleys, and 410 to center field.

1970

To make the switch between football and baseball easier, natural grass is replaced with artificial turf in the outfield only.

1973

Dimensions are reduced to 376 feet in the alleys and 404 in center.

1977

Artificial turf is installed in the infield, making Busch an all-turf park.

RIGHT: Fireballer Bob Gibson, one of the greatest pitchers in history, brought the magic to Busch Stadium in 1968. In addition to posting a 1.12 ERA, the lowest in baseball since 1914, he pitched forty-seven consecutive scoreless innings, tossed thirteen shut-outs, and helped lead the Cardinals to the World Series, where he fanned a World Series–record seventeen batters in Game 1. His blazing fastball was helped all the more by the high pitcher's mound at Busch Stadium. The next year, MLB will rule that all mounds must be reduced to 10 inches high.

October 2, 1968

Maximum Bob Bob Gibson, virtually unhittable during the regular season, continues his dominance by striking out a World Series–record seventeen batters in Game 1. Gibson defeats Detroit's thirty-one-game winner Denny McLain in the first ever Series match-up between two pitchers who will be named MVPs of their respective leagues. Gibson allows just five hits and one walk, and strikes out the side in the ninth to shatter Sandy Koufax's five-year-old record for most whiffs in a Series game. St. Louis' Mike Shannon singles in the only run Gibson needs in the fourth, but Julian Javier knocks in two more and Lou Brock homers for good measure.

Cardinals 4, Tigers 0

July 17, 1974

Three Thousand Bob Gibson becomes the first NL pitcher to strike out 3,000 career batters when he fans Cincinnati's Cesar Geronimo to end the second inning. (In the AL, only Hall of Famer Walter Johnson has fanned more than 3,000.) Gibson will finish his career in 1975 with 3,117 punchouts; Geronimo, remarkably, will also become Nolan Ryan's 3,000th strikeout victim in 1980. Gibson carries a 4-2 lead late into the game, but the Reds rally to tie, and they eventually win in the twelfth when George Foster doubles in two runs.

Reds 6, Cardinals 4

August 13, 1979

Three Thousand, Redux Lou Brock singles off the hand of pitcher Dennis Lamp for his 3,000th career hit. Fittingly, it comes against the Cubs, the team that originally signed Brock before unwisely trading him to St. Louis in 1964. The forty-year-old speedster gets a long ovation from the 44,457 spectators at Busch Stadium. Brock will retire after the season with 3,023 hits, and the *Sporting News* will name him NL Comeback Player of the Year for 1979. The Cards, meanwhile, win the game on Garry Templeton's ninth-inning sacrifice fly off Bruce Sutter.

Cardinals 3, Cubs 2

BELOW: In 1979, five years after breaking Maury Wills' single-season stolen-base record, Lou Brock enjoys another memorable moment when the crowd gives him a standing ovation for his 3,000th career hit.

RIGHT: In Game 5 of the 1985 NLCS, switch hitter Ozzie Smith (left) celebrates with third base coach Nick Leyva after hitting his first left-handed homer. Upon Busch II's closing, fans will vote this play the stadium's greatest moment.

1980 Whitey Herzog is named manager and, two months later, general manager, becoming one of the few people ever to hold both jobs simultaneously.

October 13, 1985 NL Rookie of the Year Vince Coleman gets his leg caught in an automatic tarp rolling machine before NLCS Game 4. The injury causes him to miss the rest of the playoffs.

1978

Outfield dimensions return to their original configuration.

1984

The name is shortened to simply Busch Stadium.

October 14, 1985

Go Crazy, Folks With both the NLCS and Game 5 tied 2-2, switch hitter Ozzie Smith hits the first left-handed home run of his career in the bottom of the ninth to give the Cardinals a dramatic playoff victory. The huge Monday afternoon crowd enthusiastically heeds announcer Jack Buck's advice: "Go crazy, folks. Go crazy!" The Cardinals, who lost the first two games of the NLCS in Los Angeles, head back to California with the series lead after winning all three games at Busch. Tom Niedenfuer, the reliever who gave up Smith's unlikely home run, will yield another dramatic longball to Jack Clark in Game 6 as the Cardinals capture the pennant at Dodger Stadium.

Cardinals 3, Dodgers 2

October 20, 1982

Beer Town Battle The Cardinals capture their ninth world championship, rallying from a 3-1 sixth-inning deficit to beat Milwaukee in Game 7. Hits by the St. Louis Smiths—Ozzie and Lonnie—start the Redbirds' rally, and a two-run single by Keith Hernandez ties the game. George Hendrick follows with another single to give St. Louis the lead, and Darrell Porter (the Series MVP) and Steve Braun drive home insurance runs in the ninth. Cards relief ace Bruce Sutter retires all six batters he faces, including a strikeout of Milwaukee slugger Gorman Thomas to end the Series.

Cardinals 6, Brewers 3

September 10, 1974

A Master Thief Lou Brock steals his 104th and 105th bases of the season, breaking Maury Wills' modern major league record. The two steals also give Brock 740 in his career, which pushes him past Max Carey's modern NL record of 738. However, Phillies catcher Bob Boone throws out Brock in the ninth, the twenty-ninth time he's been caught this season. Brock will finish the year with 118 stolen bases, which will stand until Rickey Henderson shatters the mark with 130 in 1982.

Phillies 8, Cardinals 2

1988 Jose Oquendo becomes the first NL player since 1918 to play all nine positions in the same season.

April 13, 1993 Cardinals closer Lee Smith records his 358th career save, breaking Jeff Reardon's major league record.

1987

The St. Louis Cardinals—the football version—play their final game at Busch before departing for Phoenix.

May 14, 1988

Now Pitching, the Second Baseman

Cardinals infielder Jose Oquendo, famed for his defensive versatility, takes things a step further when he becomes the first position player in twenty years to get a major league pitching decision. That decision goes against him, as Oquendo is the losing pitcher in a 7-5, nineteen-inning loss to the Braves. A fifteenth-inning injury to Randy O'Neal, the seventh St. Louis pitcher of the night, forces Cardinals manager Whitey Herzog to get creative. In addition to Oquendo's surprise appearance, Cards pitcher Jose DeLeon—who pitched nearly nine innings the previous night—comes in to play the outfield. Herzog tries to minimize DeLeon's chances of making a play by switching him back and forth between left and right fields depending on which side the batter hits from. Oquendo, meanwhile, survives three innings without allowing a run, despite several line drives and a runner thrown out at home plate. His luck runs out in the nineteenth when Ken Griffey Sr. delivers a two-out, two-run double. Atlanta's Rick Mahler pitches eight shutout innings of relief for the win.

Braves 7, Cardinals 5

1993

Dimensions are altered for the last time, reducing outfield distances to 372 feet in the alleys and 402 to center.

1995

The NFL's Los Angeles Rams relocate to St. Louis and play three home games at Busch before moving into the newly completed Trans World Dome.

BELOW, INSET: With two NFL teams having departed for greener pastures, Busch Stadium's artificial turf is mercifully removed on October 26, 1995. One of the turf's greatest drawbacks, highly visible here, was the crisscrossing of foul lines and hash marks that created an aesthetic nightmare for fans of both sports.

BELOW: Busch II's improvements during the mid-1990s included a beautiful new lawn, visible here through the arches, and a hand-operated scoreboard in the upper deck.

1996

With football obligations now over, measures are taken to make the park more baseball-friendly before the 1996 season. The artificial turf is replaced with real grass, center field is turned into a grassy hill that serves as a batter's eye, and a picnic area is installed in the left-field bleachers. Furthermore, almost 1,400 new luxury seats are added.

1997

New owners replace a section of seats in center field with a hand-operated scoreboard, championship flags, retired numbers, and other displays. About 7,000 seats are removed; the new capacity is around 49,000. Bullpens are moved from foul territory to behind the fences in left and right.

July 31, 1997 The Cardinals trade three prospects for Oakland slugger Mark McGwire.

2001 Twenty-one-year-old Albert Pujols makes his debut with the Cardinals. During his rookie season he will start 154 games at four different positions, bat .329, set the NL rookie record for RBIs with 130, make the All-Star Team, and win Rookie of the Year by a unanimous vote.

September 8, 1998

Big Mac Hits Number Sixty-Two After a thrilling, summer-long home run chase with Sammy Sosa, Mark McGwire reaches baseball's Holy Grail with his record-breaking sixty-second home run of the season. McGwire's low line drive off Steve Trachsel barely clears the left-field fence, giving him the long-coveted record that has been held by Roger Maris for thirty-seven years. Both Sosa and the Maris family are on hand to congratulate "Big Mac." Sosa will surpass McGwire in home runs on September 25, but McGwire will retake the single-season home run record just forty-five minutes later, and will retain the record until Barry Bonds breaks it in 2001. Baseball's memorable summer of '98 will be tarnished somewhat in 2005, when both Sosa and McGwire are subpoenaed to appear before Congress and are less than forthcoming with their testimony regarding rumors of steroid and human growth hormone use.

Cardinals 6, Cubs 3

LEFT: Mark McGwire launches one of the thirty-eight home runs he hit at Busch Stadium during his record-breaking 1998 season. McGwire was so popular with Cardinals fans that a special seating section, "Big Mac Land," was added to the upper deck in left field, where many of his home-run balls would land.

2005

On October 19, Busch Stadium hosts its final game, an NLCS Game 6 loss to the Astros that eliminates the Cardinals from the playoffs. Demolition of the park begins in November, with the third Busch Stadium opening in April 2006.

October 21, 2004

Prince Albert Reigns The Cardinals win Game 7 of the NLCS, reaching the World Series for the first time since 1987 and marking the first NL pennant won by legendary manager Tony LaRussa. The deciding game doesn't start well for St. Louis, as Houston spark plug Craig Biggio hits the first leadoff home run in any Game 7 in history, and the Astros take a 2-1 lead into the sixth inning with Roger Clemens on the mound. Clemens can't hold the lead, however, giving up a game-tying double to Albert Pujols (with first base open, no less) and a go-ahead homer to Scott Rolen. Pujols—who provided the series' most important hit with his legendary homer off Brad Lidge in Game 5—bats .500 over the seven games and is named NLCS MVP. Tonight's win is the last one of the year for the Cardinals, though, as they'll get swept in the World Series by the Boston Red Sox.

Cardinals 5, Astros 2

LEFT: The Cardinals stole Albert Pujols, who played high school and junior college baseball in Missouri, with the 402nd overall pick in the 1999 draft. He went on to become the team's best player during the final years of Busch Stadium [II].

ST. LOUIS **Cardinals**

$2.50

2003 OFFICIAL SCORECARD

Go straight to the top.

BARNES JEWISH Hospital

For a Washington University physician, call 314-TOP-DOCS (314-867-3627) or toll free 866-867-3627.

Log onto www.BarnesJewish.org for your chance to win free tickets.

BJC HealthCare™

OAKLAND–ALAMEDA COUNTY COLISEUM

Oakland, California

Athletics (AL) 1968–present

Network Associates Coliseum (1999–2004), McAfee Coliseum (2004–2008)

OPPOSITE: A's closer Huston Street throws a pitch against Kansas City in a 2005 game, which the Royals will win in twelve innings. The middling attendance of 25,834 is a fairly typical figure for the A's, who have always struggled to draw fans despite their consistently having winning teams. The situation isn't helped by "Mount Davis," the gargantuan set of upper-deck stands visible at the right side of the image. Erected in 1996 as a condition of Oakland Raiders owner Al Davis moving his team back to town, the seats are useless for baseball and serve only to block the lovely view of the Oakland hills.

The Oakland–Alameda County Coliseum was initially a pleasant place to watch a ballgame, but it never truly became a home for the Athletics. Completed in 1966 to house football's Oakland Raiders, the Coliseum added the A's as tenants when they moved to town from Kansas City two years later. Although it was home to two formidable A's dynasties (of the mid-1970s and late 1980s), the Coliseum will always be best thought of by baseball fans for its degradation at the hands of egomaniacal Raiders owner Al Davis.

Things started off well for the A's when Jim "Catfish" Hunter pitched a perfect game for Oakland in the eleventh baseball game ever played at the Coliseum. However, even though the Athletics fielded a winning team in each of their first nine seasons there, their attendance was consistently among the worst in baseball. The stadium seated 50,000, but the team averaged below 20,000 fans per game until 1981, and finished among the AL's top half in attendance only twelve times in their first forty years at the Coliseum.

Stuck in one of baseball's smaller cities (after having unsuccessfully tried to move the team to larger ones), eccentric owner Charlie O. Finley utilized a number of bizarre promotions to keep the team afloat financially. Although his schemes to use orange baseballs and yellow foul lines were kayoed by baseball's powers-that-be, Finley was allowed to install gold-colored bases for one game in 1970. He tried to make his players more colorful, too, dressing them in yellow pants and paying them bonuses to grow beards and mustaches. In 1974 Finley hired an NCAA champion sprinter, Herb Washington, to fill the newly created (and not particularly useful) role of designated runner. "Hot Pants Day," "Bald Head Night," and "Bucket of Beer Night" were only moderately more successful. The team's official mascot, a mule named Charlie O., roamed the grounds until its death in 1976.

Charlie O. notwithstanding, perhaps the most interesting of the many characters inhabiting the Coliseum during the seventies was a teenage batboy named Stanley Burrell. Finley had spotted Burrell practicing some dance moves in the Coliseum's parking lot, and decided his presence as a mascot of sorts would liven up the atmosphere. Finley liked to call him the Executive VP, but players nicknamed him "Hammer" for his resemblance to Hank Aaron. Years later Burrell, recording under the name

MC Hammer, would become a platinum-selling rap artist. Yet even Hammer's dancing failed to draw the fans, and Oakland's 1979 attendance of 306,763 earned them the record of lowest attendance for any major league team in the last half century—and resulted in their venue being nicknamed "The Mausoleum."

Because of its football-oriented construction, the Coliseum had one of the greatest amounts of foul territory in baseball, making it a pitcher's paradise. Although fans were seated farther away from the action than at most parks, they were able to enjoy a scenic view of the Oakland Hills beyond center field. This pleasant panorama was brutally destroyed in 1996. Davis' Raiders, who had abandoned Oakland for Los Angeles in 1982, agreed to move back—but only if the government agreed to renovate the Coliseum to seat 63,000. This was done largely by constructing a monstrous set of outfield bleachers that blocked the magnificent view. This hideous hunk of concrete towering high above the rest of the stadium was derisively dubbed "Mount Davis" by A's fans. In addition to the new seats, the renovation also added two 40,000-square-foot clubs for high rollers, ninety luxury suites, new scoreboards and video boards, and a 9,000-square-foot kitchen. Adding insult to injury, the construction forced the Athletics out of their own park for the first six home games of 1996, which were moved to Cashman Field in Las Vegas.

Almost as soon as the Raiders moved back in, the Athletics' new owners, the Haas family (heirs to the Levi-Strauss fortune), began agitating for a new baseball-only stadium, threatening to leave the Bay Area unless taxpayers funded such a facility. The team also considered relocating to another part of the Bay Area, such as burgeoning San Jose; however, this idea was thwarted by Major League Baseball's territorial rules, which considered San Mateo, Santa Clara, Santa Cruz, Monterey, and Marin counties to be part of Giants territory and thus off-limits to encroaching teams. In 2006, under new owner Lew Wolff, the A's set their sights on the South Bay city of Fremont, but this deal also fell apart. Oakland, meanwhile, promised to try to find a new in-town location for the A's, though Wolff has stated that the team has "no interest in covering old ground again." Until a suitable home can be found, the A's will have to make due in what their owner calls "an aging and shared facility."

November 17, 1968 The infamous *Heidi* game is played at the Coliseum, with TV network NBC pre-empting the end of a remarkable Raiders comeback to show a children's movie.

April 13, 1970 A's owner Charlie Finley installs gold-colored bases for the home opener, an innovation that is soon banned by the league.

October 14, 1972 The Athletics' Gene Tenace becomes the first player to homer in his first two World Series at-bats.

TIMELINE: OAKLAND COLISEUM

1968

The former Kansas City Athletics move into Oakland–Alameda County Coliseum, which the AFL's Oakland Raiders have already called home for two years. The baseball dimensions are 330 feet down the lines, 378 to the power alleys, and 410 to center.

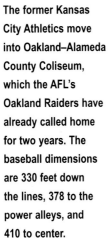

May 8, 1968

Catfish Fries Minnesota In only the eleventh game ever played at the Coliseum, twenty-two-year-old Catfish Hunter throws the first regular season perfect game in the AL since 1922. Hunter collects several more hits than the Minnesota Twins do, as his RBI bunt single breaks a scoreless tie in the seventh inning. Later he knocks a two-run single for his third hit of the day. Hunter strikes out eleven Twins, including the last two batters looking to end the game. The city of Oakland seems less than impressed with its new team, as a paltry crowd of 6,298 witnesses Hunter's feat. Still, the A's will draw 837,466 for the year, about 120,000 more than in their final season in Kansas City. The club won't top a million until 1973, the year of its second straight world championship.

A's 4, Twins 0

ABOVE: Though a cookie-cutter stadium like almost every other new park of its era, the Coliseum—pictured here in 1971—was among the best of the type when it was built.

LEFT: Catfish Hunter throws the final pitch of his 1968 perfect game. Although it is only the eleventh game ever played at the Coliseum, the panorama of empty seats behind Hunter illustrates that the Athletics' honeymoon with their new fans is already over.

CAPS: 1968, 1990.

October 21, 1973

Mets Are Muzzled Returning home just one game away from elimination, the A's capture the final two games of the World Series to win the title over the New York Mets. While Catfish Hunter beat Tom Seaver in Game 6, Game 7 features a pair of lefties facing each other for the third time in the Series. Oakland's Ken Holtzman gets the best of New York's Jon Matlack, who is knocked out in the third inning on a pair of two-run homers by Bert Campaneris and Reggie Jackson. The bombs are Oakland's only two of the Series, but they're enough to bring home a world championship. Jackson will be named MVP, but the real star of the Series is the A's bullpen. Closer Rollie Fingers pitches in six of the seven games, posting an outstanding 0.66 ERA. Southpaw Darold Knowles outdoes even that, allowing no runs while becoming the first man to pitch in all seven games of a post-season series.

A's 5, Mets 2

1976 MLB changes free agency rules, allowing players to leave their clubs once their contracts run out. Charlie Finley decides to sell off his best players before they can leave on their own, but the commissioner won't allow it. Finley later loses a court battle against MLB.

October 17, 1974

Three in a Row The A's become the second team (after the Yankees) to win three straight world championships. After the A's take an early 2-0 lead in Game 5, the Dodgers tie it back up—but Oakland's Joe Rudi provides the decisive blow with a seventh-inning solo homer. For the fourth time in five Series games, the A's emerge with a 3-2 win. Rollie Fingers, who pitches in all four wins, finishes off Los Angeles in the ninth and earns the Series MVP award. Mike Marshall, who pitched in a record 106 games during the regular season, appears in all five World Series games for the Dodgers.

A's 3, Dodgers 2

1982 Rickey Henderson steals a remarkable 130 bases, breaking Lou Brock's previous MLB record (114) by more than ten percent.

1976

Despite enjoying tremendous success with the old configuration, the A's reduce the outfield distances to 375 feet to the alleys and 400 feet to center.

1981

The Raiders play their final game in Oakland before fleeing for Los Angeles.

October 14, 1989

Stewart Stops San Francisco This 1989 Series opener is the first instance in which Oakland and San Francisco ever face off in anything other than an exhibition game. The A's don't fool around against their cross-bay rivals, having been humbled by Kirk Gibson's debilitating blow against them in Game 1 of the previous year's Series against Los Angeles. The A's will never trail at any time during the Series, and in the opening game, eventual Series MVP Dave Stewart blanks the Giants, who are playing in their first World Series since 1962. Three days later, the 7.1-magnitude Loma Prieta earthquake will strike the Bay Area just minutes before Game 3 is scheduled to start. After an eleven-day postponement, the A's will pick up where they left off and sweep the Giants.

A's 5, Giants 0

LEFT: A's first baseman Gene Tenace jumps on teammates Ray Fosse (in catcher's gear) and Darold Knowles after the final out of the 1973 World Series.

RIGHT: The always intimidating Dave Stewart throws one of the first pitches of the 1989 World Series.

1988 Oakland's Jose Canseco becomes the first player in major league history to rack up forty homers and forty steals in the same season.

January 13, 1991 Raiders (and Royals) star Bo Jackson suffers a broken hip in an NFL playoff game at the Coliseum, ending his football career.

1995

Hated owner Al Davis brings his Raiders back to Oakland, where they are received with open arms by the community and, more significantly, the stadium authority.

October 10, 1990

Clemens vs. Cooney In one of the truly bizarre moments in postseason history, Boston ace Roger Clemens is ejected in the second inning of ALCS Game 4, after getting into a brief dispute over balls and strikes with home plate umpire Terry Cooney. Cooney claims Clemens called him a "motherf--ker," which Clemens denies, but he's ejected anyway after his only walk of the day. It's a must-win game for the Red Sox, who trail three games to none, and Clemens' ejection deals them a fatal blow. Boston reliever Tom Bolton, summoned with two on and two out, allows a two-run double to ninth-place hitter Mike Gallego, giving the A's all the runs they need to take the series. Months later, a professional lip-reader hired by the players' union will review video footage of the incident and support Clemens' claim that he never said the magic words to Cooney, but will determine that he told first base ump Jim Evans, "I'll get that motherf--ker in the off-season. I'll kill him!" Clemens will be suspended for the first five games of the 1991 season.

A's 3, Red Sox 1

ABOVE: Roger Clemens offers some choice words to umpires Terry Cooney (left) and Vic Voltaggio (center) during the infamous Game 4 of the 1990 ALCS.

BELOW: The view from the press box during the 1990 World Series, in which the A's shockingly get swept by Cincinnati.

ABOVE: Rickey Henderson exults after breaking Lou Brock's modern record for most career steals. Henderson, who grew up in Oakland, is in his second of what will eventually be four stints with the A's.

May 1, 1991

"I Am the Greatest!" Rickey Henderson steals his 939th base, breaking Lou Brock's modern career record. Henderson will lead the American League in steals this year for the tenth time, and will eventually accumulate an unheard-of 1,406 career thefts. He swipes third for the record-breaking steal against the Yankees battery of Tim Leary and Matt Nokes (though Nokes has thrown him out twice during the game), and when the game is stopped to mark the event, thrusts the base over his head in front of a Wednesday afternoon crowd of 36,139. Henderson's feat and self-promoting pronouncement—"Today, I am the greatest of all time!"—will be overshadowed later in the evening by news from Texas of Nolan Ryan's seventh career no-hitter.

A's 7, Yankees 4

July 31, 1997 The A's trade Mark McGwire to the Cardinals for three prospects who never pan out.

September 9, 1999 After being diagnosed with Lou Gehrig's disease the previous year, legendary pitcher Catfish Hunter passes away.

2003 Michael Lewis' *Moneyball*, an examination of the Athletics' unique front-office philosophy, hits the nonfiction best-seller lists.

1996

The Coliseum undergoes a football-mandated makeover, forcing the A's to play their opening home games at Cashman Field in Las Vegas. The previously idyllic Oakland Coliseum is enclosed all the way around, removing much of its charm and making it a better hitter's park by blocking the wind. The massive section of eyesore bleachers in center field becomes known derisively as "Mount Davis."

1997

The distance to the power alleys is increased to 388 feet, the deepest they have ever been.

1998

A year after a court decision overturns an effort to rename it UMAX Coliseum, the park is instead branded as Network Associates Coliseum after the season ends.

RIGHT: Scott Hatteberg rounds the bases after his pinch homer gives the A's an AL-record twentieth straight win.

BELOW, LEFT: The Coliseum after construction of the "Mount Davis" upper-deck grandstand in center field.

BELOW, RIGHT: Defensive whiz Mark Ellis is one of the few players to remain with the A's throughout the tumultuous first decade of the twenty-first century. In 2008, he signed a contract extension to remain with the team through 2010.

September 4, 2002

Twenty Straight Wins Having won an AL record-tying nineteen straight games, Oakland makes its quest for number twenty a memorable one. With 55,528 rowdy fans on hand, the A's take a seemingly insurmountable 11-0 lead into the fourth inning against lowly Kansas City. But the Royals score five in the fourth, five more in the eighth, and tie it in top of the ninth on Luis Alicea's RBI single off A's closer Billy Koch. Koch, however, escapes the inning by picking Alicea off second base, and Oakland's Scott Hatteberg wins it with a pinch-hit, walk-off homer in the bottom of the inning. The A's will lose their next game and thus fall short of the MLB record of twenty-six straight wins, but they'll retire uniform number 20 in honor of their AL mark.

A's 12, Royals 11

2004

After the '04 season, the park is renamed McAfee Coliseum after the software company buys the naming rights.

2006

Seats in Mount Davis and the rest of the third deck are closed for baseball, reducing capacity by 10,000 to 34,179, the smallest capacity of any major league field.

JACK MURPHY STADIUM

San Diego, California

Padres (NL) 1969–2003

San Diego Stadium (1967–1980), Qualcomm Stadium (1997–2003)

MIKE
CALDWELL
SAN DIEGO PADRES   **PITCHER**

OPPOSITE: The sun sets on Jack Murphy Stadium on Opening Day, April 26, 1995. The baseball strike that cut short the 1994 season also delayed the 1995 opening by nearly a month, and fans were slow to return. After averaging the lowest attendance in major league history in '94, 16,734 fans per game, the Padres did even worse in '95, dropping to a 14,470 average. Note the tarpaulin over the majority of the seats in the upper deck, which were covered to decrease baseball capacity.

From time to time, the Padres tried to spruce up their concrete stadium. One of the more ill-advised attempts came in 1980 (the same year the park was renamed after Murphy), when the club hijacked Wrigley Field's traditional symbol, planting ivy at the base of the centerfield fence, where it remained until 1997.

When the first concrete-and-steel stadium, Philadelphia's Shibe Park, was built in 1909, San Diego wasn't even among the 100 most populous cities in the United States. By 1961, it had become the eighteenth-largest city in the country—primed for an influx of major sports teams. That year the American Football League's Los Angeles Chargers moved to San Diego and wanted a stadium to call home. Their cause was adopted by Jack Murphy, the influential sports editor of the *San Diego Union*, whose staunch advocacy paid off when voters passed a $27 million bond for a multipurpose stadium in November 1965. Though it was always best known as a football venue, San Diego Stadium would host major league baseball for thirty-five memorable years, witnessing the growth of the Padres from a hapless gang of also-rans into perennial contenders and two-time NL champions.

When it was completed in 1967, San Diego Stadium—which was originally going to be called All-American Stadium—immediately became home to both the Chargers and the local college football squad, the San Diego State Aztecs. More importantly, it was used as the centerpiece in the campaign to bring Major League Baseball to San Diego. Murphy took up this cause also, and although justifying a third team in Southern California was a tall order, the National League awarded San Diego an expansion franchise in 1968. Named the Padres after the city's mission heritage, the club began play in 1969.

Although San Diego Stadium was one of the massive concrete bowls that dominated stadium construction during the '60s and early '70s, it was not a carbon copy of the others. Designed in the Brutalist style by architect Gary Allen, it featured an odd, squarish shape more appropriate for football than baseball. With home plate in one of the square's four corners, the result was relatively shallow foul lines but a spacious and deep center field. The horseshoe-shaped grandstand featured a tall upper deck that wrapped around the stadium on three sides, blocking out wind from every direction except right field, where a large scoreboard was situated. As was the case with most parks of the era, the seats were distant from the field, creating an air of impersonality that was reinforced by a 17½-foot-high outfield fence. After Murphy died in 1980, the park was renamed Jack Murphy

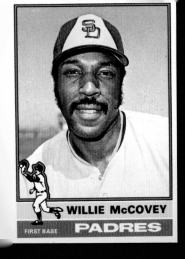

WILLIE McCOVEY
FIRST BASE
PADRES

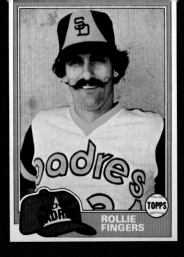

ROLLIE FINGERS

TONY GWYNN
Padres™

thrash the Arizona Diamondbacks 12-0 on September 3, 2003. San Diego reliever Brandon Villafuerte is facing D-backs catcher Robby Hammock, who will eventually draw a walk. Promising rookie Khalil Greene, at shortstop, is pictured here in his major league debut as a seventh-inning defensive replacement—scarcely a year after leading the Clemson Tigers to the College World Series.

The hapless Padres are on their way to a last-place finish in the NL West and a 64-98 record. The embarrassingly sparse crowd of 10,810 is not even their worst turnout of the year. Fortunately, the team will have only thirteen more games at this stadium before moving into brand-new Petco Park in 2004. One of the bright spots of the new season will be Greene, who will hit fifteen home runs and finish second in Rookie of the Year voting.

for its existence.

Like the stadium they played in, the Padres themselves were unremarkable. For many years their claim to fame was having the ugliest uniforms in baseball, with an unfortunate color scheme of brown and mustard. But personality finally arrived in the early '70s, when three of the most colorful personalities in team history came to town. First was Dave Winfield, the greatest athlete to enter baseball in decades, with talent so overwhelming that he was drafted in three different sports: baseball, football, and basketball. The Padres won the right to draft Winfield by posting the league's worst record in 1972, and when they signed him in 1973 they promoted him directly from the University of Minnesota to the major leagues.

However, Winfield's arrival was overshadowed by the news announced just days earlier that the Padres had been sold to a group of Washington, DC, businessmen. The new owners made plans to move the franchise to the nation's capital for 1974, and attendance at San Diego Stadium plummeted to a paltry 7,500 per game. But the relocation was nixed by the league, and a new buyer was found who promised to keep the Padres in San Diego. This was Ray Kroc, the flamboyant mogul behind the McDonald's chain, who treated the team as his personal toy—much to the delight of fans. During his first home game as owner, Kroc took over the public address system to apologize for the Padres' "stupid ball-playing." That same night, Kroc hired another man who was destined to become a San Diego baseball icon: Ted Giannoulas. Donning a yellow-and-red plush suit, Giannoulas billed himself as "The Famous Chicken" and delighted fans with his pantomime comedy routine. He became so successful that his chicken suit now resides in the Baseball Hall of Fame.

Despite the heroic efforts of Winfield and the comic relief of Kroc and the Chicken, the team on the field remained awful. The Padres posted only one winning season in their first fifteen seasons before finally capturing their first division title in 1984. That year, with an exciting young team featuring NL batting champ Tony Gwynn,

in the league in attendance six times, the Pads drew a team record 1.98 million fans in 1984 and broke two million the next year. In 1988, the stadium also hosted Super Bowl XXII, in which the Washington Redskins, behind quarterback Doug Williams, bludgeoned the Denver Broncos 42-10.

By the mid-1990s, however, Jack Murphy's 59,000 capacity was deemed too small for future Super Bowls, so the stadium was expanded in order to host the 1998 game. About 11,000 seats were added in the 1997 renovation, mostly in the upper deck, and the new-look stadium was now completely enclosed. It was also renamed Qualcomm Stadium after the telecommunications company, which paid $18 million for naming rights. This slight to Jack Murphy's memory was partially rectified in 2003, when a statue of the writer was placed in front of the stadium and the playing surface (though not the stadium itself) was dubbed "Jack Murphy Field."

Meanwhile, in 1998, the Yankees swept the Padres in the World Series, while Denver defeated Green Bay in Super Bowl XXXII at the stadium. In 2003, in Qualcomm's third Super Bowl, the Tampa Bay Buccaneers blew out the Oakland Raiders. A few months later the Padres opened what would be their final season at Qualcomm Park. As had happened in Oakland, the football renovations rendered the park even less suitable for baseball than it had already been. The Padres tried to create a more engaging atmosphere by covering some of the white elephant seats in the upper deck with a tarp, but it didn't work, and after much legal wrangling, ground was finally broken on a new park in the downtown Gaslamp District. Jack Murphy Stadium had never really been well suited for baseball, and few missed it once the Padres left for Petco Park. But as the team played out the string there in 2003, fans were nonetheless able to conjure up suitable nostalgia for the park's heyday of bumbling teams, ugly uniforms, a wacky owner, and a dancing man in a chicken suit. Though it no longer hosts baseball, Qualcomm remains in heavy use as a football venue, serving as home for the Chargers, the Aztecs, the Holiday Bowl (since 1978), and the Poinsettia Bowl (since 2005).

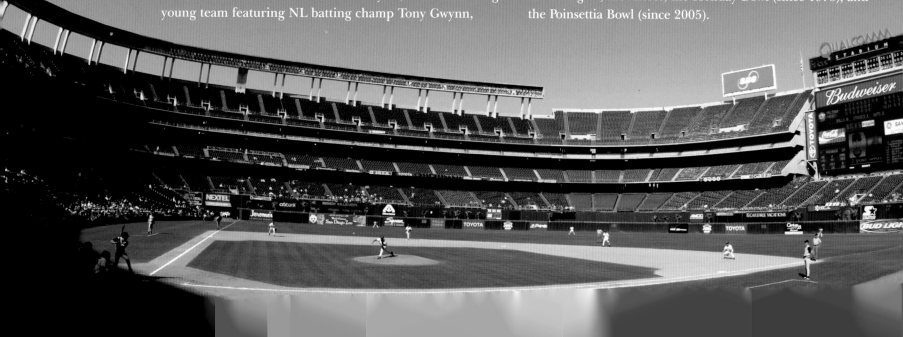

ABOVE: Jack Murphy Stadium as it appeared on April 4, 1967. The park, then called San Diego Stadium, would look like this until 1997: only three-quarters enclosed, with an open space where the right-field upper deck would later be. (Some of the football-motivated renovation can be seen by the scoreboard in the photo on the opposite page.)

Though the major league Padres didn't move into San Diego Stadium until their inaugural season of 1969,

a team named the San Diego Padres nonetheless called the stadium home in 1968. These were the minor league Padres—unaffiliated with the expansion team—who had played in the Triple-A Pacific Coast League since 1936. Although displaced by the major leagues in 1969, the Triple-A Padres won three pennants during the 1960s, and one could make a case that they were actually a better team than the 110-loss big-league club that took their place.

CAPS: 1979, 1998, 2006.

INSET: Ted Giannoulas, better known as "The Famous Chicken" or "The San Diego Chicken," poses in the stadium's upper deck on September 25, 2003, during the Padres' final home stand at the park. After a seven-year absence, the Chicken was brought back to celebrate the closing of the park that made him famous.

August 1, 1972 The Padres' Nate Colbert ties a major league record with five home runs during a doubleheader at Atlanta.

1974 McDonald's mogul Ray Kroc purchases the Padres franchise from C. Arnholt Smith.

June 30, 1984 Dodgers manager Tommy Lasorda famously quips that light-hitting Padres infielder Kurt Bevacqua "couldn't hit water if he fell out of a f--king boat."

1969

The expansion Padres begin life in a massive symmetrical stadium typical of the era. The imposing 17½-foot-high wall and dimensions of 330 feet down the lines, 375 to the alleys, and 420 to dead center don't help an inept team of castoffs.

June 12, 1970

Tied Up by Dock Pittsburgh's Dock Ellis no-hits the Padres in the first game of a doubleheader, a remarkable feat given that he will later admit to pitching the game while tripping on LSD. Ellis is wild, walking eight and hitting a batter, but he also strikes out six, including pinch hitter Ed Spiezio to end the game. Willie Stargell provides the Pirates' entire offense with two home runs. Despite San Diego Stadium having a reputation as a pitchers' park, nobody will pitch another no-hitter at the stadium until 2001 (although Pedro Martinez will pitch nine innings of no-hit ball here in 1995).

Pirates 2, Padres 0

1980

The name is changed from San Diego Stadium to Jack Murphy Stadium, after the sportswriter and editor who was instrumental in rallying local support for the expansion franchise and the stadium.

1982

The high walls are superseded by an inner fence that makes the park less formidable for batters. Center field is now only 405 feet away and the walls are only half as high, with the right-center-field fence just inches taller than the rest of the 8½-foot-high fence. About 10,000 seats are added to increase capacity to 58,000.

September 22, 1969

Willie Hits a Milestone A paltry crowd of just 4,779 witnesses Willie Mays become the second player in history (after Babe Ruth) to hit 600 career home runs. Pinch hitting for September call-up George Foster—who will eventually become quite a home run hitter himself—Mays blasts a two-run homer off San Diego's Mike Corkins. Mays's historic hit breaks a seventh-inning tie and eventually gives the Giants a victory. Also on this night, the Giants' Bobby Bonds strikes out for the 176th time this season, a new major league record.

Giants 4, Padres 2

July 29, 1983

Garvey's Streak Ends The longest consecutive-games streak in NL history comes to an end at 1,207 after Steve Garvey dislocates his left thumb in a home plate collision with Atlanta pitcher Pascual Perez. Garvey had set the NL record earlier in the year by surpassing Billy Williams' mark of 1,117 games. Even before his injury, though, the thirty-four-year-old Garvey stood little chance of surpassing Lou Gehrig's major league record of 2,130. Literally adding insult to injury, Garvey is called out at the plate while attempting to score on a wild pitch, and the Padres lose the game by one run.

Braves 2, Padres 1

RIGHT: Steve Garvey's NL-record streak of consecutive games played comes to an end in 1983, the year this photo was taken. After spending most of his legendary career with the Los Angeles Dodgers, Garvey signed with their hated rivals to the south, the Padres, before the '83 season. Ironically, the Padres would eventually retire his number while the Dodgers would not.

January 31, 1988 Jack Murphy Stadium hosts the first of three Super Bowls.

1994 Tony Gwynn bats .394, the highest average in the major leagues since Ted Williams hit .406 in 1941.

August 16, 1996 In the first MLB game ever played in Mexico, the Padres defeat the Mets 15-10 at Estadio Monterrey. Appropriately, the winning pitcher is Fernando Valenzuela.

October 7, 1984

Goose Cooks Cubs The Cubs' accursed history continues, as they blow a 3-0 lead to San Diego in a winner-take-all NLCS Game 5. Chicago manages to hold serve until the sixth inning, when two San Diego sacrifice flies make the score 3-2. In the next inning, Carmelo Martinez scores the tying run when Cubs first baseman Leon Durham boots a routine grounder, Tony Gwynn smacks a two-run double, and Steve Garvey (who will win MVP) knocks in another run for good measure. Goose Gossage pitches the final two innings to sew up the first pennant in Padres history.

Padres 6, Cubs 3

1997

In the search for extra revenue, Jack Murphy's name is stripped from the stadium and the naming rights are sold to Qualcomm, an upstart telecommunications company, through 2017. The stadium is also enclosed and expanded at the behest of the co-tenants, the San Diego Chargers.

1998

Qualcomm Stadium becomes the first facility to host a Super Bowl and World Series in the same calendar year. (The Metrodome, however, did it in a four-month span in 1991–92.)

2003

The Padres play their final game at the stadium on September 28 before moving to new Petco Park. The Chargers continue to play at "The Q," as it's known locally.

October 4, 1998

A Hitchcock Thriller The Padres polish off Houston in Game 4 of the Division Series, winning their first postseason series since 1984. The unlikely hero is journeyman lefty Sterling Hitchcock, who fans eleven Astros in six strong innings of work. The offensive spark is provided by pinch hitter John Vander Wal, who triples in two runs, and first baseman Wally Joyner, who follows with a home run. Although no official MVP awards are given in Division Series, the Padres' outstanding performer is Jim Leyritz, who hits three home runs in just ten series at-bats. The Padres will also win the NLCS before getting swept by the Yankees in the World Series.

Padres 6, Astros 1

July 25, 1990

Star-Bungled Banner In the middle of a lackluster Padres season, sitcom star Roseanne Barr sings the national anthem at Jack Murphy Stadium and turns in one of the most memorable performances of all time—and not in a good way. Barr screeches her way through an off-key rendition, capping off her performance by grabbing her crotch and spitting before a crowd of 27,285 bewildered fans. President George Bush calls the performance a disgrace, a description that could also apply to the Padres team, which will finish the year sixteen games out of first place. Tonight, though, they'll sweep the Reds in a doubleheader, with Tony Gwynn collecting five hits.

Padres 2, Reds 1
Padres 10, Reds 4

LEFT: Roseanne Barr screeches the worst version of "The Star-Spangled Banner" ever heard in baseball.

BELOW: Sterling Hitchcock hurls a pitch in 1999. The previous October, during the NLDS, Hitchcock turned in one of the finest clutch pitching performances in Padres history.

PARC JARRY

Montreal, Quebec

Expos (NL) 1969–1976

BILL STONEMAN

OPPOSITE: A former youth league field located in a municipal park, Parc Jarry had perhaps the most modest origins of any stadium in the modern major leagues. The most beloved figure in the park's early days was Rusty Staub, the hulking right fielder who hit .302 and crushed twenty-nine homers for the Expos during their debut season in 1969. The ginger-haired Staub soon learned to speak French, and was dubbed "Le Grand Orange" by local sportswriter Ted Blackman. "We come out here," one Parc Jarry fan told *Sports Illustrated*, "to have some fun, drink some beer, and of course, to see our Rusty hit the baseball."

When Parc Jarry was built in 1960, it was a nondescript community field in an idyllic public park setting, with a grandstand accommodating just a few thousand fans. By the end of the decade it had been transformed into a makeshift big league park, and hosted the first major league games ever played outside the United States. Though intended as a short-term solution, Jarry ended up serving as the home of the Montreal Expos for their first eight years of existence.

Located in the Villeray section of North Montreal, the twenty-square-block site was turned into a public park in the early twentieth century and named in honor of a former city council member, Raoul Jarry. In 1960, a community baseball diamond with a roofless grandstand, to be used for youth league games, was built among the urban oasis of trees, ponds, flowers, and fountains. Seven years later Major League Baseball decided to expand outside the United States for the first time, and a franchise was awarded to Montreal. Delormier Downs, the site where the minor league Montreal Royals had played, was dismissed as too small. After scouring the city for an appropriate temporary home for the new franchise, baseball officials decided the best solution was to expand Parc Jarry, which could at least handle the traffic the new franchise was expected to attract. (The park featured 2,600 parking spaces, and was located within a few blocks of subway, train, and bus stops.) Baseball officials weren't happy about the less-than-ideal facility, but the Expos, as the new team was called, expected to use the park for only one year until their new stadium, the Autostade, was ready.

In preparation for the Expos' arrival, the park's capacity was expanded nearly tenfold, from 3,000 to 28,450. The city paid 75 percent of the $4 million expansion cost, with the club picking up the rest. The original grandstand was extended all the way down the foul lines, a block of 7,700 bleacher seats was added in left field, and a press box was constructed as a mini upper deck behind home plate. A large scoreboard was built behind right field, and beyond that was a previously existing municipal swimming pool. On July 16, 1969, Pittsburgh slugger Willie Stargell hit what was believed to be the longest home run at Parc Jarry, a clout that landed in the pool with a gigantic splash. The pool, which still exists, is referred to by locals as *"la piscine de Willie,"* (Willie's pool).

JOHN BATEMAN

BOB BAILEY

KEN SINGLETON
MONTREAL EXPOS
OUTFIELD

BELOW: Parc Jarry, pictured here on February 13, 1969, undergoes frantic renovations to meet minimum size standards for the impending arrival of major league baseball. By June 1969, the park had been expanded from its original capacity of 3,000 to hold 28,450. Because there were bleachers in left field but not in right, the prevailing winds tended to favor balls hit toward left-center field. The stadium was built in the middle of a vibrant city park, boasting grassy fields, fountains, gardens, and even an unusual work of sculpture called *Paix des Enfants* (Children's Peace), featuring violent toys fused together.

When the Expos hosted Canada's first major league game on April 14, 1969, the expanded Parc Jarry was still a work in progress, and many fans sat on metal folding chairs since the permanent seats hadn't yet been installed. Players also complained that the playing surface was too soft, a problem caused by excess moisture in the soil from Montreal's spring thaw. By the time the game was over, home plate umpire Mel Steiner had sunk ankle-deep into the mud. The weather was unseasonably warm, in the high 60s, but the winter's snow accumulation was large enough that some fans were able to stand on massive snow piles behind right field and watch the game for free.

Although it was initially intended to be a one-year solution, the Expos ended up playing their first eight seasons at Parc Jarry. The city balked at the cost of expanding the Autostade—a multipurpose facility that had been built for the Expo '67 fair, after which the team was named—and retrofitting it for baseball. An entirely new stadium was planned, slated to open in 1972, but that too fell by the wayside. With baseball officials threatening to remove the Expos from Montreal unless a park was built, the Expos finally moved in 1977 to Stade Olympique, a new multipurpose facility built for the previous year's Summer Olympics. The stadium in Parc Jarry, meanwhile, was eventually renovated and renamed Stade Uniprix. It now hosts pro tennis tournaments. Parc Jarry itself remains one of Montreal's most popular recreation sites, featuring soccer and baseball fields, bocce and basketball courts, a bike path, a dog run, playgrounds, gazebos, and public gardens.

TIMELINE: PARC JARRY

1969

After being hastily expanded, formerly minor league Parc Jarry now holds 28,000, and 456 seats will be added during the season. The symmetrical dimensions are 340 feet down the lines, 368 to the power alleys, and 420 to center. The first game is played here on April 14, but construction continues into May.

April 14, 1969

Mack Attack The Expos win the first major league game played outside the US, beating St. Louis in front of a packed crowd of 29,184. Cardinal Curt Flood has the first major league hit in Canada, but Expo Mack Jones hits the first home run north of the border. Jones drives in the first five runs of the game, but the Cardinals rally for seven runs as Montreal commits five errors in the fourth inning. Pitcher Dan McGinn, who less than a week earlier hit the first home run in franchise history, singles in the go-ahead run in the seventh and earns the first victory on Canadian soil.

Expos 8, Cardinals 7

June 25, 1969 The Expos pull off the franchise's first triple play at Parc Jarry, with Bob Bailey and Bobby Wine teaming up on the play.

April 5, 1972 The franchise's first icon, Rusty Staub, is traded to the Mets for three players.

June 3, 1975 Andre Dawson, who will become the Expos' first homegrown superstar, is drafted out of Florida A&M University in the eleventh round.

September 29, 1971

Ouch! Montreal's Ron Hunt gains lasting fame—if not a lasting bruise—when he is drilled by a Milt Pappas pitch, the fiftieth time he's been hit this season. The figure is widely believed to be a major league record, but is actually second on the all-time list to Baltimore shortstop Hughie Jennings, who was plunked fifty-one times in 1896. Still, Hunt will get hit by more pitches than any other National League *team* in 1971. To top it off, he singles in the winning run in the bottom of the ninth.

Expos 6, Cubs 5

October 2, 1972

Aucuns Coups! Expos hurler Bill Stoneman pitches the first major league no-hitter to take place outside the United States. It's the second career no-hitter for Stoneman, who also pitched one for the Expos at Philadelphia in 1969. This time Stoneman walks seven and commits an error, but he fans nine and allows nothing even close to a hit until the ninth, when shortstop Tim Foli snags a bad-hop grounder and throws to first for the final out. Only 7,184 fans are on hand for what will be the only no-hitter ever thrown at Parc Jarry.

Expos 7, Mets 0

June 23, 1973

Brett's Hot Streak Southpaw Ken Brett dominates the Expos with a complete-game seven-hitter, but the real story is his bat. Brett goes deep in the seventh inning to put the game on ice and has now homered in four consecutive starts, a major league record. It's also Brett's fourth straight win and his third straight complete game. Ken will hit .262 for his career with ten home runs, but his younger brother George, still in the minor leagues at this point, will eventually become the family leader with 317 career homers.

Phillies 7, Expos 2

1976

The Expos host their last game here on October 2. Although most of the stands will be torn down, the original seats behind home plate will be left intact as the park is remodeled into a tennis facility called Stade Du Maurier (later changed to Stade Uniprix).

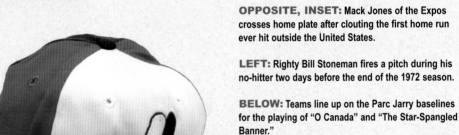

OPPOSITE, INSET: Mack Jones of the Expos crosses home plate after clouting the first home run ever hit outside the United States.

LEFT: Righty Bill Stoneman fires a pitch during his no-hitter two days before the end of the 1972 season.

BELOW: Teams line up on the Parc Jarry baselines for the playing of "O Canada" and "The Star-Spangled Banner."

CAP: Circa 1969.

THREE RIVERS STADIUM

Pittsburgh, Pennsylvania

Pirates (NL) 1970–2000

OPPOSITE: The perfectly round Three Rivers Stadium on May 17, 1992. Note the tremendous span of foul territory between the baselines and the first row of the stands. Typical of circular cookie-cutter stadiums, the layout sought almost literally to fit a square (actually, a diamond) into a round hole. Therefore even the closest seats were surprisingly far away from the action, and the cheap seats had views that were downright miserable.

Although Three Rivers Stadium got positive reviews upon its opening, Pirates fans never warmed to the huge concrete bowl on the north bank of the Allegheny River. In the thirty-one-year history of the stadium, the club ranked in the NL's top half in attendance only three times—and even then never crept higher than fifth. Those fans who did show up, however, were entertained by the prodigious power hitting of Willie Stargell and Barry Bonds, and by the final three seasons of Roberto Clemente's peerless career. But after winning two world championships and nine NL East titles in their first twenty-three years here, the Pirates' last few seasons at Three Rivers saw them embark on the longest sustained period of losing in baseball history. It was a fitting ending for a joyless stadium whose very existence was by then considered to be an unfortunate mistake by most.

The Pirates had wanted a new stadium as early as 1958, when they sold Forbes Field to the adjacent (and expanding) University of Pittsburgh. The school allowed the Pirates to stay until they could get a new park built, a wait which would turn out to be more than a decade. In 1968, ground was finally broken on a multipurpose facility to house the Pirates and the NFL's Pittsburgh Steelers. Designed by legendary stadium architects Osborn Engineering and built at a cost of $55 million, Three Rivers Stadium was supposed to be ready for Opening Day 1970. However, construction delays postponed its debut until July 16, when the Pirates played their first game at the still-not-quite-finished stadium.

Like many of its peers, Three Rivers featured movable seating blocks that eased the transition between baseball and football configurations. About 8,000 box seats along the baselines were shifted to become fifty-yard-line seats for football. The structure's round concrete shape and red-and-yellow plastic seats gave it a cookie-cutter feel, but one feature that stood out was a statue of legendary Pirates shortstop Honus Wagner, which had been moved from Forbes and placed outside the Three Rivers entrance.

In 1994 it would be joined by a statue of Clemente, the martyred star of the earliest Three Rivers teams. Despite the classical statuary, the park had a space-age feel. "Seeing the stadium for the first time from just beyond the outer walls is an experience in itself," wrote Dan Smrekar of the nearby *New Castle News*. "At first it resembles something from the future or maybe even another planet. The huge circular building with spiraling ramps makes you stop in awe."

Three Rivers Stadium also had a spectacular setting. The ballpark's name derived from its perch near the Golden Triangle, where the Allegheny and Monongahela rivers converge to form the Ohio. It was the exact spot where Exposition Stadium, the Pirates' home from 1891 to 1909 and the site of Wagner's greatest glories, had once stood. (A white pentagon painted on the parking lot pavement marked where home plate had been in the old wooden park.) The site was just across the river from downtown Pittsburgh, within walking distance for office workers, and also just a stone's throw from Fort Pitt, the colonial-era bastion from which the city derived its name. But alas, all of this scenery was invisible to those sitting in the stands, thanks to the completely enclosed upper deck necessary for football. Still, the drabness of Three Rivers initially took a backseat to the novelty, and upon its opening the park received mostly hosannas. "This sort of makes you forget about Forbes Field in a hurry," said one Opening Night attendee. Fans praised the brightness of the lighting, the completely unobstructed (albeit distant) views of the field, the large and informative scoreboard, and the short beer lines. "Three Rivers Stadium is a premier ball-park," wrote Smrekar, who had the audacity to compare the new facility favorably to Fenway Park. "It's a beaut," agreed another newspaperman, Fred Kavelak of the *Progress*. "Three Rivers Stadium stands out like a beautiful jewel in a pile of rocks."

Three Rivers was the first park to feature Tartan Turf, the 3M Corporation's version of AstroTurf. According to

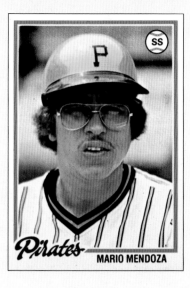

Pirates
MARIO MENDOZA

JOHN MILNER 1B-OF
PIRATES

BARRY BONDS
Pirates

Pete Rose, ground balls skipped over the Tartan Turf faster than on AstroTurf, and the newer surface was also less firm, making running more difficult. Hitters, however, found the park's symmetrical dimensions easier to deal with than the draconian Forbes, which had been a boon for triples hitters but drastically reduced home runs. (In Three Rivers' first three full seasons the Pirates hit 191 homers there, as opposed to 117 in their final three years at Forbes.) The capacity was more than 55,000, but by the 1990s ticket demand was low enough that the Pirates felt it necessary to reduce supply by covering many upper-deck sections with tarpaulins—creating yet another eyesore in a ballpark full of them. The team soon became even uglier than the ballpark, as the Pirates in 1993 began one of the longest losing streaks in the history of baseball.

Appropriately, the team ended their tenure at Three Rivers on October 1, 2000, by blowing an eighth-inning lead and losing their ninety-third game of the season. The stadium was imploded the following year on February 11, and the site is now a parking lot for the not-so-beautiful team's beautiful new home, PNC Park.

TIMELINE: THREE RIVERS STADIUM

July 16, 1970 In the first-ever game at Three Rivers, the Pirates become the first team to wear polyester double-knit jerseys instead of the traditional flannel.

1970

On July 16, the Pirates move into their first new home since 1909. Dimensions of Three Rivers Stadium are 340 feet down the lines, 385 to the power alleys, and 410 to center. The Pittsburgh Steelers will play their first game here on September 20.

1970 Playing half the season at Forbes Field and the other half at Three Rivers, Roberto Clemente bats .352.

1973 A year after winning nineteen games, the Pirates' Steve Blass becomes mysteriously unable to throw strikes, ending his career at the premature age of thirty-two.

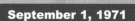

October 3, 1970

First Playoff Game Gary Nolan and Dock Ellis, the starting pitchers in the first game ever played at Three Rivers Stadium back in July, meet again for the first postseason game ever played on artificial turf. The Reds take this game, too, and will go on to sweep the NLCS in three games. Minor league umpires are used for this day's game, as the major league umps stage a one-day strike to protest low wages.

Reds 3, Pirates 0

LEFT: Construction on Three Rivers Stadium lasted more than two years, from April 1968 through July 1970.

RIGHT: Steve Blass throws a pitch during his three-hit masterpiece in Game 3 of the 1971 World Series. It was the first Fall Classic game ever played at Three Rivers Stadium.

BELOW: Al Oliver (center) is greeted by teammates Willie Stargell (left) and Roberto Clemente (right) after blowing open Game 4 of the 1971 NLCS with a three-run homer. The Bucs will win the game 9-5 to clinch the pennant.

September 1, 1971

A Victory For Diversity Pittsburgh manager Danny Murtaugh pencils in the first all-minority lineup in major league history. Six of the Pirates' starters are black and three are Latino. The historic lineup consists of second baseman Rennie Stennett, center fielder Gene Clines, right fielder Roberto Clemente, left fielder Willie Stargell, catcher Manny Sanguillen, third baseman Dave Cash, first baseman Al Oliver, shortstop Jackie Hernandez, and pitcher Dock Ellis. The Pirates hammer Phillies pitcher Woodie Fryman for five runs and send him to the showers in the first inning of a 10-7 win.

Pirates 10, Phillies 7

October 13, 1971

Adios, Daytime Baseball For the first time ever, instead of rushing home to see a World Series game after school, children are forced to bend their bedtimes or miss the finish of a Series game. To accommodate prime-time television, tonight's contest is the first World Series game ever played at night. The Orioles score three times in the first to knock out Pirates starter Luke Walker, but the Bucs' bullpen, led by Bruce Kison's 6⅓ hitless innings, stymies Baltimore the rest of the way. The Pirates take the lead in the seventh when a rare Paul Blair error keeps the inning alive and a pinch-hit single by Milt May snaps the tie. The Pirates tie up the Series at two games apiece, and will win it in seven.

Pirates 4, Orioles 3

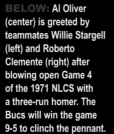

October 9, 1976 On his twenty-ninth birthday, Pirates pitcher Bob Moose dies in a head-on collision on a rain-slicked Ohio road.

May 12, 1979 Sister Sledge's disco single "We Are Family" is released. It will hit number two on the *Billboard* pop chart and become the Pirates' theme song.

1985 The Pittsburgh drug trials break open baseball's cocaine scandal, and several Pirates admit to buying cocaine in the Three Rivers Stadium locker rooms.

September 30, 1972

Exactly 3,000 Roberto Clemente collects his 3,000th career hit, a double against Mets rookie Jon Matlack. Only 13,117 attend the Thursday afternoon game to witness what nobody yet realizes will be the final regular-season hit of Clemente's career. On New Year's Eve, Clemente will die when his small chartered plane crashes shortly after takeoff from Puerto Rico on a flight intended to deliver relief supplies to earthquake-ravaged Nicaragua. The Hall of Fame will waive its regular five-year waiting period and Clemente will be enshrined after a special election in 1973.

Pirates 5, Mets 0

1973

The all-dirt infield is converted to artificial turf with dirt sliding pits.

1975

Dimensions are reduced by 5 feet down the foul lines and 10 feet in the alleys and center field. The new dimensions, 335-375-400, will remain the same for the rest of the stadium's life.

October 5, 1979

Pops Carries the Pirates After faltering in the 1972, 1975, and 1976 NLCS, the Pirates advance to the World Series for the first time since 1971 in a three-game sweep of their rivals from Cincinnati. The Pirates score in each of the first two innings on sacrifice flies, and Willie Stargell and Bill Madlock homer in the third. Stargell doubles in two more runs in the fourth, inspiring the 42,440 fans to sing and dance to the Sister Sledge disco hit "We Are Family," which Stargell and the Pirates have adopted as their theme song. The Bucs will go on to beat the Orioles in the World Series for the second time in eight years. Stargell will be voted MVP not only of the NLCS, but eventually of the World Series and the National League as well.

Pirates 7

LEFT: Roberto Clemente bats at Three Rivers Stadium in 1972, his final season before dying in a plane crash on a humanitarian mission.

May 3, 1985 Legendary broadcaster Bob Prince, terminally ill with cancer, calls his final Pirates game. He dies a month later.

1996 A group of financiers headed by Kevin McClatchy purchases the Pirates for $95 million. McClatchy will serve as lead owner and CEO until 2007.

1983

Tartan Turf is removed and AstroTurf installed. The turf will be replaced again in 1989 and 1996.

1993

Baseball capacity is reduced by 11,000 (to 48,000) as a tarp is pulled across the middle portion of the upper deck.

July 12, 1994

Moises Delivers His People The largest baseball crowd in Three Rivers Stadium history, 59,568, turns out for one of the most memorable All-Star Games. The NL ties the game on Fred McGriff's two-run homer in the ninth, and wins it on Moises Alou's clutch double in the tenth, with the portly Tony Gwynn chugging around the bases and barely sliding under the catcher's tag with the winning run. There are five lead changes in the game. Carlos Garcia, the only Pirates All-Star, collects one of the NL's twelve hits. It is the second and final Midsummer Classic at Three Rivers, the NL having won the other in 1974.

NL 8, AL 7

1994

A statue of Roberto Clemente is dedicated during the stadium's All-Star year.

2000

The Pirates play their final game at Three Rivers on October 1; the Steelers will follow suit on December 16. Three Rivers will be imploded in February 2001 to make room for a parking lot for the new football and baseball stadiums.

RIGHT: Tony Gwynn slides home with the winning run during the tenth inning of the memorable 1994 All-Star Game at Three Rivers Stadium. Missing the tag is catcher Ivan Rodriguez.

BELOW: The Pirates' John Vander Wal appears to heed the writing on the wall as he chases a home run on May 30, 2000, during the Pirates' final season at Three Rivers. Three Rivers Stadium had the dubious distinction of being one of just two non-domed stadiums to feature artificial turf throughout its lifetime. (Veterans Stadium is the other.)

July 12, 1997

Two Pitchers, No Hits With shades of Harvey Haddix's near-perfect loss in 1959 dancing through the minds of older Pirates fans, Pittsburgh's Francisco Cordova pitches nine no-hit innings, yet the game continues. It remains scoreless into the tenth as lefty Ricardo Rincon relieves Cordova and walks a batter, but retires the Astros without a hit. Pirates pinch hitter Mark Smith wins the day with a three-run homer in the bottom of the inning. The ten-inning no-hitter is the first combined extra-inning no-no in major league history, and also the first Pirates no-hitter in twenty-one years. The win ties the Pirates for first place with Houston; they'll win the next day and move into first. The two teams will remain close all year, but Pittsburgh will finish in second place, five games out at 79-83.

Pirates 3, Astros 0

RIVERFRONT STADIUM

Cincinnati, Ohio

Reds (NL) 1970–2002

Cinergy Field (1997–2002)

OPPOSITE: The Cubs and Reds line up before the Opening Day game at Cinergy Field (formerly Riverfront Stadium) on April 1, 2002. The Reds will win 5-4 on Aaron Boone's walk-off sacrifice fly in the bottom of the ninth. Cinergy and its predecessor, Crosley Field, traditionally hosted the first major league game played each season. In the 2000s, major league schedule makers put a stop to that tradition, instead scheduling the season's first game in international locales such as Tokyo or Monterrey, Mexico.

Though it was a round, completely enclosed bowl for most of its existence, Cinergy Field was partially demolished after the 2000 season to make room for the Reds' new park, constructed immediately adjacent to the old one. Accompanying this change was the replacement of the artificial turf with grass for Cinergy's final two seasons. Compare this photograph, which shows a vast open space in left and center field, to those from earlier seasons on the following pages.

The Cincinnati Reds, one of baseball's most tradition-laden teams, broke with the custom of using baseball-only fields in 1970 by moving to Riverfront Stadium, a gigantic multipurpose structure on the north bank of the Ohio River in downtown Cincinnati. It was the first time since 1884 that the Reds played their home games outside Cincinnati's West End, where Crosley Field and its predecessors had been built. The new stadium arrived just in time to greet one of modern baseball's great dynasties, the "Big Red Machine," which would capture four National League pennants and two world titles during the park's first seven seasons. However, Riverfront would never again see such heady days, as the Reds, though generally fielding winning teams, would make the World Series just once in the park's final two decades.

With seemingly every team in baseball opening a new park in the early '60s, the Reds clamored to hop on the bandwagon, and in 1962 voters passed a $40 million bond issue for a new multipurpose stadium. The main goal was to attract a pro football team to Cincinnati, but the Reds also stood to benefit, as an afterthought. After several years of delay, the American Football League awarded an expansion franchise to Cincinnati in May 1967, and construction finally began on the new stadium eight months later. A monument to unoriginal design, Riverfront had most of the same features as the dual-use stadiums that preceded it: a symmetrical concrete bowl shape, artificial turf, plastic seats color-coded according to price level, a set of movable stands on wheels, and a parking garage accommodating some 2,500 cars. But like Pittsburgh's Three Rivers Stadium, it also had an idyllic waterfront backdrop; the park was easily visible from across the Ohio River in Covington, Kentucky. On account of this cranky, unpredictable waterway, the stadium was one of the few to feature a flood wall. Among the long-before-razed buildings that had once stood on the ballpark site was the tenement birthplace of cowboy actor Roy Rogers, who liked to joke that he was born "somewhere between second base and center field."

N.L. ALL★STAR
JOE MORGAN 2B
REDS

REDS

TONY PEREZ

ERIC DAVIS

BELOW: The Reds line up for pregame ceremonies before the first contest ever played at Riverfront, on June 30, 1970. The first player along the first base line is Reds manager and future Hall of Famer Sparky Anderson (number 10), and to his right is all-time hit king Pete Rose (number 14). This is Anderson's first season as a major league manager; he will eventually manage 26 seasons and win 2,194 games, more than all but two other managers at the time of his retirement.

The Reds end up winning this game 8-4 on the strength of home runs by Johnny Bench and Tony Perez. The win bumps their record to a remarkable 72-32, nearly ten games better than any other team in baseball. Although the Big Red Machine won't truly jell until 1972, when Joe Morgan is acquired in a trade with Houston, the 1970 Reds will win 102 games and their first NL pennant in nearly a decade.

The decision to put turf in was an easy one for management, which felt compelled to keep up with baseball's latest fad. "Artificial turf will soon become a byword in sports stadia and we feel it's a must for Cincinnati," said team President Francis Dale. "It was the unanimous feeling of our people that Cincinnati's new stadium should be as modern and efficient as any in the country." The carpet cost $300,000, about $100,000 more than a traditional sod surface, although the fake grass saved the city thousands in future maintenance costs. The turf was everywhere, too. Earlier stadiums had combined AstroTurf outfields with dirt infields, but Riverfront became the first stadium in which turf covered the entire playing surface except for the pitcher's mound and small dirt cutouts around each base. "I like it; the ball hops better without the infield dirt," Reds manager Sparky Anderson said. "After they see this there won't be any infields with dirt. They'll all be this way. It's just great."

Riverfront Stadium's cost eventually mushroomed to some $40 million, and it wasn't finished in time for its planned opening at the beginning of the 1970 baseball season. Instead the Reds played their first game here on June 30, and were pounded by the Braves, 8-2. The stadium was still a work in progress. The scoreboard didn't work, there were no hot dogs because there wasn't enough electricity to cook them, and much of the parking lot remained closed. Remarkably, that night actually found more people seated in the upper deck (26,000) than the lower (25,000), a fact that neatly summarized multipurpose stadiums' greatest shortcoming: the seats

were simply too far away. But as with the similar parks in St. Louis and Pittsburgh, the opening of Cincinnati's stadium coincided perfectly with the rise of a dominant young team. The Reds drew a franchise-record 1.8 million fans during Riverfront's first season, winning the NL pennant for the first time in nearly a decade. With the Big Red Machine—a conglomeration of such stars as Pete Rose, Joe Morgan, Johnny Bench, and Tony Perez—maturing into a dynasty over the next several years, the Reds broke their attendance record four more times by 1976.

Even after the Big Red Machine's demise, the Reds usually fielded winning clubs, finishing in the first division twenty-four times in the park's thirty-three seasons. However, fans soon found that the multipurpose stadium experience left them cold, and Reds attendance reached its low point with the second-worst total in the league in 1983. Not even the 1990 world championship brought the fans back to Riverfront for good. The team tried to make the park more appealing for baseball by replacing the turf with real grass in 2001, but by then the Reds' new retro ballpark home, Great American Ball Park, was already being constructed next door. The sites were so close together that at one point the walls of the two stadiums were just twenty-six inches apart, and the encroaching construction project forced the Reds to demolish parts of Riverfront while they were still using it. The team played its final game at Riverfront Stadium— by then renamed Cinergy Field—on September 22, 2002, and what remained of the ballpark was imploded on December 29.

1970 Cincinnati fires manager Dave Bristol and hires little-known George "Sparky" Anderson to replace him.

June 30, 1970 Hank Aaron hits Riverfront Stadium's first home run—number 577 in his career.

November 29, 1971 The Reds make a trade that will transform the franchise, sending three players to Houston in exchange for Joe Morgan, Jack Billingham, Cesar Geronimo, and Ed Armbrister.

1970

The Reds christen their new multipurpose stadium, which they share with the NFL's Bengals, on June 30. Outfield distances are 330 feet down the lines, 374 to the power alleys, and 404 to center field.

INSET, TOP: Umpire Ken Burkhart, caught out of position, has to guess whether Bernie Carbo is safe or out.

INSET, BOTTOM: Pete Rose bowls over catcher Ray Fosse in the most famous play in All-Star Game history. Riverfront was the first park to host both an All-Star Game and a World Series in its inaugural season.

July 14, 1970

Rose vs. Fosse One of the most dramatic and controversial All-Star Games is played at two-week-old Riverfront Stadium. The NL trails by three entering the bottom of the ninth, but rallies to tie it on clutch RBIs by Dick Dietz, Willie McCovey, and Roberto Clemente. The deadlock lasts until the twelfth, when Pete Rose, Billy Grabarkewitz, and Jim Hickman all knock two-out singles against Clyde Wright. AL centerfielder Amos Otis fields Hickman's hit and makes a strong throw home, where the ball is waiting in catcher Ray Fosse's mitt as Rose dashes pell-mell toward the plate. Rose barrels over Fosse, knocking the ball out of his mitt and winning the game for the NL. However, the twenty-three-year-old Cleveland catcher lies on the ground writhing in pain with an injured shoulder. Although an urban legend will spring up that Rose essentially ended Fosse's career with the collision, in actuality Fosse will not miss a single game and will repeat as an All-Star next season. Only then will his promising career begin to disintegrate due to other injuries.

NL 5, AL 4

October 10, 1970

You're Out...I Think The first World Series game ever played on artificial turf is decided by a bizarre and controversial play at home plate. With the score tied 3-3 in the sixth, Cincinnati rookie Bernie Carbo charges home from third on teammate Ty Cline's chopper in front of the plate. The throw beats Carbo home, but Baltimore catcher Elrod Hendricks tags Carbo with his empty glove while holding the ball in his throwing hand. Carbo, meanwhile, clearly misses the plate. However, umpire Ken Burkhart is caught out of position with his back to the play, and ends up becoming part of the collision. After recovering his wits, Burkhart calls Carbo out, oblivious to the fact that he was never tagged. The Orioles take advantage of the gift call when Brooks Robinson, who earlier made a rally-killing play in the field, homers off Cincinnati's Gary Nolan in the seventh. Not much will go Cincy's way in the Series; the Orioles will win handily in five games.

Orioles 4, Reds 3

The stadium sits next to the Ohio River during one of its frequent floods, on March 6, 1997. Because its predecessor, Crosley Field, had often been rendered unusable by the floodwaters of the cranky Ohio, the new stadium was built on an elevated concrete platform. Just beyond the venue is the famed John A. Roebling Suspension Bridge, which at 1,057 feet was the longest suspension bridge in the world when it was completed in 1866.

October 11, 1972 The Reds win the pennant when George Foster scampers home on a Bob Moose wild pitch to end NLCS Game 5.

1977 George Foster becomes the fifth player in NL history and the first Red to hit fifty home runs in a season.

July 31, 1978 Pete Rose extends his modern NL-record hitting streak to forty-four games; however, it will be snapped the next night.

October 22, 1972

A Nail-Biting Series In an outstanding World Series that resembles a managerial chess match between Oakland's Dick Williams and Cincinnati's Sparky Anderson (and in which six of the seven games are decided by one run), the championship comes down to the ninth inning of the seventh game. The Athletics' Catfish Hunter, who has already won two Series games as a starter, enters in relief in the fifth inning and promptly gives up the tying run to Cincinnati. However, Oakland's Gene Tenace (the Series MVP) and Sal Bando wrest the lead back with an RBI double apiece in the sixth. In the eighth, with the tying runs on base for Cincinnati, Williams turns to his relief ace, Rollie Fingers. Fingers allows a sacrifice fly but escapes with no further damage, and in the ninth he gets Pete Rose to fly out for the final out of the Series. It's the first championship for the A's since 1930, when they called Philadelphia home.

A's 3, Reds 2

BELOW: A 1990 view of Riverfront Stadium and its gorgeous locale on the bank of the Ohio.

INSET: Pete Rose salutes Reds fans after collecting his 4,192nd hit.

CAP: 1998.

October 14, 1975

Obstruction of Justice? Although Carlton Fisk's home run will be the moment forever etched in history, Fenway Park isn't the only place for excitement during the 1975 World Series. The Reds take a 5-3 lead into the ninth inning of Game 3 on the strength of home runs by Johnny Bench, Dave Concepcion, and Cesar Geronimo, but Rawly Eastwick allows a two-run blast by Boston's Dwight Evans to tie it. With a runner on first in the tenth, Boston's Fisk fields an attempted sacrifice bunt by Ed Armbrister and throws the ball into center field, after which he argues unsuccessfully for an obstruction call. After an intentional walk loads the bases, Joe Morgan singles home the winning run.

Reds 6, Red Sox 5

September 11, 1985

Celebrating a Non-Record As his playing career grinds to a halt, forty-four-year-old player-manager Pete Rose keeps writing his name into the lineup as he seeks to become baseball's all-time hit leader. His single to left-center field in the first inning is the 4,192nd hit of Rose's career, sending him past Ty Cobb's official record of 4,191. However, there is overwhelming evidence that Cobb's correct total is 4,189, but MLB won't make the official change until long after Rose's record-chase is over. The crowd of 47,237 gives Rose a prolonged ovation—few realize that Rose surpassed Cobb's genuine total three days earlier in Chicago. A commemorative circle will be painted on the spot where the ball landed, but will later be painted over when Rose is banned from the major leagues for gambling.

Reds 2, Padres 0

September 16, 1988

Browning's Pitching Poetry As the Los Angeles Dodgers cruise toward the NL West title they're ambushed by Reds pitcher Tom Browning, who throws the twelfth perfect game in major league history. After a rainstorm delays the game for two hours, Browning throws 70 of his 102 pitches for strikes and fans seven, including Kirk Gibson (who's ejected for arguing) and Tracy Woodson (who fans to end the game). Tim Belcher allows just three hits for the Dodgers, and the only run of the game scores on an error by Dodgers third baseman Jeff Hamilton. Despite the setback (in front of only 16,591 fans, who held out during the rain), the Dodgers will win the World Series little more than a month later. Browning, meanwhile, will make another bid for perfection in 1989, only to have it spoiled in the ninth.

Reds 1, Dodgers 0

August 24, 1989 Reds manager Pete Rose signs an agreement that bans him from baseball for life after he's caught betting on his own team's games.

November 15, 1995 Shortstop Barry Larkin is voted NL MVP after leading the Reds to the NL Central title.

June 4, 2000 In his first season with the Reds, Ken Griffey Jr. loses control of the bat during a swing. The flying bat hits ten-year-old Christine Lindner, granddaughter of Reds CEO Carl Lindner, requiring eight stitches to her forehead.

October 17, 1990

David Slays Goliath Although popular opinion gave the Reds almost no chance to win the World Series against the vaunted Oakland Athletics, upstart Cincinnati wins its second consecutive game over the A's to take a 2-0 Series lead. Oakland knocks out Reds hurler Danny Jackson in the third inning, but Cincinnati's Billy Hatcher triples in the eighth for his seventh straight hit (a Series record) and scores the tying run on a groundout. In the tenth, the Reds knock three consecutive hits against previously invincible closer Dennis Eckersley, including the game-winning shot down the third base line by Joe Oliver. The Reds will go on to sweep the defending world champs in one of the most shocking upsets in Series history.

Reds 5, A's 4

1997

A locally based utility company, Cinergy, takes over the stadium name. Home plate, which dates back to Crosley Field, is replaced.

2000

The Bengals play their final game at Riverfront before moving to Paul Brown Stadium. With football obligations gone, the Reds switch the playing surface from artificial turf to real grass.

2001

Three decks of stands are torn down in left field to facilitate the building of the Reds' new ballpark, the floor plan of which slightly overlaps that of Riverfront. The dimensions are also changed for the first time in the stadium's history. The new asymmetrical measurements are 325 feet to left field, 370 to left-center, 393 to center, 374 to right-center, and 325 to right. To counterbalance the smaller field, the walls are raised to 14 feet high with a 30-foot-high fence in center. Capacity shrinks from almost 53,000 to 40,000.

2002

The last major league game is played here on September 22. A celebrity softball game takes place the next day, and is pointedly designated an unsanctioned event so that the banned Pete Rose can take part. The stadium is demolished on December 29.

ABOVE: Schottzie—the beloved dog of Reds owner Marge Schott and the team's unofficial mascot—was commonly seen throughout the park and was even allowed on the field before games, much to the displeasure of groundskeepers, who were usually forced to pick up after the dog. Schott, the first woman to purchase a major league team (rather than inherit it), was a controversial figure, and not just because she supposedly rubbed Schottzie's hair on manager Lou Pinella for good luck. She was beloved by fans for keeping prices at Riverfront low, but she was also a known bigot, which eventually led to her suspension by MLB.

LEFT: Oakland's Rickey Henderson leaps over a grounder during Game 2 of the 1990 World Series at Riverfront. At top is Reds hurler Scott Scudder; at bottom is second baseman Mariano Duncan (number 7), who will field the ball and retire Henderson on a force play. The Reds will go on to win the game 5-4 and sweep the Series four games to none.

The Many Faces of the Fall Classic

Since the first World Series in 1903, programs have been sold to fans looking for a lasting keepsake (besides a ticket stub and the occasional ketchup stain). World Series programs have varied greatly in look throughout the years, with a design aesthetic that frequently matches their era. For instance, those from periods of war or other politically trying times often feature overtly patriotic covers, such as the ones from 1917, 1940, 1941, 1942, and 2001. Collectible programs with an especially attractive design, or that cover a particularly historic game, can be worth hundreds of dollars. Following are the covers of some of the most interesting World Series programs of all time, including ones from the Reds dynasty.

ABOVE: World Series rings from 1940 and 1975.

BACKGROUND: Red's manager Pat Moran standing on the dugout steps during the 1919 World Series against the White Sox.

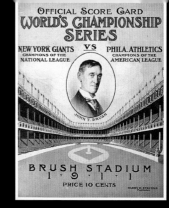

1903: Americans 5, Pirates 3

1911: Athletics 4, Giants 2

1917: White Sox 4, Giants 2

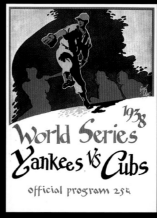

1936: Yankees 4, Giants 2

1938: Yankees 4, Cubs 0

1940: Reds 4, Tigers 3

1956: Yankees 4, Dodgers 3

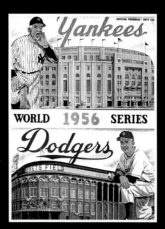

1958: Yankees 4, Braves 3

1960: Pirates 4, Yankees 3

1976: Reds 4, Yankees 0

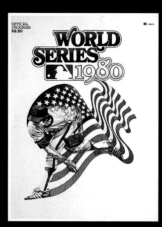

1980: Phillies 4, Royals 2

1985: Royals 4, Cardinals 3

1919: Reds 5, White Sox 3

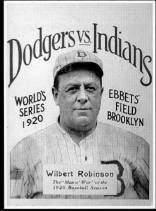

1920: Indians 5, Dodgers 2

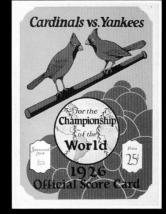

1926: Cardinals 4, Yankees 3

1931: Cardinals 4, Athletics 3

1935: Tigers 4, Cubs 2

1941: Yankees 4, Dodgers 1

1942: Cardinals 4, Yankees 1

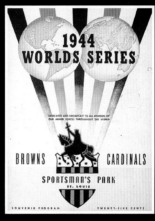

1944: Cardinals 4, Browns 2

1946: Cardinals 4, Red Sox 3

1954: Giants 4, Indians 0

1961: Yankees 4, Reds 1

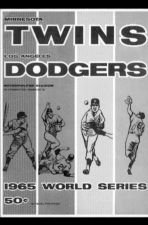

1965: Dodgers 4, Twins 3

1968: Tigers 4, Cardinals 3

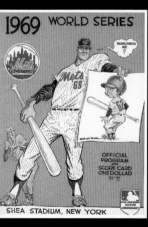

1969: Mets 4, Orioles 1

1972: A's 4, Reds 3

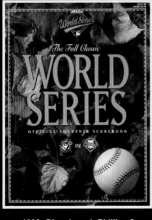

1993: Blue Jays 4, Phillies 2

1999: Yankees 4, Braves 0

2000: Yankees 4, Mets 1

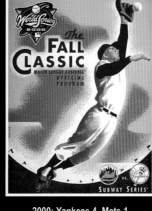

2001: Diamondbacks 4, Yankees 3

2002: Angels 4, Giants 3

VETERANS STADIUM
Philadelphia, Pennsylvania
Phillies (NL) 1971–2003

RIGHT: Given that the *New York Times* once referred to the Vet's upper deck as "a hostile tier of...public urination," these stadium workers' task of cleaning was probably envied by few.

OPPOSITE: The South Philadelphia Sports Complex as it appeared in 1971, the year Veterans Stadium (in the foreground) opened. Beyond the Vet is the Spectrum, home of the NHL's Flyers and NBA's 76ers beginning in 1967. Behind the Spectrum is John F. Kennedy Stadium, site of the annual Army-Navy football game and former home field of the Philadelphia Eagles. The historic football field was the site of a famed Jack Dempsey–Gene Tunney heavyweight fight in 1926 (attended by 120,000), as well as a concert venue for such legendary artists as the Beatles, the Rolling Stones, and Marvin Gaye. Behind JFK Stadium is the Delaware River.

Although the Sports Complex is still thriving, none of the buildings pictured here remain in use. The Wachovia Center, now the home of the Flyers and 76ers, stands on the site once occupied by JFK Stadium. The Eagles' new football stadium, Lincoln Financial Field, opened in 2003 directly east (left in the photo) of the Wachovia Center. And the Phillies' new home, Citizens Bank Park, debuted in 2004 just east of the site where the Vet once stood.

Through 1970, there was no team in baseball with a history as lackluster as that of the Philadelphia Phillies. In eighty-eight years of existence they'd managed to win just two pennants and not a single World Series. They owned the record for most consecutive losing seasons with sixteen, and had finished in last place twenty-one times. One player, Curt Flood, even filed a lawsuit to prevent his being traded to Philadelphia. It was no surprise, then, that the Phillies in 1971 seemed to shoot themselves in the foot by moving into Veterans Stadium, a concrete monstrosity that soon became a symbol of all that was wrong with modern ballparks.

When the Philadelphia A's abandoned ship in 1955, they left behind their storied ballpark, where the Phillies had been the Athletics' tenants since 1938. Originally called Shibe Park, the palatial stadium had once been baseball's crown jewel, but the Phillies allowed it to fall into disrepair, and in the late '60s they energetically hopped on the super-stadium bandwagon. The city agreed to pay for a new $42.7 million structure that would house both the Phillies and the NFL's Philadelphia Eagles. Instead of being perfectly round like most of its multipurpose brethren, Veterans Stadium was the second stadium (after San Diego's Jack Murphy Stadium) built in the shape of an octorad—that is, a square with heavily rounded corners. The Phillies tried to add a measure of color to the drab cement by installing green, yellow, and brown plastic seats, and a fountain spouting lime-green water beyond the centerfield fence. But nobody was fooled—this last of the concrete cookie-cutter parks was virtually indistinguishable from its predecessors, and just as antiseptic. Although it held more people than any other stadium of its time, most of them were far removed from the action, as the upper deck was even higher up than that of most super-stadiums. This was due in part to a block of twenty-three expansive luxury suites, which sold out despite an exorbitant rental price of $15,800 per season. For those who couldn't afford a suite, though, hot dogs and beer were more reasonably priced at 40¢ and 65¢, respectively.

Like almost all superstadiums, Veterans took longer than expected to construct, and the Phillies, who had expected to play their first game there in 1970, didn't do so until Opening Day 1971. Before the first game

a separate dedication ceremony was held, featuring speeches, dancing, and a football exhibition by the Eagles. Philadelphia fans, long famous for their boorishness, ushered in the stadium by roundly booing the city officials, the Phillies' front office delegation, and even the Eagles players. The only group that seemed to escape the crowd's wrath were the 168 scantily clad usherettes called the Fillies, 38 of whom belonged to a special group dubbed the Hot Pants Patrol.

At least everyone seemed to enjoy the newness of Veterans Stadium during its early days. "It's beautiful," utility infielder Terry Harmon said. "If you can't play here, you can't play." But one writer presciently predicted that "the Opening Day awe of the stadium will probably lessen as spring goes from summer to fall." Indeed, things began to get ugly once football season rolled around. In August,

N.L. ALL★STAR
LARRY BOWA SS
PHILLIES

PHILADELPHIA 3rd BASE
MIKE SCHMIDT **PHILLIES**

LEN DYKSTRA

games being played on a field criss-crossed with unsightly yard lines and hash marks.

Surprisingly, though, the Phillies made it work, winning seven division titles and three pennants during their thirty-three years at Veterans Stadium. In 1980, propelled by the hitting of Mike Schmidt—who led the NL in home runs and RBIs—and the pitching of Steve Carlton—who led the league in wins and strikeouts—the Phillies made it to the World Series for only the third time since their inception in 1883. In six games against the Kansas City Royals, the Phils won the first Fall Classic ever played entirely on artificial turf.

Still, the performance on the field couldn't make up for the increasingly abhorrent venue. "The Vet is a place of leaky pipes, unreliable heat and glacial elevators, a dank arena where a mouse-chasing cat once fell through the ceiling onto the desk of an assistant coach; where visiting players looked through a peephole into the dressing room of the Eagles' cheerleaders; and where the upper deck has gained a reputation as a hostile tier of taunting, public urination, fighting and general strangeness," wrote Jere Longman of the *New York Times*. Indeed, fan misbehavior was so rampant that the city was forced to open a police precinct and jail in the stadium's basement, a first for a pro sports facility. By 2003, the creaky Vet was the most deteriorated of the four facilities comprising the South Philadelphia Sports Complex, which also included the Spectrum (used for minor league hockey), the Wachovia Center (NBA and NHL), and Lincoln Financial Field (the new home of the Eagles). In 2004 the Phillies finally moved into a new ballpark next door, leaving the Vet without a tenant. A mistake almost from the moment it opened, Veterans Stadium was mercifully demolished on March 21, 2004.

when the Eagles played their first exhibition game, a traffic jam occurred, which many described as the worst in the history of the city. "The football fans acted almost rabid," one report noted. "Fistfights broke out when impatient motorists parked cars on lawns, in driveways, and even in the middle of the street." The same week, a fan died at a Phillies game when he was walking down an aisle and fell 27 feet through a hole in the concrete.

Fans and players alike soon came to realize that Veterans Stadium was a joke. Not only was the structure ill-suited for both sports it hosted, but the AstroTurf playing surface was widely reviled. With exposed seams, unsightly water stains, and dangerous dead spots, it was frequently voted the NFL's worst field, and caused career-ending injuries to at least two football players. In 2001, a game was even cancelled when the Baltimore Ravens refused to allow their players onto the unsafe field; Ravens President Joe Banner called the stadium "an embarrassment to the city of Philadelphia." Meanwhile, the turf's football markings—which at other parks were removed during baseball season—proved unable to be erased, resulting in the spectacle of major league

1972 In his first season as a Phillie, Steve Carlton enjoys one of the greatest pitching seasons of all time, going 27-10 with a 1.97 ERA in 346⅓ innings.

1976 The Phillies surpass two million in attendance for the first time in franchise history, drawing 2,480,150 fans.

1971

The Phillies open Veterans Stadium against Montreal on April 10. The playing surface is artificial turf. Dimensions at the symmetrical, hitter-friendly park will never change: 330 feet down the lines, 371 to the power alleys, and 408 to center field. The NFL's Eagles move in later in the year.

October 7, 1977

Black Friday What should have been one of the great days in Phillies history instead becomes known as Black Friday when the Phils blow a late lead, damaging their chances of winning their first NL pennant in twenty-seven years. In this NLCS Game 3, Dodgers pitcher Burt Hooton becomes unraveled by an umpire's call, walks in three runs, and gets pulled, exiting the field to a chorus of catcalls. The Phillies lead 5-3 with two outs in the ninth, but Greg Luzinski—who is usually removed for defense in the late innings—allows a potential game-ending line drive to clank off his glove. The Dodgers rally for three runs against Gene Garber and win 6-5, taking a two games to one lead in the series. Los Angeles will clinch the pennant the next night.

Dodgers 6, Phillies 5

1979

Field boxes and a picnic area are added, pushing capacity beyond 60,000. Capacity will continue to fluctuate, reaching as high as 66,000 in the mid-1980s.

BELOW: Although no actual sporting event was scheduled, on April 4, 1971, the Eagles and Phillies opened Veterans Stadium with a gala affair that included public speeches, dancing, cheer-leaders, and a football scrimmage in front of a crowd of 35,000. Though its capacity often changed, the Vet would remain one of the NL's largest venues throughout its existence.

December 5, 1978 After sixteen seasons with Cincinnati, free agent Pete Rose signs with the Phillies.

1980 Mike Schmidt is named NL MVP after hitting forty-eight home runs, a major league record for third basemen.

1983 The Phillies trade for Joe Morgan and the veteran-laden club, nicknamed "The Wheeze Kids," wins the pennant.

1980

Philadelphia deals with its notoriously rowdy fans by employing the latest in field security during the World Series, as police horses and guard dogs line the edge of the grass.

October 21, 1980

Royals are Flushed The Phillies, who won their first three games of the World Series on comebacks, lead the entire way in Game 6 to capture the first championship in franchise history. Mike Schmidt, who is named Series MVP, drives in the first two runs with a third-inning single. But the Royals, down 4-1 entering the ninth inning, load the bases. With one out, Frank White hits a foul pop-up that bounces out of Bob Boone's catcher's mitt and right into Pete Rose's glove, a play that will remain a staple of highlight reels for years to come. Tug McGraw then strikes out Kansas City's Willie Wilson (who Ks for a Series-record twelfth time) for the final out, to the delight of 65,338 screaming fans. Often derided as base-ball's laughingstock franchise since entering the league in 1883, the Phils finally are on top of the world. The final pitch to Wilson was "the world's slowest fastball," McGraw says, "because it took ninety-seven years to get there."

Phillies 4, Royals 1

August 10, 1981

Smelling Like a Rose Pete Rose, who tied the NL record for career hits the day before a player strike halted the season in June, finally breaks the mark in the first game played after the strike's end. Rose's single off St. Louis' Mark Littell is the 3,631st safety of his career, surpassing the record of Stan "The Man" Musial, who last played in 1963 when Rose was a rookie. Rose's feat is cheered on by 60,561 fans, a slightly larger crowd than the one that saw the Phillies raise their world championship banner on April 13.

Cardinals 7, Phillies 3

August 4, 1982

Double Singles Joel Youngblood, traded to the Expos earlier in the day, becomes the first player in history to collect hits for two different teams in two different cities on the same day. In an afternoon contest at Wrigley Field, Youngblood knocks a hit for the Mets, who then trade him to Montreal after the game. Youngblood hops on a plane to Philadelphia and arrives at the Vet during the Phillies-Expos game. He's sent out to play right field in the sixth inning and singles off Steve Carlton in the seventh. The Expos still lose to Carlton, however, 5-4.

Phillies 5, Expos 4

October 8, 1983

Sarge's Surge The Phillies win the NLCS, finally exacting revenge on the Dodgers—the team that beat them in both the 1977 and '78 NLCS. After being held to one run in each of the first two games, the Phillies' offense explodes, and they win Game 3 and tonight's Game 4 by identical 7-2 scores. Gary "Sarge" Matthews homers in each of the last three games of the series, and drives in just as many runs by himself as the entire Dodgers team (eight). Thirty-eight-year-old Steve Carlton wins the clinching game for this elderly club that has become known as "The Wheeze Kids." A crowd of 64,494 roars its approval as the Phillies clinch a pennant at home for the first time in the club's 101-year history.

Phillies 7, Dodgers 2

ABOVE: Pete Rose breaks the NL hit record in 1981 with career hit number 3,631.

FAR LEFT: Tug McGraw pitches the final innings of Game 6 in the 1980 World Series. McGraw will close out the Kansas City Royals to clinch the first world title in Phillies history.

CAP: 1979.

August 15, 1990 Terry Mulholland pitches the Phillies' first no-hitter at home in the twentieth century, blanking the Giants 6-0.

October 21, 1993 At the Vet, Curt Schilling pitches the first shutout in Phillies World Series history, topping Toronto 2-0.

2001 Phils rookie shortstop Jimmy Rollins leads the National League with twelve triples and forty-six stolen bases.

September 26, 1997

Phantastic Phinish In his final start of the year, Phillies hurler Curt Schilling fans six batters in seven innings, bumping his season strikeout total to 319. It's the most strikeouts for an NL right-hander in the twentieth century, six more than the record set by Houston's JR Richard in 1979. It's also six more than the total posted this year by Montreal's Pedro Martinez, who will nonetheless beat out Schilling for the Cy Young Award. In his final outing, Schilling defeats the eventual world champion Marlins. He'll again strike out more than 300 batters for the Phillies in 1998.

Phillies 5, Marlins 3

1998

After repeated disturbing incidents involving Eagles fans, a Philadelphia municipal court is established in the basement of Veterans Stadium, with a judge assigned to deal with miscreants. The court is moved off premises after the season.

2001

A new playing surface, NeXturf, is laid down, but the Baltimore Ravens cancel a preseason game against the Eagles because it is installed improperly over the baseball cutout area at third base.

2003

The Eagles play their final game at Veterans Stadium on January 19, and the Phillies follow suit on September 28.

2004

Veterans Stadium is imploded on March 21. The site is made into a parking lot for its successor, Citizens Bank Park, and stone replicas of the bases are placed where the Vet's real bases once sat.

BACKGROUND: Fireworks explode over the Vet in 2003—perhaps celebrating the news that the Phillies are about to move out of the decrepit stadium.

INSET: A work crew rips up the Vet's infamous turf in March 2001, replacing it with NeXturf, a purportedly better, more grass-like version.

ARLINGTON STADIUM

Arlington, Texas

Rangers (AL) 1972–1993

BELOW: With the Rangers off to a franchise record worst 11-26 start, outfielder Larry Parrish, left, and Doc Medich, right, don paper bags over their heads in the Arlington Stadium dugout on May 26, 1982. Both players have good reason to conceal their identities: at the time, Parrish is batting .157 while Medich is 2-5 with a 7.86 ERA. The club will finish with an abysmal 64-98 record.

OPPOSITE: The Rangers host the Baltimore Orioles at Arlington Stadium on June 1, 1974. Although both teams are struggling with records near the .500 mark, an impressive season-high crowd of 39,269 shows up in Arlington to watch the Rangers' Jim Bibby out-duel Baltimore ace Dave McNally, 4-2. Texas is propelled by homers from shortstop Toby Harrah and designated hitter Tom Grieve (who ten years later will become the team's general manager). Formerly a minor league park, Arlington Stadium by 1974 features the largest bleacher section in the majors. Unique for the era, the playing field is below street level, so all fans actually walk down to their seats upon entering. This will change when an upper deck is finally added in 1979.

Though it started life as a sleepy minor league park and ended up as a parking lot, Arlington Stadium witnessed its share of adventures during the two decades it housed the Texas Rangers, mostly at the hands of native son Nolan Ryan, who not only threw his historic 5,000th strikeout here, but also pitched his seventh and final no-hitter in the park. Located in a much less populous area than the Rangers' former home, Washington, DC, Arlington Stadium was the perfect example of a small park building a fan base in a new major league market.

In 1965, the Dallas–Fort Worth Metroplex lost one of its two minor league franchises when the Dallas Rangers relocated to Vancouver. The other local team, the Fort Worth Cats, moved into brand-new Turnpike Stadium and changed its name to the Dallas–Fort Worth Spurs. Built in the suburb of Arlington halfway between the two larger cities, Turnpike cost the city $1.5 million and held just over 10,000 fans. Its location adjacent to the state's most popular amusement park, Six Flags Over Texas, made it a frequent destination for families. In 1970, the city remodeled the five-year-old stadium and doubled its capacity in hopes of landing a big league team.

In the 1950s, after a half century of stability, major league clubs began shifting to new cities whenever the old ones weren't profitable enough. In 1972, Dallas–Fort Worth became the latest beneficiary of this version of musical

chairs when Washington Senators owner Bob Short decided to move his club to Arlington and call it the Texas Rangers. Turnpike Stadium was renamed Arlington Stadium, and its capacity expanded again to more than 35,000. (Precious few of those seats would be needed, though; average attendance didn't reach 20,000 until 1986.)

Most of the new seating was in the outfield, giving Arlington the largest bleacher section in the majors. A Texas-sized—and -shaped—scoreboard was also erected in left field. Strangely for a venue in one of the country's hottest areas, the park remained single-decked and roofless. Although the playing field was situated beneath ground level to keep the temperature cooler, Short still made a point of scheduling most games at night so fans wouldn't be subjected to the brutal Texas sun. Before the 1978 season, Arlington finally got its first shaded seats when a small upper deck was constructed over the main grandstand. Although the Rangers hardly needed the extra seating, capacity was now more than 41,000.

Pitchers loved the park, but power hitters were generally frustrated by it, as the flat suburban area's swirling winds made Arlington Stadium one of the toughest places in the league to hit home runs. In 1984, the Rangers hired sabermetrician Craig Wright, who became one of the first such baseball scientists to be employed by a club. On Wright's recommendation, the team tried to help its hitters by erecting a 30-foot wind-blocking wall behind the bleachers and a large scoreboard in right field. But by the time the Rangers developed a team with enough power to take advantage of the changes, Arlington Stadium had outlived its usefulness.

In the 1970s the Rangers had been so comically awful that they were the subject of a sarcastic memoir (Mike Shropshire's *Seasons in Hell*), but by the time they moved out of Arlington Stadium in 1994 they'd become a consistently winning team. The signing of Nolan Ryan for the 1989 season made them vastly more successful (and popular), and the Rangers soon began adding talented hitters like Juan Gonzalez, Ivan Rodriguez, and Rafael Palmeiro. In 1992, construction began on the dazzling new Ballpark in Arlington across the parking lot. The Rangers moved there in 1994, and Arlington Stadium—a minor league ballpark, all grown up—was torn down the same year.

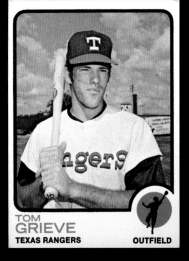

TOM
GRIEVE
TEXAS RANGERS   OUTFIELD

RANGERS

1B

PETE O'BRIEN

RANGERS   3B
BUDDY BELL

April 6, 1972 The first game in Rangers history is cancelled due to a short-lived players' strike.

1974 Jeff Burroughs becomes the first player in franchise history to win AL MVP.

April 29, 1980 The Rangers are sold to gas and oil magnate Eddie Chiles, who will own the club for nearly a decade.

1972

The Rangers play their first game at Arlington Stadium on April 21. Previously known as Turnpike Stadium when it was home to the minor league Spurs, the park has been expanded to 35,739 seats—many of which are outfield bleachers—to accommodate major league baseball. The symmetrical playing field measures 330 feet down the lines, 380 to the power alleys, and 400 to center field. Since the stadium has no roof to shield patrons from the Texas summer heat, virtually all games are played at night.

June 27, 1973

A Much-Anticipated Debut The most heralded pitching prospect in Rangers history makes his major league debut only twenty days removed from attending Houston's Westchester High School. Rushed to the majors with the team desperate for a gate attraction, eighteen-year-old lefty David Clyde walks the first two batters he faces before fanning three straight. The first overall pick in the 1973 amateur draft ends up walking seven, striking out eight, and allowing only one hit—a two-run homer—in five innings of work. The Rangers' Vic Harris and Toby Harrah drive in runs that enable Clyde to qualify for the win, and Bill Gogolewski throws four innings of stellar relief to save it for the youngster. As the Rangers had hoped, Clyde proves to be quite a drawing card, luring a crowd of 35,698 to Arlington Stadium on a Wednesday night. (The next evening the same two teams will draw just 3,992.) However, many will come to believe that Texas ruined Clyde by rushing him to the big leagues too soon; he'll go just 17-33 over the rest of his brief career.

Rangers 4, Twins 3

June 25, 1976

All Bat, No Glove Rangers shortstop Toby Harrah sets a major league record by playing a complete doubleheader without handling a single chance in the field. However, as the Texas cleanup hitter he's quite busy at the plate. Harrah drives in five runs in the opener, capped by a grand slam in the bottom of the ninth to win the game. Spitballer Gaylord Perry benefits from the late Rangers rally and notches the unlikely win. Harrah will knock in three more runs in the nightcap, a 14-9 defeat.

Rangers 8, White Sox 4; White Sox 14, Rangers 9

1979

An upper deck that extends between the first and third base lines is added. Capacity increases to more than 41,000.

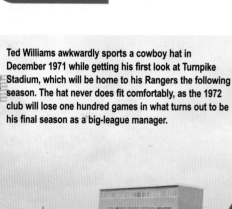

Ted Williams awkwardly sports a cowboy hat in December 1971 while getting his first look at Turnpike Stadium, which will be home to his Rangers the following season. The hat never does fit comfortably, as the 1972 club will lose one hundred games in what turns out to be his final season as a big-league manager.

David Clyde, fresh out of high school, makes the most anticipated major league debut in Rangers history.

CAP: 1970s.

December 7, 1988 The Rangers sign legendary Texan pitcher Nolan Ryan, most recently of the Astros, to a free-agent contract.

March 18, 1989 The Rangers are purchased by a group of investors that includes George W. Bush as managing partner.

April 24, 1992 Construction begins near Arlington Stadium on a new Rangers ballpark to open in 1994.

1985

Capacity is upped to 43,500 with the addition of more luxury boxes along the first and third base lines.

August 22, 1989

An Unbreakable Record The seemingly age-less Nolan Ryan strikes out Rickey Henderson, becoming the first pitcher in major league history to record 5,000 career strikeouts. (Four years earlier, he'd also become the first to reach 4,000.) Ryan is cheered madly by the 42,869 in attendance. The Ryan Express has proven to be quite a drawing card for the Rangers, who after signing him during the off-season, are on their way to drawing two million fans for the first time in franchise history. Ryan is a hard-luck loser tonight, though, on an unearned run and an RBI single by Jose Canseco. Bob Welch and Dennis Eckersley combine on the shutout for the Athletics. At age forty-two Ryan will go 16-10 on the year, capture his tenth strikeout title while fanning 300 for the sixth time, and get the win in the All-Star Game.

A's 2, Rangers 0

BELOW: It's officially "Nolan Ryan Day" at Arlington Stadium as the legendary hurler takes the mound on September 12, 1993, for the 805th of his 807 career games. Ryan takes the loss, gutting his way through 107 pitches before exiting in the sixth. Ten days later, his career will end suddenly when a tendon in his right elbow snaps during a game in Seattle.

May 1, 1991

Ryan Express: Next Stop, Toronto Nolan Ryan dramatically upstages Rickey Henderson for the second time in three years. At Oakland during the afternoon, Henderson steals his 939th career base to set the modern major league record, and proclaims himself "the greatest of all time" in an impromptu speech. In the night game at Arlington, however, something even more historic occurs: Ryan extends his own record by pitching his seventh career no-hitter, and becomes (at forty-four years, three months, and one day) the oldest pitcher ever to throw a no-no. His seven no-hitters have come against seven different teams: the Royals, Tigers, Twins, Orioles, Dodgers, A's, and now Blue Jays. Tonight's gem is the most impressive of the seven as Ryan whiffs sixteen Toronto batters, the most strikeouts ever recorded in a no-hitter, while walking only two. In an indication of Ryan's longevity, the last out of the game is made by All-Star Roberto Alomar, whose father, Sandy, played second base behind Ryan during his first two no-hitters in 1973.

Rangers 3, Blue Jays 0

1993

The Rangers play their final game at Arlington Stadium on October 3 without ever having hosted a postseason game or an All-Star Game.

1994

Arlington Stadium is razed. The Rangers now play a quarter mile away at the Ballpark in Arlington.

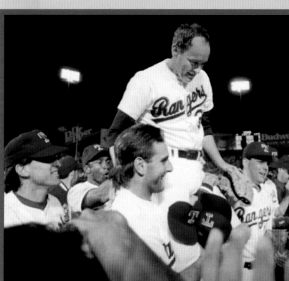

ABOVE: Ryan's teammates carry him off the field after his remarkable seventh no-hitter on May 1, 1991.

KAUFFMAN STADIUM

Kansas City, Missouri

Royals (AL) 1973–present

Royals Stadium (1973–1993)

GEORGE BRETT

Of the major league parks constructed between 1966 and 1991, all but one were virtually indistinguishable from one another. They were concrete bowls that usually featured artificial turf, symmetrical playing fields, and circular shapes that rendered them usable for both baseball and football but ideal for neither. The one glorious exception to this cookie-cutter trend was Kansas City's Royals Stadium, an oasis in the superstadium desert, which despite receiving relatively little fanfare, has remained one of baseball's crown jewels for more than thirty years.

The beautiful baseball-only facility had originally been meant for the Kansas City Athletics. In June 1967, in an attempt to keep the team in town, voters avoided the dreaded superstadium trap by passing a $43 million bond issue for two new stadiums: one for the A's and another for the city's new football team, the Chiefs. A's owner Charles O. Finley moved his team to Oakland anyway, but the AL took advantage of the already-approved stadium by awarding Kansas City an expansion franchise to begin play in 1969.

Royals Stadium and its football neighbor, Arrowhead Stadium, were originally envisioned as an audacious experiment. Chiefs owner Lamar Hunt proposed that the two parks not only be built next to one another, but that they share a single portable roof which would be placed on wheels and moved to whichever stadium had a game in progress. This pipe dream proved too costly, but the two parks were indeed built next to each other, albeit roofless, for a final cost of $70 million. Royals Stadium would prove to be a baseball oasis, but its least appealing aspect would always be its unfortunate location at what was called the Harry S. Truman Sports Complex. Located at a suburban freeway interchange some ten miles from downtown Kansas City, the area around the stadium was characterized mostly by the blazing summer sun radiating off an endless panorama of concrete and asphalt.

Royals Stadium was patterned after two Southern California ballparks built a few years earlier, Dodger Stadium and Anaheim Stadium. Like those parks, Royals Stadium eschewed the circular seating bowl that created

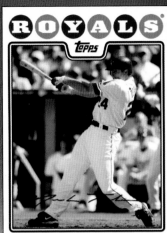

copious foul territory and placed fans far away from the action, instead featuring a more natural baseball layout in which the stands hugged the foul lines. Every seat was designed to point toward second base, and the modern tiered design meant there were no views obstructed by pillars. The park held over 40,000 fans, despite having no outfield seating. Instead, the team built a picturesque grass berm beyond the outfield walls, accompanied by an innovative fountain system that erupted in a spectacular pattern of dancing water and streaming lights between innings (or whenever the Royals homered). The fountains, which cost $750,000 and could shoot as many as 50,000 gallons into the air, became the park's signature feature. In their midst stood a 60-foot-tall scoreboard cleverly built in the shape of the Royals' crown logo.

Since Royals Stadium held fewer fans than most parks, owner Ewing Kauffman had to make up the revenue elsewhere. The average Royals ticket price was $6, far above the league norm. A luxurious stadium club was also built along the right-field line; to enter, fans had to buy a $300 annual membership and pay $25 in monthly dues. During periods when the team was winning, the park's small capacity worked in ownership's favor as the reduced supply made the Royals a hot ticket.

The park's most obvious shortcoming was a predictable one for the 1970s: artificial turf. Royals was the first AL stadium to be completely covered by synthetic grass, 3M's Tartan Turf. And although 3M's version was supposed to be more sturdy than its predecessor, AstroTurf, the artificial grass was inexpertly installed, resulting in gaps between the seams. The warning track was also made of a synthetic material that the outfielders hated. Nonetheless, Royals manager Jack McKeon believed his team's defense would benefit from the turf. "You'll see the shortstop and second baseman make more plays, because of the true hop," McKeon said. "Those two positions will be like short fielders in softball, because they'll be playing very deep." In 1975, McKeon was replaced by Whitey Herzog, one of the era's baseball visionaries, who vowed to take even better advantage of the turf than McKeon had. Herzog stocked his team with fast outfielders, stellar defenders, and base stealers, the types of players who were believed to give a team an advantage playing on the carpet. In 1976 Herzog's Royals, with a roster featuring eight players with at least twenty steals apiece, captured the franchise's first division title. They would win the AL West three years in a row before Herzog departed to work his magic in St. Louis. However, the characteristics of the team he constructed remained largely intact, and the Royals won the pennant in 1980 and the World Series in 1985.

In 1993, Ewing Kauffman, the pharmaceutical mogul who had owned the team since its inception, fell ill at the age of seventy-six. On July 2, 1993, Royals Stadium was

renamed Kauffman Stadium in honor of its benefactor, who passed away a month later. In 1995, with artificial turf having fallen out of favor in the major leagues, the Royals replaced it with natural grass. With the park's lone negative feature jettisoned, the well-kept Kauffman Stadium became as pleasant an atmosphere for baseball as exists in the majors. At the same time the team also moved the outfield fences in, making the park even more of a hitter's haven than it had previously been. By 2001, Kauffman's park factor of 110—meaning that it increased offense by ten percent over the average stadium—made it the best hitter's park in the AL.

In 2006, voters approved a sales tax increase to fund a $250 million renovation of Kauffman Stadium. The improvements, completed by Opening Day 2009, included an 8,900-square-foot high-definition video board purported to be the largest of its kind in the world. Other additions included new bullpens, widened concourses, a new press box, a food court, a Royals Hall of Fame, and a promenade encircling the stadium. In an era when most teams push for new ballparks at the drop of a hat, the Royals, like the Red Sox and Dodgers, have instead chosen to pour money into modernizing an already classic park. It is a decision for which future generations of fans will surely be grateful.

August 2, 1973 George Brett makes his major league debut at Royals Stadium, going 1-for-4 against Chicago's Stan Bahnsen.

1976 Whitey Herzog, who took over as manager in the middle of the previous season, leads the Royals to the playoffs for the first time in franchise history.

1973

Unlike other parks featuring artificial turf and symmetrical dimensions (330 feet down the lines, 375 to the power alleys, and 405 to center field), Royals Stadium is built solely for baseball. The upper deck looks like it's been carefully snipped, tapering off at an angle. With no bleachers, the venue holds just 40,000 fans, far fewer than the dual-sport stadiums built the previous decade. A fountain behind the centerfield fence starts working in time for the All-Star Game.

July 24, 1973

A National League Rout Royals starters John Mayberry and Amos Otis combine for three of the AL's five hits in the All-Star Game, but the Junior Circuit loses to the NL nonetheless. Otis' third-inning single drives in Reggie Jackson for a 1-0 lead, but Johnny Bench ties it back up with a home run leading off the fourth. Bobby Bonds, who will be named game MVP, hits a two-run homer for the NL in the fifth, and Rick Wise earns the win. Willie Mays strikes out in his final All-Star appearance.

NL 7, AL 1

BELOW: Kauffman Stadium in 1997, two years after natural grass was added, making it one of the most pleasant places in the majors to enjoy a game.

BELOW: Johnny Bench shakes hands with the Cubs' Ron Santo after hitting a solo homer to give the National League a 3-1 lead in the 1973 All-Star Game.

1978 The Royals lose their third consecutive ALCS to the Yankees despite George Brett's .389 average and three home runs.

1980 George Brett's home run off Goose Gossage at Yankee Stadium helps the Royals win their first ever AL pennant.

1983 Royals closer Dan Quisenberry sets a major league record with forty-five saves.

October 3, 1976

Down to the Wire A wild three-way race for the AL batting title comes down to the final inning of the year, with the three front-runners all playing in the same season-ending game. Minnesota's Rod Carew and Kansas City's George Brett and Hal McRae enter the final day with batting averages separated by just .001. Carew has two hits in the game, finishing at .331. Brett and McRae, meanwhile, are each 2-for-3 entering the ninth. Brett's blooper drops in front of Twins outfielder Steve Brye and skips all the way to the wall for an inside-the-park home run, bringing McRae up next needing a hit to clinch the crown. Instead McRae grounds out and loses the title to Brett, .333 to .332. An enraged McRae (who is African-American) charges the Twins with racism, alleging that Brye's misplay was deliberate.

Twins 5, Royals 3

1978

With Whitey Herzog's Royals using speed as their main weapon, the fences are pushed back 10 feet in the alleys and 5 feet in center.

BELOW, LEFT: George Brett celebrates after his bases-clearing double in the ninth inning on August 17, 1980. The hit raises Brett's average over .400 for the first time all season.

BELOW, RIGHT: Paul Splittorff throws a pitch at Royals Stadium in 1978. The franchise's all-time leader in wins and innings pitched, Splittorff enjoyed his finest season in '78, going 19-13.

August 17, 1980

King for a Day George Brett reaches the hallowed .400 mark with a 4-for-4 outburst against Toronto, capping his day with a bases-clearing double that breaks open a close game in the eighth. Brett, who has now had hits in twenty-nine straight games, receives a long ovation. His hitting streak will reach thirty before it's snapped, and his average will top .400 as late as September 20. He'll eventually drop to .390, though, failing in his attempt to become the first player to bat .400 since Ted Williams in 1941. Brett, who will miss forty-five games this year with injuries, will nonetheless win the AL MVP.

Royals 8, Blue Jays 3

October 17, 1980

It's World Series Time A raucous crowd of 42,380 packs Royals Stadium for Game 3 as the World Series comes to Kansas City for the first time. George Brett hits the first ever Series homer at the stadium, and Amos Otis adds another in the seventh to give the Royals a 4-3 lead. The Phillies tie it back up on a Pete Rose hit, though, and the game stays tied until the tenth. In the top of that inning, an outstanding defensive play by Frank White saves the Royals, and in the bottom half Willie Aikens singles in the winning run for the home team. The Royals will win again the next day, but will eventually lose the Series in six games.

Royals 4, Phillies 3

1985 Bret Saberhagen, twenty-one, becomes the youngest pitcher ever to win the Cy Young, but is supplanted two days later by twenty-year-old NL winner Dwight Gooden.

September 2, 1986 Nine months after winning the Heisman Trophy, former Auburn running back Bo Jackson makes his major league debut.

June 17, 1987 A year and a half after managing Kansas City to the world title, Dick Howser dies of a brain tumor.

October 27, 1985

Royals Inherit the Crown After winning a controversial Game 6, the Royals capture their first World Series title with an 11-0 rout of cross-state rivals the St. Louis Cardinals in Game 7 of the "Interstate 70 Series." Cardinals starter John Tudor lasts only until the third, when he's removed after suffering a bout of wildness. The Royals jump all over the St. Louis relievers, too, led by a Steve Balboni two-run single. Bret Saberhagen, Kansas City's twenty-one-year-old ace, tosses a five-hit shutout and is named Series MVP. Cardinals manager Whitey Herzog and starter Joaquin Andujar are both ejected in the fifth inning, ostensibly for arguing balls and strikes, although both are likely still peeved about the egregiously blown call by first base umpire Don Denkinger that gave the previous night's game to Kansas City.

Royals 11, Cardinals 0

September 14, 1986

Bo Knows Longballs Bo Jackson, the 1985 Heisman Trophy winner who has chosen to play baseball instead of football, launches a 475-foot homer off Seattle's Mike Moore that is the longest ball ever hit at Royals Stadium. It's the first home run of Jackson's career. After having spurned the Tampa Bay Buccaneers, who selected him with the first overall pick in the 1986 NFL draft, Jackson will later play for the Los Angeles Raiders starting in 1987. He'll also continue his baseball career, spending five memorable seasons with the Royals and becoming one of the most beloved players in franchise history. Nike's "Bo Knows" advertising campaign will make Jackson a recognized figure nationwide, but a hip injury suffered on the gridiron will cut short his career in both sports, though he will go on to play two more seasons (for two different teams) in major league baseball.

Royals 10, Mariners 3

LEFT: The introduction of interleague play revives the intrastate rivalry between the Royals and Cardinals, who'd previously met only in the 1985 World Series. Here the two teams face off at Kauffman Stadium in 2008.

ABOVE: The most heralded prospect in Royals history, Bo Jackson brought a new era of excitement to Royals Stadium after the former Heisman Trophy winner was lured away from the NFL in 1986.

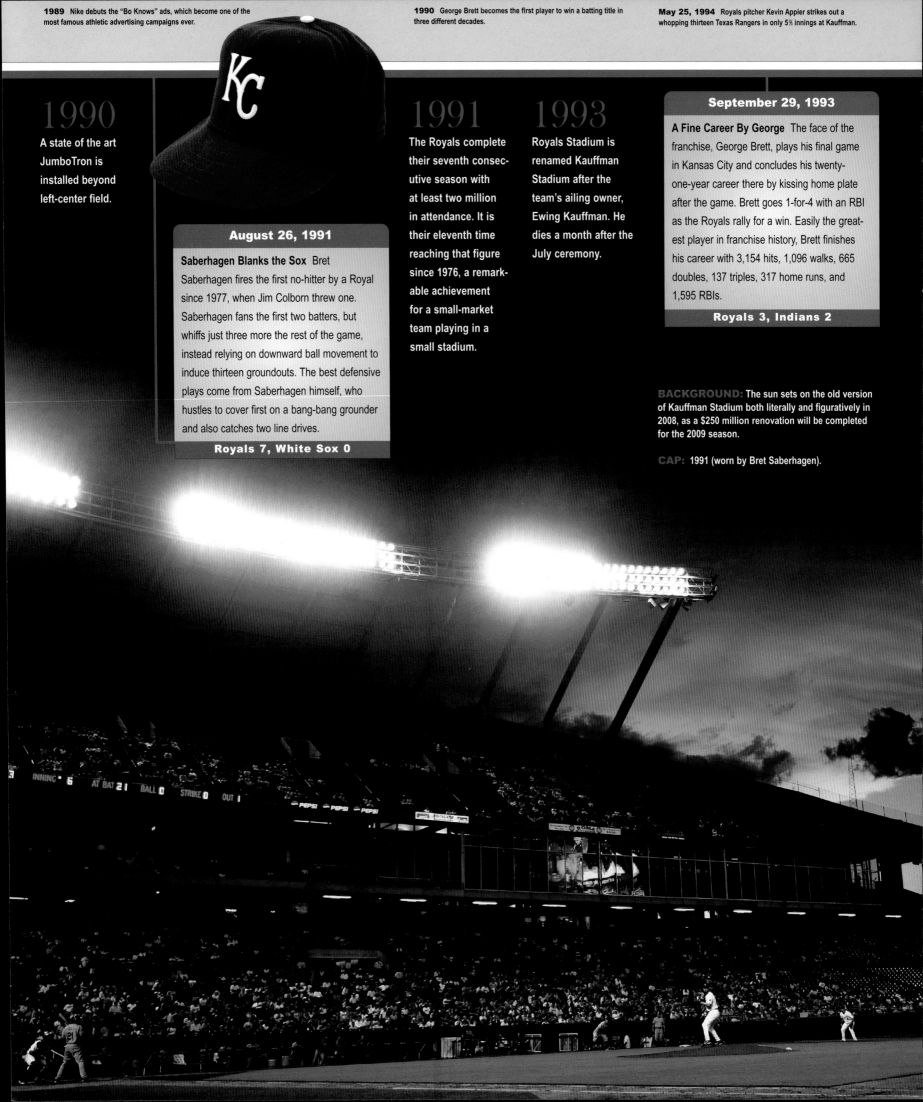

1989 Nike debuts the "Bo Knows" ads, which become one of the most famous athletic advertising campaigns ever.

1990 George Brett becomes the first player to win a batting title in three different decades.

May 25, 1994 Royals pitcher Kevin Appier strikes out a whopping thirteen Texas Rangers in only 5⅔ innings at Kauffman.

1990

A state of the art JumboTron is installed beyond left-center field.

1991

The Royals complete their seventh consecutive season with at least two million in attendance. It is their eleventh time reaching that figure since 1976, a remarkable achievement for a small-market team playing in a small stadium.

1993

Royals Stadium is renamed Kauffman Stadium after the team's ailing owner, Ewing Kauffman. He dies a month after the July ceremony.

August 26, 1991

Saberhagen Blanks the Sox Bret Saberhagen fires the first no-hitter by a Royal since 1977, when Jim Colborn threw one. Saberhagen fans the first two batters, but whiffs just three more the rest of the game, instead relying on downward ball movement to induce thirteen groundouts. The best defensive plays come from Saberhagen himself, who hustles to cover first on a bang-bang grounder and also catches two line drives.

Royals 7, White Sox 0

September 29, 1993

A Fine Career By George The face of the franchise, George Brett, plays his final game in Kansas City and concludes his twenty-one-year career there by kissing home plate after the game. Brett goes 1-for-4 with an RBI as the Royals rally for a win. Easily the greatest player in franchise history, Brett finishes his career with 3,154 hits, 1,096 walks, 665 doubles, 137 triples, 317 home runs, and 1,595 RBIs.

Royals 3, Indians 2

BACKGROUND: The sun sets on the old version of Kauffman Stadium both literally and figuratively in 2008, as a $250 million renovation will be completed for the 2009 season.

CAP: 1991 (worn by Bret Saberhagen).

September 30, 1998 Legendary Royals reliever Dan Quisenberry dies of brain cancer.

1995

The playing surface is changed to grass, and field dimensions are shortened by 10 feet in the alleys and in center, making the park a home run–hitter's haven. In 2004 the park will revert to its late 1970s dimensions.

2007

A $250 million renovation, funded by a sales tax increase, begins after the 2007 season ends. The improvements include a high-definition scoreboard, widened concourses, more restaurants, and a plaza behind the signature fountain.

ABOVE: A worker cleans the windows of the Stadium Club in 2006.

July 17, 2003

Cinderella at the Ball The upstart Royals begin the season's second half with a win over the Mariners, improving their record to 52-41 and giving them a 7½ game lead over defending AL Central champion Minnesota. After losing one hundred games in 2002 the Royals are now baseball's most improbable success story, particularly since their manager, Tony Peña, is in his first full year as a big league skipper. Tonight's winning pitcher, Jose Lima, was acquired from an independent league team in June and is now 6-0 since his return to the majors. Alas, as happens in most Cinderella stories, Kansas City soon turns back into a pumpkin. Although the Royals will remain in contention most of the season, they'll be pushed out of first place for good on August 20. The Royals will finish seven games behind the Twins, but their 83-79 record, the team's best in a decade, will earn Peña Manager of the Year honors.

Royals 7, Mariners 1

September 25, 2005

Here Comes the Sun Despite enduring another hundred-loss season, having their manager quit, and suffering through separate losing streaks of eight, nine, and nineteen games, the Royals are still able to help knock a rival out of the postseason—with a little help from the sun. With the Royals and Indians tied in the ninth, Kansas City's Paul Phillips hits a seemingly routine fly ball, but Cleveland centerfielder Grady Sizemore loses it in the sun and Angel Berroa scores to win the game. The loss starts Cleveland on a devastating final week of the season, and they'll end up missing the playoffs by one game.

Royals 5, Indians 4

LEFT: Alex Gordon, the most heralded Royals prospect since Bo Jackson, homers off Boston's Clay Buchholz in 2008.

EXHIBITION STADIUM

Toronto, Ontario

Blue Jays (AL) 1977–1989

In 1977, the big league arrived in Toronto, where the Blue Jays spent their first dozen years playing on an awkwardly converted football field where snow and freezing rain were often blown in from nearby Lake Ontario. Exhibition Stadium, the renovated home of the Canadian Football League's Toronto Argonauts, was less than ideal for baseball, but it proved popular enough with fans in the frozen north who were starving for some major league action. Despite the horrendous weather, the converted stadium attracted well over a million fans every full season until the Jays departed for the ultramodern SkyDome in 1989.

When the American League awarded Toronto an expansion franchise in March 1976, the city had just thirteen months to choose and prepare a stadium site before beginning play the following April. Since the city's Triple-A stadium had been torn down when the minor league team left town, Exhibition Stadium was identified as the most logical candidate. The site had been used as an athletic field since 1879, with the stadium structure having been rebuilt several times, most recently in 1948. It was retrofitted for football in 1959, and because Canadian football fields are 30 yards longer than American ones, Exhibition Stadium proved an even worse fit for baseball than most multipurpose stadiums. But after an $18 million renovation, the structure was rendered at least somewhat usable. The main football grandstand became the left-field bleachers, and a smaller section of seats was added around home plate. Because of this unusual configuration, it became the only major league park where the bleachers were roofed but the main grandstand was not. Some seats were as far as 820 feet from home, and others past left-center field had such terrible views for baseball that the Jays didn't even bother to offer them for sale.

The least appealing aspect of Exhibition, though, was its location just a block from Lake Ontario, which resulted in swirling winds and frequent deluges of lake-effect snow. Expecting intolerable evening temperatures,

the Blue Jays scheduled all eleven of their April 1977 home games during the daytime. The harsh weather was nonetheless in full effect on Opening Day, when the mercury crept no higher than 32°F with the wind chill below zero. Gusts of snow blew all over the park, and the Jays even had to borrow a Zamboni machine from the NHL's Maple Leafs to clear the infield between innings. The conditions enraged the visiting Chicago White Sox, who were reluctant to even take the field. "What you saw out there today was not baseball," Chicago slugger Richie Zisk said. "It was a travesty, a circus. There is no way that the game should have been played. I'm just thankful no one was injured."

But after waiting so many years for big league baseball, hardy Torontonians were not about to let some bad weather ruin their good time. They enthusiastically cheered on the new team, although they did voice one complaint in the form of a chant: "We want beer! We want beer!" Thanks to Ontario's strict liquor laws, alcohol sales were prohibited at Jays games, making Exhibition the only major league stadium not to offer beer. (The province finally relented in 1982.) Despite this shortcoming, 1.7 million fans flocked to see the Jays play in 1977, shattering the first-year attendance record of 1.2 million set by the 1969 Expos. The Jays encouraged interest by building a quality team remarkably quickly for an expansion club, posting their first winning record in 1983 and never again falling below .500 during their tenure at Exhibition. But despite the franchise's success, it was apparent from the beginning that Toronto needed a domed stadium to protect fans from the elements. The Jays played their last game here on May 28, 1989, before moving into the luxurious SkyDome, 1½ miles north. The Argonauts moved to SkyDome, too, leaving Exhibition Stadium vacant except for the occasional concert by the Rolling Stones, Pearl Jam, or Neil Young. The building was demolished in 1999 and the site is now home to BMO Field, a Major League Soccer stadium.

Jimmy Key

Jesse Barfield

DAVE STIEB

March 26, 1976 American League owners vote to award an expansion franchise to Toronto, with the team to begin play the following year.

April 22, 1978 The Blue Jays turn their first ever triple play, which is started by eventual winning pitcher Jim Clancy.

1978 The Jays convert minor league outfielder Dave Stieb into a pitcher; he'll eventually win more games than any other hurler in franchise history.

1977

Exhibition Stadium, built to host Canadian Football League games, is remodeled in time for the first Blue Jays contest on April 7. The grandstand extends far beyond the outfield fence, putting some of the 43,000 fans as far as 300 feet away from the field. Despite the odd shape of the stands, the playing field is symmetrical: 330 feet down the lines, 375 to the power alleys, and 400 to center field.

April 7, 1977

A Chilling Debut On a freezing Thursday afternoon, 44,649 fans brave the snow to witness the first AL game ever played in Canada. The first batter is the White Sox's Ralph Garr, who is walked by Toronto pitcher Bill Singer. Later in the inning, Richie Zisk homers for the first AL hit and home run north of the border. Opening Day has a happy ending for the expansion Blue Jays, however, as Doug Ault hits the first two homers of his career and leads the Jays to an epic comeback. Down 4-1 early in the game, Toronto rallies to win 9-5. Jerry Johnson gets the first win in Blue Jays history, and future Cy Young Award winner Pete Vuckovich records the first save.

Blue Jays 9, White Sox 5

BELOW: The Blue Jays–White Sox contest on April 7, 1977—the first game in Jays franchise history—is said to be the only major league game ever played on a field blanketed with snow. Below is one of the most bizarre sights ever seen on a baseball field: the grounds crew using a Zamboni machine to clear snow from the infield grass.

ABOVE: Chicago utility man Jack Brohamer spends the 1977 snow delay cross-country "skiing," using a catcher's shin guards and two baseball bats as improvised skis and poles.

1986 Jesse Barfield becomes the first Blue Jay to lead the league in homers (forty) and also the first to win a Gold Glove.

1987 George Bell is named AL MVP after piling up 47 home runs and 134 RBIs.

1987 The Jays lead the AL in attendance during their penultimate full season at Exhibition Stadium.

September 14, 1987

On a Power Trip In a season that has seen power numbers rise dramatically throughout baseball, Toronto sets a new major league record with ten home runs in one game. Six different Blue Jays go deep: Lloyd Moseby, Fred McGriff, Rob Ducey (the first of his career), George Bell (who hits two), Rance Mulliniks (who also hits two), and Ernie Whitt (who becomes the second player in franchise history to hit three in one game). Bell's second homer is his forty-fifth of the year, and although he will win the AL MVP, his power will fade as the Blue Jays unravel down the stretch and lose the division title to Detroit.

Blue Jays 18, Orioles 3

1989

The Blue Jays play their final game at Exhibition Stadium on May 28; they'll make their debut at brand-new SkyDome about a week later.

1999

Exhibition Stadium is finally demolished.

Dave Stieb, the greatest pitcher in Jays franchise history, found himself the victim of awful luck twice during the final days of the 1988 season.

ABOVE: A dumbfounded Dave Winfield looks on as a Blue Jays batboy picks up the seagull killed by an errant Winfield throw during a 1983 game. Toronto police file animal cruelty charges against the Yankees right fielder for the bird's accidental death, but the charges are dropped the next day.

CAP: 1990 (worn by Dave Stieb).

September 15, 1977

Tarp Trap? The Blue Jays are awarded a forfeit win when Baltimore manager Earl Weaver removes his Orioles from the field in the bottom of the fifth inning over an alleged safety issue. The game is scoreless until the fourth, when the Blue Jays score the only four runs of the game that actually cross home plate. In the next inning, Weaver claims that a tarpaulin held down by bricks in the left-field bullpen presents a safety hazard for Orioles left fielder Andres Mora. Weaver yanks his team off the field when umpire Marty Springstead, a longtime Weaver nemesis, refuses to remove the tarp. Jays rookie Jim Clancy, who pitched five innings, is credited with his first career shutout, while Baltimore's Ross Grimsley pitches the shortest complete game possible under baseball's official rules— a four-inning loss. The Orioles drop to 2½ games behind the first-place Yankees.

Blue Jays 9, Orioles 0 (forfeit)

September 30, 1988

Close, But No Cigars Dave Stieb becomes the poster boy for bad-luck pitchers everywhere when, for the second consecutive start, he misses a no-hitter with two outs in the ninth inning. As 32,374 fans anticipate the final out, Orioles pinch hitter Jim Traber instead bloops a ball over the head of first baseman Fred McGriff. Six days earlier in Cleveland, it was Julio Franco who broke up Stieb's gem with a bad-hop grounder past second baseman Manny Lee. Today's game is the closest anyone will ever come to throwing a no-hitter at Exhibition Stadium, but Stieb will finally get a no-no in Cleveland in 1990.

Blue Jays 4, Orioles 0

STADE OLYMPIQUE

Montreal, Quebec

Expos (NL) 1977–2004

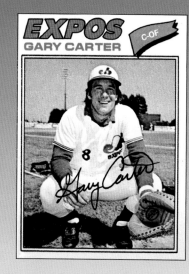

Montreal's Stade Olympique enjoyed a banner debut year, hosting a number of important events as the main stadium for the 1976 Summer Olympics. Soon afterward, though, it became a running joke, a bureaucratic money pit, and a disaster of such proportions that it eventually helped contribute to the demise of baseball in Montreal three decades later. Though Olympique hosted a promising young team in the early 1980s, a decade of incompetent ownership followed, making the Expos, like their stadium, the laughingstock of baseball until their departure for Washington, DC, in 2005.

When the major leagues expanded to Canada in 1969, the Expos' stay at makeshift Parc Jarry was expected to be a short one, but political and financial snafus kept the team playing at the converted youth league ballpark for eight years. Montreal eventually got its promised new park not because of the Expos, but because Montreal was awarded the 1976 Summer Olympics. Thanks to a special tax on cigarettes, a cool Can$134 million was budgeted for a grand domed stadium designed by French architect Roger Taillibert. The stadium was to feature a revolutionary retractable roof, which would be opened and closed by cables attached to a colossal tower. The tower, hovering 575 feet above the stadium, was reputed to be the tallest inclined structure in the world and included elevators enabling fans to ride to the top. The vast complex would also include promenade areas, a velodrome, and the Olympic swimming pool. When some expressed concern that the project would lose money, Montreal mayor Jean Drapeau famously responded that "the Olympics can no more have a deficit than a man can have a baby." But by the time the stadium was finally fully paid off in 2006, the Olympics were gone, the Expos no longer existed, and interest and repairs had driven the stunning final price tag to an estimated $1.61 billion. Initially spelled "The Big O," the stadium's nickname eventually became "The Big Owe."

Construction began in April 1973, but was beset by a number of problems, including a general building strike. By the time the Olympics rolled around, the much-ballyhooed roof still wasn't close to being finished. The still-incomplete stadium opened to the public on June 17, 1976, when it

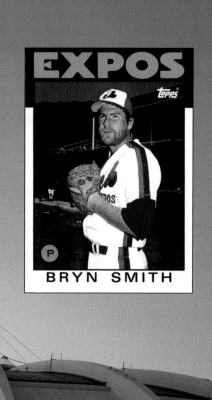

BRYN SMITH

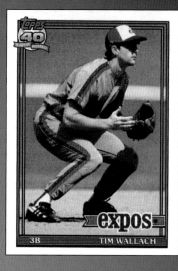

hosted the opening ceremonies. It would also be the site of the track and field, soccer, swimming, and equestrian events before hosting the closing ceremonies on August 1. With the games over, the Canadian Football League's Montreal Alouettes moved in that fall, and the Expos in April 1977.

Like most cookie-cutters, the antiseptic, cavernous park featured a seating bowl set far back from the playing surface, which was, of course, made of AstroTurf. The infamous orange Kevlar roof sat unused in a warehouse in France until 1982, and its installation was finally completed in 1987, more than a decade after the stadium's opening. The 60,000-square-foot roof was so bulky that it was unable to be used in winds of higher than twenty-five miles per hour, so the Expos occasionally encountered rain delays even after it was installed. The roof proved less than durable, too; it was soon plagued by a series of rips and leaks. In 1992, the Expos decided that opening and closing the roof wasn't worth the hassle, and decided to keep it permanently closed. Six years later, they gave up on it altogether, replacing it with a $26 million, non-retractable blue roof. This, too, proved unreliable, however, collapsing in January 1999 under the weight of accumulated snow. After that, tubes of heated water were installed underneath the roof to melt the snow atop it. However, other portions of the park were falling apart. In 1991, a 55-ton chunk of concrete fell when its support beam snapped, causing the Expos to cancel their final thirteen home dates and play the games on the road instead.

Though Stade Olympique turned out to be one of Montreal's biggest boondoggles, Expos fans nonetheless loved their team. The Quebecois proved to be louder and more enthusiastic fans than their American counterparts, and the stadium was filled with deafening cheers even in later years when the crowds grew smaller. A favorite cheer involved stomping in unison on the aluminum bleachers,

creating a tinny roar that unsettled many an opposing pitcher. In the late '70s and early '80s the Expos were a model major league franchise, with a promising farm system, a huge television deal, eager sponsors, and a deeply loyal fan base. But in the 1990s, two incompetent owners gutted the team for personal profit, drove away the fans seemingly intentionally, and put the franchise on the path to extinction. Claude Brochu, who purchased the team in 1991 to save it from a feared move to Phoenix, later declined to invest sufficient funds to build a major league–quality team. After the Expos posted the best record in baseball in 1994 only to miss the postseason due to a players' strike, Brochu ordered costs to be slashed by ridding the team of all salable players. Superstars such as Pedro Martinez, Larry Walker, Moises Alou, and John Wetteland were traded in exchange for young prospects, who themselves were similarly jettisoned once they became viable major leaguers. It became a never-ending cycle, and during their last decade in Montreal the Expos never even made a pretense of contending for the playoffs.

In 1999, the team was sold to art dealer Jeffrey Loria, a reprehensible figure who embarked on perhaps the most disastrous tenure of any owner of a major league team. Loria immediately set about alienating fans by removing the Expos from television and English-language radio, threatening to move unless a new stadium was built, and continuing to trade away all the team's good players. Loria's motives became clear two years later when it was revealed that he intended to force the team out of existence. Under an agreement with Commissioner Bud Selig, Loria planned to sell the Expos for $120 million to twenty-eight other major league teams collectively. These owners then intended to "contract" the Expos and Minnesota Twins, a euphemism for putting them out of business. Contraction was stopped by legal challenges, but Loria's sale of the team to MLB went through anyway. He took the money and bought

the Florida Marlins, while the other major league owners were left to run the Expos as a ward of the state. Loria even raided the Expos' front office on his way out the door, taking most of the team officials with him to Miami.

With MLB itself now owning the team, more attempts were made to prod taxpayers into funding a new stadium. The province of Quebec offered $100 million toward the proposed Labatt Park, but the team rejected it, insisting that the public foot the entire bill. But after the shenanigans pulled by Brochu and Loria, Montrealers had lost their sympathy for corporate welfare, and it soon became clear that the Expos' days in Quebec were numbered. MLB fired a warning shot by taking away twenty-two of the Expos' eighty-one home games in both 2003 and 2004, moving the contests to San Juan, Puerto Rico. Finally, in 2005, the hapless team was mercifully relocated to Washington, DC, and its name changed to the Nationals. Stade Olympique, meanwhile, remains as much of a white elephant as ever, hosting nothing more than the occasional CFL game, trade show, or concert. Fans and city officials alike agree that the stadium deserves to be demolished, but implosion has been deemed impossible because a subway runs underneath the structure, and the cost of alternative modes of demolition has been estimated at a prohibitive $500 million. Until the city has a reason to raise such funds, Stade Olypique stands as an empty monument to Montreal baseball, a stubborn cockroach that refuses to go away.

RIGHT: Stade Olympique, during its final major league season in 2004. The original, retractable roof was supposed to let sunshine through when open, but its many malfunctions led the Expos to replace it with this blue, unretractable version.

1979 The Expos enjoy their first winning season in franchise history, going 95-67 and finishing two games behind first-place Pittsburgh.

1977

Stade Olympique hosts its first major league game on April 15. The stadium's dimensions will remain the same throughout its twenty-eight seasons: 325 feet down the lines, 375 to the power alleys, and 404 to center field.

September 10, 1980

Gullickson Baffles the Cubs Twenty-one-year-old rookie Bill Gullickson sets an Expos franchise record by striking out eighteen Cubs in a 4-2 victory. He strikes out the side three times, and fans at least two batters in seven different innings. Chicago's Jerry Martin strikes out four times, while five other Cubs strike out more than once. The only Cub to make contact every time up is Bill Buckner, who collects three of Chicago's four hits and drives in both of its runs.

Expos 4, Cubs 2

April 13, 1984 The Expos' Pete Rose collects his 4,000th career hit.

May 2, 1987 After missing the first twenty-one games of the season due to collusion, Tim Raines gets four hits against the Mets in his season debut, including a tenth-inning, game-winning grand slam.

July 28, 1991 Montreal's Dennis Martinez throws the thirteenth perfect game in major league history.

May 10, 1981

Lea Surrenders Nothing Charlie Lea—a native of France—pitches the first no-hitter at Stade Olympique, to the delight of the French-speaking crowd of 25,343. Lea strikes out eight and walks four in his blanking of San Francisco, which gives the Expos a split of the day's doubleheader. The game is scoreless until the bottom of the seventh, when Tim Wallach leads off with a home run, sparking a four-run Expos outburst. Lea walks three batters in the next inning, but escapes without allowing a hit or a run. He retires the side in order in the ninth to finish off the third and final no-hitter that will ever be thrown by the Expos. (Bill Stoneman threw the other two.)

Expos 4, Giants 0

1984

New AstroTurf is installed.

1988

Baseball's first retractable roof debuts twelve years behind schedule. The 65-ton Kevlar dome, working like a giant umbrella, takes forty-five minutes to open. Mets slugger Darryl Strawberry hits the roof's concrete rim on Opening Day.

1991

A huge piece of concrete falls from the roof in September, forcing the Expos to change their final thirteen home games to road games.

October 19, 1981

Lundi Bleu In what will always be remembered as "Blue Monday" in Montreal, Rick Monday homers off Steve Rogers in the ninth inning of NLCS Game 5 to give the Dodgers the NL pennant. With the series tied at two and the game tied at one, Expos manager Dick Williams replaces starter Ray Burris with his ace, Rogers, who had pitched a complete game three days earlier. The fatigued Rogers retires Steve Garvey and Ron Cey leading off the ninth before giving up the fateful gopher ball to Monday. In the bottom of the ninth, Dodgers starter Fernando Valenzuela tires and is relieved by Bob Welch, who records a one-pitch save when he induces a game-ending groundout from Jerry White. Montreal will never again reach the postseason.

Dodgers 2, Expos 1

ABOVE: A sparse crowd watches one of the final home games in Expos history on September 22, 2004.

BELOW: As this 1989 photo illustrates, Stade Olympique was a much more appealing environment for baseball when the roof was opened.

July 13, 1982

Expos Dominate All-Star Game In the first All-Star Game played outside the United States, hometown ace Steve Rogers starts and gets the win at Stade Olympique. Both Rogers and AL starter Dennis Eckersley last three innings, and the key hit is a two-run homer by Reds shortstop Dave Concepcion, the game's MVP. In addition to Rogers, Montreal's Tim Raines, Andre Dawson, and Gary Carter also start the game, and Al Oliver comes off the bench to go 2-for-2. It is the NL's eleventh consecutive All-Star victory.

NL 4, AL 1

1992

"The Big O" reopens for business, but the roof remains closed at all times, which aids hitters by causing the ball to carry better.

1998

The oft-damaged roof is removed in May, and the Expos play the rest of the season under the elements.

1999

The expensive roof is replaced, and the ball-park's steadily mount-ing costs lead many to snidely refer to it as "The Big Owe."

"Domework"

Stade Olympique's ultramodern roof was supposed to open, as a *MacLean's* magazine article put it, "like a handkerchief pulled up by a string." Unfortunately, it didn't work out that way, with Montreal ultimately spending an estimated $250 million in repairs to the stadium's roof alone—almost enough for an entirely new stadium. But the allure of having the most innovative structure yet—not to mention freedom from the elements—has led many cities to attempt what in the early days of major league base-ball would have been unthinkable: an enclosed stadium.

Of course, the enclosed stadium didn't begin in Montreal, or even in Houston. The first domed structure for baseball was designed in the 1950s for the Brooklyn Dodgers. Although it was never built (with the Dodgers ultimately taking off for LA), the idea stuck, and in 1962 the ground was broken for "The Eighth Wonder of the World," the Astrodome. With Houston having worked out the inherent kinks of an enclosed park—the largest being the inability of grass to grow indoors—similar domed stadiums later popped up in New Orleans and Seattle. Montreal, however, decided to try something different.

Stade Olympique architect Roger Taillibert had never built a stadium before, but that didn't stop him from trying to improve upon a concept dreamed up when Kansas City's Kauffman Stadium was being built—a retractable roof. (The roof, designed to cover both Royals Stadium and the adjacent Arrowhead Football Stadium by rolling on rails, was eventually deemed too expensive to build.) The attempt was unsuccessful, though, and after numerous repairs, the Kevlar version was ultimately replaced with permanent fiberglass panels.

Toronto's SkyDome succeeded where its Canadian cousin failed. Architect Rod Robbie invented the first workable retractable roof by designing three sliding and rotating panels that tucked under a fourth panel to open up the stadium. Meanwhile, new stadiums in Minneapolis (the Metrodome) and Tokyo (the Tokyo Dome) used air-supported domes made of Teflon-coated fiberglass, requiring continuously operating fans to keep air pressure both consistent and greater than or equal to the pressure on the outside when closed.

Unfortunately, Stade Olympique was never able to take advantage of these new advances, and the venue is now considered by many to be a failure of modern architecture. There was one company, however, that was able to cash in—in 2000 the company that purchased the original Kevlar roof began selling small pieces of it as souvenirs, at $4.75 apiece.

LEFT, TOP: Toronto's SkyDome, which opened in 1989, featured a much more practical—and functional—retractable dome than Stade Olympique.

LEFT, BOTTOM: By the time all costs were accounted for, the city of Montreal had spent nearly $250 million on Stade Olympique's problematic roof. That amount would have been enough to build a new stadium from scratch.

September 27, 1998 St. Louis superstar Mark McGwire closes the season with two longballs against the Expos, one off Mike Thurman in the third inning and the other off Carl Pavano in the seventh, locking in a new all-time single-season home-run record at 70.

2000 The Expos play the entire season without a television contract of any kind, an unheard-of occurrence in modern baseball.

September 25, 1997

Pedro Says Goodbye Pedro Martinez becomes the first Expo to surpass 300 strike-outs, fanning nine in seven outstanding innings against the eventual world champion Marlins. It's a bittersweet moment, however, as Martinez, who was acquired in the greatest trade in Expos history, is pitching his final game for Montreal. He gets a no-decision in a 3-2 Expos win before a mere 12,094 fans. In November, Martinez will become the only Expo to win the Cy Young Award, but a few days later he will be traded to Boston because Montreal can no longer afford to pay him.

Expos 3, Marlins 2

August 6, 1999

Three Thousand Plus Three On his mother's birthday, Tony Gwynn reaches the 3,000-hit mark with a first-inning single off Montreal's Dan Smith. Fittingly, he's congratulated by first base umpire Kerwin Danley, who was Gwynn's team-mate at San Diego State two decades earlier. Smith, meanwhile, doesn't even make it through the first inning, and Padres southpaw Sterling Hitchcock lasts six innings for a 12-10 win. Gwynn goes 4-for-5, becoming the second play-er (after George Brett) to collect four hits in his milestone game. The Expos make the game interesting when Orlando Cabrera homers in the seventh to make it a one-run game, but San Diego scores twice in the eighth and twice more in the ninth to wrap up the win, even with the Expos scoring three in the bottom of the ninth.

Padres 12, Expos 10

ABOVE: The Expos' Tony Armas Jr. throws a pitch in 2001 before a typically empty Stade Olympique grandstand.

TOP: Expos owner Jeffrey Loria, who did as much as anyone to help wreck the franchise, leans over the railing during a 2001 game and observes the wreckage. To Loria's right is his stepson, and Expos executive vice president, David Samson.

BACKGROUND: Stade Olympique as it appeared shortly after its 1977 opening.

Vlad Impales the Reds Montreal tops the Reds to finish the year at 83-79, its best record since 1996. The Expos, now owned collectively by the other twenty-nine MLB teams, manage a second-place finish in the NL East. Vladimir Guerrero, batting leadoff to get more chances to bat, falls a home run short of becoming the fourth major league player with forty homers and forty stolen bases in the same season. He finishes the year with thirty-nine homers and forty steals, but his double in the finale adds to his league-leading totals in hits and total bases. The 25,178 at Stade Olympique become incensed when Guerrero is called out on a check swing in the eighth, and they litter the field with debris, forcing the Reds to take cover in the dugout. When Guerrero is replaced in the field in the ninth inning, he exits to a standing ovation.

Expos 7, Reds 2

2002 Omar Minaya leaves his post with the Mets to take over as general manager of the Expos, making him the first Hispanic GM in major league history. He'll return to the Mets two years later.

2007 The FIFA Under-20 World Cup is held at the stadium, drawing capacity crowds.

2002

A new surface, AstroGrass, is installed. Major League Baseball attempts to "contract"—a euphemism for shut down—the Expos, but is thwarted by the players' union.

2003

The Expos, struggling in attendance since Montreal voters thwarted a bid for a publicly funded stadium, announce that they will play one-fourth of their home schedule in San Juan, Puerto Rico. They will repeat the experiment in 2004.

2004

After years of speculation about when MLB would finally pull the plug on Montreal, the Expos play their last game at Olympic Stadium on September 29. The franchise moves to Washington and becomes the Nationals, while the Big O is used for concerts and conventions, and by the Montreal Alouettes of the Canadian Football League.

CAP: 2004.

LEFT, INSET: The best player in Expos history was Vladimir Guerrero, a supremely gifted five-tool talent who spent the first eight seasons of his impressive career in Montreal.

LEFT: Montreal's Terrmel Sledge takes the last major league swing at Olympique on September 29, 2004. Sledge pops up for the final out of a 9-1 loss to Florida.

KINGDOME

Seattle, Washington

Mariners (AL) 1977–1999

The Kingdome, a forgettable covered stadium that housed the Seattle Mariners during that franchise's early years, is notable mostly for its brief lifespan. Opened in 1977 and abandoned after 1999, its twenty-three years is one of the shortest tenures among parks built specifically for major league teams. The dome's tenants, meanwhile, were one of the worst teams in the major leagues until 1995, when a memorable roster featuring Ken Griffey Jr., Edgar Martinez, Randy Johnson, and Alex Rodriguez made it to the ALCS and laid the groundwork for the financing of a new stadium.

The Pacific Northwest got its first taste of the major leagues in 1969, when the Seattle Pilots, an expansion franchise, played a lone, unsuccessful season at Sicks' Stadium, a converted minor league park that dated back to 1938. However, after a disastrous season during which Sicks' proved completely unsuitable as even a temporary major league facility, it became clear that a team couldn't function in Seattle without a new park. (Funding for the Kingdome had been approved in 1968, but the stadium wouldn't be completed for another eight years.) In light of this, Pilots owner Dewey Soriano sold the team to auto dealer Bud Selig, who moved it to Milwaukee and renamed it the Brewers. The City of Seattle, King County, and Washington State then jointly sued the AL for breach of contract because the league had approved Selig's move. The suit was settled when the AL agreed to grant an expansion franchise to Seattle for the 1977 season. Thus, the Mariners were born.

Ground was broken in November 1972 on what was officially called King County Domed Stadium. The $67 million facility was built to accommodate both baseball and football, although Seattle had a team in neither sport when construction began. The dome was finished in March 1976, in time for an NFL expansion team, the Seahawks, to move in that fall. The Mariners followed in 1977 and the Seattle Supersonics, the local NBA team, joined them in 1978, making the two-year-old facility the only stadium to host all three major sports at the same time. The Sonics would play at the dome through the 1984–85 season, while both the Seahawks and Mariners would stay until the dome's demise in 1999.

The Kingdome was the second domed stadium in baseball, after the groundbreaking Astrodome more than a decade earlier. Most thought one dome was more than enough, since the structures were famous for their impersonality and lack of atmosphere. Seattle, however, was a special case; its ten inches of rainfall during the average baseball season meant a roof was necessary for the team to function. The best thing about the Kingdome was its location on the downtown Seattle waterfront, about one mile south of Pike Place Market. Of course, potentially picturesque views of Puget Sound were blocked by the roof, but more than a million fans nonetheless showed up during the Mariners' inaugural season. The customers gradually drifted away, however, when it became clear that the Mariners were going to field a perpetually non-competitive team. The club posted a losing record during each of its first fourteen seasons, and attendance dipped as low as 10,044 fans in 1983, when the M's went 60-102. Their dismal ballpark didn't help matters; the Kingdome had been dubbed "The Tomb" because it was gray and quiet. About the only thing that made noise was the dome's unusual speaker system, which featured individual speakers hung from the roof in fair territory. Every once in a while a fly ball would hit one of the low-lying speakers, and on two occasions, the ball failed to come back down. With its shallow power alleys, the Kingdome was an ideal environment for hitters, increasing offense by as much as 6 percent over the average park. Unfortunately, the opponents were generally able to take better advantage of this than the Mariners' weak hitters.

The Seattle club finally began to show signs of life in 1988, the year it drafted eighteen-year-old high school player Ken Griffey Jr., a move that would prove to save the franchise when he developed into a charismatic superstar. The team also traded for wild young left-hander Randy Johnson and developed Edgar Martinez, a Hall of Fame–caliber hitter, in its farm system. By 1995 these foundation pieces had been

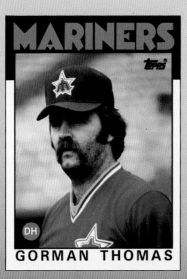

GORMAN THOMAS

KEN PHELPS

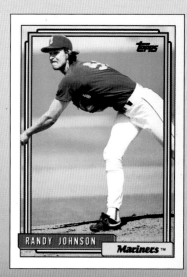

RANDY JOHNSON

Sick Stadium, Sicker Franchise

Little remembered in the annals of baseball history is Seattle's first major league team, the Seattle Pilots. More famous is their converted minor league park, Sicks' Stadium. Originally owned by Seattle beer-brewer Emil Sick, the ballpark opened in 1938 and was one of only three Pacific Coast League stadiums made of concrete and steel. Home to the Seattle Rainiers—a team formerly known as the Indians and renamed after a brand of Sick beer—the stadium may have survived as a beloved minor league park, but in 1968, the AL awarded Seattle an expansion club, the Pilots.

Of course the AL's approval hinged on the construction of a new stadium, and so the city passed a referendum that appropriated $40 million in funding to begin building a new, domed stadium while refurbishing Sicks'. Though it had been well suited to minor league ball, the small park was a bad fit for the big leagues: Only the seats from dugout to dugout were covered (despite Seattle's legendary rains), and lighting and facilities were substandard. The left-field corner stood just 305 feet from home, and both "power alleys" measured only 345 feet.

The entire affair was doomed from the start. Plans to expand Sicks' to 28,500 seats foundered due to cost disputes between the club and the City of Seattle, and work didn't even begin until late January 1969. Old outfield seats were removed, but few were replaced in time for the Pilots' April 11 home opener. Right field had no seating, and chairs beyond the left-field wall were still being installed even as the game began. Attendance for Opening Day was a sold-out, but nonetheless small, 15,014. As the season progressed, builders expanded capacity to 25,420, but the extra seats were rarely needed. The Pilots fell back in the AL West race, finishing last, and attendance sagged—which was perhaps a blessing in disguise, as the toilets in the facility tended to back up when flushed too many times.

After only one year, the club's undercapitalized owners were forced to sell the team to Milwaukee car dealer Bud Selig, who moved the Pilots to his hometown, where they became the Brewers. Sicks' Stadium stood until 1979, housing several minor league clubs before falling to the bulldozers. By then, Seattle had been awarded a new team, housed by the ultramodern Kingdome.

molded into a winning team by the addition of complementary players like Tino Martinez, Joey Cora, and Jay Buhner. The Mariners made the playoffs for the first time, and faced the New York Yankees in the AL Division Series. It was a memorable, gut-wrenching affair that would become legendary in Seattle, forever to be spoken of in reverence. When Martinez smacked a double into the left-field corner to score Griffey with the series-winning run, the future of baseball in Seattle was assured and the Kingdome's fate sealed. A month earlier voters had defeated a measure to fund a new stadium, which virtually assured that the Mariners would soon move to another city. But in the euphoria that followed the victory over the Yankees, giddy state legislators voted to allocate the funds anyway. The Mariners moved next door to Safeco Field in 2000, and the Kingdome was imploded that same year on March 26.

ABOVE: Opened in 1938, Sicks' Stadium was the second minor league park built on the site, which allowed a view of Mount Rainier from the left-field bleachers. The first, Dugdale Park, opened in 1913 and was used until 1932, when a serial arsonist named Robert Driscoll burned it down on the Fourth of July.

RIGHT: Although they must have driven the fire marshal crazy, indoor fireworks were a common sight during Mariners games at the Kingdome. The indoor explosions "never seemed like a good idea, and in fact ceiling tiles began plummeting to the ground," wrote former Mariners broadcaster Ken Levine. In July 1994, four 26-pound pieces of tile fell from the roof—this time presumably unrelated to fireworks—forcing the Mariners to play the rest of that season on the road.

April 6, 1977 The first game in Mariners history is played at the Kingdome. Seattle loses to the Angels, 7-0.

1979 The Mariners' Ruppert Jones hits a fly ball that gets stuck in the roof and never comes down; it's ruled a foul ball. Another Mariner, Ricky Nelson, will do the same thing in 1983.

1984 Mariners first baseman Alvin Davis is voted AL Rookie of the Year after hitting twenty-seven homers with a .391 on-base percentage.

1977

The year after the NFL Seahawks played their first game in the Kingdome, the stadium hosts its first baseball game, on April 6. Dimensions are 315 feet down the lines, 375 to left-center field, 405 to center, and 365 to right-center. These distances will fluctuate over the years, but it will always remain a good hitters' park.

1978

The NBA's Seattle SuperSonics join the Mariners and Seahawks as Kingdome tenants. In 1979 the Sonics will become the only team to win a championship in the building; they'll play here until 1985.

1982

The short distance in right field leads the Mariners to build a wall there that, at 23½ feet, is twice the height of the wall in left and center. It will be nicknamed Walla Walla.

July 17, 1979

Baserunners Beware With six lead changes, Seattle's first All-Star Game proves more entertaining than most Midsummer Classics in recent years, although it has a familiar ending: the NL wins. Mariners fan favorite Bruce Bochte puts the AL ahead with a sixth-inning RBI single, but the NL's Lee Mazzilli homers to tie it two innings later. In the ninth Mazzilli strikes again, walking with the bases loaded to force in the eventual winning run. The MVP, however, goes to Dave Parker, who nails two baserunners with impressive throws from the outfield—one at third base and the other at home. It's the eighth straight All-Star victory for the Senior Circuit.

NL 7, AL 6

May 6, 1982

Pitches Slippery When Wet Forty-three-year-old Gaylord Perry, the most notorious spitballer in baseball history, pitches a complete game against the Yankees for the 300th victory of his career. Perry strikes out four and walks just one, and the M's make it easier on the old man by scoring five times in the third inning against Doyle Alexander. Perry, pitching for his seventh team (he will pitch for an eighth next season), becomes the fifteenth pitcher to reach the 300 plateau and the first since Early Wynn in 1963. He's also the first to achieve the milestone indoors.

Mariners 7, Yankees 3

ABOVE: Gaylord Perry hurls a pitch during his 300th career win in 1982.

1991 The Mariners post their first winning season ever at 83-79, but nonetheless finish fifth in the AL West.

June 3, 1993 The Mariners select Miami High School shortstop Alex Rodriguez as the number-one overall pick in the draft.

1995 MLB moves from a two-division format to three divisions—each league now has a west, east, and central arm, and an extra round of playoffs is added.

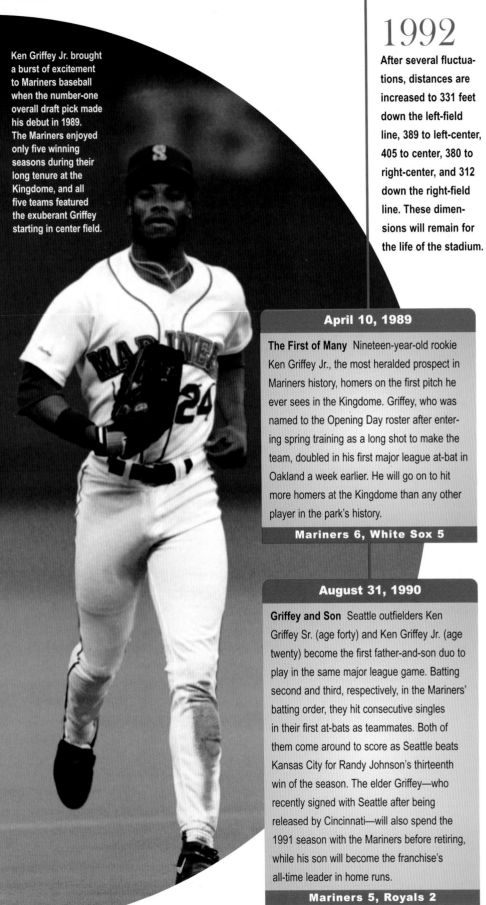

Ken Griffey Jr. brought a burst of excitement to Mariners baseball when the number-one overall draft pick made his debut in 1989. The Mariners enjoyed only five winning seasons during their long tenure at the Kingdome, and all five teams featured the exuberant Griffey starting in center field.

1992

After several fluctuations, distances are increased to 331 feet down the left-field line, 389 to left-center, 405 to center, 380 to right-center, and 312 down the right-field line. These dimensions will remain for the life of the stadium.

1994

Four ceiling tiles fall to the ground before a game with the Orioles on July 19. The series is postponed, and the Mariners are forced to play on the road until a players' strike ends the season on August 12. As a precaution, all 40,000 ceiling tiles are replaced, but on August 17 two workmen are killed due to a crane malfunction. The Seahawks, meanwhile, spend their season outdoors at the University of Washington's Husky Stadium.

October 2, 1995

Prodigal Son Returns, Loses Seattle's Randy Johnson turns in one of the greatest clutch pitching performances of all time, retiring the first seventeen Angels batters as the Mariners throttle California 9-1 in a one-game playoff to decide the AL West title. Seattle forced the playoff game by staging a furious second-half surge, going from 12½ games behind the Angels on August 20 to a flat-footed tie with them at season's end. Ironically, Johnson's pitching opponent in the playoff game is former Mariner Mark Langston, who ranked as the finest pitcher in Seattle history before Johnson came along. Like Johnson, Langston gets off to a strong start, allowing just one run through six innings; unlike Johnson, though, he unravels in the seventh. The win bumps Johnson's season record to 18-2; his .900 winning percentage is a new AL record. More importantly, the Mariners make the playoffs for the first time in franchise history.

Mariners 9, Angels 1

April 10, 1989

The First of Many Nineteen-year-old rookie Ken Griffey Jr., the most heralded prospect in Mariners history, homers on the first pitch he ever sees in the Kingdome. Griffey, who was named to the Opening Day roster after entering spring training as a long shot to make the team, doubled in his first major league at-bat in Oakland a week earlier. He will go on to hit more homers at the Kingdome than any other player in the park's history.

Mariners 6, White Sox 5

August 31, 1990

Griffey and Son Seattle outfielders Ken Griffey Sr. (age forty) and Ken Griffey Jr. (age twenty) become the first father-and-son duo to play in the same major league game. Batting second and third, respectively, in the Mariners' batting order, they hit consecutive singles in their first at-bats as teammates. Both of them come around to score as Seattle beats Kansas City for Randy Johnson's thirteenth win of the season. The elder Griffey—who recently signed with Seattle after being released by Cincinnati—will also spend the 1991 season with the Mariners before retiring, while his son will become the franchise's all-time leader in home runs.

Mariners 5, Royals 2

BELOW: Having served its purpose by bringing three major sports to Seattle, the now-obsolete Kingdome is imploded on March 26, 2000.

October 14, 1995 A special session of the state legislature approves funding for a new Seattle ballpark.

May 2, 1996 The Mariners become just the second team (after the San Francisco Giants) to postpone a game because of an earthquake. The quake, which registers 5.4 on the Richter scale, causes no structural damage to the park.

1997 Ken Griffey Jr. hits fifty-six home runs, becoming the first Mariner to win AL MVP.

October 8, 1995

The Game That Saved Baseball With the Mariners chronically struggling to draw fans, they win the AL Division Series in a thrilling Game 5 that will become widely hailed as the moment that saved baseball in Seattle. Trailing 4-2 in the eighth inning of the winner-take-all game, the Mariners tie it and then bring in Randy Johnson, who'd pitched seven innings in a victory just two nights earlier. Johnson allows a run in the top of the eleventh, but in the bottom of the inning Edgar Martinez (who bats .571 for the series) knocks a clutch double that scores Joey Cora and Ken Griffey Jr. for a walk-off victory. It's the first playoff series ever won by the Mariners, and the 57,411 fans at the Kingdome stage a wild celebration. The dramatic victory also secures the Mariners' long-term presence in Seattle, which had been in doubt after King County voters narrowly defeated a new stadium referendum in September. But the newfound baseball fervor created by the M's win will lead the County Council, in cooperation with the state legislature, to overrule the voters and allocate funds for the new stadium anyway.

Mariners 6, Yankees 5

LEFT: The Mariners mob Randy Johnson after the six-foot-ten lefty pitches the team into the 1995 postseason with a 9-1 victory over the Angels in a one-game playoff.

1999

The Mariners play their final game at the Kingdome on June 27; the Seahawks will follow suit on January 9, 2000. The Kingdome, still more than $100 million in debt, will be demolished in March 2000.

August 8, 1997

Nineteen Again For the second time this season, Randy Johnson strikes out nineteen batters in a game, falling just shy of Roger Clemens' major league record of twenty. This time, however, Johnson manages to win the game, notching his sixteenth victory of the season. (On June 24 he struck out nineteen A's, but lost 4-1.) Johnson will fan 291 batters for the season, a total that will also leave him one strikeout behind Clemens. Even worse, Clemens will beat out Johnson for the Cy Young Award. Johnson will finally tie Clemens' record with a twenty-strikeout game on May 8, 2001.

Mariners 5, White Sox 0

METRODOME

Minneapolis, Minnesota

Twins (AL) 1982–2009

RIGHT: Minneapolis' skyline becomes visible through a hole in the Metrodome roof as the covering is deflated for maintenance purposes. Made of cardboard-thin fiberglass, the roof weighs 580,000 pounds, covers 10 acres, and requires 20 fans blowing at 90 horsepower each to keep it inflated. At its peak, the roof towers 195 feet above the playing field.

OPPOSITE: Although baseball purists deride it for making a mockery of the game, the Metrodome has become one of the most renowned all-purpose facilities in the country. Much of that is due to its sheer size: at a volume of 60 million cubic feet, approximately 3,300 normal-size homes could fit inside. The playing field covers 142,515 square feet, and the structure is composed of 40,000 cubic yards of concrete and 19,000 tons of reinforced steel. The facility is used about 300 days per year and employs 3,000 people, although those numbers will surely decrease once the Twins move into their new open-air stadium.

One of the most distinctive—and least attractive—ballparks in major league history, the colossal Metrodome has been the home field of the Minnesota Twins, the NFL's Vikings, and University of Minnesota Golden Gophers football since its opening in 1982. With a capacity approaching 65,000, it has hosted many of the sporting world's most prestigious events, including Super Bowl XXVI in 1992 and the NCAA Men's Final Four in 1992 and 2001. Though the cavernous structure has always seemed ill suited for baseball, the enthusiasm of Twins fans and the dome's unusual characteristics combine to give Minnesota one of the most dramatic home-field advantages ever seen in the national pastime.

After suffering through frigid springs and autumns since moving to Minnesota in 1961, the Twins got a new ballpark in 1982 thanks to the ruthlessness of their NFL counterparts. The Vikings, wildly popular in the frozen North, threatened to move to Los Angeles unless they got a new, indoor facility. In December 1979, they got their wish as ground was broken in downtown Minneapolis for what would officially be named the Hubert H. Humphrey Metrodome. Funded by liquor and hotel taxes, the Metrodome is different from a normal dome in several ways. For one, its shape is rectangular instead of round, a circumstance that resulted in a fairly deep center field but very short measurements down the foul lines.

More intriguing is the feat of engineering used to keep the roof atop the playing field. Instead of the hard roof featured on buildings like the Astrodome, the Metrodome's cover consists of ten acres of Teflon-coated fiberglass, one-sixteenth of an inch thick. It is purported to be the largest application of Teflon in the world. The flimsy roof is kept afloat with 250,000 cubic feet per minute of air pressure, meaning that the occasional tear requires immediate repair to prevent the dome from collapsing. The thinness of the cream-colored roof also results in a harsh glare during day games, sometimes rendering it nearly impossible to see pop-ups. While the Twins play here often enough to have adapted to this phenomenon, most opponents haven't, giving the Twins a unique home-field advantage; the glare from the roof notably contributed to Oakland's loss to the Twins in the 2002 AL Division Series.

One of the park's signature features, added soon after its opening, is the loose canvas cover on the 23-foot-high right-field wall, known as "the baggie" or "the Hefty bag" because it ripples like one when a batted ball strikes it. The left-field fence, meanwhile, for many years featured a clear, 6-foot-high Plexiglas extension. This window, which was removed in the mid-1990s, was most notable for its role in Game 6 of the 1991 World Series, when Kirby Puckett crashed into it and made what remains the most memorable catch in Metrodome history. The baggie and the Plexiglas extension were both designed to thwart cheap home runs, since the Metrodome's left and right field dimensions have made the park so amenable to hitting that it was informally dubbed the "Homerdome." Typical were the stats from the 1986 season, when 223 home runs were hit at the Metrodome and just 173 in Twins road games.

The unique features of the Metrodome have combined to endow the Twins with one of the most extraordinary home-field advantages in baseball history. Through 2007, the team had posted an all-time record of 1,112-967 at the Metrodome, a .535 winning percentage. In road games, however, they went 909-1,154, an abysmal .441. There are several reasons for this, one of which is the aforementioned visibility problem created by the roof. Another is how loud the stadium gets when it's full; the dome keeps the noise inside and the Metrodome is generally regarded as the loudest stadium in both MLB and the NFL. During a 1999 football playoff game, the noise level was measured at 128.4 decibels, believed to be a record for a sports stadium. (By comparison, the loudest rock concerts are about 115 dB and a jet takeoff is about 120.) The 1987 World Series, the first played at the Metrodome, was also the first Series ever in which the home team won every game. The Twins won by virtue of having four home games to the Cardinals' three, and much credit was given to the Metrodome fans who wildly cheered on the Twins while waving their famed "Homer Hankies." In 1991, Minnesota won the World Series again, and once more every game was won by the home team.

BELOW: Located in the Downtown East section of Minneapolis, the Metrodome is mostly surrounded by industrial buildings. In recent years, however, many old warehouses and factories have been converted for residential use. Restaurants and bars have begun to spring up, much to the delight of Twins fans.

In 2003, another reason for Minnesota's longstanding home-field advantage was revealed. Dick Ericson, the stadium's superintendent until 1995, confirmed the long-whispered allegation that stadium workers systematically manipulated the Metrodome's air-conditioning system to help the Twins hit the balls farther. Whenever the Twins were batting, the stadium's fans would be turned on and made to blow toward the outfield fences, helping fly balls to carry. When the opponents came up to bat, the blowers would be turned off. "I don't feel guilty," Ericson told the *Minneapolis Star-Tribune*. "It's your home-field advantage. Every stadium has got one."

But even such a large advantage couldn't overcome a lack of talent. After the core players from the Twins' championship teams either moved on or retired, the team entered a dark period beginning in 1993 that saw them finish no better than fourth place for eight years in a row. Their owner, Carl Pohlad, who had funded the two championship clubs, now ordered a slashing of the payroll that forced the team to bid farewell to many of its best players in the prime of their careers. Though easily the wealthiest of baseball's owners (with a net worth of $3.1 billion, as estimated by Forbes in 2008), Pohlad refused to invest in player salaries until a new taxpayer-funded stadium was built. When this appeared unlikely, he then tried to put the team out of business, agreeing to sell the franchise for $200 million to Major League Baseball, which would have then "contracted" (eliminated) the team along with the Montreal Expos. A legal challenge foiled this cynical plan, but Pohlad's threat worked; he eventually got his new stadium. In 2006 Hennepin County, of which Minneapolis is the county seat, instituted a sales tax increase to pay for two-thirds of a new, $390 million, baseball-only park, with Pohlad to cover the rest. Construction began on the new park in 2007, and the Twins were expected to play their last season at the Metrodome in 2009. Whether the new stadium is designed with as many advantages for the hometown team, only time will tell.

TIMELINE: METRODOME

June 22, 1983 Carl Pohlad agrees to buy the Twins from the Griffith family, who had owned the franchise since the early years of the century.

1982

The Metrodome opens in downtown Minneapolis, and problems soon crop up with the roof and artificial turf. However, the fences are just right for hitters, leading fans to dub it the "Homerdome." Dimensions are 343 feet down the left-field line, 385 to left-center, 408 to center, 367 to right-center, and 327 to right. The right-field fence is only 7 feet high.

May 4, 1984

What Goes Up Need Not Come Down Since its opening in 1982, the Metrodome has been a haven for ground-rule doubles hopping off the bouncy artificial turf and into the stands, but tonight, Oakland slugger Dave Kingman finds a new way to perform an old trick. In the fourth inning, batting against Frank Viola, Kingman crushes a high fly ball that goes up but never comes back down. The ball enters a drainage hole in the Metrodome roof, 129 feet above home plate, and is never seen again. The umpires rule it a double. In the ninth Kingman hits a lower-trajectory drive that lands in the seats for a home run, but the Twins win nonetheless.

Twins 3, A's 1

1984 Legendary centerfielder Kirby Puckett makes his major league debut, batting .296 with twenty-five bunt singles.

July 16, 1985 The Metrodome hosts the All-Star Game, a 6-1 NL victory.

1983

Air-conditioning is switched on for the first time in July, leading to conspiracy theories regarding manipulation of the vent system to aid Twins fly balls but hinder similar hits by opponents. The fence in right is raised to 23 feet high and covered by an inelegant plastic tarp that comes to be known as "the baggie." Plexiglas is added to the fence in left and left-center to make it 13 feet high and keep balls from bouncing into the stands frequently.

August 1, 1986

Blyleven Records 3,000th Young Twins stars Gary Gaetti, Tom Brunansky, and Kirby Puckett each launch homers during a drubbing of the A's. Puckett's longball, a two-run shot in the eighth inning, makes him the seventh Twin to hit for the cycle—but the game's biggest story is a fifth-inning strikeout of Oakland's Mike Davis. It's the 3,000th career strikeout for Bert Blyleven, the well-traveled Dutch hurler. Blyleven strikes out fifteen Athletics, walks just one, and allows only two hits. He'll finish his career with 3,701 strikeouts, third of all time behind only Nolan Ryan and Steve Carlton. Those two and many others will glide into the Hall of Fame with ease, but Blyleven will still be awaiting election more than twenty years later.

Twins 10, A's 1

OPPOSITE, TOP: Frank Viola hurls a pitch during Game 7 of the 1987 World Series against the Cardinals, which he wins 4-2 to secure the title for the Twins.

BELOW: The famed blue "Hefty bag" in right field was modified during the 2000s, when the baggy covering was shortened, tightened, and adorned with advertising.

1987

New turf is installed.

CAP: 1987.

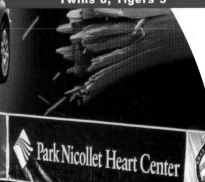

October 7, 1987

Doyle's First Defeat The Twins win their first ALCS while Doyle Alexander, who has posted a perfect 9-0 record since Detroit traded for him to bolster its pennant hopes, suffers his first loss as a Tiger. Alexander, who was acquired from Atlanta in exchange for pitching prospect John Smoltz, allows a game-tying double to Kirby Puckett in the eighth inning of the opening game of the ALCS. Then with Willie Hernandez on the hill for Detroit, late-season Twins acquisition Don Baylor singles for a 6-5 lead. Tom Brunansky doubles in two more runs to cap off the rally, and Minnesota closer Jeff Reardon retires the Tigers in the ninth for the first ALCS win in Twins history.

Twins 8, Tigers 5

October 25, 1987

Viola's Sweet Music Left-handed ace Frank Viola delivers the first world championship in Twins history, allowing just two hits over his final six innings in a Game 7 win over the St. Louis Cardinals. It's the closest game of the four Minnesota victories, as the previous three contests at the Metrodome saw the Twins outscore the Cardinals by a combined score of 29-10. The Cards take an early lead, scoring twice against Viola in the second inning, but Kirby Puckett ties it back up with a fifth-inning double. After Cardinals pitchers walk the bases loaded in the next inning, light-hitting Twins shortstop Greg Gagne singles in what will prove to be the Series-winning run off relief ace Todd Worrell. In the eighth Dan Gladden adds an insurance run with his impressive seventh RBI of the Series, but it is Viola who will be named MVP. The Series cements the Metrodome's reputation for an extreme home-field advantage, as the Twins become the first team ever to win all four Series games played on their home field—a feat they will repeat in 1991. St. Louis, playing in its third World Series in six seasons, will not play in another until 2004.

Twins 4, Cardinals 2

1988 Lefty Frank Viola wins the Cy Young Award with a 24-7 record.

September 16, 1993 The Twins' Dave Winfield singles off Dennis Eckersley for his 3,000th career hit.

September 28, 1995 Kirby Puckett suffers an ugly beaning. He will have vision problems the following spring and never play again.

1988

The second-place (but defending world champion) Twins draw a crowd of 35,952 on the last day of the season, making them the first AL club ever to reach three million in attendance. Only the Dodgers, Mets, and Cardinals, all in the NL, have reached the milestone before.

October 27, 1991

Morris' Minnesota Masterpiece The Twins and Braves may be relocated franchises playing indoors on artificial turf at night, but tonight's epic Game 7 conjures up sepia-toned images of Walter Johnson pitching in the last extra-inning Game 7—for Minnesota's predecessor, the Washington Senators, in 1924. Tonight, the two teams go through the first nine innings without scoring, thanks to superb pitching by Atlanta's John Smoltz and Minnesota's Jack Morris. A pivotal moment occurs when Atlanta veteran Lonnie Smith falls for a decoy move by Twins rookie second baseman Chuck Knoblauch, whose feint causes Smith to stay at second as the batted ball lands in left field. Smith then stays at third on a groundout and never scores the run. Meanwhile, the thirty-six-year-old Morris, who will be named Series MVP, throws ten remarkable shutout innings. Smoltz, for his part, goes eight valiant frames for the Braves, but gives way to relievers Mike Stanton and Alejandro Peña. In the bottom of the tenth, Peña gives up a leadoff double to Dan Gladden, who is sacrificed to third. Pinch hitter Gene Larkin then drives in the Series-winning run with a single over the drawn-in outfield.

Twins 1, Braves 0

1994

Plexiglas is removed from the left- and left-center-field fences, returning them to their previous height of 7 feet.

1996

The Twins honor their best players by displaying their retired numbers on a hanging curtain in the upper deck. In so doing, they eliminate some 10,000 of the stadium's worst seats, making the new capacity 44,000.

September 11, 1999

Milton in Paradise Eric Milton pitches a "rise and shine" no-hitter for the Twins, throwing the first pitch of his gem at 11:06 a.m. so the teams can vacate the Metrodome in time for a University of Minnesota football game. With September call-ups in full effect, the fourth-place Angels field a lineup consisting mostly of career minor leaguers; third baseman Troy Glaus is the only regular starter who plays. Milton strikes out thirteen batters and walks only two in front of an early-rising crowd of 11,222. Importantly, the game finishes in a brisk two hours, twenty-eight minutes, allowing plenty of time for the Golden Gophers to blank Louisiana-Monroe, 35-0.

Twins 7, Angels 0

2006

The Twins raise the upper-deck curtains for the Division Series against Oakland and set a club record with an attendance of 55,932 for Game 3.

April 15, 2000

Ripken Joins Murray in 3,000 Club In the seventh inning of this Orioles-Twins match-up, Cal Ripken singles sharply to center off Minnesota's Hector Carrasco for the 3,000th hit of his career, becoming the twenty-fourth player to reach the mark. Ripken is the third player in the last seven years to collect his 3,000th in Minnesota (after Dave Winfield and Eddie Murray), making the Metrodome the ballpark where the milestone has been reached the most often. Ripken has three hits in the game, also collecting a single to right and beating out a high chopper. After his historic hit, Ripken receives a prolonged standing ovation from the appreciative opposing crowd of 18,745. Among the first to congratulate him is Eddie Murray—Ripken's friend, former teammate, and now first base coach—who collected his number 3,000 in 1995.

Orioles 6, Twins 4

Twin-speak

Beginning in 2010—and for the next thirty years—the Twins will be the lucky tenants of a brand-new ballpark. Though its field dimensions will be similar to those of the Metrodome (339 feet to left, 404 to center, 328 feet to right, and 377 and 376 to the power alleys), the new park will be different in almost every other respect.

Designed by HOK Sport, the company responsible for Camden Yards and new parks in San Francisco and Pittsburgh, the stadium is modern retro: open-air, real grass, lots of box seats, graduated upper decks, wide concourses with great views of the field, and a glassed-in dining facility. Bullpens will be stacked in center field, and an in-play "overlook" filled with stadium seating will extend 8 feet over the right-field wall. Though the entire cost for the park (with financing) will top $517 million, budget concerns prevented the construction of a roof, a curious decision for a team often forced to play in frigid weather. However, a state-of-the-art heating system will be installed throughout the stadium and even under the playing field. As for the outside, the exterior facade of the park will be lined with 100,000 square feet of Minnesota limestone and one wall will feature "knot holes" that will allow passers-by to catch a glimpse of the action inside. Like the cherry trees at the new Nationals Park, fir trees native to Minnesota will be planted just beyond the centerfield fence.

Perhaps the biggest difference between the Twins' old and new homes is the money it stands to make for the team. Twins president Dave St. Peter estimates the park will bring in $40 to $50 million a year in new revenues, including $8 million just for the luxury suites—and with multiple high-definition TVs, 14-foot-high ceilings, and seating for twelve, the boxes may be worth the price for fans. Unlike with the Metrodome, the Twins will also be able to make money from concessions, non-baseball events held at the stadium, and selling the naming rights to the park to the nearby Target Corporation—virtually going from one of the worst leases in MLB to one of the best.

But like any real estate, the most important aspect of the Twins 40,000-seat new home is the location. Right next to Interstate 394 and a commuter rail station, the park will also feature a bike path under the stadium and a pedestrian walkway over the highway to access downtown Minneapolis. Best yet, fans will finally be able to see the city's skyline as they take in a game under the stars.

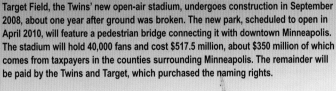

Target Field, the Twins' new open-air stadium, undergoes construction in September 2008, about one year after ground was broken. The new park, scheduled to open in April 2010, will feature a pedestrian bridge connecting it with downtown Minneapolis. The stadium will hold 40,000 fans and cost $517.5 million, about $350 million of which comes from taxpayers in the counties surrounding Minneapolis. The remainder will be paid by the Twins and Target, which purchased the naming rights.

ABOVE, INSET:
A grounds crew member sprays the pitcher's mound after it is lowered into the ground during the conversion from a baseball to football field.

BACKGROUND:
The Twins take on the Blue Jays in a 1998 game.

DOLPHIN STADIUM

Miami, Florida

Marlins (NL), 1993–present

Joe Robbie Stadium 1987–1996, Pro Player Stadium 1996–2004, Dolphins Stadium 2005

JEREMY HERMIDA

OPPOSITE: Marlins righty AJ Burnett delivers a pitch to Tampa Bay leadoff man Carl Crawford during the first at-bat of the game on July 4, 2004. Even a rare interleague match-up between two regional teams can't draw a large crowd to Dolphin Stadium (then called Pro Player Stadium) for a holiday game. Only 15,310 fans are on hand to watch the defending world champion Marlins, currently in second place, defeat third-place Tampa Bay, 4-3.

The stadium has always been decked out in the AFC Dolphins' orange and aqua, so the Marlins made a smart move by adopting a similar teal color upon the franchise's inception in 2003. Although nondescript from a baseball perspective, the octagonal Dolphin Stadium is instantly recognizable by its unique forward-leaning light towers. (Common in Latin America, particularly Cuba, this form of angled lighting has never caught on in the States.) The large area with tables just to the right of the foul pole is a picnic space available for rent to groups of fifty or more.

A massive football stadium masquerading as a baseball park, Dolphin Stadium is one of the few major league ballparks on which there is virtual unanimity. Players dislike it, fans dislike it, and above all, the Marlins owners dislike it. They dislike it so much, in fact, that they spent a decade and a half waging a public relations war against the facility, which they declare to be unsuitable for baseball. With team execs badmouthing the stadium instead of trying to attract people to it, it's little wonder that the Marlins ranked last or next to last in NL attendance eight times in nine seasons from 1999 to 2007. Even during their championship seasons of 1997 and 2003, Florida's attendance still ranked eleventh and twenty-eighth, respectively, in the majors. The park has changed names four times since hosting its first baseball game in 1993, but by any name it's been an aesthetic and business disaster.

The $115 million structure was privately financed, with most of the money coming from luxury suites and long-term football season-ticket holders. Located fifteen miles north of downtown Miami in what years later would be the city of Miami Gardens, it was named Joe Robbie Stadium, after the Dolphins owner whose tireless efforts had gotten the structure built, and it hosted its first football game in 1987.

Robbie died in 1990, after which his heirs sold 50 percent of his stadium to H. Wayne Huizenga, a video store magnate who was trying to bring baseball to South Florida. MLB awarded Huizenga an expansion franchise in 1991, and the Florida Marlins played their first season in 1993. The next year Huizenga purchased the remaining half of the stadium, which he would retain even after selling the Marlins in 1998.

Though built primarily as a football venue, Joe Robbie Stadium had also been designed with the idea of luring Major League Baseball to Miami. The field was wider than most gridirons, in order to accommodate the size of a baseball diamond, but this left football fans with sideline tickets about 90 feet away from the action. Baseball fans were no happier, as it turned out, since most seats faced the 50-yard line— which in the baseball configuration was center field. As with most multipurpose stadiums, the accommodations necessary for each sport made Joe Robbie Stadium ideal for neither.

As if to emphasize that the Marlins were guests in their own park, most of the 75,000 seats were colored Dolphins

MARLINS · Topps
JOSH WILLINGHAM

MARLINS · Topps
DAN UGGLA

MARLINS · Topps
ANIBAL SANCHEZ

orange. The tall left-field wall, which contains the main scoreboard, was dubbed the Teal Monster, although it reminded more fans of the Metrodome's garish "Baggie" than Fenway's famous wall. Still, it's the closest thing the park has to a signature element. Perhaps the best feature of the stadium is its drainage: the Prescription Athletic Turf system fends off the unpredictable Miami weather by enabling the natural grass field to be drained within half an hour of a 3-inch rainfall.

In 2006, with the facility deteriorating, Huizenga embarked on a $500 million renovation. "With architectural spaces inspired by the South Florida lifestyle, ocean hues, and nautical themes, Dolphin Stadium has been transformed into an extraordinary place for incredible experiences," said the pie-in-the-sky promotional copy issued by Dolphins Enterprises LLC. In reality, almost all the improvements were aimed at luxury areas to which only well-heeled fans had access. The main addition was a new club level that features opulent suites, private meeting rooms and restaurants, high-definition TV screens, air-conditioned VIP entrances, and private elevators. In addition, the renovations were done mostly with football in mind, as the Marlins appeared soon destined for a new home.

Although it was suitable enough on a temporary basis, Dolphin Stadium's cavernous dimensions and poor sight lines made it untenable as a permanent major league ballpark. After the turn of the century, team owners John Henry and then Jeffrey Loria began constantly harping on the need for a new publicly funded stadium, which the Florida state government consistently refused to back. By the middle of the decade, baseball's future in South Florida looked bleak, and Loria explored the option of moving the Marlins to San Antonio. In 2008, however, an ideal site was found and stadium funding was finally approved by the local government. The Miami Orange Bowl, a local landmark since 1937, was targeted for demolition and a new Marlins ballpark slated to be built on the site.

Nestled between vibrant Little Havana and the gleaming skyscrapers of downtown, the new location is an immeasurable improvement over that of Dolphin Stadium. Demolition of the Orange Bowl began in March 2008, with ground scheduled to be broken on the new stadium in July 2009 for a 2012 opening. The Marlins agreed to pay $155 million of the projected $515 million cost, with the rest coming from Miami-Dade County and the City of Miami. (Most of the Marlins' share, it is believed, will be covered by a naming rights deal.) Under the terms of their agreement, the team will rename itself the Miami Marlins upon moving into the retractable-roof facility. Like their new home, their new name seems perfect: Before MLB colonized the area, the local minor league team, which employed such memorable players as Satchel Paige, had been called the Miami Marlins. With a new, yet nostalgic moniker, a baseball-only stadium on the way, and no possibility of future rainouts, baseball in South Florida appears poised for an era of unprecedented success.

TIMELINE: DOLPHIN STADIUM

January 24, 1994 Dolphins and Marlins owner H. Wayne Huizenga, who already owns 50 percent of Joe Robbie Stadium, purchases the remaining 50 percent to give him full ownership.

May 11, 1996 The Marlins' Al Leiter tosses the first no-hitter in franchise history, blanking the Rockies 11-0 at Joe Robbie Stadium.

October 26, 1997

Advice of Counsell In a legendary Game 7, Cleveland comes within two outs of its first World Series title since 1948, only to see the upstart Marlins come from behind to win the championship. Indians closer Jose Mesa takes a 2-1 lead into the ninth, but a pair of singles and a Craig Counsell sacrifice fly enable Florida to send the game into extra innings. Cleveland brings in its best starter, Charles Nagy, in relief, but Nagy loads the bases in the bottom of the eleventh. Batting with two outs, rookie shortstop Edgar Renteria laces a line drive up the middle to win the Series for Florida, and Pro Player Stadium erupts as Counsell dances home with the winning run. Cleveland's players are devastated, particularly second baseman Tony Fernandez, whose fumble of an easy grounder prolonged the eleventh inning and allowed Renteria to come up to bat.

Marlins 3, Indians 2

1988

After having opened for football in 1987, Joe Robbie Stadium host its first baseball game, a spring-training exhibition between the Dodgers and Orioles, on March 11.

1993

The Marlins begin play, and $10 million in renovations makes the park baseball-ready. Because many upper-deck seats are not offered for sale, the listed capacity for baseball is 43,909, although future seasons will see Marlins officials constantly tinkering with this figure as ticket demand fluctuates. The pitcher-friendly dimensions are 330 feet to left field, 345 to right, 380 to the power alleys, and 404 to center. The deepest distance is 434 feet to a spot just left of center field.

1996

After having been raised to 46,238 the previous year, baseball capacity is lowered to 41,855. On August 26, the stadium is renamed Pro Player Park after a ten-year, $20 million deal is struck with the manufacturer of athletic apparel. Comically, the name lasts only two weeks; on September 10, it's changed to Pro Player Stadium.

RIGHT: Edgar Renteria smacks the second-most-famous game-winning hit of his Marlins career on September 30, 1997. This walk-off single to right field gives Florida a 2-1 win in Division Series Game 1—the first playoff game in franchise history. A month later, he will do the same thing in Game 7 of the World Series.

1997

The tarp is removed from the upper deck seats for the World Series, and Game 6 is attended by 67,498 fans, shattering the stadium's previous baseball attendance record.

April 5, 1993

Charlie the Marlin The Dodgers, who were the visiting team in the first exhibition game at Joe Robbie Stadium back in 1988, are also the guests for the first real game five years later. Forty-five-year-old knuckleballer Charlie Hough, a former Dodger, throws the first official pitch at the stadium and also becomes the winning pitcher when the Marlins outlast LA, 6-3. The Marlins' Bret Barberie knocks a single for the first hit at Joe Robbie, while the Dodgers' Tim Wallach blasts the first home run. The star of the game, however, is Jeff Conine, who in ensuing years will become Florida's most popular player and win the nickname "Mr. Marlin." In his Marlins debut, Conine goes 4-for-4 with the first stolen base in franchise history.

Marlins 6, Dodgers 3

September 30, 1997

Giant Killers The first playoff game ever held in Florida is a doozy as the Marlins and Giants remain scoreless entering the seventh inning of Division Series Game 1. Florida's Kevin Brown, who threw a no-hitter against the Giants earlier in the season, holds them scoreless today until Bill Mueller breaks through with a home run. In the bottom of the seventh, the Marlins' Charles Johnson goes deep to tie it, and the teams enter the ninth knotted at one run apiece. With the bases loaded and two outs in the bottom of the ninth, rookie Edgar Renteria wins it for Florida with a walk-off single—a preview of the way the World Series will end a month later. The Marlins will beat the Giants in the ninth inning again tomorrow en route to a three-game sweep.

Marlins 2, Giants 1

1999

Baseball capacity is raised to 42,531.

CAP: 1998.

RIGHT: As Alex Gonzalez rounds the bases after his walk-off homer in the 2003 World Series, his joyous teammates await his impending arrival at home plate. Among those pictured are Lenny Harris, Mike Lowell, Juan Encarnación, AJ Burnett, Miguel Cabrera, and Ivan Rodriguez, plus home plate umpire Jeff Kellogg.

2001

Baseball capacity is lowered drastically to 36,331.

2005

Pro Player Stadium owner H. Wayne Huizenga creates a new corporation, Dolphins Enterprises LLC, to manage and market the stadium. Huizenga begins renovations, which include additional restaurants, luxury suites, retail shops, and parking lots. As part of the reorganization, the facility is renamed Dolphins Stadium on January 10.

October 4, 2003

Can't Budge Pudge A thrilling Division Series ends with a jarring home plate collision, and Florida advances to the next playoff round when Marlins catcher Ivan "Pudge" Rodriguez emerges with the ball. Rodriguez authors the game's key offensive play, too, when in the eighth inning he scores the go-ahead run by knocking the ball loose from the mitt of Giants catcher Yorvit Torrealba. As the ball bounces away from Torrealba, Derek Lee races around to score a key insurance run. A Giants rally in the ninth cuts Florida's lead to 7-6. However, when JT Snow tries to score the tying run from second on a single, even Snow, the son of an NFL Pro Bowler, can't budge Pudge, who hangs on to end the game. Rodriguez, who also drove in the tying and go-ahead runs in extra innings in Game 3, is unquestionably the star of the series.

Marlins 7, Giants 6

October 22, 2003

Gone-zalez In what is believed at the time to be the last game of his career, the Yankees' Roger Clemens leaves the field losing to the Marlins 3-1 and receives a rousing standing ovation from Florida fans. Clemens, who has announced his retirement effective at the end of the World Series, is outpitched by the Marlins' Carl Pavano in Game 4. However, Marlins closer Ugueth Urbina fails to shut the door on the Yanks in the ninth, allowing a two-out, game-tying triple to pinch hitter Ruben Sierra. Last year's post-season hero, Aaron Boone, has two chances to win it for New York, but comes up empty in the ninth with Sierra on third, and again in the eleventh with the bases loaded. The Yankees, running out of pitchers in extra innings, leave closer Mariano Rivera unused. Instead they call on Jeff Weaver, whose disastrous regular-season performance got him demoted to mop-up bullpen duty. Weaver survives the eleventh, but gives up a walk-off homer to the first batter he faces in the twelfth, light-hitting Marlins shortstop Alex Gonzalez. The Series is now tied at two games apiece, and the Marlins will win the next two contests to capture the championship. Clemens, meanwhile, will unretire and pitch four more major league seasons.

Marlins 4, Yankees 3

In the right portion of the foreground is the rarest sight in baseball: empty seats at a World Series game. Marlins fans are known for their lackluster attendance, but it isn't their fault that these chairs sit empty during Game 3 of the 2003 World Series. The centerfield seats form part of the batter's eye, and so went unsold as per MLB rules. Despite the presence of 65,731 fans, the Marlins lose to the Yankees 6-1.

June 9, 2008 The Reds' Ken Griffey Jr. hits his 600th career home run off Marlins lefty Mark Hendrickson at Dolphin Stadium.

February 2008 Huizenga sells 50 percent of the stadium to real estate mogul Stephen Ross. Ross will purchase another 45 percent in January 2009.

January 8, 2009 The Florida Gators win college football's mythical national title at Dolphin Stadium by defeating Oklahoma 24-14 in the BCS Championship Game.

2006

The facility is given its fifth different name in a decade. In April, an "s" is dropped as Dolphins Stadium becomes Dolphin Stadium. The marked distance in the power alleys is also changed to 385 feet, although the fence is not moved.

September 6, 2006

Sanchez Skins Snakes Marlins rookie Anibal Sanchez throws the first no-hitter in the majors in two years, and the first in Miami since Al Leiter's 1996 gem. One of four rookies in Florida's starting rotation, the twenty-two-year-old Sanchez retires Eric Byrnes on a grounder to shortstop Hanley Ramirez to end the game. Sanchez is carried off the mound by his teammates as the paltry crowd of of 12,561 roars its appreciation. Both Sanchez and Ramirez came to Miami last November in a trade that sent World Series hero Josh Beckett to Boston—a deal that looks better and better for the Marlins with each passing day. The 6,364-game gap between major league no-hitters is the longest in history.

Marlins 2, Diamondbacks 0

2008

Baseball capacity is raised to 38,560.

LEFT: Rookie right-hander Aníbal Sánchez makes his next start after throwing a no-hitter on September 6, 2006. The follow-up isn't quite as successful, but Sanchez still manages to win 16-5. He's wearing an NYPD cap because the game takes place on the fifth anniversary of the September 11 attacks.

BELOW: Luis Gonzalez leads off first base during his debut game as a Marlin. As a Florida native and a Cuban-American, Gonzalez became one of Dolphin Stadium's most popular players when he signed with the Marlins at the tail end of his career in 2008.

SKYDOME

Toronto, Ontario

Blue Jays (AL) 1989–present

Rogers Centre 2004–present

OPPOSITE:
Fireworks light up SkyDome after Reed Johnson's leadoff home run off the Yankees' Mike Mussina on August 29, 2004. The Jays will win the game 6-4, but will finish in last place while the Yankees finish first.

Several of SkyDome's never-before-seen-in-baseball amenities are visible in this image, namely a Hard Rock Cafe (the row of windows above the Nikon sign in right field) and a built-in hotel (the windows ringing the upper deck just below the floodlights). In 1990, after a couple was observed in flagrante delicto during a game, signs were posted in the hotel rooms noting that "The room and its occupants are on public view" and "One should bear in mind that SkyDome caters toward a family audience."

Hailed as the vanguard of a new generation of ballparks upon its opening in 1989, Toronto's SkyDome is probably the most lavish and ambitious stadium built to date. Featuring a retractable dome, a Hard Rock Cafe, and a built-in hotel with rooms overlooking the playing field, the park attracted enough fans in its heady early days to break baseball's single-season attendance record two years in a row. But despite two Blue Jays world championships, the luster soon wore off as SkyDome proved to be more of a fad and less of a trendsetter. With the opening of Camden Yards in 1992, baseball took a decided turn toward retro ballparks, a style that encompassed everything SkyDome was not. In the late '90s attendance dropped to less than half of what it had been, and the Jays slashed payroll accordingly, settling into a comfortable mediocrity. They won between 74 and 88 games in eleven of the twelve seasons from 1996 through 2007, never once contending for the playoffs, but also never having a truly bad season.

After enduring a decade of bizarre seating arrangements and frequent snowdrifts at Exhibition Stadium, the Blue Jays in the mid-1980s began making plans for a grand dome that would set the baseball world on its ear. The eventual cost of over Can\$500 million was funded by a special corporation whose investors included a unique hodgepodge of public and private interests, including the City of Toronto, the province of Ontario, and some twenty-five private companies. About Can\$60 million was raised by pre-sales of luxury boxes, an indication of the almost limitless moneymaking ability the stadium would aspire to. Ground was broken in 1986, with the Jays planning to move in for the 1989 season. The location could not have been better. SkyDome was built in the middle of downtown Toronto, just a block from the picturesque shores of Lake Ontario and adjacent to what was then the tallest building in the world, the CN Tower. From the vantage point of the Toronto Islands as well as watercraft in Lake Ontario, SkyDome's distinctive half-moon-shaped roof would become a signature of the city's skyline, much like the Sydney Opera House.

The roof itself was designed to be retractable, an extravagance deemed necessary in light of the weather problems the nearby lake had caused at open-air Exhibition Stadium. The first retractable dome in baseball to be actually functional (Montreal's Stade Olympique featured a stillborn version), SkyDome's massive roof is a remarkable feat of engineering, and can open and close in just twenty minutes. Designed by

architects Roderick Robbie and Michael Allen, it owes much to similar roofs at concert halls, but at 310 feet high and weighing 11,000 tons, it exists on a much grander scale. Although built primarily for baseball, SkyDome is adaptable for football, track and field, concerts, conventions, and other events. Unfortunately, the shape of the structure mandated a high seating bowl, and some seats are remarkably distant from the playing field. The height of the roof also means that SkyDome, even when packed with fans, never generates the same ear-splitting noise levels as other covered structures, like the Metrodome.

What excited fans even more than the weatherproof dome was the breadth of amenities beneath it. These include what was then the largest scoreboard in the world, which cost a whopping Can$17 million. SkyDome was baseball's first "mallpark," a structure where, in the view of some, the actual game exists only as a venue through which to sell every consumer product under the sun. A Hard Rock Cafe sits high beyond the centerfield fence, allowing fans to eat at their tables while watching the game through the windows. Various other bars and restaurants dot the concourse, from upscale dining to fast-food restaurants like McDonald's, which were almost never seen at sports stadiums before SkyDome. In addition, millions of dollars worth of commissioned paintings and sculptures decorate the grounds inside and out. With a fitness club, a movie theater, and a built-in hotel added to the mix, SkyDome seems the sort of place where one might be able to live one's entire life without ever leaving the building. The hotel, located above the outfield, has 348 rooms, 70 of which contain picture windows overlooking the field (and which cost an exorbitant premium). However, it seemed that team officials never considered that while the hotel patrons could see the game through their windows, the fans in the stadium could also see inside. In 1990, when one amorous couple put on an explicit display in full view of the crowd, the hotel began requiring guests to sign an agreement upon check-in stating that they would close their curtains when necessary.

Despite its much-ballyhooed bells and whistles, at its heart SkyDome is just another domed stadium with artificial turf. *New York Times* writer Michael Janofsky compared it to "an airplane hangar or a merchandise mart or a place in which Crazy Eddie might hold a giant warehouse sale." During its early years fans were seduced by the novelty of the park, and also by the presence of an outstanding Blue Jays team that won the World Series in both 1992 and 1993. In 1991, the Jays broke baseball's all-time record by drawing just over 4 million fans; the next year, they broke it again. But just as the talented roster began to decay, fans began to weary of the giant dome. It didn't help matters that a new park, Baltimore's Oriole Park at Camden Yards, was now drawing all the attention. A natural-grass, open-air stadium that hearkened back to the golden era of baseball, Baltimore's park was everything SkyDome was not. It soon became clear that fans loved the retro style, and a stadium construction boom began in which every new park tried to mimic the feel of Camden Yards. Instead of pointing the way to the future as many had predicted, Skydome instead became an outdated anomaly less than a decade after its opening.

If anything about SkyDome began a trend in baseball, it was the way in which it marketed the game to the wealthy fan instead of the average Joe. The shops, the fancy restaurants, the expensive suites, the all-encompassing experience—all these would become staples of the new generation of retro parks. However, when it came to actually watching a game at SkyDome, the setting—the roof, the cavernous dimensions, the distant seats, the plastic grass—was something many die-hard fans wanted no part of. In 1998 the stadium's ownership corporation filed for bankruptcy, and by 2002, exactly a decade after breaking the all-time record, the Jays had sunk to eleventh out of the fourteen AL teams in attendance. In 2005 the stadium was purchased for a mere $25 million, one-twentieth of its original cost, by Rogers Communications, the Canadian media conglomerate that had also purchased the Blue Jays five years earlier. The name was changed from SkyDome to Rogers Centre, and a series of gradual refurbishments began, including the installation of a new video board and a better brand of artificial turf. These improvements, however, can do little to alter SkyDome's legacy as a park built a few years too soon and outdated nearly as soon as it opened—a space-age park in a retro era.

OPPOSITE, TOP: Although quite an attractive building from the outside, the inside of SkyDome leaves much to be desired as a baseball venue. The best atmosphere is provided when the roof is open during day games.

OPPOSITE, MIDDLE: One of SkyDome's most amusing features is its modern-day take on gargoyles, which are styled as larger-than-life baseball fans. The gold-painted sculptures hover over the northeast and northwest entrances. Collectively titled *The Audience*, the pieces were created by acclaimed Toronto-born artist Michael Snow and are indicative of the team's and architects' efforts to beautify the stadium grounds with notable works of art.

OPPOSITE, BOTTOM: Although close-ups are provided on television, there's nothing quite like soaking in a view of the ballgame while relaxing in your hotel room, as evidenced by the two fans in this 1990 photo. SkyDome was the first—and is still the only—major league park to contain a hotel with views overlooking the playing field.

ABOVE: If you ever find yourself lost in Toronto and wondering how to get to SkyDome, just head toward the famous spire of the CN Tower, once the world's tallest building, which juts 1,815 feet into the air near the northeast corner of the stadium. In this 1988 photo, work on the stadium proceeds briskly in preparation for its planned opening in April 1989. Construction delays postpone the opening until June, when the Jays hold a grandiose opening ceremony featuring six music and dance acts and hosted by sitcom star (and Ontario native) Alan Thicke.

BELOW: These drawings detail the colorful banners planned for SkyDome's exterior facade, an effort to offset its dull gray color. The final banners can be seen in the top photo on the opposite page. SkyDome was designed by architect Roderick Robbie and engineer Michael Allen. The British-born Robbie created another notable work of Canadian architecture: the Canada Pavilion, an upside-down pyramid built on Île Notre-Dame for Expo '67 in Montreal.

May 31, 1989 Cito Gaston is named Toronto's manager. He'll go on to win the only two world championships in Blue Jays history.

September 3, 1989 One week after signing for a $575,000 bonus, Washington State star John Olerud makes his debut at SkyDome without playing a single minor league game.

1989

On June 5, the Blue Jays play their first game in SkyDome, the most luxurious and state-of-the-art stadium ever built. The dimensions are the same as its predecessor, Exhibition Stadium: 330 feet down the lines, 375 to the gaps, and 400 to center. The appropriately named SkyDome has the tallest dome on earth, measuring 310 feet from top to bottom.

1991

The Toronto Argonauts of the Canadian Football League move in. Unlike American football, the CFL plays its games while baseball is in season. Converting the field takes a relatively quick ten to twelve hours.

September 30, 1989

A Division-Winning Rally The Blue Jays capture their second division title in five seasons with a victory over Baltimore. It isn't easy, though, as Toronto goes through two managers, two stadiums, and a fight to the finish against an Orioles team that lost 107 games a year earlier. The Blue Jays trail 3-1 entering the bottom of the eighth, but they rally to tie it on RBI singles by midseason pickup Mookie Wilson and first baseman Fred McGriff. George Bell then gives his Blue Jays the lead with a sacrifice fly. Tom Henke saves it for Frank Wills, who gets the win with four innings of shutout relief. It's the first postseason appearance for Jays manager Cito Gaston, who replaced Jimy Williams just before the team moved into SkyDome.

Blue Jays 4, Orioles 3

ABOVE: George Bell swings away in 1989, the year the Blue Jays moved into SkyDome.

BACKGROUND: Whatever its failings as a baseball park, SkyDome provides Toronto with an undeniably distinctive addition to the city skyline, particularly when viewed from the Toronto Islands, where this photo was taken.

July 9, 1991 SkyDome hosts its first All-Star Game, with the AL prevailing 4-2. The Jays' Jimmy Key is the winning pitcher.

April 6, 1992 Oriole Park at Camden Yards opens in Baltimore to rave reviews. The traditional and comparatively modest structure makes SkyDome immediately seem ostentatious.

October 24, 1992 Dave Winfield's eleventh-inning double in Game 6 gives the Jays their first World Series title ever.

October 2, 1991

Four Million Strong In their home finale, the Blue Jays score twice in the bottom of the ninth to clinch the AL East title in dramatic fashion. After California takes the lead on a two-out ninth-inning single by Dave Gallagher, the Blue Jays tie it back up on an Angels error. Joe Carter then wins it with a walk-off single against Angels closer Bryan Harvey in front of a crowd of 50,324. The Jays need every fan, too, as they become the first sports team to draw four million in a season, surpassing that mark by a mere 1,527 fans.

Blue Jays 6, Angels 5

October 14, 1992

Finally, Jays Win the Pennant After losing three playoff series in a six-year period, the Blue Jays finally capture their first pennant ever by pounding Oakland in ALCS Game 6. A two-run homer by Joe Carter and a three-run shot by Candy Maldonado provide the Jays with all the offense they'll need, as pitching ace Juan Guzman allows just one run in seven innings. Longtime closer Tom Henke retires Ruben Sierra for the pennant-clinching out, as 51,335 fans nearly cheer the roof off of SkyDome.

Blue Jays 9, A's 2

October 20, 1992

The Triple Play that Wasn't The first World Series contest ever played in Canada turns into a rollicking roller-coaster ride. The highlight of this Game 3 is a miraculous fourth-inning catch by Jays centerfielder Devon White that would have been a triple play if not for an umpire's blown call. With two runners on, David Justice hits a drive to deep center, which White spectacularly snags while leaping against the wall. White pegs the ball back to first baseman John Olerud, but the runner on first, Terry Pendleton, has already been called out for passing Deion Sanders on the base paths. Olerud then throws to third baseman Kelly Gruber, who makes a diving tag of Sanders for the presumed third out. But umpire Bob Davidson calls Sanders safe—a call he will later admit was incorrect. In the top of the eighth the Braves take a 2-1 lead on Lonnie Smith's single, but in the bottom of the inning Gruber ties it back up with a solo homer. After Atlanta manager Bobby Cox is ejected in the top of the ninth, he watches on the clubhouse television as his team trots out four different pitchers in the bottom of the inning. The Blue Jays mount a strange game-winning rally featuring two intentional walks, a bizarre sacrifice bunt by slugger Dave Winfield, and a walk-off single by role player Candy Maldonado.

Blue Jays 3, Braves 2

BELOW: Jays spark plug Roberto Alomar completes a double play in 1993, as the Yankees' Mike Stanley futilely slides into second.

October 23, 1993

Carter Creates a Legend With one swing Joe Carter captures a second straight championship for Toronto, joyously leaping his way around the bases after becoming only the second player in history to end the World Series with a walk-off home run. Blue Jays ace Dave Stewart takes a 5-1 lead into the seventh inning of Game 6, but Philadelphia's Lenny Dykstra makes things close with a three-run homer. Dave Hollins then ties it with an RBI single, and Pete Incaviglia's sacrifice fly off the Jays' Al Leiter brings in the go-ahead run. Phillies closer Mitch Williams, an erratic hurler who received death threats after his Game 4 meltdown, is brought in to shut down the Jays in the ninth. Williams proceeds to walk Rickey Henderson, get Devon White to fly out, and allow a single to Paul Molitor, bringing up Carter with one out and the Jays down by a run. Carter, known for his clutch hitting, lines a Williams offering just over the left-field fence, providing a moment that none of the 52,195 fans at SkyDome will ever forget. The Blue Jays are the first back-to-back world champions since the 1977-78 Yankees. Although Carter had the game's big blow, it is Molitor, with a .500 Series average, who is named MVP.

Blue Jays 8, Phillies 6

1995

The Toronto Raptors, an NBA expansion team, play their first two seasons at SkyDome. A giant curtain bisects the stadium to make the basketball setting more intimate.

ABOVE: Joe Carter half leaps, half runs to first base after his 1993 World Series–winning homer.

CAP: 2001 (worn by Tony Batista).

BELOW: The view from the upper deck during Game 2 of the 1993 World Series.

1999 After the stadium's ownership corporation goes bankrupt, it is purchased by a group of investors operating under the name Sportsco International for US$74 million.

August 3, 2001 During the third inning of a Blue Jays–Orioles game, home plate umpire Tim Welke orders the roof closed when the free bandanas given out for "Raul Mondesi Bandana Night" prove ineffective at swatting away the plague of aphids that have infested Toronto.

August 14, 2008 The Buffalo Bills play the first of what will be a series of eight regular-season and exhibition games at the SkyDome to take place over the next five years.

July 5, 1998

Rocket Reaches a Milestone Roger Clemens fans Tampa Bay's Randy Winn to become the eleventh pitcher with 3,000 career strike-outs. Tony Fernandez, mean-while, collects three hits, extending the Blue Jays career record, which he broke a day earlier with his 1,320th hit. Clemens gets a no-decision in Toronto's 2-1 win, but he will end the season atop the AL in wins, strikeouts, and ERA for the second straight year. The Rocket will also capture his second straight Cy Young Award (and the third in a row by a Blue Jay), making him the first pitcher to win the award five times.

Blue Jays 2, Devil Rays 1

2001

A malfunction during a pre-game test of the roof causes some panels to fall in left field, resulting in the first postponement in the stadium's history.

2005

Rogers Communications, the media conglomerate that owns the Blue Jays, buys the financially troubled stadium and renames it the Rogers Centre. FieldTurf, an artificial surface that more closely mimics real grass, is installed.

ABOVE: Roger Clemens throws the pitch that records his 3,000th strikeout in 1998. Though he wears a Blue Jays uniform for just two years, Clemens' stay in Toronto is a memorable one, and his 1997 season was perhaps the greatest of his career.

RIGHT: The brand-new SkyDome in 1989. Note that the lights are turned on for a game played under bright sunshine.

September 25, 2003

Delgado Goes Deep Carlos Delgado hits a record-tying four home runs in one game, becoming the fifteenth player in history to accomplish the feat—and only the sixth to do it in four consecutive at-bats. Delgado's first-inning dinger, the 300th of this career, gives Toronto a 3-0 lead; his third ties the game at 6-6 in the sixth; and his fourth evens the game at 8-8 in the eighth inning. Toronto then pushes across two more runs for a 10-8 victory. Delgado, already having a monster season before today, will lead the major leagues with 145 RBIs and finish with 42 home runs.

Blue Jays 10, Devil Rays 8

328

TROPICANA FIELD

St. Petersburg, Florida

Rays (NL) 1998–present

DELMON YOUNG

A gleaming white elephant in a tropical paradise, St. Petersburg's Tropicana Field stands on the shores of the Gulf of Mexico as a $200 million warning against counting one's chickens before they hatch. Built in 1986 in hopes of luring a major league team to Tampa Bay, the Florida Suncoast Dome (as it was originally called) stood vacant for years while teams used it as a bargaining chip to get their own new stadiums built elsewhere. By the time the expansion Tampa Bay Devil Rays came to town in 1998, the turf-infested dome was already outmoded, having been pushed into obsolescence by the popularity of Camden Yards and the retro stadiums that followed.

Constructed between 1986 and 1990 for an initial cost of $130 million, the Florida Suncoast Dome was the centerpiece of the city of St. Petersburg's plan to revitalize the community by bringing big league baseball to town. There was only one problem: they couldn't find a team willing to move in. Overtures were made to several clubs, including the Seattle Mariners and, in 1988, the Chicago White Sox. The city offered to pour $30 million more into the dome in an attempt to lure the White Sox south, but this backfired when the Sox merely used the threat of moving to Florida to extort a new stadium from the Illinois legislature. Four years later the Giants, languishing in uncomfortable Candlestick Park, became St. Pete's next suitors as they threatened to leave San Francisco. In August 1992, a consortium of Florida investors even held a press conference announcing that they had reached an agreement to purchase the Giants for $115 million and move them to the Suncoast Dome for the 1993 season. But that, too, fell through, when Giants owner Bob Lurie sold his team for $15 million less to an ownership group that promised to keep it in San Francisco. The Suncoast Dome, it seemed, was fated to serve as an eternal decoy for teams seeking new stadiums in their own hometowns.

Franchise relocation was not the only area in which Tampa Bay came up short. Throughout the 1980s and early '90s, the existence of the Suncoast Dome ensured that St. Petersburg was the first city mentioned whenever the topic of expansion came up. However, when Major League Baseball finally decided to expand in 1991, the

B.J. UPTON

ROCCO BALDELLI

CARL CRAWFORD

1998

Almost a decade after the stadium opened, baseball finally comes to Tropicana Field after a $70 million renovation is completed. The first game is played on March 31, and the dimensions from left to right are 315, 370, 410, 370, and 322 feet. Among the unintended quirks are catwalks that have two different sets of ground rules when hit by a batted ball. The slanted, translucent roof is given an orange glow whenever the Devil Rays win.

ABOVE: Rays skipper Joe Maddon scans the field during Game 2 of the 2008 World Series. As Tampa Bay made its miraculous run to the 2008 pennant, much of the media focus swirled around the team's quirky new-age manager. Maddon got attention for everything—including his affinity for Bruce Springsteen, to whom he gave partial credit for the Rays' ALCS win, as the Boss' music was playing while he made out the Game 7 lineup. Much of the recognition should go, however, to Maddon's laid-back demeanor and steady hand, which allowed his young players to grow into their abilities.

two new franchises were awarded to Denver and—worst of all insults—Miami. The modern dome in which many had invested their dreams, and in which the city had invested so much money, was swiftly becoming useless, employed infrequently for such events as trade shows and concerts. St. Petersburg eventually received a consolation prize of sorts—from the NHL. The expansion Tampa Bay Lightning began play in 1992 and spent their following three seasons at the dome, which was renamed the ThunderDome to match the team's nickname.

By the mid-1990s it was clear that with the retro stadium revolution in full effect, desirable ballparks would need to feature characteristics diametrically opposed to those of the gigantic dome. Remarkably, though, baseball's next wave of expansion—announced in 1995 and scheduled to take effect in 1998—finally bestowed a team on Tampa Bay. The Lightning moved into their own arena to make way for a $70 million, baseball-only renovation of the ThunderDome, which included the addition of dugouts and more luxury suites; the stadium's naming rights were sold to the Tropicana juice company.

However, the new baseball team, like its stadium, was a disaster right from the outset. Even its name,

Devil Rays, was so ill-conceived that it was ultimately changed after a decade. Though expansion teams are typically bad, there have been few as bad as Tampa Bay's. Thanks to incompetent management and ownership, the Devil Rays lost more than ninety games in each of their first ten years of existence. Before the 2006 season, though, an ownership change fortunately brought this nightmarish era to an end. Under a visionary game plan executed by new general manager Andrew Friedman, Tampa Bay amassed the finest collection of young talent in baseball, headlined by pitcher Scott Kazmir, outfielder BJ Upton, and third baseman Evan Longoria. In 2008 the team unveiled the new name, thus adding a literal identity change to the figurative one. They were now simply called "the Rays," a name that managed in one fell swoop to cleverly evoke two local features, fish and sunshine. With a run of winning seasons all but guaranteed, the Tampa Bay franchise appeared poised to outgrow long-since-obsolete Tropicana Field. Baseball in St. Petersburg seems to be coming full circle, with the city struggling to retain its team while distant baseball-starved communities attempt, as St. Pete once did, to poach it with the lure of a shiny new stadium.

1996 The NHL Tampa Bay Lightning move from Tropicana Field (then called the Thunderdome) to the Ice Palace to make way for the Devil Rays.

August 7, 1999

The Sweetest Kiss Two nights after Mark McGwire's 500th home run and one night after Tony Gwynn's 3,000th hit, Devil Rays third baseman Wade Boggs gives baseball a third consecutive milestone evening when he collects his 3,000th career hit. He does it in style, too, launching a sixth-inning pitch from Cleveland's Chris Haney over the right-field fence for a home run. It's just the second homer of the season for the slap-hitting Boggs, who rounds the bases, points toward the sky in memory of his late mother, and then sponta-neously kneels down to kiss home plate. He's the twenty-third player to collect 3,000 hits, but the first to reach the mark on a home run. Boggs, who's playing his second season with his hometown Devil Rays after an illustrious career with the Red Sox and Yankees, will retire after the season and win election to the Hall of Fame in 2005.

Indians 15, Devil Rays 10

August 26, 1999 Tampan Wade Boggs, playing before his hometown fans, collects the 3,010th and final hit of his career, an eighth-inning infield squibber.

2000

The turf is removed and replaced by a new kind of fake grass, FieldTurf, which is being used for the first time in the major leagues. The Devil Rays continue to have the only stadium with a dirt infield but turf everywhere else.

March 31, 1998

Better Late Than Never Tropicana Field finally hosts its first major league baseball game, eight years after being built. Things start off just fine, as southpaw Wilson Alvarez mows down the Tigers in the first, although he surrenders the first hit at Tropicana Field, a single by Tony Clark. Alvarez doesn't make it out of the third inning, and the Tigers roll to a lopsided win. Detroit outfielder Luis Gonzalez, a Tampa native, hits the first home run at the Trop. Dave Martinez, meanwhile, collects the Tampa Bay franchise's first hit, while Wade Boggs has the team's first homer and RBI.

Tigers 11, Devil Rays 6

June 22, 1998

Fish Face Off The annual interleague Sunshine State series begins, and the victors in the first all-Florida baseball game are the Marlins, who beat the Rays in an extra-inning nail-biter. In the top of the twelfth, the Marlins' Edgar Renteria alertly tags up and scores the go-ahead run on a foul pop-up to Tampa Bay first baseman Fred McGriff. The Rays mount a comeback in the bottom of the inning, loading the bases with one out, but Marlins reliever Antonio Alfonseca works his way out of the jam to preserve the win. An unimpressive (but better than normal) crowd of 25,623 comes out for the game; indeed, the Devil Rays–Marlins match-ups will continue to draw lackluster interest in the state until 2008, when both teams unexpectedly stay in first place until June.

Marlins 3, Devil Rays 2

RIGHT: Among the many regrettable ele-ments associated with the early Devil Rays were their garish uniforms, which seemed to have been borrowed from the Ringling Brothers and Barnum & Bailey Clown College—a local institu-tion that closed in 1998, the same year the Rays started up. In this 1999 photo, the home jersey can be seen on Wade Boggs, who has just had his 3,000th hit.

March 23, 2004 Tampa native Fred McGriff, owner of 491 homers, signs with his hometown team in an attempt to reach 500. He hits just two more before a July release ends his career.

April 18, 2008 The Rays shock everyone by signing rookie Evan Longoria to a six-year, $17.5 million contract after just his sixth major league game. He goes on to win AL Rookie of the Year.

2006

The second renovation to the now sixteen-year-old stadium, at a cost of $35 million, provides for repainting seats, improving the club section, and adding a large fish tank filled with actual rays.

2007

Yet another carpet is installed, this one a new and improved version of FieldTurf. Several new video boards are also added. Stadium capacity, which was 45,369 in 1998, has shrunk to 38,437 because the team chooses not to sell certain seats.

2008

Capacity shrinks again to 36,048, even as the Rays field their best team ever.

BELOW: Lefty David Price exults after inducing an ALCS-ending groundout from Boston's Jed Lowrie, clinching the 2008 pennant for the Rays. Price, the coveted prospect who until a month earlier had been plying his trade in the minors, seemed a fitting choice to finish off the key game for this rags-to-riches squad. "Price, the kid who started out in A-ball this year, to be closing out Game 7?" teammate Dan Wheeler said. "That just shows you what kind of kid he is and what kind of pitcher. The future is very bright for this kid."

October 19, 2008

Price of Greatness The Tampa Bay Rays, on the verge of having their Cinderella season turn into a pumpkin after letting a three-games-to-one lead slip away against division rival Boston, hold off the Red Sox to clinch the pennant. Rookie David Price is the last of several Game 7 heroes for the Rays in the ALCS. Price, who did not make his major league debut until September 14, goes 1⅓ innings, pitching out of a bases-loaded jam in the eighth, to save it for Matt Garza. The twenty-three-year-old Price will even make an appearance on his off-day: introducing future president Barack Obama at a campaign appearance the next day in Tampa. In the first World Series in franchise history, the Rays will lose to the Phillies, 4-1.

Rays 3, Red Sox 1

September 3, 2003

What a Way to Start St. Petersburg native Doug Waechter throws a two-hit shutout against Seattle in his first big-league start. Waechter, called up to the majors just a week earlier, is the first ever Devil Ray and ninth American Leaguer since 1970 to accomplish such a feat—and the third in that span to make his first start a complete-game shutout in his hometown. The Devil Rays will make club history again tomorrow night when Jorge Sosa goes all the way in a 1-0 victory that gives the franchise its first-ever back-to-back complete-game shutouts.

Devil Rays 7, Mariners 0

September 20, 2008

Devil May Care? One could say hell froze over: Tampa Bay has dropped the "Devil" from its name and picked up a spot in the postseason. After never winning more than seventy games in a season, Tampa Bay—now known as "The Rays"—goes 97-65 to clinch a spot in October with more than a week to spare. It'll be a few days before the Rays officially clinch the AL East title (Boston will wind up two games behind the Rays as wild card champs). It sets off a wild celebration at Tropicana Field as the Rays join the 1991 Braves as the only teams to go from the worst record in the league to a postseason berth in successive years.

Rays 7, Twins 2

TOKYO DOME

The Big-League Road Show

It turns out that not having a top-drawing stadium can have some perks. In 2003, when Major League Baseball was looking for a team to play against the Yankees at Japan's Tokyo Dome, the Red Sox, Orioles, and Blue Jays were nixed because it was thought that the teams would be unwilling to give up the large gate receipts that come with having the Yanks in town. Devil Rays owner and member of MLB's international committee Vince Naimoli, however, thought differently. "I think these games are important to the future of Major League Baseball," he told the Associated Press. And so, on March 30 and 31, 2004, the Yankees and Rays opened their seasons in one of the largest venues in Asia. It wasn't the first time the Tokyo Dome, a 55,000-seat stadium that's home to the Yomiuri Giants baseball team, had hosted American baseball—four years prior, the Cubs and Mets played their first two games of the season there in front of sellout crowds.

Not all international games have gone over so well. The first major league game played outside the United States and Canada, a Padres-Mets match-up in Monterrey, Mexico, was far from a total success. Beginning on August 16, 1996, three games were played at Estadio Monterrey, while players complained about the facilities and Mets catcher Todd Hundley came down with food poisoning. Though the players were less than thrilled, the exhibition games were seen as a much-needed PR bump after the '94–'95 work stoppage. And apparently, it worked—in addition to going back to Monterrey in 1999 (this time with the Rockies), the Padres moved into Honolulu's Aloha Stadium for three games against the Cardinals in April 1997. (No mai tai overdoses were reported.)

"Neutral sites" were once used only when a team was thinking about moving, such as the White Sox's twenty games in Milwaukee's abandoned County Stadium in the late '60s; when a stadium was undergoing repairs, like the A's 1996 six-game stint at Las Vegas' Cashman Field; or when the team was simply out of ideas, like the Expos' games in San Juan, Puerto Rico, in 2003. But the movement toward neutral sites is gaining speed as a marketing opportunity in fresh territory. The Red Sox and A's took the field at Tokyo Dome in 2007, and, hoping to expand the game farther into Asia, the Dodgers and those globe-trotting Padres held two exhibition games in March 2008 in Beijing, China. A near-capacity crowd filled Wukesong Olympic Baseball Field, snacking on peanuts, hot dogs, and beer amidst American advertisements and MLB banners. "Baseball is still a very small sport in China, so it was great to see a real game played here at last," an enthusiastic spectator told USA Today.

The next stop on MLB's international tour will most likely be Europe. Although harsh weather in the northern part of the continent may pose a problem for games early in the season, MLB officials have confirmed that they're looking at sites in London, Paris, Rome, Munich, and Amsterdam. The pump is already primed, at least on television: Britain's Five Network has hosted a major league game of the week since 1997.

TOP: Opened in 1988, the Tokyo Dome is known to Japanese fans as "The Big Egg" for the way it appears from afar. The Tokyo Dome City complex also includes shops, restaurants, the Japanese Baseball Hall of Fame, a Ferris wheel, and the Thunder Dolphin roller coaster, seen here in the foreground.

INSET: The Mets and Cubs face off at the Tokyo Dome in the second official game of the 2000 MLB season.

U.S. CELLULAR FIELD

Chicago, Illinois

White Sox (AL) 1991–present

Comiskey Park [II] 1991–2002

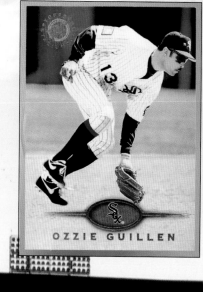

OZZIE GUILLEN

OPPOSITE: U.S. Cellular Field in 1993 (then called Comiskey Park). When the park opened, the *New York Times* called it "a hopeful beacon for the future of baseball," and as a natural grass, baseball-only stadium, it certainly provided a welcome respite from the cookie-cutter parks. But within a year of new Comiskey's 1991 debut, the rules of ballpark building were rewritten by Oriole Park at Camden Yards, leaving South Side Chicagoans to wonder what might have been had the Sox only waited a couple more years to design their stadium.

The original Comiskey Park, the grand stadium that opened on Chicago's South Side in 1910, served the White Sox well for more than eighty years. When new Comiskey Park opened in 1991, it attempted to echo the qualities fans so loved in its predecessor, while offering amenities never previously found in a Chicago ballpark. Even though it managed to strike a balance between the amusement park atmosphere of SkyDome and the utilitarian necessities of a ball field, when the retro ballpark craze swept through baseball soon afterward, the White Sox found themselves left behind, like the owner of a state-of-the-art bicycle in an age of automobiles.

Though the turning point in baseball stadium design wouldn't begin until the opening of Baltimore's Camden Yards the following year, the design of new Comiskey Park went gloriously against the grain. It was the first baseball-only park with real grass to open since Anaheim Stadium in 1966. In this respect, to the delight of fans everywhere, the White Sox set a trend: not one multipurpose baseball stadium has been built since. The rest of the park, however, didn't have much else that endeared it to fans, thanks in part to the cut-rate budget approved by the state legislature. Only $150 million had been allocated for the Sox to build a new park right next to the old one, which, by the late 1980s, was the oldest stadium in the game.

By 1988, the White Sox were in their seventy-ninth year at Comiskey, the longest any team had ever played in one stadium. It was, as the *New York Times* wrote, "a glorious, raunchy old place that has nothing picturesque about it at all." Owners Jerry Reinsdorf and Eddie Einhorn were hungry for the revenue a new park could generate, and unless they got a new taxpayer-funded stadium, vowed to move the Sox to St. Petersburg, Florida, where a brand-new dome was already under construction and only awaiting a team to inhabit it. At first it appeared the state legislature would call Reinsdorf's bluff—one of the most powerful men in Chicago sports, Reinsdorf had already purchased the Michael Jordan–fueled Chicago Bulls, and it seemed doubtful he would move his baseball team from the city. But when some pork-barrel

BELOW: While the original Comiskey Park was prized for its intimate atmosphere and outstanding sightlines, the chief complaint about new Comiskey, which seated only 751 additional fans, was that even the closest seats were too far away.

OPPOSITE, TOP: The facade of the White Sox's new ballpark echoes that of its predecessor, but the U.S. Cellular logo over the entrance doesn't have quite the same charm as "Comiskey Park" in block letters.

OPPOSITE, MIDDLE: The All-Star logo is painted on the grass in foul territory on July 11, 2003, four days before the Midsummer Classic will be held at U.S. Cellular Field.

OPPOSITE, BOTTOM: Fans view the field from the open concourse.

riders to fund the suburban Arlington Racetrack were attached to the new stadium bill, enough legislators gave in to Reinsdorf's demands. The bill passed the state senate at 11:30 p.m. and the house at 12:03 a.m., three minutes past the official deadline. In a time-honored trick, the house clock was simply set back a few minutes to make it legal.

Although it was built for a song (at only around 11 percent the cost of SkyDome), new Comiskey had no shortages of ways to generate revenue. The antithesis of its North Side neighbor, Wrigley Field, the stadium seemed to reject the patronage of the hot-dogs-and-beer crowd. With upscale concession stands and a coat check, the park also featured ninety-three luxury skyboxes that were rented out at $90,000 a year and a members-only stadium club. The bleacher seats behind right field were dubbed "reserved seating" and sold at prices significantly higher than regular bleachers—no room for "bums." "These rich people are just taking over," one fan told the *Times* on Opening Day. "You see all these people in suits. You see these limousines....I'm just a regular steelworker." Said another fan: "You feel like you need a tie to go in."

At least the team was worth seeing. Immediately after moving in, the Sox embarked on the longest sustained period of on-field success in franchise history. But with Baltimore's new retro stadium becoming the apple of every team owner's eye just a year later, new Comiskey found itself nearly obsolete just a few years after its grand opening. Despite finishing in first or second place twelve times in the park's first fifteen seasons, the Sox sunk as low as twenty-eighth out of baseball's thirty teams in attendance.

There was nothing exactly wrong with Comiskey Park; it just lacked identity. The nondescript atmosphere was exacerbated by the seating bowl, which resembled that of a multipurpose stadium in its height and distance from the field. The first row in the upper deck was actually farther away from the action than the *last* row of the upper deck at old Comiskey. The park's trademark feature was an exploding scoreboard with spinning pinwheels, a larger version of the legendary board installed by Bill Veeck at Old Comiskey. The infield dirt, too, was transported from the old park. That was the new Comiskey in a nutshell: its name and best features were borrowed from a park that itself had been deemed expendable.

In what amounted to an admission of error, the Sox announced plans for a $41 million overhaul of the park in 2001, when the facility was just ten years old. The improvements included the replacement of stadium chairs, a revamped scoreboard, a raft of trendy restaurants and shops, seven statues of Sox legends, and a new roof. Also, the ballpark's name was sold to a phone company, which paid $68 million to change the name to U.S. Cellular Field. In 2004, 6,600 seats were removed to reduce ticket supply and hopefully spur demand. The renovations certainly made it a better place to watch a game, but the park still stands as a multimillion-dollar monument to the pitfalls of poor timing. While Oriole Park at Camden Yards' retro style was mimicked in every new park built over the next fifteen years, U.S. Cellular Field reluctantly took its place in history as the last park of the superstadium era.

February 4, 1991 A rules change aimed at Pete Rose makes banned players ineligible for the Hall of Fame. The ruling also affects Sox legend Shoeless Joe Jackson, a .356 lifetime hitter.

1991

New Comiskey Park opens on April 18 in front of 42,191 fans, the first batch of a team-record 2.9 million who will attend Sox games this year. The $167 million facility is the major leagues' last symmetrical park, with dimensions of 347 feet down the lines, 375 to the power alleys, and 400 to center field.

April 9, 1993

Bo Knows Hip Replacement On the day he becomes the first man in major league history to play with an artificial hip, Bo Jackson homers on his first swing of the season. Pinch hitting for Dan Pasqua in the sixth inning, Jackson goes deep against the Yankees' Neal Heaton. Jackson will bat .232 and strike out 106 times this season, but will also hit sixteen homers and drive in forty-five runs in 284 at-bats. Despite the pedestrian numbers, Jackson's remarkable perseverance will earn him the AL Comeback Player of the Year award. The former two-sport star will play just one more season in the majors.

Yankees 11, White Sox 6

September 27, 1993

Goodbye to the West Bo Jackson's three-run homer in the sixth breaks a scoreless tie against the Mariners and helps the White Sox clinch their first AL West title since 1983. It will also be their last, since the Sox will move to the newly created AL Central in 1994. Jackson's clutch homer off Seattle's Dave Fleming gives Sox pitchers Wilson Alvarez and Kirk McCaskill all the run support they'll need in the clinching game. The White Sox will also go on to win their last three games of the season, sweeping the Indians in Cleveland before nightly crowds of more than 72,000 as they bid farewell to Cleveland Stadium.

White Sox 4, Mariners 2

February 4, 1991 A rules change aimed at Pete Rose makes banned players ineligible for the Hall of Fame. The ruling also affects Sox legend Shoeless Joe Jackson, a .356 lifetime hitter.

June 3, 1993 The Sox draft pitcher Carey Schueler (daughter of the team's general manager) in the forty-third round, making her the first woman ever drafted by MLB.

March 2, 1995 Michael Jordan, after a dalliance with baseball in the White Sox farm system, leaves the team and eventually returns to the NBA's Bulls.

RIGHT: The Cubs' Brian McRae hops back to first base ahead of the tag by White Sox first baseman Mario Valdez in the first ever regular-season meeting between the two teams on June 16, 1997. The uniforms are a throwback to models from 1911, although these modern facsimiles include numbers on the back whereas the originals did not.

BELOW: Members of the White Sox look on as their teammates bat against Cleveland in a 1993 game. Like those at most other modern ballparks, the dugouts at U.S. Cellular are gigantic, perhaps twice as large as those at old Comiskey.

June 16, 1997

An Interleague Slugfest The Cubs and White Sox face each other for the first time in ninety-one years, with the Cubs' Kevin Foster defeating the Sox's Jaime Navarro in an interleague match-up. The Cubs waste little time putting the game out of reach, scoring twice in the game's first three batters. It's the first time the crosstown rivals have met since 1906, when the "Hitless Wonder" White Sox defeated the juggernaut Cubs in the World Series. This year's interleague series, meanwhile, will draw the two biggest crowds in new Comiskey Park's history: 44,249 tomorrow and 44,204 the next day.

Cubs 8, White Sox 3

2001

After just ten years, the team decides that new Comiskey is in need of its first renovation. The bullpens are positioned parallel to the outfield fence, seats are added behind the dugouts and in the outfield, and the field is now slightly asymmetrical. The new dimensions read 330-377-400-372-335, with only center field remaining the same. Capacity increases to almost 46,000, and a picnic area is added in right field.

March 31, 1996 The White Sox, who retired uniform number 3 in honor of Harold Baines in 1989, are forced to unretire the number when Baines rejoins the team.

November 3, 2003 The White Sox hire volatile former shortstop Ozzie Guillen as their new manager.

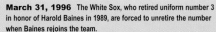

2003

U.S. Cellular buys the naming rights to Comiskey Park, and fans soon nickname the park "The Cell."

July 15, 2003

Blalock's All-Star Heroics After hosting three All-Star Games in old Comiskey Park, including the inaugural contest in 1933, the White Sox host their first Midsummer Classic at their new home. Sox fans warmly greet hometown players Magglio Ordonez, Carl Everett, and Esteban Loaiza, who is the starting pitcher for the American League. The NL looks poised for victory until the eighth inning, when Eric Gagne, the seemingly invincible Dodgers closer, surrenders a game-tying homer to the AL's Hank Blalock. Because the All-Star Game is just an exhibition, Gagne's record streak of consecutive saves remains intact, but for the first time ever, the winning league gets more than just bragging rights: the AL is awarded home-field advantage in the World Series.

AL 7, NL 6

CAPS: 1991, 1991 vintage edition.

RIGHT: New Comiskey Park gleams brilliant blue and green on a sunny South Side day in 2000. Immediately behind the park is the asphalt parking lot where the original Comiskey Park stood from 1910 to 1991. Even old Comiskey, however, was not the oldest park in the area. That distinction belongs to Armour Square Park, the small baseball diamond beyond the parking lot, which opened in 1905.

2004

The White Sox eliminate the last eight nosebleed rows of the upper deck and turn them into an amusement area, dropping capacity to 40,000. A larger roof replaces the old one, keeping many of the seats out of the sun and rain. In September, the Florida Marlins play two games against the Expos at the field, due to the threat of Hurricane Ivan.

October 12, 2005

AJ's Non-K The White Sox even the ALCS at one game apiece thanks to one of the biggest questionable calls in postseason history. In the bottom of the ninth with the score tied and a full count, Chicago catcher AJ Pierzynski swings on a pitch by Kelvim Esocbar. Though umpire Doug Eddings raises his fist in the air, supposedly calling an "out," Pierzynski thinks the ball hit the dirt, and after a moment's hesitation heads off toward first base. Pierzynski reaches first safely, and a heated argument ensues. Eddings claims he called the third strike, but not the out, a strange distinction he later admits has "never been an issue, until now." Meanwhile, catcher Josh Paul is harangued for not tagging Pierzynksi anyway, but says he never heard the customary "no catch" call. While the incident is replayed over and over from every possible angle for an incredulous viewing public, Aaron Rowand doubles in the winning run, and the Sox don't look back—they will not lose another game during the postseason, first dispatching the Angels and then sweeping Houston in the World Series.

White Sox 2, Angels 1

ABOVE: The White Sox's Tadahito Iguchi seems to be closing his eyes as he lays down a sacrifice bunt in the first inning of ALCS Game 2 on October 12, 2005. The play helps net the Sox a run. Chicago won't score again until the bottom of the ninth, when controversy erupts after the Sox's AJ Pierzynski fools umpire Doug Eddings into believing a strike three pitch hit the dirt.

October 23, 2005

An Unexpected Power Source The Houston Astros are playing in their first World Series ever, but the White Sox are playing in their first since 1959—three years before the Astros even existed. The Sox win tonight's Game 2 thanks to the clutch bat of Scott Podsednik, who after going the entire regular season without a homer, crushes a Brad Lidge pitch over the fence for a ninth-inning walk-off job. A key moment comes with Houston leading 4-2 in the seventh, when an inside pitch to Chicago's Jermaine Dye is ruled to have hit his hand, although replays show it hit the bat. Chad Qualls then enters in relief for the Astros and surrenders a grand slam to Paul Konerko. Houston ties it back up in the ninth when rookie closer Bobby Jenks gives up a two-out, two-run single to Jose Vizcaino, but Podsednik's blast in the ninth sends Sox fans home happy. It will be the last home game of the year for the White Sox, who will complete their Series sweep on the road before returning to Chicago for a victory parade.

White Sox 7, Astros 6

2006 The team changes the start time of their weekday home games to 7:11 as part of a $500,000 sponsorship deal with the convenience store 7-Eleven.

August 12, 2007 White Sox closer Bobby Jenks ties a thirty-five-year-old major league record by retiring his forty-first consecutive batter, a streak that began on July 17.

April 18, 2007

Buehrle Gets No-Hitter, New Contract Mark Buehrle throws the sixteenth no-hitter in White Sox history, but the first at U.S. Cellular Field. Buehrle allows only one baserunner—Sammy Sosa, who walks in the fifth inning—and then immediately picks him off. The veteran southpaw fans eight while facing the minimum twenty-seven batters, and also gets some defensive help from his teammates. A diving stop and throw in by third baseman Joe Crede in the third inning results in an out at first base for Jerry Hairston, and the play is so close that a disagreeing Hairston gets ejected for arguing. In the fifth, second baseman Tadahito Iguchi dives for a grounder and guns out Hank Blalock from the outfield grass. Chicago's six runs are provided by Jim Thome, who hits his 476th and 477th career home runs, and Jermaine Dye, who also connects for a grand slam. Although speculation abounds that Buehrle will leave the Sox as a free agent after the season, the team soon signs him to a four-year, $56 million contract extension.

White Sox 6, Rangers 0

RIGHT: Ken Griffey Jr., acquired in a midseason trade to bolster Chicago's lineup, singles in Game 3 of the ALDS against Tampa Bay on October 5, 2008. It is the first postseason game played at U.S. Cellular since Game 2 of the 2005 World Series. The Sox win 5-3, but it will be their only playoff victory of 2008, as the Rays will end up taking the series in four games.

BELOW: Between 2001 and 2009, a nine-stage renovation was carried out to make U.S. Cellular Field more closely resemble its modern peers. One of the first phases was the addition of the video board pictured here in dead center field, as well as the LED ribbon boards on the facing of the upper deck in left and right fields. In fact, six separate scoreboards are visible in this photograph, helping supply fans with such information as out of town scores, the batter's average, the pitcher's ERA, and the speed of each pitch. Such readily available information would likely have blown the minds of fans attending games at old Comiskey when it opened in 1910.

September 30, 2008

(Three) Fight(s) to the Finish The White Sox become the first team in history to qualify for the postseason by winning three games in three days against three different opponents. After being swept in Minneapolis to blow a 2½-game lead to the Twins, the White Sox run their losing streak to five games before winning the final Sunday of the year against the Indians. The White Sox win a makeup game in Chicago Monday afternoon against Detroit to set up the first one-game playoff in club history on Tuesday night. The game is scoreless until Jim Thome blasts a 461-foot home run for the only run of the game. John Danks pitches eight innings of two-hit ball and Bobby Jenks saves it. The defensive plays of the game come from center field. Ken Griffey Jr., acquired in a mid-season trade, throws out a runner at the plate; his replacement for defense, Brian Anderson, makes a diving catch for the final out. It is the first time the White Sox and Cubs have both qualified for the postseason in the same year since the 1906 World Series. It will, however, be an early exit for both Windy City clubs.

White Sox 1, Twins 0

CHAPTER FIVE

Retro Ballparks

1992   present

PREVIOUS PAGES: The Phillies take on the Rays during Game 4 of the 2008 World Series at Citizen's Bank Park in Philadelphia. Though Philadelphia's retro ballpark, built in 2004, has been criticized for being a copycat of Oriole Park at Camden Yards, it's still a welcome change from its much-maligned predecessor, Veterans Stadium.

RIGHT: Lucky Yankees fans get balls signed by Hideki Matsui after the team's first practice at their new stadium.

Before Oriole Park at Camden Yards opened in 1992, ballpark design was at a crossroads. Everybody realized the cookie-cutter superstadiums were disasters, but nobody knew what the alternative was. Baltimore's masterpiece answered that question in the boldest ways possible: A baseball-centric design that allowed for a few on-field quirks. Spectators close to the action and the stadium close to downtown. Natural grass. Charming features inspired by baseball's past. No longer did baseball have to suffer in bland, multipurpose arenas built for quantity over quality. "The most rabid football fan thinks little about what surrounds the gridiron; the ardent basketball fan dreams of 3-point goals, not of arenas," Paul Goldberger wrote in the *New York Times* in 1994. "But baseball is connected intimately to the place in which it is played and derives much of its aura from that place."

Baltimore's new ballpark influenced the course of stadium construction more than any other park in baseball history (with the possible exception of Shibe Park in 1909). For the next two decades, virtually every newly constructed park would have the Camden retro feel, comprising the largest architectural movement in the history of the game. When Cleveland's Jacobs Field and Texas' Ballpark in Arlington opened in 1994, they further established the characteristics of the new era of retro ballparks. Usually located in or near downtown, the baseball-only stadiums eschewed concrete for such materials as brick, stone, and wrought iron to re-create the feel of days gone by. Many details, even the small ones, were borrowed from old parks: a hand-operated scoreboard, a flagpole in play, a pitcher's path. Most important for team owners, however, were the aspects *not* borrowed from the past: The parks featured far more skyboxes and other high-priced forms of premium seating than their predecessors had, along with a variety of gourmet food stands aimed at well-heeled customers.

With dollar signs in their eyes—and urged on by Commissioner Bud Selig, who made the acquisition of taxpayer funds for private ballparks his administration's number one priority—teams bullied city, county, and state governments into forking over large amounts of cash for construction. The era of the privately funded ballpark was over. Although only one club, the Montreal Expos, switched cities during the retro ballpark era, owners nonetheless used the constant threat of relocation to coerce local governments into meeting MLB's demands. To mute taxpayer outrage, baseball owners (and the governments they partnered with) cited economic revitalization to justify the public expenditures. Retro parks were generally built in old neighborhoods near downtown that were down on their luck. Selig and company—pointing to

newly rejuvenated ballpark districts such as Baltimore's Inner Harbor and Denver's LoDo—suggested that this generated enough tax revenue to justify the building costs.

Some economists, however, viewed the owners' claims as complete fabrications. Andrew Zimbalist, a Smith College economics professor who specializes in sports, told the *New York Times*, "There really is no evidence that building a new sports stadium resurrects a downtown or a city. In cities that are investing in several downtown projects all at once, there is additional activity, but it's mostly from the transfer of income and employment from surrounding communities into the downtown area. You rarely see a great spread effect." Still, voters passed referenda to build the new parks, and when they didn't, most city councils found a way to approve the financing without having to bring the issue to the people who were paying for, on average, two-thirds of their team's new home.

The retro parks also met with criticism from those who felt that, in an attempt to mimic each other's success, the teams had simply created a new generation of interchangeable cookie-cutter parks. Asymmetrical dimensions, local cuisine trumpeted at concession stands, and anything possible to harken back to the era of classic fields made the retro era parks seem strangely similar to each other. Because of their popularity, existing structures such as old warehouses came to be sought out by architectural firms like HOK in the planning stages, so they could be used as props in creating the desired atmosphere. While the Orioles' plan to incorporate the B&O Warehouse into their design for Camden Yards was brilliant, such features at other parks seemed coldly calculated rather than spontaneous.

Features present in old ballparks due to happenstance and practicality were now consciously imitated as a way of invoking nostalgia. At the classic parks, a swimming pool or a railroad track might sit next to a ballpark by coincidence; now, pools and train tracks were built deliberately to be part of the ball-park experience. The pitcher's path, formerly a naturally worn erosion of turf between the pitcher's mound and home plate, now became a landscaper's carefully groomed creation. Irregular, asymmetrical playing fields, once a byproduct of older parks being shaped to accommodate the city blocks around them, were now carefully planned.

"That's one of the things that HOK has had to defend on numerous occasions," Jim Chibnall, chief architect of Jacobs Field and Busch Stadium [III], told the *St. Louis Post-Dispatch* about the many throwbacks to the ballparks of yesteryear. "It's the people who are involved in the projects, the clients, who request these things. I have no problem if it's done in the right context. I feel that it's absolutely appropriate for a city like St. Louis. It's not an appropriate response to put a historicist building in the middle of an open field. Jacobs Field, which takes a modern approach to design, relates to the industrial heritage of Cleveland."

Questions of architectural repetitiveness aside, there was no question that the retro ballparks were immensely popular with their most important constituents: the fans. Despite the exponentially increasing costs of going to a game, attendance boomed. In 2007, by which time more than half the teams played in retro parks, MLB attendance reached 79.5 million for an average of 32,744 fans per game—both all-time records. By comparison, the average game in 1975, at the height of the superstadium era, had drawn just 15,403 people. The exploding revenues generated by the retro ballparks drew modern baseball, ironically, into an era of big business and skyrocketing salaries. At least baseball enthusiasts have some beautiful places to watch it happen.

BELOW: Cincinnati's Great American Ball Park is lit up for a Reds-Astros game on June 18, 2003, during its inaugural season. Though it was built almost directly next to its predecessor, Riverfront Stadium, fans inside get a much better view of the river and the surrounding city in the open-air retro park, even after the 2007 addition of a scenery-blocking, two-story faux riverboat above the batter's eye in center field.

ORIOLE PARK AT CAMDEN YARDS

Baltimore, Maryland

Orioles (AL) 1992–present

It all began so innocently. In the mid-1980s the Baltimore Orioles, who had spent their entire existence playing in a nondescript football stadium, decided they wanted a new home. What they got was a palace: a ballpark that seamlessly blended into the urban landscape, and that was so jaw-droppingly beautiful that more than half the teams in Major League Baseball eventually attempted to mimic it. Built for a relatively modest $110 million and funded by the state of Maryland via a new instant lottery game, Oriole Park at Camden Yards was like nothing fans had ever seen before—and also like everything they'd seen before. In terms of influence, Camden Yards is rivaled only by Shibe Park for the distinction of most important ballpark ever constructed.

In the decade prior to Oriole Park's debut, only two new stadiums had opened in the major leagues: SkyDome, an impersonal, turf-filled behemoth in Toronto, and Comiskey Park (II), an unsuccessful attempt to rebuild Charles Comiskey's 1910 palace. Baltimore's new ballpark was completely unlike either one. Where the modern concrete bowls and domes had sealed off fans from the urban environment surrounding them, Oriole Park at Camden Yards embraced and utilized that environment. Its location, on the site of an old Baltimore & Ohio Railroad yard, had been floated as a potential stadium site before, most notably by Bill Veeck when he attempted to buy the Orioles in the 1970s. It was within walking distance of the revitalized Inner Harbor area, the Babe Ruth Museum, and the supposedly haunted gravesite of Edgar Allan Poe. It seemed the perfect spot for a ballpark, particularly since it was literally Ruth's childhood home. Before being dispatched to reform school, the young Bambino had lived with his parents in an apartment above his father's tavern, Ruth's Cafe, at 406 Conway Street. That address was smack in the middle of what would become center field at Camden Yards, and the old building's remains were unearthed during construction.

Another building on the site, this one still standing, was the B&O warehouse. Completed in 1905, the tan brick edifice was supposedly the longest building on the East Coast at 1,016 feet long (but just 51 feet deep). For many years it sheltered all manner of goods and cargo entering Baltimore via train, but the B&O had long since fallen victim to merger and relocation, and the building had been vacant for decades.

The Orioles at first viewed the warehouse as a nuisance, an obstruction that merely got in the way of their otherwise ideal plan for the site. According to architect Richard deFlon, Orioles President Larry Lucchino was adamantly opposed to leaving the building standing. "No way," Lucchino reportedly said. "This is stupid. You don't want this ugly old building." So the architectural firm hired to design the stadium—Kansas City–based Hellmuth, Obata, and Kassabaum (HOK)—created a model that involved tearing the warehouse down. But in 1987, the *Baltimore Sun* and *City Paper* both ran articles hyping a brilliant design by Eric Moss, a Syracuse University architecture student who had ingeniously incorporated the warehouse into the stadium's structure behind the right-field wall. Moss' idea became the talk of the town.

The Orioles decided to keep the warehouse, making the park, as author Peter Richmond noted, "the oldest ballpark in America, as well as its newest." It also changed the team's entire concept of what the ballpark could become. Keeping the warehouse was not only practical—the Orioles could use it as office space, and save the cost of demolishing it—but also a tribute to the urban ballparks of earlier eras, which had been squeezed into existing city blocks and thus were often surrounded by looming buildings. Huntington Avenue Grounds, the original home of the Red Sox in 1901, had featured a warehouse down the left-field line. At Philadelphia's Baker Bowl, a warehouse had sat just behind the left-field fence. Soon the Orioles were studying photographs of other old ballparks, seeking to distill the features that had made them so beloved to fans. In one remarkable memo, Orioles vice president Janet Marie Smith instructed HOK on what the team wanted done:

> [The stadium should be] compatible with the warehouse and Baltimore's civic buildings in terms of scale, configuration, and color....The outer wall of the upper roof concourse should be designed so fans can see the city. Move the upper deck closer to the playing field. Reduce the height of the second deck. Reduce the height of the third deck....Turn the upper deck seating where it abuts the warehouse to face home plate. The rail at field level should be ornamental iron work. Trees, plants, and other greenery are critical to designing this facility as a ballpark, not a stadium.

It was a memo of paramount importance. For the first time in generations, a ballpark was being constructed with the fans' experience of the game as the central consideration. Previous stadiums had focused on *amenities*—concessions, parking, souvenirs—but Camden Yards, while providing no shortage of these, focused on *aesthetics*. Above all, the park was designed to be beautiful. "If Major League Baseball offered awards for architecture, this team would win hands down," *New York Times* architecture critic Paul Goldberger wrote in 1989, as construction was about to begin. The blueprint for the park, Goldberger said, "is the best plan for a major league baseball park in more than a generation….This is a building capable of wiping out in a single gesture fifty years of wretched stadium design.…It makes every sprawling concrete dome sitting in a sea of parked cars look bloated, fat, and tired."

The facade of the new ballpark was designed with brick arches and wrought iron instead of concrete. The sides of aisle seats were adorned with ironwork designs recalling the 1890s Orioles, winners of three NL pennants. In the outfield, instead of an unnecessary deck of football bleachers, was a stunning city view including the landmark Emerson Bromo-Seltzer Tower, built in 1911. A two-tiered set of bullpens, with the Orioles' at ground level and the visitors' a story higher, was built in left-center field. Even the foul poles were designed in a unique fashion, featuring small steel bars painted yellow and aligned in a distinctive crisscross pattern.

And then there was the historic building that was actually incorporated into the ballpark design instead of being torn down. The B&O warehouse became the defining feature of the Orioles' park. Eutaw Street, the thoroughfare running between the B&O warehouse and the ballpark itself, was closed to auto traffic and turned into a pedestrian walkway. Brass, baseball-shaped plaques embedded in the ground mark the spots where home run balls have landed on the street. (The warehouse itself, 442 feet from home plate, was never hit by an actual home run ball during the park's first sixteen seasons; the only ball to reach the building on the fly was a blast by Ken Griffey Jr. during the Home Run Derby exhibition at the 1993 All-Star

Game.) On game days, Eutaw Street becomes a festive hub of activity where one might purchase souvenirs, eat hot dogs, watch batting practice, play carnival games, or relax in a shady beer garden. The Orioles Hall of Fame is located here, as is a display honoring those Baltimore players with retired uniform numbers. Near the Eutaw entrance gate is a striking statue of Babe Ruth as he appeared during his teenage years, when he played locally at St. Mary's Industrial School for Boys.

"Here, unlike other stadiums, the ads are part of the architecture," one local advertising executive told the *New York Times*. When the park opened, an antique-style clock sponsored by the local newspaper sat atop the main scoreboard. The twelve hours, instead of being represented by numbers, were represented by the twelve letters "B-A-L-T-I-M-O-R-E S-U-N." Below that, old-style lettering spelled out "THE SUN," with the H and E lighting up to denote a hit or an error. Unfortunately, this charming throwback was deemed out-of-date after just sixteen years, and was replaced by a larger one, without old-fashioned-looking detailing, in 2008.

Camden Yards was so universally praised and instantaneously beloved that team owners moved quickly to mimic it, sparking the largest and most expensive ballpark-building movement in the history of the game. By 2008, sixteen teams had built retro-style parks that attempted, with varying degrees of success, to echo the nostalgic feel of Camden Yards. Some of these new stadiums, such as PNC Park in Pittsburgh, would surpass Oriole Park in terms of sheer beauty. But Baltimore's park remains both a gem and a groundbreaker, the retro ballpark without which all the others would not have existed. "Camden Yards helped baseball fans and architects and urban designers— and municipal leaders—realize that this was a very attractive alternative to the stadium in the middle of a sea of cars," Howard Decker, curator of the National Building Museum, told the *Sun*. "It had a huge impact in helping us realize that the old-style stadiums that our parents and grandparents grew up with really represented something of extraordinary value."

October 6, 1991 After the final game at Memorial Stadium, its home plate is transplanted to the construction site of Camden Yards for use in the new ballpark.

1992 The Orioles' Mike Mussina, less than two years removed from Stanford University, wins eighteen games in his first big-league season.

1996 In one of baseball's all-time fluke seasons, Brady Anderson sets an Orioles record with fifty home runs. He never hit more than twenty-four before or after that.

1992

Amid great pomp, Camden Yards hosts its first regular-season game on April 6 and is immediately held as the gold standard of new ballpark design. It's also a hitter's paradise with asymmetrical dimensions of 333 down the left-field line, 364 in left-center, 400 in center, 373 in right-center, and 318 in right. Deepest left-center is 410.

BELOW, LEFT: Orioles hurler Rick Sutcliffe throws a pitch during the first regular-season game at Camden Yards on April 6, 1992.

BELOW: Eutaw Street, which runs between the right-field stands and the B&O warehouse, is a bustling open-air marketplace on game days.

July 13, 1993

At Least No Windows Were Broken The AL pounds the NL in the first All-Star Game played at Camden Yards, but the most memorable moment of the festivities comes during the Home Run Derby when Ken Griffey Jr. becomes the first batter ever to hit the B&O warehouse on the fly. In the game itself, Gary Sheffield, Kirby Puckett, and Roberto Alomar hit home runs, and the AL takes the lead in the fifth, on RBI singles by Griffey and Albert Belle, and never let it go. Puckett then sews up the game MVP with an RBI double. One of the more entertaining moments in All-Star history occurs when six-foot-ten lefty Randy Johnson sails a blazing fastball over John Kruk's head; Kruk, clearly fearing for his safety, proceeds to strike out on a series of increasingly feeble swings. The game also becomes infamous for the stubbornness of AL skipper Cito Gaston, who refuses to bring popular Oriole Mike Mussina into the game. Mussina, anxious to pitch, starts warming up on his own, causing the 48,147 fans to hail down a rain of boos on Gaston.

AL 9, NL 3

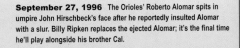

September 27, 1996 The Orioles' Roberto Alomar spits in umpire John Hirschbeck's face after he reportedly insulted Alomar with a slur. Billy Ripken replaces the ejected Alomar; it's the final time he'll play alongside his brother Cal.

September 16, 1995

Cal's Big Night Cal Ripken breaks a record long thought to be unbreakable when he plays his 2,131st consecutive game, snapping Lou Gehrig's iron-man mark. Ripken began his quest as a rookie on May 30, 1982. Streak or no streak, Ripken has enjoyed a remarkable career, with a Rookie of the Year award, two MVPs, a world championship, and two Gold Gloves. He caps this night of Cal worship by smacking a home run in the fourth inning; play-by-play on the homer is done by President Bill Clinton, who's sitting in as a guest on the broadcast. When the game becomes official in the fifth inning, play is stopped and Ripken makes numerous curtain calls and jogs a slow lap around the stadium, giving high fives to fans in the front rows. Even the Angels, who desperately need a win to hold off the hard-charging Mariners, tip their caps to the Orioles shortstop. After two seasons scarred by strike, it's the most positive moment for baseball in a long while.

Orioles 4, Angels 2

A luxury box at Camden.

The Box of Luxury

If catered meals of local delicacies, VIP parking, cushy private restrooms, big-screen TVs, and comfy leather seats spell a day at the ballpark to you, then you're clearly the lucky owner of a major league luxury suite. At Oriole Park at Camden Yards, your ample accommodations include a wet bar and two-tiered porch. At Comerica Park, you'd be provided with an in-suite photographer and a newsletter just for suite owners. Fenway Park's new boxes contain cherrywood floors and granite countertops. And at Jacobs Field, you may even be treated to a pregame shoeshine or wine tasting. But for a whopping $75,000 to $400,000 per year, these coveted boxes better have some perks!

Luxury suites may be out of reach for most fans, but they've become the quintessential way for companies to impress clients and reward employees. Providing no reason to leave their air-conditioned confines, luxury boxes are a boon to businesses—and the business of baseball. Even at price tags of hundreds of thousands of dollars, luxury suites at most stadiums sell out before a single game is ever played. They have become one of the primary reasons why a new stadium is erected—witness old Yankee Stadium's nineteen suites versus the new park's fifty-seven (each of which was previewed ahead of time in Rockefeller Center, so that fans could start salivating before the new home of the Yankees even opened).

Camden Yards wasn't the first park to have luxury suites (they've been around since the days of the Astrodome), but it did contain architectural features that made putting in the high-priced seats easier. Old parks had poles holding the upper decks in place, with the top-level spectators virtually hanging over the playing field. New parks, on the other hand, move the upper decks back (to eliminate poles blocking the views from the higher-priced, lower-level seats) and higher into the stratosphere, making room for the extra levels of skyboxes and mezzanines.

When Camden Yards was built in 1992, the Baltimore-Washington area contained fewer than 100 luxury suites. Today, that number is closer to 800. As the supply of these luxurious accommodations has gone up, and the economic downturn has provided less demand, some teams have begun allowing single game rentals of suites for groups of fans wanting a taste of the good life. Other teams, such as the Brewers and the Mariners, have torn down walls to create "clubs" that hold a hundred people or more and provide some of the amenities of a luxury box at a fraction of the price.

Camden Yards currently offers one of the widest varieties of premium seating in baseball. There are three classes of private suites, as well as several private party locations. For the right price, fans can even come to the park on non-game days and picnic in the Orioles' bullpen. Just be careful of what you do once you're there—one of Camden Yards' seventy-two luxury boxes was the famous site of much of former lobbyist Jack Abramoff's illegal wheeling and dealing.

October 24, 1997 An episode of NBC's *Homicide: Life on the Street* focuses on the fictional story of a Yankees fan murdered at Camden Yards. Orioles Scott Erickson and Armando Benitez are guest stars.

November 5, 1997 Despite a ninety-eight-win season, Orioles owner Peter Angelos forces the resignation of manager Davey Johnson—who is named AL Manager of the Year hours later.

September 20, 1998

On the 2,633rd Day, Cal Rests Cal Ripken makes news by not playing, choosing to sit out for the first time in 2,632 games. After the shock wears off, Ripken is applauded loudly by the Sunday night crowd—and the Yankees in the visitors' dugout—before the last home game of the year at Camden Yards. September call-up Ryan Minor starts in Ripken's place, goes 1-for-4, and handles four chances cleanly at third base. The official attendance is 48,013, but with the Orioles out of the pennant race, more than a few ticket holders stay home thinking the game is insignificant.

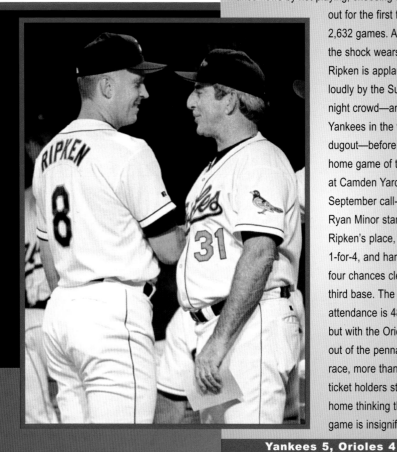

September 6, 1996

Silent Eddie Speaks Loudly With his 500th career home run, Eddie Murray joins Willie Mays and Hank Aaron as the only players with at least 3,000 career hits and 500 long-balls. A Baltimore icon in the 1980s, Murray has lately bounced around from team to team until rejoining the Orioles on July 21. His blast off Detroit's Felipe Lira ties the game, but the Tigers soon retake the lead. Baltimore ties it again in the eighth, but the Tigers eventually emerge with a twelve-inning victory, stymieing Baltimore's run at the AL Wild Card. It'll take the Orioles until the season's final weekend to clinch a playoff spot. A special orange seat will later be installed to mark the spot where Murray's home-run ball landed.

Tigers 5, Orioles 4

BELOW: The Orioles face the Yankees in a 2003 game at Camden Yards, as viewed from outside the ballpark. Note the home of the AFC Ravens, M&T Bank Stadium, peeking over the grandstand in the center of the photo. In the left portion of the foreground are Camden Station and the B&O warehouse.

Yankees 5, Orioles 4

ABOVE: Cal Ripken shakes hands with manager Ray Miller on September 20, 1998, the day he finally removes himself from the Orioles' lineup after 2,632 consecutive games in sixteen years.

2001

Dimensions are changed to 340 in left, 376 in left-center, 407 to center, 393 to right-center, and 325 in right, with the deepest corner in left-center at 376.

2001 The Orioles sue the Maryland Stadium Authority for the right to sell naming rights for Camden Yards. The team wins, but decides to keep the name for the time being.

April 4, 2001 Boston's Hideo Nomo pitches his second career no-hitter, and the first in the history of Camden Yards.

February 2007 Due to tough economic times, the Maryland Stadium Authority forgives $1.7 million in overdue rent payments owed by Orioles owner Peter Angelos.

October 6, 2001

Ripken's Farewell Cal Ripken plays in his final game. Because of an NFL game next door the following afternoon, the Orioles' final game of the year has been rescheduled for Saturday night, allowing Ripken to say goodbye in front of an adoring Camden Yards crowd and national audience. The Iron Man's uniform number 8 is retired before the game, during which he goes hitless against Boston's David Cone. In the eighth, Baltimore's Tim Raines Jr. and Tim Raines Sr. bat consecutively, becoming the second father-and-son duo (after the Griffeys) to do so in a major league game. In the ninth, with Ripken on deck hoping for one final at-bat, his best friend Brady Anderson strikes out on a 3-2 pitch that could have been ball four. The game and Cal's career are over—and so, it turns out, is Anderson's own impressive thirteen-year stint in Baltimore. He'll play a handful of games with Cleveland in 2002 before retiring.

Red Sox 5, Orioles 1

ABOVE, RIGHT: At his first game back since being placed on the disabled list fourteen days earlier, Sammy Sosa sits in the dugout as fans arrive at Camden Yards on May 24, 2005.

August 22, 2007

Three Touchdowns and Three Field Goals The hapless Orioles manage to accomplish something that's never been done in the 107-year history of the AL: allow their opponent to score thirty runs in a game. The game starts promisingly enough, as Baltimore takes a 3-0 lead in the third inning. From there, the Rangers pound the ball at a level not seen since June 29, 1897, when Chicago routed Louisville 36-7 in an NL game. Texas puts together four innings with at least five runs, including a ten-spot in the eighth. But it's the Rangers' six runs in the ninth that make the game historic; Ramon Vazquez's three-run homer provides the final margin of victory and breaks the previous AL mark of twenty-nine runs set by the Red Sox in 1950. Jarrod Saltalamacchia and Vazquez, the eighth and ninth hitters for Texas, each drive in seven runs, and grand slams are hit by Marlon Byrd and Travis Metcalf. O's reliever Paul Shuey, trying to make a comeback from retirement, allows nine runs over the final two innings. He'll be released a week later. Embarrassingly, it's the first game as a full-time manager for Baltimore skipper Dave Trembley, who has just had the "interim" tag removed. But the worst news of all for the Orioles: it's a doubleheader! The nightcap is more sporting, but the Rangers again knock around the Orioles' pitching for a 9-7 win.

Rangers 30, Orioles 3

JACOBS FIELD

Cleveland, Ohio

Indians (AL) 1994–present

Progressive Field 2008–present

albert BELLE

The opening of Cleveland's Jacobs Field in 1994, along with the Texas Rangers' Ballpark in Arlington, sent a clear signal that the retro park had become the new standard in major league baseball. Although it isn't as explicit of a throwback stadium as Camden Yards, Jacobs has the same natural grass, the same intimate feel, and most importantly, the same urban setting, making it the bustling centerpiece of rejuvenated downtown Cleveland. The Indians celebrated the opening of their park with the arrival of a masterfully constructed roster of young players developed in their farm system. Combined with increased revenues created by the new park, these homegrown stars propelled Cleveland to a decade-long run so prosperous that the Indians became baseball's most-imitated model of how to operate a franchise.

The area along Huron Road between 9th and Ontario streets had long been an eyesore in downtown Cleveland. The site had once been occupied by the Central Market, a civic landmark that had burned down in 1949, and was now dotted with vacant buildings and parking lots. In the 1980s, a multipurpose dome was proposed for the site, but the project encountered opposition because it would be funded by higher property taxes. In 1990, the Indians raised the idea of a new stadium again, and voters were asked to approve the construction of the Gateway Sports Complex, which would include a new baseball-only park for the Indians and an arena for the NBA's Cleveland Cavaliers. Nearly half of the complex's price tag (including $175 million for the ballpark) would come from a fifteen-year increase in alcohol and cigarette taxes, with the other half privately financed. Days before the vote, MLB commissioner Fay Vincent attended a city council meeting, where he not-so-subtly threatened that he would consider moving the team if voters failed to approve the funding. But Clevelanders passed the measure by a slim, 1.2 percent margin.

Built within walking distance of Lake Erie and the soon-to-open Rock and Roll Hall of Fame, Jacobs Field—which was named after Indians owner Richard Jacobs (who paid $13.9 million for the naming rights)—is an urban delight. Cleveland baseball historian Jonathan Knight noted that "the most important and impressive visual feature of the new park wasn't anything that was constructed—it was what wasn't constructed. No matter where you were in Jacobs Field, you could see some hint of the Cleveland skyline or some architectural reminder of where you were." Unlike parks in other

JIM THOME

INDIANS

KENNY LOFTON

INDIANS

GRADY SIZEMORE

Rust Belt cities, Cleveland's stadium sought to highlight the city's industrial heritage rather than hide it. The exposed steel latticework that surrounds the park (and also holds up floodlights) was intended to evoke the city's many bridges, while its granite and limestone foundation lends an aura of stability. A life-size statue of local legend Bob Feller stands in center field.

The park is triple-decked, with the second deck visually dominated by three rows of luxury skyboxes, more than a hundred skyboxes in all, which go for a minimum of $2,000 per game. Just as lavish are the ten private suites at field level, which lease for $100,000 per season. It's believed that the team makes more money from the luxury boxes than from the rest of its ticket sales combined, and many feel the suites' prominence conveys, as the *New York Times'* Paul Goldberger put it, "the sense that this park is dominated by special seating for the rich." Such ostentation seems especially inappropriate in working-class Cleveland, but has been written off by most as the cost of doing business in modern baseball.

Regular fans have found plenty to enjoy at the park, too. With extra space between seating rows, there's more leg room than at most parks. And the chairs, painted a classic dark green, are 2 inches wider than those at Cleveland Stadium were. Moreover, the seats beyond each dugout are angled toward the infield, a relatively unusual feature at the time Jacobs Field opened. When they leave their seats, fans find that the park is filled with culinary delights. Not only are fourteen kinds of beer available (most at $4.00), but a remarkable sixty-eight different food items are on the menu, including corned beef sandwiches, egg rolls, peanut-butter-and-jelly sandwiches, and chocolate éclairs. Even better, most of the concession stands are positioned so that fans can still watch the game while standing in line.

The dimensions of the park strongly favor hitters, particularly right-handed ones, with a 19-foot-high left-field wall that stands just 325 feet away from home plate. Symbolic of the era of specialized relief pitchers, each bullpen has three warm-up mounds instead of two. The natural turf, a Kentucky bluegrass blend, was grown in Indiana for a year before being transported to Cleveland. It was planted in a 12-inch deep bed of sand that sits on a 2-inch layer of loose gravel. Below that, a series of drainpipes clears water from the field at a rate of 1 foot per hour.

Cleveland's notoriously harsh spring weather threatened to spoil Jacobs Field's debut when 2 inches of snow fell on April 3, 1994, the day before the park was to be open. But the sun came out, and by game time the snow was completely gone. With President Bill Clinton in attendance, Seattle's Randy Johnson held the Indians hitless until the eighth inning, when they pounced on Johnson and three relievers, coming back to tie the game and then win it in the eleventh on a dramatic walk-off hit by journeyman outfielder Wayne Kirby.

The memorable win marked the beginning of the greatest period of success in franchise history. From 1994 to 2001, the Indians finished in first place six times and second place twice. During that period the team won two AL pennants and played a remarkable thirty postseason games at Jacobs Field, winning seventeen of them. The Indians also sold out Jacobs Field 455 consecutive times, far and away a major league record. When the sellout streak ended in 2001, the team symbolically retired uniform number 455 in honor of the rabid fans who had made "The Jake" such a phenomenon. In a city famed for sparse crowds—the Indians once drew only 365 fans, 0.5 percent of capacity, for a game at Cleveland Stadium—Jacobs Field is a revelation, demonstrating just how quickly and completely a welcoming ballpark and a winning record can reverse a team's fortunes.

TIMELINE: JACOBS FIELD

July 3, 1994 The Indians retire uniform number 14 in honor of Larry Doby, who in 1947 became the first black player in the American League.

June 12, 1995 Jacobs Field sells out for a game against Baltimore, marking the beginning of its record streak of 455 consecutive sellouts in six years.

1994

Jacobs Field opens on April 4 with a capacity crowd of 41,529. Dimensions are 325 feet to left field, 368 to left-center, 405 to center, 375 to right-center, and 325 to right. "The Jake" has little foul territory and proves to be a great place to hit.

October 24, 1995

The Fall Classic Returns Tonight is the first World Series game in Cleveland in forty-seven years, and oddly enough, it's a rematch of that 1948 Classic: Indians versus Braves. Cleveland won that one, but this year they've already dug themselves into a hole by losing the first two games in Atlanta. Tonight they jump out to a two-run lead, only to blow it in the top of the eighth. In the bottom of the inning, though, they re-tie it when a Sandy Alomar single drives in Kenny Lofton (who gets on base a remarkable six times in the game). The score remains knotted until the eleventh, when Cleveland's Eddie Murray singles home Alvaro Espinoza with the winning run.

Indians 7, Braves 6

October 11, 1997

Webster's Snooze One of the greatest pitching duels in postseason history ends with a bizarre steal of home. Playoff legend Orel Hershiser pitches scoreless ball for Cleveland, but his counterpart, Mike Mussina, allows just one run. After Baltimore scores in the ninth, the game is still tied in the twelfth, and Indians manager Mike Hargrove calls for a squeeze play. Marquis Grissom races down the third base line as Omar Vizquel attempts to bunt. But Vizquel misses, and the ball glances off catcher Lenny Webster's glove. Webster, mistakingly assuming it's foul, makes no attempt to retrieve it, allowing Grissom to cross the plate with a game-winning steal.

Indians 2, Orioles 1

ABOVE: Eddie Murray drives in the winning run during the eleventh inning of Game 3 of the 1995 World Series.

RIGHT: After recording an out on baserunner Brady Anderson, Indians shortstop Omar Vizquel throws to first to complete the double play during Game 3 of the 1997 ALCS at Jacobs Field.

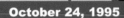

AVG .235 HR 2 RBI 18

October 22, 1997

Let It Snow The shivering Marlins, accustomed to the sunny Florida climate, are thoroughly blown out in the coldest game in World Series history. The mercury reads 38°F at the start of Game 4, but the wind chill makes it feel more like 15°. Snow flurries fall as rookie starters Jaret Wright of Cleveland and Tony Saunders of Florida take the mound, and the latter falters almost immediately, coughing up three runs to the Indians in the first. Cleveland scores three more in the third, after which the outcome is never in doubt.

Indians 10, Marlins 3

September 30, 1995 Albert Belle becomes the only player in baseball history to hit at least fifty doubles and fifty homers in the same season.

June 7, 2002 The Indians make one of their finest trades ever, pilfering future stars Grady Sizemore, Cliff Lee, and Brandon Phillips from Montreal for pitcher Bartolo Colon.

1999

With an attendance of 3.47 million, the Indians break the franchise attendance record for the fifth consecutive season.

2001

The distance to left-center field is adjusted slightly to 370 feet. On April 4, after 455 consecutive capacity crowds, the Indians finally fail to sell out a game on a chilly Wednesday night.

August 5, 2001

It Ain't Over 'Til It's Over The Mariners jump out to a twelve-run lead over the Indians only to watch it slip through their fingers as Cleveland mounts an epic comeback for a 15-14 victory. The Indians score three in the seventh, four in the eighth, and five in the ninth. The tying runs score on a bases-loaded triple by Omar Vizquel with two outs in the ninth. Cleveland's Jolbert Cabrera, brought into the game for mop-up duty when the score was 14-2, drives in the winning run with a walk-off single in the eleventh. It's the biggest comeback in the major leagues since 1925.

Indians 15, Mariners 14

RIGHT: It was so cold in Cleveland during Game 4 of the 1997 World Series that umpires made an exception to the rules and allowed pitchers (including Jaret Wright, pictured here) to blow on their hands to warm them. During normal weather, this practice is forbidden so as to deter spitballs.

RIGHT: The handsome main entrance to Jacobs Field boasts white steelwork intended to evoke the city's industrial past. The famed sign pictured here was torn down on January 18, 2008, a week after the naming rights were sold to the Progressive insurance company. The entrance now features a large Progressive logo.

ABOVE: Cleveland's young core of stars poses in the Jacobs Field dugout in 2005. From left to right: outfielder Grady Sizemore, catcher Victor Martinez, shortstop Johnny Peralta, designated hitter Travis Hafner, and outfielder Coco Crisp. Two years down the road, four of these men will play key roles in leading the Indians to the brink of a World Series appearance. Crisp, the lone exception, will by then be a member of the Red Sox team that narrowly defeats Cleveland in the ALCS.

BELOW: The Indians line up on the field before Game 1 of the ALDS against the Yankees. Cleveland will take the title after two victories at Jacobs Field and one at Yankee Stadium, in the last postseason game ever played there.

October 5, 2007

Unbearable Flying Objects A debilitating swarm of flying insects flusters Yankees reliever Joba Chamberlain in the eighth inning at Jacobs Field, enabling the Indians to take a prohibitive two-games-to-none lead in the AL Division Series. The bugs pester players on both teams, but they seem especially attracted to Chamberlain, the rookie sensation who has been entrusted with the 1-0 lead after posting a 0.42 ERA as a late-season call-up. Chamberlain, a Native American, would no doubt love to give the Indians, the lone team in baseball with an openly racist mascot, their just desserts. But the tiny midges prove too much, and even copious amounts of insecticide sprayed on the Yankees' jerseys can't keep the bugs out of the players' eyes, ears, noses, and mouths. After several delays, the distracted Chamberlain walks two batters, hits another, and uncorks two wild pitches, allowing the Indians to tie the score. Cleveland eventually wins it in the eleventh on a bases-loaded single by Travis Hafner.

Indians 2, Yankees 1

2008

The name is changed to Progressive Field after the team strikes a $57.6 million deal with an insurance company. However, the stadium will remain known to fans as "The Jake."

ABOVE: Yankees manager Joe Torre counsels pitcher Joba Chamberlain, while team captain Derek Jeter tries in vain to shoo away insects with his cap during the infamous swarm of Lake Erie midges in Game 2 of the 2007 ALDS.

BALLPARK IN ARLINGTON
Arlington, Texas
Rangers (AL) 1994–present

Ameriquest Field in Arlington 2005–2006, Rangers Ballpark in Arlington 2007–present

Though it didn't receive anywhere near the attention Camden Yards did, the Rangers' gorgeous Ballpark in Arlington was an important benchmark in the retro stadium era. Arlington and Jacobs Field were the first two stadiums to open after Baltimore's historic park did, and they sent a clear signal that the days of domes and artificial turf were gone for good. Yet despite a fantastic ballpark, a huge media market, and a loyal fan base, the Rangers have never managed to put together a great team, making the playoffs just three times in the park's first fifteen years (and each time being humiliated by the Yankees in the first round). Even with many endearing characteristics that make it one of the finest stadiums in baseball, its most interesting aspect may be how it came to be. In fact, the Ballpark's financing scheme is one of the more sordid tales in the annals of ballpark construction, with a future president as its lead character.

In the late 1980s, looking for a business accomplishment that he could tout in a future campaign for Texas governor, George W. Bush settled on one of his true loves: baseball. He decided to become a team owner, and in 1989 he joined a syndicate that purchased a controlling interest in the Texas Rangers. Nothing in his background indicated that Bush was capable of running a team, but he wasn't necessarily running it, nor did he actually own much of it. Rather, it was his name and his father's political connections that his partners were interested in. Bush spent $606,000, most of it borrowed, to buy a 1.8 percent stake in the Rangers. In return, he was made managing general partner and was presented to the public as the owner of the team.

Bush soon set about accomplishing the task he'd been hired for: getting a new stadium built with taxpayer money. First, he and his partners invoked the time-honored gambit used by virtually every team since the Dodgers left Brooklyn: They threatened to move the team elsewhere unless they were given a new stadium. "I was like a pit bull on the pant leg of opportunity," Bush later said. Properly cajoled, the City of Arlington agreed to contribute $135 million. While the deal met with vehement opposition in some corners, voters none-theless approved the required sales tax hike in January 1991. The Rangers had their ballpark, and Bush had the credibility he needed to run for office. "When all those people in Austin say, 'He ain't never done anything,'" Bush said, "well, this is it."

The most lucrative part of the deal, however, took place under the surface. With 40,000 people a night coming to the area, the real estate bordering the new ballpark site was ripe for lucrative development. And all along, Bush and his partners had been quietly buying up land in the area. In some cases, when the Rangers couldn't convince private landowners to sell, they simply directed the city of Arlington to seize the property cheaply using eminent domain, then turn it over to Bush and his partners. "The idea of making a land play," Bush admitted, "that's kind of always been the strategy." As a reward for brokering the sweetheart stadium deal, Bush's partners gave him another 10 percent stake in the team. When the group sold the Rangers in 1998, the future president reaped $14.9 million on his initial $606,000 investment—a 2,500 percent profit. The end result was, as one economist put it, that "the largest welfare recipient in the state of Texas is George W. Bush."

Regardless of what it took to get the park built, the result is a gem. The Ballpark has a larger and more enclosed feeling than Camden Yards, and steep stairways in the upper deck means those fearful of heights are best advised to sit elsewhere. Yet in most other respects, the Ballpark in Arlington echoes Baltimore's stadium in hearkening back to the classic ballparks built in the 1910s. The playing field is asymmetrical, a manually operated scoreboard adorns the left-field wall, and classical latticework lines the edge of the roof. In right field, a "Home Run Porch" reminiscent of Tiger Stadium was constructed, complete with traditional pillars. "We had to be careful," co-owner Tom Schieffer said. "We didn't want to have ivy on the walls and a green monster and an overhang in right field....Instead, we said, let's think about why those things are special in other parks and build on the ideas generated." About the only thing in the new park reminiscent of the Rangers' previous home, Arlington Stadium, are the foul poles and a small section of aluminum bleachers, both of which were salvaged from the old park before it was torn down. Meanwhile, a four-story building behind center field houses the team offices.

While most retro ballparks have been decidedly reflective of the neighborhoods they're located in, the Ballpark in Arlington is not. The park itself has an urban feel but is located in a prairie suburban setting, a part of Arlington surrounded by expansive lawns, wide-open spaces, and

corporate office parks. Featuring a red-brick exterior and classical arches lined with Texas' famous pink granite, the Ballpark towers above the flat, North Texas landscape so imposingly that one writer compared it to an Athenian palace. One would never mistake the location for Greece, though, since architect David M. Schwarz was careful to give the ballpark a Texan motif. More than thirty stone longhorn heads, each 20 feet long, adorn the exterior brickwork, and the grounds are lined with sculptures depicting scenes from Texas history. Inside, the wrought-iron detailing on the side of each row of seats features the famed Texas lone star. For a team whose very name is an indication of its desire for statewide appeal, the Ballpark in Arlington is a perfect reflection of that philosophy.

Its silly name notwithstanding, the Ballpark in Arlington has been an artistic and aesthetic success. Yet the park had at least one drawback when it opened: the prices. With tickets costing $40 for box seats and $12 for outfield bleachers, this was definitely a park aimed at the upper-class fan. Indeed, the Ballpark at Arlington was somewhat of a leader in the mallpark concept, featuring not only 122 luxury suites, but also full-service restaurants and boutiques selling high-priced souvenirs. For kids, there is a sports park, a learning auditorium, and even a Little League field across the

street. And for the history buff, there's an extensive museum with items on loan from Cooperstown. The Ballpark in Arlington was likely the first baseball stadium ever to have its own artistic director. Specially commissioned paintings were hung in the suites, many of them done by Vernon Wells Sr., the artist father of the future Blue Jays centerfielder. The Ballpark also features the largest gallery of sports art in the United States.

The park's tiny dimensions made it a paradise for sluggers like Juan Gonzalez, Ivan Rodriguez, and Rafael Palmeiro, and the Rangers managed to consistently field winning teams during their early years in the new park. The fans showed their appreciation, surpassing the old Arlington Stadium franchise attendance record eight times in the Ballpark's first ten years. However, it soon became apparent that the park was a place for pitchers to avoid at all costs. It seemed no amount of money could induce star hurlers to sign with the Rangers, and the team proved inept at producing a quality pitching staff from its farm system. Over the park's first fifteen years, the Rangers' team ERA was never better than 4.84, and one season it climbed to a ghastly 6.11. If Texas is ever to field a championship team at glorious Rangers Ballpark in Arlington (as it is now called), they will first have to figure out how to pitch there.

1994 After twenty-two years with blue as their primary color, the Rangers celebrate the new ballpark's opening by switching to a mostly red uniform. They'll switch back in 2001.

July 11, 1995 Twenty-three years after moving to Texas, the Rangers host the first All-Star Game in franchise history. The National League wins, 3-2, with every one of their hits being home runs.

September 15, 1996 Texas becomes the second of three teams to retire Nolan Ryan's number (30). The Angels did so in 1992, and the Astros will follow suit two weeks after the Rangers.

TIMELINE: BALLPARK IN ARLINGTON

1994

Completed in just twenty-three months, the Ballpark in Arlington opens on April 1 on a site just a quarter mile from the Rangers' old home, Arlington Stadium. The outfield fence features seven angles, and cozy dimensions of 334 feet to left field, 390 to left-center, 400 to center, 381 to right-center, and 325 to right.

July 28, 1994

A Wonderful Day in the Neighborhood
Rangers southpaw Kenny Rogers throws the fourteenth perfect game in major league history, a 4-0 whitewashing of the Angels. Oddly enough, the last perfect game in the AL—by California's Mike Witt in 1984—was also an Angels-Rangers match-up in Arlington. Rogers, who's in just his second season as a starter after beginning his career in the bullpen, strikes out eight Angels batters. The offense is provided by Ivan Rodriguez, who homers once, and Jose Canseco, who homers twice. The last batter of the game, California's Gary DiSarcina, hits a line drive to center field, but Texas' Rusty Greer preserves Rogers' gem by making a diving catch.

Rangers 4, Angels 0

RIGHT: Kenny Rogers salutes the crowd of 46,581 after tossing his 1994 perfect game against the Angels.

BELOW: The area behind center field at the park contains both a kid-sized field and a statue of Nolan Ryan doffing his cap after his seventh career no-hitter.

2000

An inner fence is installed in left field, reducing the distance there by 2 feet. Seats are removed from the small triangular section in the right field corner and replaced by cafe tables.

June 12, 1997

Second League, Same as the First The Rangers host San Francisco in the first regular-season interleague game in major league history, defeating the Giants 4-3 before 46,507 curious fans. Stan Javier of the Giants hits the first interleague home run ever, while Glenallen Hill becomes the first NL player to serve as a designated hitter during a regular game. Interleague play, a ploy to revive fan interest after the 1994 strike, draws well at first, but fans will soon enough grow tired of it and cease according any special significance to the games. The gimmick will persist, however, thanks to comparatively high television ratings generated by the handful of intra-city games in New York, Chicago, and Los Angeles.

Rangers 4, Giants 3

November 18, 1999   Rangers catcher Ivan Rodriguez is named AL MVP despite garnering fewer first-place votes than Boston's Pedro Martinez.

LEFT: In this aerial shot, the Nolan Ryan Expressway can be seen to the right of the stadium. Although Ryan never played at Rangers Ballpark, reminders of his legacy are everywhere. Paintings of him hang in an in-stadium art gallery, a statue of him stands behind center field, and the real-life Ryan himself can be found at nearly every game—he was named team president in February 2008 and handed the unenviable task of turning around the fortunes of the flailing Rangers franchise.

2004

On May 7, the park's name is changed to Ameriquest Field after the Rangers sign a thirty-year, $75 million deal with the company, which specializes in subprime mortgage loans to people with questionable credit.

Get Out of My Face Rangers hurler Kenny Rogers, the second-winningest pitcher in franchise history, loses his cool on the field before a game, pushing two cameramen, throwing a camera to the ground, kicking it, and making threats. One of the cameramen is sent to the hospital, and the incident becomes national tabloid fare after footage of it is shown on the local nightly news. Rogers is cited by police and fined $1,500. Commissioner Bud Selig is even harsher, handing down a $50,000 fine and a twenty-game suspension. It's one of the lengthiest suspensions in baseball history, longer even than the fifteen games Rogers' teammate Frank Francisco received a year earlier for throwing a chair into the stands at a fan. (An arbitrator, however, will reduce Rogers' suspension to thirteen games.) This isn't the first incident of the season for the hot-headed Rogers, who earlier in the month broke a bone in his non-pitching hand while punching a water cooler during a dugout tantrum. He'll still be named an All-Star, though, on the merits of his performance, which includes a 10-4 record and 2.54 ERA. However, this will prove to be his last year as a Ranger.

Rangers 7, Angels 6

April 15, 2009 In a 19-6 rout of Baltimore, the Rangers' Ian Kinsler becomes the third player in modern MLB history to collect six hits and hit for the cycle in the same game.

2007

With Ameriquest's business practices having been investigated by thirty of the fifty state attorneys general, the Rangers seek to change the embarrassing name of the ballpark. On March 19, the team agrees to an undisclosed settlement with Ameriquest to retract the naming rights, and the park is dubbed Rangers Ballpark in Arlington.

2008

The Rangers announce a $4 million makeover for their ballpark, including a new scoreboard and the addition of four big-screen TVs.

RIGHT: On July 9, 2008, catcher Gerald Laird (with his arms in the air) is among those celebrating Josh Hamilton's three-run homer, which has given Texas a 6-5 walk-off victory over Anaheim. A former number-one draft pick whose career was derailed multiple times by drug abuse, Hamilton will complete his comeback with a 32-homer, 130-RBI performance in his first season with the Rangers.

Baltimore lefty Arthur Lee Rhodes faces the Rangers on April 19, 1998, in a contest that will be won by the Orioles, 10-8. Playing third base for the O's is Cal Ripken Jr., who will collect three hits in this, his 2,494th consecutive game. The multistory building behind center field—visible at the right of the image—contains, among other things, the Rangers' team offices, a 17,000-square-foot baseball museum, and a 285-seat movie theater.

COORS FIELD

Denver, Colorado

Rockies (NL) 1995–present

In 1995 in the LoDo district of downtown Denver, the Colorado Rockies opened what immediately became the most infamous stadium in baseball. Though its retro-style architecture was deemed pleasant enough and the stadium offered scenic views of the Rocky Mountains, it wasn't these features that drew attention to Coors Field. Rather, it was the stunning frequency with which runs were scored and home runs were hit. Everybody knew the Mile High City's thin air would wreak havoc on hurlers' breaking pitches and allow batted balls to travel farther, but few were prepared for the overwhelming extent of this effect. Pedestrian hitters posted numbers worthy of legends, previously outstanding pitchers found their careers dashed, and the home team's management spent a decade stumbling around trying to figure out a way to compete in this roller-derby arena of a ballpark.

Remarkably, public stadium funding had been approved by voters in six surrounding counties before Denver had even been awarded an expansion team. Somewhat surprisingly, considering it housed a team with no history, Coors Field (so-named after the nearby Coors Brewing Company, which forked over $15 million for the naming rights) sought to capture the same old-time feel that had worked so well in Baltimore's Oriole Park at Camden Yards. Incorporated into Coors field were rusticated stone bases, a manual scoreboard, and an old-fashioned clock. The red-brick entrance rotunda recalls Shibe Park and Ebbets Field, even with a brewery built into one side of the park. Though most of the seats were painted dark green, a single row of purple chairs was incorporated in the upper deck, to mark an altitude of exactly one mile above sea level. Originally slated to seat 43,000, Coors' right-field bleachers were expanded after record-breaking attendance numbers at the Rockies' temporary home, Mile High Stadium, making the new park's final capacity 50,000. Although the park opened with most ticket and concession prices reflecting baseball's dramatic turn toward wooing the upper-class fan, tickets could still be had in the Rockpile, the centerfield bleacher section, for as little as $4.00.

In the two years the team spent playing at Mile High Stadium, about 35 percent more runs were scored than at an average park. Because of this figure and the experience of local minor league clubs, everyone was well aware that the thin air would amp up offense. Most studies concluded that batted balls travel between 7 and 10 percent farther at 5,200 feet above sea level. With this in mind, the club made Coors Field's outfield fences among the most distant in the majors, with left-center field 390 feet away and dead center 415 feet. However, this also served to drastically increase the size of the outfield, meaning that singles, doubles, and triples all had more space to fall in. During the inaugural season of 1995, there were fifty-nine triples hit at Coors, as opposed to just twenty in the Rockies' road games.

The total effect was a ballpark favoring batters to a degree unprecedented in baseball history. In 1995, Coors Field almost doubled the figures from Mile High—with the number of runs nearly 60 percent higher than the average park—and that percentage would hover between 30 and 50 for the next decade. This had the effect of making mediocre hitters look like good ones, fooling the front office, and hampering the team's success on the field. For instance, Dante Bichette, a previously average hitter, annually put up MVP-type numbers after joining the Rockies in 1993, even though he routinely batted more than a hundred points higher at Coors than on the road. Unfortunately, Rockies management was tricked into believing these high-altitude high achievers were stars, which deterred them from acquiring any *actual* star players. Another strange (and to this day, unexplained) Coors phenomenon is that many Rockies batters simply collapsed whenever they ventured away from home, becoming far worse than they had ever been at sea level. For instance, Jeff Cirillo, a career .300 hitter, batted just .239 in road games upon joining the Rockies in 2000.

Pitchers, meanwhile, found it to be a house of horrors. During Coors' first nine years, no Rockies hurler managed to pitch a full season with an ERA better than 4.00. Because the thin air offered less resistance to moving baseballs, curves and sliders didn't break as sharply. Highly touted pitcher signings backfired with regularity. Most famous was Mike Hampton, a onetime twenty-game winner who signed an eight-year, $121 million contract with the Rockies that made him the highest-paid pitcher in history. Hampton lasted just two seasons in Colorado, posting an abysmal 5.75 ERA before the team discarded him due to injuries and ineffectiveness. It became a cautionary tale for other pitchers, most of whom refused to even consider signing with the Rockies.

In such an environment, the game of baseball was barely recognizable, and Rockies management soon came to believe that the normal rules of team construction did not apply at

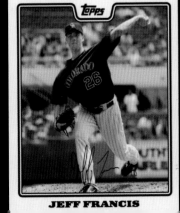

GARRETT ATKINS

JEFF FRANCIS

MATT HOLLIDAY

Coors Field. Dan O'Dowd, who took over as general manager in 1999, tried every theory under the sun, scarcely allowing one idea to play out before moving on to the next. The Rockies tried lead-footed sluggers, they tried speedsters, they tried defensive specialists. They tried curveball pitchers, strikeout pitchers, groundball specialists. None of it seemed to work, and the team was a perennial also-ran, finishing last or next to last in each of O'Dowd's first eight seasons.

The most interesting solution the Rockies tried, however, was humidifying their baseballs. Denver's arid atmosphere caused the balls to dry out, and the evaporation of moisture made the balls weigh slightly less, contributing to the way they would fly off the bat. So in 2002, the Rockies installed a humidor big enough for 4,800 baseballs in the bowels of Coors Field. The balls were kept at 70°F and 50 percent humidity, bringing them more in line with the baseballs used at sea level. Almost immediately, the level of offense dropped off noticeably, with the number of runs only about 20 percent higher than average. (Contrary to public belief, it didn't turn Coors into a pitcher's park—it was still the best hitting park in baseball.) The new environment was less extreme and more sane for everyone. "Before the humidor, the ball would get so dry that the leather would crack," Rockies reliever Mike DeJean said. "Now, the leather is supple. You can grip the ball and really throw your breaking pitches." When word got out about the humidified balls, the practice sparked a mild controversy at first. But by 2007, all thirty teams were keeping their balls in temperature-controlled environments.

Not only did the Rockies solve their ball problem, they figured out how to put together a winning team at Coors

TIMELINE: COORS FIELD

June 15, 1993 Mile High Stadium witnesses two memorable brawls after the Rockies' Andres Galarraga inflicts a nasty spiking on Los Angeles' Jody Reed. Four players are ejected.

1995

Coors Field opens on April 26. On paper, its dimensions are massive: 347 feet down the left-field line, 390 to left-center field, 415 to dead center, 375 to right-center, and 350 to right. Deepest right-center reaches 424 feet. But this is Denver, where the ball carries about 10 percent farther. Balls fly over the fences with regularity.

Field, although it had nothing to do with the humidor. It turned out to be as simple as developing a top-notch farm system and hanging on to the players. In 2007, the Rockies won the NL pennant with a roster consisting almost exclusively of homegrown talent, including Todd Helton, Matt Holliday, Garrett Atkins, Troy Tulowitzki, and Jeff Francis. The answer had been in the Rockies' backyard the whole time.

June 16, 1995 Atlanta's Tom Glavine becomes the first pitcher to throw a shutout at Coors Field. By 2008, sixteen others (including Glavine again) will have repeated the feat.

June 30, 1996 Against the Dodgers at Coors Field, Colorado's Eric Young ties a modern record by stealing six bases in one game, including second, third, and home in the same inning.

April 26, 1995

A Back-and-Forth Affair The Rockies win an exhilarating debut game at Coors Field, outlasting the Mets in a fourteen-inning roller coaster ride that includes four ties and six lead changes. New York's Brett Butler collects the park's first hit, but the Rockies score the first run when Larry Walker doubles in Walt Weiss in the bottom of the first. The tables are turned, though, when Rockies hurler Bill Swift gives up a homer to Rico Brogna and a grand slam to Todd Hundley. The Mets take the lead only to see the Rockies tie it in both the ninth and thirteenth. In the fourteenth, the Mets take another lead and blow it again, this time on a walk-off three-run homer by Colorado's Dante Bichette. The 11-9 final will be a typical Coors Field score in the years to come.

Rockies 11, Mets 9

October 1, 1995

Onward to the Playoffs In the most significant game of the franchise's first decade, Colorado forges a classic Rocky Mountain comeback to knock off the Giants and clinch the wild card playoff berth. The Rockies trail 8-2 by the middle of the third inning, but they plate four in the bottom of the frame on two-run homers by Eric Young and Larry Walker. The Rockies score another four in the fifth on three doubles and two singles, and manage to limit the Giants to just one run in a seventh-inning rally. Colorado hands a 10-9 lead to closer Curtis Leskanic in the ninth, needing just three more outs to clinch a playoff spot. Leskanic blows through the Giants with ease, and in just their third year of existence, the Rockies make the postseason—the quickest ever of any expansion team. The attendance of 48,039 brings Colorado's final total to 3.93 million for the regular season, almost a million more than any other major league team. Alas, the Rockies will be handcuffed by Atlanta in the first round of the playoffs.

Rockies 10, Giants 9

One Mile, Two Records

Like many new franchises, the Rockies began their tenure in Denver in a temporary home: Mile High Stadium. However, unlike many interim parks, Mile High had been waiting for a major league baseball team for decades.

Built in 1948 to house the minor league Bears, the park (then called Bears Stadium) was built by the Howsam family on the site of a former landfill. The team was immensely popular, and so was their home. "Bears Stadium, when it was built, was considered a showplace around the country, and in minor league baseball it was way ahead of anything at that time," Bob Howsam later told the *Rocky Mountain News*.

Still, Howsam dreamed of the major leagues. With the hope of obtaining a Continental League team, he expanded the park from 17,000 to 35,000 seats in the '50s. When the start-up league folded before a single game was played, however, Howsam was forced to find another club to play in his enormous stadium.

The club he found wasn't a baseball team, but rather the American Football League's Broncos, who became the Bears' co-tenants at the stadium in 1960. Over the years, the rag-tag team proved to be one of the more successful clubs in pro football, and Mile High—as it was renamed in 1968—was eventually expanded to hold more than 75,000 fans. For baseball games, a state-of-the-art system was developed to move the east stands outward in order to change the shape of the playing field. Hydraulic tracks filled with only .003 inches of water literally floated the three-tiered, nine-million-pound stands back and forth. The 145-foot move took nearly two hours to complete each time.

Major League Baseball finally started playing in Denver in 1993, as the city, along with Miami, was awarded an expansion team in 1991. The Bears—now called the Zephyrs—left the largest stadium in the minor leagues for Privateer Park in New Orleans, and the Rockies came to Denver. The Mile High City's first major league game was on April 9, 1993, when a regular-season record crowd of 80,227 watched the Rockies trounce Montreal 11-4. The novelty of big-league baseball brought huge crowds to the venerable park despite a gigantic foul territory and large dimensions that pushed seats far, far back. Centerfield bleachers were especially distant, but cheaply priced at just $1.00.

Though it was home to the Rockies for only two years, the stadium that always wanted a major league team will live on in the annals of baseball history: the park's enormous capacity allowed the Rockies to draw an all-time record of 4,483,350 fans in the club's first season. With no big-league park today seating more than 56,000, Mile High Stadium's hold on the single-game and single-season MLB records ought to last decades, if not forever.

Denver's Mile High Stadium, which in 1993 hosted 4.48 million fans, more than any other major league stadium before or since. Though it began as a little, 10,000-seat park, renovations over the course of a half century would transform it into one of the largest stadiums in the United States. After a two-year stay, the Rockies moved out in 1995; the Broncos followed suit in 2001. In January of the following year, demolition began—an event that was shown live on local television. The site is now a parking lot next to the Broncos' new stadium, Invesco Field.

September 17, 1996

Nomo No-No Los Angeles' Hideo Nomo, the Japanese sensation with a devastating forkball, defies the altitude and does the unthinkable by pitching the first no-hitter ever thrown at Coors Field. Taking the field after a two-hour rain delay, Nomo abandons his usual tornado windup after a few innings because it's too difficult to keep his footing on the muddy pitcher's mound. Pitching from the stretch, he walks four batters but otherwise blows through the Rockies with remarkable ease. And this is no pushover team, either: just two games earlier, Colorado broke a forty-six-year-old MLB record for most runs scored at home in a season. They'll end up leading the NL not only in runs, but also in hits, home runs, batting average, on-base percentage, and slugging percentage. Given the hitting environment at Coors and the Rockies' dominance there, Nomo's hitless game ranks as one of the most remarkable pitching performances in baseball history.

Dodgers 9, Rockies 0

RIGHT: Hideo Nomo hurls the best-pitched game in Coors Field history—a 9-0 no-hitter against the Rockies in 1996. Andres Galarraga, visible in the background on first base, was one of four Rockies to reach base on a walk.

1997

On September 6, the night portion of a day-night doubleheader against the Cardinals draws only 44,288, marking the first time since June 13, 1995— a span of 203 games— that a Rockies game has failed to sell out.

July 7, 1998

All-Star Slugfest The All-Star Game is played at Coors Field for the first time, and the result is exactly what you'd expect from two teams of baseball's best sluggers in the high-octane environment of Coors Field. The AL outslugs the NL 13-8 in the highest scoring All-Star Game ever, and the game clocks in at a slothful three hours, thirty-eight minutes, making it the longest Midsummer Classic not including extra-inning games. Baltimore's Roberto Alomar is named game MVP after hitting a homer, stealing a base, and collecting three of the AL's nineteen hits. Ironically for a team with such a strong home-field advantage, the Rockies players are the worst performers on the field. Vinny Castilla, Dante Bichette, and Larry Walker combine to go 0-for-7, while their NL teammates combine for twelve hits and a .413 average in a losing cause.

AL 13, NL 8

2001

2001 The Rockies' Larry Walker bats .350 to win the NL batting crown, marking the fourth consecutive year a Colorado player has won the title.

Coors Field tops 3 million in attendance for the seventh (and last) consecutive season.

January 2002 Demolition begins at Mile High Stadium— where, over the years, six deceased Broncos fans have had their ashes scattered.

September 28, 2006 Dodgers rookie James Loney ties a fifty-six-year-old franchise record when he collects nine RBIs in a game at Coors Field, going 4-for-5 with a grand slam.

OPPOSITE, TOP: Aisle chairs at Coors Field are adorned with the Rockies logo, which appropriately features a baseball flying deep into the mountains.

OPPOSITE, BOTTOM: As seen from the corner of Market and 20th streets in 2003, Coors Field is gorgeous at sunset, when the clouds glow golden over the High Plains and the aptness of the phrase "purple mountain majesties" becomes readily apparent.

The opening of the stadium was widely credited for revitalizing LoDo (short for "lower downtown"), Denver's oldest neighborhood, as crumbling warehouses throughout the district were renovated to house new businesses and residences. Another centerpiece of the revitalization is the historic Union Station, built in 1894, which sits four blocks southwest of the ballpark and still serves as an active Amtrak station.

September 23, 2003

A Great Day at the Old Belliard In their final home series of the season, the Rockies do something that, surprisingly, they've never done before at Coors Field: score twenty runs in a game. The star of the game isn't one of the team's myriad sluggers, but leadoff hitter Ronnie Belliard, who ties a franchise record with eight RBIs in the 20-9 throttling of Arizona. Belliard smacks a two-run single in the first (thanks to the Rockies batting around), a solo homer in the fifth, a three-run homer in the sixth, and a two-run double in the seventh. Belliard joins Larry Walker (1999) and Andres Galarraga (1996) as Rockies who have driven in eight runs in one game.

Rockies 20, Diamondbacks 9

October 1, 2007

Rocky Mountain Holliday After a remarkable late-season surge enabled them to tie San Diego for the final postseason berth, the Rockies clinch the NL wild card by winning a one-game playoff that's immediately hailed as a classic. With the score knotted at 6-6 since the eighth inning, the Padres finally break loose in the thirteenth when Scott Hairston, a journeyman playing just his thirty-first game for the Padres, blasts a two-run homer that seems the likely game-winner. San Diego puts the lead in the hands of Trevor Hoffman, the thirty-nine-year-old all-time saves leader whose blazing fastball has long since vanished. Kaz Matsui and rookie Troy Tulowitzki hit consecutive doubles off Hoffman, and NL batting champ Matt Holliday follows with a game-tying triple. After an intentional walk, the Rockies' Jamey Carroll lifts a fly ball to short right field, where Giles is waiting to try to throw out Holliday's winning run at home plate. It's a close play, but Holliday is called safe even though replays will appear to show him missing the plate. Emerging from the home plate collision with his face dripping blood, Holliday is mobbed by his teammates in celebration of the Rockies' first trip to the playoffs in more than a decade. The team will make it all the way to the World Series, but will be swept by the Red Sox.

Rockies 9, Padres 8

ABOVE: Todd Helton exults on October 15, 2007, after making the catch that clinches the first World Series appearance in Rockies history. Lying on the ground behind Helton is Arizona's Eric Byrnes, who has just grounded out to end the four-game NLCS. The 2007 Rockies, after being in fourth place with just twelve games left in the season, went on one of the most remarkable streaks in history, winning twenty-one out of twenty-two contests (including the playoffs) to reach the Fall Classic.

CAP: 2000.

TURNER FIELD

Atlanta, Georgia

Braves (NL) 1997–present

MATT DIAZ

OPPOSITE: During Turner Field's 1997 debut season, the vacant Atlanta–Fulton County Stadium was still visible behind the left-field stands throughout most of the summer, as seen in this photo. But on August 2, with the Braves on a road trip, the old stadium was imploded, clearing the way for a picturesque view of downtown Atlanta from Turner Field's stands. Although the park was full on the day this picture was taken, that was a relatively infrequent sight; attendance at Turner never quite reached the levels one might expect given the team's success.

When it comes to building ballparks, following the example of the Montreal Expos is not usually a good idea. But that's what the Braves did in 1996, taking a stadium built for the Summer Olympics—a structure that would have otherwise become a white elephant—and retrofitting it for baseball. This move had backfired on the Expos in 1976, when Stade Olympique turned out to be not only a bad stadium, but a boondoggle of staggering proportions. Atlanta learned from Montreal's mistakes, however, and Centennial Olympic Stadium was transformed into an enjoyable, if somewhat generic, place to watch a baseball game.

When Atlanta's bid to host the 1996 Summer Games was accepted, the news coincided nicely with the Braves' desire to replace Atlanta–Fulton County Stadium, the aging, multipurpose structure that had hosted many of the defining moments in superstar Hank Aaron's career. Almost immediately, plans were announced to kill two birds with one stone: the new stadium required for the Olympics would be turned over to Ted Turner's Braves once it had served its purpose. Despite strong public sentiment to rename it Hank Aaron Stadium, the building would instead be christened Turner Field. Located across the parking lot from Fulton County Stadium, the new stadium was a coup for Turner, since it was constructed almost entirely with money provided by the publicly funded Atlanta Committee for the Olympic Games.

The first thing to be built was a grandstand that, in the baseball layout, would extend from right-center field clockwise around home plate and nearly over to the left-field foul pole. To accommodate the long, oval-shaped field necessary for the Olympics, no permanent outfield seats were built. One end of the long oval was located approximately where the first-base dugout would later be. A stand of temporary bleachers— which would raise the park's capacity to the 85,000 required to meet Olympic demands, and then be torn down after the Games were over—was erected at the other end of the oval, in what would soon be deep left-center field. In addition to sold-out crowds for the opening and closing ceremonies, the stadium also hosted the track-and-field competition, in which Carl Lewis won a gold medal in the long jump and Michael Johnson did the same in the 200 and 400 meters.

JOHN SMOLTZ

CHIPPER JONES

CHUCK JAMES

CAP: 2004 (worn by Bobby Cox).

BELOW: A bird's-eye view of the Grand Entry Plaza in center field. Turner Field is atypical among major league ballparks for having its main entrance plaza in center field instead of behind the home-plate area. One of the plaza's main features is the Coca-Cola Sky Field, built atop the left-field roof and visible near the bottom right of this image. The area includes a 38-foot-tall replica of a Coke bottle and a dirt infield where kids can run the bases. Coca-Cola has offered a $1 million prize to any fan who catches a home-run ball there, but they might as well make it a billion, since at 550 feet away and 90 feet above the playing field, it's far beyond the capabilities of even the mightiest sluggers.

After the Olympics left town, the temporary stands were demolished and work began on finishing the baseball portion of the north side of the field in time for the 1997 season. The additions included outfield bleachers, a video board in dead center field, and a gigantic Coca-Cola bottle placed at the end of the upper deck as an advertisement for Atlanta's best-known corporation. A "grand entry plaza" was also built in the outfield, and includes the team's main ticket office as well as statues of such Braves legends as Aaron, Phil Niekro, and Warren Spahn. Interestingly, there's also a statue of Ty Cobb, a legendary Georgian who never played for the Braves, sliding into a base, spikes high. Along with the many boutiques and food stands in the two pavilions that make up the plaza, video games, informational kiosks, and a children's play area (which replaced the designated smoking zone) have been added to encourage fans to arrive at the game early.

Inside, the park features an admirable distribution of seats, with 28,000 at field level, 6,000 at club level (along with the usual luxury suites), and just 15,000 in an upper deck that's remarkably close to the action. The non-wrap-around nature of this top deck also means that a fantastic view of the Atlanta skyline can be had beyond center field. Though Turner Field has attempted to echo the retro style of Camden Yards, the effect is undermined by the colossal amount of advertising that inundates the senses. Ads festoon scoreboards, trash bins, food trays, and just about anything else a fan might look at, while corporations sponsor

sections of the stands, portions of the parking lot, and sometimes even the ceremonial first pitch. There's even a 40-foot, tomahawk-chopping, mechanical cow sponsored by Chick-fil-A in left field. It seems the Braves will slap an ad on anything—perhaps even the foreheads of fans who stand still for too long.

Rather than any of its physical features, though, Turner Field immediately became famous for its exorbitant prices at concession stands, which have a captive audience since the park is located amongst overpasses and not within walking distance of restaurants or other outside businesses. In the stadium's opening year, a hot dog cost $6.00 and a small soda $3.50, prices so steep that even Turner himself criticized them. According to the Fan Cost Index—a calculation representing the average cost of attending a game, including parking and concessions—a family of four attending a 1997 Braves game could expect to pay $129.16, the highest total in baseball. (By comparison, the stadium whose example the Braves had followed, Stade Olympique, was the cheapest at $80.42.) Turner Field also became one of the few stadiums to prohibit fans from bringing in their own food, although this policy was rescinded after public outcry.

The Braves club that moved into Turner in 1997 was in the middle of a full-blown dynasty, enjoying one of the greatest stretches of sustained success the sport had ever seen. However, Braves fans, most of whom were content to watch their team on Ted Turner's TBS superstation, didn't show up to the park in significant numbers. In 1997, the Braves posted the NL's best record (by a whopping nine-game margin) while playing in a brand-new stadium, but strangely didn't top the league in attendance. Things would plummet from there, even as the Braves continued their remarkable streak of eleven consecutive division titles. From 2001 to 2005, the last five years of that historic streak, their attendance became an embarrassment, ranking sixth, eighth, seventh, tenth, and then tenth again among NL teams. Even more astonishingly, they often failed to sell out their playoff games. Diminishing revenues rendered the team unable to retain many of its stars, and the Braves could only stand by and watch as legendary talents like Greg Maddux, Tom Glavine, and Andruw Jones signed lucrative free-agent contracts with other teams. The streak of division titles ended in 2006, and as Turner Field's second decade began, it appeared that only an outstanding scouting and development system could save the park from hosting a consistently losing team. Luckily for the fans who do come out to see the team in person, there's still plenty to enjoy—and purchase—at this entertainment-filled park.

July 19, 1996 Centennial Olympic Stadium hosts the Opening Ceremonies of the Summer Olympics. Soon after the Olympics end, the park will be reconfigured for baseball and its name will change to Turner Field.

October 1996 Braves owner Ted Turner merges his holdings with Time Warner, meaning the team is now owned by the largest media conglomerate in the world.

December 27, 1999 *Sports Illustrated* publishes an interview with Braves closer John Rocker, in which he makes racist, sexist, and homophobic comments. He's suspended for twelve games, and his career soon collapses.

1997

After Centennial Olympic Park is remodeled for baseball, Turner Field opens on April 4. Unlike Atlanta–Fulton County Stadium, which was dubbed "The Launching Pad," Turner is tailored to favor pitchers. Dimensions are 335 feet down the left-field line, 380 to left-center, 401 to center, 390 to right-center, and 330 down the right-field line. Capacity is 50,096.

LEFT: Centennial Olympic Stadium on June 7, 1996, about a month-and-a-half before hosting the opening ceremonies for the Summer Games. Soon after the Olympics are over, construction crews will tear down the curved section of stands in what is to become deepest left-center field. In its place they'll erect left-field bleachers and the Grand Entry Plaza. Atlanta–Fulton County Stadium, visible in the background, will become the site of a parking lot by 1998.

ABOVE: Before the first game at Turner Field on April 4, 1997, pitcher Tom Glavine places the old home plate from Atlanta–Fulton County Stadium into its new home. Braves legend Hank Aaron looks on from behind him.

October 19, 1999

Oh, Those Bases on Balls The Braves win the pennant when the Mets' Kenny Rogers, after issuing two intentional walks to load the bases in the eleventh inning, walks Atlanta's Andruw Jones to force in the winning run. The victory comes as a welcome respite for the Braves, who had watched helplessly as New York won each of the prior two games in its final at-bat. Tonight, the Braves knock Mets starter Al Leiter out of the game in the first inning, but can't hold on to their 5-0 lead. New York takes the lead in the seventh, eighth, and tenth innings of this see-saw affair, but Atlanta roars back to tie it each time. Rogers' free pass in the eleventh gives the Braves their first pennant since 1996.

Braves 10, Mets 9

2000 Tom Glavine reaches twenty wins for the fifth time in his Braves career, but misses out on his third Cy Young Award when he finishes second in the voting to Randy Johnson.

2002

The Fanplex entertainment center, featuring such diversions as miniature golf and video games, opens for business. It will lose money and eventually close its doors in early 2004.

2003

Georgia Tech and Georgia face off in the first of what will become an annual series between the two rival schools at Turner Field.

August 19, 2004 Closer John Smoltz, who has also won 159 games as a starter, records his 142nd career save to break the Braves franchise record.

July 11, 2000

No Joke: Ripken Gets Hurt Cal Ripken's streak of seventeen consecutive All-Star Games played comes to an end at Turner Field when he's sidelined due to injury. Ripken's AL teammates win anyway, despite memorable performances by hometown heroes Chipper and Andruw Jones, who contribute a game-tying homer and a run-scoring single respectively. Al Leiter of the Mets, after suffering one of the worst games of his career here the previous October, gives up a two-run single to Derek Jeter, who's named the game MVP. The AL scores three more times in the top of the ninth against Trevor Hoffman. It's the AL's fourth straight All-Star win, and the third with former Braves star Joe Torre at the helm.

AL 6, NL 3

2005

A $10 million Mitsubishi video screen is installed. At 71 by 79 feet, it is billed as the largest outdoor high-definition display in the world.

LEFT: Andruw Jones thrusts a triumphant finger into the air after winning the 1999 NL pennant with a bases-loaded walk. The method of victory was surprising, since Jones—one of baseball's most notorious free swingers—rarely accepted walks.

May 18, 2004

One Perfect Unit Forty-year-old Randy Johnson becomes the oldest pitcher ever to throw a perfect game when he retires all twenty-seven Braves batters in a 2-0 Arizona victory. It's the seventeenth perfecto in major league history and the first in the NL since 1991, when Montreal's Dennis Martinez blanked the Dodgers. Today's game is Turner Field's first no-hitter, but the second no-no of Johnson's illustrious career. (He'd thrown one with Seattle fourteen years earlier.) The light-hitting Diamondbacks manage to score just two runs, one in the second and another in the seventh, but with The Big Unit on the mound, it's more than enough. Atlanta lefty Mike Hampton suffers a complete-game loss, dropping his record to 0-5, but he'll recover to go 13-4 the rest of the year.

Diamondbacks 2, Braves 0

August 7, 2007 In San Francisco, Barry Bonds hits his 756th homer to break Hank Aaron's career record. Aaron refuses to attend the game.

2008 Chipper Jones bats .364 at age thirty-six to win his first career batting title, and the first for the Braves since Terry Pendleton's in 1991.

January 13, 2009 John Smoltz, who has won fourteen division titles in Atlanta, signs with the Boston Red Sox after spending the first twenty-one years of his career as a Brave.

October 6, 2005

McCann Launches One off Rocket In what turns out to be the final game of the season at Turner Field, Brian McCann's three-run homer off Roger Clemens helps the Braves even up the NL Division Series at one win apiece. John Smoltz pitches seven sparkling innings for his record-setting fifteenth career playoff victory. (He reclaims the record from Houston's Andy Pettitte, who had tied the mark just a day earlier in Game 1 of the series.) The Braves hope to return home for a winner-take-all Game 5, but the Astros will sweep both games in Houston to end Atlanta's season. Though nobody knows it at the time, today's contest marks the final home game in Atlanta's remarkable run of playoff appearances under Bobby Cox.

Braves 7, Astros 1

RIGHT: Tom Glavine pitches to the Braves' John Smoltz on May 24, 2007, a match-up that sparks conflicting emotions for Braves fans, as well as for the players themselves. The two were teammates for 2,266 games before Glavine departed for the Mets in 2003.

May 24, 2007

Smoltz vs. Glavine In a match-up between two of the finest pitchers in Braves history, John Smoltz defeats his close friend Tom Glavine to become the first pitcher ever with at least 200 wins and 150 saves. Smoltz, the only player to remain with Atlanta throughout its run of fourteen NL East titles in fifteen seasons, receives a long ovation from the crowd of 36,660 when he exits after seven shutout innings. His milestone win seems to be in doubt when the Mets threaten against Braves closer Bob Wickman in the ninth, but Wickman coaxes a pop-up from Jose Reyes to end the game. Glavine, in his fifth and final year with the Mets, will win his 300th game later in the season.

Braves 2, Mets 1

Atlanta fans are notorious for not selling out playoff games, including this 2004 Division Series game against the Astros, which found many seats in the upper deck empty.

BANK ONE BALLPARK

Phoenix, Arizona

Diamondbacks (NL) 1998–present

Chase Field 2006–present

Viewed from the outside, Bank One Ballpark is as unattractive a stadium as one could imagine. A rectangular box with a half-moon-shaped roof, it resembles nothing so much as a gigantic discount warehouse. Murals of baseball scenes dot the outer walls, but with no Diamondbacks franchise history to draw from, the players are faceless figures who only add to the park's generic quality. Debuting in 1998, the park featured two mainstays of Arizona life, a swimming pool and air-conditioning, but was surprisingly bereft of a third: sunshine. With high walls, a small roof opening, and steep, distant seating, it often makes fans feel as though they're watching a ballgame from the rafters of a colossal airplane hangar.

Bank One Ballpark (as it was called until September 2005, when a corporate merger rendered the name obsolete) was designed by Ellerbe Becket, a Minneapolis firm specializing in basketball arenas, but that had also designed Atlanta's Turner Field. Though Bank One certainly has its retro elements, it doesn't have the complete throwback feel of parks like Camden Yards, thanks mostly to the absence of a city skyline or other reminders of one's surroundings. Although the downtown location next to the Phoenix Suns' new arena is exhilarating, all views of the city are blocked by drab, 180-foot-high walls. The massive walls were necessary to support the retractable roof—a must thanks to the sweltering summers in Phoenix, where the average high in July is 105°F. The impressive roof, made of 9 million pounds of steel, can open or close in less than five minutes. Even with the roof fully retracted, though, the opening to the sky is small, in a manner reminiscent of Texas Stadium, the home of the Dallas Cowboys. Combined with the high stadium walls, this means that sunlight almost never covers the entire playing field even when the roof is all the way open.

The small roof opening does increase the efficiency of the stadium's high-powered air-conditioning system, however, allowing it to lower the temperature in the stands by 30° in just three hours. At first, the Diamondbacks allowed their starting pitcher for each game to decide whether the roof would stay open or closed. Curt Schilling, one of Arizona's aces from 2000 to 2003, always pitched with the roof closed because he believed home runs came easier with it open. Frequently, though, the team was forced to make concessions

CONOR JACKSON

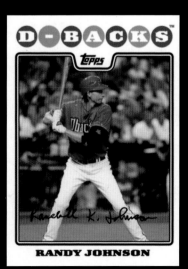

RANDY JOHNSON

ALEX ROMERO

BRANDON WEBB

to fan comfort. During one chilly night in April 1999, the crowd's chant of "Close the roof! Close the roof!" got so loud that the game was stopped so management could do exactly that. Eventually, the decision to play with the roof open or closed was taken away from the pitchers and based strictly on weather reports. Unlike most other retro parks (and very much like the previous era's superstadiums), Bank One Ballpark has a phenomenally steep upper deck and seems cavernous in its dimensions. It often resembles a lifeless echo chamber, particularly when the stands are half-empty and the roof is closed. Still, Arizona fans, at least in the beginning, embraced their first major league park with open arms, affectionately dubbing it "the BOB" after its initials.

Bank One, with a shade-tolerant grass blend, was the first stadium to permanently feature both a roof and a natural playing surface. (The Astrodome had tried this in its debut season, but the grass died, so AstroTurf was installed.) Another unique feature when the park opened was perhaps the most bizarre warning track ever constructed: a normal dirt track followed by a narrow strip of grass and then a second warning track. The dual tracks were incorporated into the field at the behest of the D-backs' first manager, Buck Showalter, who thought they would confuse opposing outfielders. A more standard warning track was installed in 2001 after Showalter was fired. Opposing outfielders, however, likely remained confused about all the balls flying over their heads, as the BOB established itself as the second-best hitter's park in baseball after Denver's Coors Field. At about 1,100 feet above sea level, it has the third-highest elevation in major league history, after Coors and Mile High Stadium.

A more successful field embellishment is the BOB's pitcher's path, a 60-foot, 6-inch strip of dirt leading from home plate to the pitcher's mound. Unseen in baseball for decades, this tradition is a throwback to the deadball era, when ballparks often featured a naturally worn dirt path between home plate and the mound, presumably due to the frequency of catchers visiting the pitcher. The version at Bank One Ballpark, though meticulously groomed, is nonetheless a well-done (and well-received) tip of the cap to baseball's early days.

Even with the quickly moving roof, easy-growing grass, and retro pitcher's path, if Bank One Ballpark has a signature feature, it is probably the swimming pool that rests just beyond the right-centerfield wall. Though many hailed it as a groundbreaking idea, the park was actually the third in the major leagues to feature a swimming area behind the outfield fence, after Philadelphia's Jefferson Street Grounds (1871–90) and Montreal's Parc Jarry (1969–76). The "RideNow Powersports Pool," which accommodates up to thirty-five fans, can be rented out for $6,500 per game. Located 415 feet from home plate, it's close enough for the occasional home run to splash down. In May 1998, the Cubs' Mark Grace—a future Diamondbacks player and broadcaster—became the first batter to launch a homer into the water.

TIMELINE: BANK ONE BALLPARK

November 18, 1997 With their first pick of the expansion draft, the D-backs select Cleveland lefty Brian Anderson. He goes 41-42 with a 4.52 ERA in five seasons with Arizona.

1998

Bank One Ballpark (so named thanks to a thirty-year, $100 million deal) opens on March 31 with a 9-2 loss to the Rockies. It's the first time since the 1977 Mariners that an expansion franchise has had a new ballpark ready for its debut season. The nearly symmetrical park can hold 49,033 patrons; dimensions are 330 feet to left field, 334 to right, 376 to the power alleys, and 407 to center.

1999

Despite unprecedented success for an expansion team—the Diamondbacks win a hundred games in just their second year of existence—attendance decreases by almost 600,000.

September 4, 1998

Lucky Number Seven Arizona is hot, and it's not just the three-digit temperature. The Diamondbacks' 3-1 win over Houston gives them seven consecutive victories, equaling the longest winning streak ever posted by a first-year expansion franchise. In a match-up of Dominican-born right-handers, Arizona's Amaury Telemaco tops the Astros' Jose Lima. The streak will end with a loss to Houston the following night.

Diamondbacks 3, Astros 1

June 25, 1999 Bank One Ballpark witnesses its first no-hitter when St. Louis rookie Jose Jimenez, owner of a 6-7 career record, handcuffs the Diamondbacks 1-0.

2001 Luis Gonzalez enjoys one of the greatest fluke seasons in baseball history when he hits fifty-seven home runs this year—twenty-six more than his previous career high.

2000

The Insight.com Bowl (the college football game formerly known as the Copper Bowl) leaves Tucson and moves to Bank One Ballpark. It will be played here through the year 2006.

May 8, 2001

Twenty Ks, No Victory Randy Johnson becomes the fourth pitcher to strike out at least twenty batters in one game, but the only one to accomplish the feat without winning the contest. Johnson ends the bottom of the ninth by whiffing Cincinnati's Juan Castro for his twentieth punchout, after which he exits with the score tied 1-1. The Big Unit allows just three hits and no walks. Cincinnati scores twice in the top of the eleventh, but the Diamondbacks come roaring back, tying the game on Mark Grace's two-run double and winning it on a bases-loaded walk. Because Johnson technically didn't strike out his twenty hitters in a nine-inning game, he doesn't officially enter the record book with Roger Clemens and Kerry Wood. However, he joins Clemens, Wood, and Tom Cheney of the 1962 Washington Senators as the only pitchers to reach twenty strikeouts in a game of any length.

Diamondbacks 4, Reds 3

RIGHT: In Game 2 of the 2001 World Series, Randy Johnson hurls a pitch during his three-hit, eleven-strikeout shutout of the Yankees. Johnson wins three Series games to share MVP honors with Curt Schilling; that November he'll also win the third of his four consecutive NL Cy Young awards.

August 6, 2004 Chairman and CEO Jerry Colangelo, in charge of the D-backs since their inception, is forced out after disagreements with the team's majority owners.

March 2006 Chase Field hosts three games in the inaugural World Baseball Classic.

October 14, 2001

Missed Squeeze Pays Off The NL Division Series comes down to a decisive Game 5 in which twenty-game winners Curt Schilling and Matt Morris face off in a memorable pitchers' duel. It's tied 1-1 entering the ninth when the Cardinals threaten, and Mark McGwire, playing the final game of his career, endures the ignominy of being pinch hit for by rookie Kerry Robinson. Robinson lays down a sacrifice bunt, but the Cardinals fail to score as Schilling pitches out of the jam. In the bottom of the ninth, Arizona puts the winning run on third and attempts a bunt of its own—a squeeze play. Tony Womack misses the bunt and the baserunner is tagged out, but Womack transforms himself from goat into hero by knocking in the series-winning run later in the at-bat. It's the first postseason series the D-backs have ever won, and they'll win two more later this month on their way to the world championship.

Diamondbacks 2, Cardinals 1

November 4, 2001

Schilling + Johnson = Championship In one of the most exciting baseball games ever played, four legendary pitchers—Roger Clemens, Curt Schilling, Randy Johnson, and Mariano Rivera—take the mound during Game 7 of the World Series, which ends with Arizona winning the championship on Luis Gonzalez's walk-off single. Clemens departs with the score tied 1-1 in the seventh, while Schilling exits after giving up a go-ahead homer to Alfonso Soriano in the eighth. The Diamondbacks refuse to go quietly, however, and Rivera puts the winning run on base in the ninth when he makes an errant throw after fielding a sacrifice bunt. Arizona's Tony Womack smacks a game-tying double and the next batter is hit by a pitch, bringing Arizona's best hitter, Luis Gonzalez, to the plate with the bases loaded. With the Series-winning run on third, the Yankees are forced to play their infield in. This backfires, however, when Gonzalez hits a soft blooper just over the head of shortstop Derek Jeter, allowing Jay Bell to scamper home with the winning run. The Diamondbacks are world champs, and the winning pitcher is Johnson, who hurls 1⅓ innings of scoreless relief just twenty-four hours after making 104 pitches in Game 6. He and Schilling are named co-MVPs, a Series first.

Diamondbacks 3, Yankees 2

LEFT: Curt Schilling fires a pitch during the first inning of one of the greatest baseball games ever played: Game 7 of the 2001 World Series.

BELOW: Arizona ace Brandon Webb faces Milwaukee's Gabe Gross in the third inning on August 22, 2007. Two innings earlier, Gross scored the first run off Webb in forty-two innings, breaking a scoreless streak that ranked twelfth on baseball's all-time list and conjured memories of Orel Hershiser's remarkable fifty-nine-inning string in 1988.

November 9, 2006 The Diamondbacks change their team color scheme, ditching bright purple and turquoise in favor of "Sedona Red" and "Sonoran Sand."

November 14, 2006 Brandon Webb wins his first Cy Young Award, which is also the first won by any Arizona pitcher other than Randy Johnson.

December 18, 2006 Chase Field suffers its first rainout—which occurs during a women's college basketball game. Arizona State is leading Texas Tech 61-45 when it starts to pour.

September 15, 2002

A Pair of Aces Arizona's Curt Schilling joins the 300-strikeout club, making him and Randy Johnson the only pair of teammates ever to whiff that many batters in the same season. Schilling punches out eight Brewers, but gets a no-decision when an error allows Milwaukee to tie the game in the ninth. Arizona eventually wins it on Tony Womack's thirteenth-inning hit. The defending world champion D-backs will go on to clinch their third division title in four years, but will be swept by St. Louis in the first round of the playoffs.

Diamondbacks 6, Brewers 5

2006

Before the 2006 season, the park is renamed Chase Field as a result of Bank One's merger with JPMorgan Chase.

2008

A $14 million high-definition video board, 46 feet tall and 136 feet wide, is installed in center field.

October 3, 2007

Cubs Caught in Arizona's Webb Two of the NL's top pitchers face off in the opening game of the playoffs, and the Diamondbacks emerge with their first postseason victory since Game 7 of the 2001 World Series. The Cubs' Carlos Zambrano and the D-backs' Brandon Webb both turn in strong performances, but Zambrano is forced to exit in the seventh. Carlos Marmol, relieving Zambrano, gives up a go-ahead homer to the first batter he faces, Mark Reynolds. Conor Jackson later brings in an insurance run on a sacrifice fly, giving the Arizona bullpen all it needs to wrap up the victory for Webb. The Diamondbacks will go on to sweep the Cubs, but will themselves be swept by Colorado in the NLCS.

Diamondbacks 3, Cubs 1

BELOW: D-backs reliever Brandon Lyon helps wrap up the victory for his fellow Brandon (Webb) in Game 1 of the 2007 NLDS against the Cubs.

SAFECO FIELD
Seattle, Washington
Mariners (AL) 1999–present

JOSE VIDRO

OPPOSITE: Adrian Beltre, one of the best free-agent signings of the Safeco Field era, faces Anaheim's John Lackey with the bases loaded on May 3, 2005. Beltre will strike out to end the inning, and the Angels will go on to win 5-2. Although there is still much to enjoy about Safeco, including dramatic sunsets and picturesque views from the stands, it is during the 2005 season that Seattle's long honeymoon with Safeco Field will finally come to an end. After three consecutive seasons of drawing more than 35,000 fans per game, attendance will sink to 33,648 in '05, and continue falling in ensuing years. Things could have been worse, though: as of 2008, the Mariners managed to finish in the top half of the AL in attendance during every year of Safeco's existence. At the Mariners' former home, the depressing Kingdome, they managed that feat only three times in twenty-two seasons.

In the warm afterglow of the first playoff series win in Seattle history—a 1995 Division Series triumph over the Yankees—the Washington legislature, brimming with baseball enthusiasm, passed a measure allocating funds for a new Mariners stadium. Voters had rejected such a ballot initiative scarcely a month earlier, but things were different now. After two decades of losing, it was clear the Mariners now meant business, and the team captured the public's affection with such stars as Ken Griffey Jr., Randy Johnson, Edgar Martinez, and even a young Alex Rodriguez. It's no exaggeration to say that the '95 Mariners saved baseball in Seattle, for relocation would have been inevitable without a new stadium. The new park, Safeco Field, was appropriately dubbed "The House That Griffey Built." Although its namesake played there for only half a season before being traded to Cincinnati, another charismatic hero, Ichiro Suzuki, soon took Griffey's place and led the Mariners to the top of the American League in both wins and attendance.

On March 8, 1997, Griffey himself helped break ground for the new park on a site immediately south of the Mariners' then-home, the Kingdome. It was a spectacular location in the heart of the city, just a block from Puget Sound and half a mile from the Bainbridge Island commuter ferry. The Mariners had to pay just $75 million of the stunning $517 million cost, with the rest coming from state lottery funds as well as increases in various taxes. (After voters rejected a .01 percent sales tax increase in the September 1995 ballot initiative, state and county officials secured funding that didn't require voter approval.)

The design created by NBBJ, a local architectural firm, called for the park to have the third retractable roof in baseball history, after Toronto's SkyDome and Phoenix's Bank One Ballpark. Although the baseball season encompasses rainy Seattle's driest months, the roof gives the team and its fans comfort in the knowledge that every scheduled game can take place as planned. The roof contains 11,000 tons of steel—enough to build a fifty-five-story skyscraper—and can be opened or closed in ten to twenty minutes. Like the retractable bleachers in many high school gyms, each section simply folds under the others until they're all piled high atop the right-field stands. The roof doesn't completely enclose the stadium even when shut. Instead it acts as a sort

Seattle Embraces Ballpark Art

Public art at baseball stadiums has come a long way since Bill Veeck hung paintings by local children in the lower concourses of Comiskey Park in the '70s. Coors Field, for example, opened in 1994, sporting a ceramic tile exhibit tracing the historical development of the ball. Rangers Ballpark in Arlington incorporates bas-relief scenes from Texas history on its outside frieze. And, of course, ballparks have long featured statues to commemorate a team's greatest players. No stadium, however, has been as artistically ambitious as Safeco Field, which spent $1.37 million during construction to commission pieces of art to display around its premises.

Much of the artwork, which was created by local talent, draws on the history of baseball in the Northwest. Bill Lawrence of the Pacific Coast League represents centerfielders in one of the nine plaques lining the third base side of the upper concourse that show the positions on the field. And the Mariners' defining moment, when Ken Griffey Jr. slid home to capture the AL West title in 1995, was not only the impetus to build Safeco Field but is the subject of a painted-steel scene just inside the left-field gate.

Outside the gate, a 3,000-pound, 9-foot-tall, bronze baseball mitt with a hole through its center gives fans a place to meet and children something to climb on. Even the parking garages have an artistic element: Mounted on every fourth support column are giant, colorful hands gripping balls, with the name of the pitch underneath. Carved into the rest of the columns are baseball idioms that have found their way into the American vernacular, such as "off base" and "out of left field."

Popular with art critics is Ross Palmer Beecher's *Baseball "Quilts"*—license plates, bottle caps, and other found metal "stitched" together with red wire to form three pieces that line the main concourse on the right-field side. "Celebrating baseball's signs and symbols, they're a glorious montage of myth and memory," *the Seattle Post-Intelligencer* raved, "[they're] among the best things this wonderful artist has ever done."

But perhaps most dazzling is the sculpture just inside the home plate gate. Called *The Tempest,* it's composed of more than a thousand bats molded from clear plastic resin hanging in a giant spiral from the ceiling. Though the bats light up for a nighttime light show, *Seattle Times* art critic Robin Updike warns, "To call it a chandelier would give it a misleading gentility. This sculpture is about power, excitement, and possible danger." The impressive piece is complemented by the floor beneath it, which is a swirl of greens, blues, and whitecaps meant to depict Puget Sound.

Though some of the installations are more successful than others—the 24-foot-long mural called *The Crowd* in the main concourse at center field has been called everything from "boring" to "creepy"—there's no debate that the .5 percent of the construction budget used for the artwork was well spent. In a time when most ballparks have advertisements on any surface a fan might see, Safeco Field's creative surroundings are a welcome change.

of umbrella covering, with wind, rain, and other elements still able to sneak in through the side.

The park—named Safeco Field after the Seattle-based insurance giant agreed to pay $36 million over twenty years—features natural grass, a traditional entrance rotunda, uniquely scaffolded light towers, a hand-operated scoreboard, and modern bullpens beyond the left-field fence. Behind the right-field fence is a kids' clubhouse and playground. In addition, a pair of museums, the Mariners Hall of Fame and the Baseball Museum of the Pacific Northwest, pay homage to the area's baseball past and provide worthwhile additions to the ballpark experience. The best feature of all, though, is the "Art in the Park" project, whereby baseball-themed works of art were commissioned from Northwest artists for a total of $1.37 million. These paintings, murals, and sculptures placed throughout the stadium add a welcome touch of beauty. And if that's not enough, there's the view of Seattle's best-known landmark, the Space Needle, which can best be seen from Lookout Landing, just a short walk from the cheap seats in the upper concourse.

The still-unfinished stadium opened on July 15, 1999, to rave reviews, and the Mariners' attendance,

ABOVE: *The Tempest,* a collaboration between local artists Linda Beaumont, Stuart Keeler, and Michael Machnic, as viewed from directly underneath. The striking sculpture, which greets fans as they enter Safeco's main gate, hangs from the ceiling and is 40 feet wide and 20 feet tall. It also functions as a source of illumination and, at night, the centerpiece of a computer-programmed strobe-light show.

which usually ranked last or next to last during the Kingdome days, shot up to fourth best in the AL. It wasn't until 2001, though, that the team and the stadium reached their zeniths. Although stung by the trades of Griffey and Johnson, and Rodriguez's departure via free agency, the Mariners put together a well-rounded club built around their electrifying new right fielder, Ichiro Suzuki. A seven-time batting champion in the Japanese Pacific League, Ichiro (popularly known known by just his first name) energized Seattle's sizable Japanese-American community and became a national sensation. In 2001 he became only the second rookie ever to win an MVP award, and led the Mariners to a major league record-tying 116 wins. All of a sudden Safeco Field was the place to be in Seattle, and the Mariners led all of baseball with an attendance of more than 3.5 million in both 2001 and 2002. Given that throughout the prior two decades the club had seemed in continual danger of going out of business, the situation demonstrated how dramatically a new stadium filled with exciting players can change a team's fortunes.

June 12, 1999 In one of the Kingdome's final games, Mariners skipper Lou Piniella becomes the fourteenth person to collect 1,000 hits as a player and 1,000 wins as a manager.

December 18, 1999 After playing ten years in Japan, closer Kazuhiro Sasaki signs with the Mariners. He saves thirty-seven games and is named the 2000 AL Rookie of the Year.

1999

Safeco Field, the first major league stadium whose retractable roof lets in outside air through side openings, opens on July 15 with a 3-2 loss to the Padres. Pitchers love the ballpark, mostly because batted balls carry poorly in the moist air, but also because of its sensible dimensions: 331 feet to left field, 390 to left-center, 405 to center, 387 to right-center, and 327 to right.

September 22, 1999

Junior's Farewell Ken Griffey Jr. homers off Kansas City's Jay Witasick for his 398th home run as a Mariner—and almost his last. Unhappy with pitcher-friendly Safeco Field, the twenty-nine-year-old Griffey will officially ask for a trade to his hometown of Cincinnati. During the off-season Seattle's star will be swapped to the Reds for four young players, including Mike Cameron, who will become a key cog in Seattle's 2001 juggernaut. Almost a decade later, Griffey will return to the Mariners receiving a hero's welcome.

Royals 12, Mariners 6

BELOW: Despite having the worst seats in the house, fans in Safeco Field's centerfield bleachers cheer wildly during the first game ever played there on July 15, 1999. With a midseason opening date that couldn't be changed, construction crews barely managed to make the stadium usable by the July 15 deadline, and work continued for another several months afterward. On Opening Night, finishing touches such as TV screens, walkways, and advertising signs had yet to be completed. That hardly mattered to M's fans, though—Safeco topped 40,000 in attendance for thirty-seven of the remaining forty-three home games that year.

December 27, 2001 The Seattle Bowl is played at Safeco for the first time, with Georgia Tech topping Stanford 24-14.

March 30, 2003 One day before the Mariners open the season in Oakland, a stadium-record 54,097 fans pack Safeco Field for WrestleMania XIX.

August 9, 2005 The most heralded pitching prospect in Mariners history, nineteen-year-old Felix Hernandez, tosses eight shutout innings in his Safeco Field debut.

October 6, 2000

The Main Squeeze The first postseason game at Safeco Field ends in exciting fashion as the Mariners sweep Chicago in the AL Division Series. With Seattle leading the favored White Sox two games to none, Mariners starter Aaron Sele holds Chicago to just three hits in 7⅓ innings. The game is tied 1-1 in the bottom of the ninth when John Olerud smacks a line drive that hits Sox pitcher Kelly Wunsch, who then throws wildly to send Olerud to second. Rickey Henderson then pinch-runs for Olerud, takes third on a sacrifice, and scores the series-ending run on a suicide squeeze bunt by Carlos Guillen.

Mariners 2, White Sox 1

October 14, 2000

Mariners Sunk by Rocket Roger Clemens pitches the best game in ALCS history, taking a no-hitter into the seventh inning before finishing with a one-hit shutout and fifteen strikeouts. Clemens' Game 4 win, the first one-hitter ever pitched in an LCS, gives his Yankees a prohibitive three-games-to-one advantage over the Mariners. Seattle's lone hit is a double by Al Martin that skips off the glove of Yankees first sacker Tino Martinez. The Mariners will win Game 5, but New York will finish off the series in Game 6 at Yankee Stadium en route to its third consecutive world championship.

Yankees 5, Mariners 0

2001

While piling up a major league record-tying 116 wins, the Mariners also rack up fifty-nine sellouts, three more than the club had during its entire 22½-year tenure at the Kingdome.

July 10, 2001

Rah-Rah for Ripken Everything comes up roses in Seattle in 2001, even the All-Star Game. Four Mariners—Ichiro Suzuki, Bret Boone, John Olerud, and Edgar Martinez—grace the AL's starting lineup, while Seattle pitchers Freddy Garcia and Kazuhiro Sasaki also get the win and the save, respectively. A couple of former Mariners have a memorable night at Safeco Field as well. Randy Johnson, now with Arizona, is the starting pitcher for the NL, while the Rangers' Alex Rodriguez, voted the starting shortstop, graciously swaps positions with third baseman Cal Ripken so the retiring iron man can play short one last time. Ripken homers, is named All-Star MVP for the second time, and gets an appreciative ovation from the 47,364 fans.

AL 4, NL 1

BELOW: With the roof closed, Safeco Field is nowhere near as pleasant as its open-air iteration—but at least the roof has open sides to allow breezes to blow through. The roof covers a 9-acre area and takes ten to twenty minutes (depending on weather conditions) to open or close. Summertime is by far the driest part of the year in Seattle, but it still rains enough that many home games would be rained out if the roof didn't exist. Due to the height of the roof and walls, the playing field is usually in the shade, even when the roof is open, and a blend of six different kinds of grass is necessary for the turf to grow properly. The grass also requires copious amounts of hot water during late winter and early spring to enable it to grow enough by Opening Day. To accomplish this, a network of plastic tubing rests underneath the playing surface.

October 1, 2004

Ichiro Passes Sisler The amazing Ichiro Suzuki, the first position player to have emigrated from Japan to the major leagues, breaks one of the oldest records in baseball: George Sisler's 1920 mark of 257 hits in a season. Ichiro singles in the first inning to tie the hallowed record, then singles again in the third to break it. Applauding in the stands is the late Sisler's eighty-one-year-old daughter, who shakes hands with Ichiro after the record knock. The Mariners star will finish the season with 262 hits and, at .372, his second batting crown.

Mariners 8, Rangers 3

LEFT: Ichiro—no surname necessary—watches the ball roll into left field for his 257th hit of the season on October 1, 2004. The hit ties George Sisler's eighty-four-year-old MLB record; Ichiro will break the mark his next time up with a single to center.

2007

Seattle's longest existing baseball team, the University of Washington Huskies, plays at Safeco for the first time on May 4. They defeat defending NCAA champion Oregon State in front of 10,421, breaking a twenty-seven-year-old Pac-10 Conference attendance mark.

COMERICA PARK

Detroit, Michigan

Tigers (AL) 2000–present

CURTIS GRANDERSON

Comerica Park's biggest problem was that it had a hard act to follow. Opened in 2000 as the successor to legendary Tiger Stadium, Comerica was one of the best entries in the series of retro ballparks built in Camden Yards' wake. The shadow of its Detroit predecessor proved difficult to escape, however. There had been a particularly vociferous fan movement for the team to remain at Tiger Stadium, and though that battle was lost, the debate raged on. Even as they bought expensive tickets to the plush new ballpark, many Detroiters continued to lament the loss of their old haunt. Not until 2006, when the Tigers fielded their first winning team at Comerica, did the city begin to embrace the new park as its own.

The Tigers had been dreaming of a new, publicly financed stadium for almost a decade, but in 1992, a ballot initiative prohibiting public funding of sports stadiums was approved at the polls by a 63-37 margin. Four years later, however, voters reversed course, passing a measure for a $300 million ballpark to be built with a combination of public and private funds. Funding was also approved for a $430 million football stadium, Ford Field, to be located adjacent to the baseball park. These projects were billed as important milestones in the revitalization of blighted downtown Detroit, which for years had been peppered with boarded-up windows as residents and businesses fled for the suburbs. Other nearby portions of the revitalization effort included an $800 million office complex, forty-seven upscale townhouses, and an MGM Grand casino.

Not everyone was happy about this plan. Tiger Stadium was still phenomenally popular among Detroit residents, even though the team's past few owners had purposely let it fall into decay, figuring that the more decrepit the old park got, the more public demand there would be for a new one. Organizations cropped up urging the public to oppose the new stadium. "It's absurd that we're spending hundreds of millions of dollars on a new ballpark when we can't keep our libraries open regular hours and our kids don't even have safe playgrounds," Frank Rashid, founder of the Tiger Stadium Fan Club, told the *New York Times*. "This city is fixated on shortcuts to revitalization that do nothing but deliver false promises."

PLACIDO POLANCO

JEREMY BONDERMAN

MIGUEL CABRERA

TOP: Comerica Park's carousel, located behind the first base stands, contains thirty hand-painted tigers on which children can ride. The ballpark also has a Ferris wheel behind the third base stands that features baseball-shaped cars.

MIDDLE: A 15-foot-tall snarling tiger greets fans at Comerica Park's main entrance. The ballpark boasts eight other tiger sculptures, all created by New York–based sculptor Michael Keropian. The two atop the giant scoreboard in left field emit growling sounds and light up their eyes whenever a Tiger hits a home run or the team closes out a victory.

BOTTOM: It's not easy to sculpt a cloud of dust, but that's exactly what artists Julie Amrany, Omri Amrany, and Lou Cella managed to do for this statue of Ty Cobb sliding into a base. Cobb, whose fierce style of play fit the Tigers' name better than anyone's, had his "number" retired by the club even though uniform numbers weren't used during his career. His statue is one of six located behind the left-field stands.

False promises or not, the stadium itself turned out to be a gem. The entrance is framed by a distinctive pair of snarling stone tiger statues. In left field a ten-story-high scoreboard, the tallest in baseball, features distinctive old-fashioned grillwork. This helps frame a picture-postcard view of the Detroit skyline beyond center field, and from the correct vantage point one can even spot the city of Windsor, Ontario, across the river. Above the left-field wall are stainless steel statues of all six players whose uniforms have been retired by the Tigers. A giant Ferris wheel stands on the concourse, featuring twelve baseball-shaped cars and offering rides for $2.00 a spin.

Most importantly to ownership, the ballpark was built with 104 luxury boxes, a colossal change from Tiger Stadium's four. These helped the price of an average Tigers ticket skyrocket to $24.83 in 2000, more than double the previous year's cost at Tiger Stadium. Fans proved willing to pay this during the debut season, more out of curiosity than any conviction that the park was an upgrade over the previous one. "There was nothing brought over from the old stadium architecturally," Tigers reliever Todd Jones lamented. "Some of the fans [at Tiger Stadium] were closer to home plate than the shortstop. In a brand-new ballpark, you have to put in the soul."

Jones and his fellow pitchers, though, loved the ballpark's layout. Instead of the massive outfield overhangs, which had caused cheap homers aplenty at Tiger, Comerica had a vast outfield and comparatively distant fences. In an era when every new ballpark sought to boost offense by pulling the fences in a little closer than the last, Comerica was an anomaly. The centerfield fence was a healthy 420 feet away, and the left-center power alley was an astonishing 395, making the park a nightmare for right-handed sluggers. During its first three seasons, Comerica rivaled Seattle's Safeco Field for the title of best pitcher's park in the league, reducing runs by about 10 percent from the average ballpark. In particular, the park frustrated two-time AL MVP Juan Gonzalez, whose home run total dropped from thirty-nine to twenty-two after signing with the Tigers in 2000. Gonzalez hated Comerica so much that he refused to re-sign with Detroit after the season. "I'd want to go to a place where it's good for a right-handed power hitter," he said. "It's incredible—one of the biggest parks in baseball. You need to hit it so hard."

Fearful that his park would get a bad name among power hitters, Tigers owner Mike Ilitch decided to abandon its refreshing dimensions. Before the 2003 season the Tigers jumped on the short-fences bandwagon, pulling in the left-centerfield wall by 25 feet. The players Detroit employed that year, though, proved unable to hit the ball out of any park, regardless of size. The woeful 2003 Tigers lost 119 games, just one shy of the major league record. Only two Detroit hitters managed more than twenty home runs, while the fly ball pitching staff fell victim to the shorter fences, giving up an astonishing 195 homers. Although the Tigers had hoped Comerica would attract fans regardless of the team's quality of play, this proved not to be the case. Even a glittering new baseball palace wouldn't attract fans to watch an awful team. Attendance dipped to 1.4 million, a figure the Tigers had topped on a nearly annual basis at Tiger Stadium.

The club responded to these woes by pouring all its resources into its farm system. Aided by a few judicious free-agent signings, the Tigers rebounded remarkably quickly. Just three years after the embarrassing 119-loss display, the Tigers cruised to the 2006 AL pennant with 95 victories. The fans returned, too, packing the stands to the tune of 2.6 million in 2006 and 3 million, a franchise record, in '07. Even weather proved no obstacle. Game 3 of the 2005 ALCS was played in intermittent snow with 24 mph winds, but a sellout crowd of more than 41,000 showed up sporting parkas, winter gloves, and thermoses full of coffee and hot chocolate. "I found out that it's a beautiful park—when it's full," team owner Ilitch said. "What a difference."

BELOW, INSET: Comerica Park's construction crews are hard at work on September 23, 1999, 6½ months before the new park's opening and 4 days before the final game at historic Tiger Stadium. Around the site are the Central United Methodist Church, built in 1867; Grand Circus Park, across the street from the church; and the thirty-five-story David Broderick Tower, the tall Beaux Arts building at the right edge of the photo. Visible behind the Comerica construction site is the cleared lot on which the Detroit Lions' Ford Field will be built between 1999 and 2002.

CAP: 2000.

2003 Tiger Todd Jones wins the Rolaids Relief Man award after making forty-two saves out of forty-six save situations.

2000

The complaints from hitters are many when Comerica opens on April 11 with pitcher-friendly dimensions of 345 feet to left field, 395 to left-center, 420 to center, 365 to right-center, and 330 to right. Only 137 homers are hit here this year, the fewest in the majors by far, but the Tigers' ERA will drop from 5.17 to 4.71 and the team's win total will increase by ten.

BOTTOM: An upper-deck seat at Comerica Park provides a fine view of the city's skyline, including the six-story Detroit Athletic Club building behind dead-center field. Note the pitcher's path between home plate and the mound. Such paths were common in the very early days of baseball, when catchers almost always caught pitches on the bounce; clearing the area of grass resulted in truer caroms. Until Comerica and Bank One Ballpark, however, the paths had been absent from the majors for the better part of a century. Another interesting touch at Comerica is the dirt cutout around the batter's box, which is shaped like a gigantic home plate.

October 7, 2006

2003

Unable to withstand the complaining, team owner Mike Ilitch orders the distance in left-center shortened by 25 feet to 370, rendering the previously in-play centerfield flagpole out of play.

2005

The bullpens are moved from right field to left field, taking advantage of the empty space created when the fence was moved inward two years earlier. The newly vacated space in right field is filled with 950 seats, raising capacity to 41,070.

Worst to First The Tigers win their first post-season series since 1984 by knocking off the heavily favored Yankees in Game 4 of the Division Series. Magglio Ordonez and Craig Monroe hit third-inning homers to chase New York starter Jaret Wright, while Tigers hurler Jeremy Bonderman lasts until the ninth. Detroit wins on the strength of its pitching, which holds four vaunted Yankees (Alex Rodriguez, Gary Sheffield, Jason Giambi, and Robinson Cano) to batting averages under .200. Worst of all is Rodriguez, whose .071 playoff average forces manager Joe Torre to drop him to eighth in the batting order. Tigers reliever Jamie Walker, a veteran of the 119-loss club of three years earlier, gets the final out to touch off a raucous celebration during which the players spray anyone they can find with champagne.

Tigers 8, Yankees 3

Justin Verlander hurls a pitch in 2006, the year he was named AL Rookie of the Year.

September 28, 2003

Whew! It's nothing to write home about, but the Tigers stay out of the history books by holding off the Minnesota Twins, 9-4. Detroit's season-ending two-game winning streak enables the Tigers to avoid the modern major league record for most losses in one season. They still set the AL mark with 119 defeats, but they fall short of the 1962 Mets' record of 120. (The overall record holder is a nineteenth-century team, the Cleveland Spiders, who lost 134 games in 1899 before going out of business.) Mike Maroth, the major leagues' first twenty-game loser since 1980, picks up the final win for the 43-119 Tigers.

Tigers 9, Twins 4

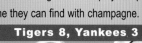

October 21, 2006 Comerica hosts its first World Series game, during which St. Louis destroys the Tigers 7-2 as rookie Justin Verlander gives up all seven runs and commits a key error.

May 25, 2007 Legendary broadcaster Ernie Harwell calls the final game of his illustrious career, temporarily coming out of retirement to fill in for the Tigers' regular analyst.

April 13, 2009 Detroit favorite Mark "The Bird" Fidrych dies tragically at the age of fifty-four when he is crushed by a truck he was working on at his Massachusetts farm.

October 14, 2006

Happy Birthday, Magglio The Tigers clinch their first pennant in twenty-two years in dramatic fashion as Magglio Ordoñez hits a three-run walk-off homer in the bottom of the ninth. Oakland, trailing in the ALCS three games to none, scores three early runs off Jeremy Bonderman in Game 4, but Ordoñez ties things with a sixth-inning homer. It's still tied 3-3 with two outs in the ninth when the Tigers scratch out two singles. Ordoñez then launches a pitch from A's closer Huston Street deep into the night, sending the crowd into a frenzy. It's just the fourth pennant-winning walk-off homer in baseball history, after Bobby Thomson, Chris Chambliss, and Aaron Boone. Ordoñez dedicates the blast to his son, Magglio Jr., who's celebrating his eleventh birthday.

Tigers 6, A's 3

BELOW: Magglio Ordoñez's takes his pennant-winning swing in Game 4 of the 2006 ALCS.

2007

High-tech improvements include a new video board on the outfield wall, 900 feet of animated fascia signage, and an additional matrix display on the left-field scoreboard.

June 12, 2007

Jinx This Justin Verlander, the reigning AL Rookie of the Year, knocks the notion of a sophomore jinx on its ear when he no-hits the Brewers. It's the first no-hitter ever at Comerica Park, the first in Verlander's career, and the first by a Tigers pitcher since Jack Morris in 1984. The young flamethrower shows no signs of fatigue, either, as his fastball reaches its fastest speeds of the game (up to 102 mph) in the ninth inning. Verlander, who's usually wild, walks four batters, but also strikes out a career-high twelve.

Tigers 4, Brewers 0

BELOW, INSET: Dontrelle Willis hurls a pitch at Comerica Park in the first game of his Tigers career on April 5, 2008.

Beginning with Jacobs Field in 1994, architects of retro ballparks would often design ornate light towers as a way of putting their unique stamp on a venue. Comerica Park's triple towers connected by crossed steel beams are among the game's most distinctive. Also note the intricate steel pattern used to support the floodlights on top of the left-field scoreboard.

PACIFIC BELL PARK

San Francisco, California

Giants (NL) 2000–present

SBC Park 2004–2005, AT&T Park 2006–present

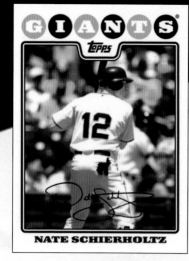

NATE SCHIERHOLTZ

OPPOSITE: Pacific Bell Park in 2005, one of the two seasons in which it was called SBC Park. Built in 2000 at a cost of $357 million, the stadium was billed as the first since Dodger Stadium to be completely financed with private funds (though that point is arguable, since Dodgers owner Walter O'Malley got considerable taxpayer assistance via a sweetheart land deal). Indeed, the city's only contribution was $15 million in tax increment financing and a relatively low $80 million in infrastructure improvements.

Howling winds and freezing weather made San Francisco's Candlestick Park one of the most dreaded venues in Major League Baseball. But in 2000, the Giants reversed course by opening spectacular Pacific Bell Park. The quirky stadium offers all the amenities fans have come to expect in a modern park, plus unique touches that make it San Franciso's own. Whether you're enjoying the game from the stands or on a boat in the nearby cove, the picturesque stadium is an appealing addition to the City by the Bay—an instant classic of the retro ballpark era.

Without a doubt, the best thing about Pacific Bell Park is its idyllic location. Situated in the South Beach section of the city, the stadium sits on San Francisco Bay's western shore at the edge of a cove that was named China Basin for the Chinese clipper ships that used to dock there in the 1860s. For years, the basin had been a warehouse district where one might encounter the wafting smells of roasting coffee or steamed crabs. Now it contains a festive public promenade, built on the narrow strip of land that separates the water from Pac Bell's right-field wall, which features elegant arched windows that non-paying fans can peek through to see the game. When the stadium opened, China Basin was renamed McCovey Cove, after Willie McCovey, who at the time was San Francisco's all-time home run leader. A statue of the famous hitter stands next to his cove, and complements a statue of Willie Mays that graces "Willie Mays Gate," the ballpark's main entrance. With a dock conveniently located about 100 yards from the center-field fence, boaters often loiter in McCovey Cove in hopes of retrieving a home run ball from the water with a fishing net.

If you're not coming by boat or ferry, there are many other transportation options. The park is also reachable by car, bus, streetcar, and the BART subway system. Moreover, it is the first stadium to feature a valet service for bicycles. Fittingly for the home park of Silicon Valley, Pac Bell is also the first park to have offered wireless internet access in the stands. Other features include a miniature baseball field that serves as a kids' play area and a giant sculpture of a 1927-model glove—billed as the largest baseball glove in the world—that stands in front of the play area and behind left field. In right-center, a real San Francisco cable car blows a foghorn whenever a Giants player homers.

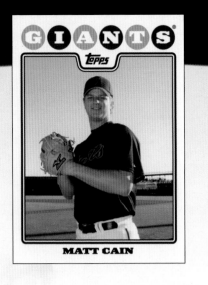

MATT CAIN

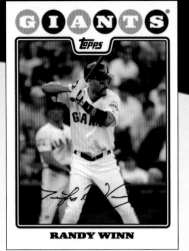

RANDY WINN

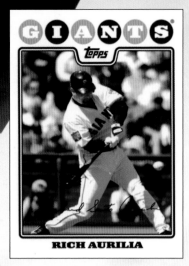

RICH AURILIA

In order to avoid the disastrous gusts off the bay that had made Candlestick Park so unpleasant, the team commissioned a comprehensive study of wind patterns before their new home was built to create just the right layout. As a result, the field faces directly east instead of northeast as Candlestick had, decreasing the wind inside to almost nothing. Only the top rows are greatly affected by gusts, and even those are protected by wind screens lining the top of the grandstand. The subtle rotation of the field deprives fans of the best views of the city skyline, but they can instead take in the panorama of San Francisco Bay, with Oakland and the Berkeley hills visible in the distance.

Upon its opening, Pacific Bell Park's history quickly became intertwined with the exploits of Barry Bonds, the controversial slugger who broke baseball's single-season and career home-run records at the park. It was Bonds who hit the first Giants homer there on Opening Day 2000, and less than a month later became the first player to homer into San Francisco Bay. Although Pac Bell has proved to be one of the most extreme pitcher's parks in baseball, and one that is especially tough on left-handed hitters like Bonds, he nonetheless continued to put up astonishing hitting numbers until he left the team in 2007.

Bonds and the rest of the Giants almost didn't see their beautiful palace by the bay get constructed. In fact, there was a time when it seemed that the San Francisco Giants would cease to exist altogether. Between 1987 and 1992, voters rejected a series of proposals for public financing of a new ballpark. Owner Bob Lurie threatened to move the team elsewhere, and in 1992 he actually agreed to sell to a group of investors who planned to move the team to St. Petersburg, Florida. Fortunately for Giants fans, though, grocery store magnate Peter Magowan swooped in at the last moment and bought the team, keeping them in San Francisco. Moreover, Magowan announced that despite the rejections at the ballot box, the Giants would in fact build a new stadium—with private funds. The Giants agreed to lease land from the Port of San Francisco and set about building their dream home.

The only negative element of the Giants' gorgeous park is its ever-changing name, which has fallen victim to corporate takeovers and rebranding. Pacific Bell paid $50 million for twenty-four years' worth of naming rights, but when the telephone utility's parent company renamed itself, the stadium was changed to SBC Park in 2004. Twenty-two months later, a merger resulted in SBC being swallowed by AT&T, and the park's name changed again to AT&T Park. It's now known mostly by its original name, Pacific Bell, although frustrated San Franciscans have come up with a number of derisive and popular nicknames like "Phone Company Park." No matter what you call it, though, Magowan and his partners succeeded in building a nearly perfect ballpark, a retro stadium that also looks toward the future.

2000 Second baseman Jeff Kent is named NL MVP, and Dusty Baker wins his third NL Manager of the Year award. The Giants won't make it to the World Series, however, as the Mets conquer them in the NLDS.

October 5, 2001 Barry Bonds beats Mark McGuire's three-year-old home-run record by hitting his seventy-third homer during a game against the Dodgers at Pacific Bell Park. He'll go on to hit two more before the season ends.

2003 Under new manager Felipe Alou, the Giants lead their division through the entire season, snagging the NL West title with 100 wins. The wild card Marlins, however, will win the NLDS.

TIMELINE: PACIFIC BELL PARK

2000

Pacific Bell Park opens on March 31 with an exhibition game against Milwaukee. It's the most pitcher-friendly park in baseball, with a deep outfield, moist air, and moderate winds that help knock down fly balls. With dimensions partly dictated by the presence of San Francisco Bay behind the right-field wall, the distances are 335 feet to left field, 364 to left-center, 404 to center, 420 to right-center, and 307 to right. Strangely, the bullpens are located on the playing field in foul territory, exposing the pitchers to line drives.

April 11, 2000

Excellent Elster In an occurrence emblematic of one of baseball's greatest rivalries, the Dodgers spoil the Giants' first game at their brand-new stadium. Adding insult to injury, the culprit is a journeyman shortstop with just seventy-four career home runs, and who has been retired from baseball for more than a year. Kevin Elster, playing in his fifth game since returning to the sport, knocks an unbelievable three homers, leading LA to a narrow victory. The hated Dodgers will go on to sweep the opening series. San Francisco won't get its first victory at Pac Bell until April 29, but will win the NL West nonetheless.

Dodgers 6, Giants 5

2001

Pac Bell fails to sell out for the first time in ninety-one games since its opening. Attendance for the Tuesday, April 24, game against Cincinnati is 40,723—336 short of capacity.

2002

Though expressly built for baseball, Pac Bell hosts the San Francisco Bowl on New Year's Eve, with Virginia Tech topping Air Force 20-13. It will become an annual game, later renamed the Emerald Bowl.

RIGHT: Shortstop Rich Aurilia makes a play during the Giants' sixteenth World Series appearance, the 2002 championship against the Anaheim Angels.

October 14, 2002

Rally Time The Giants win their first pennant in thirteen years when they stage an unlikely rally with two outs in the bottom of the ninth. NLCS Game 5 is a scoreless pitcher's duel until the seventh, when Fernando Vina's sacrifice fly gives St. Louis the lead. Barry Bonds responds with an eighth-inning sac fly of his own to tie the score. The game appears headed for extra innings, but the Giants, down to their last out, get three consecutive singles, including the game-winner by Kenny Lofton. Benito Santiago, the Giants' thirty-seven-year-old catcher, is named MVP after hitting .300 in the series.

Giants 2, Cardinals 1

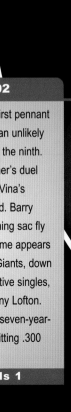

Dec. 4, 2003 Barry Bonds testifies in front of a grand jury that he used substances given to him by indicted trainer Greg Anderson, but he did not know that they were steroids and they had no impact on his game.

2004

The name is changed to SBC Park on January 1. Outfield distances are adjusted slightly to 399 feet to center, 421 to right-center, and 309 to right.

October 23, 2002

Rally Time San Francisco gets its first home game World Series win since 1962 thanks to third baseman David Bell, who singles in the go-ahead run in the eighth inning. The Giants, who had been swept in their last Fall Classic appearance in 1989, tie up the Series by winning Game 4. They initially fall behind 3-0, but catch a break in the fifth when Kirk Rueter's high chopper takes a bad hop and Kenny Lofton's bunt hugs the line. Rich Aurilia singles in a run, Jeff Kent's sacrifice fly plates another, and following an intentional walk to Barry Bonds (one of thirteen in the Series), Benito Santiago singles in the tying run. Bell provides the go-ahead tally in the eighth, and Robb Nen saves it in the ninth. The Giants will win Game 5 also, by a staggering 16-4 score, but their luck will run out when the Series returns to Anaheim.

Giants 4, Angels 3

ABOVE, INSET: After crossing the plate in the seventh inning of Game 5 of the 2002 World Series, JT Snow scoops up overzealous three-year-old batboy Darren Baker. Baker, son of Giants manager Dusty Baker, had run onto the field to fetch Kenny Lofton's bat, oblivious to David Bell quickly approaching down the third baseline. "I saw a little flash, and I knew it was him," Snow told *USA Today*. "I have a 4½-year-old, so I know how to reach them when they're trying to get away. I grabbed him by the neck of his jacket and carried him away. His eyes were huge. I don't think he knew what was going on." The near collision led MLB to adopt a minimum age requirement of fourteen for batboys.

BACKGROUND: Fans pack Pac Bell Park on a beautiful day in 2004. On the left-field grandstand the retired numbers of Bill Terry (3), Mel Ott (4), Carl Hubbell (11), Willie Mays (24), Juan Marichal (27), Orlando Cepeda (30), and Willie McCovey (44) can be seen. In 2005, pitcher Gaylord Perry's number (36) will also be retired.

2006

Telecommunications honchos continue to play musical chairs with the ballpark name. After another merger, the name is changed to AT&T Park on March 1, although few fans will call it by the official name. Also, the Giants unveil a replica of the famed Eddie Grant monument that formerly graced the Polo Grounds, placing it near an elevator in left field.

July 10, 2007

Pujols Rests The AL continues its dominance of the Midsummer Classic, winning for the fifth straight instance, this time on the strength of the first inside-the-park home run in All-Star history. With his AL club trailing 1-0 in the fifth, Ichiro Suzuki drives a ball high off the right-field wall that caroms far away from Ken Griffey Jr., enabling Ichiro to touch all four bases with ease. He leaves the game after his memorable dash, but is still named All-Star MVP. AL catcher Victor Martinez adds insurance with a two-run homer in the eighth, which turns out to be crucial. The NL stages a furious rally in the ninth, but falls short when manager Tony LaRussa, instead of sending up Albert Pujols to pinch-hit with the bases loaded, allows Aaron Rowand to make the final out.

AL 5, NL 4

2008

After years of turning Pac Bell into a shrine to Barry Bonds, with banners, murals, and home run countdown displays, the Giants play their first season here without him. With Bonds under indictment for perjury, almost all vestiges of his presence are painstakingly removed.

August 7, 2007

Seven Fifty-Six Barry Bonds ends months of anticipation—but not the controversy, which is only beginning—by hitting his 756th home run to break the record set by Hank Aaron in 1974. The historic gopher ball is served up by Washington's Mike Bacsik and caught by Matt Murphy, a fan visiting from New York. Commissioner Bud Selig, after much deliberation, is on hand for the game, but Aaron is not. He sends his videotaped congratulations instead. The national baseball press, which has vilified the notoriously media-unfriendly Bonds since the beginning of his career, gleefully leads the charge in attacking the legitimacy of his record. Bonds is singled out with a disturbing zealousness as the root of baseball's steroids problem, while other accused users, such as Roger Clemens and Mark McGwire, are accorded the benefit of the doubt. Bonds will seek to continue his baseball career in 2008, but all thirty teams—though many of them employ admitted steroid users—will refuse to sign him.

Nationals 8, Giants 6

LEFT: Sensational slugger Barry Bonds points to a sign in left field on May 28, 2006, after having hit his 715th home run—thereby surpassing Babe Ruth's record—in the previous inning. The ball flew an estimated 445 feet.

RIGHT: Seven-time MVP Barry Bonds goes up to bat for the last time as a San Francisco Giants player on September 26, 2007. Even as baseball's steroid scandal made Bonds an object of scorn and the recipient of boos wherever he went, he continued to be greeted by nothing but enthusiastic cheers from his home fans. Of the sixty homers that players crushed into San Francisco Bay at Pac Bell Park between 2000 and 2007, Bonds hit a remarkable thirty-five.

PNC PARK

Pittsburgh, Pennsylvania

Pirates (NL) 2001–present

TOM GORZELANNY

OPPOSITE: PNC Park hosts its first All-Star Game on July 11, 2006. Although the Allegheny River (foreground) is 443 feet away from home plate and has only been reached on the fly once (by Houston's Daryle Ward on July 6, 2002), five giant baseballs have floated in the river to rally boaters hoping to catch a home run ball. The Sixth Street Bridge, built in 1928 and renamed the Roberto Clemente Bridge in 1999, is closed to auto-mobiles on game days so pedestrians can get to the game. Alternatively, fans can park across the river and arrive at the game by water taxi.

The Pittsburgh Pirates enjoyed great on-field success during their tenure at Three Rivers Stadium, but the cookie-cutter concrete bowl always left much to be desired. In 2001 they finally escaped, moving into a natural-grass, baseball-only structure on the north bank of the Allegheny River. PNC Park is everything a baseball stadium could hope to be. With inspired architecture, tremendous sight lines, a breathtaking city view, and an invigorating neighborhood around it, PNC became an immediate contender for the title of best baseball park ever built. Unfortunately, this gorgeous new stadium debuted amid a seemingly endless string of losing seasons for the Pirates, prompting the satirical newspaper the *Onion* to run an article poking fun at the usual new-ballpark rhetoric: "PNC Park Threatens to Leave Pittsburgh Unless Better Team Is Built."

Real newspapers had something to say, too. "Those involved in cutting the deal to finance PNC Park," wrote the *Pittsburgh Post-Gazette*'s Robert Dvorchak, "went on a wild ride. Running counter to much of the public's senti-ment, they climbed, hurtled, dipped, careened, nearly derailed, and zoomed like they were in a roller coaster car." Citizens in the eleven-county area surrounding Pittsburgh voted down a publicly funded park in 1997, but as in so many other locales where voters nixed new ballparks, local politicians created a funding plan that sidestepped voter approval. With money coming from the county, state, PNC Bank (who purchased the naming rights for $30 million), and the Pirates themselves, a deal was finally reached and ground was broken on April 7, 1999. Twenty-three labor unions joined forces to build the park, including scuba divers, who built a sea wall to protect the park from flooding by the nearby river. The park was completed in just twenty-four months, reportedly the fastest construction time for any ballpark in the modern era.

By 2001, the retro parks that had so magnificently replaced the cookie-cutter stadiums were in danger of becoming cookie cutters themselves. Eight of the ten ballparks built after Camden Yards, for example, featured red-brick exteriors. PNC bucked this trend by using large, limestone slabs and buff-colored artificial stone with terra-cotta ornamentation. The green steel roof was designed to evoke Forbes Field, and statues of Pirates legends Honus Wagner and Roberto Clemente were salvaged from

MATT CAPPS

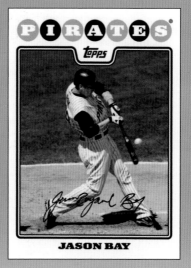

JASON BAY

FREDDY SANCHEZ

Three Rivers Stadium and placed outside the entrance. (Exposition Park, where Wagner played his glory days with the Pirates a century earlier, had been located on virtually the same site as PNC.)

The Steel City's ballpark appropriately contains artfully exposed steel beams along with detailed latticework throughout. An intricate steel frieze, similar to the copper one torn down at Yankee Stadium in 1974, rings the top of the grandstand. The beams and the seats are navy blue, another throwback to Forbes Field. Behind the left-field foul pole, a decorative canopy and walkway rises high in the air, giving fans who choose to leave their seats a unique perspective on the action. Other popular features include a brew pub in left field and a party deck overlooking the river behind the centerfield fence. In left field, the fence is only 6 feet high, making it the shortest in baseball except for Dodger Stadium, and allowing fleet-footed outfielders to leap into the stands to rob home runs. In right field, meanwhile, the 21-foot wall contains a hand-operated scoreboard that gives incredibly detailed out-of-town scores. Behind that, the Allegheny River flows just 443 feet from home plate, reachable by a long blast from a left-handed slugger. The Allegheny and the magnificent 442-foot span of the Roberto Clemente Bridge (renamed from the Sixth Street Bridge in 1999 and painted Pirates yellow) form a dazzling centerfield vista that can be seen from the grandstand.

For all its magnificence, the best thing about PNC may be its intimacy and outstanding views of the playing field. The park is tiny! It is the first major league stadium to have only two decks since Milwaukee's County Stadium debuted in 1953, and there's nothing close to a bad seat in the house—the upper deck's highest seats hover only 88 feet above the playing field. PNC is the second-smallest park in the major leagues, behind only ancient Fenway Park, and with newly added seats increasing Fenway's capacity to upwards of 39,000, PNC has the smallest number of seats at just over 38,000.

BELOW: Pirates righty Ian Snell pitches at PNC Park in 2001, when poor run support relegates him to a 9-12 record despite a fine 3.76 ERA.

August 6, 2003 PNC hosts its first rock concert when Bruce Springsteen comes to town.

2001

PNC Park opens on April 9 and is immediately hailed as one of the finest parks in the major leagues. It's a cozy ballpark, with a capacity of just 38,496 and distances of 325 feet to left field, 389 to left-center, 399 to center, 375 to right-center, and 320 to right. The deepest part of the park is the notch in left-center field where the bullpens meet the outfield wall, which stands 410 feet from home plate. The right-field wall is 21 feet high, a tribute to the uniform number worn by legendary right fielder Roberto Clemente.

April 9, 2001

Rude Houseguests The Reds, who spoiled the opening of Three Rivers Stadium in 1970, ruin the first game at PNC Park also. The Reds' Sean Casey, who spent his formative years in the Pittsburgh area, gets the park's first hit, a two-run homer off the Pirates' Todd Ritchie. Cincinnati blasts off from there, scoring six more runs off the beleaguered Pirates pitching staff. The crowd of 36,954 goes home disappointed in their team, but enthused about their gorgeous new ballpark. It will prove to be a long year, though, as the Pirates will lose 100 games for the first time since 1985. They'll get revenge in 2003, when they blast the Reds 10-1 in the debut game at Cincinnati's new park.

Reds 8, Pirates 2

OPPOSITE: The Pirates and Diamondbacks face off in a Sunday afternoon game on June 8, 2008. For years, the enclosed upper deck at Three Rivers Stadium obstructed Pirates fans' views of downtown Pittsburgh just across the river. That changed in 2001, when Pittsburgh debuted the HOK-designed gem that is arguably the finest example of a retro ballpark. With a capacity of 38,496 and its highest upper-deck seat located just 88 feet above the playing field, PNC Park is one of the coziest parks in the majors. Budgeted at $262 million—$14 million of it paid by the team—PNC Park almost never came to pass; it won approval from Allegheny County commissioners by just a single vote.

Though Pittsburghers were primed to fall in love with their spectacular new ballpark, the Pirates tried their best to make it difficult. The club lost 100 games in PNC's inaugural season of 2001, but still drew a franchise record 2.5 million fans. In the following years the stadium saw 1.5 million fans or more annually, as many or more than they'd drawn during their glory days at much larger Three Rivers Stadium. It was clear that the fans were coming for the beautiful park and not the baseball team, as the Pirates posted records well under .500 in each of PNC's first seven seasons. And who could blame them? In a 2003 ballpark review, ESPN.com rated PNC ahead of Pacific Bell Park and Camden Yards as the best stadium in baseball, even comparing it to a nearby Frank Lloyd Wright masterwork. "Fallingwater is regarded as the perfect blend of art, architecture and environment—or at least it was until PNC Park opened," ESPN's Jim Callis wrote. "Pittsburgh hasn't seen anything this beautiful since Clemente unleashed throws from right field."

May 7, 2005 A disaster drill, complete with mock explosions and 5,000 volunteer participants, is held at PNC Park to test the preparedness of Western Pennsylvania's emergency services.

2007 PNC Park becomes completely smoke-free when the Pittsburgh city council passes an ordinance banning smoking in public places.

June 26, 2001

Who Says You Can't Steal First? First-year Pirates manager Lloyd McClendon, whose team is off to a dreadful 26-47 start, blows his top in a memorable way. With the Pirates and Brewers tied in the eighth inning, Pittsburgh's Jason Kendall is called out on a close play at first base. It's the second controversial call of the evening by umpire Rick Reed, who ejects McClendon for arguing. The enraged skipper throws his hat on the ground, then pulls first base out of its anchoring and walks off the field with it, eventually heaving the base into the clubhouse tunnel. "He wasn't seeing the calls at first base, so I figured I might as well take it with me," McClendon says afterward. The game resumes after the grounds crew installs a new base, and Pittsburgh rallies to win in the twelfth inning.

Pirates 7, Brewers 6

2002

Despite having lost 100 games in their debut season at PNC, the Pirates raise ticket prices. They win eleven more games in 2002 but draw almost 700,000 fewer fans.

July 6, 2002

A Houston Rocket Houston's Daryle Ward hits a towering grand slam into the Allegheny River, becoming the first hitter to reach the river on the fly. Ward's blast off the Pirates' Kip Wells also blows the game open, doubling the Astros' lead from 4-0 to 8-0. It's the last pitch the beleaguered Wells throws in the game. Five more balls will splash into the river during the 2006 All-Star Home Run Derby.

Astros 10, Pirates 2

July 11, 2006

Trevor Is Terrible Padres closer Trevor Hoffman, who later in the season will break baseball's career saves record, blows the All-Star Game (the first held at PNC) in dramatic fashion. Hoffman and his NL teammates lead 2-1 in the bottom of the ninth, and with two outs and two strikes on the AL's Michael Young, Hoffman needs just one more strike to seal the victory. But Young rips a triple that drives home both the tying and go-ahead runs, tagging Hoffman with the loss. In the bottom of the inning Mariano Rivera slams the door on the NL, with game MVP Young appropriately catching the final out.

AL 3, NL 2

2003

A comprehensive review of all thirty ballparks by ESPN.com ranks PNC as baseball's best venue. (San Francisco and Baltimore finish second and third, respectively.) A year later, a *Reader's Digest* poll of players and sportswriters will also rank PNC number one.

2008

Minor renovations add new high-end restaurants, including an Outback Steakhouse under the left-field scoreboard and a Hall of Fame Club with outdoor patio seating. The Pirates also begin "greening" PNC Park by stepping up recycling efforts, reducing the use of non-biodegradable packaging at concession stands, and adjusting the use of lights to maximize energy efficiency.

MINUTE MAID PARK

Houston, Texas

Astros (NL) 2000–present

Enron Field 2000–2001, Astros Field 2002

In 1996, Houston's NFL team, the Oilers, announced they were leaving the Astrodome for Tennessee. Wanting to prevent a similar fate for their MLB team, voters approved funding for a new, $250 million, baseball-only stadium for the Astros. Like other venues built in the retro ballpark era, the new stadium was marked by both throwback architecture and ultramodern luxuries catering to the deep-pocketed fan. Despite going by three different names in its first three seasons, the park quickly became a favorite of fans and a centerpiece in the revitalization of downtown Houston.

From the beginning, the stadium project was deeply intertwined with the soon-to-be-disgraced Enron Corporation, the political Bush family, and the Halliburton Corporation, of which future vice president Dick Cheney was CEO. In 1997, the contract to construct the new stadium was awarded to Brown & Root, a Halliburton subsidiary. By using partially non-union labor, Halliburton was able to finish the project on time and $2 million under budget, and the appreciative Astros placed a plaque with Cheney's photograph outside the stadium's entrance gate.

With taxpayers covering $180 million of the tab, Astros owner Drayton McLane appeared to actually make a profit on the stadium when he sold its naming rights to Enron, the Houston-based energy conglomerate, for $100 million over thirty years. In addition, Enron CEO Kenneth Lay led a private partnership that contributed another $34.7 million to McLane's costs. Lay was rewarded with the opportunity to throw the ceremonial opening pitch at the stadium's first game. By the time Enron Field opened in 2000, Lay's friend, Texas Governor George W. Bush, was running for president with Cheney as his running mate. At one game, Lay orchestrated a Bush campaign stop at the ballpark, where Bush's father, the former president, held season tickets in a prominent location behind home plate.

In 2001, however, Enron imploded amid a scandal in which the company's executives used accounting trickery to line their own pockets; the resulting bankruptcy robbed thousands of Americans of their pensions, which had invested heavily in now worthless Enron stock. With the prison-bound Lay being one of the most hated men in America and the Enron brand an embarrassment, the Astros asked the corporation to remove its name from the stadium. Enron refused, however, claiming that it had kept up-to-date on its annual

payments to the Astros and therefore had the right to keep its moniker on the park. In lieu of going to court, the Astros reached an agreement whereby they paid Enron $2.1 million for the right to sell the stadium name to somebody else. The park was then known simply as Astros Field for a little more than three months until June 2002, when the Coca-Cola Company agreed to pay $170 million over twenty-eight years to name the stadium Minute Maid Park after one of its subsidiaries. Fans soon began calling it "The Juice Box."

The Enron controversy tended to overshadow the ballpark itself, which received generally favorable reviews. The design, by leading stadium architecture firm HOK, enabled the park to encompass historic Union Station, a classical-revival train station built in 1911, which sits behind the left-field wall. The station entrance was turned into the ballpark's main entry gate, and as a tribute to the site's railroad heritage, a locomotive runs on tracks behind the left-field wall, tooting its horn whenever an Astro hits a home run.

The park's most controversial feature, however, is a large embankment—dubbed Tal's Hill—at the base of the centerfield fence. It's reputed to have been the brainchild of longtime Astros General Manager Tal Smith, although Smith denied this, claiming that the architects designed it and merely named it after him. Whatever its origin, the hill is a throwback to Cincinnati's Crosley Field, which featured a left-field incline, and Boston's Fenway Park, where a hill called Duffy's Cliff once sat at the base of the giant left-field wall. To aid navigation, the warning track actually runs between Tal's Hill and the rest of the outfield, but outfielders nonetheless dread climbing the thirty-degree slope. Most fans, however, love the challenge and unpredictability that the hill offers.

Like the Astrodome, Minute Maid Park is air-conditioned to protect fans from the brutal heat that had made games so miserable in open-air Colt Stadium, the Astros' first home. Unlike the Astrodome, however, Minute Maid's roof is retractable, and the seats are located much closer to the natural-grass field. When the roof is open, the folded-back covering looms over right field, while the area above left field opens up to reveal the downtown skyline.

While the Astrodome was well known as a pitcher's park, Minute Maid immediately gained a reputation as the opposite. Due to the constrictions of the Union Station building and the surrounding city streets, the left-field wall is just

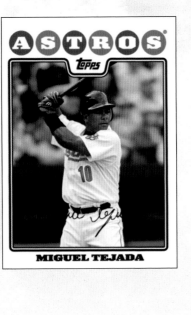

MIGUEL TEJADA

HUNTER PENCE

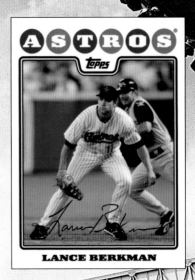

LANCE BERKMAN

316 feet away. The Astros even had to get a special exemption from the commissioner's office regarding a 1958 MLB rule that requires all outfield fences to be at least 325 feet from home plate. When the park opened, the wall featured a 21-foot-tall scoreboard, but it was nonetheless child's play for batters to knock pop flies over the fence and into the Crawford Boxes, a popular section of bleachers.

The bandbox dimensions resulted in a level of runs scored about 15 percent higher than the average major league park. The Astros stumbled to a fourth-place finish during the park's debut season, largely because their pitching staff consisted of fly-ball pitchers who had thrived in the spacious Astrodome, but proved to be fish out of water in Enron Field. The most unfortunate was Jose Lima, a twenty-one game winner with the Astros in 1999. During the park's inaugural season in 2000, Lima coughed up an NL-record forty-eight home runs en route to a disastrous 7-16 record. The stadium's extreme offensive characteristics largely disappeared after the first few seasons, though, and by 2007 Minute Maid Park had become a nearly neutral field, actually allowing slightly fewer runs than the average major league stadium. Rid of its huge pitching disadvantage and its disgraceful name, Minute Maid Park can now take its place as one of the finest parks in major league ball.

TIMELINE: MINUTE MAID PARK

2001 The Astros pick up their first postseason title ever when they win the NLDS against Atlanta, three games to two. They'll come one game shy of the World Series when they lose to the Cardinals in Game 7 of the NLCS.

2000

Enron Field opens on April 7 with dimensions that give it the feeling of a Wiffle ball field. The power alleys are just 362 feet in left-center and 373 in right-center, and though center field is extremely deep at 435, an artificial hill makes the going rough. The right-field line is a mere chip shot at 326 feet, while the left-field line is even shorter at 315 feet with a 19-foot wall.

2002

With its namesake corporation embroiled in controversy and bankruptcy, Enron Field is renamed Astros Field on February 27. On June 5, a replacement sponsor is found and the name is changed to Minute Maid Park. A new scoreboard debuts in July.

Save Streak Saved With history on the line, Los Angeles centerfielder Dave Roberts races up Tal's Hill to make perhaps the greatest defensive play in the history of Minute Maid Park. Dodgers closer Eric Gagne, with fifty-one consecutive saves under his belt, is gunning for Tom Gordon's major league record of fifty-four. With the Dodgers leading 5-3 in the eighth, the Astros get a man on base and Gagne is brought in to face slugger Lance Berkman and quell the potential rally. Berkman crushes a high drive to deepest center field, which appears headed into the stands for a game-tying homer—and a blown save that would end Gagne's streak. But the speedy Roberts scrambles up the incline, manages to keep his footing, and snatches the ball away just as it's about to clear the wall. The Dodgers tack on another run in the ninth and win 6-3. Gagne will go on to break Gordon's record, win the NL Cy Young Award, and stretch his saves streak to eighty-four before it's broken in 2004.

Dodgers 6, Astros 3

Rocket Blasted Roger Clemens, the legend who came out of retirement to pitch this year for his hometown Astros, suffers his worst outing of the year in the All-Star Game. The AL becomes the first team in All-Star history to hit for the cycle in an inning: Derek Jeter singles, Ichiro Suzuki doubles, Ivan Rodriguez triples, and Manny Ramirez and game MVP Alfonso Soriano homer. Throw in an error by the Astros' Jeff Kent, and it makes for a six-run first inning and a downed Rocket. Five other NL pitchers throw shutout innings, but their team's comeback is stymied when Carlos Zambrano allows an RBI triple to Alex Rodriguez, while Carl Pavano, the only NL pitcher to go two innings, surrenders a mammoth two-run shot to David Ortiz. Houston's Lance Berkman goes hitless; newly acquired Astro Carlos Beltran, with a single and a run scored, is the only hometown player who gives the crowd reason to cheer. Houston manager Jimy Williams, serving on the NL coaching staff, wears his Astros uniform for the last time. Phil Garner replaces him as skipper the next day.

AL 9, NL 4

December 2001 Just one year after filing a report stating that it has tripled its revenue in two years, the Enron Corporation files for bankruptcy protection and lays off almost 4,000 workers.

July 25, 2006 The foul poles are adorned with advertisements for the Chick-fil-A restaurant chain: giant cows with Astros hats. When an Astros player hits a pole, everyone in attendance wins a free chicken sandwich.

2004

The Astros make wireless internet available throughout Minute Maid Park. They also become the first major league team to offer a closed-captioning board for hearing-impaired fans.

BELOW: Octavio Dotel winds up for a pitch during a game against the Philadelphia Phillies on April 7, 2000, during his first year with the Astros. Dotel began as a starter but moved to relief, and in 2000 set an NL record for the pitcher to have the most starts as well as saves in the same season—sixteen apiece.

The Name Game

In 1953, St. Louis Cardinals owner and beer baron August Busch purchased the ballpark his team played in, Sportsman's Park. In a move that would seem obvious today, Busch decided to rename the field "Budweiser Stadium" after his best-selling beer. Other owners and baseball commissioner Ford Frick, however, thought naming the stadium after a product would be tasteless, and blocked the change. So Busch instead named the park after himself, and the next year introduced Busch beer to the market. Thus, the first stadium named after a beer was born—albeit it with a bit of reverse engineering.

Fast-forward to 1995, when Denver's new park, Coors Field, opened its gates. Coors was the first ballpark that was emblazoned with the title of a company that had nothing to do with the ownership of the team. Instead, Coors Brewing Company had shelled out $15 million for the right to put their name on the stadium. Looking for new ways to bring in revenue, ballparks in Cincinnati, Tampa Bay, San Diego, San Francisco, Oakland, and Anaheim quickly followed suit and sold their names to companies. Within ten years, eleven new parks christened with corporate identities had opened. At first, the public was just as outraged as the NL owners had been in 1953. "In any democracy worthy of the name, there ought to be a realm of civic space that remains free of the taint of commercial propaganda," media critic Mark Crispin Miller told the *Los Angeles Times*. "Whether you're talking about branded T-shirts or outright TV commercials or buildings that have been renamed by corporate sponsors, you're talking about a force that treats all citizens as nothing but consumers." But while fans have never grown to love corporate sponsorships, they have at least grown to live with them, especially when the money received for naming rights relieves part of the tax burden for the new park.

Unless, of course, the name keeps changing. AT&T Park, for instance, opened as Pacific Bell Park and was then renamed SBC Park before assuming the conglomerate's new moniker, all in the space of six years. Most fans still call it "Pac Bell Park," just as fans in Cleveland call Progressive Field "The Jake" after its original name. Enron Field learned the hard lesson of what happens when a company's reputation can turn a stadium name sour. And the Mets' new home, Citi Field, is already the object of scorn after Citigroup received federal bail-out money, laid off hundreds of thousands of employees, but are still paying $400 million to put their logo on the stadium for twenty years.

With fans refusing to use the name or resenting it, debate continues as to whether the park's namesake gets much more than a little brand recognition and the nicest luxury boxes to show off to their clients. Still, corporate naming is here to stay, and fans will continue to grumble about the long-gone days when stadiums were named for their owners, teams, or the site they were built on. It doesn't seem likely that a happy medium will be achieved anytime soon, unless, as Jim Caple of the *Seattle Post-Intelligencer* points out, "Ralph Lauren ever ponies up the money to call a stadium the Polo Grounds..."

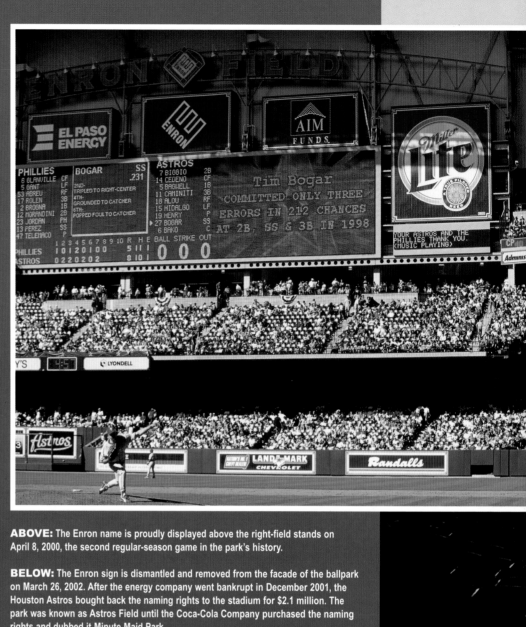

ABOVE: The Enron name is proudly displayed above the right-field stands on April 8, 2000, the second regular-season game in the park's history.

BELOW: The Enron sign is dismantled and removed from the facade of the ballpark on March 26, 2002. After the energy company went bankrupt in December 2001, the Houston Astros bought back the naming rights to the stadium for $2.1 million. The park was known as Astros Field until the Coca-Cola Company purchased the naming rights and dubbed it Minute Maid Park.

November 2, 2008 Television personality Rachael Ray hosts a mass wedding at Minute Maid Park for thirty-three couples whose wedding plans were ruined by Hurricane Ike.

December 2008 The Astros replace their sod with a new kind of genetically engineered grass called Platinum TE Paspalum, which is supposed to be a greener color and require less sunlight.

October 25, 2005

How Sweep It Is After forty-three major league seasons, the World Series finally comes to Houston—and the game, at five hours, forty-one minutes, seems almost longer than the wait was. The Astros build an early 4-0 lead, but give it back in the fifth inning when the Sox pound Houston starter Roy Oswalt for five runs. The Astros even the score in the eighth with a Jason Lane RBI double. The tie persists until the fourteenth, when White Sox reserve Geoff Blum, a former Astro, blasts a game-winning homer off Houston's Ezequiel Astacio. The fourteen innings are the longest World Series game (by time) in history, but the longest postseason game was played sixteen days earlier by the Astros and Braves. Other World Series records set are the most players used (forty-three), most pitchers used (seventeen), and most runners left on base (thirty). The next evening, Chicago will finish their sweep.

White Sox 7, Astros 5

October 18, 2004

Kent Sends Cardinals Home Jeff Kent's memorable three-run walk-off homer in NLCS Game 5 sends the Astros to St. Louis needing just one more win to reach the World Series. Houston starter Brandon Backe holds the Cardinals hitless until a two-out single by Tony Womack in the sixth. Backe and St. Louis' Woody Williams each allow just one hit and two walks with four strikeouts, although Backe pitches eight innings and Williams leaves after seven. Brad Lidge throws a perfect top of the ninth for the Astros, but in the bottom half Cardinals closer Jason Isringhausen runs into trouble. Carlos Beltran singles and steals second, after which Lance Berkman is walked intentionally, bringing up Kent. The future Hall of Famer's game-ending blow sends the frantic crowd of 43,045 home happy, but the Cards will sweep the next two games to end Houston's season.

Astros 3, Cardinals 0

July 7, 2007

Carlos in Charge Tal's Hill, which has given so many outfielders fits over the years, is conquered by a former Astro. With the Mets and Astros tied in the bottom of the fourteenth, Houston puts two runners on base with two outs. Luke Scott then crushes a pitch more than 430 feet for what seems certain to be a game-ending hit. Mets centerfielder Carlos Beltran races after it, seemingly in vain, but amazingly he manages to scale the incline, fully extend his arm while going uphill, and snag the ball for the third out. Beltran played center field for the Astros in 2004, but has been persona non grata in Houston since spurning them after that season's end. He doesn't make any new friends when he drives in the winning run for the Mets in the seventeenth.

Mets 5, Astros 3

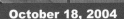

ABOVE: An enclosed Minute Maid Park on June 27, 2002. Visible on the tracks above the outfield is the park's replica nineteenth-century locomotive. The 50,000-pound train is a tribute to Union Station, which was built in 1911 and is incorporated into the park's design.

LEFT: Astros second baseman Jeff Kent hits a three-run homer in the bottom of the ninth in Game 5 of the 2004 NLCS on October 18, putting Houston ahead of St. Louis 3-2 in the series. But the Cardinals will capture the pennant after winning Games 6 and 7 in St. Louis.

MILLER PARK

Milwaukee, Wisconsin

Brewers (AL) 2001-present

OPPOSITE: Like Phoenix's Bank One Ballpark, Miller Park features a colossal retractable roof that casts a permanent shadow on the playing field regardless of whether it's open or closed. Also like the BOB, Miller attempted to offset this effect with a large section of windows underneath. The windows don't provide enough direct sunlight for grass to grow properly, but the Brewers have been resistant to putting in any fake turf. Here, Prince Fielder swings but comes up empty against Reds hurler Dave Weathers on July 12, 2008. They'll lose this game but eventually win the 2008 wild card by a one-game margin.

By 1996, Acting Commissioner Bud Selig was well on his way to becoming baseball's best-known bad cop, browbeating and threatening communities with the loss of their teams unless they agreed to build lavish taxpayer-financed stadiums. It made sense, then, that the team owned by Selig himself, the Milwaukee Brewers, finally climbed on board the gravy train with the opening of brand-new Miller Park in 2001. While the Brewers ended up with a middling retro park, the taxpayers of Wisconsin ended up with one of the most staggering boondoggles in the history of the sport.

Milwaukee's ballpark project seemed snake-bitten from the beginning. Ground was broken on October 22, 1996, in the centerfield parking lot of the Brewers' then-home, County Stadium, two miles west of downtown Milwaukee. It was scheduled to be completed by Opening Day 1999, but delays soon pushed the target date to 2000. Then on July 14, 1999, disaster struck when a gigantic crane collapsed, killing three construction workers, causing $100 million in damage, and delaying the park's opening for another year.

The baseball-only stadium had originally been budgeted at $250 million, with all but $90 million to come from a one-tenth-of-a-cent sales tax increase in Milwaukee and four surrounding counties. Taxpayers had rejected a publicly funded stadium at the ballot box, but the state legislature approved one anyway in 1995. Voters were so enraged that they recalled George Petak, the senator whose last-minute change of heart led him to cast the deciding vote. He was the first lawmaker in state history ever recalled. In addition to the state funds, $40 million was raised by selling the naming rights to the nearby Miller Brewing Company, leaving the team itself responsible for only $50 million—all of which was covered by various foundations and businesses.

Along with the construction delays came extravagant cost overruns, all of which fell to the taxpayers. By 2002, the total cost of Miller Park was $413.9 million, with an additional $72 million spent on infrastructure improvements such as walkways, lighting, and freeway off-ramps. As the total neared half a billion dollars, the stadium authority was fighting with everyone in sight. The Mitsubishi Group, builders of the retractable roof, sued for $87 million in unpaid fees. The stadium authority, a public entity, also refused to cooperate with a state audit, which later found that $10 million in insurance payouts from the crane accident was unaccounted for.

BREWERS

BEN SHEETS

BREWERS

PRINCE FIELDER

BREWERS

COREY HART

Though Wisconsinites had every reason to be upset with their lawmakers and public officials, the only thing Brewers fans cared about was that they finally had their new baseball stadium. After a staggering fifty-three months of construction, Miller Park finally opened for business on March 30, 2001, with an exhibition game against the White Sox. From an overhead vantage point, the park is shaped something like a lopsided football, with the pointed ends located at the foul poles. From ground level, outside the home plate entrance, one can see two bizarre half-moon shapes rising high above the walls, a surreal horizon line never before seen at a ballpark. These shapes are the sides of the retractable roof, capable of opening or closing in ten minutes. Unlike every other roof in baseball, the triangular seven-panel roof opens and closes in the manner of a folding fan, or a peacock spreading its feathers, fanning out from an epicenter behind home plate.

Unfortunately, the roof has proved to be unreliable. Elements of the pivoting system had to be repaired not long after the venue's opening, and the day after the 2006 season ended, the roof became stuck while partially open. Moreover, its many leaks have posed a problem during rainstorms, and its height casts a shadow on the infield throughout the day despite the presence of gigantic banks of window panes just below the roof's lip. The constant shade has prevented the grass from growing properly, leading the Brewers to explore the possibility of installing artificial turf just as the Astros did in the same predicament in 1965.

Aesthetically, Miller Park resembles another park with a retractable roof, Phoenix's Bank One Ballpark. Removed from the city and its surroundings, Miller, with its roof closed, has all the ambience of an airplane hangar. Rainy summer days often give it the hot, steamy feel of a sauna. Still, with its brick-and-glass facade, old-fashioned clock tower, and outdoor statuary, the stadium does offer many of the standbys of the retro ballpark. "A fan, upon encountering the brick facade and structural elegance, can't help but feel the reincarnation of baseball's romantic past," the team's website boasts. Plus, there is one feature distinctly absent from baseball's romantic past that has proved popular: the heating system, which on chilly nights raises the temperature inside by some 20°F.

Wisely, the Brewers transported County Stadium's two most popular features to Miller Park. Bernie Brewer, the mustachioed blond mascot famous for tumbling down a slide and into a giant mug of beer after every Brewers homer, brought his slide over to the new park but, alas, not his suds. County Stadium's wildly popular sixth-inning sausage race, wherein four team employees would dash around the bases while dressed up as a bratwurst, an Italian sausage, a Polish sausage, and a hot dog, also made the trip to Miller Park (and a chorizo was even added in 2007). Though the financial shenanigans leading to the stadium's creation were shameful, most Brewers fans found that Miller Park provided exactly what they wanted: plenty of beer and bratwurst, tolerable conditions for freezing April games, and starting in 2007, a young, exciting team that seemed a legitimate contender for the franchise's first championship.

October 25, 1999 The Brewers hire scouting director Jack Zduriencik, who over the next decade will draft such key players as Prince Fielder, Ryan Braun, Rickie Weeks, JJ Hardy, Corey Hart, and Yovani Gallardo.

September 27, 2000 Brewers farmhand Ben Sheets wins the gold medal for the United States at the Sydney Summer Olympics by hurling a three-hit shutout against juggernaut Cuba.

2001

Miller Park hosts its first regular-season game on April 6, with President George W. Bush and Commissioner Bud Selig (also the team's owner) in attendance. Measurements from left to right are 344, 371, 408, 367, and 345 feet. Much of the sod is transported from County Stadium.

2002

Attendance, which had been 2.8 million in Miller Park's first year, drops to 1.9 million, one of the most precipitous declines in baseball history.

July 19, 2002

My Kingdom for a Pitcher The most ridiculous All-Star Game in history is played at Miller Park, and ends in a ten-inning tie. All thirty players on each roster are used, and the game ends when managers Joe Torre and Bob Brenly run out of pitchers after spending most of the game unnecessarily shuttling hurlers in and out to get everyone a token appearance. The last batter, NL catcher Benito Santiago, strikes out to end the tenth with the potential winning run on second. Baseball commissioner and Brewers owner Bud Selig, who is in the stands, declares the game a tie as boos from his home fans rain down upon him, ruining what was supposed to be a grand showcase of his new stadium. NL fans, however, can at least take solace in the fact that the tie game ends their league's five-game All-Star losing streak. The embarrassment causes MLB to increase future All-Star rosters by two players, and to tie the game's result to home-field advantage in the World Series—both cursory changes that pay lip service to the problem rather than addressing it.

NL 7, AL 7

May 23, 2002

Green Means Go The Dodgers' Shawn Green feasts on Brewers pitching, setting a pile of major league records in what is likely the greatest single-game hitting performance in baseball history. Green doubles in the first inning, homers in the second, fourth, and fifth, and singles in the eighth. With two outs in the bottom of the ninth, Green stands in the on-deck circle hoping for a chance to tie the major league record of four homers in one game. Adrian Beltre homers in front of him, giving Green the opportunity to bat one last time. Amazingly, he knocks the ball deep over the right-centerfield fence for his record-tying fourth homer. Green also shatters a forty-eight-year-old record with nineteen total bases, and becomes the first man ever to collect four homers and six hits in one game. The batter after Green, Dave Hansen, also homers, making the Dodgers the first team ever to hit three consecutive home runs with two outs in the ninth. Unfortunately, few fans witness the historic performance, since it's a day game during the work week and both teams have chosen not to televise it.

Dodgers 16, Brewers 3

BELOW: Shawn Green, owner of baseball's sweetest left-handed swing, sets a heap of batting records at Miller Park on May 23, 2002. His nineteen total bases breaks the major league record, and his four homers, five extra-base hits, and six runs scored each tie records as well. Remarkably, Green homers again the next day and twice the day after that. By the time his slugging binge is finished, he'll have set or tied records for most home runs in a one-game, two-game, three-game, and one-week span.

January 13, 2005 After 12½ years as owner of the Brewers while simultaneously serving as MLB commissioner, Bud Selig finally sells the team, to banker Mark Attanasio.

July 27, 2006 The Brewers celebrate cultural diversity by adding a chorizo to the sausage race quartet of hot dog, bratwurst, Polish sausage, and Italian sausage.

May 25, 2007 Slugger Ryan Braun makes his major league debut with Milwaukee. He'll hit thirty-four homers in two-thirds of a season and win NL Rookie of the Year.

July 9, 2003

The Case of the Stumbling Sausage Brooks Kieschnick, one of the few players in modern history with major league ability as both a pitcher and hitter, picks up his first career victory in a twelve-inning Brewers win over Pittsburgh. Kieschnick pinch-hits in the eleventh, knocks a single, and then stays in the game to pitch the twelfth inning. He becomes the winning pitcher when a Wes Helms walk-off single brings in the decisive run. The most discussed incident in the game, though, occurs in the sixth inning during Milwaukee's beloved sausage race. As the four costumed wieners lope past the Pirates' dugout, Pittsburgh's Randall Simon gently strikes one of them with his bat, causing the nineteen-year-old woman inside the Italian sausage suit to trip and fall. The woman, who escapes with only a scraped knee, is given a signed bat by Simon as an apology. Nonetheless, Simon will be fined $2,000 by the commissioner's office, suspended for three games, and cited for disorderly conduct by the local sheriff's department.

Brewers 2, Pirates 1

2006

New scoreboards are erected in the outfield, as is one above home plate for fans in the bleachers. A new picnic area is also added in right field.

2007

Miller Park's problematic retractable roof is repaired at a cost of more than $13 million. Nearly 2.9 million fans attend Brewers games this year, the highest figure in the city's history. It's the fourth consecutive year attendance has increased.

BELOW: Thanks to a colossal snowstorm that wiped out most of their early-season games, the Cleveland Indians find themselves in the strange position of wearing their home whites in Milwaukee on April 10, 2007. They win two of their three "home" games against the Angels at Miller Park before returning to Cleveland on April 13.

September 29, 2007

Gwynn and Bear It On the last day of the regular season, the Padres playoff hopes are dealt a crushing blow—by Tony Gwynn Jr., the Brewers outfielder who is the son of San Diego's most beloved icon. The Brewers, whose loss to the Padres a night earlier eliminated them from playoff contention, never give up in the meaningless-for-them season finale. With San Diego just one strike away from clinching a wild card berth, legendary Padres closer Trevor Hoffman faces Gwynn in the ninth. Gwynn smacks a game-tying triple, and his Brewers win it in the eleventh on a walk-off single by Vinny Rottino. San Diego falls into a tie for the wild card with the Colorado Rockies, who will end the Padres' season the following day by defeating them in a one-game playoff.

Brewers 4, Padres 3

April 10, 2007

Shelter from the Storm After a massive spring storm dumps a foot of snow on Cleveland and threatens to wipe out a week's worth of games, the Indians borrow weather-protected Miller Park to use as their home field for a series against the Angels. Though they have no loyalty to either club, Milwaukeeans love the $10 ticket price, and 19,031 fans show up to watch Cleveland beat the Angels in a close game. It's not the first time the Indians have called Milwaukee "home," either. The classic baseball film *Major League*, featuring the hapless Indians of the 1980s, was filmed at Milwaukee's County Stadium. This year's Indians team will go on to win 96 games, the highest total in baseball.

Indians 7, Angels 6

No Place Like Home The first no-hitter is thrown at Miller Park, but it's not tossed by a Brewer or even pitched against the home team. It's by Cub Carlos Zambrano in a game that was supposed to be played in Houston. Hurricane Ike makes play at Minute Maid Park impossible, and hasty arrangements are made to play the game at vacant Miller Park, despite its designation as "Wrigley North." A decidedly pro-Cubs crowd comes ninety minutes from Chicago to see Houston's "home" game, which becomes the first no-hitter by a Cub since Milt Pappas did it at Wrigley in 1972. The next day, Cubbie Ted Lilly will throw a one-hitter—taking a no-hitter into the seventh—making it the first time in history a team has had that few hits over a two-game span. The Brewers will head to Chicago to play the Cubs at their real home two days later.

Cubs 5, Astros 0

September 25, 2007 Prince Fielder smacks his forty-ninth and fiftieth home runs, making him and father Cecil the first father-son duo to each hit fifty homers in a season.

July 13, 2008 In his second start as a Brewer, CC Sabathia does it all, pitching a complete-game 3-2 victory and hitting a home run himself to provide the margin of victory.

RIGHT: After arriving from Cleveland in exchange for prospect Matt LaPorta on July 7, 2008, CC Sabathia establishes himself as perhaps the most successful midseason acquisition in baseball history. He goes 11-2 with a 1.65 ERA, finishes in the top six in both Cy Young and MVP voting, and helps the Brewers clinch a playoff spot with a complete-game four-hitter (pictured here) on the last day of the season.

BELOW: Ryan Braun raises his fist triumphantly after his wild card–winning home run on September 28, 2008, the final day of the season. The two-run blast breaks a 1-1 tie in the bottom of the eighth, giving CC Sabathia a victory, and enabling Milwaukee to finish ahead of the Mets by one game.

The Brewers Come Back to Life After flatlining for most of September and letting the NL wild card get seemingly out of their grasp, the Brewers finish off an inspired final home stand by beating the rival Cubs to earn the team's first postseason berth in twenty-six years. As in 1982, the clinching win occurs on the last Sunday of the season by a midseason acquisition (CC Sabathia in 2008, Don Sutton in 1982). As the Brewers went 4-15 during September and replaced managers—Ned Yost in favor of Dale Sveum—they suddenly turned it on and won six of their last seven games of the season to overtake the Mets, who lose on the last day of the season to the Marlins in the final game at Shea Stadium. Sabathia goes the distance for the seventh time in seventeen starts for the Brewers. Ryan Braun hits three go-ahead home runs after the seventh, including a tiebreaker in the eighth.

Brewers 3, Cubs 1

GREAT AMERICAN BALL PARK

Cincinnati, Ohio

Reds (NL) 2003–present

KEN GRIFFEY JR.

OPPOSITE: The Reds face Houston at Great American Ball Park in 2004. The lights of Covington, Kentucky, are visible beyond center field. Three years later, this panorama will be altered by the construction of a two-story "Riverboat Deck" atop the batter's eye in dead center. The deck now serves as a promotional tool for telephone provider Cincinnati Bell, which pays the team $1 million annually for the right to house some of its offices and conference rooms at the ballpark. Unfortunately, the faux riverboat obstructs much of the ballpark's view of the Ohio River and Covington's lights on the far bank.

In 2003 the Cincinnati Reds finally replaced Riverfront Stadium, the poster child for the crime against ballpark architecture that was multipurpose stadiums, with a $325 million retro-style park. However, Great American Ball Park—named after the insurance company owned by then Reds CEO Carl Lindner—was one of the blander entries in the retro ballpark genre, and it seemed to have arrived a day late and a dollar short. Though the park itself was pleasant enough, many viewed it as emblematic of a growing problem: the new ballparks, in rejecting the aesthetics of the cookie-cutter parks of the 1970s, were now so similar to each other that they were on the verge of becoming cookie cutters themselves.

The best thing about Great American Ball Park is its stunning location in downtown Cincinnati, on the banks of the Ohio River. Directly east of Riverfront Stadium, the new structure came within 26 inches of Riverfront at its closest point, and space was cleared for construction by tearing down part of the old park's outfield stands even while the Reds were still playing there. Great American Ball Park faces southeast toward the town of Covington, Kentucky, which is visible across the glimmering river. (Home plate rests 580 feet from the river, which means that the splash-down hits of San Francisco don't happen in Cincinnati.) It's also next door to two other stadiums—US Bank Arena, a concert and minor league hockey venue, and Paul Brown Stadium, home of the NFL's Bengals—as well as one of the country's finest museums, the National Underground Railroad Freedom Center.

Great American Ball Park made strong and effective use of color, as exposed steel beams, the dominant architectural feature, were painted white, nicely offsetting the green of the playing field and the deep red of the seats. The preponderance of white means that Great American, like its predecessor Riverfront, resembles a gleaming mothership to motorists passing by at night on Interstate 71 from Kentucky.

The grounds have many of the same features as other retro parks, with a team Hall of Fame, a mosaic depicting many of the franchise's greats, and statues of team legends

JOEY VOTTO

AARON HARANG

SCOTT HATTEBERG

(in this case, Joe Nuxhall, Ernie Lombardi, Ted Kluszewski, and Frank Robinson). In 2007, the Reds built a new "Riverboat Deck," a faux steam vessel in dead center field that serves as a venue for private parties and contains office space for the local phone company, which helped pay for the structure. The stadium also features such amenities as an on-site pizza delivery service, which fans can call on their cell phones to have made-to-order pizzas delivered to their seats within twenty minutes. Such attractions, however, didn't impress critics like *New York Times* architecture guru Chrisopher Hawthorne:

> Great American's historical touches, like the reproduction riverboat smokestacks that sit behind the centerfield fence, have a bland, even rote, feel. Where it faces downtown Cincinnati, the stadium is covered in a brick facade with a stone base, a flimsy shawl of tradition that the broad-shouldered steel frame of the stadium, rising up behind, seems simply to be shrugging off....Just before the park opened, Marilyn Bauer, the art critic for the *Cincinnati Enquirer*, took six local design experts for a tour. The architect Michael McInturf provided a representative opinion when he dismissed Great American as "a theme park with a bad structure."

Nonetheless, Reds fans seem to appreciate having a new place to watch baseball. Although Great American's opening coincided with a spate of losing seasons and an era of colossal team mismanagement, Cincinnati drew at least 1.9 million fans in each of the park's first five seasons—a figure reached only twice in the final nine years at Riverfront. In 2008 a new regime began under General Manager Walt Jocketty, hoping to provide Cincinnatians with a winning team to go along with their winning ballpark.

TIMELINE: GREAT AMERICAN BALL PARK

June 20, 2004 Cincinnati's Ken Griffey Jr. hits his 500th career home run, but unfortunately for Reds fans, he does it in St. Louis.

2003

The Reds open their new park on March 31 with an embarrassing 10-1 loss to lowly Pittsburgh. The small dimensions cause hitters to lick their chops: 328 feet down the left-field line, 379 to left-center, 404 to center, 370 to right-center, and 325 to right. However, the centerfield batter's eye is actually a restaurant with darkened windows, creating a glare that will prove distracting during day games. The stadium holds 42,941, about 10,000 less than its predecessor.

August 10, 2004

Moon Shot Over Kentucky Burly Reds slugger Adam Dunn, whose thirty-five home runs lead the majors, hits a ball all the way to Kentucky—literally. His 535-foot blast off Los Angeles' Jose Lima clears the stadium, bounces on the street behind it, and finally comes to rest on a piece of driftwood in the Ohio River. Since the entire river is technically part of Kentucky, the ball actually lands in another state. Dunn's drive is all the more impressive for clearing the batter's eye in center field, which is 32 feet high and more than 425 feet from home plate. This feat doesn't help the Reds, though, as the rest of the team is baffled by Lima's kitchen-sink pitching repertoire. "He can hit a 600-foot home run, but I don't care," Lima says afterward. "There was no way I was going to walk a leadoff hitter."

Dodgers 5, Reds 2

August 3, 2004 The National Underground Railroad Freedom Center, a spectacular museum that houses an actual slave cabin, opens directly adjacent to Great American Ball Park.

2007 The Reds' Brandon Phillips hits thirty homers and steals thirty-two bases, becoming just the second second baseman to join the thirty-thirty club.

May 31, 2008 Heralded prospect Jay Bruce hits his first career homer, a tenth-inning smash that gives the Reds a 4-3 walk-off win. Bruce will bat .577 during the first week of his career.

April 4, 2005

Over and Dunn The Reds score three times in the bottom of the ninth, capped by Joe Randa's walk-off homer, to spoil Pedro Martinez's Mets debut. Martinez, the much-coveted free-agent signee, fans twelve batters in six innings, giving up a three-run homer to Adam Dunn but little else. Reliever Braden Looper, however, blows it in the ninth. Dunn's second homer of the day ties the game, and Randa follows with his game-winner, which sets off a wild celebration in Cincy. It's a memorable Reds debut for Randa, who becomes the first player since Gary Carter in 1985 to hit a walk-off homer for a new team on Opening Day. The Reds will go on to sweep the series, and new Mets skipper Willie Randolph will start his managerial career with five consecutive losses.

Reds 7, Mets 6

August 3, 2006

Masterful Maddux Forty-year-old Greg Maddux makes his Dodgers debut and, for the first time in his illustrious career, holds the opposition hitless. However, as Maddux warms up for the bottom of the seventh, the skies unleash a torrential downpour. After a forty-six-minute rain delay, manager Grady Little removes Maddux from the game, denying the living legend the opportunity to complete his no-hitter. "If it was a bigger lead, I would love to have tried it," Maddux says afterward. "But it's not about me. This was a game we needed to win." Leading 2-0, the Dodgers send lefty Joe Beimel to the mound when play resumes. Beimel gives up a hit to the first batter he faces, Scott Hatteberg, but he and two other Dodgers relievers nail the door shut on a 3-0 Los Angeles victory. Maddux, acquired a few days earlier in a deadline trade with the Cubs, will post a 6-3 record over the season's final two months and lead the Dodgers to the playoffs.

Dodgers 3, Reds 0

2007

The Riverboat Deck— a fake vessel that serves as a staging area for parties and corporate meetings— is built behind the centerfield fence. The structure generates needed revenue, but also disrupts the park's open-air feel and blocks views of the Ohio River from much of the grandstand.

CITIZENS BANK PARK
Philadelphia, Pennsylvania
Phillies (NL) 2004–present

After spending thirty-three depressing years at Veterans Stadium, baseball's version of a junked-out jalopy, the Phillies in 2004 found themselves playing in the shiniest new model in the country. Citizens Bank Park was a natural-grass retro stadium whose bandbox dimensions whipped up excitement by allowing home runs to fly out of the park at phenomenal rates. More importantly, it was nothing like Veterans Stadium. "It was absolutely fabulous to see the Vet in a pile of rubble," one joyous Phillies fan told the *New York Times* on the new park's Opening Day.

The Phillies initially wanted to build in the downtown area known as Center City, but were forced to settle for the same site where the Vet had been: the South Philadelphia Sports Complex, also home to the city's NFL, NHL, and NBA teams. Originally budgeted at $336 million, the ballpark's final cost ended up at $458 million, which was covered by a 2 percent tax bump on rental cars, $95 million for the naming rights, and a portion from the Phillies themselves.

Of all the retro parks built in the wake of Camden Yards, Citizens Bank Park is the most shameless in straightforwardly copying the features of Baltimore's gem. Both parks were built with stately red-brick exteriors, old-fashioned clocks and bi-level bullpens in the outfield, greenery behind the centerfield fence, and taller-than-normal right-field walls containing large scoreboards. Baltimore's Eutaw Street, the closed-off thoroughfare behind right field where food and souvenirs are sold, was echoed by Citizens Bank's Ashburn Alley. The Phils even mimicked the Orioles' idea of having a beloved and rotund former slugger hawk barbecue at a food stand. (In Baltimore it was Boog Powell; in Philly, Greg Luzinski.) Phillies fans, though, weren't bothered by the lack of originality. "I've been to Camden Yards plenty of times, and this place is nicer," longtime fan Tom Colonna gushed to the *Times*. "I'm excited."

The exterior of the park is the usual brick and stone with a landscaped entrance plaza at each of the four corners, but one unique aspect is a group of 50-foot-high lanterns that light the exterior at night. Because it's set 23 feet below street level, the playing field can actually be seen from several vantage points outside the park. In a tip of the cap (perhaps unintentionally) to Shibe Park, Citizens Bank features a gigantic upper deck of bleacher seats in right field only, with a much smaller seating section in left. (Shibe had contained a similarly huge and asymmetrical bleacher deck, albeit in left field.) A little more than half the seats—22,647 of 43,647—are in the upper deck, which is set much farther back from the playing field than at most retro parks. This lack of cantilevering means that the highest seats, while more distant horizontally, are closer to the ground than elsewhere. It also means that Citizens Bank's premium seats—those in the lower bowl—are largely unaffected by overhangs. Some 75 percent of the field-level seats sit underneath open skies.

One feature of the park that seemed poorly thought-out was the placement of the upper bullpen adjacent to a public concourse in the outfield, thereby subjecting the players to abuse from the notorious Philadelphia fans. This upper pen originally belonged to the Phillies, but they quickly switched to the lower one, leaving the visiting team to endure the heckles and thrown objects. To ward off potential problems, the Phillies were forced to eliminate fan access to the area once the game started.

A giant neon Liberty Bell in center field blinks whenever a home run is hit, accompanied by a bell clang booming from the loudspeakers. Since Citizens Bank Park immediately became one of the easiest home run parks in the majors, the bell seems to ring constantly. After hitting just 166 homers in their final season at the Vet, the Phillies clubbed 215 during Citizens Bank Park's inaugural year of 2004. Although they'd spent many of their early years playing at Baker Bowl, a noted home run haven, 2004 was the first time in the Phillies' 122-year history that they'd surpassed 200 homers in a season, and they did it again in '06 and '07. Before the 2006 season, the Phillies tried to temper the homer barrage by moving the left-field fence back 5 feet and making it 2½ feet taller, but pitchers still complained. "Coors Field is no longer the park pitchers talk about," Braves ace John Smoltz said. "It's the place in Philly. When you talk about pitchers' ERAs there, you can throw them right out the window."

PAT BURRELL

JIMMY ROLLINS

RYAN HOWARD

September 1, 2004 Slugger Ryan Howard, called up from Triple-A Scranton, makes his long-awaited major league debut. Seven months later, *The Office* debuts on NBC, featuring a Scranton-based character named Ryan Howard.

December 13, 2004 The Phillies select outfielder Shane Victorino from the Dodgers in the Rule 5 Draft; he'll become the spark plug for their 2008 championship team.

November 25, 2005 To make room for Ryan Howard in the lineup, the Phillies trade Jim Thome to the White Sox for outfielder Aaron Rowand.

TIMELINE: CITIZENS BANK PARK

2004

2006

Citizens Bank Park opens with cozy dimensions that appear to be inaccurately measured. Officially, the dimensions are 329 feet down the left-field line, 369 to left-center, 401 to center, 369 to right-center, and 330 to right, with one area in deepest left-center extending to 409 feet. However, pitching coach Joe Kerrigan, using a laser distance finder, determines that the spot in left-center advertised as 369 feet is actually at least 10 feet shorter, a conclusion that is supported by aerial analysis using Google Earth. The Phillies claim the "369" sign was simply placed in the wrong spot on the wall.

June 14, 2004

Thome Launches One Fan favorite Jim Thome launches his 400th career home run, an opposite-field drive to left-center in the first inning. It ties the game, and Pat Burrell follows with a home run of his own to give the Phils the lead. A downpour stops the game in the eighth inning, giving Philadelphia a rain-shortened 10-7 win. Despite the wet weather, 44,710 Philadelphians attend the Monday night game, and the total season attendance of 3.2 million will be the highest in franchise history.

Phillies 10, Reds 7

September 14, 2005

Andruw Tees Off The Braves' Andruw Jones reaches two home run milestones on one eighth-inning swing. His titanic 430-foot blast off Geoff Geary lands halfway up the upper deck, and is his 50th homer of the season, as well as the 300th of his career. The Braves are the oldest franchise in baseball, but Jones is their first fifty–home run hitter. He'll finish the year with a league-leading fifty-one, becoming the first Atlanta player to win the NL home run crown since Dale Murphy in 1985.

Phillies 12, Braves 4

After constant complaining by pitchers about the 201 home runs hit here in 2005, the Phillies remove almost 200 seats in left field and push the wall back 5 feet. They also increase its height by 30 inches. The Phillies predict this will result in as many as twenty fewer homers, but in fact thirty-two *more* homers are hit at Citizens Bank in 2007.

TOP: Jim Thome smacks his 400th career homer in 2004.

MIDDLE: The Phillies' Ramón Martinez (right) celebrates his third-inning grand slam on September 14, 2005. The game will become even more memorable for a pair of home run milestones by the Braves' Andruw Jones.

BOTTOM: Evening settles in on Citizens Bank Park in 2005. Because it's so close to I-76, the stadium can easily be seen from the highway. Especially at night, it is a striking sight while driving

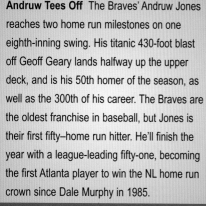

September 30, 2007

Moyer's Miracle The Phillies complete one of the greatest pennant-race comebacks in the history of baseball, roaring from seven games behind with only seventeen left to play—and helping to bury the memory of the disastrous 1964 season, when they infamously collapsed down the stretch. The Phils are in a flat-footed tie with the Mets entering today's game. Forty-four-year-old hurler Jamie Moyer, the only Phillie who was even born when the 1964 collapse occurred, allows no earned runs as his team crushes Washington 6-1. Meanwhile, at Shea Stadium, the Marlins pound Mets starter Tom Glavine to a pulp, helping the Phils clinch their first playoff appearance since 1993. It's sweet redemption for the team that earlier this season became the first ever to lose 10,000 games as a franchise.

Phillies 6, Nationals 1

November 21, 2007 Jimmy Rollins, the shortstop who spurred the Phillies to their unlikely NL East title, is named league MVP.

April 13, 2009 After forty-four years as an MLB announcer, thirty-eight of which were with the Phillies, legendary broadcaster Harry Kalas is found dead in the booth before a Phillies-Nationals game. Kalas was known for his "Outta here!" call for home runs.

BELOW: Phillies closer Brett Myers tosses his glove in the air after clinching the NL East on September 30, 2007. At far left is Washington's Wily Mo Peña, who has just struck out to end the season. The Phillies, who had been behind in the standings by seven games with seventeen to go, went on a 13-4 streak to catch the Mets.

October 29, 2008

After a Brief Intermission.... After playing into the sixth inning in a torrential downpour on Monday night, Game 5 of the Phillies' first World Series in twenty-eight years was halted minutes after Tampa Bay tied it, 2-2. When the game resumes tonight, Pedro Feliz singles in the tiebreaking run. Brad Lidge, who was perfect in forty-one save tries during the season and six so far in the postseason, gives the Phillies their first world championship since 1980 and only their second since joining the National League in 1883. Commissioner Bud Selig reveals that even if the game hadn't been tied, he'd decided that it would have been played to its conclusion, and the five-inning rain-out rule will be changed to require that all postseason and All-Star Games are played until finished. The ninety-minute postgame celebration lasts longer than tonight's action on the field. While the final play actually takes place on October 29, MLB records will date the Series winner as October 27, when Game 5 started.

Phillies 4, Rays 3

BELOW: Phillies closer Brad Lidge gets down on his knees after striking out Tampa Bay's Eric Hinske in Game 5 to end the 2008 World Series. Lidge was a perfect 48-48 in save opportunities in '08, including the regular season and playoffs.

PETCO PARK

San Diego, California

Padres (NL) 2004–present

OPPOSITE: On May 1, 2004, in the fifteenth game ever played at Petco Park, the Padres defeat the Mets. One of Petco's most interesting design features is the bleacher seating (seen in the foreground of this image), known as the Jury Box. The section juts out into the playing field next to the foul line, creating unusual caroms that cause nightmares for right fielders. The name is an homage to the famed right-field Jury Box at Boston's Braves Field, though their version didn't stick out into the field. San Diego's version is also considerably more full than the Braves' Jury Box (which once only had twelve spectators), despite a price tag of $30 per seat.

Petco Park's centerpiece is the Western Metal Supply Co. building incorporated into the left-field corner. "The environmental impact report identified it as one of the historical buildings in the area and one that needed to be preserved," Padres construction manager Bob Mueller told the *San Diego Union-Tribune*. "Because it was an unreinforced masonry building, being all brick and timbers, it was really a large challenge. We had to incorporate concrete columns and concrete shear walls to reinforce the brick, then tie the floor system together with concrete floors. The nice part is, it hasn't changed the building a lot."

After plodding through an unprecedented amount of legal red tape and construction delays, the San Diego Padres finally opened long-awaited Petco Park for the 2004 season. With a prime bayside location, brilliant architecture, and a vibrant neighborhood surrounding it, the new ballpark proved to be well worth the wait. But as pleasant an experience as it provided for the fans, the new park proved a nemesis to Padres hitters, who, in the midst of the greatest home run era in baseball history, found themselves maddeningly unable to hit the ball out of their home park.

On November 3, 1998, San Diego voters approved a new publicly funded ballpark, the proposed $411 million price tag of which included $225 million in municipal bonds, as well as funding from public sources. Ground was soon broken, but construction screeched to a halt in late 2000 when the promised city money was not delivered. With the park half-finished, the picturesque waterfront site sat idle for some fifteen months while the Padres fought off seventeen different lawsuits filed by taxpayers opposing the use of public funds for the project. To make matters worse, a city councilwoman was convicted of accepting improper gifts—in effect, bribes—from Padres owner John Moores. By 2001 the lawsuits had been dismissed, but every member of San Diego's city council that had approved the project in 1998 had been supplanted. Moores was forced to renegotiate terms with the new council, resulting in further delays.

At times it seemed as if the ballpark would never come to fruition and the Padres would move away, but the end result was not nearly so bleak: The opening date was simply pushed back from 2002 to 2004. The final bill ended up at $456 million, but the city was able to recoup some of its investment by scheduling highly successful non-baseball events at the park, such as Rolling Stones concerts, soccer games, rugby tournaments, and even bar mitzvahs for high rollers. The city also charged the Padres half a million dollars in annual rent.

Petco Park was the central feature in the redevelopment of the Gaslamp Quarter, the historic waterfront district surrounding the park. According to the *San Diego Business Journal*, "the ballpark breathed new life into Downtown, setting in motion a construction and redevelopment boom." Better yet, the ballpark itself turned out to be gorgeous. Meant to evoke the local setting as well as the Padres' team

colors, the seats are navy blue and the exposed steel beams are painted a stately white. The exterior consists of buff-colored stucco and Indian sandstone, while jacaranda trees and walls of water line the walkways leading to the entrance gates. A series of 200-foot-tall towers house luxury suites that provide sweeping views of San Diego Bay. Behind right-center field, an elevated grass park provides lawn seating for some 2,500 fans, and next door is the "Park at the Park," a kids' area featuring a playground, picnic area, faux beach, and more. Every seat in the grandstand is angled toward the pitcher, and fans are much closer to the action than they were at football-first Jack Murphy Stadium.

Like Camden Yards, Petco incorporated an existing historic building into its design—and did so even more brilliantly than Baltimore had. The four-story Western Metal Supply Co. building had been constructed in 1910, and for more than half a century it churned out horseshoes, plumbing supplies, war materiel, and various steel goods. Vacant since the company went out of business in 1976, the red-brick structure proved a boon for design firm HOK and lead architect Antoine Predock. The park was built so that the Western Metal building fits snugly in left field, where its southern corner cleverly forms the foul pole. Bleachers installed on the building's roof provide seating for 180, while balconies on the second and third floors serve as luxury suites and one on the fourth floor serves as a bar and grill. The first floor, meanwhile, hosts the Padres' team store.

Petco, like virtually every West Coast ballpark, is a pitcher's haven. In fact, it took the concept to an extreme, becoming known as the pitcher's counterpart to Coors Field. Although nobody was sure exactly why—its dimensions were not out of the ordinary—the stadium, in its first four seasons, allowed between 18 and 25 percent fewer runs than the average ballpark. During these formative years the Padres, though fielding a winning team each season, proved unable to win at home often. Particularly vexed were the team's top two sluggers: Ryan Klesko, whose home run total plummeted from twenty-three to nine, and Brian Giles, who homered just twenty-three times in his first full Petco season after hitting at least thirty-five in four consecutive seasons with Pittsburgh. "The ball just dies," Klesko told the *San Diego Union-Tribune*. "You have to change completely there. You have to take the loft out of your swing. It's not just the dimensions. The ball

hangs up in the salt air. I was surprised when I saw the park, but what are you going to do? Will they admit that they were wrong? No. Will they bring in the fences? No."

But the players' whining obscured an essential truth: The Padres' pitchers were helped to the exact degree the batters were hurt. The real reason the Padres couldn't win at Petco had nothing to do with the park itself. Indeed, San Diego was both outscored and out-homered by its opponents in Petco during each of the park's first three seasons, nullifying any home-field advantage. (During two of these three years, the Padres had a better record on the road than at home, a relative rarity in baseball.) The team simply suffered from poor planning. Though moving into a park which harmed left-handed sluggers more than any other type of player, they nonsensically pinned their offensive hopes on two left-handed sluggers, Klesko and Giles. The result was a roster uniquely unsuited to its home park, and the Padres soon set about rectifying this error by putting together a new team centered around pitching and defense.

2004 Padres righty Jake Peavy posts a 2.27 ERA to lead the major leagues. He'll do so again three years later, and win the Cy Young Award to boot.

2004

Petco Park opens on April 8 with relatively average dimensions of 334 feet to left, 367 to left-center, 396 to center, 382 to right-center, and 322 to right, with the farthest distance being 411 feet in deepest right-center. A small section of seats known as the "Jury Box" juts out into right field, making the angles difficult for outfielders and increasing the number of triples.

April 8, 2004

First Come, First Served The Padres mount a stirring come-from-behind victory in the first game ever played at Petco Park. David Wells throws the first pitch, to San Francisco's Ray Durham, in front of a full house of 41,400 (almost 20,000 fewer than the last crowd at Qualcomm Stadium). Padre Brian Giles has the park's first hit, against Dustin Hermanson in the first inning. The first home run does not come until the tenth inning, when Marquis Grissom gives the Giants a 3-2 lead. Pinch hitter Augie Ojeda's two-out double in the bottom of the inning ties the score. Sean Burroughs, who drove in the first run in the park's history and tied the game in the bottom of the ninth, knocks in the game-winner in the tenth.

Padres 4, Giants 3

September 28, 2005

How the West Was Won Despite having stumbled around .500 for most of the summer, the Padres clinch the NL West title with a lopsided win over San Francisco. Veteran hurler Pedro Astacio, released by Texas in June, picks up the win while Trevor Hoffman closes out the ninth. It's the fourth division crown for the Padres, three of which have come under manager Bruce Bochy. The Padres will tie the 1973 Mets for fewest wins, eighty-two, by a postseason team. A paltry crowd of 33,992, just 80 percent of capacity, shows up for the clincher.

Padres 9, Giants 1

July 29, 2007 Tony Gwynn enters the Hall of Fame in Cooperstown and becomes the second inductee (after Dave Winfield) to feature a Padres cap on his plaque.

2006

The 411-foot distance to right-center field is shortened by some 10 feet.

April 17, 2008

The Never-Ending Game In one of the longest major league games ever played, the Rockies outlast the Padres when Troy Tulowitzki doubles home Willy Taveras with the winning run in the twenty-second inning. It's a rematch between the teams that played a one-game playoff for the wild card berth last October, and each sends its staff ace to the mound. San Diego's Jake Peavy and Colorado's Jeff Francis both shine, and the game remains a scoreless tie through the end of nine innings. The Padres blow a golden opportunity in the thirteenth when Paul McAnulty foolishly tries to stretch a leadoff double into a triple and is thrown out easily. The Rockies finally plate the game's first run on a bases-loaded walk in the fourteenth, but the Padres tie it right back up on an RBI single by catcher Josh Bard. Seven more scoreless innings follow before Padres shortstop Khalil Greene airmails a routine throw to first, setting up Tulowitzki's go-ahead double at 1:21 a.m. A total of forty-two players, including fifteen pitchers, are used in the six-hour, sixteen-minute game.

Rockies 2, Padres 1

September 24, 2006

Trevor Time The Padres' Trevor Hoffman becomes baseball's all-time saves leader when he gets Freddy Sanchez to ground out to shortstop, breaking Lee Smith's record with his 479th career save. It's the forty-third save of the year for the thirty-eight-year-old Hoffman, who boasts a remarkable 1.95 ERA in his fourteenth season as San Diego's closer. The winning margin is provided by the longest home run to date at Petco Park, a 453-foot blast by Russell Branyan in the fourth inning. Hoffman will also get a save a week later on the last day of the season, clinching the NL West title for the Padres.

Padres 2, Pirates 1

BUSCH STADIUM [III]

St. Louis, Missouri

Cardinals (NL) 2006–present

ALBERT PUJOLS

OPPOSITE: Jose Reyes of the New York Mets is the first batter at the first 2007 game at Busch Stadium. The Cardinals have played in a "Busch" ballpark since 1954, after August Busch purchased the team. In addition to renaming the Cardinals' Sportsman's Park after himself, he built them a new stadium in 1966, also called Busch Stadium. After Busch died in 1989, his heirs sold the team, but the Anheuser-Busch corporation purchased the naming rights to the stadium. They re-signed the contract for an additional twenty years in 2004, two years before Busch Stadium [III] opened. At the announcement of the new deal, a banner that read "Thank You Anheuser-Busch" was unfurled at the construction site and each worker was given a six-pack of the brewery's famous Budweiser beer.

As the sixteenth team to build a retro-style ballpark since 1992, the St. Louis Cardinals were faced with a challenging task when planning the latest version of Busch Stadium: how to build a bold and imaginative ballpark without copying what other teams had already done. They turned to HOK, the noted firm that had designed Camden Yards, and senior designer Jim Chibnall, whose design for Cleveland's Jacobs Field had been a smashing success. "We tried to create a building that referred to the traditional buildings in downtown St. Louis," Chibnall told the *St. Louis Post-Dispatch*. Though Busch III (as it was called to distinguish it from its two predecessors) wasn't entirely successful in breaking new architectural ground, the $365 million structure did provide a pleasant locale for St. Louis's famously loyal fans to watch their beloved Redbirds.

As Chibnall intended, echoes of famed local buildings are recognizable in the design. Busch III's red brick facade echoes not only the Wainwright Building, a landmark in downtown St. Louis since 1891, but also the historic Anheuser Busch brewery. A pedestrian walkway over the arched main entrance was influenced by the Eads Bridge, an 1874 structure spanning the Mississippi. More conventionally, statues of ten Cardinals legends, including Stan Musial, are stationed near the entrance. (An eleventh statue, of Mark McGwire, was also created, but the Cardinals decided not to erect it after the once beloved home run king was fingered in baseball's steroids scandal.)

With the Cardinals enjoying a dynastic reign atop the NL Central and tickets already in high demand, the new stadium opened with a capacity of 46,861, larger than most retro parks. There's no upper deck in the outfield, however, giving fans in the grandstand a dramatic view of the city skyline and its signature Gateway Arch. From up high one might even glimpse the mighty Mississippi, just three blocks away behind the right-field fence. The effect of the city looming over the stadium is enhanced by a lower-than-street-level playing field, and the franchise's proud tradition is emphasized by the Cardinal-red seats and the dark green outfield fence.

Seats along the baselines are some 40 feet closer to the action than they'd been at Busch II, but the upper-deck

SCOTT ROLEN

JIM EDMONDS

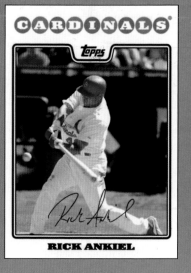

RICK ANKIEL

July 19, 2006 Just before a gam[e] high winds knock over a portable con[e] large plastic panel that was protecting[...] into the stands, injuring thirty spectato[rs]

2006

Unfinished Busch Stadium hosts its first major league game, a win over the Brewers, on April 10. Attendance at the sold-out game is 41,936, but more seats will be added throughout April. By the time the World Series is played here in October, capacity will be about 46,500, including standing room tickets. Oddly for a retro park, Busch's dimensions are nearly symmetrical: 336 feet to left field, 375 to left-center, 400 to center, 375 to right-center, and 335 to right.

ABOVE: Busch Stadium under construction on February 24, 2006. In March, natural grass will be installed. Construction will continue on the seating area after the park opens, with an eventual total capacity of around 46,500. Every game will be sold out for the stadium's debut season, for a total attendance of 3,407,104.

seats at the new park are significantly higher. In lieu of an upper deck in the outfield, the Cardinals stacked an astonishing six decks in the main grandstand, including two levels of luxury suites. Not only does every seat have an unobstructed view, but the team also took pains to integrate open spaces from which fans could watch the game while milling around. Like Pacific Bell Park, Busch III features a promenade behind the outfield fence from which fans can view the game without buying a ticket.

In Busch's inaugural season of 2006 every game was a sellout, though this resulted in only the second-highest attendance mark in franchise history, illustrating the massive difference in capacity between Busch II and Busch III. The '06 Cardinals had a strong team led by the remarkable slugging of Albert Pujols. They built a seven-game lead with twelve games remaining in the season, but then proceeded to collapse, losing nine of those twelve, and barely stumbling into the playoffs. Shockingly, the Cards then won all three of their postseason series, including the Fall Classic in five games over the dominant Detroit Tigers. Busch III thus became the first park to open with a world championship since 1912, when the Red Sox inaugurated Fenway Park in style. The Cardinals' mediocre 83-78 record made them easily the worst championship team in baseball history, but St. Louis fans couldn't have cared less. They had a brand-new ballpark with a World Series banner flying from the rafters. What could be better?

RIGHT: St. Louis' closing pitcher Adam Wainwright (right) celebrates with catcher Yadier Molina as the Cardinals win Game 5 against the Detroit Tigers to take the 2006 World Series at Busch Stadium. This is the team's tenth World Series Championship, the most any National League team has ever won, and the Cardinals' first since 1982. St. Louis and Detroit met two previous times in the World Series: In 1934, the Cardinals beat the Tigers, and in 1968, the Tigers won.

April 29, 2007 Twenty-nine-year-old Cardinals reliever Josh Hancock dies in a car accident. Cardinals players will wear his number, 32, on their sleeves for the rest of the season.

October 3, 2007 After being general manager of the Cardinals for eleven years, Walt Jocketty is let go one year before his contract expires. Assistant GM John Mozeliak will be promoted to take Jocketty's place.

June 7, 2008 The stadium hosts its first concert: Dave Matthews Band with opening act the Black Crowes.

October 27, 2006

Taming the Tigers The plucky Cardinals, written off as dead just a few weeks earlier, defeat Detroit in Game 5 of the World Series to capture the tenth championship in franchise history. Detroit takes a 2-1 lead in the top of the fourth on a Sean Casey homer, but in the bottom of the inning, Tigers pitcher Justin Verlander throws away a bunt, allowing the tying run to score. (It's the fifth error in as many games committed by the Detroit pitchers.) The next batter, eventual Series MVP David Eckstein, drives in the go-ahead run with a groundout, and the Cardinals never look back. With the tying runs on base in the ninth, Cardinals rookie closer Adam Wainwright fans Brandon Inge to give the Cards their first title since 1982.

Cardinals 4, Tigers 2

2008

Construction still has not begun on Ballpark Village, an urban renewal development surrounding Busch Stadium that the Cardinals promised the city they would help build as part of the stadium agreement. Though the team faces fines for not opening the development on time, the site remains a muddy lake filled with rainwater.

RIGHT: Cardinals first baseman Albert Pujols catches a hit off the Tigers' Curtis Granderson and tags first base to get Granderson out during the sixth inning of Game 4 of the 2006 World Series at Busch Stadium.

NATIONALS PARK

Washington, DC

Nationals (NL) 2008–present

When the second team known as the Washington Senators left for Arlington, Texas, in 1972, it marked the sixth time in a century that major league baseball had abandoned Washington. The city had lost two teams in 1885 and one in 1890, 1900, and 1961. When the Montreal Expos were purchased by the other twenty-nine major league teams, making it a ward of the baseball state, it was only a matter of time before the team moved to the nation's capital. The Washington Nationals were born in 2005, and after three years at drab RFK Stadium, moved into their idyllic new park in 2008. Situated on a river bank, surrounded by cherry trees, and within sight of a number of national landmarks, Nationals Park was the reward for patient Washingtonians who had been without major league ball for thirty-three years.

The Expos' relocation had been strenuously protested by Baltimore Orioles owner Peter Angelos, who feared added competition would hurt his nearby franchise. But the abrasive and eccentric Angelos didn't have enough clout among other owners to block the move. MLB appeased him by insuring the Orioles against lost revenue up to $130 million, and by giving him 90 percent ownership of a new cable network that would carry both O's and Nats games. The construction of a new stadium met with opposition, too. The ballpark was to be built at the city's expense, even though most of its patrons were expected to come from affluent suburbs, which didn't contribute to the financing. Public opinion polls showed that DC residents opposed the deal by as much as a 2-1 margin, and the only concession the city council could win from MLB was a promise to contribute $20 million to the $611 million price tag. After nearly two years of contentious negotiations that included accusations of bad faith on both sides, the council finally approved the new stadium on December 21, 2004, by a 7-6 vote. The path was cleared for the Montreal Expos to become the Washington Nationals, but residents took out their frustrations about the financing deal at the ballot box, voting out three of the council members who supported the project.

The park's location is ideal—in Southeast Washington on the northwest bank of the Anacostia River, just a few hundred yards downstream from the Washington Navy Yard. From the upper deck, fans have a view of the US Capitol (about a mile to the north, behind the left-field foul pole). Just a few blocks northeast of the park is the Tidal Basin,

home to the Washington Monument, Jefferson and Lincoln memorials, and various war memorials.

Local developers licked their chops at the opportunity to gentrify this waterfront area, which despite its proximity to so many tourist destinations, was dotted with vacant lots, sex clubs, and empty buildings. These would be replaced by more than a thousand hotel rooms, 785,000 square feet of retail space, and 15 million square feet of office space. "Imagine this two years from now," Michael Stevens, the project director told the *New York Times*. "[We] are literally building a brand-new downtown." Longtime neighborhood residents were not so bullish, however. "The projects are still here, the drugs are still here, the shooting is still here," business owner Eglon Daley told the *Times*. "I don't see where people on this side are getting a job over there [at the ballpark]."

Nationals Park was designed by HOK Sport, for whom the stadium was an opportunity to bounce back from the rote self-plagiarism that had characterized many of its post–Camden Yards creations. Reviews on the design, however, were mixed. Some praised the shiny steel and glass facade that eschewed the red-brick retro look, and the edifice's straight lines designed to evoke DC's public buildings, especially the East Wing of the National Gallery of Art designed by IM Pei. Others found it to be too utilitarian. "It is a machine for baseball... and it makes no apologies about its purely functional design," *Washington Post* culture critic Philip Kennicott wrote. "Although it is positioned on one of the most symbolically significant and potentially beautiful axes of the city, aligned with the Capitol and next to the Anacostia River, it all but fades into the landscape. Two disastrously situated parking garages—reserved for high-paying ticket-holders—obscure the front entrance, and its other three sides present a bland face to the world."

Parking is not the only way in which Nationals Park plays to well-heeled lobbyists and other spectators with unlimited cash flow. The park contains a whopping 4,000 club seats and 78 luxury boxes, each with its own restroom. Patrons with high-priced tickets are given access to otherwise off-limits areas of the park, including private restaurants and even the Nationals' batting cages underneath the stands.

The playing field is sunk 24 feet below street level, so 55 percent of fans walk down, not up, to their seats upon entering the park. The main interior features white-painted beams and navy blue seats (plus one section of red, padded, movie

NATIONALS™ · Topps

NOOK LOGAN

NATIONALS™ · Topps

DMITRI YOUNG

NATIONALS™ · Topps

MIKE BACSIK

BELOW: In an attempt to break free from the red bricks and rotundas that characterize most other retro-era ballparks, Nationals Park has a glass and steel facade and right angles that mimic the public buildings found throughout the DC area. Approximately 7,800 tons of steel were used to construct the park.

theater–style seats in front of a centerfield restaurant, The Red Porch). When the park hosted its first Nationals contest, patrons were immediately scandalized by the exorbitant concession prices, which included $7.00 for french fries and $10.00 for a fish taco. People seemed to enjoy other aspects of the ballpark experience, though, particularly the fourth-inning presidents race. Imported from RFK Stadium, which had adapted it from Milwaukee's sausage race, the event features presidents Washington, Lincoln, Jefferson, and Teddy Roosevelt racing around the bases (for the sake of humor Roosevelt is never allowed to win).

Teddy Roosevelt—a champion of national forests—would have been proud of Nationals Park's commitment to the environment. The first "green" sports stadium in the country, as certified by the US Green Building Council, the environmentally friendly park features energy-efficient field lighting that reduces power use by 21 percent, low-flow restroom fixtures, 20 percent recycled product in its building material, special parking for hybrid cars, battery-electric vehicles for use in stadium operations, plentiful recycling bins in the stands, a partially "green roof" that's covered with oxygen-emitting vegetation, and an intricate water runoff system to prevent the park from contaminating the nearby river.

However, the Nationals undercut their burgeoning environmental reputation by naming Exxon-Mobil the sponsor of the seventh inning stretch. The fans rebelled, especially when rumors began to swirl that the park itself was to be renamed after Exxon as part of a lucrative naming rights deal. Environmental groups organized protests, and the Exxon ads played during the seventh inning of each game were met with resounding boos. Aside from the controversy itself, the Exxon snafu emphasized the degree to which Nationals Park symbolizes its home city. It's a ballpark that seeks to be both environmentalist and industrialist, elitist and populist, retro and modern, classy and kitsch. Like Washington itself, the park is full of contradictions.

December 21, 2001 The DC City Council approves floating rate bonds to fund the construction of Nationals Park.

2008

Nationals Park opens on March 22 with a college game between George Washington University and St. Joseph's. Dimensions are 336 feet to left field, 377 to left-center, 402 to center, 370 to right-center, and 335 to right. Early indications are that the park will be neutral, favoring neither hitters nor pitchers. Capacity is 41,888, about 10 percent of which is high-end luxury box and club seating.

RIGHT: Nationals utility man Willie Harris makes a break for it in a game against the Houston Astros at Nationals Park on July 12, 2008. After the season, Harris will sign a two-year, $3 million deal to stay with the team.

BELOW: Workers pour concrete during the construction of Nationals Park, on July 11, 2007. The first sports stadium to be certified as "green" by the US Green Building Council, Nationals Park cost $611 million and took two years to complete. Built on the site of a former landfill, layers of old bricks were found 12 feet below the surface, pointing to the possibility that roads or buildings existed on the site before the landfill was created.

May 4, 2006 Using shovels made out of bats, ground is broken at the future site of the stadium.

March 30, 2008 Nationals Park holds its first regular-season game (a win against the Braves) and sets a record for the most-watched Opening Night at a ballpark on ESPN networks, with 3,656,000 viewers.

April 17, 2008 Pope Benedict XVI holds a mass at the park, which is attended by 47,000 worshippers.

March 30, 2008

Maybe He Should Change His Name to Ryan Dylan In perhaps the most exhilarating ballpark debut since the original Yankee Stadium, Nationals Park sees the home team win on a ninth-inning walk-off homer by Ryan Zimmerman, the twenty-three-year-old wunderkind who, in just his third full season, has become the face of the Nationals franchise. The Nationals score two runs in the first inning, as Cristian Guzman collects the park's first hit and Nick Johnson the first RBI. It looks as if the Nats will escape with a 2-1 win, but the Braves tie it up on a ninth-inning passed ball. The fans appear deflated until Zimmerman steps to the plate with two outs in the bottom of the ninth. ESPN.com's Jerry Crasnick describes the scene: "A ripple built into a cheer, a cheer escalated to something more, and even the understated Zimmerman felt a slight chill up his spine." Zimmerman's blast off Atlanta's Peter Moylan sends everyone home happy, and is already the fourth walk-off homer of his young career.

Nationals 3, Braves 2

BELOW: A view toward the infield from center field during a game between the Washington Nationals and the former Washington Senators, now the Texas Rangers. The outfield is made from a Kentucky bluegrass blend, while the infield dirt was imported from Maryland. The latter gets its red hue from Turface, an additive that makes the dirt absorb water faster and compact less easily.

CITI FIELD

Queens, New York

Mets (NL) 2009–present

CARLOS BELTRAN

By the twenty-first century, few ball clubs needed an upgrade more than the New York Mets, whose forty-five-year-old Shea Stadium was not much more than a shabby concrete dough-nut surrounded by parking lots and auto body shops. Not only was Shea a mediocre stadium, but it had also been the depressing site of spectacular late-season collapses in the Mets' final two years there. "Shea was old when it was new," Fox TV broadcaster Tim McCarver quipped when the Mets' most recent home opened. "I'm glad it's gone." He wasn't the only one. Mets fans now have a stadium to be proud of, from its pleasing design to the breadth of amenities inside. Better yet, they have a home field that can begin to rival that of their more glamorous westerly neighbors, the Yankees.

The Mets have long been accustomed to playing second fiddle to the Yankees, and the opening of Citi Field was no exception. Like the Yankees, in late 2001 the Mets struck a deal with outgoing mayor Rudy Giuliani to build a retractable-roof stadium—a deal that collapsed immediately upon Michael Bloomberg's taking office. Four years later, the club finally managed an agreement with Bloomberg for an open-air stadi-um next door to their existing one. Unfortunately, the Mets had the misfortune of having their new park, Citi Field, open within a week of the new Yankee Stadium, and Queens' new baseball palace was forced to share the spotlight with the House That Steinbrenner Built.

With a price tag of $800 million, Citi Field cost only half as much as new Yankee Stadium, which masks the fact that the Mets' home is still one of the most expensive stadiums ever built. Like new Yankee Stadium, the park was financed through the sale of tax-free municipal bonds. The Mets are obligated to pay $697 million back over time, but the stadium will none-theless cost taxpayers hundreds of millions of dollars in infra-structure costs and tax breaks, including waived property taxes. Though the city budget office pegged the public's portion of the cost at $138 million, an independent analysis by econo-mist Neil DeMause estimates that taxpayers will eventually pay $614 million for the stadium, while the Mets, after all their tax breaks, will be out only $134 million.

In 2006, the ballpark's naming rights were sold to one of the world's largest banking conglomerates, Citigroup, for $400 million over twenty years. By the time the stadium's doors opened in April 2009, however, Citigroup had fallen victim to the economic crisis that started in 2008 and had been

MIKE PELFREY

JOSE REYES

DAVID WRIGHT

ABOVE: As grounds crews ready the field and a marching band practices outside for Shea Stadium's final Opening Day in 2008, Citi Field undergoes construction. When the new field is complete, Shea Stadium will be razed to make room for more parking.

given a $350 billion government bailout. Taxpayers were furious that a portion of that money was going toward something as frivolous as a ballpark, and such nicknames as Bailout Park and TARP Field soon emerged for the venue.

Despite the public outcry regarding the use of bailout money, Mets fans fell in love with the new park immediately. Citi Field has a homey, informal atmosphere, with about 15,000 fewer seats than Shea Stadium had—all angled toward the infield and most much closer to the action. At Citi Field, fans finally have a reason to get out of their (2-inch wider) seats. The new ballpark features concourses with views of the field, a Mets museum, and many more restaurants than its predecessor—including longtime New York favorite the Shake Shack.

Some fans have greater reasons than others to get out of their seats. Rows 1 through 5 of the upper-deck 500 level contain many seats without views of home plate or the pitcher's mound, while thousands of fans in the bleachers are blocked from seeing vast swaths of the outfield. These partial-view seats sell for as much as $56 apiece, and like the Yankees, the Mets got caught red-handed selling them without indicating that they have obstructed views. Unlike the Yankees, however, the Mets were anything but conciliatory when fans and journalists questioned the practice. Entering the park's inaugural season, they stood by their official position that obstructed-view seats do not exist at Citi Field. "I understand that if there's a fly ball hit to the wall, you're going to lose it," Dave Howard, a Mets executive vice president, said as he understated the case to radio station WFAN. "We do have, you know, TVs, extensive high-definition televisions everywhere, you know, we do—we made that accommodation." Unfortunately for fans in the outfield seats, these ballyhooed HDTV screens are nowhere to be seen. In order to see an outfielder catch a fly ball, one has to be prescient enough to know exactly when it will be hit, and make a beeline for the concession stand where the TVs are.

No matter where a seat is located, its price is usually out of reach for the average consumer. At the beginning of the park's

inaugural season, the Mets claimed to have an average ticket price of only $37, but that figure was extremely misleading because it included only nonpremium seats; a large percentage of the stadium is actually premium seating, which had an average cost of $149 per ticket in 2009 (with the seats closest to the field running as much as $695 per game).

Citi Field was designed by the Populous firm, formerly known as HOK Sport, and like so many other HOK projects, the design sought to mask the building's insatiable commercialism through the use of old-timey touches. At its core, Citi Field is standard, paint-by numbers HOK: a brick exterior, navy-blue-painted steelwork, dark green seats reminiscent of those at the Polo Grounds, and the aping of a famed work of local architecture—in this case, the Hell Gate Bridge, which trains use to cross the East River and which is reproduced in miniature as a pedestrian walkway connecting Citi with a subway station. Unlike the Yankees, the Mets didn't want the architecture of their new stadium to echo the old one. "The Mets, having no ancient ballpark of their own to evoke, have appropriated someone else's," quipped the *New Yorker*'s Paul Goldberger. Indeed, Citi Field's nostalgic feel was achieved by mimicking one of the most beloved ballparks in New York City's history, Ebbets Field. It made sense: the Mets are the spiritual descendants of the Brooklyn Dodgers, having been created in order to fill the void in National League fandom left when the team moved to California. Most Mets fans—at least, those who are old enough—were Dodgers fans originally.

From the outside, Citi Field is virtually an exact re-creation of Ebbets, with windows galore and the same pattern of repeated red-brick archways. The right-field wall, too, echoes Ebbets' famous wall, which was a mishmash of wood, concrete, and wire that produced ricochets at an unimaginable number of angles. Citi Field's wall isn't quite as complex, but it wraps like a snake around the bullpen while also gradually getting shorter as it nears the foul line. It promises to be a daunting challenge for opposing right fielders—as well as a likely home-field advantage for any Mets right fielder who manages to learn all its nuances. "You have to take some chances on balls and hope for the best," Citi Field's first right fielder, Ryan Church, told the *New York Daily News*. "If it hits that concrete, it's shooting somewhere. It's one of those things where you have to just guess."

The park's main entrance rotunda not only echoes that of the historic Brooklyn park, it's named after Dodgers legend Jackie Robinson. Serving as a touching tribute to the groundbreaking player's life, family, and impact on baseball, the Jackie Robinson Rotunda is adorned with quotations, photographs, and reminders of the values he held dear. Robinson's name is inlaid in the marble and granite floor, and a giant sculpture of his number, 42, serves as centerpiece. "This is an overwhelming experience," Robinson's eighty-five-year-old widow, Rachel, said at the rotunda's groundbreaking ceremony on April 15, 2008. "When fans and families and children walk through that rotunda," she later told the Associated Press, "I hope they're going to reflect on not just what they see that

Jackie Robinson accomplished, but also think about themselves and say, 'What am I doing? How am I running my life? Who am I affecting? What am I doing in my community?'"

Not much followed the Mets from the old ballpark to the new one. One feature that did, though, was the home run apple, a 9-foot-tall mechanical apple that lit up and emerged from an upside-down top hat whenever a Mets player homered at Shea. The original version, a beloved kitsch landmark since its debut in 1980, was retired and placed in the Citi Field concourse. Meanwhile, a much larger version, sans top hat, was built behind the centerfield fence. The other Shea remnant that made the pilgrimage to Citi Field was its gang of feral cats. Since the early days of Shea Stadium, between twenty and forty stray felines had made the ballpark their home at any given time, according to an estimate by a local feline rescue group. The Mets took the cats to shelters whenever they were able to capture them, but the stadium's cat population nonetheless sustained itself. Questions about whether the cats would migrate with the Mets to Citi Field were answered during the new stadium's very first regular-season game, when an orange tabby jumped onto the field and dashed past startled on-deck batter David Wright. Play was briefly interrupted before the cat scampered back into the stands. It was an apt metaphor. Eternally in the shadow of the Yankees, the Mets are still the stray cats of New York baseball, spanking-new stadium or not.

LEFT: A stray cat runs on the field during the third inning on Opening Day at Citi Field. The *New York Daily News* will run a full-page photo of the cat on the front of its sports section the next day.

BELOW: Citi Field, with the impressive Jackie Robinson Rotunda visible through the front windows, took its design from Brooklyn's Ebbets Field, which was torn down in 1960. To celebrate the rotunda's opening, the Mets made a contribution to the Jackie Robinson Foundation, which provides college scholarships to economically disadvantaged minorities. The economically disadvantaged, however, could never afford a good seat inside the ballpark: Citi's cheapest infield tickets cost anywhere from $90 to $210, depending on the game.

YANKEE STADIUM [II]

The Bronx, New York

Yankees (AL) 2009–present

OPPOSITE: Yankee Stadium is the most expensive stadium ever built, and it appropriately contains several upscale dining areas—called "signature spaces"—throughout the park. The members-only Audi Yankees Club is located in the corner of left field, while the Hard Rock Cafe and NYY Steak are located by the Great Hall, an area on the right-field side of the park that pays tribute to Yankees history. Situated in dead center field is the Mohegan Sun Sports Bar, which costs $90–$95 per game for entry or $750 for a full year's membership. In addition to offering two full bars and truffle fries, it also blocks the views from 1,048 seats on either side of it. First base and right field cannot be seen from the left of the bar, and third base and left field are obstructed from the right. These undesirable seats, originally sold at regular prices to unwitting customers, were lowered to $5 after *New York Newsday* outed the Yankees for their failure to inform purchasers of the obstruction. Even before a single game was played at the new park, the *New York Times* had dubbed the area to the left of the bar "the already-notorious Section 239."

In 2009, after eighty-six memorable years in the original Yankee Stadium, baseball's most prestigious franchise abandoned the House That Ruth Built in favor of the House That Steinbrenner Built. The new edition of Yankee Stadium isn't quite baseball's largest park—with a capacity of 52,325, it ranks second to Dodger Stadium—but it is nonetheless the most lavish, ambitious, and expensive stadium ever built. At an initial cost of $1.5 billion, it was the first ballpark ever budgeted at more than a billion dollars. (The only stadium to even approach that figure previously was "The Big Owe," Montreal's Stade Olympique, which cost about Can$1.6 billion—most of it due to unanticipated repairs that took place long after the stadium opened.)

The journey of new Yankee Stadium's construction was a long one. As early as 1984—less than a decade after the completion of a Yankee Stadium renovation that was estimated to cost anywhere from $48 million to $160 million—team owner George Steinbrenner began threatening to move the Bronx Bombers to New Jersey unless taxpayers built him a brand-new park. The team also examined parts of Manhattan, with a 1996 study commissioned by the Yankees, the City, and the State and conducted by architectural firm HOK concluding that the best site for the new stadium would be between 30th and 33rd streets along the Hudson River. However, the team's options weren't explored in earnest until the 2002 expiration of Yankee Stadium's lease approached, and Steinbrenner's periodic threats to move became more and more serious.

In December 2001, with the city still reeling from the September 11 attacks, the team finally struck a deal with outgoing mayor—and noted Yankees fan—Rudy Giuliani for a new ballpark. The new Yankee Stadium was to feature a retractable roof and cost $800 million, with the cost split between the team and the City. However, when Michael Bloomberg replaced Giuliani as mayor, he killed that deal, striking a new agreement in June 2005. A total of $1.2 billion in tax-exempt municipal bonds would be sold to build the open-air stadium, to be paid back by the team over a period of forty-three years. Although the Yankees are obligated to pay for the cost of their new park eventually, it is officially owned by the City, so as to exempt the team from paying property taxes. Because of waived taxes, infrastructure improvements made by the City, and other fees, the public will end up paying for a huge portion of the park.

According to New York City's budget office, Yankee Stadium will cost taxpayers around $362 million, but estimates by economist and stadium expert Neil DeMause and the *New York Times* cite the cost as upwards of $1 billion.

New Yorkers were outraged at the project's price tag, but on August 16, 2006, ground was broken on a site immediately north of the existing stadium. (Steinbrenner's often-stated concerns about fan safety in the neighborhood—cited to the press as why he wanted to move out of the Bronx—had by now mysteriously disappeared.) After thirty months of construction, the new Yankee Stadium opened for business on April 3, 2009, with an exhibition game against the Chicago Cubs. Designed by Populous (formerly known as HOK Sport), it was easy to see how the money had been spent. It was an aesthetic marvel, hearkening back to the original Yankee Stadium—not the 1976 renovated version that took much of the soul out of the historic shrine. Most visibly, the new park contains a replica of the distinctive copper frieze that ringed Yankee Stadium's upper grandstand from 1923 to 1973. The frieze had been destroyed in the renovation, and a white-painted concrete version, less than half the size, was placed behind the outfield. The new stadium's version more closely mimics the original, albeit in much less detail, and made of steel instead of copper.

Another aspect of the original Yankee Stadium that had been discarded during the renovation was the stately engraved lettering announcing "YANKEE STADIUM" at the main entrance, which was replaced by a sign made of tacky blue plastic. Although the new park features large, blue lettering above the granite and limestone facade, the name of the park is engraved above the main entrance, accompanied by bronze eagle medallions just like the original. Another old touch is the set of three flagpoles behind the outfield fence, one of which is topped by a bronzed bat that once belonged to Lou Gehrig. The stadium has also received raves for reconnecting itself to the surrounding city. "The slot that separated the scoreboard from the right-field stands in the old stadium has been re-created, so you can still catch glimpses of the subway rumbling by—a reminder that the stadium has been carved out of the heart of a living, thriving city," wrote *New York Times* architecture critic Nicolai Ouroussoff.

Monument Park—a group of statues and plaques that commemorate great Yankees of yesteryear—was moved from the park's predecessor and situated, as at its previous

home, in dead center field. One difference, though, is that it's now directly below the high-priced Mohegan Sun Sports Bar, which itself is underneath a spectacular 59-by-101-foot video board. In contrast, old-fashioned hand-operated scoreboards stand in left and right fields. Monument Park is now complemented by the Great Hall, another tribute to Yankees history that greets fans at the main entrance.

The field's dimensions are borrowed directly from its renovated predecessor: 318 feet to left field, 399 to left-center, 408 to center, 385 to right-center, and 314 to right—albeit with slightly less foul territory. However, early indications point to the fact that it may be much easier for lefties to hit home runs than it was at the original Yankee Stadium. At the old park, the right-field fence was curved, but at the new park, the scoreboard affixed to the wall makes it much straighter. In the first five games at the new stadium, twenty-one home runs were hit, fifteen of which were to right field. Whether this is because of the new wall or is simply a fluke remains to be seen. What is noteworthy is that unlike the House That Ruth Built, this Yankee Stadium does not have dimensions tailored to suit its star slugger. Alex Rodriguez, expected to spend much of the second decade of the twenty-first century chasing Barry Bonds' career home run record, will have to do it in a ballpark that places right-handed hitters like himself at a disadvantage.

However, A-Rod is probably mollified by the quantum leap in facilities for the players. The large, oval-shaped Yankees clubhouse is significantly larger than the old, cramped one. It features, among other things, a computer at every wood-paneled locker. Manager Joe Girardi's office is a three-room

The Yankees take on the Indians on Opening Day at Yankee Stadium, April 16, 2009. The new ballpark, which has given players a huge upgrade in facilities, is a big hit with the team. "It sure is wonderful," manager Joe Girardi told the *New York Times*. "Every day we walk in, there's just a huge smile. You're excited to get to work every day."

Come for the Baseball, Stay for the Food

At early ballparks, the idea of selling prepared food would have seemed ludicrous. These ramshackle parks barely had grandstands, let alone facilities for making or storing food. For the most part, fans simply brought their own snacks, although concessions that required little or no preparation, such as popcorn, peanuts, and candy, were sold at parks (alongside cigarettes) almost from the beginning.

The quintessential baseball food—the hot dog—is alleged to have first been sold at a ballpark by Chris Von Der Ahe's American Association St. Louis Browns in the 1880s. By the early 1900s, the frankfurter was already staggeringly popular among baseball fans, and it has remained a favorite. Over the years, teams have brought in smokie links, Polish and Italian sausages, and bratwurst to supplement the basic pup. The most famous hot dog in baseball may be the "Dodger Dog," which can be purchased either grilled or steamed, and is loved and hated by Angelenos in equal amounts.

Of course, many fans need something extra to properly savor their ballpark hot dog—a little beer. In the early part of the twentieth century, the upstart American League successfully lured fans away from the National League in part because it allowed patrons to drink. In addition to buying brew there, fans could bring their own beer into the park, a tradition that lasted even into the 1980s at some stadiums. Teams soon realized, however, that many fans would pay any price to enjoy the game with a beer, especially a higher class of imported beer or a microbrew. A bottle of premium beer can top the $10 mark at some parks, with management citing the high price not as a way to make a fantastic profit but as a smart strategy to curb excessive drinking, thereby keeping the ballpark "family-friendly." However, some stadiums now serve liquor, especially in their luxury suites, and new Yankee Stadium features a martini bar.

Before the 1970s, there weren't many options for noshing at the park. Some clubs had added cheese sandwiches, hamburgers, ice cream, or cotton candy to their offerings, but the Americanness of the ballpark experience made little room for adventurous tastes. However, increased attendance from different demographic groups caused ballpark menus to expand, and Americanized "ethnic" foods, such as gourmet pizzas and nachos, began to appear at concession stands. Today, ballparks draw on diverse fan bases and local traditions to build their menus. Cincinnati sells five-way chili at Great American Ball Park, while Cleveland and Milwaukee offer special hot dog condiments (spicy brown mustard and "red sauce," respectively). Philadelphia and Pittsburgh, meanwhile, are proud of their different takes on the cheese steak. Mindful of Latino fans, San Diego and Anaheim offer quesadillas and fish tacos. Kansas City, Houston, and Baltimore each claim to have baseball's best barbecue. The garlic fries at AT&T Park are legendary, while Seattle goes all-out with sushi. Even the Yankees, long-time holdouts against a diverse menu, now offer empanadas, noodle bowls, and fresh deli sandwiches, and 70 percent of their concession stands have cooking capacity—five times that of their old park.

The one thing that remains the same with ballpark food is that healthy eating options are usually a bit hard to find, unless you don't mind a lackluster salad or a so-so veggie burger. But even if you're at AT&T Park, home of the portobello mushroom sandwich, or Safeco Field, which offers an entire "Health Hut" that has vegan options, you may be hard pressed not to use your hometown team's on-field success—or failure—as an excuse to indulge in a little Cracker Jack.

suite. Plush couches and flat-screen HDTVs are everywhere, and a training facility, weight room, spa, swimming pool, and lounge are all on-site. "I think everyone is going to be a little bit spoiled," Yankees superstar Derek Jeter told the Associated Press. "If you were sitting down and drawing out a stadium as a player, I don't think there's anything else you could add."

There are also plenty of luxuries for the fans. High-priced suites and amenities for the well-heeled consumer have become commonplace at retro-era ballparks, but with the opening of Yankee Stadium (and the Mets' new Citi Field), baseball went a step further, finally abandoning all pretense of attracting everyday fans and families. Yankee Stadium was unapologetically designed to be a park of the wealthy, by the wealthy, and for the wealthy. According to Team Marketing Report, an independent firm that researches stadium ticket prices, a family of four sitting in nonpremium seats would pay an average of $410.88—about 1 percent of the average American family's after-tax income—to attend a game at Yankee Stadium in 2009. As state assemblyman Richard Brodsky put it, "You have a stadium paid for by taxpayers that taxpayers can't afford to get into." The cheapest lower-deck ticket between the bases runs $350, while the cheapest field-level tickets are $90, in the left- and right-field corners. The worst upper-deck seats cost $23 apiece, while the distant outfield bleachers ($14 a seat) and outfield seats with half of their view of the field obstructed by the Mohegan Sun Sports Bar ($5) are a relative bargain. The stadium also contains fifty-two luxury suites costing between $600,000 and $850,000 per season. Although all fifty-two were sold out by Opening Day, in the park's opening weeks many seats close to the field—such as some of the $2,625-per-game ones between the two dugouts—didn't sell. At first, the Yankees were reluctant to lower prices, claiming they didn't want to anger those who had already bought tickets. However, less than two weeks after Opening Day, the organization reversed course by reducing prices for various premium seats, in some cases by as much as 50 percent. The club also announced that certain premium-seat season ticket holders would receive additional tickets for free—a move that would also help remedy the embarrassing display of empty blue chairs ringing the field.

The ticket situation further revealed the problem with the new Yankee Stadium (and, indeed, with all retro ballparks): It is difficult, despite all its historical flourishes, to see the new park as anything other than a gigantic, intricately constructed ATM machine spewing money into the pocket of George Steinbrenner. And as a work of architecture, an ATM machine is hard to get excited about. Time will tell if, in a harder economic climate, the money-making aspect of the retro ballparks will continue to win out over their nostalgic influences. In the meantime, scores of Yankees fans hope that their legendary team will succeed as famously as they did in the old stadium, making their second eponymous park as historic as the first.

Bibliography

Newspapers and Magazines

Alton Telegraph, The Associated Press, Baltimore Sun, Boston Globe, Bucks County Times, Cincinnati Enquirer, Dallas Morning News, Delaware County Times, Deseret News, Detroit Free Press, Detroit News, Forbes, Harper's, Hartford Courant, Japan Times, Kansas City Star, Los Angeles Times, Mansfield News Journal, Milwaukee Business Journal, Milwaukee Journal-Sentinel, Newark Star-Ledger, New York Newsday, New York Daily News, New York Times, The New Yorker, The Onion, Minneapolis Star-Tribune, Philadelphia Inquirer, Pittsburgh Post-Gazette, Rocky Mountain News, St. Louis Post-Dispatch, San Diego Business Journal, San Diego Union-Tribune, San Francisco Chronicle, Seattle Post-Intelligencer, Seattle Times, Sports Illustrated, Sporting News, Syracuse Herald-Journal, Tampa Tribune, Time, USA Today, Washington City Paper, Washington Post, Washington Times, Worcester Phoenix

Websites

baseball-almanac.com, baseball-reference.com, ballparks.com, ballparksofbaseball.com, ballparktour.com, bioproj.sabr.org, baseballhalloffame.org, ESPN.com, fieldofschemes.com, MLB.com, surveyofbuyingpower.com, teammarketing.com, walteromalley.com

Books and Articles

Axelson, Gustaf W. *"Commy": The Life Story of Charles A. Comiskey, the "Grand Old Roman" of Baseball and for Nineteen Years President and Owner of the American League Baseball Team "The White Sox."* Chicago: Reilly & Lee, 1919.

Bankes, James. *The Pittsburgh Crawfords.* Jefferson, NC: McFarland, 2001.

Benson, Michael. *Ballparks of North America: A Comprehensive Historical Reference to Baseball Grounds, Yards and Stadiums, 1845 to Present.* Jefferson, NC: McFarland, 1989.

Bruce, Janet. *The Kansas City Monarchs: Champions of Black Baseball.* Lawrence, KS: University Press of Kansas, 1987.

de Botton, Alain. *The Architecture of Happiness.* New York: Pantheon Books, 2006.

Delaney, Kevin J. and Rick Eckstein. *Public Dollars, Private Stadiums: The Battle Over Building Sports Stadiums.* Piscataway, NJ: Rutgers University Press, 2003.

Dixon, Phil with Patrick J. Hannigan. *The Negro Baseball Leagues: A Photographic History.* Mattituck, New York: Amereon House, 1992.

Enders, Eric. *Ballparks: Then and Now.* Berkeley, CA: Thunder Bay Press, 2002.

———. *The Fall Classic: The Definitive History of the World Series.* New York: Sterling Publishing, 2007.

Gershman, Michael. *Diamonds: The Evolution of the Ballpark.* New York: Houghton Mifflin, 2003.

Gillette, Gary, Pete Palmer, et al. *The ESPN Baseball Encyclopedia (Fifth Edition).* New York: Sterling Publishing, 2008.

Hattam, Jennifer. "How Green is My Ballpark?" *Major League Baseball 2008 All-Star Game Program.*

Hogan, Lawrence. *Shades of Glory: The Negro Leagues and the Story of African-American Baseball.* Washington: National Geographic, 2006.

Holway, John. *Blackball Stars.* New York: Carroll & Graf, 1992.

———. *Voices From the Great Black Baseball Leagues.* New York: Dodd, Mead, 1975.

James, Bill. *The New Bill James Historical Baseball Abstract.* New York: The Free Press, 2001.

Knight, Jonathan. *Opening Day: Cleveland, the Indians, and a New Beginning.* Kent, OH: Kent State Press, 2002.

Kuklick, Bruce. *To Every Thing a Season: Shibe Park and Urban Philadelphia, 1909–1976.* Princeton, NJ: Princeton University Press, 1993.

Leventhal, Josh. *Take Me Out to the Ballpark.* Black Dog & Leventhal. New York: 2003.

Livingston, Bill and Greg Brinda. *The Great Book of Cleveland Sports Lists.* Philadelphia: Running Press, 2008.

Lorimer, Lawrence. *The National Baseball Hall of Fame and Museum Baseball Desk Reference.* New York: DK Publishing, 2002.

Lowry, Philip J. *Green Cathedrals.* New York: Walker & Company, 2006.

McGee, Bob. *The Greatest Ballpark Ever: Ebbets Field and the Story of the Brooklyn Dodgers.* Piscataway, NJ: Rutgers University Press, 2005.

McNeil, William. *Gabby Hartnett: The Life and Times of the Cubs' Greatest Catcher.* Jefferson, NC: McFarland, 2004.

Peeler, Jodie M. "The Greatest Location In The World: A History of Atlanta Stadium." Published at www.mindspring.com/~raisingirl/location.htm, 1997; accessed January 22, 2009.

Raney, Arthur A. and Jennings Bryant. *Handbook of Sports and Media.* New York: Routledge, 2006.

Ribowsky, Mark. *A Complete History of the Negro Leagues.* New York: Carol, 1995.

Richmond, Peter. *Ballpark: Camden Yards and the Building of an American Dream.* New York: Simon & Schuster, 1993.

Ritter, Lawrence. *Lost Ballparks.* New York: Penguin, 1994.

Ruck, Rob. *Sandlot Seasons: Sport in Black Pittsburgh.* Champaign, IL: University of Illinois Press, 1993.

Shea, Stuart. *Wrigley Field: The Unauthorized Biography.* Washington: Potomac Books, 2006.

Smith, Curt. *Storied Stadiums: Baseball's History Through Its Ballparks.* New York: Carroll & Graf, 2003.

———. *Voices of Summer: Ranking Baseball's 101 All-Time Best Announcers.* Boston: Da Capo Press, 2005.

Stout, Glenn, Richard A. Johnson, and Dick Johnson. *Red Sox Century.* New York: Houghton Mifflin Harcourt, 2004.

Sutton, Jim, Marc Sandalow, John Pastier, et al. *Ballparks: Yesterday and Today.* Edison, NJ: Chartwell Books, 2007.

Wesley, Doris A., Wiley Price, and Ann Morris. *Lift Every Voice and Sing: St. Louis African-Americans in the Twentieth Century.* Columbia, MO: University of Missouri Press, 1999.

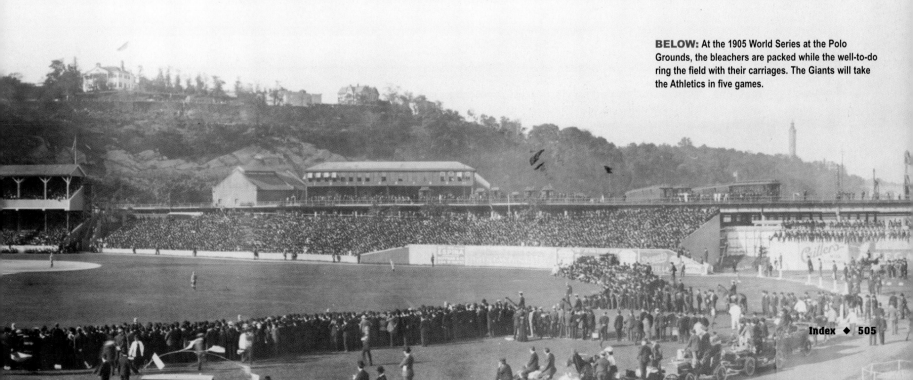

BELOW: At the 1905 World Series at the Polo Grounds, the bleachers are packed while the well-to-do ring the field with their carriages. The Giants will take the Athletics in five games.

OPPOSITE: Washington Senators infielder Germany
Schaefer tries out a newfangled camera at the Yankees'
Hilltop Park in 1911.

BELOW: The Red Sox take the field at their Huntington
Avenue Grounds during its last year of existence, 1911.

BELOW: The Red Sox take on the Yankees at Boston's Huntington Avenue Grounds in 1908.

Photography Credits

Admedia: 458–459, © Kevin R. Cooke

Alamy Photos: 236–237, © Richard Broadwell; 296, © Bill Grant; 179, © Robert Harding/Robert Harding Picture Library Ltd.

© Erik Almas: 2–3

© AP Images: 4–5, 34 inset, 70–71, 95, 106–107, 164, 168–169, 188, 189 middle right, 191 top, 196–197, 210–211, 214 top, 215 bottom, 217, 218 top, 238, 268 inset top, 280 top left, 282–283, 293 top, 300 top right, 322, 329, 335; 333 inset, © Jon Adams; 281 right, © Bill Baptist; 431 both, © John Bazemore; 349 top left, © Bill Becker; 280 bottom left, 466 bottom, © Brett Coomer; 284 middle, © Eric Draper; 382 top, © Mark Duncan; 104 bottom, 292, 488, © James A. Finley; 191 bottom, © Robert Frehm; 355 bottom, © Andre Forget; 203 top, © Gary Gardiner; 167 top, © Morry Gash; 470–471, 471, © Darren Hauck; 334, © Ron Heflin; 307 inset, © Lenny Ignelzi; 502, © Julie Jacobson; 330–331, © Joseph Kaczmarek; 137, © Rusty Kennedy; 195 bottom, 265 top left, © Mark Lennihan; 323, © Mark Lyons; 296 inset, © Kevin Manning/St. Louis Post Dispatch; 368 inset, © Jim Mone; 138, © Carlos Osorio; 131, © Piersol; 340, © Charlie Riedel; 500 top, © Frances Roberts; 330 inset right, © Amy Sancetta; 164–165, © John Swart; 320–321, © Tom Uhlman; 330 inset left, © George Wildman; 426 inset, © David Zalubowski; 345 inset top, © Ed Zurga

The Boston Society: 121, Courtesy of the Bostonian Society/Old State House Museum: Boston Streets Collection, ca. 1855–1999

Boston Public Library: 118 top, 119, 122 bottom, 170, 173 top, 173 background, 174 inset, 175 background

© Dustin Bradford: 423

The Canadian Press/La Presse: 313; 348, © Dick Loeck/Toronto Star; 348 inset, © Boris Spremo/Toronto Star

Carnegie Museum of Art, Pittsburgh: 59, © Harold Corsini. Gift of Carnegie Library of Pittsburgh

© Jeff Chevrier: 381

Chicago History Museum: 6–7 (SDN-065863), 26 (SDN-003127); 72 (SDN-008841) and 76 (SDN-008786), The Chicago Daily News

Cincinnati Museum Center-Cincinnati Historical Society Library: 31, 109 right, 109 background

Cleveland Public Library/Photograph Collection: 68 top

Cleveland State University Library Special Collections: 1, 66, 69 middle, 202

© Corbis: 38, 40–41, 48 top, 53 bottom, 55, 56–57 bottom, 61, 65 inset right, 69 top, 77 top and bottom, 78 middle and bottom, 83 bottom, 85 right, 86 bottom, 87 left, 88, 88 inset, 99 top, 100 middle and bottom, 102 bottom, 110, 114 top, 121 right, 122 top left, 122–123, 123, 133 inset, 134 top, 136, 137 inset, 140–141, 146 top and bottom, 147 inset, 149 top, 150, 151 top left, 152 inset, 153 bottom, 156, 160 left and right, 162–163 top, 164 top left, 172 right, 173 middle, 174, 175 middle, 178, 187 bottom, 193, 199 top, 201 insets, 206–207, 207 inset, 213 top, 214 bottom left, 219 top, 220 top, 227, 234 bottom, 235 top, 239, 240, 241 inset, 242 inset, 252, 253; 254 left, 254 inset, 260, 260–261 background, 261 inset right, 263 inset left, 269 top, 270, 274, 275 inset, 276–277, 277 inset bottom, 278 top and bottom right, 284 top, 286 top and bottom, 287 top, 295 right, 302 inset left, 309 inset, 317 top and bottom, 318, 323 inset left, 331, 336 left, 341 inset, 342 right, 361, 362 left, 364; 188 inset, © Art Abfier; 449, 450 top, 451 bottom right, © Andy Altenburger/Icon SMI; 126 bottom, © Walter G. Arce/ Icon SMI; 244 bottom, © Armando Arorizo/Zuma Press; 194 inset, 409 inset, 477 top, © David Bergman/Corbis; 356 top, 357 insets top and bottom, © Shaun Best/Reuters; 374, © Mike Blake/ Reuters; 350–351, © Tibor Bognár; 362 right, 363 bottom left and right © Anthony P. Bolante/Reuters; 245 left, © Matt A. Brown/Icon SMI; 243, 248, © Matt A. Brown/NewSport; 454, © BSF/NewSport; 244 top, 289, 427, © Paul Buck/epa; 457 top, © Darryl Bush/San Francisco Chronicle; 104 top, © Loren Callahan/Reuters; 255 bottom, 492 inset bottom, © Gary Cameron/ Reuters; 319 bottom, © Jason Cohn/ Reuters; 449 inset, © Rebecca Cook; 359, © Philip James Corwin; 158 bottom, © Mark Cowan/Reuters; 448 middle, © Richard Cummins; 229 top, © Lou Dematteis/Reuters; 297, © Albert Dickson/TSN/Zuma Press; 481 inset top, © Jonathan Ernst/Reuters; 338–339, © Kevin Felt/Icon SMI; 267, © Kevin Fleming; 442–443, © Natalie Fobes; 468–469, © Allen Fredrickson/Icon SMI; 125 top left, 126 top © Rick Friedman; 406 inset, 408 inset, © Joe Giza/Reuters; 456 inset top, © Carlos Avila Gonzalez/ San Francisco Chronicle; 456 background, © Philip Gould; 127, 426 top right, © CJ Gunther/epa; 367 top, © Robin Jerstad; 349 right, © Jollimore; 345 inset bottom, © Dave Kaup/Reuters; 249, © Brooks Kraft; 378 bottom, © Bob Krist; 325 bottom, © John Kuntz; 269 bottom, © Ron Kuntz; 497 top, © Justin Lane/ epa; 288, © Adrees Latif/Reuters; 485, © Stan Liu/Icon SMI; 483, © David Madison/NewSport; 410–411, © William Manning; 397 inset, © Tannen Maury/epa; 374–375, © Vick McKenzie/ NewSport; 480 inset top, © Tom Mihalek/ epa; 282 inset, © Danny Moloshok/epa; 185 inset, © John Munson/Star Ledger; 352 left and right, 354 right, 356 left, © Christinne Muschi/Reuters; 358, © Jeffry W. Myers; 319 top, © Gregg Newton; 166 middle, © Sue Ogrocki/Reuters; 496 top, © William Perlman/Star Ledger; 393 middle, 396 inset, 473, © Frank Polich/Reuters; 241, 287 bottom, © Neal Preston; 389, © Jose Fuste Raga; 284 bottom, © Kevin Reece/Icon SMI; 492, © Jason Reed/Reuters; 228 top, 301 right, © Paul Richards; 437 top right, © Rick Rickman/NewSport; 224, 316, © Charles E. Rotkin; 489, © Scott Rovak/ epa; 250–251, © Ron Sachs/CNP; 222–223, © Tony Sande; 395, © Alan Schien Photography; 375 top left, © Mark Serota/ Reuters; 366, © Richard Hamilton Smith; 125 top right, © Brian Snyder/Reuters; 228–229 bottom, 324, 368–369, 420–421 bottom, © Joseph Sohm/Visions of America; 262–263, © Shannon Stapleton/Reuters; 303 bottom right, © Dave Stephenson/Icon SMI; 400 top, © Ray Stubblebine/Icon SMI; 195 top, 263, 264 top, 265 bottom left, 265 right, © Ray Stubblebine/Reuters; 426, © Chase Swift; 389 inset, © Susumu Takahashi/Reuters; 332, © George Tiedemann; 309, © Jeff Topping/Reuters; 484, © Derrick Tuskan/Icon SMI; 439 top, © Scott Wachter/Icon SMI; 378 middle, © Nik Wheeler; 457 bottom, © Kimberly White; 167 middle, © Warren Wimmer/Icon SMI; 293 bottom, 386, © Rhona Wise/epa; 492–493, 493 bottom, © Ed Wolfstein/Icon SMI; 419 top, © David Woo/Dallas Morning News; 438 top, © Matt York/Reuters

The Detroit Public Library: 27, Courtesy of the Burton Historical Collection

© Jerry Driendl: 112–113, 128–129, 154–155, 158 middle, 163, 166–167 background, 256–257, 258–259 bottom, 333, 390–391, 394–395 bottom, 396–397, 404–405, 406–407, 408–409, 434–435, 436–437, 438–439 background, 440–441, 442 inset, 444–445, 446–447, 448 top and bottom, 450–451 bottom, 474–475, 476–477 bottom, 478, 479, 480–481 background

Ronald Einziger Collection: 259

© John Feasenmyer: 432–433

The Free Library of Philadelphia: 43

© Game Sports Venue: 277

The Gazette (Montreal): 312, 313 inset

© Getty Images: 79 bottom, 325 top; 485 inset bottom, © K.C. Alfred/San Diego Union-Tribune; 466, © Brian Bahr; 307 background, © Alan Band/ Fox Photos; 372, © Doug Benc; 342 left, © Bruce Bennett; 365, © Scott Boehm; 225, © Jon Brenneis/Time Life Pictures; 226, © Bill Bridges/Time Life Pictures; 268, © Simon Bruty; 281 inset, © Paul Buck/AFP; 153 top, © Ed Clark/ Time Life Pictures; 433 inset, © Scott Cunningham/AFP; 393 top, 472, © Jonathan Daniel; 337 inset, © Louis DeLuca/MLB Photos; 220 middle, © Diamond Images; 271 inset, © John Dickerson/AFP; 124–125 bottom, 176–177, 184–185, 246–247, 264–265 bottom, 400–401 bottom, 452–453, © Jerry Driendl; 341, © Stephen Dunn; 378 top, © John Edwards; 111, 214 bottom right, 295 left, 323 inset right, 324 inset, © Focus on Sport; 414 bottom, © Elsa Garrison; 413 inset, © Otto Greule, Jr.; 363 top, © Therese Frare/ AFP; 414 top, 432, © Jeff Haynes/AFP; 278 left, © Andy Hayt/Sports Illustrated; 203 bottom, 315, © Jeff Hixon; 261 inset left, © Walter Iooss, Jr./Sports Illustrated; 303 top right, 451 top, Jed Jacobsohn; 353, © Charles Laberge; 394 top, © Vincent Laforet/AFP; 255 inset, © Mitchell Layton; 308, © Bill Livingston/ MLB Photos; 304–305, © V.J. Lovero/ Sports Illustrated; 343 left, © G. Newman Lowrance; 387, © Andy Lyons; 380–381, © Alan Marsh/First Light; 417, 419 bottom, 421 top, 464, 465, 467 top, © Ronald Martinez; 105, © David Maxwell/ AFP; 495, © Chris McGrath; 79 top, © Al Messerschmidt; 376–377, © Peter Mintz/First Light; 306, © Donald Miralle; 124, 354 left, 425, © Ronald C. Modra/Sports Imagery; 384–385, © Doug Pensinger; 337, 499, © Rich Pilling/ MLB Photos; 101 bottom, 108, © Robert Riger; 412–413, © Joe Robbins; 370–371, © Eliot J. Schechter; 375 bottom, © Mark Serota; 415 bottom, 415 inset right, © Gregory Shamus; 344–345, © Jamie Squire; 379 top, 380 inset, 382 bottom, 383, © Rick Stewart; 415 top left, © Al Tielemans/Sports Illustrated; 86 top, Transcendental Graphics; 500, © Rob Tringali/ SportsChrome; 336 right, © Tony Triolo/ Sports Illustrated; 343 right, © Ron Vesely; 89, © Hank Walker/Time Life Pictures; 355 top, © Frank Whitney; 373, © Rhona Wise/AFP

© Otto Greule: 360–361

© Chris Harrell: 367 bottom

© Mark Hertzberg/Racine Journal Times: 208–209, 209

The Historical Society of Western Pennsylvania: 60 bottom

© Paul Hitz: 139 inset

IBI Group: 379 © Rod Robbie & Mike Allen/Robbie/Young + Wright/ IBI Group Architects

Icon SMI: 460, 461, © Andy Altenburger; 470 inset top, © John Biever/SI; 455, © John Cordes; 413, © Robert Dickson/ TSN/Zuma Press; 481 inset bottom, © Philadelphia Daily News/Zuma Press; 467 bottom, © San Antonio Express-News/Zuma Press; 388, © Cliff Welch; 491, © Ed Wolfstein

© James Idiart: 258

© David Kohrman: 138–139 bottom

© Robert Landau: 393 bottom

© Landov: 294; 496 bottom, © John Angelillo/UPI; 297 top inset, © Mike Blake/Reuters; 445 top, © Andy Clark/ Reuters, 497 bottom, © Lucas Jackson/ Reuters

Library of Congress: 8–9, 13, 16, 20–21, 26–27 bottom, 28 top, 28–29 bottom, 30 top and bottom, 34–35, 36–37, 39 top and bottom, 42, 42 inset, 43 top, 44–45, 46, 46–47, 47, 48 bottom, 49, 52–53 top, 58, 62 top, 63 top, 68–69 bottom, 76 top, 77 background, 82, 83 top, 85 left, 92, 93, 94 top and bottom, 96 top, 96–99 bottom, 98 top, 102 top, 109 left, 114–115 bottom, 116 top, 116–117 bottom, 117 top, 117 middle, 118 bottom, 129 middle, 130; 134–135 bottom, 142–143, 144, 145, 148, 149 bottom, 159 inset, 160–163 bottom, 172 left, 179 top, 182 top right, 182–183 bottom, 183 top, 198–201 background, 218–219 bottom, 501 bottom left, 504–505, 506, 507, 508, 509, 510–511

Minneapolis Historical Society: 234 top, 235 bottom; 232, 233, © Minneapolis Star Journal Tribune; 230–231, Norton & Peel

Museum of History & Industry, Seattle: 360, Post Intelligencer Collection

National Baseball Hall of Fame: 32, 33 top, 35 inset, 50–51, 52 bottom, 54, 56 inset, 60, 62–63 bottom, 67, 73, 86 middle, 151 top right, 158 top, 159, 187 top, 189 top and middle left, 192, 213 bottom, 221 bottom, 245 right, 347; 215 top, © Kevin Allen; 56 top, 57 top, 87 right, 101, 200 inset, © AP Images; 310–311, © Bier; 161 inset, © George Brace; 56 inset, 90–91, 102 middle, 279, Cleveland State University Library; 190, 212, 301, © Corbis; 156–157, © Steve Green; 65, 80–81, 275, 356–357 background, © National Baseball Library; 300, © Oakland Tribune; 302 inset right, © Photofile; 166 top, © Steven Schwab

Mike Nola Collection: 68 inset

NYY Steak: 501 top and bottom right, © George Barnes

Photolibrary: 392, © Visions of America

© Marc Piscotty: 424–425

Private Collection: 33 bottom, 48 center, 64, 72–73, 74 inset, 78 top, 119 top, 135 inset, 164 top right, 221; 102–103, 146 middle, 182 top left, 186 left, 186–187, National Baseball Hall of Fame

Redux Pictures: 190 top, © G. Paul Burnett/The New York Times; 138–139 top, © Fabrizio Constantini/The New York Times; 147 bottom, © Andrew Gombert/The New York Times; 147 top, © WOR/The New York Times

Reuters Pictures: 254–255, © Jonathan Ernst; 480 inset bottom, © Tim Shaffer

© Julia Robertson: 180–181, 268 inset middle, 290–291, 303 left, 398–399, 403, 420 top

SportsChrome: 430, © Scott Cunningham; 194–195, © Tom DiPace; 120, © Mike Kullen; 74–75, © C. Rydlewski; 132–133, 192–193, 271, 302, 428–429, 463, © Rob Tringali, Jr.

© 2009 Star Tribune/Minneapolis-St. Paul: 369, David Brewster

SuperStock: 272–273, © Steve Vidler

Transcendental Graphics: 10–11, 17, 18–19, 23, 83 middle, 84, 97 top, 100 top, 129 top, 138 background, 151 bottom, 152–153, 161 top, 171, 175 top, 205, 220 bottom, 221 top, 326–327 (Fall Classic Programs)

University of Pittsburgh: 326–327 inset

© Anthony Warnack: 299

© Joshua Eli Young: 418, 486–487

© Tom Zimmerman: 242–243

Unless otherwise noted, all baseball caps, pennants, and other memorabilia appear courtesy of the National Baseball Hall of Fame.